The Great Golden Spoon

The most comprehensive Italian cookbook

The Great Golden Spoon

The most comprehensive Italian cookbook

FOOD EDITORE

The Great Golden Spoon

© 2008 Food Editore Srl

Published originally under the title "Il Grande Cucchiaio D'Oro"
© 2006 Food Editore
Via Bordoni, 8 - 20124 Milano, ITALY
Via Mazzini, 6 - 43100 Parma, ITALY
www.foodeditore.it

Photographs
Davide Di Prato, Alberto Rossi
Recipes
Licia Cagnoni, Simone Rugiati
English Translation
Traduzioni Culinarie
English Layout
Gi.Mac Savigliano (CN)

Thanks to
Marco Bistarelli (www.jre.it)
I love my house, Parma
Artefiore, Parma

Printed in China
ISBN-10: 88-6154-088-0
ISBN-13: 978-886154-088-0

contents

e believe that cuisine is never static and fixed, not even classic, if that means something opposed to modernity and innovation. If for no other reason, this is because cuisine is something created in kitchens every day as part of ordinary life. Because where there is a kitchen there are hands kneading and mouths tasting, wafting aromas and bright colours, timers ticking away and pots and pans bubbling and sizzling. All the senses are on alert, and this means cuisine is always made in the present, even when it might reference tradition. At the risk of upsetting orthodox gastronomical traditionalists, we can say that cuisine is always innovative, thanks to its infinite capacity to locate itself in the present.

It makes us smile when we look at the grand culinary and cultural heritage which makes up Italian regional cuisine, and we see how, in every corner of the country, there are stories and anecdotes to explain the invention of regional dishes which have gone on to national and international fame. It makes us think about how dishes created in the individual kitchens of restaurants or homes have shaped our country's gastronomic panorama, crossing borders and dissolving social or cultural differences. The amazing thing is that, at least in legend, these new dishes often come about by accident or the mistaken interpretation of great classics. Just one example is the story of *pan de Toni*, Toni's bread: how, according to popular tradition, panettone was born out of the desperation of a pastry cook's assistant who burned the dessert for an important lunch. Skillfully he mixed together a few simple, leftover ingredients and created a delicious cake which soon became famous all over Italy as panettone.

Cooking does not only delight and stimulate the senses. It is an art, one which offers a strict set of rules to be scrupulously followed, but also allows the expert hand to subvert the very rules on which tradition is based.

For this reason our wide-ranging new book is unique in offering not only traditional recipes but also new creations invented by talented chefs dedicated to research and experimentation. The fruit of the many years of experience of a culinary publishing company which has produced both books and magazines, we believe this collection of recipes is of great importance to Italian cuisine. Typical recipes deeply rooted in the past can be found alongside surprises and bold innovations. In short, we are presenting a creative and youthful cuisine, able to reinvent tradition with taste and harmony, showcasing the finest quality ingredients and the best techniques.

We thank you for having chosen this new book from Food Editore, a collaborative effort from editors, graphic designers, photographers and chefs, inspired by our passion for the great food of Italy.

It is all very well to write and read about cooking, but direct practical experience is always best. And so I'll finish by wishing you good work and happy eating: *Buon lavoro e buon appetito!*

Editor
Paolo Dalcò

Readers' Guide

This is the first English translation of this Italian collection of recipes which form an important compilation of both traditional and innovative Italian cuisine.

The recipes are organized by season—Autumn, Winter, Spring and Summer—to highlight the importance of using seasonal ingredients, which are generally tasty, easy to find, cheap and environmentally sustainable. The chapters include Starters, *antipasti*, to whet the appetite; First Courses, *primi*, the soups, pastas, risottos and other dishes which Italians typically eat in small portions before the entrée; Main Courses, *secondi*, meat, poultry, fish or vegetarian; Vegetables, *contorni*, sides to round out the meal; and finally Desserts, *dolci*, for a sweet finish.

A chapter of festive menus suggests dishes for Christmas, New Year's Eve, Easter and St. Valentine's Day.

Over 200 of the recipes are identified as traditional to one of Italy's 20 regions, offering the reader a coherent overview of the country's cuisine, a blend of international influences and a strongly rooted sense of identity.

Almost every recipe includes a drink pairing, and at the back you'll find a guide to some of Italy's best-known wines, to help you choose the perfect bottle for a meal. Hopefully, you will be able to find these Italian wines at wine cellars and stores, and Italian foodstores, but if not the guide may help you find a suitable alternative wine that is available locally.

For every recipe you'll find approximate preparation and cooking times. These are just guidelines, given how ability and experience can vary. Never forget that speed is not always a virtue in the kitchen.

The difficulty rating for the recipes is also approximate, and is indicated by little chef's hats:

♗ easy   ♗♗ intermediate   ♗♗♗ difficult

Over the next few pages you'll find an Ingredient Glossary, including conversions and translations for various terms and measurements, and explanations of some of the more unusual Italian ingredients used in the recipes.

This is followed by an overview of what fruits and vegetables are at their best season by season.

Italian recipes tend to be more spare than English-language ones, leaving room for creativity and variation; they often give less-detailed instructions, and assume a greater level of knowledge on the cook's part. This is not a cookbook for complete beginners in the kitchen, but with a few basic skills and consultation of our various glossaries and appendices, we are sure that home cooks everywhere will find great success — even if some adaptation and experimentation is required.

Precise measurements are given for herbs, spices, salt and pepper only when necessary for the success of the recipe. When they are not specified, let taste be your guide.

All recipes serve four people, unless otherwise stated.

Some recipes require reference to the basic recipes in the back of the book, for example for pasta dough or pesto.

Recipes traditional to a specific region are identified by the name of the region and a little outline of the region.

In the back you can also find a guide to utensils and cooking techniques, tips on how to host successful dinner parties, with ideas for original centrepieces and menu planning and suggestions for wine pairings, followed by a list of some of the best-known Italian wines, giving a taster of the wide diversity and high quality available from the country's vineyards.

Ingredients, **Glossary** *and* Conversions

Here you'll find a list of some of the more unusual Italian ingredients and terms used in this book, including alternative names for certain ingredients. While many of the ingredients, including the various cheeses, cured meats and breads, can now be found at markets and at Italian delicatessens and food-stores, the descriptions for each should assist you in finding substitute ingredients should they not be available in your local area. Also included is information to help you convert measurements and temperatures from metric to imperial, and vice versa.

10

Abate pears Italian variety, with smooth yellow skin and a reddish-orange tinge, known for their sweetness.

Alchermes Sweet, red liqueur made with cinnamon, cardamom, cloves and vanilla. Widely used in Italian desserts.

Altamura-style bread Crusty, durum-wheat bread, baked in a wood-fired oven and traditionally made in the Puglia region of southern Italy.

Aluminum foil = tin foil

Arugula = rocket

Asiago cheese Sharp, semi-hard or hard cow's milk cheese from the Veneto region.

Baccalà Cod which has been dried or preserved in salt. Technically *baccalà* is the name for salted cod, while dried cod is called *stoccafisso*.

Bitto Aged, semi-hard cow's milk cheese made in the mountainous Valtellina area of northern Italy. Traditionally a small amount of goat's milk is added to this farmhouse cheese.

Bottarga Pressed and salted tuna or mullet roe. A salty condiment used in small doses, often grated over pasta. Tuna bottarga comes from the Egadi Islands off Trapani in Sicily, while mullet is from the Tuscan coast.

Bresaola Air-dried, cured beef from Lombardy.

Broil = grill

Burrata A rich Puglian cheese with an outer shell of mozzarella and almost-liquid interior of cream and mozzarella shreds.

Butter
1 tablespoon butter = 0.5 oz = 14 g
1/2 cup butter = 8 tablespoons = 1 stick = 4 oz = 113 g
1 cup butter = 16 tablespoons = 2 sticks = 8 oz = 225 g

Cacciatore Italian for hunter, this term refers to foods, usually meat, braised with mushrooms, onions and tomatoes.

Caciocavallo Mild, slightly salty and firm cow's milk cheese. It is a *pasta filata* cheese, meaning that the cheese is stretched and shaped by hand. When aged it becomes grainy and ideal for grating over pasta or rice.

Caciotta Semi-aged pecorino cheese traditionally produced in the Marche, made with the addition of some cow's milk.

Castelmagno Sharp cow's milk cheese from Piedmont, with a crumbly texture and blue veins.

Catalogna chicory Dark, bitter, leafy green with long, serrated leaves.

Chioggia radicchio Most common radicchio variety, round with tightly packed leaves.

Cicerchie Wild chickpeas, also known as grass peas, from the Marche.

Confectioners' sugar = icing or powdered sugar

Cookies = sweet biscuits

Coppa A cured meat made of pressed, cured, boneless pork neck.

Corn pasta Pasta made from corn, with a longer cooking time and a slightly sweeter taste than wheat pasta.

Cornstarch = cornflour

Cotechino Fresh, fatty pork sausage from Modena in Emilia-Romagna, often containing pork rind.

Crackers = savoury biscuits

Cranberry beans = borlotti beans

Crescenza Soft, mild and creamy cow's milk cheese from Lombardy, with a fresh, acidic flavour and a buttery texture.

Cups 1 US cup = 236 ml = 8.5 fl oz

Cuttlefish Cephalopod similar to a large squid.

Decana pear Large, thick-skinned pear known for being sweet and juicy.

Dogfish A small shark, known as *palombo* in Italian, with lean, firm flesh and the ability to stand up to strongly flavoured sauces.

Eggplant = aubergine

Farro The Italian term for emmer wheat, used in soups and salads or ground into flour and used to make pasta.

Fava beans = broad beans

Finocchiona Tuscan cured salami flavoured with fennel seeds.

Fiore Sardo Flavoursome sheep's milk cheese (pecorino) from the island of Sardinia, used for grating when aged.

Fontina Traditionally from Valle d'Aosta, a mild, soft, cow's milk cheese often used melted, for example in the rich cheese and egg-yolk sauce fonduta.

Frosting = icing

Gelatin sheets Commonly used in Europe to set aspics, mousses etc. Can be replaced by powdered gelatin (wich must sprinkled over a liquid to soften before use). 4 gelatin sheets = 1 package powdered gelatin

Gianduia chocolate Sweet hazelnut chocolate from Piedmont.

Green beans = French beans

Ground meat = minced meat

Guanciale Salted and cured pig cheek and jowl, used like pancetta.

Heavy cream = double cream

Involtini Stuffed rolls, typically of thinly sliced meat or fish, cabbage leaves or sliced vegetables like eggplant or zucchini.

Kitchen towel = tea towel

Lampascioni Wild hyacinth bulbs, common in Puglia and often pickled.

Lardo A type of cured pork or boar meat made from the layer of back fat just under the skin and cured with salt, herbs and spices.

Lardo di Colonnata a type of lardo made in and around the town of Colonnata in Tuscany. The pork fat is seasoned with a mixture of sea salt, herbs and spices and layered into individual marble tubs. The meat is aged in the tubs for 6-10 months in a cave or cellar.

Latteria Semi-hard, mild, white cow's milk cheese with small regular holes, made in the Friuli region of northern Italy.

Limoncello Lemon liqueur from Sicily and the Amalfi coast.

Lonzino Cured lean pork loin.

Lupini beans Large, flat yellow beans of the lupin plant, commonly preserved in a salty brine.

Luganega sausage Long, thin pork sausage from the Garda area of northern Italy.

Mâche = lamb's lettuce.

Mesclun = mixed baby lettuce leaves.

Mirto Aromatic Sardinian liqueur made with myrtle berries and leaves.

Montasio Mild cow's milk cheese from Friuli-Venezia Giulia.

Mostarda Spicy preserved fruit seasoned with mustard.

Mozzarella Fresh white cheese made from cow's or buffalo's milk. Cow's milk mozzarella, *fiordilatte*, has less moisture than *mozzarella di bufala*, buffalo mozzarella.

'Nduja Spicy, soft, spreadable cured pork from Calabria, seasoned with salt and chile pepper.

Nero di seppia Squid or cuttlefish ink, used to flavour and colour foods like rice or pasta.

Originario rice Short-grain, round rice often used in desserts.

oven temperature conversion table

Gas Mark	Fahrenheit	Celsius
1/4	225	110
1/2	250	130
1	275	140
2	300	150
3	325	170
4	350	180
5	375	190
6	400	200
7	425	220
8	450	230
9	475	240

Pancetta Cured pork belly, much like bacon.

Pandoro Literally "golden bread", a sweet, yellow, yeast cake traditionally eaten at Christmas.

Pane carasau Paper-thin, twice-baked Sardinian flatbread, sometimes called *musichiera* (musical paper) due to the noise it makes when broken.

Panettone A fluffy, sweet, cake-like bread studded with candied citrus and raisins, enjoyed around Italy particularly during Christmas and New Year.

Parchment paper = baking paper

Pecorino Sheep's milk cheese. Can be aged for varying periods of time. Pecorino Romano is from Lazio while Pecorino Sardo is from Sardinia.

Plastic wrap = cling film

Provola Mild, semi-soft cow's milk cheese from the south of Italy, sometimes smoked.

Ragusano Mild, provolone-like cow's milk cheese, made near Ragusa in Sicily.

Renette apples Small, yelllowish, tart apples often used for cooking.

Ricotta salata Dry, firm, salty ricotta, often grated over pasta.

Riso carnaroli A medium grain rice native to the region of Piedmont. Carnaroli rice is favored for risotto because of its high starch content and firm texture and because it holds its shape better than other rice varieties during slow cooking.

Robiola Soft, creamy cow's milk cheese. Robiola di Roccaverano, from Piedmont, is made with a mix of goat's, sheep's and cow's milk.

Romanesco Greenish-yellow cauliflower with distinctive fractal-like florets.

Salame Cotto A type of salami which is cooked or smoked before or after the curing process.

Salami Cooked or uncooked cured sausages, which can be made with various seasonings like fennel and garlic.

Salumi Cured meats (charcuterie), such as salami, prosciutto, mortadella, coppa etc.

San Marzano tomatoes Flavoursome red Neapolitan plum tomato.

Scamorza Southern Italian cow's milk cheese similar to mozzarella, aged about two weeks and sometimes smoked.

Shrimp = prawns

Snow peas = mangetout

Spaghetti alla chitarra Quite thick, square, egg spaghetti, traditionally cut on a stringed box called a *chitarra* (guitar).

Spring onions = green onions or scallions

Squaquerone Fresh, soft and tangy cow's milk cheese.

Squash Summer squash have an edible rind and seeds, like zucchini, while winter squash have a harder rind and big, hard seeds, like pumpkin.

Strega liqueur Spirit with a liquorice flavour, commonly drunk as a digestif, made from over 70 different herbs.

Tablespoon 1 US tablespoon = 15 ml = 0.5 fl oz

Taggiasca olives Small, brownish-black olives traditionally grown on the Ligurian coast, preserved in oil or brine.

Teaspoon 1 US teaspoon = 5 ml = 0.16 fl oz

Tomato sauce Usually tomatoes cooked down until thick with onion and/or garlic and other seasonings. Not ketchup.

Tropea onion Sweet red onion, grown in southern Italy for over 2,000 years. Often eaten raw.

Treviso radicchio Typically grown in the Veneto region, a mild radicchio variety that looks similar to a red Belgian endive.

Truffles A subterranean fungus highly prized for its distinctive aroma, used to flavour foods like rice, eggs and pasta. Black truffles are often cooked, while white truffles should be added to dishes just before serving.

Tomini Small, fresh forms of tuma cheese.

Tub gurnard A delicately flavoured white fish with firm flesh, *gallinella* in Italian.

Tuma cheese Also known as toma, a firm cow's milk cheese from northern Italy, aged anywhere between 3 to 18 months.

Tuscan-style bread Crusty, unsalted bread.

Umbrine Mediterranean fish similar to sea bass.

Valtellina Casera Delicately flavoured, white cow's milk cheese from Lombardy, aged for varying periods of time.

vanilla bean = vanilla pod

wax paper = greaseproof paper

whole-wheat = wholemeal

wild fennel Wild fennel has smaller bulbs than cultivated fennel, and the long, feathery leaves, similar to dill, are commonly used as an herb.

vin santo Sweet Tuscan dessert wine, made from partially dried grapes.

Zolfini beans Small, white beans from Tuscany.

zucchini = courgette.

Fruits *and* Vegetables *in* SEASON

These days we have an abundance of choice in our supermarkets, with greenhouse cultivation and air freight giving us everything at all times of year. But this huge selection has its price. Fruit and vegetables which do not ripen naturally or which are shipped around the world in refrigerated containers have a less intense flavour, more watery flesh and are grown using more chemicals. Buying produce only when it's in season is not just about buying better quality food, it's also about protecting our health.

Below is a calendar following the natural ripening times of some common fruits and vegetables.

Spring

This is the season of the first early harvests, and the fresh *asparagus* is excellent. Buy the spears when firm, with tightly closed tips, and before cooking snap off the woody part of the stalk and peel the lower half. Spring is also a good season for sweet new *carrots*, as a base flavouring in mirepoix with onions and celery or to use in salads, soufflés, flans and soups. Another typical spring vegetable is the *onion*, and of course the *spring onion*, both of which can be eaten raw in mixed salads or sautéed as a base for soups and sauces. Peel off the papery skin and trim away the root and shoot ends before using. Green *peas* are legumes, rich in vitamins, proteins and minerals, perfect as a side dish or in flans or quiches. Available year-round but best in the spring, *lettuces* include romaine, with long green leaves and a central white rib; tender leaf lettuces; and round, spherical heads of crisp iceberg. Spring *radishes* are a true delight, crunchy and slightly spicy, to be sliced into salads or eaten whole dipped in olive oil and salt.

For fruit, this is the time for *strawberries, rhubarb* and *apricots, to mention just a few*.

Summer

This is the best time of year for juicy *cucumbers*, which should be peeled if they have thick skin. Black, purple or white *eggplant* can be round, oblong or elongated; to test freshness make sure they are firm and shiny. Before cooking they can be sprinkled with coarse salt to draw off their bitter liquid. Sweet *bell peppers* are at their best in late summer: Green ones have a sharp, pungent taste; yellow have sweet and creamy flesh; while red are fragrant and full of flavour. They are excellent raw, thinly sliced in mixed salads or marinated as an antipasto. Peppers can sometimes be hard to digest, but removing the skin helps. The *tomato* is one of the kitchen's most versatile vegetables (though technically it's a fruit). Tomatoes can be eaten raw or stuffed and make an excellent base for many kinds of sauces. Thinly sliced, raw *zucchini* are good in various kinds of salads. If they are going to be cooked, quick methods which maintain their crunchiness and firm flesh are the best. They are excellent roasted, fried or sautéed.

Peaches, nectarines, plums, cherries, watermelons, canteloupes and *honeydew melons* are just a few example of juicy and delicious summer fruit.

Autumn

Not so rich in nutrients but full of flavour, *mushrooms* can be used in many dishes. Some varieties, like porcini or white button mushrooms, can be eaten raw in salads when young, dressed with oil, lemon juice and pepper. Another allium, *leeks* taste similar to onions but are sweeter and more aromatic. They can be used as a flavour base or stand on their own in soups, flans and gratins. Orange, yellow, white and green *winter squash* like acorn, butternut and Kabocha and sweet orange *pumpkins* are rich in vitamin A and antioxidants. They are very versatile and can be used in sauces, purees, flans or savoury tarts.

Autumn fruit includes late-harvest *figs* and *grapes*.

Winter

In Italy, the meaty, flavoursome *artichoke* flower is eaten in many ways: raw, grilled, stuffed, stewed or fried. A close relative, *cardoons* also have purifying and detoxifying properties. They can be eaten raw with an olive oil dip or broiled in a gratin. Highly nutritious *cabbages*, whether white, red or dark-green Savoy, are typical of the winter. This is also the season for crunchy white bulbs of *fennel*, with an anise flavour, and *potatoes*, rich in starch, minerals and vitamins. To appreciate the flavour of potatoes steam or roast them, without too much added fat. Yellow-fleshed potatoes, like Yukon Gold, are firmer and best for salads and frying, while white-fleshed potatoes tend to be more floury and are better suited for mashing and dishes which use mashed potato, like gnocchi. Small new potatoes are excellent pan-fried. One of the most nutritious vegetables is dark-green leafy *spinach*, packed full of vitamins A and C and iron. The winter varieties are the most common, but there are also spring varieties with tender leaves perfect raw in salads with a little oil and lemon juice. Another winter leaf vegetable that can be cooked or eaten raw is *radicchio*, grown in darkened sheds to give it its typical deep red colour. Round Chioggia is the most common variety, while Treviso has elongated leaves like endive.

For fruits there are *apples*, *pears* and *citrus*, while winter is also the season when *dried fruit* like figs and prunes come into their own.

autumn

Vibrant soups to highlight the flavours of autumn vegetables. Nutritious and substantial pastas and risottos to cheer up a grey rainy day. Hearty roasts to pair with a robust red wine, and soft, creamy desserts to comfort during the first chilly evenings. Tempting ideas to taste the foods of the season in many original ways.

Whole-Wheat Toasts
with Caponata and Mozzarella

Preparation time 15 minutes
Cooking time 30 minutes
Wine *Inzolia*

1/2 onion, minced
2 tbsps extra-virgin olive oil
1 wedge pumpkin or Kabocha
 squash, peeled, deseeded
 and chopped
1 celery stalk, diced
1/2 eggplant, diced
1 garlic clove, smashed
salt and pepper
5 cherry tomatoes, sliced
2 small potatoes, boiled,
 peeled and sliced
1/2 whole-wheat baguette
5.5 oz (150 g) cow's milk
 mozzarella, sliced

Preheat oven to 400°F (200°C).
Sauté the onion in the olive oil in a large frying pan. When brown, add the pumpkin and celery, cook for a few minutes, then add the eggplant. Add the garlic, salt and pepper to taste and a few tablespoons of water. Let simmer until the vegetables are soft, then add the tomatoes, potatoes and salt and pepper to taste. Set aside.
Slice the baguette and place on a baking sheet. Cover each slice of bread with a thin slice of mozzarella and a generous spoonful of the vegetable mixture. Bake for 3 minutes or until the mozzarella begins to melt. Serve hot.

Asiago and Mushroom Croquettes

Preparation time 35 minutes
Cooking time 25 minutes
Wine *Fiano di Avellino*

1 knob of butter
1/2 shallot, finely diced
1¼ cups (9 oz or 250 g)
 Carnaroli rice
4.5 oz (130 g) Asiago cheese,
 shaved
1 tbsp extra-virgin olive oil
1 garlic clove, smashed
5 mushrooms, thinly sliced
parsley, finely chopped
salt and pepper
1 egg
3/4 cup (3.5 oz or 100 g)
 breadcrumbs
sunflower oil for frying

24

Melt the butter in a large pan, and sauté the shallot until soft, then add the rice and stir well. Let toast briefly then gradually add hot water to the rice, stirring frequently and letting the water absorb before adding more. Cook about 18-20 minutes. When the rice is nearly cooked, add the Asiago and stir well. Set aside.
In a frying pan heat the olive oil and add the garlic. Add the mushrooms and cook over high heat until softened. Add the parsley and salt and pepper to taste. Stir the mushroom mixture into the cooled risotto. With damp hands form small balls of risotto, set them on a baking sheet and chill in the refrigerator. Meanwhile beat the egg in a bowl and pour the breadcrumbs onto a large plate. Dip the chilled rice balls in the egg mixture and then roll in breadcrumbs. Heat the sunflower oil in a large frying pan. When the oil is hot but not smoking, fry the croquettes until they are browned on all sides. Once cooked, place on paper towels to absorb excess oil. Salt and serve hot.

Chestnut-Polenta Dumplings Wrapped in Savoy Cabbage

Preparation time 35 minutes
Cooking time 35 minutes
Wine *Alto Adige Sylvaner*
♟ ♟

DUMPLINGS
1 cup (250 ml) water
1¼ cups (300 ml) milk
salt
1/2 cup (3.5 oz or 100 g)
 instant polenta
3 tbsps chestnut flour
pepper
1 pinch ground cinnamon
2 tbsps grated Parmesan

12 Savoy cabbage leaves
2 tbsps extra-virgin olive oil

CHEESE SAUCE
1 knob of butter
1 tbsp plain flour
1¼ cups (300 ml) milk
4 oz (120 g) Bitto cheese, grated
1 egg yolk
nutmeg, grated
salt and pepper
rosemary, finely chopped

Preheat oven to 350°F (180° C).
Bring and the water and milk to a boil with 1/2 teaspoon of salt.
Whisk in the polenta and chestnut flour. Cook for 10 minutes,
stirring frequently. Add pepper to taste, the cinnamon and the
Parmesan cheese. Mix well and let cool.
Bring a large pot of salted water to boil. Immerse each cabbage
leaf in the water briefly then pat dry with a clean kitchen towel.
Fill each cabbage leaf with 1 tablespoonful of polenta. Fold the
longest sides in and then fold into thirds to form a dumpling. Place
the dumplings in an oiled baking dish.
Melt the butter in a saucepan and stir in the flour. Add the milk
and whisk continuously. When the mixture begins to thicken add
the Bitto cheese and egg yolk. Continue whisking until a smooth
cream forms. Add nutmeg, salt and pepper to taste.
Pour the cheese sauce over the dumplings and sprinkle with the
rosemary. Bake for 15-20 minutes. Serve hot.

autumn

Finocchiona Salami with Figs

Preparation time 5 minutes

6 green figs
12 slices of finocchiona salami

Clean the figs, cutting away
any dark spots on the skin and
cutting off the stem.
Cut the figs in half and
wrap each half in a slice of
finocchiona.
Secure each one with a
toothpick or small skewer.
Refrigerate until serving.

Note *These little skewers
make a good accompaniment
to* aperitivi *(pre-dinner drinks).
The fig and finocchiona rolls can
also be alternated on a skewer
with cubes of a mild, semi-aged
pecorino.*

26

Beef Carpaccio with Pears

Preparation time 15 minutes
Cooking time 10 minutes
Wine *Roero Arneis*

1 pear, thinly sliced
juice of 1 lemon
6.5 oz (180 g) Gorgonzola cheese,
 chopped
4 tbsps milk
3 tbsps heavy cream
2 tbsps extra-virgin olive oil
9 oz (250 g) beef tenderloin,
 thinly sliced
salt
white pepper
1 head frisée lettuce, shredded
1/3 cup (1.5 oz or 40 g) chopped
 walnuts

Brush the pear slices with lemon
juice. Melt the Gorgonzola
cheese with the milk and cream
in a saucepan. Oil 4 plates.
Alternate slices of beef and pear
around the outside of each plate
to form a circle, then sprinkle
with salt and pepper to taste.
Place some frisée in the centre
of each plate and salt to taste.
Drizzle with the Gorgonzola
cream and sprinkle with the
walnuts.

Crispy Polenta
with Speck Ham and Walnuts

Preparation time 15 minutes
Cooking time 20 minutes
Wine *Alto Adige Santa Maddalena*

POLENTA
8 cups (2 l) water
3 cups (1 lb or 500 g)
 instant polenta
salt
extra-virgin olive oil
3 tbsps butter

TOPPING
1/2 cup (2 oz or 60 g) ohopped
 walnuts
9 oz (250 g) ricotta
salt and pepper
chives, chopped
7 oz (200 g) speck ham,
thinly sliced

Bring the water to a boil with a little salt. Sprinkle in the polenta,
whisking constantly, and cook for a few minutes. Pour into
an well-oiled, rectangular baking dish. Press down well to form
an even layer, cover with plastic wrap and leave to cool.
Mix the walnuts into the ricotta. Add salt and pepper to taste and
the chives.
Cut the cooled polenta into triangles. Heat the butter in a large
frying pan, then add the polenta triangles and brown them on both
sides until a golden crust forms.
Place the triangles on a serving dish then top each one with a
spoonful of the ricotta mixture and 2 slices of speck ham.

Panzarotti
(CAMPANIA)

Preparation time 40 minutes
Cooking time 20 minutes
Wine *Greco di Tufo*

DOUGH
2¼ cups plus 2 tbsps (10.5 oz
 or 300 g) plain flour
salt
1½ tbsps lard

FILLING
1 egg
parsley, chopped
pepper
3.5 oz (100 g) ricotta, sieved
2 oz (50 g) cow's milk
 mozzarella, cubed
5 tbsps grated Parmesan
3.5 oz (100 g) prosciutto,
 cubed
sunflower oil

28

Mound the flour on a work surface, and make a well in the centre.
Add the salt and lard, then mix a smooth and uniform dough by
adding warm water to the centre of the flour. Knead the dough
well and form a ball, then let it rest for 1 hour.
Beat the egg and add the parsley and a pinch of pepper. Mix in
the ricotta, and then the mozzarella, Parmesan and prosciutto.
Roll out the pasta dough with a rolling pin to form a thin sheet.
Place equally spaced spoonfuls of the ricotta mixture along one
side of the dough, then fold it over and press down between the
filling with fingertips. Cut the dough with a ravioli or cookie cutter
or a knife to form the ravioli. Heat the oil in a large pan and fry
them. As soon as they turn golden, drain and dry on paper towels,
then serve immediately.

Roman-Style Panzerotti
(LAZIO)

Preparation time 40 minutes
Cooking time 20 minutes
Wine *Bianco dei Colli Albani*

FILLING
3.5 oz (100 g) Gruyère cheese,
 diced
3.5 oz (100 g) prosciutto,
 finely chopped
2 tbsps of grated Parmesan
1 egg
salt and pepper

DOUGH
3/4 cup plus 1 tbsp (3.5 oz
 or 100 g) plain flour
salt
3½ tbsps butter, at room
 temperature
2 egg yolks
frying 7 tbsps lard

29

Mix together the Gruyère, prosciutto, Parmesan and egg with
pinches of salt and pepper.
Mound the flour on a wooden board, make a well in the middle
and mix in a pinch of salt, the butter, egg yolks and enough water
to make a smooth and uniform dough. Roll out the pasta with a
rolling pin to make a not-too-thin sheet. Use a cookie cutter to cut
out disks, and in the centre of each one place a spoonful of the
cheese and prosciutto filling. Fold each disk over to make a half-
moon and press around the edges with a fork.
Melt the lard, and when it is hot fry the panzerotti. As soon as
they are golden drain them with a slotted spoon and dry on paper
towels, then serve immediately.

Tuscan Crostini

Note *The term* crostino *in Italian can refer to different preparations, such as small canapés of sliced bread in different shapes, slices of toasted crusty bread spread with various toppings or even small cubes of toasted bread used to garnish soups and fondues.*

Preparation time 25 minutes
Cooking time 10 minutes
Wine *Rosso di Montalcino*

10.5 oz (300 g) chicken livers
7 tbsps white vinegar
1 yellow onion, minced
4 tbsps extra-virgin olive oil
sage, chopped
red wine
1¼ cups (300 ml) hot
 vegetable broth
salt and pepper
10-15 capers, rinsed
5 anchovy fillets in oil
8 slices of crusty bread

Wash the chicken livers and place them in a bowl with the vinegar and a little water and let sit for 10 minutes. Drain and rinse, then set aside.
Sauté the onion with the oil and sage until golden, then add the chicken livers. Brown them briefly then add some red wine and let reduce for 2 or 3 minutes. Add the broth, salt and pepper and reduce.
Take off the heat, add the capers and anchovies and blend the mixture in a food processor. Let it rest for 20 minutes.
If it is too thick heat the mixture up with a little broth.
Toast the slices of bread under the broiler or in the oven for a few minutes, then spread with the chicken-liver mixture and serve.

Fig and Proscuitto Toasts

Preparation time 10 minutes
Cooking time 15 minutes
Wine *Collio Pinot Bianco*

8 slices of crusty bread
2 tbsps water
1 tbsp sugar
8 ripe figs, peeled and halved
3 tbsps balsamic vinegar
freshly ground pepper
4 oz (120 g) prosciutto,
 thinly sliced

Preheat oven to 400°F (200°C).
Toast the bread in the oven for
a few minutes. In a frying pan,
heat the water and the sugar,
add figs and sauté over high
heat. When the figs begin to
caramelize add the balsamic
vinegar.
Place figs on top of the toasted
bread and drizzle the pan
juices over the figs, then top
with freshly ground pepper.
Place 1 slice of prosciutto on
each piece of toast and serve
immediately.

Chickpea and Prawns Croquettes

Preparation time 15 minutes
Cooking time 15 minutes
Wine *Metodo Classico
Franciacorta Brut*

2 tbsps extra-virgin olive oil
1 shallot, minced
2/3 cup (5.5 oz or 150 g) drained
 canned chickpeas
thyme leaves
1 egg
salt and pepper
20 small prawns, partially peeled
 leaving the tail intact
3/4 cup (3.5 oz or 100 g)
 breadcrumbs
sunflower oil

Heat olive oil in a large frying
pan, add shallot and sauté. Add
chickpeas and thyme. Let cook
for 5 minutes. Puree the mixture
using a food processor. When
the puree is cool add the egg,
salt and pepper and mix well.
Add prawns to the chickpea
puree and toss to coat. Roll each
prawns in breadcrumbs to coat.
Heat sunflower oil in a large
frying pan and fry the prawns.
When golden-brown drain with a
slotted spoon and dry on paper
towels, then serve immediately.

31

Chestnut and Cabbage Rolls with Parmesan Sauce

Preparation time 20 minutes
Cooking time 50 minutes
Wine *Fiano di Avellino*

FOR ROLLS
2/3 cup (3.5 oz or 100 g) dried
 chestnuts, soaked overnight
1.5 oz (40 g) lardons
1 bay leaf
2 tbsps grated Parmesan
salt and pepper
12 Savoy cabbage leaves
5.5 oz (150 g) speck ham, thinly
 sliced
1 knob of butter

FOR CHEESE SAUCE
7 tbsps heavy cream
6 tbsps grated Parmesan
2 egg yolks
salt and pepper

32

Preheat oven to 400°F (200°C)
In a large pot, boil chestnuts, lardons and bay leaf until chestnuts are soft. Drain and transfer mixture to a bowl, removing bay leaf. Mash chestnuts with a fork, add Parmesan cheese and season with salt and pepper to taste.
Bring a large pot of salted water to a boil. Immerse each cabbage leaf for a few minutes, and dry on a clean kitchen towel. Place 1 slice of speck ham and 1 spoonful of chestnut filling in the centre of each cabbage leaf. Fold the longest sides in and then fold into thirds to form a dumpling. Place the dumplings in a buttered baking dish.
Place all of the sauce ingredients in a double boiler and cook, whisking constantly, until a smooth cream forms. Adjust salt and pepper to taste.
Top each roll with a spoonful of Parmesan sauce and let brown in the oven for 5-10 minutes. Serve immediately.

Crescenza Tarts
with Taggiasca Olives

Preparation time 20 minutes
Cooking time 15 minutes
Wine *Metodo Classico*
Franciacorta Brut

CRUST
1/2 tsp dried yeast
1 cup (250 ml) lukewarm water
1 tsp honey
1 cup plus 3 tbsps
 5.3 oz or 150 g) plain flour
2 tbsps sesame oil
1 tsp salt

FILLING
9 oz (250 g) crescenza or other
 fresh cow's milk cheese
zest of 1 lemon
1 tbsp extra-virgin olive oil
salt and pepper

GARNISH
15 pitted Taggiasca olives in oil

33

Preheat oven to 375°F (190°C).
Dissolve yeast in the water with honey. Let sit 10 minutes.
Mound the flour on a work surface, make a well in the centre and
add sesame oil. Sprinkle salt around the outer border of the flour.
Pour the yeast mixture into the centre of the well and mix to make
a smooth and uniform dough. Roll out the dough and cut out
circles using a glass or a cookie cutter. Place rounds on a baking
sheet lined with parchment paper and bake for 15 minutes. Let
cool.
Mix the crescenza with the lemon zest, oil and salt and pepper to
taste. Spread cheese mixture over tarts and decorate with olives.

Rice and Savoy Cabbage Rolls

Note *Roma is a variety of short-grain rice, with particularly round, fat grains which give off a lot of starch during cooking. Roma rice absorbs flavours very well, and is often used for risottos.*

Preparation time 25 minutes
Cooking time 1 hour 10 minutes
Wine *Verdicchio dei Castelli di Jesi*

Serves 6

4 tbsps extra-virgin olive oil
2 onions, diced
1 carrot, diced
1 bell pepper, diced
3/4 cup (5.5 oz or 150 g)
 Roma rice
7 oz (200 g) ground beef
3.5 oz (100 g) tomato paste
1 egg
salt and pepper
1 Savoy cabbage

In a large frying pan heat the olive oil, then add the onions, carrot, and bell pepper. Cook for 5 minutes.
Add rice, stir and remove from heat. Add beef, tomato paste, egg, salt and pepper and stir well.
Bring a large pot of salted water to a boil. Immerse each cabbage leaf for a few minutes, then drain and cool on a clean kitchen towel.
Place 1 spoonful of filling on each cabbage leaf and roll up each leaf tightly, fixing with a toothpick if necessary.
Place the rolls in a pan with salted water and bring to a boil. Let cook for 40 minutes.
Drain and serve immediately.

Crostini with Black Truffle Cream

Note *Fresh truffles need to be cleaned thoroughly before use. Dirt should be removed with a small, stiff brush and any spoiled parts cut away with a sharp paring knife. The truffle should then be wiped with a damp cloth.*

Preparation time 15 minutes
Cooking time 10 minutes
Wine *Dolcetto di Dogliani*

3/4 cup plus 1 tbsp (200 ml) milk
1 pinch salt
1 knob of butter
1 tbsp plain flour
1 medium-sized black truffle,
 cleaned and finely diced
8 slices of crusty bread

Preheat oven to 400°F (200°C).
Heat the milk in a small saucepan with the pinch of salt.
Melt the butter in another small saucepan. Remove the melted butter from the heat and add the flour, mixing well with a fork or small whisk.
Whisk the flour-butter mixture into the boiling milk and stir with a wooden spoon until the liquid thickens. Stir in the diced truffle and pour the béchamel into a bowl, stirring frequently to prevent a skin forming on the surface.
Toast the bread in the oven for a few minutes and then spread with the truffle sauce.
Serve the crostini immediately.

Spicy Crostini with Sausage

Preparation time 15 minutes
Cooking time 15 minutes
Wine *Morellino di Scansano*

5.5 oz (150 g) luganega sausage
1 clove of garlic, peeled and
 minced
1 red chilli pepper, minced
3 tbsps extra-virgin olive oil
3/4 cup plus 1 tbsp (200 ml)
 canned crushed tomatoes
basil, chopped
ground cumin
parsley, chopped
salt and pepper
8 slices of crusty bread

Preheat oven to 400°F (200°C).
Remove the sausage from
its casing and break it up
into small pieces. In a small
saucepan heat oil and add
garlic and chilli. After 1 minute
add sausage. Let cook for a
few minutes until the fat begins
to render and then add the
crushed tomatoes. Let simmer
until the sauce thickens. Add
basil, cumin, parsley and salt
and pepper to taste. Toast
bread in the oven for a few
minutes. Spread each slice of
toasted bread with sauce.

Melted Brie and Porcini Crostone

Preparation time 10 minutes
Cooking time 5 minutes
Wine *Alto Adige Pinot Nero*

4 slices crusty bread
10 oz (280 g) Brie, sliced
2 tbsps extra-virgin olive oil
4 or 5 medium-sized fresh
 porcini mushrooms, thinly sliced
salt and pepper

Preheat oven to 400°F (200°C).
Place bread on a baking sheet.
Lay Brie slices next to one
another on the bread, being
careful not to let the cheese
overlap.
Heat olive oil in a large frying
pan, add mushrooms and sauté
for 1 minute. Season with salt
and pepper to taste.
Spoon mushrooms on top
of the Brie and toast in the
oven until the cheese melts.
Serve immediately.

Truffled Egg Canapés

Preparation time 20 minues
Cooking time 5 minutes
Wine *Teroldego Rotaliano*

2 eggs
salt and pepper
1 tbsp extra-virgin olive oil
8 slices of Altamura-style bread,
 crusts removed
3 tbsps truffle butter

Beat eggs, salt and pepper in a small bowl.
Heat oil in a non-stick frying pan and pour in egg mixture.
Let cook for about 1 minute, flip and let cook for 1 more minute.
Let the omelette cool and cut into thin slices.
Spread truffle butter on each slice of bread and then cut bread into small triangles.
Top with omelette slices.

Note *Altamura bread comes from the Puglia region of southern Italy and is made with hard wheat semolina. It can be replaced by any crusty bread, preferably baked in a wood-fired oven.*

Mini Panini with Crescenza

Preparation time 20 minutes
Wine *Prosecco di Conegliano*

5.5 oz (150 g) crescenza or soft
 cow's milk cheese
salt and pepper
2 tbsps truffle oil
1 small black truffle, cleaned
 and finely diced
8 small butter rolls
8 slices of prosciutto,
 thinly sliced
1 fresh porcini mushroom,
 cleaned and thinly sliced

Mix the crescenza with a little salt and pepper and the truffle oil.
Add the diced truffle.
Cut the rolls in half and spread each side with the cheese mixture.
Place 1 slice of prosciutto and 3 slices of mushroom on half of each roll. Place the top on each sandwich and press down slightly.

Potato and Ricotta Flan
with Radicchio Sauce

38

Preparation time 15 minutes
Cooking time 1 hour 15 minutes
Wine *Greco di Tufo*

FLAN
1 medium potato, boiled
 and peeled
10.5 oz (300 g) ricotta
2 eggs
2 egg whites, beaten to soft peaks
salt and pepper
nutmeg, grated
3 tbsps butter
breadcrumbs

SAUCE
2 tbsps extra-virgin olive oil
2 heads Treviso radicchio, chopped
1 tbsp plain flour
1¼ cups (300 ml) vegetable broth
salt and pepper

GARNISH
Treviso radicchio, sliced

Preheat oven to 350°F (180°C).
Mash the potato with the ricotta in a bowl. Stir in eggs and fold in the beaten egg whites. Add salt, pepper and nutmeg.
Butter 6 aluminum ramequins and coat with breadcrumbs. Pour potato mixture into ramequins and bake for 20 minutes.
Heat the olive oil in a large frying pan. Add the radicchio and cook for 2-3 minutes until wilted. Sprinkle over the flour, stir and add broth, salt and pepper. Simmer for 10 minutes. Puree radicchio in a food processor or with an immersion blender. Remove flans from the oven, cut around each ramequin to loosen the flan and invert onto a serving plate. Cover with radicchio sauce and garnish with slices of radicchio.

Mini Pizzas with Spinach and Tomatoes

Note *There are several stories that tell how fontina cheese was named. Some say that fontina comes from the name of the pasture "fontin" where the cows whose milk was used grazed. Others say that the name comes from the Italian word* fondere, *meaning to melt, because the cheese melts so easily.*

Preparation time 30 minutes
Cooking time 25 minutes
Wine *Prosecco di Conegliano e Valdobbiadene Brut*

4 cups (1 lb or 500 g) whole-wheat flour
8 tbsps extra-virgin olive oil
1 lb (500 g) spinach
2 tbsps butter
8 oz (200 g) canned whole tomatoes, pureed or crushed
3.5 oz (100 g) fontina cheese, cubed
salt and pepper

39

Preheat oven to 350°F (180°C).
Sift flour and mound it on a work surface. Make a well in the centre and pour in olive oil and a little water. Mix to form a smooth and uniform dough. Roll out dough and using a cookie cutter cut out several circles. Place rounds on an oiled baking sheet.
Bring a large pot of salted water to boil and blanch spinach for a few minutes in boiling water. Meanwhile in a large frying pan melt the butter and when the spinach is cooked, drain and transfer to the frying pan. Sauté for a few minutes. Season with salt and pepper to taste.
Place 1 spoonful of tomatoes, 1 spoonful of spinach and a few cubes of fontina on each pizza round. Sprinkle with salt and pepper.
Bake the pizzas for 15 minutes. Serve immediately.

Crescioni
(Emilia Romagna)

Note *Italian flatbread*
is usually called **piadina***.*
It is a simple unleavened
bread which is cooked
and then filled with a mixture
of greens or herbs. Crescioni
differ slightly from piadina
because the edges are
closed like a ravioli, while the
piadina is simply folded over.
Variations on this recipe are
endless: Crescioni can be
filled with squash, potatoes,
tomatoes, cabbage or
cheese, for example.

40

Preparation 30 minutes
Cooking time 30 minutes
Wine *Colli Piacentini Gutturnio*

DOUGH
4 cups (1 lb or 500g)
 plain flour
5 tbsps lard
salt
milk

FILLING
7 oz (200 g) lardo
1 garlic clove
1 pinch of pepper
9 oz (250 g) spinach
salt

Mound flour on a wooden board and make a well in the centre.
Add lard and a pinch of salt to the centre and mix. Gradually add
enough milk to form a smooth and uniform dough. Work quickly
otherwise air pockets may form during cooking. Cover with a clean
kitchen towel and let rest for about an hour.
Meanwhile mince the garlic and lardo together with the pepper.
Bring a large pot of salted water to a boil. Add spinach and boil for
2 to 3 minutes. Drain and squeeze out excess water and chop the
spinach. In a large frying pan render the lardo and garlic mixture
and then add the spinach. Salt to taste.
On a floured surface roll out the dough into 8-inch (22 cm) circles.
Place a few spoonfuls of filling on each circle and fold in half.
Using a fork press the dough closed. The crescioni can either be
baked, fried or grilled until both sides are golden-brown.

Savoury Spinach Tart
(Trentino-Alto Adige)

Preparation time 15 minutes
Cooking time 40 minutes
Wine *Trentino Müller Thurgau*

FILLING
4 tbsps butter
1 onion, diced
3.5 lb (1.3 kg) spinach chopped
salt
2 eggs
2/3 cup (150 ml) heavy cream
6 tbsps grated Trentingrana
  cheese

DOUGH
1 10-oz (300 g) roll of puff-pastry
  dough

Preheat oven to 400°F (200°C).
Melt butter in a large frying pan and add onion. When the onion
begins to brown, add chopped spinach. Salt and let cook for a
few minutes.
In a mixing bowl beat the eggs and add heavy cream.
Roll out the dough and cut out two 8-inch (22 cm) rounds. Place
one of the rounds in an 8-inch (22 cm) pie pan. Evenly distribute
the spinach over the dough. Sprinkle cheese over the spinach.
Pour cream mixture over the tart and cover with the remaining
dough round.
Bake for 30 minutes. Serve warm.

Potato and Porcini Croquettes

Note Gomasio *is a misture of toasted sesame seeds and salt. Toast sesame seeds and when they begin to brown add salt. Continue cooking for a few minutes.*
The proportions are 1 tcaspoon of salt for every 15 teaspoons of sesame seeds.

Preparation time 25 minutes
Cooking time 1 hour
Wine *Rossese di Dolceacqua*

3 tbsps extra-virgin olive oil
2 shallots, minced
1/2 red chilli pepper
4 potatoes, boiled and peeled
2 rosemary sprigs
4 fresh porcini mushrooms,
 cleaned and sliced
parsley, finely chopped
salt and pepper
1 tbsp of grated Parmesan
2 tbsps gomasio (see note)

42

Preheat oven to 350°F (180°C).
Heat 2 tablespoons oil in a large frying pan. Add 1 shallot and the chilli pepper. Using a potato ricer mash the potatoes directly into the pan. Add whole rosemary sprigs. Let cook over low heat for about 5 minutes. Remove the rosemary.
In another frying pan heat the remaining olive oil. Add the remaining shallot and then the mushrooms. Cook over high heat until mushrooms soften. Add salt, pepper and parsley.
Add Parmesan cheese to potato mixture and divide the dough into 4 parts. Make a hole in each ball of dough and fill with 1 spoonful of mushrooms. Roll dough into a ball and coat with gomasio.
Place the 4 balls on a baking sheet and bake for 20 minutes. Serve immediately.

Truffle and Porcini Mushroom Omelette

Preparation time 15 minutes
Cooking time 10 minutes
Wine *Alto Adige Santa Maddalena*

1 tbsp extra-virgin olive oil
1 garlic clove, smashed
2 small to medium-sized fresh
 porcini mushrooms, cleaned
 and sliced
salt and pepper
2 eggs
1/2 tbsp grated Parmesan
1 tbsp truffle oil

Heat olive oil in a large pan and add the smashed garlic clove.
Sauté for 1 minute, until golden-brown.
Add the sliced porcini mushrooms and season to taste with salt
and pepper. Sauté until soft.
Transfer the cooked mushrooms to a cutting board and dice.
In a mixing bowl beat the eggs and Parmesan cheese together,
then whisk in the truffle oil.
Coat a medium-sized non-stick frying pan with a little olive oil and
add the egg mixture. Let cook for a few minutes and then flip the
omelette and let cook another few minutes until browned evenly
on both sides.
Cut the omelette into small squares. Place each square on a
teaspoon and top with the sautéed mushrooms.
Serve immediately.

Pear and Parmesan Strudel

Preparation time 15 minutes
Cooking time 20 minutes
Wine *Trentino Talento Brut*

1 9-oz (250 g) roll of puff
  pastry or phyllo dough
5.5 oz (150 g) unaged pancetta,
  thinly sliced
1/3 cup (50 g) walnuts, coarsely
  chopped
2 Decana pears
2 oz (60 g) Parmesan cheese,
  shaved
salt and pepper
2 tbsps extra-virgin olive oil
melted butter
fennel seeds

44

Preheat oven to 350°F (180°C).
Peel, core and thinly slice the pears.
Roll out the puff pastry or phyllo. Cover the dough with slightly
overlapping slices of pancetta and sprinkle over the walnuts. Place
the pear slices on top of the pancetta and walnuts, sprinkle with
Parmesan cheese shavings and season with salt and pepper.
Drizzle with oil.
Fold in the sides and roll up the pastry. Pinch the outside edges
shut, making sure they are well sealed.
Brush with melted butter and sprinkle a few pinches of fennel
seeds over the top.
Bake for 20 minutes and serve warm.

Gorgonzola Grape Skewers

Preparation time 15 minutes
Wine *Malvasia Istriana*

♟

1 bunch green grapes
1 bunch red grapes
10.5 oz (300 g) Gorgonzola
 cheese

Cut each grape in half
lengthwise and, using a sharp
knife, remove the seeds.
If using a seedless variety of
grape, scoop out a little of the
pulp with a sharp knife.
In a small bowl beat the
Gorgonzola until it becomes
creamy and soft.
Fill each grape half with the
softened Gorgonzola and
reassemble the grape halves.
Thread the stuffed grapes
onto short wooden skewers or
toothpicks, alternating red and
green grapes.

Mushroom Toasts

Preparation time 20 minutes
Wine *Bardolino Chiaretto*

♟

8 white button mushrooms,
 chopped
juice of 1/2 lemon
3 tbsps extra-virgin olive oil
salt
black pepper
5 chives, finely chopped
1 bunch parsley, finely chopped
1 garlic clove, minced
8 slices of white bread

Preheat oven to 400°F (200°C).
Place chopped mushrooms
in a bowl and mix with lemon
juice, olive oil, salt and pepper.
Add chopped herbs and garlic.
Refrigerate 30 minutes.
Meanwhile, toast bread in the
oven. Spoon mushroom mixture
over toasted bread. Serve
immediately.

45

Stuffed Squash Blossoms
(Piedmont)

Preparation time 25 minutes
Cooking time 15 minutes
Wine *Freisa di Chieri*

46

Serves 6

3.5 oz (100 g) crusty bread
7 tbsps milk
7 oz (200 g) roast beef, minced
3.5 oz (100 g) salame cotto,
  broken into small pieces
2 tbsps grated Parmesan
2 garlic cloves, minced
parsley, finely chopped
4-5 sage leaves, finely chopped
mint, finely chopped
1 egg
1 small black truffle, minced
24 squash blossoms
5 tbsps butter
salt

Soak the bread in the milk. Let soften, then drain, squeezing out
all of the excess milk.
In a large bowl mix the bread with the roast beef, salame cotto,
Parmesan cheese, garlic, parsley, sage and mint. Add egg and 1/2
the truffle. The mixture should be quite thick.
Carefully stuff the squash blossoms with the filling.
Melt butter in a large frying pan, add squash blossoms and fry
until golden. Drain on paper towels and salt them. Place on a
serving plate and garnish with remaining truffle.
Serve immediately.

Norcina Crostini
(UMBRIA)

Preparation time 15 minutes
Cooking time 30 minutes
Wine *Colli del Trasimeno Rosso*

Serves 6-8

6 tbsps extra-virgin olive oil
1 garlic clove
1 anchovy packed in salt,
 rinsed and chopped
2 oz (50 g) black truffle, grated
3.5 oz (100 g) chicken livers,
 minced
1/2 garlic clove, minced
1 tbsp capers in vinegar, minced
juice of 1 lemon
salt and pepper
1 loaf crusty bread,
 sliced and toasted

47

Heat 4 tablespoons of the olive oil in a small saucepan and add
the whole garlic clove. Sauté until golden-brown.
Remove from heat and discard the garlic clove. Add the anchovy
and grated truffle and stir well to obtain a smooth, uniform, creamy
mixture.
In a frying pan heat the remaining 2 tablespoons of olive oil and
add the minced chicken livers, the minced garlic and capers.
When the chicken livers are cooked, remove from heat and stir in
the truffle-anchovy mixture. Add lemon juice, salt and pepper and
mix well.
Spread the mixture on toasted bread. Serve immediately.

Polenta and Asiago Flans

Preparation time 15 minutes
Cooking time 20 minutes
Wine *Cabernet di Breganze*

1/2 cup plus 2 tbsps
 (3.5 oz or 100 g) instant polenta
3 tbsps butter
3 oz (80 g) Asiago cheese,
 diced
salt and pepper
1 small black truffle, minced
1 egg, beaten
breadcrumbs

Preheat oven to 400°F (200°C).
In a saucepan bring water to
a boil with the butter. Whisk in
polenta and cook for 5 minutes,
stirring constantly. Add cheese
to polenta and continue stirring
until the cheese melts. Remove
from heat. Add salt, pepper and
truffle and let cool.
Stir in the egg.
Butter 4 ramequins and coat
with breadcrumbs. Transfer
polenta mixture to ramequins
and bake for 20 minutes or until
the tops begin to brown. Let
cool 5 minutes and invert onto
serving plates.

Canapés with Walnut Sauce

Preparation time 15 minutes
Cooking time 10 minutes
Wine *Val D'Aosta Pinot Grigio*

2 cups (7 oz or 200 g) walnuts
3 tbsps butter
3 sage leaves
1 tbsp heavy cream
3.5 oz (100 g) sheep's milk
 ricotta
salt and pepper
8 slices of brioche bread

Grind the walnuts in a food
processor.
Melt butter in a small saucepan,
add sage and continue to cook
until the butter browns. Add
ground walnuts and let toast
briefly. Remove sage leaves and
pour a little water into the pan.
Let cook for 5 minutes and
then add the cream. Remove
from heat and let cool.
Add ricotta cheese, salt and
pepper. Mix well. Spread the
cream on the sliced brioche
bread.
Serve immediately.

48

Pork Terrine
with Savoy Cabbage and Carrots

Preparation time 20 minutes
Cooking time 50 minutes
Wine *Nebbiolo d'Alba*

2 tbsps raisins
1/2 cup (120 ml) Marsala wine
4 Savoy cabbage leaves
14 oz (400 g) ground pork
4 oz (120 g) soft salami, diced
3 tbsps extra-virgin olive oil
salt and pepper
3 carrots, peeled, boiled and
 julienned
7 tbsps cooked grape must

Preheat oven to 375°F (190°C).
Soak raisins in the Marsala.
Bring a large pot of salted water to boil and briefly blanch the
Savoy cabbage leaves. Let cool.
In a bowl mix the pork, salami, drained raisins, oil, salt and pepper.
Line a loaf pan with parchment paper. Spread a third of meat
mixture in pan, and layer half of the carrots and cabbage leaves
on top. Cover with meat and then layer the rest of the carrots and
cabbage leaves and cover with the last third of the meat. Press
down firmly to form an even layer. Place a weight on top of the
terrine. Set loaf pan in a large baking dish and fill with hot water.
Transfer dish to oven and bake for 20 minutes. Remove from the
oven and let cool for a few minutes. Invert onto a serving dish and
drizzle with grape must.

Stuffed "Coccoi Prena" Bread

(SARDINIA)

Note *Fiscidu is an aged goat's milk cheese from the island of Sardinia. It is made from leftover acidic curds. The curds are left to dry for two days and then matured in brine for a few days.*

Preparation time 25 minutes
Cooking time 40 minutes
Wine *Carignano del Sulcis Rosato*

50

DOUGH
2 tbsps (0.9 oz or 25 g) dried yeast
1/2 cup (120 ml) warm water
4 cups (1 lb or 500 g) plain flour
salt

FILLING
2 small potatoes, boiled and peeled
1 onion, diced
1 garlic clove, minced
3 tbsps extra-virgin olive oil
4 tbsps fiscidu cheese, grated
mint, torn into small pieces

Preheat oven to 400°F (200°C).
Disolve yeast in water. Mound flour on a wooden board. Make a well in the centre and add dissolved yeast and salt. Mix to form a smooth and uniform dough, adding more water if necessary. Cover and let rise for 1 hour.
Mash potatoes into a mixing bowl using a potato ricer. Add onion, garlic, oil, cheese and mint. Mix until smooth.
Roll dough into a thin sheet and place on an oiled baking sheet. Spread filling over half the dough and fold over to close.
Pinch edges to seal.
Bake for 40-50 minutes. Slice and serve immediately.

Tirtlen
(Trentino-Alto Adige)

Preparation time 40 minutes
Cooking time 30 minutes
Wine *Sorni Rosso*

DOUGH
1¼ cups (7 oz or 200 g) rye flour
1½ cups plus 1½ tbsps (7 oz or
 200 g) plain flour
salt
1 tbsp extra-virgin olive oil
milk

FILLING
7 oz (200 g) spinach,
 blanched and chopped
7 oz (200 g) ricotta
salt
sunflower oil for frying

Sift the flours on a work surface and add salt. Make a well in the centre of the flour and add olive oil and milk. Mix to form a soft and uniform dough, adding more milk if necessary. Form dough into a ball and let rest for 30 minutes.
Roll dough into a log, slice into rounds and roll out each round.
In a mixing bowl, combine spinach, ricotta and salt. Mix well.
Place 1 tablespoon of filling in the centre of each dough round and cover with another round of dough. Using a fork, press to seal the edges.
Heat sunflower oil in a deep frying pan and fry the tirtlen until they are golden-brown. Remove with a slotted spoon and drain on paper towels. Serve immediately.

Rosemary Breadsticks

Preparation time 10 minutes
Cooking time 4 minutes
Wine *Elba Bianco*

1 cup plus 3 tbsps (5.3 oz
 or 150 g) plain flour
4 tbsps sunflower oil
2 tbsps extra-virgin olive oil
2 rosemary sprigs, minced
4 tbsps warm water
sea salt

52

Preheat oven to 485°F (250°C).
Mound the flour on a work surface and make a well in the centre.
Add the sunflower oil and olive oil to the centre of the well. Add
the minced rosemary and warm water. Mix to combine, forming a
ropey, coarse dough.
Knead the dough vigorously by hand on a floured surface, adding
more flour if the dough seems too sticky. Continue kneading until
the dough becomes smooth and elastic.
Wrap the dough in plastic wrap and let it rest in the refrigerator for
20 minutes.
Remove from the refrigerator and divide into smaller portions. Roll
each portion into a long stick. Lay on a baking sheet and bake for
4 minutes.
Let cool before serving. Serve as pre-dinner snacks with drinks.

Provola and Vegetable Strudel

Preparation time 40 minutes
Cooking time 30 minutes
Wine *Sicilia Chardonnay*
♟ ♟

Serves 8

DOUGH
2 cups (8.8 oz or 250 g)
 plain flour
1 egg
3 tbsps butter
3½ tbsps water
salt

FILLING
1 red bell pepper
1 yellow bell pepper
3 zucchini, julienned
2 tbsps butter
4 tbsps grated Parmesan
thyme leaves
salt and pepper
5.5 oz (150 g) smoked provola
 cheese, thinly sliced

53

Preheat oven to 400°F (200°C).
Mix dough ingredients together in a large bowl or mixer to form
a smooth and uniform dough. Form a ball, wrap in plastic wrap
and let rest in a cool place.
Roast bell peppers, peel, deseed and remove pith. Let dry on a
clean kitchen towel. When dry, slice thinly.
Bring a pot of salted water to boil and blanch zucchini briefly.
Remove with a slotted spoon and let dry on paper towels.
Roll out dough into a large rectangle. Brush the edges with melted
butter and sprinkle 1 tablespoon of Parmesan in the centre. Cover
with a layer of zucchini, sprinkle with 1 tablespoon Parmesan,
thyme, salt and pepper. Add a layer of provola. Cover provola with
a layer of roasted pepper and sprinkle with Parmesan, thyme, salt
and pepper. Add a final layer of provola. Roll up the strudel and
seal the ends. Place on a baking sheet. Brush with melted butter
and poke small holes in the top. Bake for 25-30 minutes. Let cool
for 5 minutes.

Truffle and Vin Santo Pâté

Preparation time 20 minutes
Coooking time 15 minutes
Wine *Verduzzo di Ramandolo*

10.5 oz (300 g) chicken livers
3 tbsps white vinegar
7 tbsps butter
1/2 onion, minced
1/2 cup (120 ml) vin santo
2 sage leaves
1 black truffle, shaved
salt and pepper
toasted bread
basil leaves

54

Let chicken livers soak in cold water with the vinegar for 5 minutes, then rinse and pat dry.
Heat 2 tablespoons butter in a large frying pan, add onion and sauté until onion is transparent. Add chicken livers and vin santo. Let wine evaporate. Add sage leaves, truffle and salt and pepper to taste.
Let cook 2-3 minutes.
Remove sage leaves. Remove from heat and puree the mixture with the rest of the butter cut into small pieces. Let cool. Serve with toasted bread, garnished with basil leaves.

Mushroom and Bell Pepper Toasts

Preparation time 15 minutes
Cooking time 10 minutes
Wine *Ribolla Gialla*

1 bell pepper
3 large white button mushrooms,
 finely sliced
juice of 1/2 lemon
2 tbsps extra-virgin olive oil
salt
parsley, minced
pepper
8 slices bread

Preheat oven to 400°F (200°C).
Roast or grill the bell pepper, either in a hot oven, under the broiler, over an open flame or in a cast-iron grill pan until the skin is blackened. Place in a plastic bag and close. Let steam for at least 10 minutes, then peel, remove the white pith, deseed and chop finely.
In a small bowl mix the sliced mushrooms, lemon juice, olive oil and a pinch of salt. Add the roast bell pepper, minced parsley and pepper to taste.
Using a circular cookie cutter, cut out rounds from the bread slices.
Toast the bread rounds in a hot oven or under the broiler until golden-brown and top with mushroom-pepper mixture. Serve immediately.

Spicy Chicken Wings

Preparation time 15 minutes
Cooking time 8 minutes
Wine *Terre di Franciacorta Rosso*

16 chicken wings
1/2 tsp garlic powder
1/2 tsp cayenne pepper
paprika
parsley leaves
salt and pepper

Singe the chicken wings over an open flame to remove any feathers. Rinse the wings and pat dry with paper towels.
Preheat a barbecue or grill.
Mix the garlic powder, cayenne pepper, paprika, parsley leaves and salt and pepper to taste.
Sprinkle the spice mixture over the chicken wings. Refrigerate for 10 minutes.
Place the chicken wings on the grill and let cook for 4 minutes on each side, turning twice during the cooking. Serve immediately.

Asiago, Ricotta and Ham Bites

Preparation time 15 minutes
Cooking time 3 minutes
Wine *Alto Adige Gewürztraminer*

12 oz (350 g) ricotta
salt and pepper
extra-virgin olive oil
3.5 oz (100 g) Asiago cheese, diced
7 oz (200 g) ham, diced
breadcrumbs (optional)
sesame seeds, toasted

Beat the ricotta until it becomes creamy. Stir in salt, pepper and a little olive oil.
Add the Asiago cheese and ham and mix well. If the mixture seems to thin, add a few tablespoonfuls of breadcumbs.
Form small balls of the cheese mixture, roll each ball in the toasted sesame seeds and place on a serving plate.
The cheese bites may be served with toasted bread.

58

Baked Winter Squash with Green Beans and Goat's Cheese

Preparation time 20 minutes
Cooking time 1 hour
Wine *Aprilia Bianco*

SQUASH
1.3 lb (600 g) sweet winter
 squash, peeled
2 tbsps plain flour
3 tbsps grated Parmesan
2 egg whites
nutmeg, grated
salt and pepper
1 knob of butter
2 tbsps breadcrumbs

GREEN BEANS
7 oz (200 g) green beans,
 blanched
4 tbsps extra-virgin olive oil
1 tsp cumin seeds
salt

GARNISH
8.5 oz (240 g) goat's cheese,
 sliced
pepper
thyme leaves

Preheat oven to 350°F (180°C).
Slice squash into wedges and place in a well-oiled baking dish.
Cover with aluminum foil and bake until the squash is soft. Puree
squash and transfer to a mixing bowl. Add flour, Parmesan
cheese, egg whites, nutmeg, salt and pepper and mix well.
Butter a baking dish and coat with breadcrumbs. Pour in squash
mixture and level off using a damp spatula. Bake for 35 minutes.
Meanwhile, dress green beans with olive oil, cumin and salt.
Remove squash from the oven and slice into wedges. Serve with
green beans and a slice of goat's cheese. Sprinkle with pepper
and thyme leaves.

Chicken Liver and Mushoom Terrine on Mixed Greens

Preparation time 25 minutes
Cooking time 1 hour
Wine *Alto Adige Gewürztraminer*
♟

TERRINE
2 small yellow-fleshed
 potatoes, boiled and peeled
9 oz (250 g) chicken livers
7 tbsps white wine vinegar
3 tbsps extra-virgin olive oil
1 onion, minced
salt and pepper

1 garlic clove, minced
$2^2/_3$ cups (7 oz or 200g) thickly
sliced mushrooms
parsley, chopped
1 egg

GREENS
mixed salad leaves
extra-virgin olive oil
vinegar
salt

60

Preheat oven to 350°F (180°C).
In a large mixing bowl mash potatoes with a fork.
Meanwhile, soak chicken livers in cold water and vinegar. Rinse
well. Heat 1 tablespoon olive oil in a large frying pan, add onion
and let cook over low heat. Add livers and sauté for 5 minutes.
Add salt and pepper. Remove from heat and let cool.
Heat 2 tablespoons olive oil in a frying pan. Add garlic, mushrooms
and parsley. Sauté until mushrooms soften.
Add mushroom mixture to potatoes, then add liver mixture and
egg. Mix well. Line a loaf pan with parchment paper and fill with
terrine mixture. Bake for 20 minutes.
Let cool. Unmold terrine and slice. Serve on a bed of mixed greens
dressed with olive oil, vinegar and salt.

Chestnut, Ricotta and Speck Ham Tartlets

Preparation time 25 minutes
Cooking time 18 minutes
Wine *Alto Adige Santa Maddalena*

DOUGH
1 cup plus 3 tbsps (5.3 oz or
 150 g) plain flour
5 tbsps butter, diced
1 egg yolk
salt

FILLING
5.5 oz (150 g) ricotta cheese
salt and pepper
1 sprig thyme, minced
1 tbsp light extra-virgin olive oil
4 tbsps (2 oz or 60 g) finely
 chopped cooked chestnuts
2 oz (50 g) speck ham, thinly
 sliced and minced

Preheat oven to 325°F (170°C).
Mound flour on a wooden board. Make a well in the centre and add butter, egg yolk, salt and a little ice water. Quickly mix the dough, gradually adding a little more water if necessary. As soon as the dough comes together wrap it in plastic wrap and refrigerate for 30 minutes.
Meanwhile, beat the ricotta with salt, pepper, thyme and olive oil. Add the chestnuts (reserve some for garnish) and speck ham. Set aside in a cool place.
Roll out the dough and use it to line miniature tart tins. Place a few dried beans in each tartlet to avoid air bubbles while baking. Bake for 18 minutes or until golden-brown. Remove from the oven and let cool. Fill tartlets with ricotta cream. Garnish with chopped chestnuts.

Mini Skewers with Clams and Polenta

Preparation time 25 minutes
Cooking time 20 minutes
Wine *Trentino Müller Thurgau*

12 oz (350 g) clams
salt
**3/4 cup (5.5 oz or 150 g) instant
 polenta**
3 tbsps extra-virgin olive oil
1 garlic clove, minced
1/2 red chilli pepper, minced
5-6 cherry tomatoes, diced
parsley, chopped
sunflower oil

Wash the clams in cold water, drain, then let them soak in cold salted water for 30 minutes.
Meanwhile bring salted water to a boil in a saucepan.
Whisk in polenta and cook, stirring constantly. Pour polenta into a square or rectangular baking dish.
Heat olive oil in a frying pan and add garlic and chilli. Add the clams and cover. Cook over high heat for 3 minutes. Add cherry tomatoes and parsley.
Cut polenta into small cubes.
Heat sunflower oil in a frying pan and fry polenta cubes until they are just brown.
Skewer the polenta cubes and clams, alternating them.
Strain the clam cooking liquid and serve in small bowls with skewers.

Chanterelle Flan

Preparation time 20 minutes
Cooking time 40 minutes
Wine *Ribolla Gialla*

2 tbsps extra-virgin olive oil
1 garlic clove, smashed
3 cups (9 oz or 250 g) chanterelle
 mushrooms, cleaned
 and chopped
parsley, minced
salt and pepper
1¼ cups (300 ml) water
3/4 cup (5.3 oz or 150 g)
 semolina flour
5 tbsps butter
2 eggs
1 tbsp grated Parmesan
breadcrumbs

63

Preheat oven to 375°F (190°C).
Heat oil in a large frying pan, add garlic clove, mushrooms and parsley. Sauté until mushrooms soften. Add salt and pepper to taste.
Bring water to boil in a small pot with a pinch of salt. Whisk in semolina flour. Let cook for a few minutes, stirring constantly. Add 3 tablespoons of butter and the cooked mushrooms. Remove from heat and continue stirring while the mixture cools.
Beat eggs and Parmesan cheese in a small bowl. Add to mushroom mixture and mix well. Butter 4 ramequins with remaining butter and coat with breadcrumbs. Fill the ramequins with the mushroom mixture.
Bake for 25 minutes. Serve immediately.

Potato Fritters with Lumpfish Caviar

Preparation time 30 minutes
Cooking time 30 minutes
Wine *Metodo Classico*
Franciacorta Rosè

2/3 cup (150 ml) water
2 tbsps butter
salt
3/4 cup (3.2 oz or 90 g)
 plain flour
2 eggs
1 small starchy potato (4 oz or
 125g), boiled, peeled and
 mashed with a potato ricer
juice of 1 lemon
1/2 cup (120 ml) heavy cream
4 cups (1 l) peanut oil
2 oz (50 g) lumpfish caviar
 chives, chopped

64

Cut out 4-inch (10 cm) squares of wax paper and lightly butter them.
Bring water, butter and a pinch of salt to a boil in a saucepan.
Add flour and stir vigorously with a wooden spoon until the mixture pulls away from the sides of the pan. Let cool. Add eggs one at a time, mixing well, and then add mashed potato. Transfer mixture into a pastry bag with a star tip and form rounds on the parchment paper squares.
Place lemon juice and a pinch of salt and pepper in a mixing bowl. Add cream and whisk into soft peaks. Refrigerate.
Heat peanut oil in a high-edged frying pan. When very hot, add potato rounds on the wax paper. Once immersed in oil remove wax paper. Fry potato rounds until golden brown. Drain with a slotted spoon onto paper towels.
Place potato fritters on a plate and top with whipped cream and lumpfish caviar. Sprinkle with chives.

Fried Polenta
with Wild Mushroom Ragù

Preparation time 20 minutes
Cooking time 40 minutes
Wine *Bardolino Chiaretto*

2 cups (500 ml) water
salt and pepper
1 cup plus 2 tbsps (7 oz or 200 g)
 instant polenta
3 tbsps extra-virgin olive oil
1/2 yellow onion, finely diced
1 celery stalk, finely diced
1/2 carrot, finely diced
2 sage leaves, minced
4 cups (10 oz or 280 g) diced
 honey mushrooms or other
 wild mushrooms
7 tbsps hot vegetable broth
4 tbsps tomato paste
parsley, chopped
sunflower oil

Bring salted water to a boil in a small pot and whisk in instant
polenta. Continue to whisk and let cook for 25 minutes.
Line a loaf pan with parchment paper and pour in the polenta. Let
cool for 3 hours.
Heat olive oil in a frying pan and add onion, celery, carrot and
sage. Add mushrooms and boiling broth. Let simmer for 10
minutes. Add tomato paste, parsley, salt and pepper. Reduce until
ragù becomes thick and remove from heat. Let cool 20 minutes.
Meanwhile, slice polenta and fry in sunflower oil until golden-brown
on both sides. Remove with a slotted spoon and let dry on paper
towels. Sprinkle salt over the fried polenta.
Spoon mushroom ragù onto the fried polenta slices and serve
immediately.

Potato Salad with Yellow Pepper Cream

Note *The burrata can be replaced by feta or shavings of ricotta salata.*

Preparation time 15 minutes
Cooking time 60 minutes
Wine *Lagrein Rosato*

SALAD
4 red onions
1 potato, boiled, peeled
 and chopped
1 burrata cheese, sliced
extra-virgin olive oil
pepper

YELLOW PEPPER CREAM
2 tbsps extra-virgin olive oil
1 garlic clove, sliced
1 anchovy fillet in oil, chopped
2 yellow bell peppers, roasted
 and peeled
1 cup (180 ml) cold water
salt and pepper

Preheat oven to 350°F (180°C).
Roast onions on a baking sheet for 30-40 minutes, until they are soft. Cool, peel and slice.
Make the pepper cream: Heat the oil in a frying pan and add the garlic and anchovy. Add bell peppers and water. Let simmer 20 minutes, stirring frequently. Remove from heat and puree.
Add salt and pepper to taste.
Place 1 spoonful of pepper cream on each plate and top with potatoes, onions and burrata cheese. Drizzle with olive oil and sprinkle with freshly ground pepper.

Endive Tarts with Ham

Preparation time 20 minutes
Cooking time 35 minutes
Wine *Lambrusco di Sorbara*

2 heads of Belgian endive
3 tbsps butter
1/2 garlic clove
salt and pepper
2 eggs
3/4 cup (180 ml) milk
1 tbsp cornstarch
9 oz (250 g) pie crust dough
 (p. 1093)
butter
ham, sliced

Preheat oven to 350°F (180°C).
Bring a large pot of salted water to a boil. Add endive leaves and blanch for a few minutes. Drain and dry on a clean kitchen towel. Melt butter in a frying pan and add the garlic clove. Let brown and then remove. Add endive and let cook 5 minutes. Add salt and pepper.
In a mixing bowl whisk eggs, milk, cornstarch and a pinch of salt together.
Roll out the dough and cut out 4 rounds. Butter and flour 4 small tart tins. Place dough in tins and pierce with a fork. Pour endive mixture into tarts and then pour egg mixture over the endive. Bake for 20 minutes. Serve immediately with a few slices of ham.

Truffle, Porcini and Pine Nut Spread

Preparation time 20 minutes
Cooking time 20 minutes

1 cup plus 2 tbsps (5.3 oz
 or 150 g) butter, diced
1 shallot, minced
3 large fresh porcini mushrooms,
 cleaned and chopped
salt and pepper
2 tbsps pine nuts
1 egg, hard-boiled
1/2 black truffle, shaved
4 slices Tuscan-style bread,
 cut into quarters

68

Heat 1/2 of the butter in a medium-sized frying pan, add the minced shallot and let cook until soft. Add mushrooms and sauté for 10 minutes. Season with salt and pepper to taste.
Toast the pine nuts in a non-stick frying pan and stir them into the mushroom mixture. Let cool.
Puree the cooled mushroom mixture with the remaining butter, the crumbled hard-boiled egg and truffle shavings.
Pour mixture into a ceramic bowl and refrigerate.
Toast the Tuscan-style bread slices until golden-brown on both sides.
Remove the spread from the refrigerator 20 minutes before serving to bring to room temperature.
Spread on toasted bread and serve immediately.

Colourful Tartlets

Preparation time 20 minutes
Cooking time 10 minutes

Serves 6

Dough
2 cups (8.8 oz or 250 g)
 plain flour
1 cup plus 1 tbsp (4.4 oz
 or 125 g) butter, diced
1 egg yolk
1 pinch of salt
2 tbsps water

FILLING
7 oz (200 g) Asiago cheese,
 cubed
1/2 onion, diced
1/2 red bell pepper, chopped
1/2 yellow bell pepper, chopped
1 slice (about 3 oz or 80 g)
 ham, chopped
3 tbsps diced celery
2 tbsps chopped cornichons
salt and pepper
4 tbsps extra-virgin olive oil
chives, chopped
parsley, chopped

Sift flour onto work surface. Place butter, egg yolk and salt in the centre and mix. When the dough has a coarse consistency add water and quickly mix to form a smooth and uniform dough. Wrap in plastic wrap and refrigerate for 30 minutes.
Preheat oven to 350°F (180°C).
Roll out dough into a thin sheet, cut dough into rounds and place in tart tins. Pierce with a fork and fill with pie weights or dried beans. Bake for 15 minutes. Remove from oven and let cool.
Mix Asiago cheese, onion, bell pepper, ham, celery and cornichons. Add salt, pepper, olive oil and chopped chives. Toss to coat.
Fill tart shells with ham and pepper mixture. Garnish with chopped parsley and serve.

Bucatini with Guanciale (LAZIO)

Preparation time 5 minutes
Cooking time 30 minutes
Wine *Cerveteri Rosso*

salt and pepper
3½ tbsps butter
1 onion, diced
4 oz (120 g) guanciale
 or pancetta, chopped
12.5 oz (350 g) bucatini pasta
3 tbsps grated pecorino
3 tbsps grated Parmesan
parsley, chopped

70

Bring a large pot of salted
water to a boil.
Meanwhile, heat the butter
in a frying pan. Add the onion
and brown. Add guanciale.
Boil bucatini until they are
cooked but still firm (al dente).
Drain, reserving a few spoonfuls
of the cooking water.
Add pasta and cooking water
to the guanciale and sauté
for a few minutes.
Sprinkle pasta with the pecorino,
Parmesan, pepper and chopped
parsley. Serve immediately.

Emilian Egg Soup

Preparation time 15 minutes
Cooking time 10 minutes
Wine *Lambrusco di Sorbara*

3 eggs
nutmeg, grated
salt
1 cup (5.5 oz or 150 g)
 breadcrumbs
2 cups (7 oz or 200 g) grated
 Parmesan, plus extra for garnish
beef broth

Beat the eggs, nutmeg and salt
in a mixing bowl.
Add the breadcrumbs and mix.
Add Parmesan cheese and
mix. The mixture should be
smooth but firm. Add broth or
breadcrumbs if necessary.
Pass the mixture through
a potato ricer to form long
ropes of pasta.
Bring the beef broth to a boil,
add the pasta and boil.
The pasta is cooked
when it rises to the surface.
Serve in soup bowls with
grated Parmesan cheese.

Carcerato
(Tuscany)

Note *Tuscan bread is traditionally crusty and unsalted. The lack of salt dates back to times when bread was made at home and salt was an unaffordable luxury. This unsalted bread is a staple of modern Tuscan recipes like* pappa al pomodoro, *Tuscan bread and tomato soup.*

Preparation time 25 minutes
Cooking time 3 hours 20 minutes
Wine *Parrina Rosso*

10.5 oz (300 g) tripe
3/4 cup (3.5 oz or 100 g)
 diced onion
3/4 cup (3.5 oz or 100 g)
 diced carrot
3/4 cup (3.5 oz or 100 g)
 diced celery
mixed herbs
6 cups (1.5 l) water
10.5 oz (300 g) Tuscan-style
 bread, sliced
2 tomatoes, peeled and deseeded
salt and pepper
extra-virgin olive oil
aged pecorino cheese, grated

Wash the tripe, rinse well under running water, cook briefly and let soak again in clean water overnight.
Boil tripe, onion, carrot, celery and herbs in the water for 3 hours to make a broth. Strain the broth.
Place sliced bread in a large saucepan. Pour broth over the bread. Add tomatoes, salt and pepper and let cook over low heat until the soup is smooth. Adjust salt and pepper.
Pour soup into bowls and drizzle with olive oil. Sprinkle with pecorino cheese and serve.

Creamy Chanterelle and Potato Soup

Note *Chanterelle mushrooms are small and yellow. They usually grow at the base of pine trees from late summer through fall.*

Preparation time 15 minutes
Cooking time 35 minutes
Wine *Friuli Latisana Chardonnay*
♟ ♟

6 tbsps extra-virgin olive oil
1/2 onion, finely diced
1 large starchy potato, diced
4 cups (1 l) vegetable broth
salt and pepper
3 tbsps grated Parmesan
1 garlic clove
2 cups (7 oz or 200 g) chanterelle
  mushrooms, cleaned and chopped
1 tbsp mixed herbs
  (parsley, rosemary, thyme), minced

Heat 2 tablespoons oil in a large frying pan. Sauté onion. Add potato and broth. Add salt to taste and let cook 20-25 minutes. Add Parmesan cheese and puree.
Heat the rest of the oil in a frying pan and add garlic clove and mushrooms. Let cook for 5 minutes. Add salt, cover and cook for another 5 minutes. Remove garlic clove. Add minced herbs.
Pour puree into bowls. Place a spoonful of mushrooms in the centre. Drizzle with olive oil and freshly ground pepper.
Serve immediately.

Chestnut Soup

Preparation time 15 minutes
Cooking time 1 hour
Wine *Alto Adige Schiava*

5.5 oz (150 g) dried chestnuts,
 soaked overnight
4 cups (1 l) water
salt
4 cups (1 l) milk
3 tbsps cornmeal
5.5 oz (150 g) crusty bread, cubed
3 oz (80 g) lardo, thinly sliced
rosemary, minced
cinnamon, ground

Boil chestnuts in 4 cups (1 l)
of lightly salted water for
40 minutes. Add milk and
bring back to a boil. Whisk in
cornmeal, stirring continuously.
Cook for 20 minutes.
Wrap each cube of bread in
half a slice of lardo. Place on a
baking sheet and sprinkle with
rosemary. Broil for 2-3 minutes.
Pour soup into bowls and top
with the lardo croutons and a
pinch of cinnamon.
Serve immediately.

Leek Soup with Croutons

Preparation time 20 minutes
Cooking time 30 minutes
Wine *Ribolla Gialla*

1 tbsp extra-virgin olive oil
1 large leek, cleaned and thinly
 sliced
4 cups (1 l) vegetable broth
2 small potatoes, cleaned,
 peeled and thinly sliced
1 tbsp rice miso
3 slices crusty bread, diced

Heat oil in a saucepan, add leek
and cook over low heat until
transparent. Add 1 tablespoon
vegetable broth. Add potatoes
and the rest of the broth,
reserving 1 tablespoon. Cook
for 20 minutes and puree.
Dissolve miso in reserved
spoonful of hot broth. Add to
soup and mix.
Toast bread under the broiler.
Pour soup into bowls and
top with croutons. Serve
immediately.

73

Cream of Spinach Soup with Mushrooms and Pine Nuts

Note *Due to their high fat content, pine nuts can easily become rancid. It is best to buy bulk pine nuts that can be sampled before purchasing.*

Preparation time 15 minutes
Cooking time 30 minutes
Wine *Ribolla Gialla*

4 tbsps extra-virgin olive oil
1 onion, diced
1 lb (450 g) spinach
4 cups (1 l) vegetable broth
salt
1 garlic clove
2 cups (9 oz or 250 g) oyster
 mushrooms, cleaned
 and chopped in irregular pieces
6 slices French bread, diced
1/4 cup (1 oz or 20 g) pine nuts
pepper
nutmeg, grated
3 tbsps grated Parmesan

Heat 1/2 the oil in a large frying pan and add the onion. Sauté until soft. Add spinach and cover with broth. Bring to a boil, add salt and cook for 20 minutes.
Heat the remaining oil in another frying pan. Add the garlic clove and mushrooms. Sauté for a few minutes, adding a little water if necessary.
Toast bread and pine nuts in a non-stick frying pan.
Puree spinach mixture and add salt, pepper, nutmeg and Parmesan cheese. Puree again for 1 minute.
Pour soup into bowls and place a spoonful of mushrooms in the centre. Serve the toasted pine nuts and croutons on the side.

Porcini Cappelletti in Truffle Broth

Preparation time 40 minutes
Cooking time 25 minutes
Wine *Gutturnio Classico*

CAPPELLETTI
1¾ cups (7.7 oz or 220 g)
 plain flour
2 eggs
salt
2 cups (500 ml) chicken broth

FILLING
2 tbsps extra-virgin olive oil
1 shallot, minced

3 fresh porcini mushrooms,
 cleaned and diced
thyme leaves
salt and pepper
1 egg
1 tbsp grated Parmesan
1 tbsp breadcrumbs

GARNISH
1 small black truffle

Mound flour on work surface and make a well in the centre. Break eggs into the well and add a pinch of salt. Mix to form a smooth and uniform dough. Cover with plastic wrap and refrigerate for 30 minutes.
Heat oil in a large frying pan. Add shallot and cook until soft. Add mushrooms and cook until tender. Add thyme leaves, salt and pepper to taste and a few tablespoons of hot water. Let cool.
Puree mixture with the remaining egg, Parmesan cheese and breadcrumbs.
Using a pasta machine, roll dough into long, paper-thin rectangles. Place 1/2 teaspoon of filing at 2 inch (5 cm) intervals on the pasta. Cover with a second sheet of pasta and seal edges. Cut out cappelletti using a rolling cutter.
Bring chicken broth to a boil and cook cappelletti for 1-2 minutes. Serve cappelletti in broth with shaved truffle.

Pancetta and Rice Soup

Preparation time 10 minutes
Cooking time 25 minutes
Wine *Albana di Romagna*

4 tbsps extra-virgin olive oil
5.5 oz (150 g) unaged pancetta,
 diced
1 onion, diced
1½ cups (10.5 oz or 300 g) rice
4 cups (1 l) vegetable broth
salt and pepper
1/2 head butter lettuce, washed
 chopped
parsley, minced
3.5 oz (100 g) crusty bread,
 diced and toasted

Heat 2 tablespoons oil in a
frying pan. Add pancetta and
brown.
Heat remaining oil in a large
saucepan and sauté the
onion. Add rice and toast for 2
minutes. Add 1 ladleful of broth
and salt and pepper to taste.
Bring to a boil. Lower heat and
cook for 15-18 minutes, adding
broth little by little.
Add pancetta and lettuce. Stir
and sprinkle with parsley and
croutons. Serve immediately.

Asiago Cream with Croutons

Preparation time 25 minutes
Cooking time 20 minutes
Wine *Friuli Carso Terrano*

6 tbsps butter
1/2 onion, diced
1 garlic clove, minced
2 tbsps plain flour
3½ cups (850 ml) beef broth
5.5 oz (150 g) Asiago cheese,
 shaved
7 tbsps heavy cream
salt and pepper
extra-virgin olive oil
2½ cups (2 oz or 50 g) arugula
3.5 oz (100 g) crusty bread, diced

Heat 1/2 the butter in a
saucepan. Sauté onion and
garlic. Sprinkle with flour and
stir. Pour in broth and bring to
a boil. Cook for 15 minutes.
Add cheese and return to boil.
Remove from heat and add
cream, salt and pepper.
Heat the oil in a frying pan. Add
arugula and sauté briefly.
Heat the remaining butter in a
frying pan and brown the bread.
Pour soup into bowls and top
with croutons and arugula.

Cream of Winter Squash Soup

Preparation time 15 minutes
Cooking time 30 minutes
Wine *Malvasia Istriana*

1 tbsp sesame oil
1/2 onion, diced
1 lb (450 g) winter squash,
 peeled and diced
1 rosemary sprig
2 cups (500 ml) vegetable broth
salt and pepper
2 oz (60 g) sliced bread
nutmeg, grated

Heat sesame oil in a large
saucepan. Add onion and then
squash and rosemary sprig.
Sauté for 5 minutes. Remove
rosemary, add broth and salt
and pepper to taste. Let cook
for 20 minutes over medium
heat.
Toast bread.
Puree the soup until smooth.
Pour into bowls and garnish
with nutmeg. Serve with
toasted bread.

Leek and Oatmeal Soup

Preparation time 10 minutes
Cooking time 25 minutes
Wine *Alto Adige Santa Maddalena*

4 cups (1 l) vegetable broth
1 potato, diced
3 carrots, diced
1 leek, thickly sliced
2½ cups (9 oz or 250 g)
 rolled oats
salt and pepper
parsley, minced

Bring broth to a boil in a large
pot. Add potato, carrots and
leek. Cook for 25 minutes. Add
rolled oats and cook for another
10 minutes until the soup
becomes thick. Add salt and
pepper to taste.
Garnish with parsley and serve
immediately.

Note *For a more flavourful soup,
use beef broth instead
of vegetable broth.*

Winter Squash Soup with Prawns

Preparation time 10 minutes
Cooking time 20 minutes
Wine *Ribolla Gialla*

SOUP
3 tbsps extra-virgin olive oil
1/2 onion, diced
14 oz (400 g) winter squash,
 peeled and chopped
7 tbsps dry white wine
2/3 cup (150 ml) fish broth
salt and pepper
2/3 cup (150 ml) heavy cream

PRAWNS
3 tbsps extra-virgin olive oil
6.5 oz (180 g) prawns, cleaned,
 deveined and shelled
parsley, chopped
salt and pepper

78

Heat the oil for the soup in a large frying pan. Add the diced onion and chopped squash. Sauté for 5 minutes, then add the white wine and reduce slightly.
Add broth and let cook for 10 minutes. Season with salt and pepper to taste and add the heavy cream. Let cook over high heat for 1 minute. Puree with the squash mixture with an immersion blender or in a food processor.
Heat the olive oil for the prawns in a large frying pan. Add the prawns to the frying pan together the chopped parsley and salt and pepper to taste. Let cook for a few minutes.
Add prawns to the soup and serve immediately.

Turbot and Mushroom Soup

Preparation time 15 minutes
Cooking time 1 hour
Wine *Alto Adige Chardonnay*

6 tbsps extra-virgin olive oil
1/2 onion, diced
1 carrot, diced
1 celery stalk, diced
1 tsp curry powder
2 turbot, filleted reserving
 head, tail, bones and skin
3/4 cup (180 ml) dry white wine
2 tomatoes, chopped
parsley, chopped
1 bay leaf
2 garlic cloves, minced
5 cups (14 oz or 400 g) sliced
 mushrooms
1½ tbsps plain flour
4 cups (1 l) water
salt and pepper

Heat 1 tablespoon olive oil in a large pot and add the onion, carrot
and celery. Sauté. Add curry and fish head, tail, bones and skin to
the pot and let brown. Add wine, tomatoes, parsley and bay leaf.
Cover with water and cook for 30 minutes.
Meanwhile, in a large frying pan heat 2 tablespoons oil and add
garlic and mushrooms. Sprinkle with flour and let cook for 10
minutes.
Strain the fish broth and add to the mushrooms. Let boil for 20
minutes.
Meanwhile, heat remaining oil in a large frying pan. Add turbot
fillets and cook for 3-4 minutes. Add salt and pepper to taste.
Puree 1/3 of the soup and return it to the pan.
Serve hot with the turbot fillets.

Winter Squash Soup with Chickpeas and Cavatelli Pasta

Note *To check the ripeness of winter squash, immerse the squash in a container full of water. If the squash floats it is not yet ripe, and if it sinks it is ready to eat.*

Preparation time 20 minutes
Cooking time 40 minutes
Wine *Val d'Aosta Bianco*

CHICKPEAS
3/4 cup (5.5 oz or 150 g)
  dried chickpeas
2 celery stalks with leaves, diced
1 onion, diced
6 sage leaves
cloves

SOUP
7 oz (200 g) winter squash,
  sliced into 1-inch (2 cm) wedges
salt and pepper
2 tbsps extra-virgin olive oil
1/2 yellow onion, diced
1 oz (30 g) pancetta, diced
1 dried red chilli pepper
2/3 cup (3 oz or 80 g) peas
1½ tbsps white wine
broth
4.5 oz (130 g) cavatelli pasta

80

Soak chickpeas for 12 hours. Boil chickpeas with celery, onion, sage and cloves until tender (1 hour 30 minutes in a pressure cooker). Preheat oven to 350°F (180°C).
Place squash on a baking sheet, salt and bake for about 20 minutes. Remove and discard the skin of the squash and dice the pulp.
Heat olive oil in a large pot. Add onion, pancetta and whole chilli pepper. Add the squash, peas and wine. Cook for 10 minutes over low heat. Add the chickpeas and 3 ladlefuls of broth. Continue cooking for 7-8 minutes, adding broth if necessary. Add cavatelli pasta directly to the soup and cook for 8-10 minutes (or according to directions on the pasta package). Add salt and pepper to taste. Serve immediately.

Rustic Mixed Grain Soup

Preparation time 10 minutes
Cooking time 25 minutes
Wine *Lagrein Dunkel*

3 tbsps extra-virgin olive oil
1 onion, diced
1 celery stalk, diced
1 fennel bulb, outer leaves
 removed, diced
thyme leaves
4 cups (1 l) vegetable broth
1 cup (7 oz or 200 g) mixed grains
 (spelt, rice, barley)
salt and pepper
8 slices of crusty bread
2 tbsps smoked ricotta, grated
1 fresh bay leaf, minced
dried red chilli pepper flakes

Heat oil in a large pot. Add onion, celery and fennel and sauté. Add thyme leaves and broth. Bring to a boil and cook for a few minutes. Add mixed grains, salt and pepper and cook for 20 minutes.
Toast the bread.
Pour soup into bowls and garnish with smoked ricotta, bay leaf and chilli flakes.

Carrot and Onion Soup

Preparation time 10 minutes
Cooking time 30 minutes
Wine *Bianco D'Alcamo*

extra-virgin olive oil
2 large onions, thinly sliced
5 large carrots, chopped
1/2 cup (3 oz or 80 g)
 Roma rice
3 cups (700 ml) water
salt
4 slices French bread, diced
 and toasted
oregano

Heat the oil in a large pot. Add the onions and carrots. Sauté for a few minutes.
Add rice, water and salt. Let cook over low heat for 30 minutes, adding water if necessary. Puree the soup.
Place croutons in bowl and sprinkle with salt and oregano. Drizzle with oil. Toss to coat. Serve soup with croutons.

Tagliatelle with Truffles
(UMBRIA)

Note *To make fresh
tagliatelle at home,
mix 4 cups (1 lb or 500 g)
plain flour with 4 eggs to
form a smooth dough. Roll
out the dough with a pasta
machine. Roll up strips of
dough and cut into 1/5-inch
(1/2 cm) slices with a sharp
knife.*

Preparation time 5 minutes
Cooking time 20 minutes
Wine *Torgiano Rosso*

3 tbsps extra-virgin olive oil
2 garlic cloves, peeled
2 oz (50 g) white truffle, shaved
salt
12 oz (350 g) tagliatelle
parsley, minced

Heat the olive oil in a large frying pan. Add the peeled garlic cloves
and sauté until golden-brown. Remove and discard the garlic
cloves and add 3/4 of the truffle shavings. Mix well and remove
from the heat.
Bring a large pot of salted water to a boil. Add the tagliatelle and
cook until just al dente.
Drain and add to the frying pan with the truffles and oil. Toss the
tagliatelle until well coated with the sauce.
Garnish with minced parsley and the remaining shaved truffle.
Serve immediately.

Brescian-Style Ravioli
(LOMBARDY)

Preparation 40 minutes
Cooking time 10 minutes
Wine *Valcalepio Rosso*

1 egg
3 tbsps breadcrumbs
3 tbsps grated Parmesan
ground cinnamon and nutmeg
salt and pepper

FILLING
1 celery stalk, chopped
1 carrot, chopped
5 cups (7 oz or 200 g) Swiss
 chard, shredded
3½ tbsps butter
2 garlic cloves, minced
1 onion, diced
7 oz (200 g) roast beef
2 oz (50 g) prosciutto, sliced
2 oz (50 g) mortadella, sliced

PASTA DOUGH
4 cups (1 lb or 500 g)
 plain flour
3 eggs
2 tbsps extra-virgin olive oil
1 pinch of salt

SAUCE
3½ tbsps butter
sage leaves

Blanch celery, carrot and chard for a few minutes. Drain and puree.
Melt butter in a frying pan. Add garlic, onion and pureed vegetables.
Sauté for a few minutes and transfer to a bowl.
Puree roast beef, prosciutto and mortadella in a food processor and
add to the bowl with the egg, breadcrumbs, Parmesan, spices, salt
and pepper. Mix until smooth.
Mound flour on a work surface and make a well in the centre. Add
the eggs, oil, salt and enough water to form a smooth and uniform
dough. Let rest 30 minutes.
Roll out into a thin sheet and cut into squares. Place 1 spoonful of
filling on each and fold into a triangle. Seal the edges with the tines
of a fork.
Bring a large pot of salted water to boil and cook ravioli for a few
minutes, until they rise to the surface.
Melt butter in a frying pan. Add sage and brown the butter. Transfer
ravioli to the pan and toss to coat. Sprinkle with Parmesan.

Leek and Ricotta Cannelloni with Walnut Sauce

Preparation time 40 minutes
Cooking time 10 minutes
Wine *Alto Adige Gewürztraminer*

PASTA DOUGH
2 cups (8.8 oz or 250 g)
 plain flour
1/3 cup (1.7 oz or 50 g)
 chestnut flour
2 eggs
1 egg yolk
3 tbsps butter, diced
2 tbsps extra-virgin olive oil

FILLING
1 tbsp extra-virgin olive oil
2 large leeks, sliced
2 tbsps water
10.5 oz (300 g) ricotta
5 tbsps grated Parmesan
nutmeg, grated
salt and pepper
3 tbsps butter

SAUCE
1/4 cup (1 oz or 25 g) chopped
 walnuts
3½ tbsps heavy cream
salt and pepper

84

Preheat oven to 350°F (180°C).
Sift the flours onto a work surface and make a well in the centre.
Add eggs, egg yolk, butter and oil and mix to form a uniform
dough. Roll out into a thin sheet and cut into large rectangles.
Heat the oil for the filling in a frying pan; add leeks and water and
cook until tender. Transfer to a bowl to cool. Set aside some leeks.
Mix ricotta and Parmesan with remaining leeks. Add nutmeg, salt
and pepper to taste. Transfer to a pastry bag without the tip.
Bring a large pot of salted water to boil. Cook the pasta rectangles
for 3 minutes. Drain and let cool on a kitchen towel.
Spread the filling along the long side of each rectangle and roll up.
Slice diagonally into 1-inch (2½ cm) slices.
Arrange the slices in a buttered baking dish and brush with melted
butter. Bake for 3-4 minutes.
Meanwhile, mix walnuts, cream, salt, pepper and a little warm
water. Bring to a simmer over low heat. Pour sauce over cannelloni
and garnish with reserved leeks. Serve immediately.

Crêpes with Spinach, Ricotta and Taleggio

Preparation time 30 minutes
Cooking time 20 minutes
Wine *Erbaluce di Caluso*

CRÊPES
2 egg yolks
1½ cups plus 1½ tbsps
 (7 oz or 200 g) plain flour
4 cups (1 l) milk
salt
butter, melted

FILLING
5.5 oz (150 g) ricotta
3 cups (3.5 oz or 100 g) spinach,
 steamed and chopped
salt and pepper
3.5 oz (100 g) taleggio cheese,
 chopped

Preheat oven to 350°F (180°C).
Beat egg yolks and flour in a mixing bowl. Slowly whisk in the milk to form a thin batter. Add salt to taste and let sit 10 minutes.
Heat a 6-inch (15 cm) diameter non-stick pan. Brush the pan with melted butter and add 1 ladleful of batter to the pan. Swirl the pan to form a uniform layer. Flip and cook briefly. Continue making crêpes until the batter is finished.
Mix ricotta and spinach in a bowl. Add salt and pepper to taste.
Fill each crêpe with 2 tablespoons of filling and fold into quarters. Place crêpes in a baking dish and cover with Taleggio cheese. Bake for 20 minutes. Serve immediately.

Radicchio and Amarone Rice Cups

Preparation time 30 minutes
Cooking time 20 minutes
Wine *Amarone della Valpolicella*

CHEESE SAUCE
3 tbsps butter
1 tbsp plain flour
1¼ cups (300 ml) milk
3.5 oz (100 g) Montasio cheese,
 diced
1 egg yolk
salt

RICE
4 tbsps butter
1 onion, thinly sliced
7 oz (200 g) Treviso radicchio,
 sliced
1 tbsp sugar
salt and pepper
3/4 cup (180 ml) Amarone wine
1¼ cups (8.8 oz or 250 g)
 Vialone Nano rice
4 cups (1 l) beef broth
1 cup (3.5 oz or 100 g) grated
 Parmesan

For the cheese sauce, melt the butter in a saucepan. Just as it begins to brown add flour and mix with a wooden spoon. Add milk and Montasio cheese. Bring to a boil. Remove from heat, add egg yolk and puree. Salt the cheese sauce and set aside.

Heat 2 tablespoons butter in a large pan. Add onion and let soften. Add radicchio and sprinkle with sugar and season with salt and pepper. After a few minutes, add the wine and let evaporate. Pour in rice and add broth little by little, cooking for 13-14 minutes. Remove from heat and add the remaining butter and Parmesan cheese. Mix well and add salt and pepper to taste.

Fill 4 small bowls with rice mixture. Let sit for a few minutes, then invert bowls onto plates. Remove bowl and cover rice with cheese sauce. Serve immediately.

Chestnut Dumplings
with Rosemary Pesto

Preparation time 30 minutes
Cooking time 45 minutes
Wine *Bosco Eliceo Bianco Secco*

DUMPLINGS
2 large starchy potatoes, boiled
 and peeled
3/4 cup (3.5 oz or 100 g)
 chestnut flour
1/3 cup (1.7 oz or 50 g) cornstarch
1 egg
salt

PESTO
2 tbsps (1 oz or 30 g)
 pine nuts, plus extra for garnish
rosemary, chopped, plus extra
 for garnish
4 tbsps extra virgin-olive oil
5 tbsps grated pecorino
salt and pepper

Mash the potatoes using a potato ricer. Let cool.
Add the chestnut flour, cornstarch, egg and a pinch of salt to the cooled mashed potatoes. Mix to obtain a uniform dough.
Form the dough into small dumplings and place on a floured work surface or tray.
Using a mortar and pestle or a blender, blend the pine nuts, chopped rosemary, olive oil and grated pecorino. Season with salt and pepper to taste.
Bring a large pot of salted water to a boil. Add the dumplings and boil until they rise to the surface.
Drain and place in a large bowl. Add pesto. Toss to coat. Garnish with rosemary and pine nuts. Serve immediately.

Thyme and Porcini Lasagnas

Preparation time 10 minutes
Cooking time 20 minutes
Wine *Lagrein Rosato*

4 tbsps extra-virgin olive oil
1 shallot, minced
2 large yellow-fleshed potatoes,
 peeled and diced
rosemary, chopped
salt and pepper
1/2 cup (120 ml) mushroom
 or vegetable broth
3 fresh porcini mushrooms,
 cleaned and diced
thyme leaves
16 sheets dry lasagna pasta

Heat oil in a saucepan.
Add shallot and sauté.
Add potatoes, rosemary and
salt and pepper to taste,
add broth then cook for 7-8
minutes. Add mushrooms
and thyme.
Bring a large pot of salted
water to a boil. Boil lasagna
sheets and drain.
Form individual lasagnas on
each plate by alternating layers
of pasta and potato-mushroom
sauce.
Serve immediately.

Broccoli-Bottarga Spaghettini

Preparation time 20 minutes
Cooking time 25 minutes
Wine *Cirò Bianco*

13.5 oz (380 g) spaghettini
1 head of broccoli,
 chopped into florets
3 tbsps extra-virgin olive oil
1 garlic clove, smashed
1 white spring onion, sliced
15 fresh anchovies,
 heads and backbones removed
2 San Marzano or plum
 tomatoes, diced
1 tsp bottarga
salt and pepper

Bring a large pot of salted
water to boil. Blanch broccoli
for a few minutes. Drain, with
sloted spoon, add spaghettini
and cook until al dente.
Meanwhile, heat oil and sauté
garlic and spring onion. Add
broccoli and salt. Sauté for 5-6
minutes and add anchovies,
tomatoes, a few spoonfuls of
pasta cooking water, salt and
pepper. Drain pasta and sauté
in the pan. Grate over the
bottarga.

88

Risotto with Arugula

Preparation time 10 minutes
Cooking time 20 minutes
Wine *Val d'Aosta Pinot Grigio*

1 tbsp extra-virgin olive oil
1 garlic clove, smashed
6 large button mushrooms,
 sliced
parsley, chopped
3 tbsps butter
1 yellow onion, minced
1⅓ cups (9 oz or 260 g)
 Vialone Nano rice
4 cups (1 l) hot broth
2 tbsps grated Parmesan
1 bunch arugula, shredded
salt and pepper

Heat the oil in a non-stick frying pan and add garlic, mushrooms and parsley. Sauté until tender. Remove half of the mushrooms and continue cooking remaining mushrooms until crispy.
Heat butter in a pan, add onion and sauté until soft. Add rice and toast over high heat. Add hot broth and less-cooked mushrooms. Add broth little by little, cooking 13-14 minutes. Add Parmesan, arugula and crispy mushrooms. Season with salt and pepper to taste.

Porcini Tagliatelle with Swordfish

Preparation time 20 minutes
Cooking time 20 minutes
Wine *Ribolla Gialla*

3 tbsps extra-virgin olive oil
2 cloves garlic
2 small porcini mushrooms,
 cleaned and thinly sliced
thyme, minced
7 oz (200 g) swordfish fillet,
 skinned and chopped
1/2 red chilli pepper
salt
11 oz (320 g)
 cornmeal tagliatelle

Bring a large pot of salted water to a boil.
Heat oil in a large frying pan and add garlic and mushrooms. Add thyme and swordfish. Add a little of the boiling salted water for the pasta, chilli pepper and salt and simmer for 5 minutes.
Boil tagliatelle until al dente. Drain. Add to the sauce and toss in the pan for 1 minute. Serve immediately.

89

Potato Crêpes
with Broccoli and Mozzarella

Preparation time 10 minutes
Cooking time 40 minutes
Wine *Marino Superiore*

CRÊPES
2 eggs
salt
2 tbsps butter, melted
1/4 cup (3 oz or 80 g)
 plain flour
1 tsp (0.3 oz or 10 g)
 dry active yeast
3/4 cup plus 2 tbsps (200 ml) milk
1 small potato, boiled,
 peeled and mashed
1 knob of butter

FILLING
3 cups (10.5 oz or 300 g)
 broccoli florets
1 tbsp extra-virgin olive oil
1 red chilli pepper
5 tbsps grated Parmesan
3.5 oz (100 g) mozzarella, diced
salt and pepper

90

Preheat oven to 350°F (180°C).
Mix eggs, a pinch of salt and melted butter in a large bowl. Add
flour and yeast dissolved in a little bit of warm milk. Add remaining
milk. Add mashed potato and mix well. Let rest for 20 minutes.
Meanwhile, bring a large pot of salted water to a boil. Blanch
broccoli and chop into large pieces.
Heat oil in a large frying pan. Add red chilli pepper and broccoli.
Add Parmesan cheese, mozzarella and salt and pepper to taste.
Brush a small pan with butte. When hot add 1 small ladleful of
crêpe batter. Let cook 1 minute, flip and cook for 1 more minute.
Repeat until all the batter has been used.
Fill each crêpe with 1 tablespoon of filling and fold in half.
Place crêpes in a baking dish and bake for 5-6 minutes. Serve
immediately, serve with tomato sauce, if desired.

Buckwheat Dumplings
with Savoy Cabbage and Speck Ham

Preparation time 40 minutes
Cooking time 20 minutes
Wine *Alto Adige Santa
Maddalena*

BUCKWHEAT ROLLS
2¼ cups (8.8 oz or 250 g)
 buckwheat flour
2¼ cups (8.8 oz or 250 g)
 plain flour
1 egg
salt
warm water

FILLING
1 knob of butter
1/2 onion, minced

3.5 oz (100 g) speck ham, diced
1 tbsp plain flour
3½ cups (9 oz or 250 g) blanched
 and diced Savoy cabbage
1/2 cup (120 ml) heavy cream
nutmeg, grated
salt and pepper
1 tbsp grated Parmesan

SAUCE
3 tbsps soft butter
1 bunch mixed herbs
 (marjoram, thyme, sage, parsley),
 minced
Parmesan cheese, grated

Sift buckwheat flour and plain flour onto a work surface, make a
well in the centre and add egg, a pinch of salt and enough warm
water to form a smooth and uniform dough. Let rest 1 hour.
Heat butter in a large frying pan. Sauté the onion and speck
ham and sprinkle with flour. Add cabbage, cream, nutmeg, salt
and pepper to taste and Parmesan cheese. Roll out pasta into
thin sheets using a pasta machine. Cut pasta sheets into small
squares. Place 1 tablespoon of filling in the centre of each pasta
square and fold in corners to form a dumpling. Bring a large pot of
salted water to a boil. Add dumplings and boil for 4 minutes.
Meanwhile, mix butter and herbs. Melt herb butter and add
dumplings. Garnish with Parmesan cheese.

Fresh Fettuccine with Asiago, Mushrooms and Tomatoes

92

Preparation time 30 minutes
Cooking time 20 minutes
Wine *Cabernet di Breganze*

PASTA
2⅓ cups plus 1 tbsp (10.5 oz
 or 300 g) plain flour
2 eggs
4 egg yolks
salt

SAUCE
3 tbsps extra-virgin olive oil
1/2 onion, diced
3½ cups (10.5 oz or 300 g)
 chanterelle mushrooms,
 cleaned and halved
parsley, chopped
2 yellow tomatoes, blanched,
 peeled and diced
2 red tomatoes, blanched,
 peeled and diced
salt and pepper
3.5 oz (100 g) Asiago cheese,
 grated

Mound flour on a work surface and make a well at the centre. Add eggs, egg yolks and salt to the centre of the well. Mix to form a smooth and uniform dough. Refrigerate 1 hour. Roll out pasta dough with a pasta machine and cut using the fettuccine attachment. Place fettuccine on a floured baking sheet to dry.
Heat oil in a large frying pan and add the onion. Add the mushrooms and parsley. Sauté for 3 minutes, stirring frequently. Add tomatoes and salt and pepper to taste. Let cook for 10 minutes. Meanwhile, bring a large pot of salted water to boil. Add fettuccine and boil until al dente. Drain and add pasta to the sauce. Sauté 1 minute and sprinkle with Asiago cheese. Serve immediately.

Polenta Dumplings with Gorgonzola Cheese

Preparation time 15 minutes
Cooking time 1 hour 10 minutes
Wine *Teroldego Rotaliano*

DUMPLINGS
7 cups (1.75 l) water
1 tbsp sea salt
**3 cups (1 lb or 500 g) instant
 cornmeal polenta**
butter

SAUCE
3 tbsps butter
5 tbsps plain flour
2 cups (500 ml) hot milk
salt and pepper

**7 oz (200 g) mild Gorgonzola
 cheese, diced**
nutmeg, grated
3 tbsps grated Parmesan

Preheat oven to 400°F (200°C).
Bring water and salt to a boil in a large pot. Whisk in cornmeal polenta and continue to stir with a wooden spoon until the polenta is thick. Pour polenta into a damp surface and spread into a 1/2-inch (1 cm) thick layer.
To make the sauce, melt the butter in a saucepan. Add flour, stir and after a few minutes add hot milk. Add salt to taste and cook for 5-10 minutes, stirring frequently. Add Gorgonzola, nutmeg and pepper to taste. Let cook for a few minutes.
Cut polenta into circles using a round cookie cutter and place the dumplings in a buttered baking dish. Pour Gorgonzola sauce over the polenta dumplings and sprinkle with Parmesan cheese. Bake for 20 minutes. Serve immediately.

Lasagna with Ricotta and Meatballs

Preparation time 25 minutes
Cooking time 45 minutes
Vino *Gutturnio Classico*
♟

MEATBALLS
10.5 oz (300 g) ground beef
5 tbsps grated Parmesan
5 tbsps breadcrumbs
2 eggs
parsley, minced
1 garlic clove, minced
nutmeg, grated
salt
extra-virgin olive oil

LASAGNA
2 tbsps extra-virgin olive oil
1 onion, minced
3 cups (1.5 lb or 700 g)
 tomato sauce
7 oz (200 g) ricotta
salt
1 lb (500 g) pre-cooked lasagna
 pasta sheets
7 oz (200 g) cow's milk
 mozzarella, sliced
5.5 oz (150 g) prosciutto, diced

94

Preheat oven to 350°F (180°C).
Mix together all of the meatball ingredients except for the olive oil
and roll into balls. Heat oil in a saucepan and fry meatballs until
golden-brown. Drain on paper towels.
Heat the oil for the lasagna in a large frying pan and add onion.
Sauté for a few minutes. Add tomato sauce and reduce until sauce
thickens. Add meatballs to the sauce. Let cook for a few minutes.
Remove from heat and remove meatballs from the sauce.
Mix ricotta, salt and a little water to form a smooth cream.
Spread a small amount of tomato sauce on the bottom of a baking
dish. Lay lasagna pasta over sauce. Alternate layers of ricotta,
sauce, mozzarella, prosciutto and pasta. Bake for 30 minutes. Serve
with reheated meatballs.

Porcini and Hazelnut Risotto

Preparation time 15 minutes
Cooking time 20 minutes
Wine *Rossese di Dolceacqua*

3 tbsps butter
1 onion, minced
3-4 fresh porcini mushrooms,
 cleaned and chopped
salt and pepper
1½ cups (12.5 oz or 350 g)
 Vialone Nano rice
6 cups (1.5 l) boiling
 vegetable broth
10 hazelnuts, finely chopped
2 tbsps grated Parmesan
parsley, chopped

Heat butter in a large
saucepan. Add onion and
sauté until golden. Add 1/2 the
mushrooms and season with
salt and pepper. Add the rice
and let toast for a few minutes.
Add boiling broth little by little,
letting the broth absorb before
adding more. Add hazelnuts.
Halfway through the cooking
time add the remaining
mushrooms. When rice is
cooked add Parmesan cheese
and mix well. Sprinkle with
parsley. Serve immediately.

Rigatoni with Porcini

Preparation time 15 minutes
Cooking time 20 minutes
Wine *Lago di Caldaro*

4 tbsps extra-virgin olive oil
2 garlic cloves, smashed
1 shallot, sliced
3-4 fresh porcini mushrooms,
 cleaned and sliced
salt and pepper
12.5 oz (350 g) rigatoni pasta
2 tbsps grated Parmesan
2 tbsps chopped mixed herbs
 (parsley, rosemary, thyme)

Heat oil in a large pan; add
garlic and shallot and sauté
until soft. Add mushrooms
and salt and pepper to taste
and cook over high heat for 5
minutes. Remove garlic. Puree
the mushroom sauce.
Bring a large pot of salted
water to a boil. Add pasta and
boil until al dente. Drain pasta,
leaving some of the cooking
liquid. Add to sauce and mix.
Add Parmesan cheese and
garnish with mixed herbs and
pepper. Serve immediately.

95

Winter Squash and Porcini Lasagna

Preparation time 40 minutes
Cooking time 20 minutes
Wine *Cesanese di Affile*

PASTA DOUGH
2⅓ cups plus 1 tbsp (10.5 oz
 or 300 g) plain flour
2 eggs
2 egg yolks
1 tbsp extra-virgin olive oil

FILLING
4 tbsps extra-virgin olive oil
1 leek, sliced
1 2-lb (1 kg) winter squash,
 peeled and diced
1¼ cups (300 ml) milk
1/2 cup (120 ml) water
5 tbsps grated Parmesan
nutmeg, grated
salt and pepper
1 garlic clove
2-3 fresh porcini mushrooms,
 cleaned and sliced
2 tbsps butter

96

Preheat oven to 400°F (200°C).
Mound flour on a work surface and make a well in the centre.
Add eggs, egg yolks and oil and mix to form a smooth dough.
Cover and let rest for 20 minutes.
Heat 2 tablespoons oil in a frying pan. Add leek and sauté for
a few minutes. Add squash, milk and water. Cover and cook until
the squash is soft. Puree and add 4 tablespoons of Parmesan
and nutmeg, salt and pepper to taste.
In another frying pan heat remaining oil with the garlic.
Add mushrooms and cook for a few minutes. Remove garlic
and add mushrooms to squash mixture.
Bring a large pot of salted water to a boil.
Meanwhile, roll out dough with a pasta machine and cut into
rectangular sheets. Boil for a few minutes. Drain and let cool
on a kitchen towel.
Layer pasta and squash mixture in a buttered baking dish. Finish
with a sheet of pasta and brush with melted butter. Sprinkle with
the remaining Parmesan. Bake for 10 minutes. Serve hot.

Baked Penne
with Porcini and Four Cheeses

Preparation time 15 minutes
Cooking time 20 minutes
Wine *Alto Adige Pinot Nero*

10 basil leaves, minced
6 sage leaves, minced
oregano leaves, minced
marjoram leaves, minced
3.5 oz (100 g) ricotta
salt and pepper
3 fresh porcini mushrooms,
  cleaned and sliced
11 oz (320 g) penne rigate
4 tbsps grated Parmesan
3 tbsps melted butter
2 oz (50 g) Emmenthal cheese,
  grated
1 oz (30 g) Gorgonzola
  cheese, chopped
2 oz (50 g) mild provolone
  cheese, grated

97

Preheat oven to 425°F (220°C).

Mix basil, sage, oregano and marjoram with the ricotta. Add salt
and pepper to taste. Add mushrooms.

Bring a large pot of salted water to a boil. Add pasta and boil until
al dente. Drain and stir in ricotta mixture and Parmesan cheese.
Line an oval baking dish with a large sheet of parchment paper.
Make sure that the parchment sheet is large enough to close over
the top of the dish. Do not trim extra paper. Brush the parchment
paper with butter and add half the pasta, sprinkle with half the
Emmenthal, Gorgonzola and provolone cheeses. Add remaining
pasta and sprinkle with remaining cheeses and melted butter.
Close parchment paper over the top of the pasta and bake for 5
minutes. Serve immediately.

Semolina Dumplings with Finnochiona Salami and Stilton

Note *Finnochiona is a typically Tuscan soft salami. Pork meat is ground with wild fennel seeds, garlic, salt and pepper and then aged between 6 months and a year. Due to its large size and unique flavour, finnochiona is easily recognizable.*

Preparation time 20 minutes
Cooking time 15 minutes
Wine *Nero d'Avola*

DUMPLINGS
3 cups (700 ml) water
salt and pepper
1¾ cups (7 oz or 200 g)
  semolina flour
2 tbsps butter

SAUCE
5.5 oz (150 g) finocchiona salami,
  thinly sliced
3.5 oz (100 g) Stilton cheese,
  crumbled
1 tbsp breadcrumbs
salt and pepper

Preheat broiler.
Bring 3 cups (700 ml) salted water to a boil in a saucepan. Whisk in semolina flour. Add butter and cook for 5 minutes. Add salt and pepper to taste. Remove from heat and pour into a damp baking dish. Spread semolina to form an even 1/2-inch (1½ cm) layer. Refrigerate.
Using a cookie cutter, cut out 8 circles of semolina. Using a sharp knife, remove the starchy film from the top of the semolina circles. Make 4 sandwiches with the semolina circles and finnochiona. Return sandwiches to the baking dish and cover sandwiches with Stilton. Broil for 4 minutes, until the cheese melts and begins to brown.

98

Porcini Ravioli
with Bell Pepper Cream

Preparation time 45 minutes
Cooking time 25 minutes
Wine *Trentino Marzemino*

5.5 oz (150 g) ricotta
2 tbsps grated Parmesan
1 tbsp chopped mixed herbs
salt and pepper

PASTA DOUGH
2⅓ cups plus 1 tbsp (10.5 oz
 or 300 g) plain flour
3 eggs
1 tbsp extra-virgin olive oil
salt

BELL PEPPER CREAM
2 tbsps extra-virgin olive oil
2 red bell peppers, roasted,
 peeled and sliced
1/4 cup (60 ml) heavy cream
1/2 cup (120 ml) water
2 tbsps grated Parmesan
salt and pepper
0.7 oz (20 g) black truffle, shaved

FILLING
2 tbsps extra-virgin olive oil
1 garlic clove, smashed
2-3 fresh porcini mushrooms,
 cleaned and thinly sliced

Mix flour, eggs, oil and salt and mix to form a smooth dough. Cover and refrigerate for 30 minutes.

Heat oil for the filling in a frying pan with garlic. Add mushrooms and sauté for 5 minutes. Let cool then stir in ricotta, Parmesan, herbs and salt and pepper to taste. Set aside.

Heat oil for the pepper cream in a saucepan then add the bell peppers, cream and water and cook over low heat for 12-15 minutes. Puree together with 1/2 the Parmesan. Add salt and pepper to taste.

Using a pasta machine roll out dough into long sheets. Place 1/2 teaspoon of filing at 2-inch (5 cm) intervals on the pasta. Cover with a second sheet and seal edges. Cut out ravioli.

Bring a large pot of salted water to a boil. Boil ravioli until they float to the surface. Drain and place in a serving dish. Add bell pepper cream and sprinkle with remaining Parmesan and the truffle.

Winter Squash Ravioli
(VENETO)

Preparation time 30 minutes
Cooking time 40 minutes
Wine *Lison-Pramaggiore
Sauvignon*

PASTA DOUGH
4 cups (1 lb or 500 g)
 plain flour
2 egg yolks
1 tbsp extra-virgin olive oil

FILLING
7 tbsps butter
1/4 onion, chopped

1.3 lb (600 g) winter squash,
 peeled and chopped
5 egg yolks
3 tbsps grated Parmesan
1 tsp sugar
cinnamon, ground

SAUCE
poppy seeds
butter

100

Mound flour on a work surface and make a well in the centre. Add
egg yolks and oil to the well. Mix to form a smooth and uniform
dough. Cover and let rest 30 minutes.
Melt butter in a frying pan. Add onion and sauté until it begins
to brown. Add squash and cook until soft, stirring occasionally.
Puree the squash and mix with the egg yolks, Parmesan cheese,
cinnamon and sugar.
Using a pasta machine roll out the pasta dough into long sheets.
Cut into rounds and place 1 teaspoon of filling on each round.
Fold pasta over and press down edges to seal.
Bring a large pot of salted water to a boil. Add ravioli and boil
briefly. Drain.
Meanwhile melt the butter for the sauce in a saucepan. Pour
melted butter over ravioli and sprinkle with poppy seeds. Serve
immediately.

Cerinole Pasta with Sausage and Mushrooms (UMBRIA)

Note *This type of pasta is called* umbricelli *in Perugia and Tavernelle. Around Terni and Spoleto the same dough is used to make* stringozzi *or* strangozzi *(meaning shoelace). The pasta is thicker and rougher than the more common* tagliatelle.

Preparation time 25 minutes
Cooking time 15 minutes
Wine *Chardonnay*

1 oz (30 g) dried mushrooms
1/2 cup (120 ml) warm water
1 knob of butter
7 oz (200 g) sausage meat, diced
2 tbsps heavy cream
4 tbsps grated Parmesan
1 lb (500 g) cerinole (or bucatini)
salt

101

Soak mushrooms in the warm water for a few minutes. Squeeze out excess water and dry mushrooms on a paper towel.
Melt butter in a large frying pan. Add sausage and mushrooms. Brown sausage and remove from heat. Add cream and Parmesan cheese.
Bring a large pot of salted water to boil. Add pasta and boil until al dente.
Drain pasta and add to sauce. Sauté 1 minute.
Serve immediately.

Reginette with Hare Ragù

Note *Try reginette with walnut and truffle sauce. Melt 1 knob of butter, add 1 tablespoon flour and whisk in 1⅔ cups (400 ml) milk. Salt and pepper to taste. Stir until the mixture comes to a boil. Add 3.5 oz (100 g) chopped fontina cheese and 3.5 oz (100 g) chopped taleggio cheese, 5 chopped walnuts and 1 egg yolk. Mix well. Boil the reginette (or other fettuccine-type pasta) until al dente. Sauté with sauce for 1 minute. Garnish with shaved truffle and chopped parsley and serve immediately.*

Preparation time 20 minutes
Cooking time 40 minutes
Wine *Chianti Classico*

1/2 hare or rabbit
vinegar
3 tbsps extra-virgin olive oil
1 small onion, minced
1 celery stalk, minced
1 small carrot, minced
1 tbsp pine nuts
1/2 cup (120 ml) red wine
salt and pepper
1/2 cup (3.5 oz or 100 g) diced
  canned tomatoes
3/4 cups plus 2 tbsps (200 ml)
  vegetable broth
1 tbsp tomato paste
1 tsp ground spices (cloves,
  juniper berries, nutmeg)
14 oz (400 g) reginette pasta

Wash the hare in water and vinegar. Rinse well.
Heat oil in a large heavy-bottomed pot. Add onion, celery and carrot and sauté. Add hare and pine nuts and brown for 5 minutes. Add wine and salt to taste. Let cook for another 3-4 minutes. Remove from heat and let cool. Remove the meat from the hare, dice and return to the pot. Return to heat and add tomatoes, broth and tomato paste. Add spices. Cook for 30 minutes. Season with salt and pepper to taste.
Bring a large pot of salted water to a boil. Add reginette and boil until al dente. Add pasta to ragù and serve immediately.

102

Penne with Salt Cod

Preparation time 20 minutes
Cooking time 15 minutes
Wine *Alto Adige Pinot Nero*

6.5 oz (180 g) pre-soaked salt cod
2 egg whites
5 tbsps breadcrumbs
parsley, chopped
salt and pepper
6 tbsps extra-virgin olive oil
1 garlic clove, smashed
1 dried red chilli pepper
1-2 fresh porcini mushrooms,
 cleaned and sliced
2 tomatoes, peeled and diced
14 oz (400 g) penne pasta

Puree the salt cod, egg whites, breadcrumbs, parsley, salt and pepper. Roll into small balls. Heat a third of the oil in a frying pan. Fry balls until golden. Drain on paper towels. Heat remaining oil in a frying pan with garlic and chilli. Add mushrooms and sauté over high heat. Add tomatoes and fish balls. Salt to taste. Bring a large pot of salted water to a boil. Add penne and boil until al dente. Drain and add to sauce. Garnish with parsley. Serve immediately.

Provolone and Barley Flan

Preparation time 15 minutes
Cooking time 40 minutes
Wine *Ribolla Gialla*

1 head Treviso radicchio, sliced
2 tbsps extra-virgin olive oil
1/2 onion, diced
1½ cups (10.5 oz or 300 g)
 pearled barley, rinsed
4 cups (1 l) vegetable broth
7 oz (200 g) mild provolone
 cheese, diced
salt and pepper

Preheat oven to 400°F (200°C). Separate the white part of the radicchio from the red. Heat olive oil in a saucepan. Add onion and white part of the radicchio and cook for a few minutes over high heat. Add barley and toast for a few minutes. Add broth and let cook for 30 minutes over medium heat. Add reserved red radicchio halfway through cooking. When barley is cooked add provolone cheese and salt and pepper to taste. Butter 4 small ramequins and fill with barley mixture. Bake for 5 minutes. Unmold onto serving plates and serve immediately.

Pear and Ricotta Ravioli with Pecorino

104

Preparation time 1 hour
Cooking time 10 minutes
Wine *Bianco d'Alcamo*

DOUGH
5 eggs
1 tbsp extra-virgin olive oil
salt
4½ cups (1lb or 500 g)
 plain flour

FILLING
1 lb (500 g) ricotta
1 pear, peeled and diced
2 egg yolks
1 cup (3.5 oz or 100 g) grated
 Parmesan

SAUCE
10.5 oz (300 g) semi-aged
 pecorino cheese, shaved
10 tbsps (5.2 oz or 150 g) melted
 butter
1 pear, peeled and thinly sliced

GARNISH
poppy seeds

Beat eggs in a large bowl then add oil, salt and flour a little at a
time. Mix to form a smooth and uniform dough. Let rest 30 minutes.
Mix together ricotta, pear, egg yolks and Parmesan.
Roll out dough with a pasta machine. Cut dough into 4-inch (10 cm)
rounds. Place 1 tablespoon of filling on each circle and fold in half.
Press down edges to seal.
Bring a large pot of salted water to boil. Boil ravioli for a few minutes
and drain carefully. Place ravioli on a serving dish. Top with pecorino
shavings, pear and butter. Sprinkle with poppy seeds and serve
immediately.

Brown Rice Risotto with Walnuts and Winter Squasha

Preparation time 15 minutes
Cooking time 50 minutes
Wine *Val d'Aosta Pinot Grigio*

RISOTTO
1 tbsp extra-virgin olive oil
1/2 shallot, minced
1¾ cups (12.5 oz or 350 g)
 brown rice
vegetable broth
2/3 cup (3 oz or 80 g) chopped
 walnuts
2 tbsps heavy cream

105

SQUASH CREAM
2 tbsps extra-virgin olive oil
1/2 shallot, minced
1 lb (500 g) acorn
 or Kabocha squash, peeled
 and diced
thyme leaves, chopped
salt

Heat oil in a large saucepan. Add shallot and sauté briefly. Add rice and toast for a few minutes. Add broth little by little and let cook 40 minutes.
Meanwhile, heat the oil for the squash cream in a large saucepan. Add shallot and squash, sauté briefly. Add thyme leaves and salt to taste. Cover with water and let cook for 20 minutes. Remove from heat and puree.
Add walnuts and cream to the risotto and stir. Let sit for 10 minutes. Pour squash cream into bowls and top with risotto.

Quail Risotto with Radicchio and Truffles

Preparation time 25 minutes
Cooking time 30 minutes
Wine *Amarone della Valpolicella*

2 tbsps extra-virgin olive oil
1/2 onion, diced
1/2 carrot, diced
1 celery stalk, diced
2 quails, cleaned
1/2 cup (120 ml) broth
1¼ cups (9 oz or 250 g)
 Vialone Nano rice
1 knob of butter
1/2 head Treviso radicchio,
 finely sliced
1 tbsp grated Parmesan
1/2 small black truffle, sliced
salt and pepper

Heat oil in a large pot. Add onion, carrot and celery and let cook for a few minutes. Add quail and a little broth and let cook 5-6 minutes. Remove from heat and let cool. Remove meat from quail and chop the meat.
Add rice to the pan juices and toast, stirring constantly, over high heat.
Add the rest of the broth little by little and after 10 minutes add the quail meat. Salt to taste.
Heat butter in a frying pan. Add radicchio and sauté for a few minutes. Remove from heat and add to risotto.
When rice is cooked, add Parmesan cheese and truffle, season with salt and pepper to taste and serve immediately.

Whole-Wheat Pasta with Chickpeas and Sausage

Preparation time 30 minutes
Cooking time 1 hour
Wine *Cabernet del Piave*
👨‍🍳 👨‍🍳

PASTA DOUGH
1 cup plus 3 tbsps (5.3 oz or
 150 g) plain flour
3/4 cup (3.5 oz or 100 g)
 whole-wheat flour
2 eggs
1 tbsp extra-virgin olive oil
salt

SAUCE
3/4 cup (5.5 oz or 150 g) dried
 chickpeas, soaked 12 hours
1 bay leaf
salt and pepper
4 tbsps extra-virgin olive oil
2 garlic cloves, smashed
rosemary, chopped
3.5 oz (100 g) sausage meat
 diced
3 tbsps grated Parmesan

Sift the flours onto a work surface and make a well in the centre.
Add eggs, oil and a pinch of salt to the well. Mix to form a smooth
and uniform dough, adding water if necessary. Cover and let rest
30 minutes in a cool place.
Boil chickpeas with the bay leaf and a pinch of salt until they are
soft. Drain.
Heat oil in a large frying pan. Add garlic, rosemary and sausage.
Add chickpeas and sauté for 10 minutes.
Roll out dough using a pasta machine and cut the pasta into
irregular diamond shapes.
Bring a large pot of salted water to boil. Cook the pasta for
3-4 minutes. Drain and add to sauce. Sauté for 1 minute, add
Parmesan cheese and season with salt and pepper to taste.
Serve immediately.

Fried Spaghetti with Wild Mushroom Ragù

Preparation time 20 minutes
Cooking time 1 hour
Wine *Blanc de Morgex et de La Salle*

10.5 oz (300 g) thin spaghetti
salt and pepper
4 tbsps extra-virgin olive oil
3/4 cup (3.5 oz or 100 g) diced onion
3/4 cup (3.5 oz or 100 g) diced celery
3/4 cup (3.5 oz or 100 g) diced carrot
1 dried red chilli pepper
3 cups (10.5 oz or 300 g) mixed wild mushrooms, (porcini, chanterelles, honey mushrooms), cleaned and chopped
1/2 cup (3 oz or 80 g) crushed tomatoes
1 tsp tomato paste
parsley, chopped
10 cherry tomatoes
3 garlic cloves

Preheat oven to 325°F (170°C).
Line a rectangular baking dish with parchment paper.
Bring a large pot of salted water to a boil and cook the spaghetti until still very al dente. Drain and place pasta in the baking dish.
Cover pasta with a sheet of parchment paper and place another baking dish on top of the pasta.
Heat 2 tablespoons oil in a large frying pan. Add onion, celery, carrot and chilli pepper. Sauté briefly. Add mushrooms and sauté for another 7-8 minutes. Remove from heat and drain any excess liquid. Dice the mixture. Place in a saucepan with the tomatoes, tomato paste, parsley and salt and pepper to taste. Cook over low heat until thickened.
Place cherry tomatoes on a baking sheet with garlic cloves and 1 tablespoon oil. Roast for 30 minutes.
Remove pasta block from baking dish and slice. Heat remaining oil in a large frying pan and fry pasta slices. Top pasta slices with ragù and tomatoes and serve immediately.

Strozzapreti with Leek Sauce

Preparation time 10 minutes
Cooking time 30 minutes
Wine *Valcalepio Rosso*

2 tbsps extra-virgin olive oil
4-5 leeks, sliced
2 oz (50 g) speck ham
7 tbsps milk
1 vegetable stock cube, crumbled
salt and pepper
11 oz (320 g) egg strozzapreti
 (can be substituted with
 egg pasta of choice)
1 knob of butter
3 tbsps grated Parmesan
ground cinnamon

Heat oil in a large frying pan.
Add leeks and speck ham and
sauté. Add milk little by little
and the crumbled stock cube.
Meanwhile, bring a large pot
of salted water to a boil and
cook the pasta until al dente.
Drain and add pasta and butter
to the leeks. Add pepper,
Parmesan cheese and a pinch
of cinnamon and mix well.
Remove from heat and serve
immediately.

Tagliolini with Radicchio

Preparation time 10 minutes
Cooking time 10 minutes
Wine *Colli di Conegliano Verdiso*

3.5 oz (100 g) fontina cheese,
 diced
7 tbsps heavy cream
4 tbsps extra-virgin olive oil
10.5 oz (300 g) Treviso radicchio,
 julienned
salt and pepper
1 tbsp truffle paste or cream
11 oz (320 g) egg tagliolini
2 tbsps grated Parmesan

Soak fontina cheese in cream
for 10 minutes. Pour into a small
saucepan and melt cheese over
low heat. Stir constantly until
smooth.
Heat oil in a large frying pan
and add radicchio. Sauté for 5
minutes. Add salt and pepper
to taste and stir into the fontina
sauce. Mix in the truffle paste.
Bring a large pot of salted water
to a boil. Add tagliolini and cook
until al dente. Drain, reserving a
few spoonfuls of cooking water,
and add tagliolini to sauce.
Mix in the cooking water and
Parmesan. Serve immediately.

Quail and Prune Ravioli

Preparation time 45 minutes
Cooking time 20 minutes
Wine *Trentino Marzemino*

PASTA DOUGH
1 cup plus 3 tbsps (3 oz or 150 g)
 plain flour
4 egg yolks
extra-virgin olive oil
salt

FILLING
3 tbsps butter
1 tsp juniper berries
2 small quails
1/2 cup (120 ml) vegetable broth
cornstarch
salt and pepper
4 soft prunes, pits removed,
 diced
2 tbsps heavy cream

110

Preheat oven to 425°F (220°C).
Mix the flour, egg yolks, oil and salt to form a smooth and uniform dough. Cover with plastic wrap and let rest in a cool place.
Heat butter and juniper berries in an oven-proof saucepan. Add quail and brown for 6-7 minutes. Add broth and place in the oven. Bake for 10 minutes. Remove quail from the pan and remove the meat from the bones. Chop and set aside.
Strain the cooking liquid and return to the saucepan. Add cornstarch and season with salt and pepper to taste. Set aside.
Add prunes and cream to the quail meat and mix well. Use a wooden spoon to form small balls.
Roll out pasta dough into thin sheets using a pasta machine. Place the balls of filling at 1-inch (2½ cm) intervals along the pasta. Cover with a second sheet of pasta and press down to seal. Use a cookie cutter or a glass to cut out the ravioli.
Bring a large pot of salted water to boil. Add ravioli and cook for 2 minutes. Drain and add to the reserved sauce, sautéing briefly. Serve immediately.

White Tortelli with Figs, Ricotta and Prosciutto

Preparation time 1 hour
Cooking time 15 minutes
Wine *Trebbiano di Romagna*

👨‍🍳 👨‍🍳

PASTA DOUGH
1 cup plus 3 tbsps (5.3 oz or
 150 g) plain flour
6 tbsps milk
salt

FILLING
2 black figs, peeled
6.5 oz (180 g) ricotta
3 oz (80 g) prosciutto, minced

1 tbsp breadcrumbs
1 tbsp grated Parmesan
salt and pepper

GARNISH
1/2 cup (3 oz or 80 g) instant
 polenta cornmeal
1 tbsp extra-virgin olive oil
1 knob of butter
1 oz (20 g) prosciutto, julienned

111

Mix flour, milk and salt to form an elastic dough. Cover with plastic
wrap and refrigerate for 30 minutes.
Place figs in a mixing bowl and smash them with a fork. Add
ricotta, prosciutto, breadcrumbs, Parmesan cheese and salt and
pepper to taste. Mix well and refrigerate.
Roll out pasta into thin sheets using a pasta machine. Place the
balls of filling at 1½-inch (3 cm) intervals along the pasta. Cover
with a second sheet of pasta and press down to seal. Use a round
cookie cutter to cut out the ravioli. Pinch together the two
opposite sides of the ravioli.
Bring a small saucepan of salted water to a boil. Whisk in polenta
and add oil. Stir constantly.
Fry the prosciutto strips in a saucepan until browned and crispy.
Meanwhile bring a large pot of salted water to a boil. Boil ravioli
for a few minutes. Drain and sauté with butter for 1 minute. Serve
ravioli on top of the polenta and garnish with the prosciutto.

autumn

Mint and Pecorino Ravioli in Tomato Sauce (SARDINIA)

Preparation time 20 minutes
Cooking time 10 minutes
Wine *Torbato di Alghero*

FILLING
3 potatoes, boiled, peeled
 and mashed
1 egg
4 tbsps chopped mint
salt and pepper
2 cups (7 oz 200 g) grated
 pecorino cheese
5.5 oz (150 g) hard goat's milk
cheese, grated

SAUCE
2 tbsps extra-virgin olive oil
1 onion, diced
2.2 lb (1 kg) tomatoes, diced
basil, chopped
parsley, chopped

PASTA DOUGH
1¾ cups (7 oz or 200 g)
 semolina flour
2⅓ cups plus 1 tbsp (10.5 oz
 or 300 g) plain flour
2 eggs
salt

GARNISH
4 tbsps grated pecorino cheese

112

Mixed the cooled mashed potatoes with the egg and mint. Add salt
and pepper to taste, and the cheeses. Mix well and set aside.
Heat olive oil in a frying pan. Add onion and sauté. Add tomatoes,
basil and parsley. Let simmer until sauce thickens.
Sift flours onto a wooden board and add eggs, salt and enough
water to form a smooth and uniform dough. Let rest 30 minutes.
Roll out dough into a thin sheet and cut out circles. Holding the
dough over thumb and forefinger, stretch each dough circle. Place
1 teaspoon of filling on the dough and close the dough by folding
inward, alternating left and right to form a fluted ridge. Pinch dough
closed.
Bring a large pot of salted water to a boil. Cook the ravioli until they
rise to the surface. Drain and place in serving bowls. Add tomato
sauce and sprinkle with pecorino cheese. Serve immediately.

FIRST COURSES

Campofilone Pasta in Capon Broth (MARCHE)

Preparation time 20 minutes
Cooking time 2 hours
Wine *Bianchello del Metauro*
♟ ♟

BROTH
1 capon (about 1.5 lb or 700 g)
1/2 onion
1 carrot
1/2 celery stalk
1 bunch of herbs, chopped
salt

PASTA DOUGH
1½ cups plus 1½ tbsps (7 oz or 200 g) plain flour
2 eggs

DUMPLINGS
1 tbsp breadcrumbs
3 tbsps grated Parmesan

GARNISH
8 spears of wild or pencil asparagus, sliced
1/4 cup (1 oz or 20 g) shaved pecorino di fossa or other aged pecorino cheese
8 cherry tomatoes, blanched, peeled, seeded and chopped

Place capon, onion, carrot, celery and herbs in a large pot and cover with water. Bring to a simmer and let cook. When broth is cooked add salt to taste.

Meanwhile, mix flour and eggs to form a smooth and elastic dough. Roll dough into a thin sheet and slice into very thin spaghetti.

Remove capon from broth, take the leg meat off the bone and chop finely. Add breadcrumbs and Parmesan cheese. Roll mixture into small balls to form dumplings. Chop the remaining capon meat into small cubes.

Bring broth to a boil and add asparagus. When it is nearly cooked add pasta.

Pour soup into bowls, add dumplings and remaining capon and serve with pecorino and tomatoes.

Tagliatelle with Porcini Ragù

Note *Porcini ragù is a classic autumn sauce. It goes well with all egg pastas, but is best with tagliatelle and pappardelle. For a variation on this recipe, try eliminating the tomato and substituting the mint with parsley.*

Preparation time 30 minutes
Cooking time 10 minutes
Wine *Rossese di Dolceacqua*

PASTA
2⅓ cups plus 1 tbsp (10.5 oz or 300 g) plain flour
3 eggs
salt

SAUCE
2 tomatoes
2 tbsps extra-virgin olive oil
2 garlic cloves
1/2 dried red chilli pepper
3 fresh porcini mushrooms, cleaned and diced
parsley, chopped
salt and pepper

Mix flour, eggs and a pinch of salt to form a smooth and elastic dough. Wrap in plastic wrap and refrigerate for 30 minutes.
Blanch tomatoes and place them immediately in ice water. Peel and quarter. Remove seeds and chop.
Heat olive oil in a large frying pan. Add garlic cloves and chilli pepper. Sauté briefly and add mushrooms. Sauté for another 3 minutes and add parsley, tomatoes and salt to taste.
Using a pasta machine, roll out the pasta into thin sheets. Fold sheets in half and then in half again and slice into very thin strips.
Bring a large pot of salted water to a boil and cook tagliatelle for 2 minutes. Drain pasta and add to the mushroom sauce. Sauté for 1 minute over high heat and add pepper to taste. Serve immediately.

Mushroom and Leek Lasagna

Preparation time 20 minutes
Cooking time 30 minutes
Wine *Val Venosta Riesling*

3 tbsps extra-virgin olive oil
1 leek, thinly sliced
1/2 cup (120 ml) hot vegetable
 broth
1 garlic clove
4 cups (1 lb or 450 g)
 wild mushrooms, cleaned
 and chopped
5.5 oz (150 g) goat's milk cheese
7 tbsps heavy cream
salt and pepper
10 squares pre-cooked lasagna
 pasta made with egg

Preheat oven to 375°F (190°C).
Heat 1 tablespoon oil in a large
frying pan and add the leek.
Sauté briefly and add hot broth.
Let cook for 10 minutes.
In another pan heat the
remaining oil with garlic. Add
mushrooms and sauté until soft.
Add the mushrooms to leeks and
then mix in cheese, cream and
salt and pepper to taste.
Layer the pasta and sauce in a in
a baking dish. Drizzle with olive
oil. Bake for 25 minutes, until the
surface is crusty.

Mushroom Tagliatelle

Preparation time 10 minutes
Cooking time 10 minutes
Wine *Alto Adige Merlot*

1/2 cup (3.5 oz or 100 g)
 butter, softened
thyme, minced
chives, minced
3-4 fennel seeds, pounded
8 cups (2 l) light broth
 (chicken or vegetable)
14 oz (400 g) mushroom-flavoured
 tagliatelle
1/2 cup (1.5 oz or 40 g) chopped
 almonds

Spread butter on a piece of
parchment paper to form an
even, thin layer. Sprinkle herbs
and fennel seeds over the
butter and roll up the paper.
Place roll in the refrigerator.
Bring broth to a boil in a large
pot. Add tagliatelle and boil until
al dente.
Meanwhile, remove butter roll
from the refrigerator, take butter
the parchment paper and break
into little pieces.
Drain pasta and add herb
butter. Garnish with almonds.
Serve immediately.

Orzotto with Amarone and French Plums

Preparation time 10 minutes
Cooking time 25 minutes
Wine *Amarone della Valpolicella*

3 tbsps butter
1 shallot, minced
1½ cups (10.5 oz or 300 g) pearl barley
2 cups (500 ml) Amarone della Valpolicella wine
2 French plums, pitted and sliced
sugar
salt and pepper
1 tbsp grated Parmesan

Heat 2 tablespoons butter in a saucepan, add the minced shallot and sauté until soft.

Add the barley and toast for a few minutes over high heat, stirring constantly. Add some wine and let it evaporate. Continue adding wine little by little, stirring frequently.

Meanwhile, heat the remaining butter in a frying pan and add the sliced plums and a pinch of sugar. Sauté briefly until the sugar begins to caramelize.

Add half of the plums to the barley and season with salt and pepper to taste.

Continue cooking until the barley is tender, adding water when the wine is finished.

When barley is cooked, stir in the remaining plums and grated Parmesan cheese. Serve immediately.

Rice with Herb Pesto and Apples

Preparation time 10 minutes
Cooking time 12 minutes
Wine *Val Venosta Riesling Renano*

1 bunch thyme, finely chopped
1 bunch marjoram, finely chopped
1 bunch basil, finely chopped
1 bunch parsley, finely chopped
1 rosemary sprig, finely chopped
1/2 Granny Smith apple, peeled
 and sliced
zest and juice of 1/2 organic lemon
4 anchovies packed in oil
extra-virgin olive oil
salt
2 cups (12.5 oz or 360 g)
 brown rice
chives, chopped
2 tbsps grated ricotta salata
1/2 red apple, sliced

Blend together the thyme,
marjoram, basil, parsley,
rosemary, apple sliced, lemon
zest and juice and anchovies
in a food processor. Continue
blending and add olive oil and
salt to taste.
Boil the rice in a large pot.
Drain and dress with the herb
pesto. Add chives and ricotta
salata. Garnish with red apple
slices.

Tagliatelle with Spinach

Preparation time 10 minutes
Cooking time 15 minutes
Wine *Roero Arneis*

6 cups (7 oz or 200 g) spinach
5 tbsps butter
1 garlic clove
salt and pepper
10.5 oz (300 g) tagliatelle
8 tbsps grated Parmesan

117

Blanch spinach for 1 minute.
Drain and immerse in cold
water, then drain again.
Melt butter in a large frying
pan. Add garlic and sauté for 1
minute. Add spinach and sauté
2-3 minutes. Add salt and
pepper to taste.
Bring a large pot of salted
water to a boil and add
tagliatelle. Cook until al dente.
Drain and add to the spinach.
Stir in Parmesan cheese and
mix carefully. Serve immediately.

Roman Semolina Dumplings
(LAZIO)

Preparation time 20 minutes
Cooking time 1 hour
Wine *Velletri Bianco*

4 cups (1 l) milk
6 tbsps butter
salt
1½ cups (8.8 oz or 250 g) semolina flour
1¼ cups (4.5 oz or 125 g) grated Parmesan

118

Preheat oven to 400°F (200°C).

Heat the milk, 3 tablespoons butter and a pinch of salt in a saucepan. Bring to a boil and whisk in semolina flour. Cook for 30 minutes, stirring constantly. Remove from heat and add 1 cup (3.5 oz or 100g) Parmesan cheese. Pour semolina into a damp baking dish and spread to form a thin, even layer. Let cool. Using a round cookie cutter cut semolina into small circles.

Melt remaining butter in a small saucepan. Butter a baking dish and place the leftover semolina cuttings on the bottom. Pour half of the melted butter over the semolina and sprinkle with Parmesan cheese. Cover with semolina circles and top with remaining butter and Parmesan cheese.

Bake until golden-brown and serve immediately.

Winter Squash Dumplings
(LOMBARDY)

Preparation time 10 minutes
Cooking time 10 minutes
Wine *Colli Morenici Mantovani del Garda Rosato*

salt
2.2 lb (1 kg) winter squash
 or pumpkin, peeled and chopped
4 cups (1 lb oz or 500 g)
 plain flour
1 egg
3 tbsps grated Parmesan,
 plus extra for garnish
nutmeg, grated
butter
tomato sauce (see p. 1099)

Bring a large pot of salted water to boil. Add the chopped squash and boil until soft. Drain and let cool.
Puree the cooled squash and stir in the flour, egg and Parmesan cheese. Mix well until smooth. Add grated nutmeg and season with salt to taste.
Bring a large pot of salted water to boil. Drop spoonfuls of dough into the boiling water and let cook until the dumplings rise to the surface. Drain using a slotted spoon. Arrange in a buttered baking dish.
Top dumplings with tomato sauce and Parmesan cheese. Serve immediately.

119

Maltagliati with Pheasant and Vernaccia Ragù

Preparation time 40 minutes
Cooking time 30 minutes
Wine *Vernaccia di S. Gimignano*

3/4 cup (180 ml) Vernaccia wine
1/2 cup (3.5 oz or 100 g) crushed tomatoes
1/2 cup (100 ml) chicken broth
salt and pepper

RAGÙ
3 tbsps extra-virgin olive oil
1/2 onion, diced
1/2 celery stalk, diced
1/2 carrot, diced
1/2 pheasant, cut into pieces
1 tbsp raisins, soaked in water and drained
2 tbsps pine nuts
1 rosemary sprig

PASTA
2$\frac{1}{3}$ cups plus 1 tbsp (10.5 oz or 300 g) plain flour
2 eggs
3 egg yolks
salt

120

Heat olive oil in a large pan; add onion, celery, and carrot. Sauté for 1 minute. Add the pheasant, raisins, pine nuts and rosemary, and let brown. Add wine and let evaporate. When the pheasant is almost cooked, remove it and let cool. Add tomatoes and broth to the pan juices.
Remove the meat from the bones and chop the meat. Return meat to the pan and reduce the sauce over low heat, then season with salt and pepper.
Meanwhile, combine flour, eggs, egg yolks and salt. Mix to form a smooth and uniform dough. Refrigerate for 20 minutes. The dough may be prepared 1 day in advance.
Using a pasta machine, roll the dough into thin sheets. Cut the sheets of dough into irregular squares (maltagliati).
Bring a large pot of salted water to a boil. Add pasta and cook for 3-4 minutes. Using a slotted spoon transfer pasta directly into the ragù. Mix and serve immediately.

Eggs Benedict on Rye Bread

Preparation time 10 minutes
Cooking time 10 minutes
Wine *Alto Adige Sauvignon*
♟ ♟

4 egg yolks
3/4 cup (6 oz or 175 g) butter
2 tbsps water
2 tbsps white wine vinegar
4 slices rye bread
8 slices ham
4 cups (1 l) water
8 eggs
salt and pepper

Melt the butter in a double boiler. Place the egg yolks, water and
1 tablespoon vinegar in a blender or food processor, and gradually
pour in the butter while mixing to emulsify, forming a thick sauce.
Toast the bread on both sides and lay 2 slices of ham on each
slice of bread.
Bring the water to a boil in a large pan, add the remaining
tablespoon of vinegar, and as soon as it starts boiling, poach the
eggs by breaking them one at time onto a plate and adding them
to the water after swirling the water with a spoon so that the egg
white wraps itself around the yolk. As soon as they are cooked,
drain them and immerse in cold water, then drain and pat dry.
Lay 2 eggs on each slice of bread, season the sauce with salt and
pepper to taste, and pour over. Serve immediately.

Rabbit with Chestnuts and Wild Fennel

Note *Chestnuts get their name from a ancient city in Thessalia, an region in northern Greece. In the past the chestnut was a staple food for many poor people in Italy, who used the nuts as a bread substitute. Chestnuts have a higher energy value than bread.*

Preparation time 10 minutes
Cooking time 1 hour
Wine *Cirò Rosso*

5 tbsps extra-virgin olive oil
3½ tbsps butter
1 rabbit, cleaned and cut into pieces
1 bunch wild fennel or 1 fennel bulb, cut into chunks
2 cups (14 oz or 400 g) chestnuts, peeled
salt and pepper
3/4 cup (180 ml) water
4 bay leaves
2 cloves
wild fennel or fennel leaves, minced

124

Melt the olive oil and butter in a heavy-bottomed saucepan and then brown the rabbit pieces, turning them so that all sides become evenly browned.
Add the fennel, chestnuts, salt, pepper and water and stir. Cover the pot and let cook for 30 minutes, then add the bay leaves, cloves and minced wild fennel leaves, reserving some for garnish. Cook, covered, for another 20 minutes.
Serve the rabbit hot with the fennel and chestnuts, with minced wild fennel leaves sprinkled on top.

Lamb Chops with Red Wine Sauce

Preparation time 15 minutes
Cooking time 50 minutes
Wine *Cannonau di Sardegna*
ⵜ ⵜ

SAUCE
3 tbsps butter
1 shallot, minced
1 sprig thyme
1 sprig rosemary
1 bottle red wine
2½ tbsps cornstarch
2 tbsps cold water
salt

LAMB
12 lamb chops
salt and pepper
2 tbsps minced mixed herbs
 (rosemary, thyme, marjoram,
 oregano)
4 tbsps extra-virgin olive oil

SPRING ONIONS
3 tbsps (1.4 oz or 40 g) butter
12 spring onions
salt and pepper
1/2 cup (120 ml) water

Melt the butter for the sauce in a saucepan and add shallot, thyme, rosemary and red wine. Reduce to two-thirds of original volume.

Dissolve cornstarch in the water. Stir into wine and cook for a few minutes until thickened. Strain, salt to taste and keep warm.

Melt the butter for the spring onions in a saucepan and add the spring onions. Brown for 5-6 minutes, add salt, pepper and water and cook for 15 minutes.

Salt and pepper the lamb and sprinkle with herbs. Heat the olive oil in an frying pan and sauté lamb for 2-3 minutes per side.

Drizzle chops with the wine sauce and serve the spring onions on the side.

Stuffed Roast Beef

Preparation time 20 minutes
Cooking time 1 hour 20 minutes
Wine *Teroldego Rotaliano*

FILLING
3.5 oz (100 g) ground beef
3.5 oz (100 g) sausage meat,
 crumbled
1 egg
2 tbsps grated Parmesan
parsley, minced
1 garlic clove, minced
nutmeg, grated
salt and pepper

BEEF
1 lb (500 g) beef flank steak
3.5 oz (100 g) ham
3 tbsps butter
1 tbsp extra-virgin olive oil
1/2 onion, minced
1/2 cup (120 ml) white wine
beef broth

Mix the ground beef, sausage meat, egg, Parmesan, parsley and
garlic and season with nutmeg, salt and pepper.
Lay the beef on a work surface and lightly flatten it with a meat
pounder. Cover it with slices of ham and spread over the filling
mixture. Roll up the beef and tie it with kitchen string.
Melt the butter and oil in a saucepan and brown the onion, then
add the meat and the wine. Once the wine has evaporated add
the broth. Cover and cook for around 1 hour 15 minutes, basting
with more broth if the meat gets too dry.
When it is cooked through, untie the meat and serve sliced with its
cooking juices.

Beef Entrecôte
with Artichokes and Scamorza

Preparation time 25 minutes
Cooking time 12 minutes
Wine *Oltrepò Pavese Pinot Nero*

1 garlic clove
8 tbsps extra-virgin olive oil
5 small artichokes, trimmed
 of hard external leaves,
 and sliced
salt and pepper
thyme leaves
parsley, minced
4 beef entrecôtes
 (around 2 lb or 900 g)
1 rosemary sprig
3-4 sage leaves
5.5 oz (150 g) scamorza cheese,
 cut into strips

Preheat oven to 350°F (180°C).
Brown the garlic clove in a pan with 4 tablespoons oil. Add the
artichokes and sprinkle with salt, pepper and thyme, then cook
for 5 minutes. Take the pan off the heat and stir in the parsley. Set
aside.
Lay the entrecôtes on a tray and lightly salt and pepper them. Heat
the rest of the oil in an oven-proof fryng pan with the rosemary and
sage, then add beef steaks and brown them on both sides for a
couple of minutes.
Remove from heat, spread the artichokes over the beef and top
with the scamorza.
Bake in the oven for 5 minutes, then serve hot.

Warm Beef Carpaccio

Preparation time 10 minutes
Cooking time 10 minutes
Wine *Barbera Oltrepò Pavese*

1 fennel bulb, sliced
1 carrot, diced
1 white turnip, diced
vegetable broth
chives, minced
tarragon, minced
parsley, minced
1 tsp extra-virgin olive oil
juice of 1/2 lemon
salt and pepper
9 oz (250 g) sirlion steak,
  thinly sliced

Steam the fennel, carrot and
turnip separately for 5 minutes
each.
Bring the vegetable broth to a
boil.
Meanwhile mix the herbs with
the oil, lemon juice, salt and
pepper, toss the steamed
vegetables with this dressing
and spread them on a serving
plate.
Blanch the beef fillet slices very
quickly in the boiling broth, then
lay them over the vegetables.
Serve immediately.

Braised Rabbit

Preparation time 30 minutes
Cooking time 50 minutes
Wine *Dolcetto d'Asti*

1 rabbit, cut into pieces
salt and pepper
2 tbsps plain flour
5 tbsps extra-virgin olive oil
1/2 onion, minced
1 carrot, diced
1 celery stalk, diced
2 garlic cloves
rosemary sprigs
3 cups (9 oz or 250 g)
  chopped mixed mushrooms
3/4 cup plus 1 tbsp (200 ml) broth
1/2 cup (120 ml) white wine
parsley, minced

Salt, pepper and flour the
rabbit. Brown evenly in 4
tablespoons of oil. Pat dry.
Brown the onion, celery, carrot,
garlic and rosemary in the
remaining tablespoon of oil.
Add the rabbit, pour over the
wine and let it evaporate.
Add the mushrooms and broth,
cover and cook for 35-40
minutes.
Salt and pepper to taste and
garnish with parsley. Serve hot.

128

Chicken Thighs with Chestnuts

Preparation time 25 minutes
Cooking time 1 hour 10 minutes
Wine *Colli di Luni Rosso*

2½ cups (1 lb or 500 g)
 chestnuts, shelled
1 garlic clove
1 tbsp extra-virgin olive oil
1 carrot, finely diced
1 onion, minced
2 oz (50 g) lardo, finely chopped
1 bay leaf
rosemary, chopped
thyme leaves
4 chicken thighs
salt and pepper
1/2 cup (120 ml) white wine
8 spring onions

Boil the chestnuts for 25
minutes, drain and peel.
Brown the garlic in the oil then;
add the carrot, onion, lardo and
herbs. Sauté for a few minutes
then add the chicken and
season with salt and pepper.
Brown the chicken evenly. Add
the wine, let evaporate, then
cook, covered, for 20 minutes.
Add the chestnuts and spring
onions and cook for another 20
minutes.

Guinea Hen with Decana Pears

Preparation time 1 hour
Cooking time 50 minutes
Wine *Lagrein Dunkel*

10 chestnuts, peeled
salt
1 guinea hen, plucked
 and entrails removed
3 tbsps extra-virgin olive oil
2 garlic cloves
2 Decana pears, washed,
 cored and cut into chunks
2 bay leaves
white wine
salt and pepper

129

Preheat oven to 400°F (200°C).
Boil the chestnuts in lightly
salted water until al dente, then
drain.
Place the guinea hen in a well-
oiled baking dish and place the
garlic, pears, chestnuts and
bay leaves around it. Roast for
around 40 minutes, frequently
stirring the pears and
chestnuts. After 10 minutes
sprinkle with some wine.
Salt and pepper, and serve cut
into pieces over the pears and
chestnuts.

Braised Rabbit with Vegetables and Grilled Polenta

Preparation time 20 minutes
Cooking time 30 minutes
Wine *Refosco dal Peduncolo Rosso*

POLENTA
1 cup (5.5 oz or 150 g)
 instant polenta
2 cups (500 ml) water

RABBIT
4 tbsps extra-virgin olive oil
1 carrot, roughly chopped
1 celery stalk, roughly chopped
1 shallot, roughly chopped
1 garlic clove, halved

2 saddles of rabbit, boned
 and cut into bite-size pieces
1/2 cup (120 ml) white wine
1 sprig thyme
salt and pepper
1/4 head of Savoy cabbage,
 julienned
10 cherry tomatoes, quartered

Bring the water to a boil and sprinkle in the polenta, whisking continuosly. Continue cooking, stirring constantly, for 15 minutes. Spread it out on a tray, let cool and cut into slices. Set aside.
Heat 2 tablespoons of the olive oil and sauté the carrot, celery, shallot and garlic for about 5 minutes.
Add the rabbit and pour over the white wine, then add the thyme, salt and pepper.
Meanwhile sauté the cabbage in a frying pan with the remaining 2 tablespoons of oil and season with salt and pepper.
Squeeze some of the liquid out of the tomatoes, then add them to the rabbit, and after a few minutes add the sautéed cabbage. Salt and pepper to taste.
Grill the polenta slices on a very hot cast-iron griddle.
Serve the rabbit with the vegetables and polenta.

Pork Tenderloin with Fig Sauce

Preparation time 20 minutes
Cooking time 30 minutes
Wine *Sangiovese di Romagna*

FIGS
1 knob of butter
1 tsp raw sugar
6 ripe figs, quartered
3/4 cup (180 ml) Amarone di
 Valpolicella wine or other red wine
salt

PORK
1.25 lb (550 g) pork tenderloin
salt
peppercorns, crushed
4 tbsps extra-virgin olive oil
2 garlic cloves
2 bay leaves

Melt the butter and the sugar, add the figs and then the wine. Cook, stirring constantly, until figs are coated. Salt to taste. Cut the tenderloin into 4 pieces and season with salt and peppercorns. Brown the pork with the oil, garlic and bay for 6-7 minutes, browning the outside well but leaving the inside pink. Serve the tenderloin pieces cut in half with a few fig wedges and their cooking juices.

Turkey with Spring Onions

Preparation time 15 minutes
Cooking time 1 hour
Wine *Rosso del Conero*

4 turkey drumsticks
salt and pepper
4 tbsps extra-virgin olive oil
3/4 cup (180 ml) white wine
10 spring onions, trimmed
 and peeled
1 sprig rosemary
3/4 cup (180 ml) broth
3 tbsps balsamic vinegar

Salt and pepper the turkey drumsticks.
Heat the oil in a saucepan, and brown the turkey. Pour over the white wine and let evaporate. Cook for 20 minutes.
Add the spring onions and rosemary and pour over the broth. Cover and cook for 30 minutes.
Sprinkle with balsamic vinegar and finish cooking at high heat so that the onions caramelize. Serve immediately.

Braised Veal Ossobuco
(LOMBARDY)

Note *This traditional recipe from around Como for* ossobuchi, *veal shank steaks, is usually paired with risotto or polenta. You can enrich the dish by adding some tomatoes halfway during the cooking. The secret to making this dish so flavoursome is the gremolada, a mixture of chopped garlic, parsley, rosemary and lemon zest.*

132

Preparation time 20 minutes
Cooking time 1 hour 20 minutes
Wine *Valtellina Rosso*

3½ tbsps butter
2 tbsps extra-virgin olive oil
1/2 onion, minced
2 garlic cloves
3 sage leaves, minced
4 ossobuco steaks
 (veal shank steaks)
3 tbsps plain flour
1/2 cup (1220 ml) white wine
vegetable broth
parsley
rosemary
grated zest of 1 lemon
salt and pepper

Sauté the onion, 1 garlic clove and the sage in the butter and oil in a saucepan until transparent.
Lightly dust the shanks with flour and add them to the saucepan, turning on all sides until evenly brown. Pour over the white wine, let it reduce, lower the flame and cook, covered, for around an hour, adding a little broth when necessary.
Mince the parsley, other garlic clove, a little rosemary and the lemon zest together to make the gremolada. As soon as the meat starts to pull away from the bone, season with salt, pepper and the gremolada. Let the flavours absorb for a few minutes then serve the steaks hot, sprinkled with minced parsley.

Valtellina-Style Steak (LOMBARDY)

Preparation time 20 minutes
Cooking time 2 hours
 20 minutes
Wine *Valtellina Superiore Sassella*

4 steaks, deboned
salt and pepper
8 tomatoes, blanched, peeled
 and chopped
4 fresh porcini mushrooms,
 cleaned and sliced
1/2 cup (3.5 oz or 100 g) butter
vegetable broth
25 spring onions, trimmed
 and peeled

Preheat the oven to 375°F
(190°C).
Salt and pepper the steaks
and lay one on top of the other,
with layers of tomatoes and
mushrooms in between. Tie with
kitchen string.
Melt the butter in a saucepan
and brown the steak. Transfer
to the oven and bake for 1 hour
30 minutes, adding spring onions
halfway through. Baste with a
little vegetable broth if necessary.

Kid Goat Alla Cacciatora (SARDINIA)

Preparation time 20 minutes
Cooking time 45 minutes
Wine *Cannonau*

2 lb (1 kg) kid goat
 (shoulder and back)
salt and pepper
2 tbsps extra-virgin olive oil
1 onion, thinly sliced
1/2 cup (120 ml) white wine
5 tomatoes, peeled
4 cups (10.5 oz or 300 g)
 sliced mushrooms
parsley, minced (optional)

133

Cut the meat into pieces and
salt and pepper them.
Heat a frying pan and add the
olive oil. Sauté the onion until
golden then add the meat and
cook for around 5 minutes,
turning so that it browns evenly
on all sides. Pour in the wine,
let it evaporate and lower the
heat. Add the tomatoes and let
cook for 30 minutes, adding the
mushrooms near the end of the
cooking time.
Serve the goat very hot,
sprinkled with some minced
parsley if desired.

Pork Tenderloin with Glazed Onions

Note *Onions are without doubt one of the fundamental basics of Italian cooking, used in many different ways, whether in side dishes or as a flavouring. Cultivated for over 5,000 years, onions have had an important role to play in both peasant and aristocratic cuisine throughout history.*

Preparation time 10 minutes
Cooking time 25 minutes
Wine *Lagrein Dunkel*

PORK
1.3 lb (600 g) pork tenderloin
salt and pepper
rosemary, minced
4 tbsps extra-virgin olive oil
1 garlic clove, unpeeled
1 bay leaf

ONIONS
4 tbsps extra-virgin olive oil
20 pearl onions, peeled
1 tsp sugar
1 tbsp balsamic vinegar
salt

Cut the pork tenderloin into 8 medallions and sprinkle them with a little pepper and the rosemary. Drizzle with olive oil. Set aside. Heat 4 tablespoons olive oil in a saucepan and add the pearl onions. Sprinkle with sugar and let them brown over high heat. After 5 minutes sprinkle over the balsamic vinegar and a little hot water, then salt to taste.
Meanwhile heat a wide aluminum frying pan with the other 4 tablespoons of oil, the garlic clove and bay leaf. Add the pork medallions and brown them over high heat, seasoning with salt and pepper. Leave the inside pink, and serve with the glazed onions.

Grilled Ostrich Fillets
with Porcini Flans

Preparation time 25 minutes
Cooking time 30 minutes
Wine *Carema*

👨‍🍳

OSTRICH
4 ostrich fillets (3 oz or 80 g each)
8 thin slices of Colonnata lardo
salt and pepper

LEEKS
3 tbsps extra-virgin olive oil
1 leek, finely sliced
3/4 cup (180 ml) white wine
salt and pepper

FLAN
3-4 fresh porcini mushrooms,
 cleaned and roughly chopped
3 tbsps extra-virgin olive oil
1 garlic clove, smashed
thyme leaves
5.5 oz (150 g) ricotta
1 egg
1 tbsp breadcrumbs
1 knob of butter
7 oz (200 g) taleggio cheese,
 cubed

Preheat oven to 400°F (200°C).
Wrap each ostrich fillet in 2 slices of lardo and tie with kitchen
string into a round shape.
Sweat the leek in a frying pan with the oil and add the white wine.
Reduce and season with salt and pepper to taste.
To make the flan, sauté the porcini in a frying pan with the oil,
garlic and thyme. Once cooked, let them cool then remove
the garlic clove and mix in the ricotta and egg, adding some
breadcrumbs if the mixture is too thin.
Butter 4 ramequins and sprinkle with breadcrumbs, then fill each
halfway with the mushroom mixture. Place a few cubes of taleggio
in the middle of each flan. Cover with the rest of the mushroom
mixture then bake for 20 minutes.
Lightly salt and pepper the ostrich fillets then grill them. Serve with
the leeks and the porcini flans.

Goose Breast with Radicchio Flan and Balsamic Vinegar

Preparation time 25 minutes
Cooking time 50 minutes
Wine *Refosco dal Peduncolo Rosso*
👨‍🍳👨‍🍳

GOOSE

1 goose breast
peppercorns
juniper berries
1 bay leaf
1/2 onion, roughly chopped
2 garlic cloves, smashed
1 rosemary sprig
red wine
sea-salt flakes (such as Maldon)

FLAN

1/2 white onion, minced
2 tbsps extra-virgin olive oil
2 yellow-fleshed potatoes, peeled
 and finely sliced
1¾ cups (400 ml) vegetable broth
salt and pepper
1 garlic clove
1 head of Treviso radicchio,
 chopped
1 egg
1 tbsp heavy cream
1 knob of butter

GARNISH

1 tbsp balsamic vinegar

Preheat the oven to 375°F (190°C).
Place the goose in a terrine dish with the peppercorns, juniper berries, bay leaf, onion, garlic and rosemary and cover with red wine. Marinate overnight.
Soften the onion for the flan in a saucepan with 1 tablespoon oil and brown the potatoes. Cover with boiling broth and let cook for about 10 minutes, then season with salt and pepper.
Heat a non-stick pan with the remaining oil and garlic and sauté the radicchio over high heat, adding a little salt.
Puree the potatoes and stir in the radicchio, egg and cream.
Butter 4 ramequins and fill with the mixture. Bake for 25 minutes.
Drain the goose and pat dry, salt with the sea salt and cook on a hot grill, starting with the skin side. Turn over and cook for 2 minutes then let rest on a cutting board for another 2 minutes. Serve goose cut into thin slices with the flan. Drizzle with balsamic vinegar.

Pork Tenderloin in a Citrus Crust with Chanterelles

Preparation time 25 minutes
Cooking time 30 minutes
Wine *Terrano*

PORK
1.3 lb (600 g) pork tenderloin
salt and pepper
grated zest of 1 organic orange
grated zest of 1 organic lemon
3/4 cup (3.5 oz or 100 g)
 breadcrumbs
1 egg
clarified butter

VEGETABLES
2 tbsps extra-virgin olive oil
1 shallot, minced
4 cups (12.5 oz or 350 g)
 chanterelle mushrooms
1 bunch bitter greens, washed
 and stalks removed
1 garlic clove, smashed
4 slices Colonnata lardo, minced

GARNISH
parsley, minced

Trim the pork well, removing any external veins or fat, then salt and pepper it.
Mix the citrus zests with the breadcrumbs by hand.
Beat the egg with a little pepper. Cut the pork into medallions and dust the pieces with flour, pass them in the egg and then the citrus breadcrumbs, pressing the crumbs so they stick. Chill.
Heat 1 tablespoon of oil in a saucepan and add the shallot, soften then add the mushrooms. In another saucepan sauté the greens with the other tablespoon of oil, garlic, lardo and a little water.
Brown the pork medallions in a non-stick pan with a little clarified butter. Serve them sliced with the mushrooms and greens, sprinkled with parsley.

Roast Spring Chickens Wrapped in Vine Leaves

Preparation time 25 minutes
Cooking time 45 minutes
Wine *Cabernet di Breganze*

SPRING CHICKENS
4 grapevine leaves
2 spring chickens, around 10 oz
 (300 g) each
salt and pepper
3 garlic cloves
3 sprigs rosemary
2 oz (60 g) pancetta, thinly sliced
6 tbsps extra-virgin olive oil
3/4 cup (180 ml) Marsala wine
1½ cups (350 ml) white wine

138

GRAPE SAUCE
3 tbsps (1.4 oz or 40 g) butter
2 cups (10.5 oz or 300 g) green
 and red grapes, halved

Preheat oven to 350°F (180°C).
Blanch the vine leaves in boiling water for 2-3 minutes. Drain and cool.
Salt and pepper the chickens and insert a garlic clove and rosemary
sprig into each cavity. Place the pancetta on each breast and then
lay over 2 vine leaves each. Tie with kitchen string and lay in a baking
dish. Drizzle with oil, add the remaining garlic and rosemary to the
dish and place in the oven.
After 10 minutes baste with the Marsala. When it has evaporated,
baste with the white wine. Continue cooking for 40-45 minutes.
Remove from the oven, strain the cooking juices and reserve.
Melt the butter in a saucepan, add the grapes and sauté for 2
minutes. Add the chicken cooking juices and cook for another 2
minutes. Remove the string from the chickens and cut in half. Serve
with the grapes.

Chicken and Grape Salad

Preparation time 15 minutes
Cooking time 25 minutes
Wine *Bardolino Chiaretto*

1 lb (500 g) chicken breasts
1/2 cup (120 ml) white wine
salt and pepper
3 oz (80 g) smoked pancotta,
 thinly sliced
1 small head lettuce
3 celery stalks, sliced
1/2 cup (3.5 oz or 100 g)
 green grapes, halved and seeds
 removed
1/2 cup (3.5 oz or 100 g)
 red or black grapes, halved
 and seeds removed
4 oz (120 g) smoked provola
 cheese, cut into strips
3 tbsps extra-virgin olive oil
1 tbsp white wine vinegar

Place the chicken breasts in a saucepan, pour over the wine, add
salt and pepper and cook, covered, for 15-20 minutes. Let them
cool and cut into cubes.
Lay the pancetta on a baking tray and place under the broiler for a
few minutes until crisp, then crumble into small pieces.
Divide the lettuce leaves between 4 plates.
In a bowl, mix together the chicken, celery, grapes and provola
cheese. Dress with olive oil, vinegar and salt and pepper to taste.
Serve over the lettuce leaves, sprinkled with the pancetta.

140

Flavoursome Braised Rabbit

Preparation time 15 minutes
Cooking time 45 minutes
Wine *Aprilia Sangiovese*

♟ ♟

Serves 6

1 rabbit, cut into pieces
2 tbsps plain flour
salt and pepper
6 tbsps extra-virgin olive oil
3/4 cup (180 ml) white wine
2 garlic cloves, 1 whole
 and 1 minced
parsley, minced
4 sage leaves, minced
4 anchovies in oil, minced
1 tbsp capers in brine, minced
7 tbsps red wine vinegar
3 tomatoes, diced

Dust the rabbit with flour, salt
and pepper. Brown them in
the oil with 1 garlic clove for 10
minutes. Add the wine and let
evaporate. Cook for 25 minutes,
adding water if necessary.
Mix together the parsley, sage,
anchovies, minced garlic, capers
and vinegar.
Halfway through the cooking add
the tomatoes, and 5 minutes
before the end of cooking add
the herb mixture.

Beef and Pecorino Involtini

Preparation time 15 minutes
Cooking time 18 minutes
Wine *Trentino Marzemino*

♟ ♟

8 Savoy cabbage leaves
8 minute steaks
 (around 12 oz or 350 g)
salt and pepper
16 sage leaves
3.5 oz (100 g) pecorino cheese,
 cut into small sticks
2 tbsps extra-virgin olive oil

Preheat oven to 400°F (200°C).
Blanch the cabbage leaves in
boiling water then dry them well
with a clean kitchen towel. Cut
out the hard stalk and lay the
leaves on a cutting board.
Lightly pound the steaks,
and lay each one on top of a
cabbage leaf. Salt and pepper
the meat, lay 2 sage leaves
on each slice and add some
cheese to each one.
Roll up the cabbage leaves,
drizzle with olive oil and wrap
each one in aluminum foil.
Place in a baking dish and bake
for 15 minutes. Unwrap the
involtini before serving.
Serve very hot.

Pork Loin with Apple Sauce

Preparation time 15 minutes
Cooking time 1 hour and 40 minutes
Wine *Barbaresco*

PORK
2.5 lb (1.2 kg) pork loin
salt
2 tsps curry powder
breadcrumbs
2 tbsps extra-virgin olive oil

SAUCE
6 Renette or other baking apples,
  cored and thinly sliced
3½ tbsps butter

Preheat oven to 375°F (190°C).
Salt the pork loin. Mix together
the breadcrumbs and curry and
roll the loin in the mixture. Place
in a lightly oiled baking dish.
Drizzle with olive oil and bake
for 1 hour 30 minutes.
Place the butter and apples in
a saucepan and cook, covered,
for around 10 minutes. Mash
them with a fork or puree with a
handheld blender.
Serve the apple sauce with
slices of the roast pork.

Veal with Leeks and Potatoes

Preparation time 25 minutes
Cooking time 15 minutes
Wine *Rossese di Dolceacqua*

4 slices of veal fillet
 (around 2.5 oz or 70 g each)
1 tbsp plain flour
salt and pepper
1 knob of butter
thyme sprigs
1 small leek, sliced into rounds
1/2 cup (120 ml) white wine
6 tbsps extra-virgin olive oil
1 medium potato, peeled
 and diced

141

Dust the veal fillets with flour
and season with salt and
pepper. Melt the butter in a
frying pan and add the thyme,
then brown the fillets on both
sides for around 4 minutes.
Add the leeks, sauté for a few
minutes, then pour over the
wine and cook for another 3-4
minutes.
Heat the oil in another frying
pan and fry the potato for 5-6
minutes.
Lay the veal fillets on plates,
and serve with the leek sauce
and fried potatoes.

Pork Loin with Milk and Hazelnuts
(EMILIA-ROMAGNA)

Preparation time 20 minutes
Cooking time 1 hour
Wine *Colli Bolognesi Barbera*

1.75 lb (800 g) pork loin
mixed aromatic herbs (thyme,
  parsley, rosemary), finely chopped
salt
1 knob of butter
1 tbsp extra-virgin olive oil
2 juniper berries
1/2 cup (120 ml) white wine
1 bouquet garni (bay, thyme,
  parsley), well tied
4 cups (1 l) hot milk
1/2 cup (2 oz or 50 g) hazelnuts,
  toasted and coarsely chopped
plain flour
parsley, minced (optional)

142

Cut the pork loin open like a book, and sprinkle in the chopped
herbs and a pinch of salt. Close the meat and tie it tightly with
kitchen string.
Heat the butter, olive oil and the juniper berries in a saucepan. Add
the pork loin and brown evenly on all sides over high heat. Pour in
the wine and reduce. Lower the heat slightly and add the bouquet
garni, then the hot milk.
Salt to taste and then add the hazelnuts. Lower the heat and cook
for around 40 minutes, adding more milk if the pork dries out.
Once cooked remove the pork and set aside. Remove the bouquet
garni, and thicken the sauce with a little flour.
Serve the pork sliced with the sauce and some minced parsley, if
desired.

Umbrian Rabbit Alla Cacciatora

Preparation time 20 minutes
Cooking time 2 hours
Wine *Rubesco*

2 lb (1 kg) rabbit, or hare
 cut into pieces
1 carrot, finely chopped
1 celery stalk, finely chopped
1 onion, finely chopped
1 bay leaf
1 thyme sprig, minced
1 clove
peppercorns
salt
1 cup (250 ml) red wine
2 tbsps extra-virgin olive oil
2 tbsps plain flour

143

Wash the rabbit pieces under cold running water and pat dry with paper towels.
Place the rabbit in a large bowl or container with the carrot, celery, onion, bay leaf, thyme, clove, peppercorns, salt and wine. Cover, refrigerate and leave to marinate for 12 hours.
Remove the rabbit from the marinade, then strain and reserve the liquid.
Heat the olive oil in a saucepan and brown the rabbit pieces for a few minutes over high heat. Add the marinade, season with salt and lower the flame. Cover and cook for around 1 hour 45 minutes.
Remove the rabbit and thicken the sauce with the flour.
Serve the rabbit very hot, with the sauce poured over.

Porcini-Stuffed Pork Fillet

Preparation time 20 minutes
Cooking time 25 minutes
Wine *Alto Adige Santa Maddalena*

PORK
1 lb (500 g) pork fillet
salt and pepper
6 tbsps extra-virgin olive oil
1/2 cup (120 ml) white wine

STUFFING
2 garlic cloves, minced
2 tbsps olive oil
1/2 dried red chilli pepper
3 fresh porcini mushrooms, sliced
parsley, minced

GARNISH
mixed salad leaves

144

Preheat oven to 425°F (220°C).
Butterfly the pork loin, pound it with a meat tenderizer to obtain an even thickness and season with salt and pepper.
Sauté the garlic in a frying pan with the 2 tablespoons of oil and the chilli. Add the porcini and sauté over high heat for 5 minutes, then add the parsley and remove from the heat.
Place the mushroom mixture on the meat and roll it up. Tie with kitchen string, season with salt and pepper and place in a baking dish. Drizzle with the 6 tablespoons olive oil and bake for around 20 minutes. Halfway through the cooking time baste with white wine.
Remove the string and serve the fillet immediately, cut into slices and served with the salad leaves.

Duck Breast with Honey and Figs

Preparation time 20 minutes
Cooking time 40 minutes
Wine *Oltrepò Pavese Barbera*

2 tbsps balsamic vinegar
3 tbsps honey
1/2 cup (120 ml) orange juice
2 tbsps extra-virgin olive oil
salt and pepper
1.3 lb (600 g) duck breast
1 cup (3.5 oz or 100 g) green
 beans, trimmed
3 cups (7 oz or 200 g) snow
 peas (mangetout), trimmed
6 figs, peeled and halved
1/2 cup (3.5 oz or 100 g) butter
parsley, minced

Mix together the balsamic vinegar, honey, orange juice, olive oil, salt
and pepper. Add the duck breast and leave to marinate for 1 hour.
Steam the green beans for about 8-10 minutes, then using the
same water steam the snow peas for about 5 minutes.
Remove the duck from the marinade and reserve. In a frying pan,
brown the duck breast evenly on all sides, then set aside. Add the
figs and cook for 2 minutes, then set aside. Skim the fat off the
juices left in the pan, then pour in the reserved marinade. Bring to
a simmer over a low heat. Add 3 tablespoons of the butter and
pinches of salt and pepper, and stir with a whisk.
In another frying pan melt the rest of the butter, then add the green
beans and snow peas, season with salt and pepper, sprinkle with
the parsley and cook for around 4 minutes.
Slice the duck and serve with vegetables, figs and marinade sauce.

Turkey and Mushroom Rotolini

146

Preparation time 25 minutes
Cooking time 15 minutes
Wine *Val d'Aosta Pinot Bianco*

4 tbsps extra-virgin olive oil
1 garlic clove, smashed
5 mushrooms, thinly sliced
parsley, minced
salt and pepper
4 slices turkey
 (3.5 oz or 100 g each)
1 tbsp plain flour
1 lemon, juiced and zest
 julienned
1/2 cup (120 ml) white wine

Heat 2 tablespoons olive oil with the garlic clove in a non-stick
frying pan. Add the mushrooms and sauté over high heat for
7-8 minutes. Sprinkle over the parsley and season with salt and
pepper. Reserve a few slices for garnish, then finely chop the rest
of the mushrooms.
Pound the turkey slices between 2 pieces of parchment paper,
then salt them lightly. Place some mushroom mixture on each one
and roll it up. Tie with kitchen string or fix with a toothpick.
Dust each roll with flour, then brown them in a frying pan. Sprinkle
over the lemon juice and then the wine, add salt and pepper and
let cook for around 6 minutes.
Serve the rotolini cut in half, garnished with the reserved
mushroom slices and julienned lemon rind.

Stuffed Veal Breast

Preparation time 40 minutes
Cooking time 3 hours
Wine *Castel del Monte Rosso*

👨‍🍳 👨‍🍳

Serves 6

STUFFING
3/4 cup (3.5 oz or 100 g)
  breadcrumbs
4 tbsps broth (from a stock cube)
salt and pepper
nutmeg, grated
9 oz (250 g) ricotta
1 egg, beaten
1⅓ cups (4.5 oz or 130 g)
  grated Parmesan

VEAL
1 veal breast (around 2 lb or 1 kg)
4 tbsps extra-virgin olive oil
3 garlic cloves, smashed
1 cup (1.8 oz or 50 g) herbs,
  minced
2 medium potatoes, sliced
1 rosemary sprig
salt
3/4 cup plus 1 tbsp (200 ml)
  broth (from a stock cube)

147

Preheat oven to 350°F (180°C).
Mix together the breadcrumbs and the 4 tablespoons of broth in a
small saucepan, and heat, stirring, until a compact mixture forms.
Season with salt, pepper and nutmeg to taste. Remove from the
heat, and mix in the ricotta, then the egg, then the Parmesan cheese.
Stuff the veal breast with the breadcrumb mixture and sew it up
using kitchen string. Lay the meat in a baking dish oiled with olive
oil. Add the garlic cloves, the minced herbs, the potatoes and the
rosemary and season with salt. Place in the oven and roast for
around 3 hours, basting every so often with a little broth.
Serve hot together with the potatoes.

Ham en Crôute
(FRIULI-VENEZIA GIULIA)

Note *This recipe for ham cooked in a bread crust is typical of Friuli-Venezia Giulia, and like many of the region's specialities has its origins outside Italy, in this case from Czechoslovakia.*

Preparation time 20 minutes
Cooking time 1 hour 15 minutes
Wine *Isonzo Tocai Friulano*

Serves 6-8

2 tbsps (0.9 oz or 25 g) dried
 active yeast
8 cups (2 lb or 1 kg) plain flour
bay leaves
salt
peppercorns
1 cooked ham (around 4.5 lb or 2 kg)

148

Preheat the oven to 350°F (180°C).
Dissolve the yeast in some warm water. Place the flour in a bowl and mix in the salt and the yeast. Mix with as much water as needed to form a smooth and uniform dough. Shape it into a ball and leave to rise, covered with a clean kitchen towel, for around 1 hour.
Knead the dough further, then let rise again until it has doubled in volume.
Roll out the dough into a sheet about 3/4-inch (2 cm) thick, large enough to cover the ham. Scatter some peppercorns and the bay leaves over the dough, then place the ham in the centre and wrap it completely with the dough, wetting the borders and pressing them together well to create a tight seal.
Place the ham in a baking dish and bake for around 15 minutes, then lower the heat and cook for another hour.
Remove from the oven and serve cut into thick slices.

Turkey with Chestnuts
(ABRUZZO)

Preparation time 50 minutes
Cooking time 3 hours 20 minutes
Wine *Abruzzo Rosato*

Serves 8

4.5 lb (2 kg) chestnuts
1 turkey (around 6.5 lb or 3 kg)
salt and pepper
parsley, minced
2 garlic cloves, minced
rosemary, minced
1.5 oz (40 g) lard
3/4 cup plus 2 tbsps (200 ml)
 white wine

Preheat oven to 325°F (170°C).
Cut an X in the chestnut shells, then roast them over an open
flame in a pan with holes for chestnut-roasting, or in the oven. Peel
and let cool.
Clean the turkey well and season the cavity with salt, pepper and a
mixture of the parsley, garlic and rosemary. Add half the chestnuts
and half the lard in small pieces. Tie the turkey up well with kitchen
string, sewing closed the cavity.
Use the rest of the lard to grease a roasting pan and place the
turkey on it, then roast in the oven for around 3 hours.
Meanwhile grind the remaining chestnuts in a mortar and pestle.
Put them in a saucepan with some of the cooking liquid from the
turkey and the white wine. Bring to a boil and reduce.
Remove the turkey from the oven, carve it and serve with the
chestnut sauce.

149

Roast Beef with Salt

Preparation time 20 minutes
Cooking time 20 minutes
Wine *Friuli Collio Merlot*

BEEF
1.75 lb (800 g) beef loin
3 tbsps extra-virgin olive oil
2 egg whites, beaten
2 lb (1 kg) coarse salt
1 bunch mixed herbs (rosemary,
 thyme, marjoram), minced

SAUCE
3 tbsps balsamic vinegar
salt and pepper
5 tbsps extra-virgin olive oil
1 garlic clove, smashed
rosemary, minced

150

Preheat oven to 425°F (220°C).
Brush the beef with olive oil and brown on all sides in a frying pan.
In a large bowl beat egg whites until foamy, and stir in the salt and
herbs. Place a layer of the salt mixture on the bottom of a baking
dish, then place the beef on top and cover with the rest of the salt
mixture. Bake for 30 minutes.
Meanwhile heat the balsamic vinegar in a small saucepan and add
salt and pepper to taste, then mix in the oil, garlic and rosemary
and heat through.
Remove the roast beef from the oven. The salt crust should be
hard and darkened. Break the crust, and remove the meat. Serve it
sliced with the balsamic-vinegar sauce.

Roast Pork with Potatoes

Preparation time 20 minutes
Cooking time 40 minutes
Wine *Nebbiolo d'Alba*

thyme, sage and rosemary,
 minced
salt and pepper
1 pork shank
3 tbsps extra-virgin olive oil
5 potatoes, peeled and sliced
1 knob of butter
1 shallot, minced
1¼ cups (300 ml) hot vegetable
 broth
1 truffle, minced

Preheat oven to 375°F (190°C).
Mix herbs, salt and pepper
together. Rub into the pork,
place on a baking sheet and
drizzle with olive oil. Roast, turning often, until cooked through.
Trim the potatoes with a knife to
form teardrop shapes.
Melt the butter in a frying pan,
add the shallot and sauté. Add
potatoes and cook for 3 minutes
until golden. Add a little broth
and truffle. Cook, adding hot
broth little by little.
Serve the pork, sliced, with the
potatoes.

Steak with Chestnuts

Preparation time 15 minutes
Cooking time 30 minutes
Wine *Sicilia Cabernet-Sauvignon*

15 chestnuts
1 beef steak, 3/4-inch (2 cm) thick
coarse salt
1 bunch arugula, shredded
2 oz (60 g) Parmesan cheese,
 shaved
3 tbsps extra-virgin olive oil

Cut an X in the chestnuts and
cook them in a heavy-bottomed
steel saucepan over very low
heat, shaking the pan often.
When cooked through, peel
and crumble the chestnuts.
Trim any external fat from the
steak. Heat a cast-iron grill
pan. Sprinkle the grill pan with
coarse salt, and then lay on the
steak. After 3 minutes salt the
uncooked top then turn and
cook for another 3-4 minutes.
Slice the meat and return to the
grill pan for 20 seconds.
Serve the steak slices covered
with arugula, chestnuts and
Parmesan shavings and drizzle
with olive oil.

Cheese Tart with Chicken and Mushrooms

Preparation time 35 minutes
Cooking time 50 minutes
Wine *Alto Adige Santa Maddalena*

4 fresh porcini mushrooms
3 tbsps extra-virgin olive oil
2 leeks, dark green leaves
 removed, sliced
1 garlic clove, smashed
1 chicken breast, diced
2 sprigs mint
salt and pepper
9 oz (250 g) puff pastry
7 oz (200 g) pecorino cheese,
 diced

152

Preheat oven to 375°F (190°C).
Clean the porcini with damp paper towels and remove the dirty part of the stalk, then slice.
Sauté the leeks with 1 tablespoon olive oil over a low flame for around 15 minutes.
In another frying pan heat 1 tablespoon of oil and sauté the garlic briefly, then add the chicken and a few minutes later the mushrooms. Add the mint and season with salt and pepper.
Roll out the puff pastry and line a pie dish, reserving a piece for the top. Poke holes in the bottom with a fork.
Mix together the leeks, the chicken and mushroom mixture and the pecorino. Pour the whole mixture into the pie dish and cover with the remaining puff pastry, rolled out thin. Oil the top with the remaining tablespoon of oil. Poke some more holes in the top with a fork to let steam escape, and bake for around 40 minutes. As soon as the top is golden, remove. Serve warm.

Roast Lamb Chops

Preparation time 20 minutes
Cooking time 25 minutes
Wine *Taurasi*

12 lamp chops
2 cups (500 ml) milk
breadcrumbs
3 tbsps grated Parmesan
salt and pepper
2 eggs
1/2 cup (120 ml) white wine

153

Preheat oven to 400°F (200°C).
Trim any excess fat from the lamb chops, then place in a bowl
and cover with milk. Refrigerate for at least 12 hours. Drain and
pat dry.
Mix together the breadcrumbs, Parmesan and pepper in a bowl.
In another bowl, beat the eggs and add salt.
Dip the lamb chops in the egg and then the breadcrumb mixture
and press well so that it sticks.
Line a baking tray with parchment paper and lay the lamp chops
on it, with a little oil drizzled on both sides. Bake for 10 minutes,
turn over, and cook for another 10 minutes. Sprinkle with a little
white wine and return to the oven for a few more minutes.
Serve the lamp chops very hot, with a side dish of steamed
vegetables if desired.

Spiced Beef Kebabs with Speck Ham and Herb Mayonnaise

Preparation time 20 minutes
Cooking time 15 minutes
Wine *Alto Adige*
Santa Maddalena

1 garlic clove, smashed
2 tbsps extra-virgin olive oil
12.5 oz (350 g) lean
 ground beef
2 oz (50 g) speck ham, finely
 chopped
1 egg yolk
ground cumin
ground coriander
parsley, minced
salt and pepper
2 tbsps herb mayonnaise

154

Sauté the garlic in the olive oil for a few minutes until golden-brown, then remove from the heat and let cool.
Remove and discard the garlic clove and pour the oil into a bowl with the beef.
Add the speck ham, egg yolk, parsley, cumin, coriander, salt and pepper to the beef. Mix thoroughly by hand until all the ingredients are incorporated.
Form small balls with the meat mixture and thread them onto wooden skewers. Shape the balls into flattened oval shapes.
Grill the kebabs on both sides.
Serve with the herb mayonnaise.

Gratinéed Scallops

Preparation time 20 minutes
Cooking time 15 minutes
Wine *Alto Adige Pinot Bianco*

8 large scallops, with scallop
 shells, washed
8 thin slices of Colonnata lardo
1 sprig of rosemary
3 tbsps extra-virgin olive oil
1 shallot, minced
4 medium white-fleshed potatoes,
 peeled and diced
3/4 cup plus 1 tbsp (200 ml)
 vegetable broth or hot water
1 egg yolk
salt and pepper

Preheat oven to 400°F (200°C).
Wrap each scallop in a slice of lardo with one rosemary leaf.
Heat oil in a large saucepan. Add shallot and sauté. Add potatoes
and broth and let cook until potatoes are soft. Puree the mixture,
adding egg yolk and salt and pepper to taste.
Fill the scallop shells with the potato mixture and bake
for 5 minutes.
Place the scallops wrapped in lard on top of the potato puree
and bake for another 7 minutes. Remove from the oven and serve
immediately.

Swordfish with Spinach

Preparation time 20 minutes
Cooking time 15 minutes
Wine *Torgiano Bianco*

2.2 lb (1 kg) spinach
1 cup (250 ml) heavy cream
1 egg yolk
nutmeg, grated
salt and pepper
parsley, chopped
2 tbsps extra-virgin olive oil
1.3 lb (600 g) swordfish fillet,
 chopped
3½ tbsps white wine
juice of 1 lemon
parsley, chopped

Blanch spinach briefly.
Simmer the cream and reduce.
Beat egg yolk with nutmeg, salt,
pepper and parsley. Add yolk
and spinach to cream and mix.
Heat olive oil in a frying pan.
Add swordfish and sauté for
4 minutes. Season with salt
and pepper. Add wine and let
evaporate, then add lemon juice
and cook for 2 minutes, then
add parsley.
Place spinach on a serving
plate, top with swordfish and
drizzle pan juices over the fish.

Sole with Green Grape Sauce

Preparation time 20 minutes
Cooking time 15 minutes
Wine *Bolgheri Bianco*

12 sole fillets
salt and pepper
1 tbsp plain flour
2 tbsps extra-virgin olive oil
2 shallots, minced
3/4 cup (180 ml) white wine
3 tbsps heavy cream
1 bunch green grapes

Lightly pound the fish with a
meat tenderizer. Salt, pepper
and flour the fillets.
Heat oil in a large frying pan and
add fish. Sauté for 1 minute on
each side. Keep warm.
Heat the shallots, wine and
cream together in a saucepan.
Smash half of the grapes and
add them to the sauce. Simmer
for 10-15 minutes. Add salt
and pepper to taste. Sieve
the sauce. Slice the remaining
grapes in half and add to the
sauce. Bring sauce to a boil for
1 minute.
Place fillets on individual
plates and top with sauce.
Serve immediately.

158

Sautéed Prawns

Preparation time 12 minutes
Cooking time 18 minutes
Wine *Metodo Classico Franciacorta Brut*

4 tbsps extra-virgin olive oil
6 spring onions, peeled and
 sliced
6 large white button mushrooms,
 cleaned and sliced
1.3 lb (600 g) prawns, peeled
 and deveined
salt and pepper
parsley, chopped

Heat oil in a large frying pan.
Add spring onion and sauté for
a few minutes. Add mushrooms
and sauté over high heat for
3-4 minutes. Add prawns and
season with salt and pepper.
Sprinkle with parsley and serve
immediately.

Swordfish with Broccoli

Preparation time 15 minutes
Cooking time 20 minutes
Wine *Trebbiano d'Abruzzo*

4 tbsps extra-virgin olive oil
fresh dill, chopped
2 garlic cloves, smashed
salt and white pepper
4 swordfish fillets
 (4 oz or 120 g each)
2 heads of broccoli,
 cut into florets
1 lime (1/2 juiced, 1/2 cut
 into wedges)

159

Preheat oven to 375°F (190°C).
Mix 1/2 the oil, dill, 1 garlic
clove, salt and pepper in a
baking dish. Add fish and cover.
Refrigerate for 2 hours.
Heat remaining oil in a frying pan
and sauté 1 garlic clove. Add
broccoli and sauté for 5 minutes.
Add a little hot water and salt
and pepper to taste. Let cool
and chop finely.
Transfer swordfish from
marinade to a baking dish. Pour
lime juice over the fish and bake
for 10 minutes. Serve fish with
broccoli, a drizzle of olive oil and
lime wedges.

Baked Monkfish

Note *Due to the low yield of saffron flowers, the spice is famously expensive. In fact, it takes thousands of saffron flowers to make just one kilogram of saffron. It is possible to find another similar spice which made from the safflower plant.*

160

Preparation time 15 minutes
Cooking time 10 minutes
Wine *Colli di Luni Bianco*

MONKFISH
14 oz (400 g) monkfish steaks
parsley leaves
chives, chopped
thyme leaves
1 shallot, diced
6 tbsps extra-virgin olive oil
salt
3 tbsps brandy

HERB BUTTER
7 tbsps butter
parsley, chives and thyme, minced
white pepper

GARNISH
dried saffron pistils

Preheat oven to 350°F (180°C).
Beat the butter, parsley, chives and thyme together.
Add white pepper to taste. When the butter and herbs are smooth wrap in parchment paper and refrigerate.
Cut out 4 large rectangular pieces of parchment paper. Brush a little oil over each rectangle. Place paper on a baking sheet. Place herbs and shallot on each piece of paper and then top with the monkfish steaks. Brush fish with oil and season with salt. Bake for 5 minutes; pour brandy over fish and bake for another 5 minutes. Remove fish from the oven and top with a pat of herb butter and a few saffron pistils. Serve immediately.

Tuna Rösti

Note *Rösti is a traditional Swiss potato cake. Typically the potatoes are boiled and sliced one day in advance, then they are sautéed with pieces of cured lard and mashed in the pan. Once the potatoes are golden-brown the pan is inverted onto a serving plate.*

Preparation time 25 minutes
Cooking time 10 minutes
Wine *Metodo Trento Talento Brut*

14 oz (400 g) tuna fillet
3 tbsps extra-virgin olive oil
salt and pepper
2 yellow-fleshed potatoes,
 peeled and grated
1/2 garlic clove
2 tbsps Taggiasca or other small
 black olives in oil
parsley, finely chopped

Preheat oven to 400°F (200°C).
Cut the tuna into 4 pieces. Brush with olive oil, season with salt and pepper and cover. Leave to marinate in the refrigerator.
Place grated potatoes in a large bowl and season with salt and pepper.
Heat olive oil in a large frying pan, add the garlic and sauté for 1 minute. Remove garlic and add potatoes. Press down potatoes with a spatula and cook for 2 minutes. Flip the potato cake and cook for another 2 minutes. Remove from heat and cut into 8 slices or rounds.
Place tuna on top of 1 potato rösti and top with another. Press down to close the potato around the tuna, then place on a baking sheet and bake for 3 minutes.
Meanwhile, blend parsley and oil from the olives. Pour parsley oil over the rosti and top with olives. Serve immediately.

Mediterranean Grilled Swordfish with Polenta

Note *Swordfish can be substituted with tuna or dogfish fillets. To make a more flavoursome sauce add 10 black olives to the Mediterranean sauce.*

Preparation time 15 minutes
Cooking time 20 minutes
Wine *Etna Bianco*

2 cups (500 ml) water
salt
3/4 cup plus 2 tbsps (5.5 oz
 or 150 g) instant polenta
1 lb (500 g) swordfish fillets
oregano leaves
pepper
6 sun-dried tomatoes preserved
 in oil, drained and chopped
10 salted capers, rinsed
 and chopped
basil, chopped
3 tbsps extra-virgin olive oil

Salt the water and bring to a boil in a saucepan. Whisk in polenta. Cook over low heat, stirring constantly with a wooden spoon until polenta is cooked. Pour into a rectangular baking dish and let cool.
Cut the swordfish fillets into smaller pieces and sprinkle with oregano and pepper.
Mix tomatoes, capers, basil and 1 tablespoon olive oil in a bowl.
Cut polenta into equal-sized pieces and place on a pre-heated grill or grill pan. Let cook for 5 minutes and flip. Add fish to the grill and cook 3 minutes per side.
Serve swordfish and polenta with tomato-caper sauce.

Sole Sautéed in White Wine

Preparation time 25 minutes
Cooking time 20 minutes
Wine *Trebbiano d'Abruzzo*

4 sole, filleted
1 tbsp plain flour
3 tbsps butter
1 shallot, minced
1 bay leaf, chopped
thyme leaves, chopped
parsley, chopped
salt and pepper
1/2 cup (120 ml) white wine

Lightly coat the fish fillets with
flour.
Heat 1 tablespoon butter in a
large frying pan and add the
minced shallot. Let soften and
add fish fillets, herbs and salt
and pepper to taste.
Melt the remaining butter. Add
melted butter and wine to the
fish. Let cook for 20 minutes.
Serve fish immediately, with the
pan juices.

Sturgeon with Chickpeas

Preparation time 20 minutes
Cooking time 15 minutes
Wine *Bianchello del Metauro*

2 cups (500 ml) water
2 green tea bags
2 cinnamon sticks
1 bunch mint
9 oz (250 g) sturgeon fillet,
 cut into 2-inch (5 cm) slices
1¼ cups (10.5 oz or 300 g)
 canned chickpeas, drained
2 tsps ground turmeric
1 egg white
salt
poppy seeds
4 sprigs rosemary
1/2 cup (120 ml) sunflower oil

163

Boil water with green tea,
cinnamon and half the mint.
Salt the sturgeon and steam in
a steaming basket over the tea
infusion for 10 minutes.
Heat chickpeas in a frying pan
with the turmeric, remaining mint
and a little water.
Beat egg white with a pinch of
salt. Dip rosemary sprigs in the
egg white, then in the poppy
seeds and fry in sunflower oil.
Serve sturgeon with chickpeas,
garnished with rosemary sprigs.

Codfish Croquettes with Pesto and Olives

Preparation time 15 minutes
Cooking time 20 minutes
Wine *Verdicchio di Matelica*
♟

PESTO
1 bunch of basil
1 tbsp pine nuts
3 tbsps extra-virgin olive oil
salt

CROQUETTES
3 tbsps extra-virgin olive oil
1 shallot, minced
14 oz (400 g) codfish (or half
 codfish and half soaked salt cod)
2 slices French bread
7 tbsps milk
5 Taggiasca or other small
 black olives
1 egg
salt and pepper
1/2 cup (2 oz or 50 g)
 breadcrumbs

GARNISH
mixed greens
5 Taggiasca or other small
 black olives

164

Heat 3 tablespoons oil in a large frying pan and add the shallot.
Let soften, add codfish and season with salt and pepper.
Soak bread in milk until soft. Squeeze excess milk out of bread
and place, the bread in a food processor. Add the fish, a few
olives, the egg, salt and pepper. Blend and add a few tablespoons
of breadcrumbs to bind the mixture.
Pour the remaining breadcrumbs on a plate. Roll fish mixture into
balls and coat with breadcrumbs.
Place croquettes on a hot grill or grill pan and cook slowly, turning
frequently.
Meanwhile, blend basil, pine nuts, oil and salt to taste in a food
processor. Set aside.
Place greens on a serving plate, add croquettes and top with
pesto and remaining olives.

Tuna Fillet with Fried Pears

Preparation time 20 minutes
Cooking time 20 minutes
Wine *Metodo Classico
Franciacorta Dosaggio Zero*

TUNA
2 tbsps extra-virgin olive oil
1 garlic clove
14 oz (400 g) tuna fillet,
 cut into 4 pieces
1 sprig of thyme

PEARS
2 Decana pears
1 tbsp plain flour
1 egg, beaten
5 tbsps breadcrumbs
1/3 cup (1 oz or 30 g)
 hazelnuts, finely chopped
sunflower oil

SAUCE
3 tbsps soy sauce
1 tbsp rice oil
1 tbsp extra-virgin olive oil
1 tbsp water

165

To make the tuna, heat the olive oil in a large frying pan; add garlic
and sauté for 1 minute. Add tuna and thyme and cook for
2 minutes per side. Keep hot.
Using a melon baller, make pear balls. Roll the balls in the flour,
then the egg and then the breadcrumbs mixed with the hazelnuts.
Heat sunflower oil in a small saucepan and fry the pear balls.
Meanwhile mix the soy sauce, rice oil, olive oil and water.
Place tuna and pear balls on a serving dish. Serve soy dressing
in a small bowl on the side.

Sole with Winter Squash Cream

Preparation time 25 minutes
Cooking time 1 hour 10 minutes
Wine *Bianchello del Metauro*

SOLE
4 sole fillets, sliced
 into strips
2 tbsps extra-virgin olive oil
1/2 tsp thyme
salt

WINTER SQUASH CREAM
4 tbsps extra-virgin olive oil
1/3 leek, julienned
1 winter squash, 1/4 diced,
 3/4 sliced into thin wedges
7 tbsps heavy cream
3/4 cup (180 ml) water
juice of 1/2 lemon
1 tbsp chopped herbs
 (parsley, rosemary, thyme)
salt
5 tbsps Taggiasca olives

Preheat oven to 400°F (200°C).
Place sole on an oiled baking sheet. Brush with oil and sprinkle with thyme leaves and salt, then set aside.
Heat 1 tablespoon olive oil in a large frying pan and add leek. Sauté for 1 minute and add the diced squash, cream, and water. Cover and cook for 15 minutes. Smash with a fork or puree to form a cream.
Place remaining squash on a baking sheet and bake for 3-4 minutes. Bake the fish for 3-4 minutes.
Meanwhile whisk remaining olive oil, lemon juice, herbs and salt to taste in a small bowl.
Place squash cream on individual serving plates. Top with fish, squash wedges and olives. Drizzle with lemon-herb dressing. Serve immediately.

Hake with Mixed Beans

Preparation time 15 minutes
Cooking time 40 minutes
Wine *Colli di Luni Bianco*

4 cups (1 l) water
1/2 cup (4 oz or 120 g) mixed
 legumes (lentils, cannellini and
 borlotti beans), soaked
1 hake fillet (about 14 oz or 400 g),
 butterflied
thyme leaves, chopped
6 tbsps extra-virgin olive oil
salt and pepper
1 garlic clove, halved

Boil legumes until they are just
cooked in 4 cups (1 l) of salted
water.
Place hake fillet in a steaming
basket and top with thyme, 1
tablespoon oil, salt and pepper.
Steam for 15 minutes.
Heat remaining oil in a large
frying pan. Add garlic clove,
legumes and a few tablespoons
of water. Cook until heated
through.
Serve the steamed hake with
lentils and beans.

Sea-Bream Sandwiches

Preparation time 15 minutes
Cooking time 8 minutes
Wine *Bianco d'Alcamo*

5-6 sun-dried tomatoes in oil
7-8 salted capers, rinsed
1 egg white
4 small sea bream, cut into 8 fillets
2 slices French bread
1 tbsp black olive tapenade
2 tbsps extra-virgin olive oil
salt and pepper

Place tomatoes, capers,
bread and egg white in a food
processor and blend to form
a thick sauce.
Spread the sauce on 4 fillets.
Place another fillet on top to
form sandwiches. Wrap each
sandwich in plastic wrap and
steam in a steaming basket
for 8 minutes.
Dilute the olive tapenade with
olive oil. Pour into a small
serving dish.
Remove sea-bream sandwiches
from the steamer, unwrap and
slice. Place on a serving dish
and serve with tapenade.

167

Spinach and Buffalo Mozzarella Omelette

Note *Buffalo's milk mozzarella is best stored in its own liquid in a cool place up until it is ready to be eaten. If stored in the refrigerator the cheese may be brought to room temperature 30 minutes before serving.*

Preparation time 15 minutes
Cooking time 10 minutes
Wine *Greco di Tufo*

4 eggs
salt and pepper
1 tbsp grated Parmesan
3 cups (3.5 oz or 100 g) fresh
  spinach, blanched
3 tbsps extra-virgin olive oil
1 buffalo's milk mozzarella, diced
1 bunch mixed greens (arugula,
  chicory, watercress), washed

168

Beat eggs, salt and pepper in a bowl. Add Parmesan cheese and spinach.
Heat oil in a small non-stick pan and pour in a quarter of the egg mixture. Let cook for 30 seconds and swirl the egg in the pan to make a uniform layer. Shake the pan so that the omelette rolls up, using a fork to help if necessary. Continue cooking the omelette by rolling it in the pan so that it cooks uniformly on all sides and remains soft in the centre, about 3 minutes. Repeat 3 times with remaining egg mixture.
Fill the omelettes with mozzarella and serve on a bed of mixed greens.

Mixed Cheese Plate

Preparation time 10 minutes
Cooking time 10 minutes
Wine *Amarone della Valpolicella*

♟

1 bunch green grapes,
 peeled and seeded
3.5 oz (100 g) buccia di rospo
 or other sheep's milk cheese
3.5 oz (100 g) goat's milk cheese,
 aged in grape pomace
3.5 oz (100 g) cow's milk cheese,
 aged in walnut leaves
2 tbsps orange blossom honey
2 tbsps acacia blossom honey
2 tbsps chestnut blossom honey

Slice the cheese into irregular
wedges and place on a serving
plate, dividing the cheese by
type.
Place one grape on or beside
each slice of cheese and drizzle
with honeys.

Note *Buccia di rospo is a
sheep's milk cheese made
in Tuscany. Its name, meaning
toad skin, comes from the rough
texture of the rind.*

Grilled Provola with Truffles

Preparation time 10 minutes
Cooking time 5 minutes
Wine *Rossese di Dolceacqua*

♟

4 thick slices mild provola
 cheese, sliced in half
2 tbsps extra-virgin olive oil
1 truffle
salt and pepper
French bread

Heat a grill pan until nearly
smoking.
Place slices of provola cheese
on the grill and cook 2 minutes
on each side.
Arrange the slices on a serving
dish.
Slice the truffle directly onto the
cheese, drizzle with oil. Season
with salt and pepper to taste.
Serve with French bread.

Note *This recipe can be made
with black truffles or the more
aromatic white variety.*

Mushroom-Stuffed Squash Blossoms

Preparation time 20 minutes
Cooking time 15 minutes
Wine *Metodo Classico*
Franciacorta Extra Brut

FILLING
2 tbsps extra-virgin olive oil
1 garlic clove, smashed
4 wild mushrooms,
 cleaned and thinly sliced
salt and pepper

SQUASH BLOSSOMS
16 squash blossoms,
 washed and pistil removed
3/4 cup (3.5 oz or 100 g)
 plain flour
2/3 cup (3.5 oz or 100 g) rice flour
1½ cups (350 ml) very cold
 sparkling water
sunflower oil
parsley leaves

170

Heat oil in a large non-stick pan and add garlic clove. Add
mushrooms and sauté until soft and liquid has evaporated.
Add salt and pepper to taste. Let cool then chop mushrooms.
Fill each squash blossom with 2 spoonfuls of mushrooms and
twist the top of the blossom to close.
Mix flour and rice flour in a mixing bowl. Slowly add sparkling
water to form a smooth batter.
Heat sunflower oil in a saucepan until very hot.
Meanwhile, dip squash blossoms into the batter. Fry squash
blossoms until golden-brown. Drain on paper towels. Season
with salt, garnish with parsley leaves and serve immediately.

Cheese Crisp
(FRIULI-VENEZIA GIULIA)

Note *This cheese crisp
from the northeastern
region of Friuli-Venezia
Giulia is known as* frico.
*It is usually served with
polenta. There are several
richer versions of* frico
*made with eggs, potatoes
and speck ham.*

Preparation time 5 minutes
Cooking time 20 minutes
Wine *Grave del Friuli Cabernet
Franc*

1/2 cup (3.5 oz or 100 g) butter
1 onion, thinly sliced
7 oz (200 g) hard white cheese,
 thinly sliced
3.5 oz (100 g) aged Montasio
 cheese, thinly sliced
salt and pepper

Heat butter in a large frying pan. Add the sliced onion and sauté
until it begins to brown.
Add the cheese slices and mix. Continue cooking until the cheese
melts, forming a uniform layer. Add salt and pepper to taste.
When the cheese forms a golden crust on the bottom, flip
the frico.
Cook until both sides have formed a golden-brown crust.
Remove from the pan and place on paper towels to absorb
excess oil.
Slice into wedges and serve immediately.

Rustic Pizza

Note *For a thicker crust, plain flour may be substituted with the same quantity of bread flour.*

Preparation time 20 minutes
Cooking time 40 minutes
Beer *German Weizen*

172

DOUGH
4 cups (1 lb oz or 500 g)
 plain flour
1 small potato, boiled,
 peeled and mashed
7 tbsps water
7 tbsps light beer
2 tbsps (0.9 oz or 25 g) dry
 active yeast
3 tbsps extra-virgin olive oil
salt

TOPPING
1¼ cups (10.5 oz or 300 g)
 canned borlotti beans, drained
5 cherry tomatoes, halved
5.5 oz (150 g) smoked pancetta,
 diced
3 tbsps extra-virgin olive oil
2-3 garlic cloves, sliced
parsley, chopped
salt

Place flour in a large mixing bowl. Add potato, water, beer and mix.
Add yeast, oil and salt and knead to form a smooth and elastic
dough. Let rise for 2 hours in a warm place.
Preheat oven to 400°F (200°C).
Oil a rimmed baking sheet and flatten out the dough to cover
the entire surface with a uniform layer.
Mix beans, tomatoes, pancetta, oil, garlic, parsley and salt in a bowl.
Spread the topping over the pizza dough. Drizzle with oil and
season with salt.
Bake for 30-40 minutes. Serve immediately.

Pizza with Truffle Oil

Preparation time 10 minutes
Cooking time 10 minutes
Beer *English Pale Ale*

10.5 oz (300 g) prepared
 pizza dough (see p. 1093)
3 tbsps truffle oil
salt
9 oz (250 g) cow's milk
 mozzarella, diced
2 fresh porcini mushrooms,
 cleaned and sliced
5.5 oz (150 g) Parmesan, shaved

Preheat oven to 450°F (230°C).
Cut pizza dough into 4 rounds.
Oil each round with truffle oil
and season with salt.
Top with mozzarella and porcini
mushrooms. Sprinkle over the
Parmesan cheese.
Bake pizzas for 8 minutes
and serve immediately.

Note *If fresh porcini mushrooms
are unavailable they may be
substituted with white button
mushrooms.*

Ham and Truffle Pizza

Preparation time 10 minutes
Cooking time 12 minutes
Beer *German Weizen*

10 oz (280 g) prepared
 pizza dough (see p. 1093)
9 oz (250 g) mild provolone,
 shredded
3.5 oz (100 g) cow's milk
 mozzarella, shredded
salt
2 tbsps extra-virgin olive oil
6.5 oz (180 g) ham, diced
1 small black truffle

173

Preheat oven to 475°F (240°C).
Roll out pizza dough on a floured
surface. When the dough is very
thin transfer to a baking sheet.
Sprinkle with shredded cheese
and salt. Drizzle with oil and
scatter over the ham.
Bake for 8 minutes. Transfer to a
serving dish and shave truffle over
the pizza. Serve immediately.

Eggs with Fontina Cheese

(Valle d'Aosta)

Note *A simple white bread can also be made at home using the following recipe: 1 oz or 30 g yeast, 2.2 lb or 1 kg flour, 3.5 oz or 100 g butter, olive oil, water and salt. The secret to good home-made bread is in the rising time, in this case about 1 hour 30 minutes.*

Preparation time 10 minutes
Cooking time 20 minutes
Wine *Valle d'Aosta Rosato*

Serves 6

8 slices white bread
3/4 cup (180 ml) milk
7 oz (200 g) fontina cheese, sliced
3 tbsps butter, diced
4 eggs
salt and pepper

174

Preheat oven to 400°F (200°C).
Soak bread in milk for 5 minutes. Squeeze out excess liquid.
Butter a rectangular baking dish and cover with bread slices.
Cover each slice with slices of fontina cheese and butter. Bake until the butter melts.
Crack eggs over the bread and cheese, making sure that eggs are not too near each other. Cover each yolk with a slice of fontina cheese.
Return to the oven for 15 minutes. Season with salt and pepper and serve immediately.

Emmenthal and Potato Croquettes

Preparation time 15 minutes
Cooking time 30 minutes
Wine *Alto Adige Müller Thurgau*

2 medium potatoes,
 boiled and peeled
3.5 oz (100 g) Emmenthal
 cheese, diced
1/3 cup (1 oz or 30 g)
 hazelnuts, chopped
3/4 cup (5.5 oz or 150 g)
 finely ground cornmeal
2 eggs
parsley and chives, chopped
salt and pepper
1¼ cups (300 ml) peanut oil

Mash potatoes in a large bowl. Add Emmenthal cheese, hazelnuts,
1/4 cup (2 oz or 50 g) cornmeal and 1 egg. Mix well and then add
parsley, chives and salt and pepper to taste.
Form small balls with the potato mixture.
Beat remaining egg and pour remaining cornmeal on a plate.
Dip potato balls in egg and then coat with cornmeal.
Heat peanut oil in a saucepan. Add croquettes and fry until
golden-brown.
Drain on paper towels and salt to taste. Serve immediately.

Stuffed Phyllo Triangles

Note *Several types of goat's milk cheese are readily available, from very fresh to aged. For a subtle variation, fresh goat's milk cheese can be marinated in aromatic oil or with fresh herbs.*

Preparation time 10 minutes
Cooking time 5 minutes
Wine *Metodo Trento Talento Brut*

3.5 oz (100 g) mortadella
1/2 cup (2 oz or 50 g)
 pistachios
2 oz (50 g) fresh goat's
 milk cheese
1/2 roll of phyllo dough
1 egg, beaten
sunflower or sesame oil

176

Place mortadella and pistachios in a food processor and blend to form a compact, granular mixture. Add goat's milk cheese and mix well. Set aside.
Unroll phyllo dough and stick 2 sheets of dough together using a little egg wash. Cut out several 2-inch (4 cm) squares.
Place 1 teaspoon of filling in the centre of each square and fold over to form a triangle. Seal the edges with egg.
Heat the oil in a saucepan and fry phyllo triangles until golden-brown. Drain on paper towels and salt to taste. Salt and serve immediately.

Polenta Sandwiches with Cheese

Preparation time 40 minutes
Cooking time 20 minutes
Wine *Alto Adige Santa Maddalena*

POLENTA
1 cup (5.5 oz or 160 g)
 inctant polenta cornmoal
sunflower oil
1 egg
salt

FILLING
5.5 oz (150 g) fresh cow's milk
 cheese, diced
3.5 oz (100 g) smoked ham, diced
marjoram leaves

TOPPING
1 egg
white pepper
1 black truffle

Bring salted water to a boil and whisk in polenta. Continue whisking until the polenta begins to thicken. Pour polenta into a damp rectangular baking dish. Using a spatula form an even layer 1/2 inch (1½ cm) thick. Refrigerate.
Mix cheese, ham and marjoram in a bowl and set aside.
Cut polenta into 4 large rectangles and slice each rectangle horizontally into 3 very thin sheets. Discard centre sheet.
Beat egg in a small bowl. Brush the edges of 4 polenta sheets with egg and top with ham and cheese mixture. Top with remaining four polenta sheets. Brush edges with egg and press down to seal. Refrigerate for 5 minutes.
Heat oil in a large frying pan and fry polenta rectangles until golden brown. Drain on paper towels.
Beat remaining egg in a small bowl. Heat a non-stick pan and scramble the egg.
Top polenta sandwiches with scrambled egg and white pepper. Shave truffle over the sandwiches and serve immediately.

Autumn Vegetables with Chestnuts

178

Preparation time 40 minutes
Cooking time 55 minutes
Wine *Valle d'Aosta Bianco*

3 tbsps butter
1.3 lb (600 g) fresh chestnuts,
 roasted and peeled
1 tbsp sugar
3 small carrots, chopped
2 large celery stalks, chopped
thyme
1 bay leaf
1 tbsp fennel seeds
salt and pepper
3/4 cup (180 ml) water
10.5 oz (300 g) Savoy cabbage
2 red onions

Preheat oven to 350°F (180°C).
Heat butter in a large saucepan. Add chestnuts and sugar and caramelize, without letting the sugar brown. Add carrots, celery, thyme, bay leaf and fennel seeds. Add salt and pepper to taste. Add water, cover and let simmer for 20 minutes.
Meanwhile, bring a large pot of salted water to a boil. Blanch cabbage leaves. Drain and slice. Add cabbage to the simmering vegetables. Continue cooking another 10 minutes.
Bake whole onions for 10 minutes. Remove from the oven, peel and cut into wedges. Add onions to vegetables. Season with salt and pepper to taste. Serve immediately.

Chard, Porcini and Fontina Tart

Preparation time 25 minutes
Cooking time 40 minutes
Wine *Trentino Nosiola*

Serves 6-8

DOUGH
2 cups (8.8 oz or 250 g)
 plain flour
1 egg
1/2 cup (120 ml) water
5 tbsps melted butter
salt

FILLING
7 oz (200 g) Swiss chard
salt and pepper
3 tbsps extra-virgin olive oil
2 fresh porcini mushrooms,
 cleaned and sliced
3.5 oz (100 g) fontina cheese,
 diced
2 eggs
7 tbsps milk
7 tbsps heavy cream
3 tbsps grated Parmesan

179

Preheat oven to 350°F (180°C).
Pour flour onto a work surface and make a well in the centre. Add egg, water, butter and salt. Mix the dough and then knead for 10 minutes. Cover and let rest for 30 minutes.
Blanch the Swiss chard in boiling salted water, drain and chop.
Roll out dough into a very thin sheet. Butter a pie pan and line the pan with dough leaving an ample border.
Heat olive oil in a frying pan. Add mushrooms and sauté until soft.
In a large bowl, mix chard, mushrooms, fontina, salt and pepper. Spread the mixture evenly over the crust.
Beat eggs, milk, cream, Parmesan and salt to taste. Pour over the vegetables and fold extra dough over the top of the filling to form a crust. Brush the crust with milk.
Bake for 35-40 minutes. Let cool slightly and serve.

Truffled Potato Gratin

Note *Provolone cheese is made from cow's milk and is characterized as a* pasta filata *or string cheese. The curd is stretched during the cheese-making process. Provolone is aged for several months. Although it originated in southern Italy, most provolone cheese is now made in the Lombardy region of northern Italy. Spicy and smoked varieties of provolone are readily available.*

Preparation time 10 minutes
Cooking time 55 minutes
Wine *Bianchello del Metauro*

4 potatoes
1/2 cup (120 ml) heavy cream
3 oz (80 g) provolone cheese, sliced
4 tbsps grated Parmesan
2 tbsps butter
2 black truffles
salt and pepper

Preheat oven to 350°F (180°C).
Boil the potatoes, drain, peel and thinly slice.
Butter individual ramequins (or a large baking dish) and layer potatoes and provolone cheese, sprinkling each layer with Parmesan, salt and pepper.
Pour cream over the final layer and sprinkle with Parmesan, salt and pepper.
Bake for 10-15 minutes until cheese melts and begins to brown.
Shave truffles over hot potato gratin and serve.

Potato and Goat's Cheese Flan

Preparation time 25 minutes
Cooking time 1 hour
Wine *Bardolino Chiaretto*

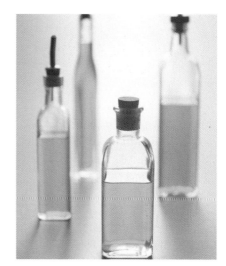

1.6 lb (750 g) potatoes
7 oz (200 g) fresh goat's milk
cheese
3 tbsps grated pocorino cheese
salt and pepper
2 eggs, separated
extra-virgin olive oil

Preheat oven to 350°F (180°C).
Boil, peel and mash the potatoes and mix with goat cheese
and 2 tablespoons pecorino in a bowl. Season with salt and
pepper and let cool.
Stir in the egg yolks and a little milk if necessary into the potato
mixture. Beat egg whites into stiff peaks and fold into the potato
mixture.
Pour potato mixture into a well-oiled baking dish or soufflé dish
and sprinkle with remaining pecorino. Bake for 20-25 minutes.
Remove from oven and let cool completely before serving.

Zucchini and Ricotta Strata

Preparation time 20 minutes
Cooking time 30 minutes
Wine *Alto Adige Terlaner*

extra-virgin olive oil
1 lb (500 g) zucchini, sliced
1 garlic clove, sliced
salt and pepper
1 onion, diced
12.5 oz (350 g) tomatoes, peeled and chopped
basil leaves, torn
3.5 oz (100 g) ricotta
4 tbsps grated pecorino cheese

Preheat oven to 400°F (200°C). Oil a baking dish and add zucchini, garlic, salt and pepper. Bake for 15 minutes. Remove from the oven and set aside.
Meanwhile, heat olive oil in a large frying pan, add onion and sauté. Add tomatoes and salt and pepper to taste. Add basil and sauté briefly.
Oil a baking dish and make layers of zucchini, tomatoes, ricotta and pecorino. Repeat layers until the ingredients are finished. Bake for 20 minutes. Serve immediately.

Potato and Sesame Croquettes

Preparation time 20 minutes
Cooking time 40 minutes
Wine *Ribolla Gialla*

4 potatoes
1/2 cup (2 oz or 60 g) sliced almonds, toasted
thyme
salt and pepper
2 tbsps sesame seeds
sunflower oil

Boil, peel and mash potatoes, and mix with almonds and thyme leaves. Add salt and pepper to taste.
Form balls and roll in sesame seeds.
Heat sunflower oil in a saucepan and fry croquettes until golden brown.
Serve immediately, with a green salad if desired.

182

Quick Pickled Onions

Preparation time 25 minutes
Cooking time 45 minutes
Wine *Nobile di Montepulciano*

2 tbsps sunflower oil
1 lb (500 g) pearl onions,
 washed and peeled
salt
2 tbsps white wine vinegar
1 tbsp rice malt syrup
1 tbsp soy sauce
parsley, chopped

Heat sunflower oil in a
saucepan and add onions.
Sauté over medium heat for a
few minutes, add salt, cover
with water and simmer for
35-40 minutes. Drain and set
aside.
Mix vinegar, rice malt and soy
sauce in a small bowl.
Pour dressing over onions and
let sit for 5 minutes. Sprinkle
with parsley and serve with
meat or cheese main dishes.

Potato and Savoy Cabbage Moulds

Preparation time 20 minutes
Cooking time 20 minutes
Wine *Cinque Terre*

2 yellow-fleshed potatoes,
 boiled and peeled
2 tbsps extra-virgin olive oil
thyme
salt and pepper
2 tbsps black olives, chopped
4 Savoy cabbage leaves,
 blanched
juice of 1/2 lemon
mustard
2 tbsps extra-virgin olive oil

183

Mash potatoes with olive oil,
thyme and pepper. Add olives
and mix well.
Line 4 ramequins with cabbage
leaves and fill with potato
mixture. Fold leaves over the top
of the potato mixture. Cover with
plastic wrap and refrigerate for
20 minutes. Remove from the
refrigerator and unmould.
Whisk lemon juice and mustard
in a small bowl. Add olive oil and
beat until emulsified.
Drizzle dressing over cabbage
moulds and serve at room
temperature.

Endive Gratin with Raisins and Pine Nuts

184

Note *Endive and other winter greens are perfect for blanching or grilling due to their robust texture. Dried fruit and nuts balance the bitter taste of the greens and provide a unique flavour. Endive can also be served with cheese.*

Preparation time 10 minutes
Cooking time 10 minutes
Wine *Trentino Müller-Thurgau*

1 tbsp raisins
3 tbsps extra-virgin olive oil
2 garlic cloves, smashed
1 tbsp pine nuts
4 heads Belgian endive, quartered
salt
2 tbsps vinegar
1/2 cup (120 ml) hot vegetable broth
3 tbsps breadcrumbs
thyme

Soak the raisins in a little hot broth until soft. Drain and squeeze out excess liquid.
Heat olive oil in an oven-proof frying pan and add garlic. Sauté until golden-brown. Add the drained raisins, pine nuts and endive and salt to taste. Sauté for 5-6 minutes and add vinegar. Let evaporate and add hot broth.
Cover and simmer until endive is tender. Remove from heat, sprinkle with breadcrumbs and broil until golden-brown. Add thyme and serve immediately.

Tartlets with Bell Peppers and Potatoes

Preparation time 15 minutes
Cooking time 30 minutes
Wine *Sicilia Chardonnay*

1 red bell pepper
1 large yellow-fleshed potato,
 boiled and peeled
3 tbsps extra-virgin olive oil
thyme
salt and pepper
2 sheets phyllo dough
2 tbsps melted butter

Preheat oven to 400°F (200°C).

Slice bell pepper in half, remove seeds and white membrane and brush with olive oil. Place cut side down on a baking sheet and roast for 5 minutes, turn over and roast for another 5 minutes. Remove from the oven and place in a plastic bag for 10 minutes. Peel pepper halves.

Place cooled potato, bell pepper, thyme and salt and pepper to taste in a food processor. Blend and add remaining olive oil to form a cream.

Roll out the phyllo dough. Brush with butter and sprinkle with salt. Cut out circles and line 8 stainless-steel ramequins with phyllo dough. Bake for 5 minutes and remove from the oven. Remove phyllo shells from the ramequins and let cook. Fill with potato-bell pepper cream.

185

Green Beans in Tomato Sauce
(Lombardy)

Note *This recipe can also be made using a mix of snow peas (mangetout) and green beans.*

Preparation time 20 minutes
Cooking time 1 hour

1 knob of butter
4 spring onions, thinly sliced
1 oz (20 g) pancetta, diced
1.75 lb (800 g) green beans,
 topped and tailed
2 tomatoes, chopped
salt and pepper

186

Melt the butter in a large frying pan. Add the sliced spring onions and sauté until golden.
Add the pancetta and sauté for a few minutes.
Stir in the green beans and tomatoes, cover and cook until green beans are tender. Add water if necessary.
Season with salt and pepper to taste. Serve immediately.

Roman-Style Spinach
(LAZIO)

Note *This spinach recipe can also be used to make croquettes. Roll spinach into balls, dip in beaten egg and coat with breadcrumbs. Fry until golden-brown in sunflower oil and serve immediatcly.*

Preparation time 10 minutes
Cooking time 40 minutes

salt
2.2 lb (1 kg) spinach
1 tbsp raisins
4 tbsps butter
2 tbsps extra-virgin olive oil
1 garlic clove
1 tbsp pine nuts

Bring a large pot of salted water to a boil. Blanch the spinach and then drain. Squeeze out excess water and chop.
Soak the raisins in warm water for a few minutes and then drain and squeeze out excess water.
Heat butter and oil in a large frying pan and add garlic. Sauté garlic until golden-brown. Remove and discard garlic.
Add spinach, raisins and pine nuts. Sauté for a few minutes.
Season with salt to taste. Serve immediately.

Pumpkin and Mozzarella Croquettes

Preparation time 20 minutes
Cooking time 20 minutes
Wine *Pinot Grigio del Piave*

2 tbsps extra-virgin olive oil
1 onion, diced
1 lb (500 g) pumpkin or other
   winter squash, peeled and
   chopped
salt and pepper
1 egg
1 cup (5.5 oz or 150 g)
   breadcrumbs
1 buffalo mozzarella, chopped
sunflower oil

188

Heat olive oil in a large frying pan and add onion. Sauté until transparent. Add squash and let cook over medium heat, adding water when necessary. Add salt and pepper to taste and cook until the squash is soft and liquid has evaporated.
Blend squash in a food processor. Add egg and breadcrumbs to form a thick dough. Roll the dough into balls and stuff each ball with a piece of mozzarella. Roll croquettes in breadcrumbs.
Heat sunflower oil in a saucepan and fry croquettes until golden-brown. Drain on paper towels and salt to taste. Serve immediately.

Julienned Vegetables with Curry Sauce

Note *Curry was first sold in Europe at the end of the eighteenth century. The English name curry actually refers to a mix of ground spices commonly used in southern Asia.*

Preparation time 15 minutes
Cooking time 15 minutes
Wine *Lagrein Rosato*

3 potatoes, julienned
5 asparagus spears, julienned
3 zucchini, julienned
3 carrots, julienned
salt and pepper
2 tbsps butter
1 shallot, minced
3 tbsps milk
1 tsp curry
cornstarch
3 slices crusty bread

Steam all of the vegetables and season with salt and pepper. Heat 1 tablespoon butter in a large frying pan and add shallot. Sauté over low heat. Add milk, curry and a pinch of salt. Let simmer for 4 minutes.

Meanwhile, mix cornstarch in 1 tablespoon of softened butter. Whisk butter and cornstarch into the curry and pour over the steamed vegetables. Serve with toasted bread.

Stuffed Artichokes

Preparation time 25 minutes
Cooking time 20 minutes
Wine *Sorni Rosso*

6 tbsps extra-virgin olive oil
1 garlic clove, minced
1 pork shank, cooked
 and deboned
3/4 cup (180 ml) white wine
salt and pepper
1 red bell pepper, diced
8 large artichokes
juice of 1 lemon
1/2 cup (2.5 oz or 70 g) black
 olives, diced
parsley, minced

190

Preheat oven to 425°F (220°C).

Heat half the olive oil in a large frying pan and add garlic. Sauté briefly and add pork. Sauté for 2 minutes and add wine and salt and pepper to taste. Keep warm.

Heat remaining olive oil in another frying pan. Add bell pepper and sauté for 4-5 minutes. Season with salt and pepper.

Bring a large pot of salted water to a boil.

Meanwhile, slice the artichokes in half and remove the choke. Soak them in cold water and lemon juice.

Blanch artichokes for 3-4 minutes and let cool.

Mix pork, peppers, olives and parsley. Fill artichokes with the pork mixture. Place on a baking sheet and bake for 10 minutes. Serve warm.

Mushroom Tart

Preparation time 25 minutes
Cooking 50 minutes
Wine *Colli Tortonesi Cortese*

Serves 6

3 tbsps butter
2 onions, sliced
5 fresh porcini mushrooms,
 cleaned and sliced
1/2 cup (120 ml) white wine
salt and pepper
parsley, chopped
7 tbsps heavy cream
1 tbsp plain flour
1 9-oz (250 g) roll of puff pastry

Preheat oven to 350°F (180°C).
Heat the butter in a large frying pan. Add the onions and sauté
until soft. Add the mushrooms and sauté over high heat until all
the liquid has evaporated. Add the white wine and season with
salt and pepper. Let cook for another 10 minutes and then add the
parsley and the cream. Remove from heat, mix well and let cool.
Butter and flour a pie dish. Roll out the puff pastry and layer it into
the pie dish. Pierce the dough with a fork and then pour in the
mushroom filling.
Bake for 40 minutes. Remove from the oven and serve
immediately.

Cannellini Beans in Tomato Sauce

Preparation time 25 minutes
Cooking time 10 minutes
Wine *Dolcetto d'Asti*

4 cups (1.75 lb or 800 g) dried
 cannellini beans
4 tbsps extra-virgin olive oil
2 garlic cloves, smashed
2-3 sage leaves
salt and pepper
1⅔ cups (14 oz or 400 g) tomato
 sauce

Soak the beans overnight. Boil
for 30 minutes then drain.
Heat olive oil in a saucepan.
Add the garlic and sage
leaves, then add beans, salt
and pepper. When most of the
cooking liquid has evaporated
add the tomato sauce. Stir and
cover. Let cook for 20 minutes.
Serve hot with toasted bread, if
desired.

Sweet and Sour Fennel

Preparation time 15 minutes
Cooking time 20 minutes
Wine *Malvasia Istriana*

1 tbsp raisins
1/2 cup (120 ml) vin santo or
 other sweet wine
2 tbsps extra-virgin olive oil
1 tbsp pine nuts
2 bay leaves
3 peppercorns
3 fennel bulbs, sliced into
 wedges
3 tbsps white wine vinegar
1 pinch of sugar
salt

Soak raisins in vin santo for 15
minutes. Drain the raisins.
Heat the olive oil in a large
frying pan. Add the pine nuts,
bay leaves and peppercorns
and toast for 1 minute. Add the
fennel and sauté for 3 minutes.
Add the vinegar, raisins, sugar,
salt and a little water. Cover
and let cook for 10 minutes.
Serve immediately.

192

Vegetable Rösti

Preparation time 10 minutes
Cooking time 10 minutes
Wine *Lagrein Rosato*

1 large starchy potato, peeled
 and julienned
1 small zucchini, julienned
2 small carrots, julienned
parsley, minced
curry powder
nutmeg, grated
salt and pepper
2 tbsps extra-virgin olive oil

Toss the vegetables in a bowl
with parsley, curry, nutmeg and
salt and pepper to taste.
Heat olive oil in a large frying
pan and place spoonfuls of
vegetable mixture in the pan.
Spread the vegetables to
cover the bottom of the pan
and press down to adhere.
Let cook for 6-7 minutes and
then carefully flip and cook for
another 6-7 minutes.
Repeat until the vegetables are
finished.
Place vegetable rösti on a plate
and serve immediately.

Beet Salad

Preparation time 10 minutes
Winet *Trentino Nosiola*

2 oz (60 g) ricotta
juice of 1 lemon
1/2 tsp ground cumin
1/2 tsp mustard
1 tbsp sunflower oil
2 large beets, roasted, peeled
 and grated
1 green apple, peeled and grated
fresh ginger, peeled and grated
8 lettuce leaves

Beat the ricotta until smooth.
Add lemon juice, cumin,
mustard and oil and mix well.
Mix beets, apple and ginger in
a bowl.
Place the lettuce leaves on a
serving dish, top with beets and
apple and drizzle with ricotta
dressing.

Truffled Potato and Cheese Fritters

Note *Bitto cheese gets its name from the Bitto River, a tributary of the Adda. It is produced almost exclusively in the area around Sondrio and is usually served at the end of a meal with a hearty wine like Valtellina Superiore or Grumello.*

Preparation time 20 minutes
Cooking time 30 minutes
Wine *Metodo Classico Franciacorta Dosaggio Zero*

3 yellow-fleshed potatoes, boiled and peeled
1/2 cup (120 ml) milk
1 medium black truffle, shaved
3 oz (80 g) Bitto cheese, grated
2 eggs
1 tbsp heavy cream
nutmeg, grated
thyme
salt and pepper
3 tbsps clarified butter

194

Mash the potatoes in a saucepan with the milk and add truffle, reserving a few shavings for garnish. Cook over low heat stirring frequently. Transfer potatoes to a bowl and let cool.
Beat eggs and cream in a small bowl.
Add Bitto cheese to the potatoes and then stir in the egg and cream mixture. Add a pinch of nutmeg and the thyme and season with salt and pepper. Let the mixture rest for 10 minutes.
Heat butter in a large frying pan. Drop spoonfuls of the potato mixture into the pan and fry for 4 minutes on each side. Garnish with shaved truffle and serve immediately.

Green Salad with Apples and Almonds

Preparation time 15 minutes
Cooking time 5 minutes
Wine *Riesling Renano*

2 green apples, peeled
juice of 1/2 lemon
1 knob of butter
4 tbsps extra-virgin olive oil
1 tbsp acacia honey
3 tbsps ground almonds
parsley, chopped
nutmeg, grated
salt and pepper
4 slices crusty bread
3 oz (80 g) semi-aged goat's
 milk cheese, sliced into
 4 wedges
7 oz (200 g) mâche
5.5 oz (150 g) frisée
4 tbsps sliced almonds, toasted

195

Quarter one of the apples and set aside. Dice the other apple and sprinkle with a little lemon juice.
Heat butter in a frying pan and add the apple quarters. Sauté for a few minutes.
Mix olive oil, remaining lemon juice, honey, ground almonds, parsley and nutmeg together in a small bowl. Season with salt and pepper. Set aside.
Place the bread slices on a baking sheet. Place one slice of sautéed apple on each slice of bread and top with the cheese. Broil the crostini for 2 minutes.
Mix the mâche, frisée, chopped apples and toasted almonds. Dress with the honey-lemon vinaigrette. Serve salad with goat's cheese crostini.

Potato and Mushroom Gratin

Note *Either fresh or frozen mushrooms of a mix of varieties can be used for this dish. Freezing mushrooms is a great way to preserve them. Although fresh mushrooms give a better result, there are excellent frozen mushrooms available at specialty stores.*

196

Preparation time 25 minutes
Cooking time 40 minutes
Wine *Lugana*

4 cups (1 l) water
3 tbsps extra-virgin olive oil
salt and pepper
2 medium potatoes, peeled and sliced
2 cups (5.5 oz or 150 g) sliced mushrooms
1/2 onion, minced
parsley, chopped
1/2 cup (120 ml) heavy cream
5 tbsps grated Parmesan
3 tbsps butter

Preheat oven to 425°F (220°C).
Bring water to a boil with 1 tablespoon oil and salt. Add the potato slices and blanch for 1 minute. Drain and dry on paper towels.
Heat 2 tbsps olive oil in a frying pan and add the mushrooms and onion and sauté for 5 minutes. Season with salt and pepper and add the parsley.
Mix the cream and 3 tablespoons Parmesan in a small bowl.
Butter a baking dish and line with 1 layer of potatoes. Top with 1 uniform layer of mushroom mixture and pour the over the cream.
Add another layer of potatoes.
Sprinkle with remaining Parmesan and small pieces of butter. Bake for 30 minutes.
Serve warm.

Braised Fennel with Saffron

Preparation time 10 minutes
Cooking time 15 minutes
Wine *Pinot Grigio di Breganze*

4 tbsps extra-virgin olive oil
1 garlic clove, halved
1/2 dried red chilli pepper
2 large fennel bulbs, thinly sliced
salt and pepper
1/2 cup (120 ml) vegetable broth
1 tsp saffron
sesame seeds, toasted

Heat olive oil in a wide saucepan. Add the garlic and chilli pepper. Sauté for a few minutes. Add the fennel and sauté until it begins to colour. Season with salt and pepper and add the broth. Let cook over low heat. Dissolve the saffron in a little bit of broth and add to the fennel. When the fennel begins to turn yellow, raise the heat and let the excess cooking liquid evaporate. Transfer to a serving plate and garnish with sesame seeds. Serve immediately.

Mâche with Sabayon Sauce

Preparation time 10 minutes
Cooking time 5 minutes
Wine *Cabernet di Breganze*

2 hard-boiled eggs, hard boiled,
 yolks only
1 tsp mustard
1/2 tsp balsamic vinegar
2 tbsps extra-virgin olive oil
2 tbsps beef broth
salt and pepper
3 cups (2 oz or 50 g) mâche
0.5 oz (10 g) white truffle,
 shaved

Blend the egg yolks, mustard, balsamic vinegar, olive oil, broth and salt to form a smooth sauce.
Place mâche on a serving plate and season with salt and pepper. Dress the salad with sabayon sauce and shave the truffle over the top.

Bell Pepper and Porcini Tarts

Preparation time 20 minutes
Cooking time 30 minutes
Wine *Rossese di Dolceacqua*

198

3 tbsps extra-virgin olive oil
1 shallot, minced
1/2 red bell pepper, seeded and
chopped
2 fresh porcini mushrooms
cleaned and chopped
mint and parsley, chopped
salt and pepper
1 tbsp goat's milk cheese
9 oz (250 g) puff pastry

Preheat oven to 400°F (200°C).
Heat olive oil in a large frying pan and add the shallot. Sauté until soft. Add bell pepper and sauté for another 10 minutes.
Add the mushrooms, mint and parsley to the pan and season with salt and pepper. Cook the mixture until the liquid has evaporated. Remove from heat and add the cheese. Mix well.
Roll out puff pastry and cut out 8 circles of dough.
Butter and flour 4 small tart tins and line them with 1 circle of puff pastry each. Fill with mushroom mixture and cover with a second layer of puff pastry. Poke holes in the top layer of pastry to let the steam out while baking.
Bake for 18 minutes. Remove from the oven and serve immediately.

Calabrian Bean Salad

Preparation time 20 minutes
Cooking time 1 hour 20 minutes
Wine *Cirò Rosso*
♟ ♟

1⅓ cups (5.5 oz or 150 g)
  dried borlotti beans, soaked
  overnight
2 bay leaves
salt and pepper
4 tbsps extra-virgin olive oil
2 garlic cloves
1 red onion, sliced
3 potatoes, peeled and cubed
1 red bell pepper, diced
1 yellow bell pepper, diced
parsley, chopped
oregano leaves
crushed red chilli pepper
4 slices Altamura-style bread,
  toasted

Place beans in a pot and cover with water. Add bay leaves and a pinch of salt and cook for 40 minutes.
Heat olive oil in a large pan and add the garlic. Sauté for a few minutes and add the onion. Continue to cook until onion softens and then add the potatoes and peppers.
Drain the beans with a slotted spoon and transfer them directly to the vegetables. Reserve the cooking liquid. Season with salt and pepper and cook for 30 minutes, adding cooking liquid from the beans if necessary.
Sprinkle the beans with parsley, oregano and chilli and stir. Let sit for a few minutes and serve with toasted bread.

Swiss Chard with Mushrooms

Note *Chard grows wild in Italy, almost like a weed. Due to its availability chard is used frequently in Italian cooking. There are two main varieties, a large-leaf meaty type and a more delicate spinach-like type.*

Preparation time 10 minutes
Cooking time 35 minutes
Wine *Malvasia Istriana*

extra-virgin olive oil
2 garlic cloves, peeled and sliced
2½ cups (9 oz or 250 g)
 chopped mushrooms
1 lb (500 g) Swiss chard,
 chopped
salt and pepper
vegetable broth
thyme leaves

200

Heat olive oil in a saucepan and add the garlic. Sauté for a few minutes until golden-brown.
Add the mushrooms and sauté briefly. Reduce heat, cover and cook for 15 minutes.
Add the chard to the pan and season with salt and pepper to taste. Add a little vegetable broth and continue cooking for 15 minutes.
Before serving, garnish with thyme leaves.

Carrot, Fennel
and Bell Pepper Salad

Preparation time 15 minutes
Wine *Gambellara*
♟

4 tbsps extra-virgin olive oil
1 garlic clove, smashed
1 large fennel bulb, thinly sliced
1/2 cup (120 ml) vegetable broth
1/2 tsp ground saffron
salt and freshly ground pepper
2 red or yellow bell peppers,
 thinly sliced
3 carrots, peeled and thinly
 sliced
1 head frisée

Heat olive oil in a frying pan and add the garlic. Sauté briefly until
golden and add the sliced fennel.
Sauté the fennel for 2 minutes over high heat and then add the
broth and saffron. Season with salt and pepper.
Continue cooking until the fennel is tender. Add the sliced bell
peppers and carrots and remove from heat.
Place frisée on a serving plate and top with fennel-pepper mixture.
Season with freshly ground pepper.

Gorgonzola and Walnut Salad

Preparation time 25 minutes
Cooking time 15 minutes
Wine *Orvieto Classico*

2 sheets of cracker bread
2 bunches of mesclun
4 oz (120 g) mild Gorgonzola
 cheese, diced
3 tbsps walnuts, chopped
3 tbsps pine nuts
1/3 cup (1.5 oz or 40 g) raisins
salt and pepper
8 tbsps balsamic vinegar
8 tbsps extra-virgin olive oil

Preheat oven to 350°F (180°C).
Soak cracker bread in water for
a few minutes.
Place 4 small oven-proof teacups upside-down on a baking
sheet. Squeeze the excess
water out of the cracker bread
and mould the bread around the
tea-cups. Bake for 15 minutes.
Remove from the oven and let
cool completely.
Tear the mesclun and mix it
with the gorgonzola, walnuts,
pine nuts and raisins. Season
with salt and pepper and dress
with balsamic vinegar and olive
oil. Transfer to bread cups and
serve.

Zucchini and Escarole Tart

Preparation time 20 minutes
Cooking time 25 minutes
Wine *Vermentino di Gallura*

2 tbsps extra-virgin olive oil
1 garlic clove
1 head of escarole,
 roughly chopped
salt and pepper
2 zucchini, sliced lengthways
9 oz (250 g) phyllo dough

Preheat oven to 400°F (200°C).
Heat olive oil in a frying pan
and add garlic. Sauté for a
few minutes and add escarole.
Cook for 10 minutes. Remove
garlic, drain excess liquid and
season with salt and pepper.
Lightly oil a baking dish and line
with 3 sheets of phyllo dough.
Spread escarole evenly over
the phyllo dough and top with
zucchini slices. Drizzle with oil,
season with salt and pepper
and cover with 2 sheets
of phyllo.
Bake for 12-15 minutes. Serve
hot.

202

V E G E T A B L E S

Winter Squash and Chickpea Strudel

Preparation time 20 minutes
Cooking time 40 minutes
Wine *Riviera Ligure
di Ponente Pigato*
♟

Serves 6

2 tbsps extra-virgin olive oil
1/2 onion, minced
3 cups (14 oz or 400 g) chopped
 winter squash
1¼ cups (300 ml) hot vegetable
 broth
2/3 cup (5.5 oz or 150 g) canned
 chickpeas, drained
thyme leaves
salt and pepper
9 oz (250 g) puff pastry dough
butter, melted

Preheat oven to 375°F (190°C).
Heat oil in a frying pan and add onion. Let cook until soft. Add
the squash and a little hot broth. Let cook for 10 minutes. Add
the chickpeas and thyme leaves and season with salt and pepper.
Cook for another 5 minutes until the squash is tender and the
mixture is creamy.
Roll out the puff pastry and spread the squash mixture over the
dough. Fold in the sides and roll up the dough.
Brush with melted butter and make a few incisions along the top
of the strudel.
Bake for 30 minutes. Let cool slightly, slice and serve.

Kabocha Squash with Fried Polenta

Preparation time 15 minutes
Cooking time 15 minutes
Wine *Metodo Classico*
Franciacorta Extra Brut

POLENTA
salt
3/4 cup plus 2 tbsps (150 g)
 instant polenta cornmeal
2 tbsps extra-virgin olive oil
rosemary

SQUASH
1 lb (500 g) Kabocha squash,
 peeled and diced
2 thyme sprigs
2 tbsps extra-virgin olive oil
salt and pepper

204

Bring about 3 cups (750 ml) of water and a generous pinch of salt
to a boil in a saucepan. Whisk in the cornmeal and stir until the
polenta begins to thicken. Continue stirring with a wooden spoon
until the polenta pulls away from the sides of the pan. Pour into a
damp rectangular baking dish and spread into a 3/4-inch (2 cm)
layer. Refrigerate.
Steam squash with thyme until tender. Remove thyme and transfer
squash to a mixing bowl. Mash squash with the olive oil and
season with salt and pepper.
Using a round cookie cutter make 4 squash cakes on individual
serving plates.
Cut the polenta into small squares and pan-fry in oil until golden-
brown.
Top squash with fried polenta and garnish with rosemary.
Serve immediately.

Grilled Winter Squash with Pancetta and Pistachios

Preparation time 10 minutes
Cooking time 20 minutes
Wine *Metodo Classico
Franciacorta Brut*

1.3 lb (600 g) winter squash,
 very thinly sliced
5 oz (140 g) slice of pancetta,
 diced
rosemary
salt and pepper
1/2 cup (2 oz or 50 g) unsalted
 pistachios, finely chopped

Grill the squash slices for 8 minutes on each side, using
a cast-iron grill pan or the broiler.
Meanwhile, heat a non-stick pan. Add the chopped pancetta and
sauté until golden-brown and crunchy. Add the rosemary sprig.
Place the grilled squash on a serving plate and season with salt
and pepper.
Top the squash with the sautéed pancetta and chopped
pistachios. Serve immediately.

205

Swiss Chard and Mushroom Croquettes

Preparation time 20 minutes
Cooking time 15 minutes
Wine *Alto Adige Santa
Maddalena*

14 oz (400 g) Swiss chard, blanched
2 eggs
2 tbsps grated Parmesan
3/4 cup (3.5 oz or 100 g)
 plain flour
2 tbsps extra-virgin olive oil
1 garlic clove
2 cups (7 oz or 200 g) mushrooms
nutmeg, grated
salt
3 tbsps plain flour
3/4 cup (3.5 oz or 100 g)
 breadcrumbs
1¾ cups (400 ml) peanut oil

206

Chop the chard and mix it with 1 egg, Parmesan and flour.
Heat olive oil in a large frying pan and add the garlic clove.
Add mushrooms and sauté over high heat for 10 minutes.
Season with salt. Drain mushrooms and chop them coarsely.
Add mushrooms to the chard mixture and season with nutmeg
and salt.
Beat 1 egg in a small bowl. Pour the flour onto a plate and the
breadcrumbs onto another.
Form small balls of the spinach-mushroom mixture. Roll each
ball in the flour then dip in the egg wash and finally roll in the
breadcrumbs.
Heat peanut oil in a saucepan. When the oil is very hot fry the
croquettes until golden-brown. Drain on paper towels and serve
immediately.

Chickpea and Eggplant Dip

Preparation time 15 minutes
Cooking time 30 minutes
Wine *Lacryma Christi Bianco*

DIP
1 cup (7 oz or 200 g) dried
 chickpeas, soaked for at least
 12 hours
1 bay leaf
1 garlic clove
2 large eggplants, halved
 lengthways
3 tbsps extra-virgin olive oil
1 tbsp sesame oil
parsley, chopped
salt and pepper

GARNISH
1 red bell pepper
1 yellow bell pepper
4 slices of crusty bread

Preheat the oven to 350°F (180°C).
Boil chickpeas with the bay leaf and garlic until they are tender.
Make parallel incisions along the cut sides of the eggplant. Place
the eggplant, cut side down, on a baking sheet and bake
for 30 minutes.
Scoop out the eggplant pulp and puree in a food processor
with the drained chickpeas. Transfer to a bowl and add olive oil,
sesame oil and parsley. Season with salt and pepper. Set aside.
Roast peppers over high heat on the stove. Place the peppers
in a plastic bag and let sit for 20 minutes. Peel, seed and julienne
the peppers.
Transfer the eggplant spread to small serving dishes. Garnish
with julienned peppers and serve with toasted bread.

Ricotta-Stuffed Onions

Preparation time 15 minutes
Cooking time 25 minutes
Wine *Fiano di Avellino*

**4 onions
10.5 oz (300 g) goat's
 milk ricotta
1 egg, separated
1 tbsp grated Parmesan
salt and pepper
4 tbsps breadcrumbs
extra-virgin olive oil**

208

Preheat oven to 350°F (180°C).
Blanch the whole onions in boiling salted water for 8-10 minutes.
Drain and cut off the top third. Scoop out the inner part of the
onions without breaking the outer layers.
Chop the inner part of the onions and mix with the ricotta, egg
yolk and Parmesan. Beat the egg white until stiff and fold into
the onion mixture. Season with salt and pepper.
Fill the onions with the ricotta mixture and sprinkle with
breadcrumbs. Drizzle with olive oil and bake for 10 minutes,
then broil to form a golden crust. Serve immediately.

Mediterranean Onion Tart

Preparation time 20 minutes
Cooking time 40 minutes
Wine *Prosecco di Conegliano
e Valdobbiadene Extra Dry*

extra-virgin olive oil
1 lb (500 g) onions, thinly sliced
**1¾ cups (8.8 oz or 250 g) pitted
 black olives, chopped**
basil leaves, chopped
oregano
salt and pepper
3 tbsps grated Parmesan
9 oz (250 g) puff pastry

209

Preheat oven to 400°F (200°C).
Heat olive oil in a non-stick frying pan and add the onion. Sauté
until tender and remove from heat. Add olives, basil, oregano,
Parmesan, salt and pepper and mix well.
Roll the puff pastry out into a very thin sheet.
Line a pie dish with parchment paper and then with the puff pastry.
Fill with the onion mixture. Fold the extra puff pastry over the
top of the tart to close. Cut out small flowers with any remaining
dough and place them on top of the tart.
Bake for 25-30 minutes and serve hot or warm.

White Velvet Potatoes

Preparation time 20 minutes
Cooking time 30 minutes
Wine *Lugana Riserva*

**1.3 lb (600 g) potatoes,
 peeled and diced
1 onion, finely diced
2 red bell peppers, diced
1/2 tsp salt
1/2 tsp ground pepper
3/4 cup plus 1 tbsp (200 ml)
 coconut milk
1¼ cups (300 ml) chicken
 or vegetable broth
fresh coriander (cilantro) or basil,
 julienned**

210

Place the diced potatoes, onion, bell peppers, salt, pepper
and coconut milk in a large saucepan. Mix well and add the broth.
Bring to a boil, cover and cook until the potatoes are tender.
If there is excess liquid when the potatoes are cooked, raise
the heat and cook uncovered until the liquid has evaporated.
Place in a serving dish and garnish with the julienned coriander
or basil.

Swiss Chard
with Bagna Cauda Sauce

Preparation time 10 minutes
Cooking time 20 minutes
Wine *Roero Arneis*

3 tbsps extra-virgin olive oil
1 spring onion, minced
1 hard-boiled egg
2 anchovy fillets in oil
6 tbsps heavy cream
pepper
1 bunch Swiss chard

Heat olive oil in a frying pan and add the minced spring onion.
Sauté over low heat until soft.
Add anchovies and dissolve by smashing them with a fork.
Remove from heat and place the spring onion mixture, hard-boiled egg, cream and a small pinch of pepper in the blender.
Puree and keep warm.
Steam the Swiss chard until tender, then chop.
Place chard on a serving plate and top with sauce.

Winter Squash, Carrot and Zucchini Tarts

Preparation time 25 minutes
Cooking time 50 minutes
Wine *Gambellara*

3 zucchini
2 tbsps extra-virgin olive oil
2 tbsps butter
1 onion, minced
2 carrots, peeled and diced
1/4 winter squash, peeled
 and chopped
salt and pepper
hot vegetable broth
1 egg
thyme leaves, chopped
14 oz (400 g) pie crust dough
 (see p. 1093)
1 tbsp plain flour
1/3 cup (2 oz or 50 g) pumpkin
 seeds

212

Preheat oven to 375°F (190°C).
Remove the seeds from the zucchini and dice.
Heat olive oil and butter in a saucepan and add the onion. Sauté
until soft, add carrots, then squash. Sauté for a few more minutes
and season with salt and pepper. Add the boiling broth, cover
and let simmer for 7 minutes. Add the zucchini and simmer until
tender. Let cool.
Transfer the vegetables to a bowl and add egg and thyme to the
vegetables.
Roll out the dough. Flour a tart pan and line the pan with the
dough. Pierce the dough with a fork. Pour vegetable mixture over
the dough. Sprinkle pumpkin seeds over the tart and bake
for 40 minutes. Remove from the oven and serve immediately.

Swiss Chard and Chestnut Tart

Preparation time 20 minutes
Cooking time 25 minutes
Wine *Trentino Nosiola*

Serves 6

2 tbsps extra-virgin olive oil
1/2 onion, sliced
1 large bunch of Swiss chard,
 blanched and chopped
salt and pepper
10 dried chestnuts, soaked
9 oz (250 g) ricotta
nutmeg, grated
1 knob of butter
9 oz (250 g) pie crust dough
 (see p. 1093)

Preheat oven to 375°F (190°C).
Heat olive oil in a frying pan and
add onion. Sauté until soft. Add
the chard and season with salt
and pepper. Add the chestnuts
and finally the ricotta. Mix well
with a fork and cook for
10 minutes.
Puree and add grated nutmeg.
Roll out the dough.
Butter a tart pan and line with
dough. Pierce the dough with a
fork and pour in the filling. Bake
for 35 minutes. Remove from the
oven, let cool slightly and serve.

Carrots with Nuts and Raisins

Preparation time 15 minutes
Cooking time 20 minutes
Wine *Alto Adige Gewürztraminer*

2 tbsps extra-virgin olive oil
1½ cups (9 oz or 250 g)
 chopped shallots
1 lb (500 g) carrots, thinly sliced
thyme leaves
salt
2/3 cup (3.5 oz or 100 g) raisins,
 soaked in water and drained
20 almonds, chopped

213

Heat olive oil in a frying pan.
Add shallots, carrots, thyme
and salt to taste. Sauté for
10 minutes.
Add the raisins and the
almonds and let cook for
another 5 minutes. Serve
immediately.

Note *This delicate side dish
is an ideal pairing for steamed
white fish. The salad may also
be garnished with fried daikon
slices.*

Porcini, Roasted Tomato and Ricotta Salad

Preparation time 15 minutes
Cooking time 1 hour 20 minutes
Wine *Lagrein Rosato*

4 firm but ripe tomatoes
salt and pepper
2 garlic cloves, sliced
1 sprig of thyme
4 tbsps extra-virgin olive oil
juice of 1/2 lemon
9 oz (250 g) baked ricotta,
thinly sliced
3-4 fresh porcini mushrooms,
cleaned and sliced
1 bunch of chervil, minced
1 head of lettuce

214

Preheat oven to 210°F (100°C).
Slice tomatoes into 4 equal slices.
Line a baking sheet with parchment paper and place tomatoes on
the baking sheet. Sprinkle with salt and top with garlic and thyme
leaves. Bake for 1 hour 20 minutes.
Meanwhile, whisk oil and lemon juice with a pinch of salt.
Dress mushrooms with lemon vinaigrette and sprinkle with chervil.
Divide lettuce between individual plates and top with roasted
tomatoes, ricotta slices and mushrooms. Drizzle with olive oil
and season with salt and pepper.

Potato, Bell Pepper and Asiago Cakes

Preparation time 25 minutes
Cooking time 10 minutes
Wine *Bardolino Chiaretto*

3 eggs
4 tbsps heavy cream
6 tbsps plain flour
salt and pepper
3 potatoes, peeled and thinly
 sliced
1 red bell pepper, diced
1 green bell pepper, diced
1 yellow bell pepper, diced
1 onion, minced
1 garlic clove, minced
3 oz (80 g) speck ham, chopped
5.5 oz (150 g) Asiago cheese,
 chopped
5 tbsps extra-virgin olive oil
butter

Mix the eggs, cream and flour in a bowl and set aside.
Bring a large pot of salted water to a boil and blanch the potato
slices. Drain and let dry on a kitchen towel. Add the potatoes, bell
peppers, onion, garlic, speck ham and Asiago to the egg mixture.
Mix well and season with salt and pepper.
Heat olive oil and butter in a small frying pan. Drop spoonfuls
of the potato mixture into the pan and fry until golden-brown.
Drain on a paper towel and serve immediately.

Savoury Tart with Ricotta and Radicchio

Preparation time 15 minutes
Cooking time 35 minutes
Wine *Riviera Ligure
di Ponente Pigato*

216

Serves 6-8

3 tbsps extra-virgin olive oil
2 heads Treviso radicchio, sliced
9 oz (250 g) ricotta
3 tbsps heavy cream
2 eggs
4 tbsps grated Parmesan
salt and pepper
9 oz (250 g) pie crust dough
 (see p. 1093)
1 knob of butter
1 tbsp plain flour
2 oz (60 g) aged ricotta, shaved

Preheat oven to 350°F (180°C).
Heat olive oil in a large frying pan. Add radicchio and sauté
for 3-4 minutes.
Mix the ricotta, cream, eggs, Parmesan and radicchio in a bowl.
Mix well and season with salt and pepper.
Roll out the dough into a thin sheet. Butter and flour a tart pan
and line the pan with the dough. Pour in the filling and pinch the
edges of the dough to finish.
Bake for 30 minutes. Remove from the oven, let cool slightly
and garnish with shaved ricotta.

Fava Flan with Onion Sauce

Preparation time 15 minutes
Cooking time 50 minutes
Wine *Colli Orientali del Friuli Tocai*
♟ ♟

FLAN
3 tbsps extra-virgin olive oil
1 garlic clove
1½ cups (7 oz or 200 g) dried
 fava beans, chopped
1¼ cups (300 ml) hot vegetable
 broth
1 egg
1 cornstarch plain flour

ONION SAUCE
3 tbsps extra-virgin olive oil
1 red onion, peeled and diced
3/4 cups plus 1 tbsp (200 ml)
 hot vegetable broth
salt and pepper
2 tbsps heavy cream

GARNISH
3 oz (80 g) pancetta, diced

Preheat oven to 350°F (180°C).
Heat olive oil in a large frying pan. Add garlic and sauté briefly. Add beans and sauté for 5 minutes. Add broth, cover and cook until the beans are tender.
Puree and stir in egg and cornstarch.
Flour 4 ramequins and pour in the bean puree. Place ramequins in a baking dish and fill it halfway with hot water.
Bake for 20 minutes.
Heat olive oil in a frying pan and add onion. Sauté over low heat, adding hot broth, until the onion is transparent. Season with salt and pepper. Puree with the cream and let cool.
Sauté the pancetta until crispy then drain on paper towels.
Unmould flans onto serving plates and top with onion sauce.
Garnish with pancetta and serve.

Honey and Pistachio Cassata with Grape Salad

Note *This dessert can also be garnished with almond brittle or crumbled torrone (nougat). For a rich Christmas dessert, try cassata with chocolate sauce.*

Preparation time 20 minutes
Cooking time 1 minute
Wine *Moscato Passito di Pantelleria*

1/2 cup (2 oz or 50 g) organic pistachios
8 tbsps honey
13.5 fl oz (400 ml) whipping cream
ground cinnamon
3 egg whites
2 tbsps (1 oz or 30 g) sugar
10 walnut halves
1½ cups (7 oz or 200 g) green grapes

Blanch the pistachios in boiling water for 1 minute. Drain, peel and chop the nuts.
Mix 5 tablespoons honey with a little cream and set aside.
Whip the remaining cream and a pinch of cinnamon into stiff peaks. In a separate bowl beat the egg whites and sugar into stiff peaks. Fold the honey and cream into the whipped cream and then fold in the egg whites. Finally fold in the pistachios. Transfer the mixture to a rectangular terrine or loaf pan. Cover and freeze for 6-8 hours.
Dilute the remaining honey in a few tablespoons of warm water. Chop the walnuts. Slice the grapes in half and mix the grapes, nuts and honey in a serving bowl.
Invert the cassata onto a plate and slice. Plate the cassata and garnish with grape salad.

Chestnut Puddings
with Chocolate Sauce

Preparation time 15 minutes
Cooking time 15 minutes
Wine *Oltrepò Pavese*
Moscato Passito

PUDDING
3/4 cup (4.2 oz or 120 g)
 chestnut flour
1/2 cup (3.5 oz or 100 g) sugar
8.4 fl oz (250 ml) milk
8.4 fl oz (250 ml) whipping cream

ALMOND BRITTLE
1/3 cup (2.4 oz or 70 g) sugar
1 cup (3.1 oz or 90 g) sliced
 almonds

CHOCOLATE SAUCE
1/2 cup (1.4 oz or 40 g) cocoa
 powder
1/4 cup (1.7 oz or 50 g) sugar
1 tbsp corn flour
8.4 fl oz (250 ml) milk

Mix the chestnut flour, sugar and milk in a bowl. Let sit for a few
minutes and transfer to a saucepan. Add cream and bring to a
simmer stirring constantly. Let cook for 5 minutes.
Pour the mixture into ramequins and refrigerate for 2 hours.
Oil a baking sheet.
Pour sugar into a small frying pan and let caramelize over medium
heat. Let cook without stirring until the sugar turns a deep amber
brown. Add the almonds and remove from heat. Pour the brittle
onto the baking sheet and smooth using a buttered spatula. Let
cool completely. When cool, break into small pieces.
Whisk the cocoa, sugar, corn flour and milk in a small saucepan.
Make sure that the mixture is smooth, working out any lumps
with the back of a spoon. Bring to a boil over low heat stirring
constantly. Cook until the mixture thickens. Remove from heat and
let the sauce cool.
Invert the chestnut puddings onto individual serving plates, top
with the chocolate sauce and garnish with almond brittle.

Moscato and Concord Grape Jelly

Preparation time 15 minutes
Cooking time 10 minutes
Wine *Asti Moscato Spumante*

JELLY
1½ cups (7 oz or 200 g) concord
 grapes
2 tbsps sugar
2 tsps water
3.4 fl oz (100 ml) sweet
 Moscato wine
1 tsp powdered agar agar

GARNISH
whole concord grapes
mint leaves

220

Blend the grapes, sugar and water in a food processor. Strain the
mixture, pushing any larger pieces through the strainer with the
back of a spoon.
Bring the wine to a simmer in a small saucepan. Remove from
heat and dissolve the agar agar in the wine. Add the strained
grape juice. Mix well.
Pour into 4 triangular, silicon moulds or aluminum moulds lined
with plastic wrap.
Refrigerate for 2 hours. Invert the jellies onto individual serving
plates and garnish with concord grapes and mint leaves.

Pear and Calvados Tart Tatins with Acacia Honey

Preparation time 25 minutes
Cooking time 20 minutes
Wine *Zibibbo*

2 Williams pears
3 tbsps (1.7 oz or 50 g) butter
3 tbsps acacia honey
3 tbsps Calvados
10.5 oz (300 g) puff pastry
ground cinnamon
crème anglais (optional)

Preheat oven to 400°F (200°C).
Peel and quarter the pears and then slice each quarter into thirds.
Heat butter in a non-stick frying pan and add the pears. Sauté for
1 minute and add the honey. Sauté for another 2 minutes or until
the pears begin to brown. Sprinkle with Calvados and let the liquid
evaporate. Let the pears cool.
Roll out the puff pastry and cut out circles just slightly larger than
the tart tins.
Place the caramelized pears in concentric circles in the bottom of
4 small round (not fluted) tart tins. Cover with pastry rounds.
Bake for 15-18 minutes and remove from the oven. Let cool
slightly. Invert the tarts onto individual serving plates and garnish
with a little cinnamon or crème anglais if desired.

Chantilly Cream Cups with Chocolate Cookies

Note *We suggest using langues-de-chat or cat's tounge cookies for this recipe. The cookies can be made by whipping butter and sugar together until creamy and then thinning the batter with egg whites. They are traditionally served with tea or hot chocolate but can also accompany coffee or dessert wines.*

224

Preparation time 25 minutes
Cooking time 15 minutes
Wine *Marsala Dolce*

4 egg yolks
2/3 cup (4.4 oz or 125 g) sugar
1 tsp vanilla extract
1/3 cup plus 2 tbsps (1.7 oz or 50 g) plain flour
17 fl oz (500 ml) milk
1.6 fl oz (50 ml) whipping cream
5.2 oz (150 g) semi-sweet chocolate
15-20 thin, crispy cookies
1 tbsp pine nuts, toasted

Beat the egg yolks with a whisk until foamy and then add the sugar and vanilla and mix well. Add the flour and mix well.
Bring milk to a boil in a saucepan. Whisk boiling hot milk into the egg mixture. Return the mixture to the saucepan and cook over low heat for 5 minutes to thicken. Remove from heat, pour into a bowl and refrigerate.
Whip the cream and refrigerate.
Melt the chocolate in a double boiler and dip the cookies in the chocolate. Let cool on a tray lined with parchment paper. Reserve some melted chocolate for decorating.
When the pastry cream is cool, fold in the whipped cream with a wooden spoon.
Layer the chantilly cream and the remaining melted chocolate in dessert cups or small bowls. Top with toasted pine nuts and serve with chocolate-coated cookies.

Chocolate Mousse
with Marron Glacé

Note *The sponge cake crust may be substituted with ladyfingers soaked in a few teaspoons of rum.*

Preparation time 20 minutes
Cooking time 10 minutes
Wine *Ruby Port*
🍴 🍴

1 gelatin sheet
2 tbsps water
1 egg, separated
1/4 cup (1.5 oz or 45 g) sugar
4.2 fl oz (125 ml) boiling milk
3.5 oz (100 g) semi-sweet
 chocolate
1 tsp vanilla
5 fl oz (150 ml) whipping cream
salt
2 strips of sponge cake
5 marrons glacé

Soak the gelatin sheet in cold water. Remove the gelatin and squeeze out the excess water. Place in a small saucepan with the water and dissolve the gelatin over low heat.

Meanwhile, in a saucepan, beat the egg yolk with the sugar until it becomes a pale yellow color and has thickened. Bring the milk to a boil and whisk into the egg mixture. Return to the saucepan and cook over low heat until the cream thickens.

Remove from heat and add the gelatin, chocolate and vanilla. Let cool.

Whip cream and fold into the cooled chocolate mixture.

Beat the egg white and a pinch of salt to form stiff peaks. Fold into chocolate mousse.

Line the bottom of a serving bowl or trifle bowl with the sponge cake strips or lady fingers. Pour the chocolate mousse over the cake and refrigerate for at least 2 hours. Garnish with marrons glacé.

Chestnut Pudding

Preparation time 20 minutes
Cooking time 15 minutes
Wine *Zibibbo*

1 cup (5.6 oz or 160 g) dried
 chestnuts
6.7 fl oz (200 ml) milk
1/4 cup (1.7 oz or 50 g) sugar
1.6 fl oz (50 ml) rum
1½ gelatin sheets
2 tbsps whipping cream
1 basket raspberries
2 tbsps raw sugar
1.6 fl oz (50 ml) dessert wine

Boil the chestnuts until tender and drain. Chop or crumble the chestnuts into small pieces.

Heat the milk and sugar in a saucepan. Add the chestnuts and rum. Bring to a boil.

Meanwhile, soak the gelatin sheets in cold water for a few minutes. Squeeze out the excess water and add the sheets to the milk mixture. Dissolve the gelatin and remove from heat. Puree until creamy and let cool.

Whip the whipping cream until it holds soft peaks and fold into the chestnut cream. Pour the chestnut cream into 4 ramequins and refrigerate for 2 hours.

Cook the raspberries, sugar and wine in a small saucepan for 8 minutes. Puree. If the sauce seems too thick add a few tablespoons of water.

Invert the chestnut puddings onto plates and top with raspberry sauce.

Chestnut Shakes

Preparation time 15 minutes
Cooking time 20 minutes
Wine *Piemonte Moscato Passito*

1 cup (4.5 oz or 130 g) chestnuts
1 tsp sugar
5 fl oz (150 ml) whole milk
10 fl oz (300 ml) whipping cream
2 tbsps icing sugar
vanilla
ice cubes
semi-sweet chocolate, shaved

Make an X-shaped incision on each of the chestnuts and boil them in lightly sugared water until tender.
Drain and let cool. Peel the chestnuts.
Place chestnuts, milk, cream, powdered sugar and vanilla in a blender. Add a few cubes of ice and blend. Serve the chestnut shake in martini glasses with chocolate shavings.

Apple Mousse with Calvados

Preparation time 15 minutes
Cooking time 15 minutes

3 gelatin sheets
4 green apples
1/2 cup (120 ml) milk
1 cup (250 ml) water
3 tbsps Calvados
1/3 cup (2.8 oz or 80 g) sugar
2 egg whites
3.4 fl oz (100 ml) whipping cream
1/3 cup (2 oz or 50 g)
 mixed berries

Soak the gelatin sheets in cold water for a few minutes. Drain and squeeze out the excess water.
Peel and chop the apples.
In a saucepan, cook the apples, milk, water, Calvados and half the sugar over medium heat. Remove from heat when the apples are tender and add the gelatin. Mix well and let cool. Meanwhile, whip the egg whites and remaining sugar to form stiff peaks. Fold into the apple mixture. Whip the cream. Divide the mousse between 4 serving bowls and garnish with whipped cream and berries.

Mascarpone and Fig Tart

Preparation time 20 minutes
Cooking time 5 minutes
Wine *Marsala Dolce*

Serves 6-8

7 oz (200 g) graham crackers
1/2 cup (3.5 oz or 100 g) sugar
4 tbsps (2.1 oz of 60 g) butter
2 sheets of gelatin
2 fl oz (60 ml) sweet Marsala or rum
3 eggs, separated
10.5 oz (300 g) mascarpone
6 figs, peeled and halved
3 tbsps honey

228

Blend the graham crackers, 3 tablespoons of sugar and the butter in a food processor. Press the mixture evenly into the bottom of a spring-form pan.
Soak the gelatin in cold water for a few minutes. Squeeze out excess water and dissolve gelatin in the Marsala.
Beat the egg yolks and remaining sugar and then add the mascarpone and the Marsala gelatin.
Beat the egg whites to stiff peaks and fold into the mascarpone mixture.
Pour the mixture over the graham cracker crust and smooth with a spatula. Refrigerate.
Mix the figs with the honey. Place them on a parchment paper-lined baking sheet. Broil until the figs begin to caramelize, turning them carefully with a spatula.
Let the figs cool slightly and decorate the tart with figs.

Monte Bianco

Preparation time 30 minutes
Cooking time 1 hour
Wine *Trentino Vin Santo*

2.2 lb (1 kg) chestnuts
salt
1¼ cups (8.8 oz or 250 g)
 confectioners' sugar
1 tsp vanilla
2 tbsps cocoa powder
1 cup (250 ml) milk
2 tbsps rum
6.7 fl oz (200 ml) whipping cream
semi-sweet chocolate shavings

Boil the chestnuts in salted water for about 1 hour. Drain and peel.
Using a potato ricer, mash the chestnuts.
Transfer the chestnuts to a saucepan and add the sugar, vanilla,
cocoa powder and milk. Bring to a simmer over low heat and stir
constantly until the mixture begins to pull away from the sides of
the pan. Let cool and add the rum.
Push the mixture through the potato ricer again, letting the
vermicelli-like strings fall directly onto a serving plate to form a
mountain.
Whip the cream and cover the chestnut strings. Sprinkle with
shaved chocolate.

Chestnut Cream with Meringues

Preparation 20 minutes
Cooking time 45 minutes
Wine *Asti Moscato Spumante*

2 cups (10.5 oz or 300 g)
  chestnuts
1½ cups (10.5 oz or 300 g)
  sugar
4 tbsps (60 ml) rum
12.3 oz (350 g) ricotta
whipping cream
4 marrons glacé
cocoa powder
semi-sweet chocolate, shaved
8 meringues

230

Boil the chestnuts for 45 minutes, drain and peel. Push the chestnuts through a potato ricer. Transfer the chestnut puree to a saucepan and add the sugar.
Cook over low heat, stirring constantly until the mixture is quite thick. Remove from heat, add rum and let cool. Once the chestnut mixture has cooled, add the ricotta and mix to form a smooth cream.
Whip the whipping cream.
Push the cream through a potato ricer directly onto individual serving plates. Top with 1 marron glacé and a dollop of whipped cream. Sprinkle with cocoa powder and chocolate shavings. Place 1 meringue on either side of the chestnut cream and serve.

Fig and Green Grape Sorbet

Preparation time 20 minutes
Cooking time 20 minutes
🎩

Serves 6

3.4 fl oz (100 ml) water
3 tbsps sugar
1 tsp glucose syrup
1 bunch (1 lb or 450 g)
 green grapes
3 green figs
whole grapes and fig slices
 for garnishing

Boil the water and sugar for 5
minutes, then add the glucose
syrup. Place the syrup and
grapes into the blender and
puree. Filter the mixture through
a sieve and pour into a bowl.
Peel and chop the figs. Add the
figs to the grape mixture and
freeze for 2 hours.
Break the grape ice into cubes
with an ice pick and place the
cubes in the blender. Blend to
form a smooth sorbet.
Serve immediately, garnishing
with grapes and fig slices.

Chocolate-Rum Pudding

Preparation time 20 minutes
Cooking time 20 minutes
Wine *Marsala Soleras*
🎩 🎩

Serves 6-8

10 fl oz (300 ml) milk
6.7 fl oz (200 ml) whipping cream
3 egg yolks
1/3 cup plus 2 tbsps (2.8 oz
 or 80 g) sugar
1 tsp aged rum
1/4 cup (0.7 oz or 20 g) cocoa
 powder
7 oz (200 g) milk chocolate
3 gelatin sheets

Simmer the milk and cream.
Beat egg yolks and sugar then
add the rum and cocoa powder.
Chop the chocolate, add to the
milk and cream and let melt.
Soak the gelatin in a little
water. Squeeze out excess and
dissolve in the chocolate.
Remove the chocolate mixture
from the stove and let cool.
Whisk into the egg yolks.
Line a Bundt pan with plastic
wrap and pour the mixture into
the pan. Refrigerate for at least
1 hour. Unmould and serve.

Fig Sandwiches with Malaga Gelato

Preparation time 35 minutes
Cooking time 40 minutes
Wine *Ruby Port*

FIG SANDWICHES
3.4 fl oz (100 ml) port wine
1 tbsp sugar
2 large figs
1 tbsp raw sugar

GELATO
1 vanilla bean
11.8 fl oz (350 ml) whole milk
3 egg yolks
1/2 cup (3.1 oz or 90 g) sugar
1/3 cup (1.7 oz or 50 g) raisins
1 fl oz (30 ml) dark rum
1 egg white
6.7 fl oz (200 ml) whipping cream

232

Slice vanilla bean open and scrape out the seeds with the tip of a sharp knife. Add seeds to the milk and heat in a small saucepan. When the milk is hot but not boiling remove from heat and let infuse for 10 minutes.

In a bowl, beat the egg yolks and sugar. Whisk in the hot milk and continue stirring. Return the mixture to the saucepan and bring to a very low simmer. Cook until the mixture coats the back of a spoon. Remove from heat and let cool.

Soak the raisins in the rum for 10 minutes.

Whip egg whites into soft peaks. Add whipping cream and egg whites to the milk and egg mixture. Mix in raisins and rum.

Pour the mixture into an ice cream or gelato machine and follow manufacturers' instructions for making ice cream or gelato.

Reduce the port and sugar in a small saucepan over low heat. Let cool.

Thickly slice the figs. Toss the figs with the sugar and arrange them on a parchment paper-lined baking sheet. Broil for a few minutes until caramelized.

Place a scoop of gelato between 2 fig slices and drizzle with port reduction.

Rice Pudding
with Candied Fruit

Note *Candied fruit may be substituted with dried figs and apricots in this recipe. The rice pudding may also be served with chocolate sauce.*

Preparation time 20 minutes
Cooking time 1 hour
Wine *Alto Adige Moscato Rosa*

1 vanilla bean
33 fl oz (1 l) milk
8.8 oz (250 g) Originario
 or Balilla rice
1¼ cups (8.8 oz or 250 g) sugar
3/4 cups (2.6 oz or 75 g) sliced
 almonds
3 tbsps (1.7 oz or 50 g) butter
4 eggs, separated
1.7 oz (50 g) candied citron
1.7 oz (50 g) candied orange
1.7 oz (50 g) candied cherries
2 fl oz (60 ml) cognac
salt
orange marmalade sauce (optional)

Preheat oven to 350°F (180°C).
Slice open the vanilla bean, scrape out the seeds and add to the milk. Bring the rice, milk and sugar to a boil in a saucepan.
Meanwhile toast the almonds and dice the candied fruit.
When the rice has absorbed all of the milk, remove from heat and add the butter, egg yolks, almonds, candied fruit and Cognac. Mix carefully and let cool.
Beat egg whites and a pinch of salt into stiff peaks and fold into the rice.
Butter a Bundt pan or pudding mould and pour in the rice mixture. Bake in a bain marie for 40 minutes. Let cool completely. Serve cold with orange marmalade sauce if desired.

Poached Pears with Hazelnuts

Preparation time 15 minutes
Cooking time 20 minutes

234

PEARS
4 pears
1/2 cup (120 ml) white wine
1/2 cup (3.1 oz or 90 g) sugar
juice and zest of 1 lemon
2 cinnamon sticks
2/3 cups (1.7 oz or 50 g) ground
 hazelnuts

CHOCOLATE SAUCE
3.5 oz (100 g) dark chocolate
10 fl oz (300 ml) milk
1 egg
1/3 cup (2.1 oz or 60 g) sugar
1 tsp corn flour

GARNISH
icing sugar
whole hazelnuts

Peel the pears, leaving them whole. Place them in a saucepan with
the wine, half the sugar, the lemon juice and zest and cinnamon
sticks. Cook over medium heat for 15 minutes. Remove from heat
and let cool.
Meanwhile, chop the chocolate. Heat the milk to a boil.
Beat the egg, sugar and corn flour and slowly whisk in the boiling
milk. Add chocolate pieces and return to heat. Cook over low heat
until the mixture coats the back of a wooden spoon.
Place the pears on 4 serving plates. Top with chocolate sauce,
icing sugar and hazelnuts.

Mocha Panna Cottas

Preparation time 20 minutes
Cooking time 10 minutes
Wine *Marsala Dolce*

Serves 8

6.7 fl oz (200 ml) milk
6.7 fl oz (200 ml) whipping cream
3 tbsps sugar
2 sheets gelatin
2 fl oz (60 ml) sweetened
 espresso coffee
7 oz (200 g) dark chocolate

Bring the milk, cream and sugar to a boil in a saucepan.
Soak the gelatin in cold water for a few minutes, drain and squeeze out excess water.
Add the gelatin and espresso to the mixture. Mix well and let cool slightly.
Meanwhile, finely chop the chocolate and whisk it into the warm cream mixture. Stir until the chocolate melts. Pour the mixture into 8 ramequins lined with plastic wrap. Refrigerate for 3 hours.
Unmould the panna cottas and serve.

Apple Strudels with Marsala

Preparation time 15 minutes
Cooking time 20 minutes
Wine *Marsala Dolce*

2 Golden Delicious apples
1 tbsp raisins
3/4 cup (180 ml) Marsala wine
2 tbsps raw sugar
ground cinnamon
8.8 oz (250 g) puff pastry
7 tbsps (3.5 oz or 100 g) butter

235

Preheat oven to 375°F (190°C). Peel and chop the apples and mix with raisins and Marsala. Let marinate for 2 hours. Drain and reserve marinade.
Roll out the pastry and cut into 4 rectangles. Place a few spoonfuls of apple in the centre of each rectangle. Fold in the outer edges and roll up the strudels. Place on a parchment paper-lined baking sheet and brush with melted butter. Bake for 20 minutes.
Meanwhile, reduce the reserved marinade with sugar and a pinch of cinnamon over low heat.
Remove strudels from the oven. Place them on individual serving plates. Slice the strudels in half and top with Marsala reduction.

Dark Chocolate Cake

Preparation time 20 minutes
Cooking time 1 hour 20 minutes
Wine *Malvasia delle Lipari*

4 medium potatoes
7 tbsps (3.5 oz or 100 g) butter
1 cup plus 2 tbsps (7.9 oz
 or 225 g) sugar
1 tsp vanilla
1 cup (3.5 oz or 100 g) ground
 almonds
zest of 1 orange
4 eggs, separated
4.4 oz (125 g) dark chocolate
salt

Preheat oven to 350°F (180°C).
Boil the potatoes. Drain, peel and mash the potatoes with a ricer.
Let cool.
Melt the butter and add it to the potatoes. Mix well. Add the sugar,
vanilla, almonds and orange zest. Mix well. Add the egg yolks.
Shave the chocolate into the batter.
Beat the egg whites and a pinch of salt to stiff peaks. Fold the
whites into the batter. Pour the mixture into a buttered Bundt pan.
Place the pan in a baking dish and fill half-full with hot water. Bake
for 45 minutes.
Let the cake cool slightly and invert onto a serving dish.

Chestnut Tart
with Dark Chocolate

Preparation time 30 minutes
Cooking time 3 hours
Wine *Cartizze*

Serves 8

FILLING

1¾ lb (800 g) chestnuts
8.8 oz (250 g) dark chocolate
10 fl oz (300 ml) milk
1/2 cup (3.5 oz or 100 g) sugar
4 tbsps mascarpone

CRUST

2¾ cups (12.3 oz or 350 g)
 plain flour
1 egg
4 tbsps (2.8 oz or 80 g) butter
 softened
3/4 cup (5.2 oz or 150 g) sugar
1 tsp vanilla

Preheat oven to 350°F (180°C).
Boil the chestnuts until soft. Drain, peel and mash with a potato ricer. Chop the chocolate.
Mix the chestnut puree with the milk and sugar in a saucepan and cook for 10 minutes. Add the chocolate and cook for another 10 minutes. Add mascarpone and cook for 2 more minutes. Remove from heat and let cool.
Mound flour on a work surface and make a well in the centre. Add the egg, softened butter, sugar and vanilla. Mix to form an elastic dough. If the dough seems to dry add a few teaspoons of warm water. Divide the dough in half. Roll out half the dough into a sheet and place in a pie dish. Fill with chestnut cream and roll out the remaining dough. Cover the filling with the second sheet of dough, tuck the top sheet over the filling and fold the edges of the bottom sheet over to seal. Prick the top of the tart with a fork and bake for 45 minutes.
Remove from oven and let cool.

Honey Focaccia

Note *The color, taste and consistency of honey varies depending on the type of flower that it is made from. Some common single flower honeys are acacia, orange blossom, lavender, heather and eucalyptus. The millefiori variety refers to honey made from the nectar of many different types of flowers.*

238

Preparation time 25 minutes
Cooking time 45 minutes
Wine *Asti Moscato Spumante*
♟

Serves 6-8

8-9 tbsps milk
3 tbsps (1.4 oz or 40 g) butter
6 tbsps honey
1⅓ cups (5.2 oz or 150 g)
 plain flour
1/4 cup (1.7 oz. or 50 g)
 whole-wheat flour
1 tsp active dry yeast
1 egg
zest and juice of 1/2 lemon
salt
icing sugar

Preheat oven to 400°F (200°C).
Heat the milk and butter in a saucepan over low heat without boiling. Add the honey and stir for 2 more minutes. Remove from heat and let cool.
Sift the flours together in a large mixing bowl. Add the yeast, egg, lemon zest and juice and a pinch of salt. Mix well. Slowly add the milk and honey mixture. Mix to form a soft dough.
Line a baking sheet with parchment paper and spread the dough onto the baking sheet.
Bake for 45 minutes, let cool and sprinkle with icing sugar.

Plum Jam Tart

Preparation time 20 minutes
Cooking time 20 minutes
Wine *Colli Albani Bianco Dolce*

1¾ cups (7 oz or 200 g)
 plain flour
1/4 cup (1.7 oz or 50 g) sugar
7 tbsps (3.5 oz or 100 g)
 softened butter
2 egg yolks
1 jar plum jam

Preheat oven to 350°F (180°C).
Mix together the flour, sugar,
butter and egg yolks. When the
dough comes together, knead
to form a smooth and elastic
ball. Cover with plastic wrap
and refrigerate for 30 minutes.
Butter and flour a 8-inch (22
cm) tart pan.
Roll out the dough into a thin
sheet and line the tart pan with
the dough. Spread a thick layer
of jam over the dough.
Bake for 20 minutes. Remove
from the oven and cool
completely before serving.

Cornmeal Cake

Preparation time 15 minutes
Cooking time 30 minutes
Wine *Gewürztraminer Passito*

2 egg yolks
1 egg
1/2 cup (3.5 oz or 100 g) sugar
6 tbsps melted butter
1 tsp vanilla
1/2 cup plus 2 tbsps (3.5 oz
 or 100 g) cornmeal
3/4 cup (3.5 oz or 100 g)
 plain flour
1⅓ cups (3.5 oz or 100 g)
 hazelnuts
1.8 oz (50 g) chocolate chips
icing sugar

Preheat oven to 350°F (180°C).
Beat the egg yolks, egg and
sugar together in a large mixing
bowl. Add the butter and the
vanilla. Sift the 2 flours into the
egg mixture and mix well.
Finely chop half the hazelnuts.
Add to the batter with the
chocolate chips.
Chop remaining hazelnuts.
Butter and flour a cake pan and
pour in the batter. Top with the
remaining hazelnuts. Bake for 30
minutes. Dust with confectioners'
sugar before serving.

Neapolitan Ricotta Tart

240

Preparation time 30 minutes
Cooking time 15 minutes
Wine *Albana Passito*

Serves 6

CRUST
7 tbsps (3.5 oz or 100 g) butter
1/2 cup (3.5 oz or 100 g) sugar
1 egg
1 egg yolk
2¼ cups (8.8 oz or 250 g)
 plain flour

FILLING
1/2 cup (120 ml) milk
3/4 cup (5.2 oz or 150 g)
 cooked wheat
2 tbsps orange blossom water
1 egg yolk
2 tbsps sugar
4.2 oz (120 g) ricotta

Preheat oven to 350°F (180°C).
Beat together the butter, sugar, and egg and egg yolk. Add the flour and mix to form a smooth and elastic dough. Let rest for 20 minutes.
Roll out the dough and line 6 miniature tart tins.
Heat the milk and add the cooked wheat and orange blossom water. Let simmer for 5 minutes. Remove from heat and let cool.
In a mixing bowl beat the egg yolk with the sugar and then add the ricotta. Add the cooked wheat mixture. Pour the filling into the tart tins and bake for 25 minutes. Let cool completely before serving.

Chestnut and Ricotta Roll

Preparation time 20 minutes
Wine *Prosecco di Valdobbiadene Dry*

8.4 fl oz (250 ml) water
3 tbsps sugar
2 tbsps rum
1 sheet of sponge cake
8 oz (230 g) ricotta
2 tbsps icing sugar
1 tsp vanilla
6.3 oz (180 g) canned chestnuts
3.4 fl oz or (100 ml) whipping
 cream
1.7 oz (50 g) dark chocolate chips
cocoa powder

Bring the water and sugar to a boil to make a syrup, then add rum. Let cool.
Place the sponge cake on a foil-lined baking sheet. Brush one side of the sponge cake with the sugar syrup, turn over and brush the other side.
Mix the ricotta, icing sugar and vanilla. Drain and chestnuts and puree them with the cream. Add the chestnut mixture to the ricotta and then stir in the chocolate chips. Spread the filling onto the sponge cake and even out the layer with a spatula.
Tightly roll up the sponge cake like a jelly roll. Close the foil around the roll and refrigerate for 2 hours.
Slice the roll and dust with cocoa powder.

Honey Tart

Preparation time 30 minutes
Cooking time 50 minutes
Wine *Gewürztraminer
Vendemmia Tardiva*
♟ ♟

Serves 6-8

CRUST
10 tbsps (5.2 oz or 150 g) butter
1 egg
2 tbsps sugar
2¼ cups (8.8 oz or 250 g)
 plain flour

FILLING
3/4 cup (4.2 oz or 120 g) raisins
2 eggs, separated
6.7 fl oz (200 ml) plain yogurt
1 cup (7 oz or 200 g) fresh fruit
 puree
1/2 cup (6 oz or 170 g) honey
ground cinnamon and nutmeg

242

Preheat oven to 350°F (180°C).
Mix the butter, egg, sugar and flour together to form a smooth dough.
Refrigerate for at least 30 minutes.
Soak the raisins in a little warm water for 5 minutes. Drain and squeeze
out excess water.
Beat the egg yolks and add the yogurt, fruit puree, honey and raisins.
Season to taste with cinnamon and nutmeg.
Beat the egg whites to stiff peaks and fold into the batter.
Butter and flour a tart tin. Divide the chilled dough in 2 portions. Roll out
1 portion into a thin sheet. Line the tart tin with the dough. Pour in the
filling. Roll the remaining dough into another thin sheet. Cover the filling
with the second sheet of dough, tuck the top sheet over the filling and
fold the edges of the bottom sheet over to seal. Bake for 50 minutes.

Almond Cake

Preparation time 10 minutes
Cooking time 50 minutes
Wine *Campania Malvasia
Passita*

Serves 8

5 eggs
1 cup (7 oz or 200 g) sugar
3 cups (10.5 oz or 300 g)
 ground almonds
1/2 cup (120 ml) Amaretto liqueur
10.5 oz (300 g) dark chocolate
7 tbsps (3.5 oz or 100 g) butter
2 tsps baking powder
2 tsps vanilla
1 tsp almond extract
3 tbsps corn flour
icing sugar

Preheat oven to 350°F (180°C).
Mix the eggs, sugar, ground
almonds and Amaretto.
Melt the chocolate and butter in
a double boiler. Whisk into the
egg mixture.
Add the baking powder, vanilla,
almond extract and corn flour.
Mix until smooth. Butter and
flour a cake pan. Pour batter
into the pan. Bake for 50
minutes. Remove from oven
and dust with powdered sugar.

Chocolate Torte

Preparation time 10 minutes
Cooking time 35 minutes
Wine *Vin Santo*

Serves 6

3.5 oz (100 g) dark chocolate
7 tbsps (3.5 oz or 100 g) butter
2/3 cup (4.2 oz or 120 g) sugar
1½ cups (4.9 oz or 140 g
 ground almonds
3 eggs, separated
1 tbsp breadcrumbs
icing sugar

Preheat oven to 350°F (180°C).
Melt the chocolate in a
saucepan over low heat. Add
the butter, sugar and ground
almonds. Remove from heat
and let cool. When cool, stir in
egg yolks.
Beat the egg whites to stiff
peaks and fold into the
chocolate mixture.
Butter a tart tin and coat with
breadcrumbs. Pour the batter
into the tart tin and bake for 35
minutes. Remove the tart from
the oven, let cool and dust with
icing sugar.

243

Pear Tart with Amaretto Cream

Preparation time 20 minutes
Cooking time 50 minutes
Wine *Soave Recioto Spumante*

CRUST
2¼ cups (8.8 oz or 250 g)
 plain flour
1/2 cup (3.5 oz or 100 g) sugar
8 tbsps (4.2 oz or 120 g) butter
3 egg yolks
1 tsp vanilla
salt

PEARS
2.2 lbs (1 kg) Kaiser pears
1 knob of butter
1/4 cup (1.7 oz or 50 g) sugar
3 tbsps white wine

FILLING
5 egg yolks
1¾ cups (5.2 oz or 150 g) sugar
2/3 cups (2.8 oz or 80 g) corn flour
25 fl oz (750 ml) milk
3.5 oz (100 g) amaretto cookies
3/4 cup (180 ml) Amaretto liqueur

244

Preheat oven to 350°F (180°C).
To make the crust, quickly mix the flour, sugar, butter, egg yolks, vanilla and salt together to form an elastic dough. Cover with plastic wrap and refrigerate for 30 minutes.
Peel, core and dice the pears.
To make the pears, melt the butter and sugar in a saucepan, add the pears and cook for a few minutes. Add the wine and cook over high heat for 5 minutes.
To make the filling, beat the egg yolks with the sugar in a sauce-pan, add the corn flour and warm milk. Cook over low heat until the mixture thickens. Remove from heat and add the amaretto cookies and liqueur.
Butter a tart tin. Roll out the dough and line the tart tin with the dough. Pour amaretto cream over the crust, then top with the pears. Bake for 40 minutes.
Remove from the oven, cool completely and serve.

Apple Pie with Orange Marmalade

Note *This pie may be served with a light vanilla cream sauce, if desired.*

Preparation time 25 minutes
Cooking time 50 minutes
Wine *Malvasia di Lipari*

CRUST
1 1/4 cups (7 oz or 200 g)
 whole-wheat flour
2 tbsps (1 oz or 30 g) butter,
 softened
salt
2 tbsps agave juice

FILLING
2 Golden Delicious apples
1 tsp ground cinnamon
2 tbsps orange marmalade

Preheat oven to 350°F (180°C).
Mix the flour, softened butter, salt and agave juice to form a smooth dough. Let rest for 20 minutes.
Peel and dice the apples and sauté for a few minutes. Season with cinnamon and set aside.
Divide the dough in half. Roll out halfinto a thin sheet. Line a pie pan with the sheet of dough. Pierce the dough with a fork and fill with half the apples. Top with 1 tablespoon of marmalade, then add remaining apples and top with remaining marmalade.
Roll the remaining dough into a thin sheet and cover the pie with the dough. Flute the edges and pierce the top layer of dough with a fork.
Bake for 40-50 minutes. Remove from the oven and cool slightly.

Pineapple Cake with Pine Nuts

Preparation time 20 minutes
Cooking time 40 minutes
Wine *Moscato Passito*

Serves 8

4 eggs
3/4 cups (5.2 oz or 150 g) sugar
grated zest of 1 lemon
2 tbsps milk
3 tbsps (1.7 oz or 50 g) pine nuts
1¼ cups (3.5 oz or 100 g)
 graham crackers, crushed
4 tbsps plain flour
1 tsp baking powder
1 corn flour
2 tbsps melted butter
2 tbsps sunflower oil
1/4 pineapple, peeled and sliced

Preheat oven to 375°F (190°C).
Beat eggs, sugar and lemon
zest in a bowl. Whisk in milk,
pine nuts and graham crackers.
Sift and mix in the flour, baking
powder and corn flour. Add
melted butter and oil.
Arrange a layer of pineapple in a
spring-form pan. Pour over half
the batter. Add another layer of
pineapple and rest of batter. Top
with the remaining pineapple
slices. Bake for 40 minutes.

Hazelnut Cake

Preparation time 15 minutes
Cooking time 50 minutes
Wine *Passito di Pantelleria*

5 eggs
1 cup (7 oz or 200 g) sugar
4 cups (10.5 oz or 300 g) ground
 hazelnuts
1 cup (250 ml) espresso coffee
10.5 oz (300 g) dark chocolate
7 tbsps (3.5 oz or 100 g) butter
2 tsps baking powder
2 tsps vanilla
3 tbsps corn flour
6.7 fl oz (200 ml) milk

Mix the eggs, sugar, hazelnuts
and 1/4 cup (60 ml) of the
espresso in a mixing bowl.
In a double boiler melt the
chocolate and butter. Whisk the
chocolate into the egg mixture.
Add the baking powder, vanilla
and corn flour. Stir carefully to
form a smooth batter.
Pour the batter into a buttered
cake pan and bake for 50
minutes.
Meanwhile, prepare
cappuccinos with the hot milk
and the remaining espresso.
Serve the cake and cappuccino
together.

Caramelized Fig Tart

Preparation time 10 minutes
Cooking time 30 minutes
Wine *Erbaluce di Caluso Passito*

6 tbsps (2.8 oz or 80 g) butter
2.2 lbs (1 kg) figs
1 cup (7 oz or 200 g) sugar
1 tsp vanilla
3 tbsps (50 ml) whisky
8.8 oz (250 g) puff pastry
2.7 fl oz (80 ml) whipping cream

Preheat oven to 350°F (180°C).
Melt the butter in a baking dish.
Place the figs in the baking dish
and sprinkle with sugar, vanilla
and whisky. Place the puff
pastry over the figs and bake
for 30 minutes.
Remove from the oven and
invert onto a serving plate.
Whip the cream.
Serve the tart warm with whipped cream.

Red Wine Cake

Preparation time 20 minutes
Cooking time 45 minutes
Wine *Aleatico*

1 cup (8.8 oz or 250 g)
 butter, softened
1¼ cups (8.8 oz or 250 g) sugar
1 tsp cinnamon
1 tsp cocoa powder
salt
4 eggs
2¼ cups (8.8 oz or 250 g)
 plain flour
1 tbsps vanilla sugar
2 tsps baking powder
3/4 cup (180 ml) red wine

247

Preheat oven to 350°F (180°C).
Mix the softened butter, sugar,
cinnamon, cocoa powder and a
pinch of salt in a bowl.
Beat the eggs and then add
them to the butter mixture. Add
the flour, vanilla sugar, baking
powder and the red wine. Mix
well and pour into a cake pan.
Bake for 45 minutes. Let cool
and serve.

Carrot Cake with Yogurt Cream

Note *Carrots are low in calories (42 per 100 grams) and rich in vitamins A, B1, B2 and PP. They also contain important minerals like calcium, iron and magnesium.*

Preparation time 20 minutes
Cooking time 50 minutes

1½ cups (7 oz or 200 g) peeled almonds
1¼ cups (8.8 oz or 250 g) sugar
14 oz (400 g) carrots
4 eggs
1 cup (3.8 oz or 110 g) plain flour
1 tsp baking powder
salt
grated zest of 1 lemon
2/3 cup (5.2 oz or 150 g) yogurt
1 tsp icing sugar
1 tbsp whipping cream

248

Preheat oven to 320°F (160°C).
Blend the almonds and sugar in a food processor into a fine cornmeal consistency.
Grate the carrots and add them to the almond mixture. Mix in the eggs and then sift in the flour and baking powder. Mix well and add a pinch of salt and lemon zest.
Butter and flour a 10-inch (24 cm) diameter pan. Pour the batter into the pan and bake for 12 minutes. Raise the oven temperature to 350°F (180°C) and continue baking for 30 minutes.
Mix the yogurt and confectioners' sugar together. Whip the whipping cream and fold into the yogurt. Refrigerate.
Remove the cake from the oven and invert onto a wire rack. Let cool completely. Serve with yogurt cream.

Saint-Honoré with Grapes

Note *This cake was inverted by pastry chef Chiboust in 1846 in his shop on the Rue Saint Honoré in Paris. Today the cake is made with many variations.*

Preparation time 30 minutes
Cooking time 10 minutes
Wine *Malvasia di Lipari*
👨‍🍳 👨‍🍳

17 fl oz (500 ml) milk
4 egg yolks
3/4 cup (5.2 oz or 150 g) sugar
3/4 cup (3 oz or 90 g)
 plain flour
7 oz (200 g) sponge cake
orange blossom water
2 tbsps ground hazelnuts
1½ cups (7 oz or 200 g)
 green grapes
1½ cups (7 oz or 200 g)
 concord grapes
6.7 fl oz (200 ml) whipping cream

Heat milk in a saucepan.
Mix the egg yolks, sugar and flour in another saucepan. Whisk in the hot milk, being careful not to let lumps form. Bring the mixture to a boil and let cook for 2 minutes stirring constantly. When the mixture coats the back of a wooden spoon, remove from heat.
Meanwhile, cut the sponge cake into 3 rounds. Brush each round with orange blossom water.
Spread a third of the cream over 1 sponge cake round. Place the second round on top of the filling. Spread cream over the second layer of cake and top with the final layer of sponge cake and top with remaining cream, making sure to spread the cream over the sides of the cake as well. Stick the hazelnuts to the sides of the cake.
Slice the grapes in half and cover the top of the cake with grape halves. Decorate with whipped cream. Refrigerate the cake for at least 30 minutes and serve.

Imperial Chocolate Cake

Preparation time 45 minutes
Cooking time 45 minutes
Wine *Montefalco Sagrantino Passito*

Serves 6-8

CAKE
1/3 cup (1.4 oz or 40 g)
 plain flour
1/3 cup (1.4 oz or 40 g) corn flour
4 tbsps cocoa powder

1 tsp baking powder
4 tbsps (2.1 oz or 60 g) butter
1/2 cup (3.5 oz or 100 g) sugar
3 eggs, separated
3.5 oz (100 g) dark chocolate

FROSTING
3/4 cup (2.6 oz or 75 g)
 cocoa powder
2 tsps icing sugar
8.4 fl oz (250 ml) whipping cream
3.5 oz (100 g) gianduia chocolate

Preheat oven to 325°F (170°C).
Sift the flour, corn flour, cocoa powder and baking powder together.
Cream the butter in a mixing bowl. Add 1/4 cup (1.8 oz or 50 g) sugar to the butter and cream until fluffy.
Melt the chocolate in a double boiler. Add chocolate to the butter and sugar and then add the egg yolks.
Beat the egg whites and remaining sugar to stiff peaks. Fold the egg whites into the chocolate mixture.
Butter and flour a cake pan and pour in the batter.
Bake for 40-45 minutes. Remove the cake from the oven and cool completely.
Mix the cocoa powder and icing sugar together. Add the whipping cream and whip the mixture.
Slice the cake in half horizontally to form 2 rounds. Frost 1 round with half of the cocoa cream and then place the second round on top. Frost the top and the sides of the cake. Shave gianduia chocolate over the top of the cake.

Pear Gratin with Whisky Gelato

Preparation time 50 minutes
Cooking time 30 minutes

GELATO
6.3 oz (180 g) pre-made
 gelato base
3 tbsps whisky
3 tbsps water

PEARS
3 Williams pears
2 tbsps sugar

CARAMEL
1/2 cup (3.5 oz or 100 g) sugar
2 tbsps water
1 tsp balsamic vinegar

GARNISH
whisky cream liqueur

251

Remove the gelato base from the refrigerator and prepare the gelato
in an ice-cream machine following the manufacturer's instructions.
Before the final mixing, add the whisky and water. Let the machine
finish its cycle and then freeze the gelato.
For pears, preheat the broiler. Peel the pears and thinly slice them.
Fan the pear slices over the individual oven-proof serving plates.
Sprinkle with sugar.
Place the plates under the broiler for 1 minute or until the sugar
begins to color.
For the caramel, pour the sugar in a saucepan and add the water
and balsamic vinegar and cook over medium heat.
Prepare an ice-water bath in the sink. When the syrup turns
golden, remove the saucepan from the heat and place the pan in
the ice-water bath.
Place 1 scoop of gelato on the pears and drizzle with caramel and
whisky cream liqueur. Serve immediately.

Chocolate Mousse with Mandarin Sauce

Preparation time 35 minutes
Cooking time 5 minutes
Wine *Barolo Chinato*

Serves 6-8

MOUSSE
8.8 oz (250 g) dark chocolate
1 gelatin sheet
2 egg whites
1 tbsp sugar
salt
5 fl oz (150 ml) whipping cream
5 tsps dark rum
2 tbsps pistachios, chopped

SAUCE
2 mandarin oranges
1 knob of butter
raw sugar
white rum

252

Melt the chocolate in a double boiler.
Soak the gelatin sheet in cold water for a few minutes. Drain and squeeze out excess water. Dissolve the gelatin in a small saucepan over low heat.
Whip the egg whites, sugar and a pinch of salt into stiff peaks. Whip the whipping cream into stiff peaks.
Transfer the chocolate to a bowl, fold in the whipped cream, then the gelatin, rum and finally the egg whites. Refrigerate for 2 hours.
Meanwhile, peel the mandarins and separate the segments.
Melt the butter in a frying pan with the raw sugar. Add the mandarin segments and let caramelize slightly. Add the white rum and let evaporate. Add a little hot water and reduce the sauce by half. Puree and strain the sauce.
Spoon the mousse into 6 small bowls and drizzle with mandarin sauce. Sprinkle with pistachios and serve.

Almond Cakes
with Cinnamon Gelato

Preparation time 35 minutes
Cooking time 1 hour 20 minutes
👨‍🍳 👨‍🍳 👨‍🍳

Serves 6-8

ALMOND CAKE
3.5 oz (100 g) dark chocolate
3 cups (10.5 oz or 300 g)
 ground almonds
14 tbsps (7 oz or 200 g) butter
6 eggs, separated
1½ cups (300 grams) sugar
7 tsps cocoa powder
white chocolate

GELATO
2 egg yolks
1/3 cup (2.4 oz or 70 g) sugar
1 tsp dextrose
9 fl oz (270 ml) whole milk
1.6 fl oz (50 ml) whipping cream
1 tsp glucose syrup
1/4 cup (0.8 oz or 25 g)
 powdered milk
4 cinnamon sticks

Preheat oven to 350°C (180°C).
Chop the chocolate and add to the ground almonds. Melt the butter.
Beat the egg yolks and sugar until they are thick. Add the chocolate
and almonds, the butter and cocoa powder.
Beat the egg whites to stiff peaks and fold into the batter.
Pour the batter into cake pan and bake for 40 minutes. Invert the
cake onto a wire rack and let cool. Decorate with melted white
chocolate.
Beat the egg yolks, sugar and dextrose until thick and pale yellow.
In a saucepan heat the milk, cream and glucose syrup. Whisk in
the powdered milk. Break up the cinnamon sticks and add them to
the milk mixture. When the milk begins to boil, remove from heat.
Strain the milk mixture and whisk it into the egg and sugar. Return to
heat and cook, stirring constantly until it reaches 185°F (85°C). Cool
quickly and pour into the ice-cream machine. Follow manufacturer's
instructions to finish the gelato.
Cut out 8 small rounds of cake and serve with cinnamon gelato.

Calvados Pears

Note *Chestnut honey
is characteristically dark
brown, with a strong,
spicy flavour with bitter
understones.
It is said to have the highest
mineral content of all
single-variety honeys.*

Preparation time 15 minutes
Cooking time 5 minutes
Wine *Moscato Passito
di Pantelleria*

2 small firm pears
juice of 1 lemon
7 oz (200 g) ricotta
5 tbsps Calvados
7-8 walnut halves
2 tsps chestnut honey

254

Peel, core and quarter the pears.
Soak the pears in cold water with the lemon juice.
Whip the ricotta and then using 2 spoons make quenelles. Place
the quenelles in the middle of a serving plate.
Heat the Calvados in a saucepan. Let the alcohol evaporate and
then add a little water. Place the pears in a metal steaming basket
and set over the Calvados. Steam the pears for 3 minutes.
Chop the walnuts.
Slice the pears into very thin slices and place them around the
ricotta quenelles. Sprinkle the pears with walnuts and drizzle with
honey.

winter

Rich, filling dishes based on meat, fish, cheeses and vegetables, to show off the best of winter foods from the land and the ocean. Sophisticated appetizers to start holiday feasts, fragrant and tasty filled pastas, luxurious desserts and many more ideas to make winter cooking a joy.

Radicchio Crostini
with Ricotta Cream

Note *Radicchio's deep red colour indicates a high antioxidant content. It is rich in vitamins A and C as well as iron. When buying radicchio it is important to make sure the leaves are not wilted or wet, which means it is not fresh.*

Preparation time 15 minutes
Cooking time 10 minutes
Wine *Colli di Conegliano Verdiso*

1/2 baguette
2 tbsps extra-virgin olive oil
2 shallots, minced
1/2 head red Chioggia radicchio,
 finely shredded
1 tbsp balsamic vinegar
salt
5.5 oz (150 g) ricotta
chives, minced
1 tsp grated ginger

259

Slice the bread and toast it in the oven for a few minutes.
Heat olive oil and sauté shallots until soft. Stir in the radicchio, then add the balsamic vinegar and a pinch of salt and cook over low heat for 5 minutes.
Using a fork, beat the ricotta into a cream then mix in the chives and ginger.
Make the crostini by spreading the ricotta cream on the toasts and topping with a spoonful of radicchio.

Spiced Lentil Pâté

Preparation time 30 minutes
Cooking time 35 minutes
Wine *Sorni Rosso*

1 cup (7 oz or 200 g) dried lentils
6 tbsps extra-virgin olive oil
1 garlic clove
1 cup (4 oz or 120 g) minced
 celery, carrot and onion
1 tsp curry powder
1 tsp tomato paste
2 cups (500 ml) hot vegetable
 broth
salt and pepper
parsley, chopped

260

Rinse the lentils under running water and soak them in cold water
for 2 hours.
Heat olive oil in a saucepan and sauté the garlic, celery, carrot and
onion. Add the lentils, curry powder and tomato paste. Cook for a
few minutes then add hot broth and cook for 30 minutes until the
lentils are soft and the liquid has evaporated.
Blend in a food processor to obtain a thick puree and season with
salt and pepper, then mix in the parsley.
Divide the lentil pâté between individual bowls and leave to cool to
room temperature.
Serve with toasted bread, if desired.

A P P E T I Z E R S

Polenta Shapes with Vegetables

Preparation time 35 minutes
Cooking time 20 minutes
Wine *Rossese di Dolceacqua*

6 tbsps extra-virgin olive oil
1 carrot, peeled and diced
1 zucchini, green part only, diced
1 celery stalk, diced
salt
1½ cups (8.8 oz or 250 g) instant
 polenta cornmeal
2 tbsps Taggiasca or other small
 black olives in oil
3 tbsps diced tomatoes
fresh oregano leaves
1 fresh porcini mushroom, diced
1 garlic clove, smashed
thyme
salt and pepper

Heat 1 tablespoon of olive oil in a saucepan and sauté the carrot, zucchini and celery for 2 minutes.
Bring to a boil a pan of salted water. Add 2 tablespoons of oil and sprinkle in the polenta, stirring constantly with a whisk. While still liquid, pour two-thirds into a plastic container to create a layer 1/2-inch (1½ cm) thick. Stir the vegetables into the remaining polenta and set aside.
Sauté the olives, tomato and oregano with 1 tablespoon oil in a small frying pan.
Heat 1 tablespoon oil in another frying pan and sauté the mushrooms with the garlic, thyme, salt and pepper.
Cut the cooled polenta into circle and triangle shapes with cookie cutters. Fry the triangles in 1 tablespoon olive oil and top with the olive mixture. Brown the circles in a non-stick pan and top with the porcini mixture.
Using an ice-cream scoop form 4 balls of the polenta and vegetables.
Compose individual plates with the different polenta shapes.

Lardo and Tomato Crostini

Preparation time 10 minutes
Cooking time 10 minutes
Wine *Rosso di Montalcino*

4 thick slices of country-style
 bread
1 tbsp extra-virgin olive oil
1 San Marzano or plum tomato
salt and pepper
5.5 oz (150 g) Colonnata lardo
 thinly sliced
rosemary leaves

Preheat oven to 425°F (220°C).
Oil the surface of the bread and
cut into quarters. Toast in the
oven until golden-brown.
Blanch tomato for 1 minute,
then immerse in iced water.
Peel, deseed and dice. Season
with salt and pepper and set
aside.
Place 1 slice of lardo on each
toast then top with some
tomato and a rosemary leaf.
Sprinkle with pepper and serve.

Pumpkin and Pea Parcels

Preparation time 30 minutes
Cooking time 30 minutes
Wine *Alto Adige Terlaner*

2 tbsps extra-virgin olive oil
1/4 onion, diced
1/2 pumpkin, peeled, deseeded
 and cubed
3/4 cup plus 1 tbsp (200 ml)
 vegetable broth
salt
2 cups (10.5 oz or 300 g) peas
9 oz (250 g) puff pastry
1 tsp poppy seeds
1 egg, beaten

Preheat oven to 400°F (200°C).
Heat the olive oil in a heavy-
bottomed pan then sauté the
onion, adding a little water.
Add pumpkin and pour over
the vegetable broth. Salt to
taste then add peas. Cook over
medium heat for 10 minutes
then leave to cool.
Cut puff pastry into squares
and place a spoonful of the
vegetable mixture on each
one. Pinch together at the top
to form little packages. Brush
with beaten egg and sprinkle
with poppy seeds. Bake for 15
minutes and serve immediately.

262

Chickpea Farinata with Radicchio

Preparation time 20 minutes
Cooking time 30 minutes
Wine *Prosecco di Conegliano
e Valdobbiadene Brut*

2¾ cups (8.8 oz or 250 g)
 chickpea flour, sifted
3 cups (700 ml) water
salt
1 tsp dry active yeast
5 tbsps extra-virgin olive oil
1 shallot, minced
1 head Treviso radicchio,
 shredded
1 tsp honey

Preheat oven to 350°F (180°C).
Whisk chickpea flour into water and add salt, yeast and
3 tablespoons oil. Set aside to rest for 30 minutes.
Put the radicchio in a saucepan and cover with cold water. Bring
to a boil and drain, then repeat. This helps remove some of the
radicchio's bitterness.
Heat the remaining 2 tablespoons oil and sauté the shallot, then
add the radicchio and honey. Let it caramelize over a low heat for
2 minutes.
Pour the farinata batter into a baking dish and bake for
25 minutes. Leave to cool and cut into circles.
Serve with the radicchio, reheated if necessary.

Goat's Cheese and Smoked Salmon Puffs

Note *For a flavoursome alternative, try filling the puffs with a cream made from 5.5 oz (150 g) ricotta blended with 2 oz (50 g) mild Gorgonzola cheese. Garnish with chopped walnuts.*

264

Preparation time 1 hour
Cooking time 30 minutes
Wine *Metodo Classico Franciacorta Rosé*
♟ ♟

PUFFS
1 cup (4.4 oz or 125 g) plain flour
salt
2 tsps sugar
1/2 cup (3.5 oz or 100 g) butter
1 cup (250 ml) water
4 eggs

FILLING
7 oz (200 g) fresh goat's cheese
2 oz (50 g) robiola cheese
4 oz (120 g) smoked salmon, chopped
1 tbsp heavy cream
salt
pink pepper

GARNISH
wild fennel leaves

Preheat oven to 400°F (200°C).
Sift the flour, salt and sugar together.
Melt the butter in a saucepan with the water and bring to a boil.
Remove from the heat, add the flour and stir quickly until the
batter pulls away from the sides of the pan. Leave to cool for
5 minutes then add the eggs one at a time and mix well. Put the
batter in a pastry bag with a plain tip and form little mounds of
batter on a baking sheet. Bake for 15-20 minutes.
Mix together the goat's cheese, robiola, smoked salmon, cream,
a pinch of salt and some ground pink pepper in a food processor,
then put the mixture in a pastry bag. Fill the puffs with the salmon
cream and garnish with wild fennel.

Cauliflower with Parmesan Crisps

Preparation time 20 minutes
Cooking time 20 minutes
Wine *Prosecco
di Conegliano Brut*

CAULIFLOWER CREAM
4 cups (1 l) vegetable broth
1/2 cauliflower, cut into florets
1 tbsp extra-virgin olive oil
thyme leaves
salt

CRISPS
9 oz (250 g) puff pastry
salt
3 tbsps extra-virgin olive oil
1 tbsp grated Parmesan
sesame seeds

Preheat oven to 400°F (200°C).
Bring broth to a boil and boil
cauliflower until tender. Drain
and cool. Puree with olive oil,
thyme and a little salt.
Roll the puff pastry out thinly, salt
and lightly oil. Pierce the dough
and sprinkle with Parmesan and
sesame seeds. Cut into triangles
and lay on an oiled parchment
paper-lined baking sheet. Bake
for around 10 minutes. Serve the
cauliflower with the crisps.

Pecorino and Mostarda Crostini

Preparation time 10 minutes
Cooking time 4 minutes
Wine *Chianti Classico*

4 slices country-style bread,
  cut into 1/3-inch (1 cm) strips
9 oz (250 g) semi-aged mild
  pecorino, cut into 1/3-inch
  (1 cm) strips
2 tbsps fruit mostarda, finely
  chopped

Preheat the broiler.
Lay the bread strips on a baking
sheet and top each one with a
strip of pecorino. Broil until the
cheese is melted, then sprinkle
over the mostarda. Serve
immediately.

Note *Mostarda is a spicy
preserve from northern
Italy particulary the town of
Cremona. Mixed whole fruit is
preserved in a syrup flavoured
with mustard.
For a variation of this recipe,
use fresh goat's cheese instead
of pecorino.*

Creamy Leek Spread

Preparation time 15 minutes
Cooking time 10 minutes
Wine *Alto Adige Santa Maddalena*

1 tsp sunflower oil
2 oz (50 g) smoked speck ham, diced
1/4 onion, minced
1 leek, thinly sliced
1/2 red chilli pepper, deseeded and finely chopped
salt and pepper
9 oz (250 g) ricotta
12 slices Tuscan-style bread

Heat the oil in a frying pan and brown the speck ham and onion for 2-3 minutes. Add the leeks and chilli and sauté for another 5-6 minutes. Season with salt and pepper and let cool.
Once cool, stir in the ricotta and season with salt and pepper.
Toast the bread slices for a few minutes under the broiler, spread with the leek cream and serve immediately.

Prawn and Potato Croquettes

Preparation time 20 minutes
Cooking time 40 minutes
Wine *Metodo Classico Franciacorta Dosaggio Zero*

1/2 cup (4.2 oz or 120 g) butter
1 small onion, minced
1 lb (450 g) prawns, peeled, deveined and roughly chopped
parsley, chopped
3 yellow-fleshed potatoes, peeled
salt and pepper
3 tbsps milk
3 tbsps plain flour
2 tbsps extra-virgin olive oil

Melt a knob of the butter in a frying pan and sauté the onion, then add prawns and parsley and continue cooking until prawns are cooked through.
Boil and mash the potatoes, season with salt and pepper, then stir in some milk to create a smooth mixture. Let cool.
Stir the prawn mixture into the potatoes and form small balls. Flour them and fry in the butter and olive oil.
Serve the croquettes immediately, accompanied by a crunchy salad if desired.

266

Mini Onion Pies

267

Note *There are many kinds of onions: flat, round, white, red, yellow. Violet onions have a very intense flavour, white ones are more delicate, while the red onions of Tropea are the sweetest. To avoid tears while peeling onions, rinse them under running water.*

Preparation time 30 minutes
Cooking time 15 minutes
Wine *Bianco d'Alcamo*
♟ ♟

FILLING
1/2 cup (120 ml) extra-virgin
 olive oil
2.2 lb (1 kg) onions, thinly sliced
3 tomatoes, diced
salt and pepper
3.5 oz (100 g) feta cheese,
 crumbled
olive oil

PASTRY
4 cups (1 lb or 500 g)
 plain flour
4 tbsps extra-virgin olive oil
juice of 1 lemon
7 tbsps water
1/2 tsp salt

Heat the olive oil in a large saucepan and add the onions. Cook until golden, then add the tomatoes, salt and pepper. Simmer until the sauce thickens, then add the feta.
To make the pastry, mix the flour, olive oil, lemon juice, water and salt to form a dough, then roll out to 1/5-inch (1/2 cm) thick.
Cut out circles 4 inches (10 cm) in diameter and place a teaspoon of onion filling on each one. Fold over the circles to create semi-circles and press around the edges with a fork.
Heat the olive oil and fry the pies until golden-brown on both sides. Drain on paper towels.

Borlenghi
(Emilia-Romagna)

Preparation time 20 minutes
Cooking time 5 minutes
Wine *Colli Bolognesi Barbera*

2⅓ cups plus 1 tbsp (10.5 oz or 300 g) plain flour
salt
2 oz (50 g) lardo, minced
1 garlic clove, minced
rosemary, minced
2 oz (50 g) pork rind
9 tbsps grated Parmesan

In a bowl, mix the flour with a pinch of salt and enough water
to obtain a loose batter.
Mix together the lardo, garlic and rosemary.
Heat a frying pan, and oil it with the pork rind. When very hot add
a ladleful of the batter and spread it out with the back of the ladle
to cover the bottom of the pan, creating a kind of flat tortilla.
Cook for a few seconds then turn as soon as it starts to colour.
When browned on both sides remove from the pan, spread with
some of the lardo mixture, sprinkle over some Parmesan, fold
in quarters and keep warm. Continue until the batter has run out.
Serve hot.

268

Nervetti with Beans
(LOMBARDY)

Preparation time 30 minutes
Cooking time 3 hours 20 minutes
Wine *Valcalepio Rosso*

NERVETTI
6 pig's trotters,
 cleaned and scraped
salt
1 onion, peeled
1 celery stalk
parsley, chopped
1 carrot
aromatic herbs (thyme and bay)
1 knob of butter

BEANS
1/2 cup (3.5 oz or 100 g)
 cooked butter beans
sage
salt and pepper
3 tbsps heavy cream
Parmesanì, grated
nutmeg, grated

Place the pig's trotters in a large pan and cover with salted water.
Add the onion, celery, parsley, carrot and herbs. Bring to the boil
and cook for 3 hours.
As soon as the trotters are soft, remove them from the cooking
liquid with a slotted spoon. Remove the meat from the bone and
cut it into pieces.
Melt the butter in a frying pan and add the meat. Brown for
10 minutes, then add some of the cooking liquid.
Meanwhile put the beans in another frying pan with some sage
leaves, let cook for 5 minutes, season with salt and pepper, then
add the cream, Parmesan and a sprinkling of nutmeg.
Mix the beans with the nervetti and serve hot.

Radicchio Flan
with Balsamic Vinegar

Preparation time 20 minutes
Cooking time 30 minutes
Wine *Colli Orientali del Friuli Tocai*

2 tbsps butter
2 yellow onions, minced
2 heads Treviso radicchio,
 cut into pieces
3 tbsps balsamic vinegar
7 tbsps white wine
salt and pepper
7 oz (200 g) sheep's milk ricotta
2 tbsps grated Parmesan
nutmeg, grated
1 egg
5 tbsps breadcrumbs

270

Preheat oven to 375°F (190°C).
Melt a knob of butter in a saucepan and sauté the onion. When transparent add the radicchio, then the balsamic vinegar. When it has evaporated, add the wine.
Cook over low heat for 10 minutes and season with salt and pepper to taste.
Mix the ricotta with the Parmesan, nutmeg and egg, stir in the radicchio and mix well. Stir in the breadcrumbs to create a compact mixture.
Butter 6 ramequins and coat with breadcrumbs. Fill with the radicchio mixture up to 1/2 inch (1½ cm) from the top.
Bake the flans in the oven for around 20 minutes, until the top is well browned. Remove from the oven and serve hot.

Potato Focaccia
with Scamorza

Preparation time 15 minutes
Cooking time 50 minutes
Wine *Aglianico del Vulture*
♟

FOCACCIA
1 small potato
3 cups plus 3 tbsps (14 oz or 400 g)
 plain flour
2 tbsps lard
1 tbsp extra-virgin olive oil
2 tbsps (0.9 oz or 25 g)
 dry active yeast
3/4 cup (180 ml) water
1 tsp salt

TOPPING
9 oz (250 g) sausage meat,
 crumbled
5.5 oz (150 g) smoked scamorza,
 cubed
3 tbsps extra-virgin olive oil
rosemary, minced
pepper

Preheat oven to 350°F (180°C).
Boil the potato, peel and pass through a vegetable mill or potato ricer.
Mix together the potato puree with the other focaccia ingredients to obtain a smooth and uniform dough.
Roll out the dough and form a rectangle, then transfer to a baking sheet well oiled with olive oil. Cover with plastic wrap and leave in a warm place for 45 minutes.
When the dough has risen, sprinkle on top the sausage, scamorza and rosemary and a generous amount of pepper and drizzle with olive oil. Bake for 20 minutes, remove from the oven and serve immediately.

Roquefort Soufflés

Preparation time 15 minutes
Cooking time 30 minutes
Wine *Alto Adige Pinot Grigio*

3 tbsps butter
1 spring onion, finely chopped
4 tbsps plain flour
3/4 cup plus 1 tbsp (200 ml)
 hot milk
salt
nutmeg, grated
3 egg yolks
3.5 oz (100 g) Roquefort cheese,
 cubed
4 egg whites
Parmesan, grated

272

Preheat oven to 375°F (190°C).
Melt the butter in a small frying pan and add the spring onion.
Sauté for a few minutes. Stir in the flour and cook for a few more
minutes. Add the hot milk and stir until the sauce thickens.
Remove from the heat and season with salt and a pinch
of nutmeg.
Stir in the egg yolks one at a time and then the Roquefort.
Beat the egg whites into soft peaks, then fold gently into the
cheese mixture.
Butter 4 small soufflé molds, sprinkle with grated Parmesan and
fill them three-quarters-full full with the batter. Bake in a bain-marie
for 20 minutes then serve immediately.

Ricotta and Potato Fritters

Preparation time 10 minutes
Cooking time 35 minutes
Wine *Metodo Classico Franciacorta Brut*

1 large yellow-fleshed potato, paeled
salt and pepper
6.5 oz (180 g) ricotta
10 sage leaves, finely chopped
1 egg, beaten
breadcrumbs
sunflower oil for frying

Boil the potato until it is tender all the way through. While still hot, mash it and stir in the salt, pepper, ricotta and chopped sage. Chill the mixture in the refrigerator.
Once cool, form cherry-sized balls. Dip the balls in the egg, shake off the excess, then dip in breadcrumbs.
Heat the sunflower oil and fry the balls when the oil is very hot.
Drain on paper towels, lightly sprinkle with salt and serve immediately.

Squash with Parmesan Cream

Preparation time 20 minutes
Cooking time 10 minutes
Wine *Ribolla Gialla*

1/2 Kabocha squash, peeled and cubed
salt and pepper
1 tbsp extra-virgin olive oil
1 cup (3.5 oz or 100 g) grated Parmesan
saffron
4 thin slices prosciutto

Preheat oven to 350°F (180°C). Steam the squash cubes for 6 minutes, leaving them quite firm. Toss with a little salt, pepper and oil.
Place the Parmesan in a bowl then pour in a little boiling water, whisking constantly, to obtain a smooth cream. Mix in a pinch of saffron.
Heat a non-stick pan and brown the prosciutto slices on both sides, then dry them in the oven for 3 minutes. Once cooled, chop finely.
Serve the squash over the Parmesan cream, sprinkled with the crispy prosciutto.

Mortadella Soup
with Onion Crostoni

Preparation time 20 minutes
Cooking time 40 minutes
Wine *Morellino di Scansano*

SOUP
2 tbsps extra-virgin olive oil
1 cup (4 oz or 120 g) minced
 celery, carrot and onion
1 garlic clove
1 bay leaf
5.5 oz (150 g) mortadella,
 cut into small cubes
1¾ cups (400 ml) vegetable broth

CROSTONI
2 tbsps extra-virgin olive oil
2 sweet red onions, cut into rings
1 tsp peppercorns
1/2 cup (120 ml) vin santo
 or other dessert wine
salt
4 slices Altamura-style or other
 crusty bread

GARNISH
1/3 cup (1.5 oz or 40 g) shelled
 pistachios, finely chopped

274

To make the soup, heat the oil and sauté the celery, carrot, onion,
garlic and bay leaf. When soft, add the mortadella and cook for
4 minutes. Add the vegetable broth and cook over low heat for
15 minutes. Remove the garlic and bay and blend the soup,
seasoning with salt and pepper to taste.
Heat the oil for the crostoni in a saucepan and add the red onions
and peppercorns. Add the vin santo and reduce, then cook over a
low heat, adding a little hot water if necessary, until the onions are
soft. Add salt to taste.
Toast the bread and divide the onions between the 4 slices.
Serve the soup topped by the with the onion crostoni, sprinkled
with pistachios.

Potato and Pancetta Tart

Preparation time 20 minutes
Cooking time 45 minutes
Wine *Prosecco di Conegliano e Valdobbiadene*

3 tbsps extra-virgin olive oil
2 medium potatoes, sliced
1 shallot, minced
2 cups (500 ml) boiling
 vegetable broth
3 oz (80 g) pancetta, diced
salt and pepper
1 egg, beaten
3 tbsps grated Parmesan
9 oz (250 g) puff pastry
1 tbsp sesame seeds

Preheat oven to 400°F (200°C).
Heat 2 tablespoons olive oil and sauté the potatoes with the shallot until golden. Cover with boiling broth and cook until tender. Blend them into a puree and season with salt and pepper.
Sauté the pancetta in a frying pan with 1 tablespoon olive oil until crispy.
Mix the pancetta and potatoes together and stir in the egg, Parmesan and a little pepper.
Line a pie dish with parchment paper and fill with the potato mixture. Top with puff pastry and poke holes with a fork to let the steam escape. Sprinkle with sesame seeds and bake for around 35 minutes.

Salmon and Escarole Mousse

Note *The escarole in this recipe gives the mousse greater volume, and its bitterness contrasts well with the sweetness of the other ingredients.*

276

Preparation time 25 minutes
Cooking time 10 minutes
Wine *Orvieto Classico*

MOUSSE
3 tbsps butter
1 shallot, minced
1 red chilli pepper, deseeded
 and minced
1 head escarole, coarsely chopped
14 oz (400 g) salmon, cut into
 chunks
2½ tbsps white wine
1/2 cup (2 oz or 60 g) black olives,
 pitted
4 tbsps capers in salt, rinsed
4 tbsps mayonnaise
salt and pepper

GARNISH
4 black olives
1 fillet red bell pepper preserved
 in oil, cut into strips
1 baguette, sliced and toasted

Melt the butter in a frying pan and sauté the shallot and chilli pepper. Add the escarole and cook, covered, for 5 minutes, until it reduces in volume.
Add the salmon and wine and reduce. Stir in the olives and capers and cook until the salmon is cooked through, then remove from the heat and let cool.
Once cool blend the mixture in a food processor with mayonnaise, salt and pepper. Fill a mold with the mousse and refrigerate for 2 hours.
Unmold and decorate with olives and strips of bell pepper. Serve with toasted bread.

Scallops with Salted Butter

Preparation time 20 minutes
Cooking time 10 minutes
Wine *Alto Adige Gewürztraminer*

8 large scallops, with shells
1/4 cup (2 oz or 60 g) salted butter
1 shallot, thinly sliced
2 tbsps Traminer wine
salt and pepper
1 tbsp extra-virgin olive oil
2 slices country-style bread, cubed

Clean the scallops and wash the shells well.
Melt a little of the butter and sauté the shallot, adding a little water, until the shallot is transparent and soft.
Heat a non-stick pan with the rest of the butter and sauté the scallops. Add the wine and let evaporate.
Mince the cooked shallot, coarsely chop the scallops and mix together. Season with salt and pepper and divide between the scallop shells. Heat the oil in a frying pan and sauté the bread cubes. As soon as they are crispy remove from the pan and chop finely. Sprinkle the bread over the scallops and gratinée under the broiler for 3 minutes.

Turkey Mousse

Preparation time 15 minutes
Cooking time 15 minutes
Wine *Alto Adige Pinot Bianco Riserva*

9 oz (250 g) puff pastry
1 tbsp extra-virgin olive oil
1 garlic clove
thyme and rosemary, chopped
4.5 oz (120 g) turkey breast, cut into bite-size chunks
1 tbsp heavy cream
salt and pepper
1 pomegranate

277

Preheat oven to 350°F (180°C).
Cut the puff pastry into small circles and bake in the oven for around 6-8 minutes until lightly golden, then cool.
Heat the oil in a frying pan and add the garlic and herbs. Add the turkey and brown.
Lower the heat and cook, covered, for 7-8 minutes.
Blend the turkey into a puree with the cream and season with salt and pepper. Put the mousse in a pastry bag with a star tip, and decorate the pastry circles with it. Garnish with pomegranate seeds.

Citrus Trout Crostini

Preparation time 30 minutes
Cooking time 3 minutes
Wine *Malvasia Istriana*

1 salmon trout
(around 1 lb or 500 g),
 cleaned and filleted
juice of 2 lemons
1 tsp coarse salt
1 tsp peppercorns, crushed
6 tbsps extra-virgin olive oil
thyme, finely chopped
1 bay leaf, finely chopped
rosemary, finely chopped
zest of 1 organic lemon,
 cut into strips
zest of 1 organic orange,
 cut into strips
1/2 baguette

Place the trout fillets in a bowl and pour over the lemon juice. Sprinkle with coarse salt and crushed peppercorns and refrigerate for around 12 hours.
Remove the fillets from the marinade and rinse briefly then pat dry. Place in a bowl and cover with olive oil.
Mix together the thyme, bay leaf, rosemary and lemon and orange zest, then add to the trout, cover with plastic wrap and marinate for another 12 hours in the refrigerator. Preheat oven to 350°F (180°C). Slice the bread and toast for 3 minutes. Cut the trout fillets into thin slices along the diagonal then lay the slices on the toasted bread. Garnish with the strips of citrus zest and drizzle over a little of the marinade. Serve immediately.

Salmon Cannoli

Preparation time 20 minutes
Cooking time 15 minutes
Wine *Cartizze*

14 oz (400 g) smoked salmon,
 sliced
chives, chopped
3.5 oz (100 g) fresh soft cheese
2 tbsps butter, softened
juice of 1 lemon
salt
5 tbsps extra-virgin olive oil
1/2 tsp paprika
9 oz (250 g) puff pastry

Preheat oven to 400°F (200°C).
Blend half the salmon with the chives, cheese, butter and lemon juice to form a smooth cream. Season with salt to taste and refrigerate.
Sprinkle the rest of salmon with 1/2 teaspoon salt, oil and paprika and set aside.
Cut the puff pastry strips 3/4-inch (2 cm) wide and 5-inches (12 cm) long.
Drain the salmon from the marinade and cut into strips the same size as the pastry strips. Lay a strip of salmon on each piece of pastry and roll each one around a buttered cannoli mold.
Line a baking sheet with parchment paper and place the cannoli on it. Bake for 15 minutes, turning halfway through so they cook evenly.
Remove from the oven, let cool and remove from the molds. Fill the cannoli with the salmon cream and serve on a bed of green salad, if desired.

Spiced Saffron Bread
(TUSCANY)

Preparation time 30 minutes
Cooking time 1 hour

Serves 6-8

2 cups (12.5 oz or 350 g) raisins
8 cups (2.2 lb or 1 kg) flour
1 tbsp plus 1 tsp (0.5 oz or 15 g)
 dry active yeast
1/2 cup (120 ml) warm water
1 tbsp ground mixed spices
 (coriander, juniper, cloves)
1 tsp saffron
5 tbsps extra-virgin olive oil
salt and pepper

Soak the raisins in a bowl with the warm water.
Mound the flour on work surface and make a well in the centre.
Dissolve the yeast in the warm water and pour into the centre
of the flour. Add a pinch of salt, ground spices, saffron, oil and mix
with enough warm water to form a smooth and uniform dough.
Drain the raisins and squeeze out excess water, then knead them
quickly into the dough, working it by hand so that the raisins are
evenly distributed.
Leave the dough to rise for 1 hour in a warm place, covered
by a clean kitchen towel and a woolen cloth.
Preheat oven to 350°F (180°C).
Place the dough in a baking tin and bake for 1 hour. Remove
from the oven and let cool slightly.
Serve immediately.

Walnut Rolls
(MARCHE)

Preparation time 45 minutes
Cooking time 30 minutes
Wine *Verdicchio di Matelica Spumante*
♟ ♟

Serves 6

1 lb (500 g) walnuts
2 cups (500 ml) milk
2 tbsps (0.9 oz or 25 g)
 dry active yeast
8 cups (2.2 lb or 1 kg)
 plain flour
1 tsp salt
1 tsp pepper
7 tbsps extra-virgin olive oil
6½ tbsps lard
7 oz (200 g) pecorino cheese,
 cubed
1 knob of butter
1 egg, beaten

281

Pour boiling water over the walnuts and soak for 5 minutes. Drain and rub with a clean kitchen towel to remove the skins.
Warm 3/4 of the milk and dissolve the yeast in it. Mound half the flour on a work surface, make a well in the centre and pour in the milk with the yeast, little by little. Mix to form a smooth and soft dough, then cover with a clean kitchen towel and leave to rise in a dry place for 30 minutes.
Place remaining flour in a bowl and mix in salt, pepper, remaining milk, oil and lard, then mix in the risen dough. Work vigorously to obtain a soft dough, then leave to rise for 30 minutes.
Form the dough into small rolls and in the centre of each one insert a cube of pecorino cheese and a few walnut halves. Leave the rolls to rise for 2 hours.
Preheat oven to 400°F (200°C).
Butter a baking sheet and set the rolls on it, then brush them with beaten egg. Bake for around 30 minutes. Serve warm.

Gratinéed Scallops with Almonds and Thyme

Note *Scallops are one of the world's most common mollusks. If fresh they must have a firm consistency and smell good, with no hint of spoilage.*

Preparation time 10 minutes
Cooking time 5 minutes
Wine *Metodo Classico Franciacorta Rosé*

4 large scallops, shelled
1/2 cup (3 oz or 80 g) almonds,
  coarsely chopped
lemon thyme, minced
salt and pepper
2 tbsps extra-virgin olive oil
mixed baby salad leaves

282

Preheat the broiler to the highest setting.
Wash the scallops well to remove any sand, then pat dry and place in a baking dish.
Sprinkle the scallops with thyme, salt and a little pepper.
Top with some almonds, drizzle over the oil and broil for 5 minutes.
Serve the scallops over the mixed salad leaves.

Scallops over Fennel

Preparation time 25 minutes
Cooking time 10 minutes
Wine *Riviera Ligure di Ponente Vermentino*

8 scallops, cleaned, with shells
4 tbsps extra-virgin olive oil
salt and pepper
thyme leaves
1 fennel bulb
2 tbsps balsamic vinegar
1 tsp minced chives
1 garlic clove, unpeeled

Toss the scallops with
1 tablespoon oil, salt and thyme
and refrigerate for 20 minutes.
Finely chop the fennel bulb, and
soak in cold water until ready
for use.
Drain the fennel and toss with
2 tablespoons oil, salt, pepper,
balsamic vinegar and chives.
Heat 1 tablespoon oil in a frying
pan with the garlic clove and
sauté the scallops briefly.
To serve place some fennel
salad in each scallop shell and
top with a warm scallop.

Prawns in Brandy Sauce

Preparation time 30 minutes
Cooking time 20 minutes
Wine *Bianco d'Alcamo*

2 tbsps extra-virgin olive oil
1 shallot, minced
3 tbsps water
1.3 lb (600 g) jumbo prawns
1/2 oup (120 ml) brandy
1 cup (180 ml) white wine
2 ripe tomatoes, blanched,
 peeled and chopped
salt and pepper
7 tbsps heavy cream
parsley, finely chopped

283

Heat the oil and sauté the
shallot together with the water.
Add the prawns and coat with
the shallots, then pour over the
brandy. When evaporated, add
the wine and reduce by half.
Add the tomatoes, season with
salt and pepper and cook for
10 minutes.
Remove the prawns and set
aside. Add the cream to the
pan and reduce over high
heat. Season to taste with salt
and pepper, sprinkle over the
parsley, and toss the prawns
with the sauce.

Prawn Cocktail with Cicerchie Cream

Note *Cicerchie, sometimes known as grass peas, are a kind of wild chickpea of Egyptian origin. They are very rich in calcium and phosphorous, but are rarely used in Italy as they are hard to cultivate and require a long cooking time. They can be substituted with regular chickpeas.*

Preparation time 20 minutes
Cooking time 40 minutes
Wine *Verdicchio di Matelica*

4 oz (120 g) cicerchie
 or chickpeas
1 garlic clove
2 tbsps extra-virgin olive oil
1 shallot, minced
3/4 cup plus 1 tbsp (200 ml)
 fish broth
1 pinch saffron
salt and pepper
parsley, minced
9 oz (250 g) prawn tails, shelled

Soak the cicerchie for a day, then boil in salted water with the garlic clove for around 40 minutes, until soft.
Heat the oil in a saucepan and sauté the shallot, then add the drained cicerchie. Cover with fish broth, add the saffron and cook for a few minutes. Blend with an immersion blender to obtain a smooth cream, season to taste with salt and pepper and sprinkle with a little parsley. Keep warm.
Steam the prawns for 5 minutes. Divide half between martini glasses, top with the cicerchie cream, then garnish with the remaining prawns. Serve immediately.

284

Individual Prawn and Leek Quiches

Preparation time 45 minutes
Cooking time 30 minutes
Wine *Friuli Collio Tocai*

👨‍🍳 👨‍🍳

PASTRY

2 cups (8.8 oz or 250 g)
 plain flour
1/2 oup (4.4 oz or 120 g) butter
1 egg yolk
salt

FILLING

3.5 oz (100 g) smoked speck ham,
 diced
1/2 onion, minced
1 garlic clove, minced
1 leek, sliced
7 oz (200 g) small prawns,
 cleaned and shelled

CREAM SAUCE

3/4 cup plus 1 tbsp (200 ml)
 heavy cream
2 tbsps aromatic herbs
 (thyme, rosemary), minced
3 eggs
salt
white pepper
3 oz (80 g) Gruyère cheese,
 diced

Preheat oven to 400°F (200°C).
Mix together pastry ingredients to obtain a uniform dough, wrap in
plastic wrap and leave to rest in the refrigerator.
Brown speck ham in a frying pan, add onion, garlic and leek, sauté
for a few minutes then remove from the heat.
Mix together the cream, aromatic herbs and eggs, season with salt
and pepper, and stir in the Gruyère cheese.
Roll the pastry dough out thinly. Butter individual aluminum tart
dishes and line them with the dough. Poke holes in the base with
a fork and divide the vegetable and ham mixture between them.
Divide the prawns between them then pour over the cream sauce.
Bake for 20-25 minutes, until the surface is crispy. Serve warm.

Baked Pineapple with Ham

Preparation time 20 minutes
Cooking time 15 minutes
Wine *Friuli Annia Sauvignon*

1/2 pineapple, peeled
2 cloves
pepper
1 bunch arugula
3 tbsps extra-virgin olive oil
1 tbsp balsamic vinegar
salt
7 oz (200 g) roasted ham,
 sliced and cut into strips

286

Preheat oven to 375°F (190°C).
Place the pineapple on a
baking sheet lined with wax
paper. Stick the cloves into the
pineapple and sprinkle with a
little pepper. Bake for around
15 minutes.
Meanwhile wash the arugula
and soak it for a few minutes in
iced water to make it crunchy.
Drain, dry and shred. Toss with
oil, balsamic vinegar and salt.
Roll up the ham strips. Cut the
pineapple into wedges and
serve over the arugula with the
ham strips.

Ham Baguette

Preparation time 20 minutes
Wine *Lambrusco di Sorbara*

12.5 oz (350 g) ham, cubed
3.5 oz (100 g) preserved
 vegetables in oil, minced
1 bunch arugula, finely chopped
2/3 cup (5.3 oz or 150 g) butter,
 softened
salt and pepper
2 French baguettes

Mince the ham in a food
processor. Mix it with the
preserved vegetables, arugula
and butter, and season with salt
and pepper.
Remove some of the soft
crumb from the baguettes and
fill them with the ham mixture.
Wrap in plastic wrap and chill in
the refrigerator before serving.
Cut into diagonal slices to
serve.

Chanterelle and Borage Mousse in Baskets

Preparation time 20 minutes
Cooking time 10 minutes
Wine *Dolcetto di Dogliani*

♟ ♟

MOUSSE
6 tbsps extra-virgin olive oil
1 garlic clove, smashed
1 medium potato, peeled
 and diced
2 cups (5.5 oz or 150 g)
 chanterelle mushrooms
1/2 cup (120 ml) white wine
1/2 cup (2 oz or 50 g) borage,
 roughly chopped
3/4 cup (180 ml) hot water
1/4 cup (2 oz or 60 g) butter
salt and pepper

BASKETS
2 egg whites
2½ tbsps icing sugar
3/4 cup (3.5 oz or 100 g)
 plain flour
saffron
8 tbsps melted butter
salt

GARNISH
1 black truffle, minced
pine nuts, toasted (optional)

287

Preheat oven to 425°F (220°C).
Heat the oil in a frying pan, sauté the garlic, then add the potato and cook for 5 minutes. Add the mushrooms and pour over the wine. Stir in the borage, add the hot water and cook, covered, for 5 minutes.
Beat the egg whites with the sugar, then beat in the flour and a pinch of saffron. Continue beating and pour in the melted butter in a thin stream. Add salt.
Line a baking sheet with parchment paper, then use the batter to make 4 circles of 4 inches (10 cm) in diameter. Bake until golden, remove from the oven, place each one over the bottom of glass to form a basket shape and leave to cool.
Blend the mushroom mixture, butter, salt and pepper in a food processor. Fill the baskets with the mousse using a pastry bag.
Sprinkle over the truffle and garnish with toasted pine nuts if desired.

Gratinéed Swiss Chard Rolls

Note *Rice can be used as a filling for many different kinds of rolls. Slices of grilled eggplant can be stuffed with cooked rice and mozzarella cubes, covered with tomato sauce and baked in a 350°F (180°C) oven for 10 minutes.*

Preparation time 20 minutes
Cooking time 25 minutes
Wine *Soave*

1/2 small leek, minced
1 knob of butter
1¼ cups (8.8 oz or 250 g) Vialone Nano rice
1/2 cup (120 ml) white wine
hot vegetable broth (optional)
12 Swiss chard leaves
1 tbsp grated Parmesan
salt and pepper
2 tbsps extra-virgin olive oil
1 tbsp breadcrumbs

288

Sauté the leek in a small saucepan with the butter. Add the rice and toast, stirring constantly. Add the wine, cook for a few minutes, then add the hot vegetable broth or water and continue cooking.
Meanwhile blanch the Swiss chard leaves in boiling water, then immerse in a bowl of iced water.
When the rice is cooked, stir in the Parmesan and season with salt and pepper to taste.
Preheat the broiler.
Drain and dry the Swiss chard leaves and lay them out on a cutting board or work surface. Place 2 tablespoons of rice on each one and roll up. Place the rolls in a baking dish and drizzle with olive oil. Sprinkle with breadcrumbs and gratinée under the broiler for 3 minutes.

A P P E T I Z E R S

Scallops with Belgian Endive

Preparation time 30 minutes
Cooking time 20 minutes
Wine *Val d'Aosta Pinot Grigio*

3½ tbsps sugar
1½ tbsps water
1½ tbsps raspberry vinegar
1/2 cup (120 ml) Moscato Rosa wine
2 heads Belgian endive, chopped
salt and pepper
14 oz (400 g) scallops
8 grapefruit segments, peeled
chervil leaves

Heat the sugar and water in a pan until caramelized, add the vinegar and reduce. Add the wine and cook until it reaches a syrupy consistency. Remove from the heat and cool.
Sauté the endive briefly in a pan, then divide between individual plates. Season with salt and pepper to taste.
Grill the scallops under the broiler, arrange on the endive and garnish with 2 grapefruit segments.
Drizzle over the wine syrup and sprinkle with chervil. Serve immediately.

289

Crispy Polenta with Spicy Octopus

Preparation time 20 minutes
Cooking time 30 minutes
Wine *Greco di Tufo*

POLENTA
2 cups (500 ml) water
salt
3/4 cup (5.5 oz or 150 g)
 instant polenta cornmeal
sunflower oil for frying

OCTOPUS
9 oz (250 g) baby octopus or squid
3 tbsps extra-virgin olive oil
2 garlic cloves, halved
1 chilli pepper, chopped
1/2 cup (120 ml) white wine
parsley, finely chopped
10 ripe cherry tomatoes, quartered
salt and pepper

290

Bring water to a boil with a little salt and sprinkle in the polenta, whisking constantly. Continue cooking, stirring with a wooden spoon, for 5 minutes. Line a rectangular cake pan with plastic wrap, pour in the polenta and cool in the refrigerator.
Wash the octopus, detaching the heads and removing the central bone. Roughly chop the heads and tentacles, and wash them again.
Heat the oil in a saucepan and sauté the garlic and chilli pepper. Add the octopus and sauté for 1 minute, then add the wine. Add the parsley and tomatoes. Cook over low heat for around 15 minutes, then season to taste with salt and pepper.
Unmold the polenta and cut into slices. Fry them in hot sunflower oil and drain on paper towels. Serve the crispy polenta topped with the octopus.

Pecorino and Pear Skewers with Honey and Walnuts

Note *Pecorino is a strongly flavoured, hard cheese made from sheep's milk. The name cames from the Italian for sheep,* pecora. *Pecorino can be less aged and milder or more aged and sharper. A semi-aged cheese would work well for this recipe.*

Preparation time 10 minutes
Cooking time 2 minutes
Wine *Nobile di Montepulciano*
♟

7 oz (200 g) pecorino cheese
2 Williams pears
pepper
2 tbsps acacia honey
7-8 walnut halves, coarsely chopped

Preheat the grill or barbecue.
Cut the pears and pecorino into cubes of the same size. Thread them onto wooden skewers, alternating pear and cheese cubes. Sprinkle with pepper.
Grill or broil for 30 seconds on each side, not too close to the heat, and lay them on serving plates.
Drizzle with honey and sprinkle with walnuts.

293

294

Langoustines with Orange

Preparation time 15 minutes
Cooking time 10 minutes
Wine *Terlaner Riserva*

2 oranges, 1 juiced
 and 1 cut into supremes
 (peeled segments)
juice of 1 lemon
salt and pepper
16 medium langoustines
1 fennel bulb, diced
2 carrots, diced
3 tbsps extra-virgin olive oil
basil, shredded

Mix the orange and lemon juice
with salt and pepper and divide
between 2 bowls.
Remove part of the langoustine
shell, leaving the tail, and place
the langoustines in one of the
bowls. Toss with the juices and
marinate for 20 minutes.
Meanwhile soak the fennel and
carrot in ice water.
Grill the langoustines, and
remove the rest of the shell.
Drain the vegetables and toss
with the remaining citrus juice.
Add the orange segments, basil
and a little oil.
Serve the langoustines over the
vegetable salad.

Smoked Swordfish with Citrus

Preparation time 15 minutes
Wine *Metodo Classico
Franciacorta Extra Brut*

1 bunch arugula
2 oranges, 1 juiced and 1 cut into
 supremes (peeled segments)
2 tbsps extra-virgin olive oil
salt and pepper
7 oz (200 g) smoked swordfish,
 sliced
1 tsp pink peppercorns, crushed
1 bunch wild fennel leaves or dill,
 chopped

Soak the arugula in ice water
for 10 minutes to make it
crunchy.
Whisk together the orange
juice, olive oil, salt and pepper
to make a dressing. Set aside.
Drain, dry and shred the
arugula, then arrange on
serving plates.
Lay the swordfish over the
arugula and sprinkle with pink
pepper. Garnish with orange
segments and drizzle over the
orange dressing. Sprinkle with
wild fennel leaves.

Salmon Roll with Lemon Sauce

Preparation time 20 minutes
Cooking time 15 minutes
Wine *Blanc de Morgex et de La Salle*

ROLL
12.5 oz (350 g) Norwegian
 salmon fillet
salt and pepper
6-7 lettuce leaves, blanched

SAUCE
3½ tbsps butter
1 tsp peppercorns
juice and zest of 1 organic lemon
1 bay leaf
4 tbsps heavy cream
2 tbsps extra-virgin olive oil
salt and pepper

295

Remove the skin and any bones from the salmon and cut horizontally to obtain 2 rectangular fillets. Place them between 2 sheets of plastic wrap and gently flatten. Season with salt and pepper and lay the lettuce leaves on top, then roll up the fillets tightly, closing each end with more plastic wrap. Steam the rolls for around 8-10 minutes. Meanwhile melt the butter and sauté the peppercorns, then add the lemon juice and a little water, or a broth made from salmon scraps. Add the bay leaf and cook for a few minutes. Strain, then beat in the cream with a little oil to even out the consistency. Season with salt and pepper to taste.
Unwrap the rolls and slice, then serve with the lemon sauce. Garnish, if desired, with thin strips of lemon zest.

Fried Piadina
(Emilia-Romagna)

Note *The name piadina
means "little plate".
This grilled or fried flatbread
is typical of Romagna,
the eastern part
of Emilia-Romagna.
It is traditionally eaten with
cheeses or cured meats.*

Preparation time 30 minutes
Cooking time 15 minutes
Wine *Colli Bolognesi Bianco
Frizzante*

Serves 6-8

2½ tsps (0.4 oz or 10 g) dry
 active yeast
8 cups (2.2 lb or 1 kg)
 plain flour
1 egg
salt
1 tbsp extra-virgin olive oil
sunflower oil for frying

296

Dissolve yeast in a little warm water. Mound the flour on a work
surface, make a well in the middle and break the egg into it. Add a
pinch of salt, the oil and the dissolved yeast. Mix by hand to create
a smooth and uniform dough, adding water when necessary, and
making sure there are no lumps.
Divide the dough into many small balls and leave them to rise in
a dry place, covered with a clean kitchen towel.
Roll each dough ball out with a rolling pin to form a thin disk. Heat
abundant sunflower oil in a pan, and when it is very hot fry the
disks until they turn golden-brown. Drain with a slotted spoon and
dry on paper towels. Serve them hot, with sliced cured meats like
salami and prosciutto.

Red Cabbage
and Goat's Cheese Tart

Preparation time 20 minutes
Cooking time 30 minutes
Wine *Friuli Isonzo Sauvignon*
♟ ♟

CRUST
3 cups plus 3 tbsps
 (14 oz or 400 g) plain flour
4 eggs
salt

FILLING
10.5 oz (300 g) fresh goat's cheese
salt and pepper
4 tbsps extra-virgin olive oil
2 garlic cloves, unpeeled
 and halved
1/4 head red cabbage, shredded
1 tbsp balsamic vinegar

Preheat oven to 350°F (180°C).
Prepare the crust by mixing together the flour, eggs and salt.
Knead for 10 minutes then roll out into a thin sheet.
Bring a large pan of salted water to the boil. Cut the dough into
8-inch (20 cm) rectangles and blanch them in the boiling water.
Beat the goat's cheese with the pepper, salt and 2 tablespoons oil
until creamy then fill a pastry bag with it.
Heat 1 tablespoon oil in a saucepan and sauté garlic until golden.
Remove garlic and add cabbage. Cook over medium heat, adding
the vinegar and letting it evaporate. Add a little water if necessary,
and season with salt to taste.
Layer a sheet of dough with goat's cheese piped from the pastry
bag and the hot cabbage, and continue until all the sheets have
been used. Drizzle of olive oil and a grinding of pepper. Bake for
20 minutes. Remove from the oven and let rest for 20 minutes
before serving.

Tigelle
(EMILIA ROMAGNA)

Note *These savoury snacks are a traditional accompaniment to a plate of cheeses and cured meats. This particular recipe, in which they are filled with a flavoursome pesto, is from the town of Modena.*

Preparation time 25 minutes
Cooking time 15 minutes
Wine *Lambrusco Salamino di Santa Croce*

TIGELLE
2 tbsps (0.9 oz or 25 g) dry active yeast
4¾ cups (1.3 lb or 600 g) plain flour
4 tbsps lard
salt
3/4 cup plus 1 tbsp (200 ml) heavy cream

PESTO
7 oz (200 g) lardo, minced
1 garlic clove, minced
rosemary, minced
2 tbsps grated Parmesan
pepper

298

Dissolve the yeast in a little warm water. Mix the flour well with the yeast, lard and a pinch of salt, then add the cream and knead to create a smooth and uniform dough. Leave to rest for 1 hour.
Once the dough has rested, form cylinders around 1 inch (2½ cm) in diameter then tear off pieces of the same lenght. Form them into balls, then flatten them, creating a hollow on one side. Let them rest for 30 minutes on a clean kitchen towel.
Preheat oven to 350°F (180°C).
Once the tigelle have rested, press them out to form circles 4 inches (10 cm) in diameter and 1/5 inch (1/2 cm) thick. Bake in the oven until golden.
Meanwhile make the pesto by grinding the lardo with garlic, a little rosemary, Parmesan and a pinch of pepper in a mortar and pestle.
Serve the tigelle hot, opened and filled with the pesto.

Ricotta with Radicchio and Honey

Note *Picolit is a grape variety used for the prized DOC wine of the same name. It has an intense straw-yellow colour, a slightly sweet flavour and a strong persistency on the palate.*

Preparation time 15 minutes
Cooking time 20 minutes
Wine *Picolit*

1 head Treviso radicchio
1 knob of butter
2 tbsps acacia honey
5.5 oz (150 g) ricotta
2 oz (60 g) soft cheese
2 tbsps heavy cream
1 Williams pear
5 tbsps Picolit wine

Wash the Treviso radicchio, dry it well and remove the white stalks. Julienne the red leaves. Blanch them in boiling water then immerse immediately in ice water.
Melt the butter with 1 tablespoon honey in a saucepan, then add the drained radicchio and cook over a low heat until caramelized.
Beat the ricotta, soft cheese and cream with a wooden spoon until smooth.
Reserve a few slices of pear for decoration and chop the rest of it very finely, until almost minced. Mix the pear into the cheese cream, and with an ice-cream scoop form 4 balls. Refrigerate for 10 minutes.
Meanwhile reduce the wine with the remaining honey, then cool.
Serve the cheese and pear balls with the radicchio, a slice of fresh pear and the Picolit reduction.

Creamed Mushrooms with Croutons

Note *There are two kinds of button mushrooms, white and chestnut. The latter are darker in colour and more flavoursome. Choose the size of mushrooms based on use: Small, young mushrooms are better in raw salads, the tiny ones are good for preserving in oil and the largest should be cooked.*

300

Preparation time 10 minutes
Cooking time 15 minutes
Wine *Friuli Collio Ribolla Gialla*

2/3 cup (150 ml) extra-virgin olive oil
1 shallot, minced
2⅔ cups (7 oz or 200 g)
 sliced mushrooms
1/3 cup (80 ml) white wine
1/2 cup (120 ml) vegetable broth
1/3 cup (80 ml) heavy cream
salt and pepper
2 slices crusty bread, cubed
5.5 oz (150 g) smoked bacon,
 julienned
parsley, chopped

Heat 2 tablespoons of the oil and sauté the shallot. Add the mushrooms and sauté for 2 minutes. Add the wine and let it evaporate. Add the broth and cream and cook for 5 more minutes, then season to taste with salt and pepper.
Drizzle the bread with a little olive oil and toast under the broiler, then pat dry on paper towels.
Broil the bacon until crispy and pat dry.
Whisk the mushroom mixture for 2 minutes while adding the remaining olive oil in a thin stream.
To serve, pour some of the mushroom cream on a plate, top with bacon and parsley and garnish with the croutons. Serve immediately.

Chickpea and Sausage Soup

Preparation time 25 minutes
Cooking time 1 hour
Wine *Chianti Classico*

1 cup (7 oz or 200 g)
 dried chickpeas, soaked
1 bay leaf
2 garlic cloves
4 tbsps extra-virgin olive oil
1 cup (4 oz or 120 g) minced
 celery, carrot and onion
1 dried red chilli pepper
1/2 cup (120 ml) red wine
vegetable broth
salt
5 oz (150 g) sausage, crumbled
8 slices bread

Boil chickpeas with bay and
1 garlic clove for 40 minutes.
Smash the other garlic clove
and sauté in the oil with the
minced vegetables. Add chilli
and chickpeas and cook for
3-4 minutes. Add wine, cover
with broth and cook for
20 minutes. Puree a third of the
of soup and mix with the rest.
Salt to taste.
Top the bread slices with
sausage meat and grill under
the broiler for a few minutes.
Serve the soup topped with
2 slices of bread per serving.

Onion Soup with Croutons

Preparation time 20 minutes
Cooking time 15 minutes
Wine *Elba Bianco*

4-inch (10 cm) piece kombu
 seaweed
2 cups (500 ml) water
5 onions, sliced
1 tsp extra-virgin olive oil
crusty bread, cubed
5 tsps white miso
parsley, chopped

Place the seaweed in a
saucepan, cover with the water
and bring to a boil. Lower the
heat and simmer for
15 minutes.
Remove the seaweed and add
the onions. Cook until very soft.
Heat the oil in a frying pan and
toast the bread cubes.
Dissolve the miso in a little of
the onion cooking liquid, then
add to the soup. Simmer for a
few minutes.
Serve the soup garnished with
parsley and croutons.

301

Cabbage and Fontina Soup

Preparation time 15 minutes
Cooking time 1 hour
Wine *Rossese di Dolceacqua*

1 Savoy cabbage
6 cups (1.5 l) beef broth
salt and pepper
parsley, chopped
3 tbsps butter
1 tbsp extra-virgin olive oil
10 slices bread
10.5 oz (300 g) fontina cheese,
  sliced

Remove and discard the outer
leaves of the cabbage and shred
the inner leaves.
Bring the broth to a boil, season
with salt and pepper, add the
shredded cabbage and cook
for 40 minutes, then add the
parsley.
Preheat oven to 350°F (180°C).
Heat the butter and oil in a frying
pan and toast the bread slices.
Lay the bread in a baking dish.
Top with slices of half the fontina
and some pepper. Pour over the
cabbage and broth. Cover with
the remaining cheese. Bake for
20-25 minutes. Remove from
oven and serve immediately.

Leek, Potato and Rice Soup

Preparation time 25 minutes
Cooking time 30 minutes
Wine *Alto Adige Pinot Nero*

1 leek, finely sliced
2 slices lardo, minced
2 tbsps extra-virgin olive oil
2 medium potatoes
1 cup (7 oz or 200 g) Roma rice
hot vegetable broth
salt and pepper

Heat the olive oil in a saucepan
and sauté the leek with a little
water for 5 minutes, then add
the lardo.
Peel the potatoes, cut into thick
slices and then small cubes.
Add to the leeks.
Sauté for 2-3 minutes and add
the rice. Cover with hot broth
and cook for 18-20 minutes.
Season with salt and pepper.
Serve hot.

FIRST COURSES

Savoy Cabbage, Potato and Pumpkin Soup

Note *Savoy cabbage is a flavoursome cabbage with a round head of tightly packed green leaves. Choose one with a heavy head and crisp-fresh leaves.*

Preparation time 25 minutes
Cooking time 40 minutes
Wine *Rossese di Dolceacqua*

1/4 pumpkin
4 tbsps extra-virgin olive oil
1 onion, thinly sliced
I garllc clove, unpeeled
1 carrot, peeled and sliced
1 celery stalk, sliced
1 yellow-fleshed potato, peeled and sliced
salt and pepper
6 cups (1.5 l) vegetable broth (optional)
1/2 Savoy cabbage, julienned
4 slices crusty bread

Peel the pumpkin, discard the seeds and cube the flesh.
Heat the olive oil in a saucepan and sauté the onion and garlic for a few minutes. Remove the garlic and add the pumpkin, carrot, celery and potato. Brown for a few minutes then season with salt and pepper.
Add the vegetable broth or hot water and cook for 20 minutes.
Add the cabbage and continue cooking for another 20 minutes.
Toast the bread and serve with the soup.

Ciciones
(SARDINIA)

Preparation time 10 minutes
Cooking time 40 minutes
Wine *Carignano del Sulcis
Rosato*

CICIONES
2 cups (14 oz or 400 g)
 semolina flour
salt

SAUCE
3 oz (80 g) lardo, diced
1/2 onion, minced
10.5 oz (300 g) ground pork
2 tomatoes, diced (optional)
saffron
salt
4 tbsps grated pecorino cheese

304

Mound the flour on a work surface, add a pinch of salt and mix
in enough warm water to obtain a smooth, uniform and compact
dough. Form into ropes by hand, then cut into pieces the size of a
chickpea. Lay out to dry on a clean kitchen towel.
Brown the lardo in a saucepan for a few minutes. Add the onion,
cook until transparent, then add the ground pork. Cook for
30 minutes over low heat, stirring occasionally and adding water if
necessary. If desired, add chopped tomatoes. Season with a pinch
of saffron and salt to taste.
Bring a large pot of salted water to the boil and cook the ciciones.
Drain and add to the sauce. Serve immediately, sprinkled with
grated pecorino.

Seuppa
(VALLE D'AOSTA)

Preparation time 15 minutes
Cooking time 1 hour
Wine *Valle d'Aosta Pinot Nero*

2.2 lb (1 kg) dry crusty bread
10.5 oz (300 g) fontina cheese,
 sliced
10.5 oz (300 g) mild white
 cheese, sliced
1½ cups (10.5 oz or 300 g)
 butter, cut into pieces
2 cups (500 ml) hot beef broth

Cut the bread into thick slices.
In a large, ovenproof saucepan,
create alternating layers of
bread and slices of cheeses
with pieces of butter, starting
with bread and finishing with
cheese and butter. Cook over
moderate heat, adding ladlefuls
of broth until all the bread is
covered. Cover and cook for an
hour, finishing in a hot oven to
brown the top. Serve very hot.

Chickpea Soup
(MARCHE)

Preparation time 5 minutes
Cooking time 30 minutes
Wine *Colli Maceratesi Bianco*

1½ cups (11 oz or 320 g)
 chickpeas
salt and pepper
2 oz (50 g) lardo, chopped
1 garlic clovo, minocd
2 tbsps tomato sauce
bread (optional)

Soak the chickpeass overnight.
Drain and boil in abundant
salted water until soft.
Heat the lardo in a frying pan,
sauté the garlic until soft then
add the tomato sauce and
pinches of salt and pepper.
Drain the chickpeas and add to
the frying pan. Cook for around
10 minutes over moderate heat.
Puree half of the chickpeas in a
blender and return to the soup
pot.
Serve hot, with slices of toasted
bread if desired.

Porcini and Potato Soup

Preparation time 15 minutes
Cooking time 30 minutes
Wine *Alto Adige Pinot Nero*

2 medium potatoes
 (around 7 oz or 200 g)
2 fresh porcini mushrooms
1 knob of butter
3 tbsps extra-virgin olive oil
1 large shallot, minced
ground chilli pepper
6 cups (1.5 l) hot vegetable broth
1 thyme sprig
salt and pepper
2 slices crusty bread, cubed

306

Peel the potatoes and slice them thinly. Clean the mushrooms with damp paper towels and remove the earthy part of the stalk.
Heat the butter and 2 tablespoons oil in a saucepan and add the shallot. Add a dash of chilli pepper and the potatoes and brown, stirring frequently. Slice the mushrooms and add to the potatoes.
Cook for 3 minutes and cover with hot broth. Cook over medium heat for around 20 minutes.
Add thyme leaves and puree the soup in a blender. Season with salt and pepper to taste.
Toast the bread cubes in a hot oven or a non-stick pan.
Serve the soup in individual bowls with a drizzle of olive oil and the croutons.

Fava Soup with Prosciutto

Preparation time 15 minutes
Cooking time 40 minutes
Wine *Lagrein Rosato*

7 oz (200 g) dried fava beans
1 yellow-fleshed potato
4 tbsps extra-virgin olive oil
1/2 onion, minced
salt and pepper
4 cups (1 l) hot vegetable broth
1 rosemary sprig
3.5 oz (100 g) prosciutto

Soak the fava beans over night. Blanch in boiling water for
10 minutes, drain and peel (if necessary).
Peel and thinly slice the potato.
Heat the oil in a saucepan and sauté the onion. Add the potatoes
and sauté for 2 minutes.
Add the fava beans and a little salt. Cover with hot broth and cook
over low heat for 25 minutes. Add the rosemary and cook for
another 5 minutes.
Remove the rosemary and puree the soup with an immersion
blender. Season with pepper to taste.
Cut the prosciutto into thin strips and brown in a non-stick frying
pan until crispy.
Serve the soup topped with prosciutto strips.

Oil-Mill Soup with Beans and Farro

Note *This soup is traditionally made during the crushing period at the olive mills in November and December. This recipe calls for farro, an ancient wheat also known in English as emmer.*

Preparation time 20 minutes
Cooking time 40 minutes
Wine *Nobile di Montepulciano*

1 cup (7 oz or 200 g) dried
 borlotti beans
4 tbsps extra-virgin olive oil
1 carrot, minced
1 celery stalk, minced
1/2 onion, minced
salt
3 rosemary sprigs
2 garlic cloves, smashed
1 cup (7 oz or 200 g) pearled
 farro (emmer wheat)
red chilli pepper flakes
parsley, minced

308

Soak the beans overnight.
Heat 1 tablespoon oil in a pressure cooker and sauté the carrot, celery and onion for a few minutes. Add the drained beans, salt, rosemary and cover with water. Bring to a boil, close the pot and cook for 30 minutes from when the cooker starts whistling. Remove from the heat, remove the rosemary and puree two-thirds of the soup. Set aside the whole beans.
Heat 1 tablespoon oil and brown the garlic. Add the pureed soup. Add the farro and cook for 25 minutes. Add the whole beans and let sit for 20 minutes. Serve the soupe drizzled with olive oil and garnished with chilli flakes and minced parsley.

Red Lentil and Kale Soup

Preparation time 15 minutes
Cooking time 25 minutes
Wine *Gutturnio Classico*

5 tbsps extra-virgin olive oil
1/2 onion, minced
8-10 leaves black kale, chopped
3/4 cup (5 oz or 150 g) red lentils
vegetable broth
1 tbsp arame seaweed
2 slices crusty bread, cubed

Heat 4 tablespoons olive oil in a saucepan and sauté the onion until soft. Add the kale, cook for a few minutes then add the lentils. Cover with vegetable broth and simmer over low heat until lentils are soft.
Soak the seaweed in cold water and add to the soup just before the end of cooking.
Toast the bread cubes in a frying pan with 1 tablespoon olive oil.
Serve the lentil soup in individual serving bowls, garnished with the croutons.

Leek, Potato and Pumpkin Soup

Preparation time 30 minutes
Cooking time 35 minutes
Wine *Trentino Marzemino*

3½ tbsps butter
1/2 leek, sliced
1 large potato, peeled and
 thinly sliced
salt and pepper
hot vegetable broth
2 tbsps extra-virgin olive oil
1 garlic clove, smashed
3 cups (10.5 oz or 300 g) cubed
 pumpkin or winter squash
1 cup (7 oz or 200 g) Roma rice
2 oz (50 g) aged peppercorn
 pecorino, shaved

Heat the butter in a saucepan and sauté the leek. Add the potato slices, season with salt and pepper and cover with hot broth. Simmer over low heat until potatoes are soft, then puree.
Heat the oil in a saucepan and sauté the garlic. Add the pumpkin and salt and sauté until soft.
Cook the rice in the pureed soup and serve garnished with the pumpkin cubes and shavings of pecorino.

Bean and Grain Soup

Preparation time 20 minutes
Cooking time 50 minutes
Wine *Alto Adige
Santa Maddalena*

1/2 cup (3 oz or 80 g) dried
  chickpeas
1/2 cup (3.5 oz or 100 g) dried
  borlotti beans
3 garlic cloves
3 rosemary sprigs
salt
2 slices lardo
1½ cups (7 oz or 200 g) minced
  celery, carrot and onion
4 tbsps extra-virgin olive oil
1/4 cup (2 oz or 50 g) pearled
  farro (emmer wheat)
1/4 cup (2 oz or 50 g) pearled
  barley
4 cups (1 l) vegetable broth
1/3 cup (3 oz or 80 g) lentils

310

Soak the chickpeas and beans for 8 hours. Place in a pressure
cooker with 1 garlic clove, 1 rosemary sprig and salt and cover
the beans with 1inch (2½ cm) of water. Close and cook for
25-30 minutes after the cooker begins to whistle.
Finely chop the lardo together with 1 rosemary sprig and 2 garlic
cloves, then sauté in the olive oil with the celery, carrot and onion.
Add the farro and barley and lightly toast for a few minutes, then
add a little broth. Add the lentils and 1 rosemary sprig.
Drain half the chickpeas and beans and set aside. Remove the
garlic and rosemary and puree the rest together with the cooking
liquid. Add the puree to the farro, barley and lentils, and cook until
they are soft, thinning with broth to desired consistency.
Add the reserved chickpeas and beans.
Serve hot with a sprinkling of pepper.

Anolini and Tortelli with Parmesan

Preparation time 45 minutes
Cooking time 30 minutes
Wine *Lambrusco delle Terre
Verdiane*

ANOLINI
7 oz (200 g) egg-pasta dough,
 made with yolks only (see p. 1094)
5 oz (150 g) cooked beef,
 chopped
2 oz (50 g) prosciutto, chopped
2 cups (500 ml) beef broth

PUMPKIN TORTELLI
1 knob of butter
1 tbsp minced onion

1/4 pumpkin, cubed
vegetable broth
2 tbsps grated Parmesan
2 amaretti cookies, crumbled
salt and pepper
7 oz (200 g) egg-pasta dough
 (see p. 1094)

GARNISH
grated Parmesan
1 slice spalla cotta or cooked ham,
 julienned

SAUCE
3/4 cup (200 ml) Lambrusco wine
1 shallot, sliced
1 tsp sugar

Roll out pasta dough and form anolini filled with beef and prosciutto.
Melt the butter and sauté the onion, then add the pumpkin. Pour
over a little broth and cook for 15 minutes over low heat. Puree the
pumpkin and add Parmesan, amaretti, salt and pepper. Roll out pasta
dough and make tortelli with the pumpkin mixture, cutting them with
a serrated roller.
Melt the grated Parmesan in a non-stick pan, turn out onto a cold
surface and cut out 4 disks.
Reduce the wine, shallot and sugar in a saucepan over very low heat.
Boil the tortelli in salted water and toss them with melted butter.
Boil the anolini in the beef broth.
Sauté the spalla cotta strips in a frying pan until crunchy.
Serve the anolini in a glass with hot broth. Serve the tortelli with the
Lambrusco reduction, some grated Parmesan, the Parmesan wafer
and the spalla cotta.

Brown Rice Ring with Pears

RICE
4 tbsps butter
1/2 onion, minced
1 Kaiser pear
1¼ cup (8.5 oz or 240 g)
 brown rice
3/4 cup (180 ml) white wine
vegetable broth
3.5 oz (100 g) blue cheese
1 tbsp grated Parmesan
salt
white pepper

GARNISH
1 pear, sliced
grated nutmeg

312

Preparation time 15 minutes
Cooking time 30 minutes
Wine *Friuli Collio Merlot*

Melt 3 tablespoons butter in a saucepan and sauté the onion over
low heat for 10 minutes.
Meanwhile, core the pear and cut into cubes. Add half the pear
to the onion and cook for 5 minutes. Add the rice, toast and then
add white wine.
Add the rest of the pear cubes and cook until the rice is done,
adding vegetable broth little by little.
Meanwhile melt the blue cheese over a double-boiler.
When the rice is done stir in the rest of the butter and the grated
Parmesan. Season with salt and pepper.
Butter individual ring moulds and fill with the rice. Let sit 5 minutes
then unmould on serving plates. Fill the centre with melted blue
cheese. Garnish with pear slices and sprinkle over the nutmeg.

Broccoli Carbonara

Preparation time 20 minutes
Cooking time 20 minutes
Wine *Friuli Isonzo Sauvignon*

2 heads broccoli
1 garlic clove, smashed
2 tbsps extra-virgin olive oil
1 egg
1 tbsp heavy cream
1 tbsp grated Parmesan
1 tbsp grated pecorino cheese
salt and pepper
12 oz (350 g) bucatini

Cut the broccoli into florets and blanch in boiling water.
Heat the olive oil in a frying pan and add the smashed garlic. Remove after a few minutes and add broccoli.
Beat the egg with the cream, cheeses and pepper in a bowl.
Bring a large pot of salted water to boil. Boil bucatini until al dente. Drain, toss with broccoli and place in a bowl. Pour over the egg mixture, mix well and serve.

Macaroni with Walnut Sauce

Preparation time 10 minutes
Cooking time 10 minutes
Wine *Bolgheri Bianco*

1 cup (3.5 oz or 100 g) walnuts
1/2 garlic clove, minced
parsley, minced
1 tbsp barley miso
3½ tbsps heavy cream
1 tbsp extra-virgin olive oil
salt and pepper
11 oz (320 g) corn macaroni

Toast the walnuts in a frying pan for a few minutes. Grind with a mortar and pestle to make a paste. Stir in the garlic, parsley and miso, dilute with cream and olive oil and season to taste with salt and pepper.
Bring a pot of salted water to the boil and cook the macaroni until al dente. Drain, leaving a little cooking water, and toss with the walnut sauce. Let sit for 2-3 minutes before serving.

313

Paccheri with Vernaccia and Pheasant Ragù

Preparation time 30 minutes
Cooking time 20 minutes
Wine *Nero d'Avola*

1 pheasant
3 tbsps extra-virgin olive oil
1¼ cup (5.5 oz or 150 g) minced
 celery, carrot and onion
1 garlic clove, smashed
3 sage leaves, minced
2.5 oz (70 g) ground pork
3/4 cup (180 ml) Vernaccia wine
salt and pepper
1/2 tsp tomato paste
1/2 cup (120 ml) beef broth
2 tbsps chopped tomatoes
14 oz (400 g) Gragnano paccheri

314

Clean the pheasant, removing the entrails, and cut into pieces.
Heat the oil in a saucepan and sauté the celery, carrot, onion,
garlic and sage until soft. Add the pork, then the pheasant pieces.
Pour over the wine and cook over high heat for 10 minutes.
Season with salt and pepper. Dissolve the tomato paste in a little
broth and add together with the tomatoes to the sauce. Remove
from the heat.
Take out the pheasant pieces, let cool and remove the meat from
the bones. Chop the meat and return to the pan. Add the broth,
season with salt and pepper and cook over low heat until the
sauce thickens.
Bring a large pot of salted water to the boil and cook the paccheri
until al dente. Drain them and toss gently with the ragù. Serve
immediately.

Fresh Tagliolini with Radicchio and White Truffle

Note *Cream comes from skimming the fat off of milk, and different kinds vary in their fat content. Cream can suffocate the flavours of individual ingredients, so it should be used only when absolutely necessary and in small quantities.*

Preparation time 30 minutes
Cooking time 12 minutes
Wine *Dolcetto di Dogliani*

PASTA
2 cups (9 oz or 250 g)
 plain flour
2 eggs
1 tbsp extra-virgin olive oil

SAUCE
12 oz (350 g) Treviso
 radicchio
3 tbsps extra-virgin olive oil
7 tbsps heavy cream
truffle oil
1 knob of butter
5 tbsps grated Parmesan
salt and pepper
1 oz (25 g) white truffle

315

Mix together the pasta ingredients to form a firm and elastic dough. Form into a ball, cover with plastic wrap and refrigerate for 20 minutes.
Roll out into a thin sheet, dust with flour, fold the sheet in half and then in half again and slice into thin strips to make tagliolini.
Julienne the radicchio. Heat the oil in a frying pan and sauté the radicchio for 5 minutes. Add the cream and a drizzle of truffle oil, cover and cook for 2 minutes.
Bring a large pot of salted water to the boil and cook the tagliolini until al dente. Drain and mix with the radicchio, together with a little of the pasta cooking water.
Stir in the butter, Parmesan and a pinch of pepper. Serve the pasta topped with shavings of white truffle.

Radicchio Ravioli
with Gorgonzola Sauce

Preparation time 1 hour
Cooking time 10 minutes
Wine *Primitivo di Manduria*

PASTA
2⅓ cups (10.5 oz or 300 g)
 plain flour
3 eggs
salt

FILLING
2 tbsps extra-virgin olive oil
2 tbsps minced onion
1 garlic clove, minced

9 oz (250 g) Treviso radicchio,
 shredded
1 egg
6 tbsps grated Parmesan
7 oz (200 g) ricotta
nutmeg, grated
salt and pepper

SAUCE
9 oz (250 g) Gorgonzola cheese
7 tbsps heavy cream
salt and pepper
chives, snipped

316

Combine the pasta ingredients to form a smooth dough, cover
with plastic wrap and let rest.
Heat the oil in a frying pan and brown the onion and garlic. Add
the radicchio and sauté for 4-5 minutes, then remove from heat.
Add the egg and quickly mix into the radicchio. Pour the mixture
into a bowl and stir in the Parmesan, ricotta, nutmeg, salt and
pepper.
Roll out the dough, form a long thin strip and divide horizontally
into 2 equal pieces. Place spoonfuls of the radicchio mixture on
one strip at 1-inch (2-3 cm) intervals. Cover with the other strip,
press around the filling to seal the dough and cut out the ravioli.
Break the Gorgonzola into pieces and heat in a saucepan with the
cream to obtain a smooth sauce. Season with salt and pepper.
Bring a large pot of salted water to the boil and cook the ravioli.
Serve tossed with the Gorgonzola sauce and sprinkled with chives.

Fusilli with Chickpeas

Preparation time 10 minutes
Cooking time 15 minutes
Wine *Sicilia Cabernet Sauvignon*

1 oz (25 g) dried porcini
4 tbsps extra-virgin olive oil
1 spring onion, sliced
1¼ cups (8.5 oz or 240 g)
 canned chickpeas, drained
1 cup (9 oz or 250 g) tomato puree
salt and pepper
2 cups (500 ml) broth
6 tbsps grated Parmesan
parsley, minced
10.5 oz (300 g) fusilli

Soak the porcini in hot water for 10 minutes, drain and chop. Heat the oil in a frying pan and brown the spring onion. Add the porcini and the chickpeas, cook for a few minutes, then add the tomato puree. Season with salt and pepper, then add the broth and simmer until the sauce has thickened. Meanwhile bring a large pot of salted water to the boil and cook the fusilli until al dente. Drain and add to the sauce. Stir in the Parmesan and parsley and serve immediately.

Emperor's Penette

Preparation time 10 minutes
Cooking time 15 minutes
Wine *Elba Bianco*

6 tbsps extra-virgin olive oil
1 medium onion, sliced
9 oz (250 g) shelled prawns
9 oz (250 g) crab meat
salt and white pepper
1/4 cup (60 ml) Cognac
7 oz (200 g) ricotta
3/4 cup (200 ml) heavy cream
12 oz (350 g) pennette or penne
parsley, minced
1 tbsp almond slivers, toasted

Heat the oil in a saucepan and brown the onion. Add prawns, crab, salt and pepper and sauté for a few minutes. Add Cognac and remove from heat.
Bring a large pot of salted water to the boil and cook the pennette until al dente. Meanwhile, sieve the ricotta. Just before the pennette are done, add the ricotta and cream to the prawns and crab.
Drain the pennette and toss with the sauce, adding parsley and pepper. Serve topped with almond slivers.

Valpelline-Style Soup
(VALLE D'AOSTA)

Note *This is a traditional soup of the Valle d'Aosta, made only in the winter. It represents the* cucina povera, *or poor cooking of the mountains, and is celebrated during a local festival.*

318

Preparation time 20 minutes
Cooking time 1 hour 20 minutes
Wine *Valle d'Aosta Nus Rosso*

salt and pepper
1 Savoy cabbage, shredded
12 slices dry bread
3.5 oz (100 g) salted lardo,
 thinly sliced
9 oz (250 g) fontina cheese,
 thinly sliced
4 cups (1 l) beef broth
ground cinnamon
2 tbsps butter, cut into pieces

Preheat oven to 350°F (180°C).
Bring a large pot of salted water to the boil.
Boil the shredded cabbage in the salted water until tender, then drain.
Toast the bread in the oven until golden-brown on both sides.
Sauté the lardo in a frying pan to render some of the fat and make it crispy.
In an oven-proof terracotta baking dish, make alternating layers of bread slices, shredded boiled cabbage, sautéed lardo and fontina cheese slices, finishing with a layer of bread slices.
Mix some ground cinnamon into the broth to taste, add pepper and pour the seasoned broth over the bread layers. Bake for at least 1 hour. Halfway through cooking, top with pieces of butter.

Canederli Soup with Speck Ham
(Trentino-Alto Adige)

Note *The smooth green leaves of chives have a garlicky taste and are rich in vitamin C. Chives are often used in Trentino to flavour the classic canederli dumplings and soups in general, as well as other savoury dishes.*

Preparation time 30 minutes
Cooking time 25 minutes
Wine *Alto Adige Santa Maddalena*

5 oz (150 g) crusty bread
1/2 cup (120 ml) milk
3.5 oz (100 g) speck ham, diced
2 oz (50 g) salami, diced
1/2 onion, minced
parsley, minced
3 eggs
salt
1/2 cup (2.5 oz or 70 g)
 plain flour
hot beef broth

319

Cube the bread and soak in half the milk, together with half the speck ham and half the salami.

Brown the remaining speck ham in a frying pan together with the minced onion and parsley and then add to the bread and milk mixture.

Beat the eggs with the remaining milk and a pinch of salt, then stir into the bread and milk mixture. Stir in the flour and mix thoroughly to obtain a thick and uniform mixture. Form the mixture into little balls by hand.

Bring a large pot of salted water to the boil and cook the canederli for 15 minutes. Drain and serve in hot broth, sprinkled with some more minced parsley.

Trofie with Green Apple, Salama and Goat's Cheese

Note *Salama is a specialty of Ferrara, in Emilia-Romagna. A cured sausage of pork, spices and wine, it is often eaten cooked, in pasta sauces.*

Preparation time 25 minutes
Cooking time 20 minutes
Wine *Cirò Rosato*

5 oz (150 g) semi-aged salama
2 ripe tomatoes
1 green apple
1 garlic clove
3 tbsps extra-virgin olive oil
3.5 oz (100 g) fresh goat's cheese
 (preferably in ash)
salt and pepper
13 oz (380 g) fresh trofie pasta

320

Cut the salama into thin strips and keep chilled.
Quarter the tomatoes, remove the seeds and cut into fillets.
Cut the apple into wedges and remove the seeds, then thinly slice.
Bring a large pot of salted water to the boil and cook the trofie
until al dente.
Meanwhile heat a non-stick pan and sauté the garlic and tomatoes
in the oil. Add the salama and cook for 1 minute. Add the apple
slices and a little of the pasta cooking water, cook for a few
minutes then stir in the goat's cheese. Toss the trofie in the sauce,
season with pepper and serve.

Barley with Squash and Crispy Cabbage

Preparation time 15 minutes
Cooking time 30 minutes
Wine *Alto Adige Pinot Nero*

1/4 Savoy cabbage
3 tbsps butter
1/2 yellow onion, minced
2 cups (9 oz or 250 g) cubed
 winter squash
salt and pepper
1½ cups (10.5 oz or 300 g)
 pearled barley
6 cups (1.5 l) vegetable broth
2 tbsps plain flour
sunflower oil

321

Set aside 2 whole green cabbage leaves and julienne the rest.
Melt the butter and sauté the onion, then add the squash and
cook for 5 minutes. Add salt and barley and toast briefly.
Add the broth and after 5 minutes the julienned cabbage.
Cook for 30 minutes over low heat.
Meanwhile cut the 2 reserved cabbage leaves into thin strips.
Dust with flour and leave to sit in a colander to remove any excess
water.
Just before serving heat the sunflower oil and when very hot, fry
the cabbage strips until crispy. Drain on paper towels and use
to garnish the barley. Sprinkle with a pinch of pepper.

Crêpes with Ricotta and Gorgonzola

Preparation time 1 hour
Cooking time 15 minutes
Wine *Val d'Aosta Chardonnay*

CRÊPES
3 1/2 tbsps butter
3 eggs
1¼ cups (300 ml) milk
3/4 cup (3.5 oz or 100 g)
 plain flour
salt

FILLING
10 cups (10.5 oz or 300 g)
 spinach
8.5 oz (240 g) ricotta

1 cup (3.5 oz or 100 g)
 grated Parmesan
salt and pepper

SAUCE
1 cup (250 ml) milk
parsley sprigs
5 peppercorns
2 tbsps butter
1/4 cup (1 oz or 30 g)
 plain flour
1/2 cup (120 ml) heavy cream
3.5 oz (100 g) Gorgonzola cheese
salt and pepper
Parmesan, grated

Preheat oven to 300° F (150°C).
To make the crêpes, melt 1½ tablespoons butter. Beat the eggs
with the melted butter, milk, flour and salt. Melt the rest of the
butter in a non-stick frying pan and make 12 crêpes.
Blanch, drain, squeeze out and finely chop the spinach. Mix with
ricotta, Parmesan, salt and pepper.
Fill crêpes with the spinach mixture and roll up like cannelloni.
Place the milk, parsley and peppercorns in a saucepan. Bring to
the boil, remove from heat and let sit for 10 minutes. Strain.
Melt the butter in a saucepan, add the flour and stir well. Add the
milk little by little, and simmer until thick. Stir in cream and pieces
of Gorgonzola, season with salt and pepper.
Pour half the cheese sauce in a buttered baking dish, arrange
the crêpes and pour over the rest of the sauce. Sprinkle with
Parmesan and bake for 8 minutes.

Farro Pasta with Cauliflower

Preparation time 15 minutes
Cooking time 20 minutes
Wine *Orvieto Classico*

1 small cauliflower
salt
12 oz (350 g) farro spaghetti
1 shallot, minced
3 tbsps extra-virgin olive oil
I tbsp capers
10 green olives, pitted
chives, snipped
basil, shredded

Cut the cauliflower into florets
and blanch for a few minutes in
boiling salted water.
Bring a large pot of salted
water to the boil and cook the
farro pasta for 10 minutes.
Meanwhile sauté the shallot in
the oil in a frying pan together
with the capers and olives. Add
the cauliflower.
Drain the pasta and add to the
sauce. Cook for a few minutes
then drizzle with olive oil and
sprinkle with chives and basil.

Sausage Risotto

Preparation time 10 minutes
Cooking time 20 minutes
Wine *Barbera*

1¼ cups (300 ml) red wine
2/3 cup (5,5 oz or 150 g) butter
1 spring onion, minced
2½ cups (1 lb or 500 g)
 Carnaroli rice
salt
hot beef broth
3 tbsps grated Parmesan
10.5 oz (300 g) sausage meat

Heat 1 cup (250 ml) wine in a
small saucepan and reduce to
half cup (120 ml).
Melt half the butter and sauté
the spring onion. Add the rice
and toast, stirring. Add the
reduced wine and evaporate.
Adjust salt and add 1 ladleful
hot broth, stir, and continue
adding broth, little by little, until
the rice is almost cooked. Just
before the rice is done, add the
remaining butter and Parmesan
and stir well.
Meanwhile sauté the sausage
with the rest of the wine.
Serve the risotto with the
sausage and its pan juices.

Walnut and Arugula Linguine

Preparation time 15 minutes
Cooking time 15 minutes
Wine *Val d'Aosta Pinot Grigio*

1/2 cup (2 oz or 50 g) walnuts
1 tbsp extra-virgin olive oil
salt
1/2 cup (120 ml) vegetable broth
11 oz (320 g) linguine
1 bunch arugula, shredded

Chop the walnuts coarsely with a mezzaluna or knife.
In a small frying pan toast the walnuts with the oil and a pinch of salt. Add the broth and reduce.
Bring a large pot of salted water to the boil and cook the linguine until al dente. Drain and toss with the arugula, then add to the walnuts in the frying pan. Serve hot.

Gorgonzola and Pine Nut Reginette

Preparation time 15 minutes
Cooking time 20 minutes
Wine *Bardolino Chiaretto*

2 tbsps butter
1 shallot, minced
3/4 cup (200 ml) heavy cream
3.5 oz (100 g) Gorgonzola cheese, chopped
2½ tbsps pine nuts
salt and pepper
12 oz (350 g) reginette

Melt 1½ tablespoons butter and sauté the shallot, then add the cream and Gorgonzola.
Sauté the pine nuts with 1/2 tablespoon butter until golden-brown and add them to the sauce. Season with salt and pepper and simmer until thick and creamy.
Bring a large pot of salted water to the boil and cook the pasta until al dente. Drain and toss with the sauce, sprinkle over some pepper and serve immediately.

324

Risotto with Treviso Radicchio, Porcini and Truffle

Note *Truffles are fungi which grow underground, much appreciated by the Ancient Greeks and Romans, who believed them to be aphrodisiacs. They were believed to be of divine origin, born out of lightning, which was sacred to the god Jupiter.*

Preparation time 10 minutes
Cooking time 20 minutes
Wine *Umbria Cabernet Sauvignon*

3½ tbsps butter
1 onion, minced
1 Treviso radicchio, shredded
2 cups (10.5 oz or 350 g) Carnaroli rice
hot vegetable broth
2-3 fresh porcini mushrooms
1 garlic clove, smashed
2 tbsps extra-virgin olive oil
salt
thyme, minced
4 tbsps grated Parmesan
1 small black truffle

Melt the butter in a saucepan and sauté the onion. Add the radicchio and cook for 5 minutes. Add the rice, turn up the heat and toast. Add the hot broth little by little, stirring frequently.
Clean the porcini with damp paper towels and remove the earthy part of the stalk. Cut into pieces.
Heat the oil in a frying pan with the garlic and sauté the mushrooms.
Halfway through the rice cooking time, add the mushrooms.
When the rice is done, salt to taste and stir in thyme and Parmesan. Serve with shavings of black truffle.

Vegetable and Bean Soup with Bread (TUSCANY)

326

Note *For more flavour, cook the soaked beans with 3 garlic cloves, 1/2 tomato and 2-3 sage leaves.*

Preparation time 20 minutes
Cooking time 1 hour 15 minutes
Wine *Chianti Classico*

1¼ cup (9 oz or 250 g) dried cannellini beans, soacked and cooked
1¼ cup (9 oz or 250 g) dried borlotti beans, soacked and cooked
6 tbsps extra-virgin olive oil
1 garlic clove, minced
1 onion, minced
1/2 tbsp tomato paste
2 large carrots, chopped
2 small potatoes, chopped
4 celery stalks, chopped
4 cups (1 l) water
1/4 Savoy cabbage, chopped
5 Swiss chard leaves, chopped
2 heads black kale, chopped
salt and pepper
dry Tuscan-style bread

Puree two-thirds of the cannellini and borlotti beans.
Heat 3 tablespoons oil in a large saucepan and brown the garlic and onion. Dilute the tomato paste in a little water, then add it to the pan together with the carrot, potatoes and celery. Add the pureed beans and the water. Stir in the Savoy cabbage, Swiss chard and black kale. Season with salt and pepper and cook, covered, for 1 hour over low heat.
Add the whole beans and cook for another 10 minutes.
Fill a soup tureen with cubes or slices of dry bread. Pour the soup on top. Serve hot, with a drizzle of extra-virgin olive oil and a grinding of black pepper if desired.

Spaghetti with Chianti Classico

Note *Chianti Classico is a red wine, possibly the most famous Italian wine, made in Tuscany from Sangiovese grapes.*

Preparation time 15 minutes
Cooking time 25 minutes
Wine *Chianti Classico*

1/2 small leek, minced
1 knob of butter
3/4 cup (180 ml) Chianti Classico
 winc
1 tbsp sugar
salt
11 oz (320 g) spaghetti
2 oz (50 g) aged pecorino, shaved

327

Reserve a little of the minced leek for garnish and blanch the rest in boiling water.

Melt the butter in a saucepan and sauté the blanched leek over low heat, adding a little water to soften it. Add the wine and sugar and simmer for 15 minutes to reduce the mixture and obtain a syrupy sauce.

Bring a large pot of salted water to the boil and cook the spaghetti until al dente. Drain.

Shape the spaghetti into 4 nests using a fork and a cup, rolling the spaghetti around the fork inside the cup, and arrange the nests on serving plates.

Drizzle over the Chianti sauce and garnish with shavings of pecorino and the minced leek.

Gnocchi alla Bava
(VALLE D'AOSTA)

Preparation time 40 minutes
Cooking time 1 hour 30 minutes
Wine *Valle d'Aosta Pinot Grigio*

GNOCCHI
2.5 lb (1.2 kg) potatoes
salt
1¾ cups (8 oz or 220 g)
 plain flour

SAUCE
7 oz (200 g) fontina cheese
6 tbsps butter
1 garlic clove, crushed
4 tbsps grated Parmesan

328

Bring a pot of water to the boil add the potatoes, boil until tender
and drain. Peel, and while still hot, pass through a potato ricer or
mash with a fork.
Mix a pinch of salt and 1½ cups plus 1½ tablespoons (7 oz or 200 g)
of the flour into the mashed potatoes to obtain a soft dough with
no lumps.
By hand, form the dough into cylinders 1/2-inch (1 cm) thick. Dip a
knife in flour and use it to cut little pieces from the cylinders, then
squash them gently with the tines of a fork. Lay on a floured work
surface or tray and let rest.
Meanwhile cut the fontina into little cubes. Melt the butter in a
small saucepan and brown the garlic, then remove and discard.
Bring a large pot of salted water to the boil and cook the gnocchi.
As they rise to the surface, remove with a slotted spoon and
transfer to serving plates. Immediately top with fontina cubes,
grated Parmesan and some of the garlic butter. Serve hot.

Agnolotti
(PIEDMONT)

Preparation time 40 minutes
Cooking time 1 hour 30 minutes
Wine *Grignolino d'Asti*

FILLING
3½ tbsps butter
1 onion, minced
1 garlic clove, minocd
1 rosemary sprig, minced
1 bay leaf, minced
9 oz (250 g) veal
9 oz (250 g) pork
2 cups (500 ml) vegetable broth

2 tbsps extra-virgin olive oil
1 small cabbage, chopped
1 egg
1 cup (3.5 oz or 100 g)
 grated Parmesan
salt and pepper
nutmeg

PASTA
4 cups (1 lb or 500 g)
 plain flour
5 eggs
1 tbsp extra-virgin olive oil
salt

329

Melt the butter in a saucepan and sauté the onion, garlic,
rosemary and bay. Add the meat and brown evenly on all sides,
add broth and continue cooking until cooked through. Remove the
meat, chop finely and place in a bowl. Reserve the cooking liquid.
In another saucepan heat the olive oil and sauté the cabbage. Add
to the meat. Mix in the egg, Parmesan, pinches of salt and pepper
and a grating of nutmeg. Stir well.
Make the pasta by mixing the flour with the eggs, oil and a pinch
of salt to obtain a smooth and uniform dough. Form a ball and let
rest, covered in plastic wrap, for around 30 minutes.
Roll out the dough and distribute spoonfuls of filling on half. Fold
over the other half and press around the filling to seal. Cut with a
roller into ravioli shapes.
Bring a large pot of salted water to the boil and cook the agnolotti.
Serve with the reserved cooking liquid.

Truffled Rice Ring

330

Note *White truffles are rarer and more expensive than black. To maintain their fragrance, we recommend keeping them in a dry place, or storing them in rice or in a clay container, once they have been carefully cleaned of all dirt.*

Preparation time 15 minutes
Cooking time 30 minutes
Wine *Bardolino Chiaretto*

3½ tbsps butter
1/2 white onion, minced
1⅓ cups (9 oz or 260 g)
 Vialone Nano rice
8 cups (2 l) hot vegetable broth
1 small white truffle
salt and pepper
1 oz (30 g) Parmesan, shaved
2 small Caesar's mushrooms
 or button mushrooms
1 tbsp extra-virgin olive oil

Preheat oven to 425°F (220°C).
Melt the butter in a saucepan and sauté the onion over low heat, adding a little hot broth to stop it becoming too brown. Add the rice and toast over high heat, stirring often, until it starts to stick to the pan. Add a little hot broth and stir until it is absorbed, then add a little more and continue until the rice is cooked. Meanwhile mince half the white truffle and stir in at the end, together with salt, pepper and grated Parmesan.
Butter 4 small ring moulds and fill with rice. Bake for 4 minutes.
Slice the mushrooms finely and toss with oil, salt and pepper.
Unmould the rice on serving plates and top with mushrooms, shavings of Parmesan and white truffle.

Pipe Pasta with Brussels Sprouts

Preparation time 15 minutes
Cooking time 20 minutes
Wine *Colli di Luni Bianco*

4 cups (14 oz or 400 g) Brussels
 sprouts
salt and pepper
4 tbsps extra-virgin olive oil
1 spring onion, sliced
1/2 cup (100 ml) broth
10.5 oz (300 g) pipe, lumache
 or conchiglie pasta
3 tbsps grated Parmesan
3.5 oz (100 g) fontina cheese,
 cubed
parsley, minced

Boil the Brussels sprouts in
salted water for 10 minutes.
Drain and cut into wedges.
Heat the oil in a saucepan,
sauté the spring onion and then
add the Brussels sprouts and
broth. Simmer for 4-5 minutes,
then add salt and pepper.
Bring a large pot of salted water
to the boil and cook the pasta
until al dente. Drain and add to
the Brussels sprouts. Add the
Parmesan and fontina and stir
well. Sprinkle with parsley and
serve immediately.

Taleggio Risotto

Preparation time 10 minutes
Cooking time 17 minutes
Wine *Bianco d'Alcamo*

1 organic orange
3 tbsps butter
2½ tbsps minced onion
1/4 cup (60 ml) brandy
1½ cups (10.5 oz or 300 g) rice
4 cups (1 l) vegetable broth
3 oz (80 g) taleggio cheese,
 chopped
chives, thinly sliced

331

Zest the orange and cut the
zest into strips.
Melt half the butter in a
saucepan and sauté the onion
and the orange zest for a few
minutes. Remove from the heat
and add brandy. Return to
heat and flambé. Add the rice
and toast for a few minutes.
Add some broth and continue
cooking for 12 minutes, adding
broth little by little as it absorbs.
When the rice is cooked, add
the taleggio and remaining
butter and stir until melted.
Sprinkle over the chives and
serve.

Tuscan Farrotto with Fossa Cheese

332

Nota *Farrotto is a variation on risotto, using farro (emmer wheat) instead of rice.*
Fossa cheese is made using an ancient production method, with the cheese forms placed inside cloth bags and then aged with straw and reeds in holes (fosse) around 3 meters deep, dug out of the tuff rock.

Preparation time 10 minutes
Cooking time 30 minutes
Wine *Morellino di Scansano*

1 knob of butter
1 onion, minced
6 cups (1.5 l) hot vegetable broth
1½ cups (10.5 oz or 300 g) pearled farro (emmer wheat)
3 baby artichokes, trimmed and sliced
2 tbsps new peas
2 oz (60 g) Colonnata lardo, minced
2 mint leaves, minced
2 oz (60 g) fossa cheese, chopped
1 tbsp extra-virgin olive oil
salt and pepper

Melt the butter and sauté the onion with a little broth until soft.
Add the farro and toast over high heat, stirring frequently.
Add the artichokes and peas, stir, then add the hot broth and continue cooking until the farro is tender. Halfway through add the minced lardo, reserving a small amount.
When the farro is cooked stir in the remaining lardo and the mint together with the cheese and olive oil. Stir until the cheese is melted. Adjust the salt, sprinkle with pepper and serve.

Whole-Wheat Broccoli Ravioli with Prawns

Preparation time 1 hour
Cooking time 20 minutes
Wine *Trentino Nosiola*

Serves 6

FILLING
1.3 lb (600 g) broccoli florets
3 tbsps extra-virgin olive oil
dried red chilli pepper flakes
salt and pepper

DOUGH
4¾ cups (1.3 lb or 600 g)
 plain flour

3 cups plus 3 tbsps (14 oz or
 400 g) whole-wheat flour
6 eggs
7 egg yolks

SAUCE
20 prawns
1 bay leaf
3 tbsps extra-virgin olive oil
1 garlic clove
4 tomatoes, chopped
10 Taggiasca olives, pitted
salt and pepper
3-4 tbsps butter

Boil the broccoli until tender, drain and puree in a food processor with the oil, chilli, salt and pepper.
Mix the 2 flours with the eggs and yolks to make a smooth dough. Divide the dough in half and roll out into 2 thin sheets. Place spoonfuls of the broccoli puree at regular intervals on the first sheet, and brush between them with water. Lay over the second one and press down between the broccoli. Cut out ravioli.
Shell and devein the prawns, reserving the shells. Boil the shells in water with the bay leaf to make a broth, then strain.
Chop the prawns and sauté them in the oil with the garlic, tomatoes and olives. Add a little of the prawn broth and adjust salt and pepper.
Bring a large pot of salted water to a boil and cook the ravioli. Drain and add to the sauce with the butter. Sauté until the sauce becomes creamy. Serve hot.

Venere Rice with Champagne and Scallops

Note *The Venere rice variety was developed in the Po River plain, Italy's top rice-growing region. Named for Venus, the goddess of love, it is a whole-grain rice with an ebony colour. Venere rice has a longer cooking time than white varieties (about 40 min). It pairs well with fish, seafood and meat.*

334

Preparation time 20 minutes
Cooking time 30 minutes
Wine *Metodo Classico Franciacorta Rosé*

3½ tbsps lightly salted butter
1 shallot, minced
1¼ cups (9 oz or 250 g) Venere rice
2/3 cup (150 ml) Champagne
3 tbsps instant polenta cornmeal
10.5 oz (300 g) scallops
1 tbsps extra-virgin olive oil
salt and pepper
lemon thyme leaves
parsley, minced

Preheat oven to 325° F (170°C).
Melt half the butter in a saucepan and sauté the shallot until soft.
Add the rice and toast briefly over high heat. Add the Champagne and evaporate. Start adding hot water little by little, stirring frequently and adding more when necessary.
In a small saucepan prepare the polenta by whisking it into a little boiling water. Spread it with a spatula on parchment paper and dry in the oven for 10 minutes, then cut out 4 rounds.
Toss the scallops with oil, salt, pepper and lemon thyme.
As soon as the rice is cooked al dente, stir in the remaining butter.
Fill 4 oiled individual moulds with the rice and let rest 1 minute.
Sear the scallops in a non-stick pan without adding extra oil.
To serve, unmould the rice and serve with scallops, the polenta wafer and a sprinkling of parsley.

Walnut Cappellacci with Chanterelles

Preparation time 30 minutes
Cooking time 15 minutes
Wine *Alto Adige Pinot Bianco*

♟ ♟ ♟

PASTA

1½ cups (7 oz or 200 g)
 plain flour
2 egg yolks
salt
1 egg, beaten

FILLING

1¼ cups (4 oz or 120 g) walnuts
2 tbsps sesame oil
6 oz (180 g) ricotta

1 tbsp mascarpone
1 tbsp grated Parmesan
salt and white pepper

SAUCE

3 cups (10.5 oz or 300 g)
 chanterelle mushrooms
4 tbsps extra-virgin olive oil
1/2 red chilli pepper, minced
1 garlic clove, unpeeled and halved
mint
salt
1 knob of butter

Mix a smooth dough with the flour, egg yolks and salt. Wrap in plastic wrap and refrigerate.

Toast the walnuts in a frying pan with the sesame oil and mince them in a food processor. Mix the walnuts with the ricotta, mascarpone and Parmesan and season with salt and pepper to taste.

Roll out the dough, not too thinly, and cut out 8 circles 3 inches (8 cm) in diameter. Brush the borders of 4 circles with the beaten egg and divide the ricotta and walnut mixture between them.

Lay the other circles on top, press around the edges to seal and trim with a serrated rolling pasta-cutter.

Wash the chanterelles and soak in cold water for 5 minutes. Trim off the base of the stem and quarter the mushrooms.

Heat the oil in a frying pan with the chilli and the garlic. Sauté the mushrooms and mint for 5 minutes over medium heat and add salt.

Bring a large pot of salted water to the boil and cook the cappellacci. Drain, toss with the mushrooms and a knob of butter, and serve.

Amarone Risotto

Preparation time 10 minutes
Cooking time 25 minutes
Wine *Oltrepò Pavese Chardonnay*

3½ tbsps butter
1 yellow onion, minced
1⅓ cup (5 oz or 150 g)
 chopped winter squash
6 cups (1.5 l) hot vegetable broth
2 Renette apples, sliced
1¼ cup (8.5 oz or 240 g)
 Carnaroli rice
1¼ cups (300 ml) Amarone wine
4 tbsps grated Parmesan
salt

Melt the butter in a saucepan
and sauté the minced onion.
Add the squash and 1 ladleful of
hot broth. Add the apple slices
and cook for 5 minutes. Add
the rice, turn up the heat and
add the wine. Stir frequently.
Continue cooking, adding a little
broth whenever the rice gets
dry, until it is cooked through.
Stir in the grated.
Parmesan and season with salt
to taste. Serve very hot.

Risotto with Veal and Mushrooms

Preparation time 5 minutes
Cooking time 15 minutes
Wine *Friuli Isonzo
Cabernet Sauvignon*

2 tbsps extra-virgin olive oil
3 tbsps butter
1 spring onion, minced
1¼ cups (3.5 oz or 100 g)
 chopped mushrooms
4 oz (120 g) ground veal
1½ cups (10 oz or 280 g)
 Carnaroli rice
1/2 cup (120 ml) white wine
4 cups (1 l) vegetable broth
2 tbsps grated Parmesan
salt and pepper
parsley, finely chopped

Heat the oil and half the butter
in a saucepan. Sauté the spring
onion. Add mushrooms and veal
and brown for 5 minutes. Add
rice and toast for a few minutes,
stirring often, then add the wine
and let evaporate. Cook the rice
for 15 minutes, adding the broth
little by little when necessary.
When the rice is cooked, add the
rest of the butter and Parmesan,
season with salt and pepper and
stir until creamy. Top with parsley.

Taleggio Gnocchi with Squash and Walnuts

Preparation time 35 minutes
Cooking time 40 minutes
Wine *Ribolla Gialla*

GNOCCHI
salt and pepper
1 yellow-fleshed potato
 (about 9 oz or 250 g)
2 oz (50 g) taleggio cheese
2 oz (50 g) walnut flour
5 tbsps (1.5 oz or 40 g)
 plain flour

2 tbsps grated Parmesan
2 eggs

SAUCE
3½ tbsps butter
1/2 yellow onion, minced
1 slice aged spalla or prosciutto
1/4 winter squash, cubed
hot vegetable broth
salt and pepper
sage, minced
6 walnuts, minced

Boil the potato in salted water until tender.
Chop the taleggio into small pieces and spread on a tray, then place in the freezer.
Melt a little of the butter for the sauce in a saucepan and sauté the onion. Add the slice of spalla and cook for a few minutes. Add the squash and cook for 5 minutes, then cover with hot broth and cook until tender.
Meanwhile peel the potato and mash it. While still warm, stir in the flours, Parmesan, eggs and salt and pepper and work vigorously to make a smooth dough. Once cooled, form the gnocchi and insert a piece of taleggio into the centre of each one.
Remove and discand the slice of spalla from the squash. Puree the squash. Season with salt and pepper.
Bring a large pot of salted water to the boil and cook the gnocchi. Meanwhile melt the remaining butter with the sage and walnuts in a pan. When the gnocchi rise to the surface, drain with a slotted spoon and add to the pan with the butter.
Serve the gnocchi over the squash puree.

Buckwheat Polenta with Cheese
(LOMBARDY)

Note *This kind of polenta, known as* tucch, *is typical of the area around Bellagio on Lake Como. It is traditionally served in the middle of the table, and everyone helps themselves to spoonfuls, rolling them into balls before eating them.*
Use whatever kind of cheese you prefer for this recipe, preferably one not too high in fat and which melts well.

338

Preparation time 10 minutes
Cooking time 50 minutes
Wine *Valtellina Rosso*

salt
8 cups (2 l) water
1½ cups (9 oz or 250 g)
  coarse cornmeal polenta
2 cups (9 oz or 250 g)
  buckwheat flour
3/4 cup (7 oz or 200 g) butter,
  cut into pieces
1 lb (500 g) cheese, sliced

Salt the water and bring to a boil in a large, deep saucepan. Whisk in the cornmeal polenta and buckwheat flour little by little.
Cook, stirring constantly with a wooden spoon to avoid lumps forming, over moderate heat. After 25 minutes take the polenta off the heat and stir in pieces of butter, then return to the heat and continue cooking for at least 25 more minutes.
When the polenta is cooked, add the slices of cheese and stir well. Pour the hot polenta onto a cutting board and serve immediately.

Pansoti with Walnut Sauce
(LIGURIA)

Preparation time 40 minutes
Cooking time 20 minutes
Wine *Riviera di Ponente Ormeasco*

PASTA
4 cups (1 lb or 500 g)
 plain flour
3 eggs
salt
white wine
extra-virgin olive oil

FILLING
10.5 oz (300 g) Swiss chard
 and borage

3 eggs
6 tbsps grated pecorino cheese
3.5 oz (100 g) quagliata
 (fresh, soft cheese)
salt

SAUCE
3½ tbsps butter
2 cups (7 oz or 200 g) walnuts
3 sage leaves
3.5 oz (100 g) sheep's milk ricotta
1 tbsp heavy cream
salt
grated Parmesan (optional)

339

Mound the flour on a work surface and mix in the eggs and a pinch
of salt. Work well, adding wine as necessary, to create a smooth
and uniform dough. Form into a ball, cover with plastic wrap and set
aside.
Boil the Swiss chard and borage in water. Drain, squeeze out excess
water and chop finely.
Beat the eggs for the filling and mix with the chard, borage, cheeses
and salt.
Roll the dough out thinly and cut out 4-inch (10 cm) squares. Place
1 tablespoon of filling in the centre of every piece then fold from
corner to corner to create a triangle and press the edges to seal.
Prepare the walnut sauce according to the recipe on p. 1099.
Bring a large pot of salted water to the boil and cook the pansoti,
adding a drizzle of oil to the water so they don't stick. Drain and serve
with the walnut sauce and grated Parmesan if desired.

Gnocchi with Rabbit, Apples and Saffron

Preparation time 20 minutes
Cooking time 50 minutes
Wine *Alto Adige Sauvignon*

GNOCCHI
2 large yellow-fleshed potatoes
salt
3 tbsps grated Parmesan
1/2 cup (2 oz or 60 g)
plain flour
1 egg
1 egg yolk

SAUCE
1/2 rabbit
3 tbsps extra-virgin olive oil
1 shallot, minced
1/2 Golden Delicious apple, cubed
salt and pepper
1 ladleful vegetable broth
saffron
1 tbsp crescenza cheese

340

Place the potatoes in a saucepan with cold salted water and bring
to a boil. Cook until soft in the centre and drain. Peel, mash, and
stir in the grated cheese, flour, egg yolk and salt. Quickly mix into
a smooth dough.
Form thick ropes with the dough and cut into small pieces. Roll on
the back of a fork and lay on a tray, then keep cool.
Debone the rabbit and cut the meat into small pieces.
Heat the oil in a frying pan and sauté the shallot. Add the rabbit
and cook for 10 minutes.
Sauté the apple cubes in a non-stick pan with salt and pepper.
Add them to the rabbit and add the broth and the saffron and
cook for a few more minutes.
Bring a large pot of salted water to the boil and boil the gnocchi.
Drain and add to the sauce. Mix in the crescenza and serve.

Bucatini with Sardines

Note *Bucatini is a long pasta, similar to spaghetti but hollow. This recipe would work with other long pastas like spaghetti or linguine also.*

Preparation time 15 minutes
Cooking time 25 minutes
Wine *Grecanico*
♟

6 fresh sardines
4 tbsps extra-virgin olive oil
1 onion, minced
3 anchovies in oil
1⅓ cup (9 oz or 250 g)
 peeled tomatoes
salt
12 oz (350 g) bucatini
freshly ground black pepper

Clean the sardines, remove the head, the backbone and the entrails. Wash well and pat dry.

Heat the oil in a saucepan or large frying pan and sauté the onion. Add the anchovies and break them up by squashing with the back of a fork. Add the sardines to the pan and sauté to brown them evenly on all sides. Add the tomatoes, breaking them up with a fork, and cook for about 10 minutes.

Bring a large pot of salted water to the boil and cook the bucatini until al dente. Drain.

Add the bucatini to the pan with the sardines. Toss to coat well with the sauce, season with salt to taste, grind over some black pepper and serve immediately.

Farinata with Black Kale
(Tuscany)

Note *Cornmeal is often called* farina gialla (*yellow flour*), *in Italy. It is used in some well-known Italian regional specialties, like* taragna polenta, *which is made with cornmeal and buckwheat flour.*

Preparation time 15 minutes
Cooking time 1 hour 20 minutes
Wine *Bolgheri Rosato*

1 head black kale
3 tbsps extra-virgin olive oil
1 sweet red onion, thinly sliced
2 slices lardo
4 cups (1 l) beef broth
salt and pepper
6½ tbsps (2.5 oz or 70 g)
  instant polenta cornmeal

342

Trim off the white stalks of the kale and discard. Roughly chop and reserve the green leaves.
Heat 1 tablespoon of oil in a saucepan and sauté the onion with the lardo slices. Add the chopped kale and continue cooking until it wilts.
Cover with broth and season with salt and pepper to taste.
When the cabbage is cooked through, add the polenta little by little, stirring continuously so lumps do not form. Cook for around 15 minutes.
Season with salt and pepper to taste and serve garnished with a drizzle of extra-virgin olive oil.

Novara-Style Risotto
(Piedmont)

Note *This traditional dish, called* paniscia, *comes from the Piedmontese town of Novara. Grated Parmesan is never added, and ideally it should be made with the typical Piedmontese salame d'la duja, a soft, spiced salami cured in lard.*

Preparation time 20 minutes
Cooking time 3 hours
Wine *Gattinara*

1/2 head Savoy cabbage, chopped
1 carrot, diced
1 celery stalk, diced
1 cup (7 oz or 200 g) dried
 borlotti beans
3½ tbsps butter
1 onion, thinly sliced
2 oz (50 g) lardo, minced
2.5 oz (70 g) pork rind
1 small, soft salami, chopped
1 teaspoon tomato sauce
1¾ cups (13 oz or 360 g)
 Carnaroli rice
3/4 cup (180 ml) red wine
pepper

Boil the cabbage, carrot and celery with the beans in abundant salted water for around 3 hours.
Meanwhile melt half the butter in a saucepan and add the onion, lardo, pork rind, salami and tomato sauce. Cook for a few minutes, then add the rice and toast for 1 minute, stirring. Add the red wine and when evaporated, start adding little by little the cooking liquid from the beans, together with the cooked vegetables.
When the rice is cooked through stir in the rest of the butter and any remaining beans and vegetables. Finish with a sprinkling of pepper.

Artichoke and Scallop Risotto

Preparation time 25 minutes
Cooking time 30 minutes
Wine *Elba Bianco*

5 baby artichokes
juice of 1 lemon
4 cups (1 l) vegetable broth
6 tbsps extra-virgin olive oil
1 shallot
1½ cups (10.5 oz or 300 g)
 Carnaroli rice
3/4 cup (180 ml) white wine
12 scallops
salt and white pepper
2 tbsps butter
parsley, finely chopped

344

Trim the artichokes, cutting off and reserving the stalk and hard external leaves and leaving only the tender inner part. Cut into wedges and place in a bowl. Cover with cold water and lemon juice.
Wash the artichoke stalks and external leaves and boil them in the vegetable broth.
Meanwhile heat 5 tablespoons oil in a saucepan, sauté the shallot then add the drained artichoke wedges. Cook for 2 minutes, add the rice and toast for a few minutes, stirring constantly. Add the wine and let evaporate.
Strain the broth and keep warm. When the wine has evaporated start adding the broth to the rice little by little, letting it absorb completely before adding more and stirring frequently.
Rinse the scallops and pat dry. Heat the remaining oil in a frying pan and sear the scallops for 1-2 minutes each side. Season with salt and pepper.
When the rice is cooked through stir in the butter and parsley. Serve on warm plates topped with 3 scallops per serving, sprinkled with a little white pepper.

Fonduta Risotto

Preparation time 20 minutes
Cooking time 25 minutes
Wine *Fiano di Avellino*

♟ ♟

FONDUTA
10.5 oz (300 g) fontina cheese,
 chopped
1 garlic clove, smashed
1 cup (250 ml) milk
1 knob of butter
3 egg yolks

RISOTTO
3½ tbsps butter
1/2 onion, minced
2 cups (14 oz or 400 g)
 Vialone Nano rice
2/3 cup (150 ml) white wine
4 cups (1 l) beef broth
salt

345

Place the cheese and garlic in a bowl, cover with milk and
refrigerate overnight.
Drain the cheese and place in a saucepan with the butter. Cook
over low heat, stirring continuously, until melted, then whisk in the
egg yolks one at a time.
Melt the butter in a saucepan and sauté the onion. Add the rice
and toast over high heat. Add wine, let evaporate, then add the
broth little by little.
Cook for 15 minutes and salt to taste.
Serve the rice in shallow bowls, topped with the fonduta.

Crispy Amarone Risotto with Quails

Preparation time 25 minutes
Cooking time 40 minutes
Wine *Amarone della Valpolicella*
👨‍🍳 👨‍🍳

3½ tbsps butter
1/2 yellow onion, minced
1¼ cups (9 oz or 250 g) Carnaroli rice
1½ cups (350 ml) Amarone della Valpolicella wine
4 cups (1 l) hot vegetable broth
3 tbsps extra-virgin olive oil
2 garlic cloves, unpeeled
3 sage leaves
1 rosemary sprig
4 quails
salt and pepper

346

Melt 1 tablespoon butter in a saucepan and sauté the onion over low heat, without browning it. Add the rice and toast over high heat, stirring frequently. Add 1 cup (250 ml) wine and let evaporate.
Start adding the hot broth little by little, adding more when it has been absorbed.
When the rice is cooked al dente, stir in the remaining butter. Pour into 4 round moulds and let cool.
Heat 2 tablespoons oil in a saucepan with the garlic. Add the sage and rosemary and brown the quails. As soon as they are evenly browned, add remaining wine and cook for 10 minutes. Season with salt and pepper.
Heat a large non-stick pan with a 1 tablespoon oil. Unmould the risotto and sear in the pan to obtain a crunchy crust on the out-side.
Cut the quails into pieces and serve over the rice, drizzled with the cooking liquid.

Maltagliati with Quails, Truffle and Porcini

Preparation time 20 minutes
Cooking time 30 minutes
Wine *Gattinara*

SAUCE
3 tbsps extra-virgin olive oil
1/2 yellow onion, minced
1/2 celery stalk, minced
1/2 carrot, minced
sage leaves
3.5 oz (100 g) ground pork
2 quails, quartered
1/2 cup (120 ml) white wine
1/2 tbsp raisins
1/2 tbsp pine nuts
salt and pepper
1 large porcini mushroom, sliced
1 garlic clove, unpeeled
1/2 black truffle, shaved

MALTAGLIATI
1 lb (450 g) fresh egg pasta
  dough (see p. 1094)

Heat 2 tablespoons oil in a saucepan and sauté the onion, celery and carrot with the sage. Add the pork and brown for 5 minutes. Add the quails and wine, let evaporate and cook for 15 minutes.
Soak the raisins in water, then drain and squeeze out excess water. Remove the quails from the saucepan, debone and chop the meat. Return it to the pan with raisins and pine nuts and season with salt and pepper.
Heat 1 tablespoon oil in a frying pan and sauté the mushrooms slices with the garlic. Season with salt and pepper.
Roll out the egg pasta dough and cut into irregular shapes. Bring a large pot of salted water to the boil and cook the pasta until al dente. Drain, add to the pan with the quail and toss.
Serve the maltagliati topped with the sautéed mushrooms and truffle.

Trentino-Style Canederli Dumplings

Note *You can substitute the salami with sausage meat or brined tongue, or the canederli can be sauced with sauerkraut or tomato sauce. Before cooking them all, it is a good idea to cook one to check the consistency. If it falls apart, add more breadcrumbs or flour to the dough.*

348

Preparation time 40 minutes
Cooking time 15 minutes
Wine *Sorni Rosso*

1 lb (500 g) dry crusty bread
4 eggs, separated
1¼ cups (300 ml) milk
1 garlic clove, smashed
salt
1 knob of butter
2 oz (50 g) lardo, diced
1 onion, minced
parsley, minced
aromatic herbs, minced
3.5 oz (100 g) salami, chopped
plain flour
hot vegetable broth
4 tbsps grated Parmesan

Cut the bread into cubes and place in a bowl. In another bowl beat the egg yolks with the milk and pour over the bread. Add garlic and a pinch of salt and let sit for 2 hours.
Melt the butter in a frying pan and brown the lardo. Add the onion and cook until soft, then add the parsley and herbs.
Stir the onion mixture into the bread and add the salami.
Beat the egg whites into soft peaks and fold them into the bread mixture, then add enough flour to make a firm dough.
Form the dough into balls by hand and cook in boiling broth for around 15 minutes.
Serve hot in the broth with grated Parmesan.

Acquasale Soup
(BASILICATA)

Preparation time 10 minutes
Cooking time 40 minutes
Wine *Castel del Monte Rosato*

2 tbsps extra-virgin olive oil
1 onion, thinly sliced
1 hot red chilli pepper, chopped
salt
4 eggs
4 slices crusty bread
3.5 oz (100 g) aged ricotta salata,
 grated

Heat the oil in a large frying pan
and sauté the onion. Add the
chilli pepper and cook for a few
minutes, then add warm water,
season with salt and break in
the eggs, stirring well with a
wooden spoon.
Cut the bread into cubes and
divide between shallow bowls.
Pour over a ladleful of soup and
top with grated ricotta salata.

Egg Soup
(LOMBARDY)

Preparation time 20 minutes
Cooking times 15 minutes
Wine *Oltrepò Pavese Cortese*

1½ cups (6.5 oz or 180 g)
 breadcrumbs
6 cups (1½ l) beef broth
3 tbsps butter
3 eggs
3 tbsps grated Parmesan

Soak the breadcrumbs in a
saucepan with the broth for
about 10 minutes.
Add the butter and bring
to a boil, then simmer for
15 minutes.
Meanwhile break the eggs into
a bowl and beat them with the
Parmesan.
Pour the eggs into the broth,
stirring constantly. Serve very
hot.

349

Lobster Tortelli with Mushrooms

350

FILLING
1 small lobster
 (around 2.5 lb or 1.2 kg)
vegetable stock (optional)
2 tbsps breadcrumbs
1 egg yolk
2 tbsps extra-virgin olive oil
salt and white pepper

DOUGH
2¹/₃ cups (10.5 oz or 300 g)
 plain flour
7 tbsps milk
salt

SAUCE
3 tbsps extra-virgin olive oil
1 garlic clove, minced
3-4 fresh porcini mushrooms,
 sliced
thyme leaves
salt and pepper

Preparation time 25 minutes
Cooking time 30 minutes
Wine *Metodo Trento Talento*
Extra Brut

Boil lobster in stock or water for 15 minutes. Drain and cool. Shell the
meat, mince it, mix with breadcrumbs, egg yolk, oil, salt and pepper
and refrigerate for a few hours.
Mix the flour, milk and salt into a smooth dough, roll out thinly and
make tortelli with the lobster filling.
Heat the oil in a frying pan and sauté the garlic. Add mushrooms
(reserving a few slices), thyme, salt and pepper. Sauté for 3-4 minutes.
Bring a large pot of salted water to the boil and cook the tortelli for
2 minutes. Drain and toss with the mushrooms, sautéing over high heat
for 1 minute. Sprinkle with thyme and top with a few raw mushroom slices.

Risotto with Sea Bass

Preparation time 20 minutes
Cooking time 20 minutes
Wine *Torbato di Alghero*
♟

1 sea bass (around 1.75 lb or 800 g)
1¼ cup chopped celery, carrot,
 onion and leek
6 cups (1.5 l) water
salt
1 leaf Swiss chard
1 bunch parsley
5 tbsps breadcrumbs
4-5 tbsps extra-virgin olive oil
pepper
3 tbsps butter
1/2 onion, minced
1½ cups (11 oz or 320 g)
 Vialone Nano rice
1/2 cup (120 ml) white wine
3 tbsps grated Parmesan

Preheat oven to 350°F (180°C).
Descale, wash, skin and fillet the sea bass, washing and reserving the
spine and head.
Place the fish scraps and chopped vegetables in a saucepan, add
water and bring to the boil. Add salt, simmer for 15 minutes, and strain.
Blend the chard, parsley, breadcrumbs, oil, salt and pepper in a food
processor.
Cut the sea bass fillets into strips, dip in the breadcrumb mixture and
lay on a parchment paper-lined baking sheet.
Melt the butter in a saucepan, sauté the onion, add the rice and toast
over high heat. Add the wine and let evaporate, then continue cooking
adding the broth little by little.
Just before the rice is done, bake the sea bass fillets for 5 minutes.
When the rice is cooked, remove from the heat, stir in the Parmesan
and divide between serving plates. Top with the fish and serve.

Oyster, Champagne and Orange Risotto

Note *Oysters are often eaten raw, so it is important to check they are still alive when opened (see if they react to being touched). They are easily digested, so the normal serving size (6 per person as a starter) can be increased without any ill effects.*

Preparation time 20 minutes
Cooking time 15 minutes
Wine *Champagne Extra-Brut Riserva*

♟ ♟

1 knob of butter
1/2 onion, minced
1½ cups (10.5 oz or 300 g)
 Vialone Nano rice
3/4 cup (180 ml) Champagne
8 oysters
1 organic orange
3.5 oz (100 g) sheep's milk ricotta
lemon thyme
salt and white pepper

Melt the butter in a saucepan and sauté the onion over low heat, adding a little water to soften it. Add the rice, increase heat and toast. Add Champagne and when evaporated start adding hot water little by little, stirring often.
Shuck the oysters over a bowl to collect the liquid, then add the liquid to the rice.
Grate a little orange zest. Peel the orange with a sharp knife and cut out the segments between the membranes.
Beat the ricotta until creamy.
When the rice is cooked stir in the orange zest and thyme, season with salt and pepper and divide between serving plates. Top with a spoonful of ricotta, orange segments and the oysters, which will cook slightly from the heat of the risotto.

Parsley Ravioli

Preparation time 20 minutes
Cooking time 15 minutes
Wine *Val d'Aosta Pinot Grigio*

♟ ♟

PARSLEY PASTA
1½ cups (3.5 oz or 100 g) parsley
1⅓ cups (5.5 oz or 150 g)
 plain flour
1/2 cup (3.5 oz or 100 g)
 semolina flour
2 eggs

FILLING
2 small carrots, minced
1 small turnip or kohlrabi, minced

1 zucchini, minced
1 small cauliflower, cut into florets
4 tbsps extra-virgin olive oil
2/3 cup (150 ml) heavy cream
salt and pepper

SAUCE
4 tbsps grated pecorino
1 tbsp grated Parmesan
1 knob of butter (optional)

Boil the parsley in water until it floats, then drain and chop finely.
Mix the 2 flours, add the eggs, a little water and the parsley and
mix well to form a smooth dough. Cover with plastic wrap and let
rest for at least 30 minutes.
Meanwhile, boil the carrot and turnip separately in salted water
until tender. Sauté the zucchini in 1 tablespoon olive oil. Boil the
cauliflower in the cream and puree.
Mix together all the vegetables and the rest of the oil and season
with salt and pepper.
Roll out the pasta and make ravioli with the vegetable filling.
Cut the ravioli with a round cutter.
Bring a large pot of salted water to the boil and cook the ravioli.
Serve them tossed with the grated cheeses and a little butter, if
desired.

Radicchio Risotto
(VENETO)

Note *For this typical dish from the Veneto region, the Carnaroli rice can be replaced by Vialone Nano, preferably Veronese IGP (protected geographical indication).*

Preparation time 25 minutes
Cooking time 25 minutes
Wine *Gambellara*

Serves 6

1 lb (500 g) Treviso radicchio
7 tbsps butter
2 oz (60 g) pancetta, cubed
2 onions, minced
1 garlic clove, minced
salt and pepper
2¾ cups (1.25 lb or 550 g)
 Carnaroli rice
1/2 cup (120 ml) red wine
4 cups (1 l) vegetable broth
6 tbsps grated Parmesan cheese

354

Remove any external wilted leaves from the radicchio and cut the rest into thin strips.
Melt 3 tablespoons butter in a large saucepan, brown the pancetta, then sauté the onions and garlic. As soon as they are golden add the radicchio, let wilt and season with salt and pepper. Cook, covered, for 10 minutes over moderate heat.
Add the rice and toast for 1 minute. Add the wine and as soon as it evaporates add the broth little by little, stirring frequently, until the rice is cooked.
Stir in the remaining butter and Parmesan. Serve hot, topped with more Parmesan if desired.

Pavia-Style Soup
(LOMBARDY)

Preparation time 5 minutes
Cooking time 15 minutes
Wine *Oltrepò Pavese Cortese*

Serves 6

4 cups (1 l) beef broth
crusty bread
6 eggs
watercress
6 tbsps grated grana cheese

Heat the broth in a large
saucepan.
Slice the bread and toast the
slices in a non-stick frying pan
or under the broiler.
Break 1 egg into each serving
bowl and add a few leaves of
watercress. Pour over 1 ladleful
of hot broth, which will cook
the egg.
Sprinkle the grated cheese over
the top and serve the soup hot
with the bread.

Wild Hops Soup
(LOMBARDY)

Preparation time 10 minutes
Cooking time 25 minutes
Wine *Lambrusco Mantovano*

Serves 6

2 lb (1 kg) wild hops or wild
 asparagus
salt
1½ cups (10.5 oz or 300 g)
 Padano rice
4 cups (1 l) vegetable broth
1 garlic clove
parsley
1 knob of butter
6 tbsps grated grana cheese

Blanch the wild hops or
asparagus in boiled salted
water for a few moments.
Cook the rice in the vegetable
broth, stirring every so often.
When the broth is boiling, add
the hops or asparagus.
Minced the garlic and parsley
together, then add to the soup
when the rice is almost cooked,
together with butter and grana.
Salt to taste, cook for a few
more minutes then serve.

Arezzo-Style Bean Soup
(Tuscany)

Preparation time 20 minutes
Cooking time 1 hour 5 minutes
Wine *Chianti Classico*

**3/4 cup (5.5 oz or 150 g)
 black-eyed peas
2 ripe tomatoes
2 tbsps extra-virgin olive oil
1 bay leaf
2 garlic cloves
salt and pepper**

356

Soak the beans for 12 hours or overnight in cold water. Drain and rinse well.

Blanch the tomatoes in boiling water, drain and immerse in cold water. Peel, deseed and chop.

Place the soaked beans in a saucepan with 1 tablespoon oil, chopped tomatoes, bay leaf and whole garlic cloves. Cover with water and bring to a boil over moderate heat. Cook, covered, over medium heat for around 1 hour. Season with salt and pepper to taste after 30 minutes.

Before serving remove the garlic and bay leaf. Serve hot, drizzled with oil and sprinkled with pepper.

Beef and Chicken Terrine with Sangiovese Sauce

Preparation time 20 minutes
Cooking time 1 hour 30 minutes
Wine *Alto Adige Gewürztraminer*

TERRINE
10.5 oz (300 g) chicken for boiling
chicken bones for broth
2 celery stalks, chopped
3 carrots, chopped
1 yellow onion, chopped
2 bay leaves

salt and peppercorns
3/4 cup (180 ml) Gewürztraminer
 wine
7 oz (200 g) lean beef
7-8 green beans, trimmed
2 sheets gelatin

SAUCE
2 cardamom seeds, smashed
3/4 cup (180 ml) Sangiovese wine
1 tsp sugar

Remove the meat from the chicken and place the carcass with the extra bones in a large saucepan. Add the celery, 1 carrot, onion, bay, some peppercorns, a pinch of salt and the Gewürztraminer. Cover with cold water and bring to a boil. Cook for 1 hour, skimming off the foam if necessary.

Add the beef and chicken meat and lower the heat. When cooked through, remove and cut into pieces. Place in a bowl with a little broth and let cool.

Boil the remaining carrots and beans separately until tender. Let cool. Strain the remaining broth and cook down, reducing to 1 cup (250 ml) liquid. Strain again. Soak the gelatin in a little water, drain and squeeze out the excess water, then dissolve in the broth.

Remove the meat from the broth and place it with the carrots and beans in a terrine mould lined with plastic wrap. Pour in the broth with the gelatin and refrigerate until firm.

Place the cardamom with the Sangiovese wine and sugar in a saucepan. Cook down until it reaches a syrupy consistency. Set aside.

Unmould the terrine, slice and serve with a drizzle of the wine reduction.

Wild Boar
with Buttered Chestnuts

Preparation time 1 hour
Cooking time 2 hours
Wine *Barolo*

Serves 6-8

2.2 lb (1 kg) wild boar meat
2 onions
4 carrots
2 garlic cloves
parsley, bay, thyme, juniper
salt and pepper
1 bottle red wine
1/2 cup (120 ml) red-wine vinegar
5.5 oz (150 g) pancetta, diced
2 tbsps extra-virgin olive oil
10 tbsps (5 oz or 140 g) butter
2 tbsps plain flour
1¼ cups (9 oz or 250 g) dried
  chestnuts

360

Cut the meat into pieces and place in a bowl. Add 1 onion and 2 carrots cut into pieces, 1 garlic clove, parsley, bay, thyme, crushed juniper berries, salt and pepper. Pour the wine and vinegar over and let marinate overnight.
Mince together 1 onion, 1 garlic clove and 2 carrots. Mix with the pancetta. Heat the oil and a third of the butter in a saucepan and sauté the vegetable-pancetta mixture until soft.
Drain the meat from the marinade and add to the saucepan. Strain the marinade. Brown the meat evenly, then sprinkle over the flour, add the marinade and cook, covered, for around 2 hours.
Meanwhile rinse the chestnuts and soak for 1 hour.
Boil the chestnuts until tender.
Melt the remaining butter in a frying pan, add the chestnuts and sauté for 5 minutes.
Serve the boar with the chestnuts.

Speck Ham and Asiago Involtini

Preparation time 15 minutes
Cooking time 20 minutes
Wine *Alto Adige Santa Maddalena*

1 lb (500 g) sirloin tip steaks
salt and pepper
5.5 oz (150 g) speck ham, sliced
5.5 oz (150 g) Asiago cheese,
 chopped
3 tbsps extra-virgin olive oil
1 knob of butter
3/4 cup (180 ml) white wine

Lightly pound out the steaks,
lay them out on a work surface
and sprinkle with salt and
pepper.
Top each steaks with 1 slice of
speck ham and some pieces of
Asiago. Roll up the steaks and
close with a toothpick.
Heat the oil and butter in a
frying pan and brown the
involtini for a few minutes.
Add the white wine and let
evaporate. Continue cooking
the involtini for another 20
minutes. Serve hot.

Boiled Beef Salad

Preparation time 15 minutes
Cooking time 15 minutes
Wine *Bardolino Chiaretto*

1 bunch spinach
parsley
6 tbsps extra-virgin olive oil
1 garlic clove
salt and pepper
2 large potatoes, boiled, peeled
 and cubed
12.5 oz (350 g) boiled beef,
 thinly sliced
2 boiled beetroot, cubed
10 walnuts, crumbled

Blanch the spinach in boiling
water. Drain, squeeze out excess
water and place in a food
processor with parsley and 5
tablespoons oil. Remove the
green shoot from the garlic and
add to the food processor. Blend
to a smooth consistency and
season with salt and pepper.
Mix together the beef, potatoes
and beetroot and arrange on
plates topped with some
walnuts. Drizzle with the
spinach dressing and a little oil
and serve.

Rabbit with Wild Fennel

Preparation time 30 minutes
Cooking time 1 hour 10 minutes
Wine *Montepulciano Cerasuolo*

1 rabbit (around 2.5 lb or 1.2 kg)
3 garlic cloves
salt and pepper
2 cups (500 ml) Tocai Friuliano wine
2 bay leaves
1 sprig rosemary
1 bunch wild fennel
2 cups (500 ml) water
2 oz (50 g) prosciutto
1.5 oz (40 g) smoked pancetta
3 tbsps extra-virgin olive oil
roasted potatoes (if desired)

362

Preheat oven to 325°F (170°C).
Clean the rabbit, reserving the liver. Wash well, dry and rub with
1 garlic clove, salt and pepper. Place in a container and marinate
with 1¼ cups (300 ml) wine, bay and rosemary.
Place the green fennel leaves in a small saucepan with 1 garlic
clove and water and cook for 20 minutes over moderate heat.
Remove the garlic, drain the fennel (reserving cooking liquid) and
chop finely.
Mince together the prosciutto, pancetta and rabbit liver. Mince the
remaining garlic clove. Heat 2 tablespoons oil in a saucepan and
sauté the prosciutto, pancetta, liver and garlic. Add the fennel
leaves and cook for 5 minutes. Season with salt and pepper.
Stuff the rabbit with the mixture and tie or sew up well with kitchen
string. Rub with oil, place in a baking dish and bake in the oven for
30 minutes. Baste with white wine then continue cooking for another 40 minutes, basting with the fennel cooking liquid and turning
every so often.
Serve the rabbit cut into pieces with the pan juices, accompanied
by roast potatoes if desired.

Bollito

Preparation time 15 minutes
Cooking time 20 minutes
Wine *Rosso di Montalcino*

4 tbsps extra-virgin olive oil
2 slices Colonnata lardo,
 minced
1 garlic clove
3/4 cup (180 ml) Sangiovese wine
1 lb (500 g) boiled beef
1 bay leaf
sugar
salt
3/4 cup (3.5 oz or 100 g)
 chopped celery, carrot and onion

Heat the oil in a saucepan and
sauté the lardo with the garlic
until it melts. Add a little wine
and let evaporate.
Meanwhile cut the beef into
thick strips, then add to the
saucepan. Add the bay and
the rest of the wine, a pinch
of sugar and a little salt. Let
reduce over low heat, then add
the celery, carrot and onion.
Cook over very low heat to
reduce the liquid but without
toughening the beef.
Remove from the heat and let
sit for 20 minutes. Serve the
beef with the pan juices.

Guinea Hen with Pumpkin

Preparation time 10 minutes
Cooking time 25 minutes
Wine *Trentino Marzemino*

1 guinea hen (around 2.2 lb or 1 kg)
salt and pepper
nutmeg, grated
2 tbsps extra-virgin olive oil
3/4 cup (180 ml) brandy
9 oz (250 g) pearl onions, peeled
3½ cups (14 oz or 400 g)
 chopped pumpkin
rosemary, sage
2 garlic cloves, smashed
3/4 cup (180 ml) broth

363

Preheat oven to 350°F (180°C).
Cut the guinea hen into pieces
and season with salt, pepper
and nutmeg.
Heat the oil and brown the
guinea hen. Sprinkle with brandy
and transfer to a baking dish.
Sauté the onions in the same
pan for a few minutes, season
with salt and add to the guinea
hen.
Add the pumpkin, rosemary,
sage, garlic and broth. Season
with salt and pepper, cover with
aluminum foil and bake for 20
minutes. Remove the foil and
continue cooking for 10 minutes.

Cotechino Sausage in Puff Pastry

Preparation time 50 minutes
Cooking time 3 hours
Wine *Gutturnio Riserva*

3/4 cup (5.5 oz or 150 g) lentils
3 tbsps extra-virgin olive oil
1 shallot, minced
3 tbsps white wine
1/2 cup (120 ml) beef broth
1 cotechino sausage
 (around 4.5 lb or 2 kg)
1 lb (500 g) spinach
9 oz (250 g) puff pastry

364

Soak the lentils in cold water overnight.
Heat the oil in a saucepan, sauté the shallot until soft, then add lentils and wine. Let the wine evaporate then add broth, cover and cook for 20 minutes.
Poke holes in the cotechino with a fork and place in a large saucepan. Cover with cold water and boil over moderate heat for at least 1 hour 30 minutes.
Preheat oven to 350°F (180°C).
Blanch the spinach in boiling water for a couple of minutes, drain and squeeze out excess water.
Lay the puff pastry out on a baking sheet, top with a layer of spinach and then the whole cotechino, taking care not to break it. Roll up in the pastry, trimming any excess, and press closed to seal. Bake for around 30 minutes.
Remove from the oven, slice carefully and serve with the lentils.

Roast Pork with Truffled Potatoes

Preparation time 20 minutes
Cooking time 40 minutes
Wine *Nebbiolo d'Alba*

thyme, sage, rosemary
1 pork leg
salt and pepper
3 tbsps extra-virgin olive oil
5 potatoes
1 knob of butter
1 shallot, minced
1¼ cups (300 ml) hot vegetable
 broth
1 truffle, sliced

365

Preheat oven to 375°F (190°C).
Minced the thyme, sage and rosemary together, then massage the
pork leg with the herbs and salt and pepper. Drizzle with oil and
roast in the oven, turning often, until cooked through.
Peel the potatoes and cut into thick slices. Turn with a sharp knife
to form teardrops or sticks with a rounded end.
Heat the butter in a non-stick frying pan, sauté the shallot then
add the potatoes and cook for 3 minutes, lightly browning them.
Add a little hot broth, then add the truffle. Continue cooking,
adding the broth little by little, until potatoes are tender.
Serve slices of pork with the potatoes.

Braised Duck with Savoy Cabbage
(LOMBARDY)

Preparation time 30 minutes
Cooking time 2 hours
Wine *Capriano del Colle Rosso*

Serves 8-10

4 tbsps butter
duck liver and kidneys, minced
3.5 oz (100 g) chicken livers,
 minced
1 celery stalk, minced
1 carrot, minced
1 onion, minced
1 garlic clove, minced

parsley, minced
5.5 lb (2.5 kg) Savoy cabbage,
 chopped and blanched
dry bread
3/4 cup (200 ml) milk
9 tbsps grated Parmesan
2 eggs
grated nutmeg
salt and pepper
1 duck (around 4.5 lb or 2 kg),
 cleaned
2 tbsps extra-virgin olive oil
vegetable broth
cloves

366

Heat three-quarters of the butter in a saucepan and sauté the
duck liver and kidneys, chicken livers, celery, carrot, onion, garlic
and parsley until the meat is cooked through. Remove from the
heat and let cool.
Soak the dry bread in the milk until soft. Squeeze out excess milk
and place bread in a bowl with Parmesan, eggs, a little nutmeg, a
pinch of salt, pepper and the liver mixture. Mix well.
Stuff the duck with the bread mixture then close well with kitchen
string.
Heat remaining butter and oil in a large saucepan and brown the
duck well, adding a little broth now and then.
Add the Savoy cabbage, cloves and more broth and continue
cooking until duck is done.
Serve hot with the cabbage.

Liver and Sweetbread Skewers
(LIGURIA)

Preparation time 20 minutes
Cooking time 20 minutes
Wine *Rossese di Dolceacqua*

Serves 6

1 knob of butter
7 oz (200 g) chicken livers,
 roughly chopped
7 oz (200 g) sweetbreads,
 roughly chopped
3 cups (10.5 oz or 300 g)
 mushrooms, roughly chopped
1 small black truffle

3/4 cup (200 ml) béchamel sauce
 (see p. 1096)
5 tbsps grated Parmesan
2 oz (50 g) prosciutto, minced
parsley, minced
2 egg yolks
1 tbsp plain flour
1 egg, beaten
breadcrumbs
sunflower oil for frying
salt

Heat the butter in a saucepan. Sauté the chicken livers until
cooked through and remove. Sauté the sweetbreads until cooked
through and remove. Sauté the mushrooms until cooked through
and remove.
Thread alternating chicken liver, sweetbread and mushroom pieces
on wooden skewers.
Use a mandoline to thinly slice the truffle.
Mix the béchamel, Parmesan, prosciutto, parsley and egg yolks in
a bowl and add the truffle shavings.
Dip the skewers in the sauce so that they are well coated, then lay
them carefully on a work surface.
When they are cool, dip each into flour, then beaten egg, then
breadcrumbs.
Heat the sunflower oil and fry the skewers. Drain, dry on paper
towels, salt to taste and serve.

Breaded Beef with Nuts

Preparation time 20 minutes
Cooking time 25 minutes
Wine *Enfer d'Arvier*

4 yellow onions
14 oz (400 g) beef rump, sliced
3/4 cup (3.5 oz or 100 g)
 almond flour
2 eggs, beaten
3/4 cup (3.5 oz or 100 g)
 breadcrumbs
thyme, minced
3 tbsps grated Parmesan
salt and pepper
2 tbsps extra-virgin olive oil
sunflower oil
2 tbsps almonds, minced
2 tbsps pistachios, minced

368

Peel the onions, cut in half and boil for 20 minutes.
Pound out the beef slices and dip them first in the almond flour,
then the eggs and then the breadcrumbs.
Preheat the broiler or oven.
Drain the onions and lay on a baking sheet. Sprinkle with thyme,
Parmesan and salt, drizzle over the oil and gratiné for 10 minutes
under the broiler or in the oven.
Heat the sunflower oil and fry the meat slices. Drain on paper
towels and season with salt and pepper.
Mix together the almonds and pistachios.
Serve the beef sprinkled with the nuts, with the onions on the side.

Beef Stew with Speck Ham and Onions

Preparation time 10 minutes
Cooking time 1 hour 30 minutes
Wine *Alto Adige Lagrein Dunkel*

1.75 lb (800 g) beef for stewing
3 tbsps extra-virgin olive oil
3.5 oz (100 g) speck ham, diced
6 carrots, sliced
10.5 oz (300 g) pearl onions, peeled
2 cups (7 oz or 200 g) mushrooms
2 cups (500 ml) dry white wine
1/4 cup (60 ml) brandy
salt and pepper
2 cups (500 ml) broth

Cut the beef into large cubes.
Heat the oil in a frying pan and
brown the speck ham. Add the
beef and brown evenly on all
sides.
Place the meat in a saucepan
and add the carrots, pearl
onions, mushrooms, wine,
brandy salt and pepper. Stir
well then cook for 1 hour 30
minutes, covered, adding a little
broth when necessary.
Serve the stew directly from the
saucepan.

Brisket with Barolo and Blueberries

Preparation time 40 minutes
Cooking time 30 minutes
Wine *Barolo*

1 beef brisket
 (around 1.3 lb or 600 g)
salt and pepper
1/2 bottlo (375 ml) Barolo wine
1 shallot, halved
1 tablespoon sugar
3 tbsps extra-virgin olive oil
1 basket blueberries

369

Preheat oven to 400°F (200°C)
Tie the brisket with kitchen string,
not too tightly, and season with
salt and pepper.
Place the wine in a small
saucepan with sugar and shallot
and cook until reduced by half.
Heat the oil in an oven-proof
saucepan and brown the meat
evenly. Remove the shallot from
the wine and add the wine to the
meat. Add the blueberries and
cook for 5 minutes, turning the
meat often.
Place in the oven and bake for
20 minutes, basting often with
the cooking liquid.
Serve thickly sliced, drizzled with
the pan juices.

Chicken Kebabs

Preparation time 20 minutes
Cooking time 30 minutes
Wine *Alto Adige Sauvignon Riserva*

1 garlic clove, sliced
1 red chile pepper, desdeed
 and sliced
2 shallots, minced
saffron
1 tsp grated ginger
2/3 cup (0.5 oz or 10 g) lemon balm
salt
7 tbsps water
2 potatoes, peeled and cubed
1 lb (500 g) pumpkin, peeled
 and cubed
2 cups (450 ml) chicken broth
3 tbsps coconut milk
1.3 lb (600 g) chicken breast
6 tbsps extra-virgin olive oil

370

Place the garlic, chile, shallots, a pinch of saffron, ginger, lemon balm, salt and water in a saucepan and bring to the boil. Cook for a few minutes then add the potatoes, pumpkin and broth. Return to the boil then cover and cook for 5 minutes. Add the coconut milk and let thicken.
Cut the chicken into pieces and thread onto wooden skewers. Heat the oil in a frying pan and sauté the chicken until browned and cooked through. Serve hot with the vegetables.

Pheasant with Pears

Preparation time 25 minutes
Cooking time 25 minutes
Wine *Nebbiolo d'Alba*
♟ ♟

3 cups (700 ml) water
1 cup (7 oz or 200 g) sugar
zest and juice of 1 organic lemon
2 Williams pears
1 pheasant (around 2.2 lb or 1 kg)
3 tbsps sunflower oil
salt and white pepper
3½ tbsps butter
1 onion, sliced
3/4 cup (180 ml) white wine
3/4 cup (180 ml) Port wine
1 tsp corn flour

Bring the water to a boil with the sugar and lemon zest.
Peel the pears, cut in half and remove the core. Poach in the boiling water for 10 minutes. Drain and set aside.
Cut the pheasant into pieces. Heat the sunflower oil in a frying pan and brown the pheasant evenly on all sides. Season with salt and pepper. Remove the pheasant from the pan and pour off the fat. Add the butter and sauté the onion, then return the pheasant to the pan and cook for 2 minutes. Add the wines, cook for a few minutes then cover and cook for 12 minutes.
Add the lemon juice and cook for another 3 minutes.
Arrange the pheasant on a serving plate, together with the pears.
Mix the corn flour in a little water, then add it to the sauce left in the pan and stir well, cooking over high heat until thickened.
Pour the sauce over the meat and serve immediately.

Roman-Style Oxtail
(LAZIO)

Note *Guanciale, cured pig cheek, is sometimes added to this dish, which is called coda alla vaccinara. The sauce can also be used to make an excellent pasta.*

Preparation time 20 minutes
Cooking time 3 hours 20 minutes
Wine *Cesanese del Piglio*

Serves 6-8

1 oxtail (around 3.3 lb or 1.5 kg)
2½ tbsps lard
2 oz (50 g) lardo, minced
1 carrot, minced
1 onion, minced
2 garlic cloves, minced
parsley, minced
salt and pepper
1/2 cup (120 ml) white wine
tomato sauce
2 cups (500 ml) water
vegetable broth

If necessary, trim the oxtail (removing any bristles and washing well), then cut into pieces. Melt the lard in a saucepan and add the lardo, carrot, onion, garlic and parsley. Sauté briefly then add the oxtail and brown evenly over high heat, stirring often. Season with salt and pepper, add wine and let evaporate.
Mix the tomato sauce with the water and pour over the oxtail. Cook for 3-6 hours over a very low heat, adding a little vegetable broth when necessary.
Once cooked through, serve hot.

Lamb with Egg and Cheese (Abruzzo)

Preparation time 20 minutes
Cooking time 40 minutes
Wine *Montepulciano d'Abruzzo Riserva*

1 leg of lamb
extra-virgin olive oil
1 garlic clove
1 rosemary sprig
3/4 cup (180 ml) white wine
4 eggs
8 tbsps grated pecorino cheese
juice of 1 lemon
1 slice country-style bread,
 crusts removed
salt

Debone the leg of lamb and cut
into pieces.
Heat the oil in a frying pan with
the garlic and rosemary then
brown the lamb pieces.
Add the wine and evaporate,
then remove the rosemary.
Meanwhile beat the eggs with
the pecorino, lemon juice, the
crumbled bread and salt.
Pour the mixture over the lamb
and cook until the sauce is
thickened.
Serve hot.

Valle d'Aosta-Style Beef with Fontina

Preparation time 20 minutes
Cooking time 1 hour 30 minutes
Wine *Valle d'Aosta Rosso*

Serves 6-8

6 cups (1.5 l) water
salt
1 garlic clove
sage
2.2 lb (1 kg) beef
1 medium cabbage
3.3 lb (1.5 kg) potatoes
9 oz (250 g) fontina cheese
1/2 cup (3.5 oz or 100 g) butter

Salt the water and bring to a
boil with the garlic and sage.
Meanwhile cut the meat into
chunks, shred the cabbage
and cube the potatoes, then
add them to the boiling water.
Cook, covered, for 45 minutes,
skimming off the foam when
necessary.
Preheat oven to 350°F (180°C).
Slice the fontina. In a baking
dish layer the beef and
vegetable mixture with fontina.
Melt the butter and pour over.
Bake for a few minutes. Serve
very hot.

Pork Chops with Apples

Preparation time 15 minutes
Cooking time 1 hour
Wine *Dolcetto d'Acqui*

1.3 lb (600 g) pork chops
8 juniper berries
2 cups (500 ml) apple cider
1/2 cup (4.2 oz or 120 g) butter
1½ tbsps plain flour
1 garlic clove
salt
12.5 oz (350 g) Renette apples
3 tbsps Calvados

374

Cut the pork chops into pieces, place in a bowl with the juniper berries and apple cider and marinate overnight.
Melt two-thirds of the butter in a saucepan with the juniper berries from the marinade. Drain the pork chops (reserving the marinade), dip in flour and lay in the saucepan together with the garlic. Brown on both sides for 5-6 minutes, then pour over half the marinade and cook, covered, for 40 minutes. Season with salt and cook for another 20 minutes uncovered.
Cut the apples into wedges. Melt the remaining butter in a frying pan and sauté the apples for 3-4 minutes. Remove from the heat, add the Calvados and let sit.
Serve the chops with the marinade sauce and apple wedges.

Peppered Pork Fillet

Preparation time 15 minutes
Cooking time 15 minutes
Wine *Ghemme*

4 pork tenderloin steaks
salt
1 tsp mixed peppercorns
 (black, white, green and pink),
 oruchod
powdered garlic
2 tbsps peanut butter

Season the pork chops
with salt, mixed pepper and
powdered garlic.
Heat a cast-iron grill pan or a
grill until very hot, then cook the
chops, turning only once.
Serve topped with a little cold
peanut butter, which will melt
and create a contrast between
hot and cold.

Note *Black, white and green
peppercorns all come from
the same plant, while pink
peppercorns are from the Baies
rose plant.*

Pork Chops with Tabasco

Preparation time 20 minutes
Cooking time 15 minutes
Wine *Taurasi*

3/4 cup (180 ml) red wine
1 tsp Tabasco or other hot sauce
1 sprig rosemary
16 small pork chops
3½ tbsps salted butter
1 tbsp aromatic herbs
salt and pepper
2 sweetcorn cobs, cooked

375

Mix the wine, Tabasco and
rosemary, pour over the chops
and marinate for 30 minutes,
refrigerated.
Blend the butter with the herbs,
form into a roll in wax paper
and refrigerate.
Drain the pork chops, season
with salt and pepper and grill
on a cast-iron grill pan or grill,
melting the fat and flavouring
the meat without burning it.
Grill the corn and cut into
rounds.
Serve the chops with the corn
topped with the herb butter.

Chicken Breasts Stuffed with Endive and Brie

Note *Belgian endive is a kind of chicory, grown underground or indoors with no exposure to sunlight, so the leaves stay white and do not open up. It has a slightly bitter taste. The whiter the leaves the less bitter they are. The inner core must be removed before using.*

376

Preparation time 15 minutes
Cooking time 15 minutes
Wine *Barbera d'Alba*

3 tbsps (1.4 oz or 40 g) butter
1/2 head Belgian endive, sliced
salt and pepper
parsley, minced
4 chicken breasts
 (around 4 oz or 120 g each)
3 oz (80 g) Brie, chopped
2 tbsps plain flour
3 tbsps extra-virgin olive oil
1/2 cup (120 ml) white wine

Melt half the butter and sauté the endive for 3-4 minutes. Season with salt and add parsley.
Cut the chicken breasts in half horizontally without completely detaching the 2 halves. Salt and pepper the insides and lay 2 pieces of Brie and 2 slices of endive inside each one. Reclose the chicken and fix with a couple of toothpicks. Dust with flour.
Melt the rest of the butter and the oil and brown the chicken breasts on each side for around 5 minutes. Add the wine, lower the heat to the lowest possible setting and continue to cook, covered, for 5-7 minutes, reducing and thickening the wine. Serve hot.

Guinea Hen
with Turnip Gratin

Note *Guinea hen meat is halfway between turkey and pheasant. The breast meat is quite pale while the legs are much darker. In Italy guinea hen is considered a white meat.*

Preparation time 30 minutes
Cooking time 20 minutes
Wine *Colli Euganei Merlot*

1.3 lb (600 g) guinea hen breasts
salt and pepper
8 tbsps (4.2 oz or 120 g) butter
1/2 cup (120 ml) red wine
3/4 cup (200 ml) chicken broth
1 medium turnip
7 tbsps heavy cream
nutmeg, grated

377

Salt and pepper the guinea hen breasts. Melt three-quarter of the butter in a frying pan and brown the breasts on the skin side for 5 minutes, then turn and cook for another 2-3 minutes. Remove from the pan and keep warm.
Pour excess fat from the pan and add red wine. Reduce, add the broth and cook down until thickened. Whisk in the remaining butter then return the breasts to the pan.
Preheat the broiler.
Slice the turnip into rounds. Bring the cream to a boil, add salt, pepper and nutmeg, then the turnips, and cook for 10 minutes. Drain, reserving the cream, and arrange in a buttered baking dish. Pour the cream over and brown under the broiler.
Slice the guinea hen breasts, arrange in fan shapes on serving plates, and serve with the wine sauce and gratinéed turnips.

Wild Boar alla Cacciatora
(UMBRIA)

Preparation time 20 minutes
Cooking time 40 minutes
Wine *Montefalco Rosso Riserva*

Serves 6

MARINADE
4 cups (1 l) red wine
1 onion, minced
1 carrot, minced
1 celery stalk, minced
1 sprig rosemary
1 garlic clove, sliced
1 bunch parsley, minced
1 bay leaf
mint, sage, wild fennel

WILD BOAR
2.2 lb (1 kg) wild boar meat
2 tbsps extra-virgin olive oil
1 knob of butter
3.5 oz (100 g) lardo (cured lard), minced
1 onion, minced
1 carrot, minced
1 celery stalk, minced
chile flakes
salt and pepper
3 tbsps tomato sauce

Mix together the marinade ingredients. Add the wild boar, cut into pieces. Marinate for 24 hours.
Drain the boar, reserving the marinade, and rinse under cold running water.
Heat oil, butter and lardo, and sauté onion, carrot and celery.
Add wild boar and season with salt, pepper and chile flakes. Add tomato sauce and simmer, covered, until cooked through.
Meanwhile strain the marinade and boil for a few minutes.
Serve the boar with its own cooking liquid and the marinade.

Beef Stew with Barolo
(PIEDMONT)

Preparation time 35 minutes
Cooking time 2 hours 30 minutes
Wine *Barolo*
♟

Serves 10

3.3 lb (1.5 kg) beef for stewing
4 cups (1 l) Barolo or Barbera
 d'Asti wine
7 oz (200 g) lardo
1/2 celery stalk
4 onions, minced
3 carrots

3 bay leaves
3 garlic cloves
3 cloves
10 juniper berries
thyme, sage, marjoram, tarragon,
 savoury
3 tbsps sugar
1/2 cup (120 ml) Marsala wine
3 tbsps extra-virgin olive oil
3½ tbsps butter
1 tbsp plain flour
ground cinnamon
salt and pepper

379

Cut the beef into pieces of about 50 g (2 oz) each, then place in
a bowl with Barolo, the lardo cut into 4 pieces, celery, onions and
carrots. Add the bay leaves, garlic cloves, cloves, juniper berries,
thyme, sage, marjoram, tarragon, savoury, 2 tablespoons of sugar
and Marsala. Let sit for at least 2 hours or overnight.
Drain the vegetables, mince them and sauté with the oil and butter
in a large saucepan.
Drain the pieces of beef and lardo, pat dry, dust with flour and
brown in the saucepan with the vegetables.
Strain the marinade and add to the meat together with salt,
cinnamon and the remaining sugar. Cook, covered, over a
moderate heat for 2-3 hours.
Remove the meat and lardo and set aside. Puree the cooking
liquid and vegetables with an immersion blender. Mince the lardo.
Return the beef and lardo to the cooking liquid. Serve hot,
accompanied by boiled potatoes or polenta, if desired.

Pork Stew with Cannellini Beans

Note *Cannellini beans have a distinctive long shape and delicate flavour. They are very versatile, and can be used in side dishes, sauces and salads. They are rich in protein and fiber.*

Preparation time 20 minutes
Cooking time 4 hours
Wine *Chianti Classico Riserva*

2.5 lb (1.2 kg) pork for stewing
1½ cups (350 ml)
 Chianti Classico wine
1 cup (9 oz or 250 g) dried
 cannellini beans
3 garlic cloves
1 dried red chile pepper
rosemary, bay
salt and pepper
3 tbsps extra-virgin olive oil
2 oz (50 g) prosciutto fat, minced
1/2 onion, minced
1/2 cup (120 ml) pureed tomato
parsley and basil, minced

Cut the pork into pieces and marinate overnight in the wine with a little water.
Soak the beans in cold water for 12 hours.
Place the pork with its marinade in a large saucepan and add 2 garlic cloves, chile, rosemary, bay, salt and pepper. Cook for 4 hours.
Meanwhile, boil the beans until soft.
Heat the oil and sauté the prosciutto fat, onion and 1 garlic clove.
Add the drained beans, salt and tomato and cook for 20 minutes.
Add pepper and the minced parsley and basil and serve hot with the pork stew.

380

Braised Goose

Preparation time 20 minutes
Cooking time 1 hour
Wine *Teroldego Rotaliano*

rosemary, sage
1 garlic clove
1 tsp ground mixed spice
 (pepper, cardamom, cinnamon,
 nutmeg)
4 tbsps extra-virgin olive oil
4 goose legs
1/4 cup (60 ml) brandy
1 Savoy cabbage
1/4 cup (1.5 oz or 40 g) raisins
1 bay leaf
salt

Mince the rosemary and sage
with the garlic, mix with the
spices and rub into the goose
legs.
Heat the oil in a saucepan and
brown the goose. Sprinkle with
brandy and cook over low heat
for 20 minutes.
Chop the cabbage and blanch
in boiling water for 5 minutes.
Add to the goose together
with raisins, bay, salt and some
water. Cover and cook for 40
minutes.
Serve the goose sliced, with the
cabbage.

Stuffed Pork Fillet

Preparation time 30 minutes
Cooking time 20 minutes
Wine *Trentino Marzemino*

1 knob of butter
1 Abate pear, peeled and cubed
3 sage leaves, minced
salt and pepper
2 crackers, crumbled
2 oz (60 g) semi-aged pecorino,
 diced
1 pork tenderloin
 (around 1 lb or 500 g)
pork caul fat
2 tbsps extra-virgin olive oil

381

Preheat oven to 400°F (200°C)
Melt the butter and sauté the
pear with the sage, salt and
pepper. Mix in the crackers and
let cool, then add the pecorino.
Butterfly the pork fillet (or ask the
butcher to prepare a
butterflied pork tenderloin) and
fill it with the stuffing. Close and
wrap tight in the caul fat. Trim
any excess. Heat the oil in a
frying pan and brown the pork
on all sides. Pour off any excess
fat then roast in the oven for
around 10 minutes. Let sit for 2
minutes then cut into thick slices
and serve.

Florentine-Style Stewed Beef
(TUSCANY)

Note *For a variation,
before placing the meat
in the saucepan, cut slits
and fill with carrot sticks
and cubes of pancetta.
Salt and pepper the meat
and tie with kitchen string
before proceeding with
the recipe.*

Preparation time 30 minutes
Cooking time 3 hours
Wine *Chianti Classico*

Serves 6

2 tbsps extra-virgin olive oil
1 onion, minced
1 celery stalk, minced
1 carrot, minced
3.5 oz (100 g) pancetta, diced
2.2 lb (1 kg) lean beef for stewing
3/4 cup (180 ml) red wine
1 lb (500 g) tomatoes, peeled,
 deseeded and chopped
salt and pepper

382

Heat the oil in a saucepan and sauté the minced onion, celery and
carrot. Add the diced pancetta then the beef. Add the wine and let
reduce.
Add the chopped tomatoes and season with salt and pepper to
taste.
Cover the saucepan and cook over low heat for around 2 hours,
adding a little warm water every so often if necessary.
Serve the beef very hot, in its own cooking liquid.

Roman-Style Tripe (LAZIO)

Preparation time 20 minutes
Cooking time 5 hours
Wine *Cesanese di Affile*

2.2 lb (1 kg) tripe
salt
1 onion, minced
1 celery stalk, minced
1 carrot, minced
extra-virgin olive oil
2 tbsps butter
1 garlic clove
bay, basil
3/4 cup (180 ml) white wine
1½ cups (10.5 oz or 300 g)
 peeled tomatoes
vegetable broth
pepper

Rinse the tripe, cut into pieces
and place in a saucepan with
salted water, onion, celery and
carrot. Bring to a boil and cook
for 5 hours, skimming every so
often.
Once cooked, cut into strips then
rinse again.
Heat a little oil with the butter,
then add the garlic, bay and basil,
then the tripe. Add wine, reduce,
then add tomatoes, a little broth,
salt and pepper and cook until the
sauce thickens. Serve very hot.

Florentine-Style Tripe (TUSCANY)

Preparation time 20 minutes
Cooking time 1 hour 30 minutes
Wine *Chianti Classico Riserva*

Serves 6

2.2 lb (1 kg) tripe
2 tbsps extra-virgin olive oil
1 red onion, minced
2 carrots, minced
2 celery stalks, minced
1½ cups (10.5 oz or 300 g)
 chopped tomatoes
salt and pepper
6 tbsps grated Parmesan
parsley, minced (optional)

Clean the tripe well and cut into
strips. Heat the oil and sauté
the onion, carrots and celery.
As soon as the onion softens
add the tripe and stir with a
wooden spoon. Cook for 15-20
minutes then add tomatoes.
Season with salt and pepper
then cook for 1 hour over
low heat, until the sauce has
reduced.
Serve very hot with a sprinkling
of Parmesan and parsley, if
desired.

383

Truffled Beef Involtini

Preparazione 20 minuti
Cottura 15 minuti
Vino *Bardolino Chiaretto*

3 oz (80 g) fontina cheese
8 beef sirloin tip steaks
2 oz (60 g) ham or prosciutto,
 sliced
1 black truffle, grated
3 tbsps extra-virgin olive oil
1 shallot, minced
1/2 cup (120 ml) white wine
salt and pepper
2 tbsps heavy cream
parsley, minced

384

Cut the fontina into strips. Pound out the beef steaks, lay them out on a work surface and top each one with fontina and ham slices. Sprinkle with grated truffle and roll up the slices, securing them with toothpicks.
Heat the oil, sauté the shallot then brown the involtini on all sides. Add the wine, season with salt and pepper and let reduce. Cook for around 10 minutes, then add cream and mix well. Sprinkle with parsley.
Serve very hot with their cooking liquid.

Pomegranate Chicken

Preparation time 20 minutes
Cooking time 40 minutes
Wine *Chianti Classico*

1 small chicken
 (around 2.2 lb or 1 kg)
1 pomegranate
grated **zest and juice**
 of 1 organic lemon
5 tbsps extra-virgin olive oil
2 rosemary sprigs
sage
salt and pepper
2 oz (50 g) pancetta, julienned

Preheat oven to 400°F (200°C).
Cut the chicken into pieces. Finely chop the liver and set aside.
Squeeze the juice from half the pomegranate, strain and mix with
the grated zest and juice of the lemon.
Lay the chicken pieces on a baking sheet and drizzle with 2
tablespoons oil, sprinkle with herbs, salt and pepper.
Roast for around 30 minutes, basting halfway through with some
of the pomegranate and lemon juices.
Heat the remaining oil, and sauté the pancetta and liver. Add
the remaining pomegranate and lemon juices and cook for 5-10
minutes.
Arrange the chicken on a serving plate. Strain the pan juices and
add to the pancetta mixture.
Serve the chicken drizzled with the sauce and topped with the
seeds from the remaining pomegranate.

Savoy Cabbage with Pork

Note *This dish is called
verzolata in Italian, after
verza, Savoy cabbage.*

Preparation time 15 minutes
Cooking time 20 minutes
Wine *Teroldego Rotaliano*

4 tbsps extra-virgin olive oil
1 garlic clove
1 red onion
3 cups (7 oz or 200 g)
 shredded Savoy cabbage
2 pork chops
 (around 7 oz or 200 g each)
salt and pepper
1 tbsp plain flour
2 sausages (7 oz or 200 g each)
1/2 cup (120 ml) white wine
4 sage leaves
2 tbsps white wine vinegar

386

Heat the oil in a saucepan and sauté the garlic and onion.
Salt, pepper and flour the chops. Prick the sausage with a fork.
Add the chops and sausage to the saucepan and brown for 5-6
minutes. Add the wine and let reduce, then add the cabbage, salt,
sage and vinegar and cook, covered, for around 15 minutes. Add
a little water if necessary.
Remove the meat, chop the sausage and thinly slice the chops.
Arrange the cabbage on serving plates, top with meat and serve
immediately.

Beef, Mushroom and Olive Stew

Preparation time 20 minutes
Cooking time 1 hour
Wine *Valdadige Rosso*

Serves 6

4 tbsps extra-virgin olive oil
1 garlic clove
2.2 lb (1 kg) beef for stewing,
 cubed
3 tbsps red wine vinegar
3 carrots, diced
bay, tarragon and parsley,
 minced
12 black olives, pitted
salt and pepper
4 cups (1 l) hot broth
2 cups (7 oz or 200 g) mushrooms
3 tomatoes

Heat 3 tablespoons oil with the garlic and brown the meat.
Sprinkle the meat with the red wine vinegar then add the diced
carrots, minced herbs, olives and salt and pepper to taste.
Cover with hot broth and cook, covered, for 1 hour.
Meanwhile cut the mushrooms into wedges. Deseed the tomatoes
and cut into chunks.
Heat the remaining oil in a frying pan and sauté the mushrooms
for 5 minutes, until browned. Add the tomatoes and salt and cook,
covered, for a few minutes.
Just before the meat is done mix in the mushrooms and tomatoes
and some parsley.
Serve hot.

Beans with Cotechino
(FRIULI-VENEZIA GIULIA)

Note Muset *is a traditional cotechino from Friuli, prepared with fatty and lean pork spiced with cinnamon, pepper and chile. It is often cooked with* brovade, *turnips fermented in grape pomace (what's left after the wine has been pressed).*

Preparation time 10 minutes
Cooking time 1 hour
Wine *Carso Terrano*

3/4 cup (7 oz or 200 g)
 dried beans
2 tbsps extra-virgin olive oil
2 tbsps butter
1 onion, minced
salt and pepper
1 "musetto" cotechino
 (around 1.75 lb or 800 g)

Soak the beans overnight in abundant water. Drain, cover with water in a saucepan and boil for around 20 minutes over moderate heat.
Heat the oil and butter in a frying pan and sauté the onion. Season with salt and pepper. Add to the beans, then continue cooking for another 20 minutes.
Pierce the cotechino with a fork and boil in a large saucepan with abundant water. As soon as it is cooked through drain and wipe off any excess fat. Add to the pot with the beans.
Serve the cotechino sliced with the drained beans.

Tongue with Botticino
(LOMBARDY)

Preparation time 30 minutes
Cooking time 3 hours 30 minutes
Wine *Botticino*

1 beef tongue
2 tbsps plain flour
2 tbsps extra-virgin olive oil
2 onions, thinly sliced
1 garlic clove, peeled
1 cup (7 oz or 200 g) chopped
 tomatoes
4 cups (1 l) Botticino wine
2 cups (500 ml) veal broth
bay leaves, cinnamon stick,
 cloves
salt

389

Boil the tongue in abundant water for around 1 hour 30 minutes.
Drain, peel, dry and lightly dust with flour.
Heat the oil in a saucepan and sauté the onions and garlic. Brown
the tongue, then add the tomatoes and wine.
When it comes to a boil lower the heat and continue cooking.
Place the bay, cinnamon and cloves in a piece of fabric and tie
closed with kitchen string. Add to the saucepan. Continue cooking
the tongue, adding broth when necessary.
After 2 hours remove the tongue, discard the bag of spices and
puree the rest of the cooking liquid with an immersion blender.
Continue cooking until thickened, adding a little flour if necessary.
Season with salt and serve with thick slices of tongue.

Lemon Verbena-Steamed Monkfish

Preparation time 20 minutes
Cooking time 15 minutes
Wine *Gambellara*

FISH
14 oz (400 g) monkfish
1 sprig lemon verbena

SPINACH
1 tsp raisins
1 tsp pine nuts
2 tbsps extra-virgin olive oil
1/2 onion, minced
vinegar
7 tbsps white wine
2 bunches spinach
salt and pepper

390

Cut the fish into bite-sized pieces, removing the skin and central bone.
Soak the raisins in a little warm water for a few minutes. Drain and squeeze out the excess water and set aside. Toast the pine nuts. Heat the olive oil in a small saucepan and add the onion. Sauté the onion until soft and then add the raisins, pine nuts and vinegar. Let the vinegar cook off for 1 minute and then add the wine, spinach and a little water. Cook for 2 minutes and remove from heat. Season with salt and pepper and puree.
Fill a pot with 1 inch (2½ cm) of water. Chop the verbena and add to the water. Bring to a boil. Place the fish in a metal steaming basket and place in the pot. Cover and steam the fish until cooked through and tender.
Place a few spoonfuls of spinach puree on each plate and top with fish. Serve immediately.

Grilled Octopus Salad

Preparation time 20 minutes
Cooking time 30 minutes
Wine *Verduzzo del Piave*
♟ ♟

1¼ cups (5 oz or 150 g)
 chopped onion, celery and carrot
1 dried red chilli pepper
2 sprigs rosemary
1 small octopus
3 yellow-fleshed potatoes
1/2 cup (3.5 oz or 100 g) red lentils
1 red onion, sliced
2 tomatoes, diced
3 tbsps extra-virgin olive oil
salt and pepper

Bring a pot of water to a boil with the onion, celery and carrot.
Add the chilli pepper and rosemary to the broth and then the
whole octopus. Cover and let cook for 30 minutes.
Remove from the heat and let the octopus cool completely
in the broth.
Meanwhile, boil the potatoes in salted water. Drain, peel and dice
the potatoes.
Boil the lentils in salted water until tender.
Preheat the grill.
Cut the octopus into pieces and then grill for 3 minutes, turning
frequently. Place the grilled octopus on a plate and cover with
plastic wrap. Let rest for 5 minutes.
Meanwhile, place the potatoes on a serving dish; add the octopus,
lentils and red onion. Garnish with the tomatoes and season with
salt and pepper. Drizzle with oil and serve immediately.

Bagna Caoda (PIEDMONT)

Note *Bagna caoda is a traditional peasant food of Piedmont. Its simplicity and convivial nature make it a great dish to serve with many friends. Any and all available winter vegetables can accompany bagna caoda. The bagna caoda can also be served in a fondue pot.*

394

Preparation time 20 minutes
Cooking time 25 minutes
Wine *Carema*

BAGNA CAODA
5 garlic cloves
1¼ cups (300 ml) milk
7 oz (200 g) salted anchovies
white wine
3/4 cups (200 ml) extra-virgin olive oil
5 tbsps butter
3 tbsps heavy cream

VEGETABLES
a selection of the following:
 Savoy cabbage, red cabbage, celery, fennel, carrots, escarole, endive, cardoons, potatoes, leeks, cauliflower, Jerusalem artichokes, white turnips, butternut squash, bell peppers, beets, onions

Preheat oven to 375°F (190°C).
Chop cabbage, celery, fennel, carrots, escarole and endive into bite-sized pieces. Chop cardoons and soak in cold water and lemon juice. Blanch potatoes, leeks, cauliflower, Jerusalem artichokes and turnips until just barely tender then cut into bite-size pieces. Roast the peppers, peel, deseed and slice. Cut squash, beets and onions into bite-sized pieces and roast for 45 minutes.
Slice the garlic and soak in the milk for 1 hour. Rinse the anchovies and soak in the wine. Drain the garlic and the anchovies, place in a heavy-bottomed saucepan and cover with oil. Cook over low heat for 10 minutes, stirring to dissolve the ingredients. Add butter and cook, stirring, for another 10 minutes. Stir in the cream. Bring the saucepan to the table and divide the sauce between individual terracotta serving bowls set over candles. The sauce should simmer continually throughout the meal. Serve the vegetables to be dipped into sauce.

Stuffed Squid with Tomato Sauce

Preparation time 40 minutes
Cooking time 55 minutes
Wine *Vermentino di Gallura*
♟ ♟

SQUID
12 medium squid
3.5 oz (100 g) fresh caciotta cheese
1 cup (5.2 oz or 150 g) breadcrumbs
parsley, chopped
1 garlic clove
3 tbsps extra-virgin olive oil
salt and pepper
3/4 cup (180 ml) white wine

TOMATO SAUCE
3 tbsps extra-virgin olive oil
1 shallot, minced
1 dried red chilli pepper
14 oz (400 g) peeled, canned
 tomatoes
salt and pepper
oregano

Preheat oven to 400°F (200°C).
Clean and wash the squid under running water. Remove a third of the
tentacles and chop them. Finely chop the caciotta cheese and mix
with the squid in a bowl. Add the breadcrumbs, chopped parsley, the
whole garlic clove and 1 tablespoon of olive oil. Season with salt and
pepper and add just enough wine to bring the mixture together.
Fill the squid with the stuffing and sew closed with kitchen string.
Place the stuffed squid in a baking dish and season with salt and
pepper. Add the remaining wine. Bake for 40 minutes.
Heat the remaining olive oil in a frying pan and add the shallot and
chilli pepper. Sauté briefly and than add the tomatoes, salt and
pepper. Let cook for 15 minutes. Puree the tomato sauce. Season
with oregano, salt and pepper and keep warm.
Serve the squid with the tomato sauce.

Grilled Stuffed Salt Cod

Preparation time 20 minutes
Cooking time 30 minutes
Wine *Friuli Collio Sauvignon*

1/2 red bell pepper
2 yellow-fleshed potatoes
2 tbsps milk
parsley
4 basil leaves
salt and pepper
1 lb (450 g) salt cod fillet, soaked

Preheat the grill.
Remove the seeds from the pepper and cut in half. Roast the pepper and then close in a plastic bag for 15 minutes. Peel and chop.
Boil the potatoes in salted water. Drain, peel and place the potatoes in a saucepan. Mash the potatoes with a fork and add the milk. Cook for a few minutes and add the parsley, basil and bell pepper. Season with salt and pepper.
Remove any bones from the fish and cut it into 8 rectangles. Spread the potato cream over 4 pieces of fish and then top with another piece of fish. Grill the fish for 7 minutes on each side and serve immediately.

Grouper with Mushrooms

Preparation time 15 minutes
Cooking time 20 minutes
Wine *Bianco d'Alcamo*

3 tbsps butter
3 cups (9 oz or 250 g) sliced white mushrooms
1/2 cup (120 ml) white wine
salt and pepper
1 lb (450 g) grouper fillets

Melt half of the butter in a non-stick pan and add the mushrooms. Sauté over low heat for 2 minutes. Add the wine and season with salt and pepper.
Heat the rest of the butter in another frying pan and add the grouper. Season with salt and pepper and sauté until cooked. Transfer the fish to the mushroom pan. Serve the fish and mushrooms with steamed new potatoes, if desired.

396

Sea Bream with Walnuts and Broccoli

Preparation time 40 minutes
Cooking time 30 minutes
Wine *Cirò Bianco*

4 sea bream (9 oz or 250 g each)
salt and pepper
2 tbsps plain flour
2¾ cups (7 oz or 200 g)
 broccoli florets
1 potato
1¼ cups (4 oz or 120 g) walnuts
2 garlic cloves
3 tbsps sunflower oil
1 tbsp apple vinegar
1 tsp lemon juice
1/3 cup (3.5 oz or 100 g)
 plain yogurt
2 tbsps extra virgin olive oil
2 tbsps butter
1 spring onion, chopped

Clean and rinse the fish. Dry with a paper towel and sprinkle with salt and pepper. Dust with flour and shake off any excess.
Blanch the broccoli until tender, drain and set aside.
Peel the potato and boil in salted water. Drain and mash with a potato ricer.
Chop the walnuts and garlic and add to the potato. Add the sunflower oil, vinegar, lemon juice and yogurt to the potato mixture. Season with salt and pepper and mix well.
Heat the olive oil and butter in a large frying pan. Add the fish and sauté for 5-6 minutes turning once. Set the cooked fish on paper towels.
Place the fish on individual serving plates with the broccoli. Top with a spoonful of walnut sauce and garnish with spring onion.

Baccalà with Olives and Anchovies

Note *In most of Italy*
baccalà *refers to Atlantic*
cod which has been
dried or preserved in
salt. However, baccalà
is actually the name for
cod preserved in salt,
while dried cod is called
stoccafisso. *Regardless of*
whether the fish has been
preserved in salt or dried,
it is necessary to wash
the fish well and then let it
soak, changing the water
frequently, before use.

398

Preparation time 20 minutes
Cooking time 35 minutes
Wine *Alto Adige Gewürztraminer*

1 lb (450 g) salt cod
1/2 cup (1.7 oz or 50 g)
 plain flour
1 sweet red onion
1/2 cup (2 oz or 60 g)
 pitted black olives
1 garlic clove
2 tbsps extra-virgin olive oil
2 tbsps butter
3 anchovy fillets in oil
1¼ cups (300 ml) milk
parsley, minced
salt

Rinse the salt cod in cold water to remove the salt. Soak the fish for
at least 2 days changing the water at least twice a day so that the
fish re-hydrates. Drain the cod and rinse it one more time. Pat the
fish dry and then dust with flour. Set aside.
Slice the onions and olives and smash the garlic clove.
Heat the olive oil and butter in a large pan. Add the onion, garlic,
olives and anchovies.
Add the salt cod to the pan and sauté for 3-4 minutes. Pour the
milk over the fish slowly and cover the pot. Lower the heat and let
simmer for 30 minutes. Season with salt and parsley.

Sea Bass
with Radicchio

Preparation time 20 minutes
Cooking time 20 minutes
Wine *Cinque Terre Bianco*

2 heads Treviso radicchio,
 quartered lenghtwise
6 tbsps extra-virgin olive oil
oregano
salt and pepper
4 sea bass fillets

Preheat oven to 400°F (200°C).
Place the radicchio in an oiled
baking dish and season with
oregano, salt and pepper. Drizzle
with olive oil and bake for 15
minutes.
Turn the oven down to 350°F
(180°C).
Line a baking sheet with
parchment paper and place the
fillets, with their skin still on, on
the tray. Drizzle the fish with oil,
season with salt and pepper and
bake for 10 minutes. Serve with
the radicchio.

Hake with
Potatoes and Beets

Preparation time 15 minutes
Cooking time 30 minutes
Wine *Elba Bianco*

2 yellow-fleshed potatoes
salt and pepper
1 hake
1 lemon, sliced
2 roasted beets, thinly sliced
parsley, minced
6 tbsps extra-virgin olive oil
2 tbsps rinsed capers

Boil the potatoes in salted water
until tender. Drain, peel and slice.
Clean the fish, dry and salt
lightly. Fill the body cavity of the
fish with lemon slices and steam
for 15 minutes. Debone the fish.
Toss the potatoes with salt,
pepper and parsley.
Puree the olive oil and capers
to form a sauce.
Plate the beets and potatoes,
top with fish and drizzle with
caper sauce. Season with salt
and pepper. Let rest 15 minutes
before serving.

Umbrine with Potatoes

Preparation time 20 minutes
Cooking time 20 minutes
Wine *Cinque Terre Bianco*

2 yellow-fleshed potatoes
6 tbsps extra-virgin olive oil
1/2 red onion
4 umbrine fillets
salt and pepper
mâche (lamb's lettuce)

Preheat oven to 400°F (200°C).
Peel and thinly slice the potatoes using a mandoline. Oil a baking
dish and spread the potatoes, slightly overlapping, on the bottom
of the dish to form 4 rectangles. Season with salt and pepper.
Thinly slice the onion and place on top of the potatoes.
Drizzle with olive oil and bake for 5 minutes.
Lower the oven temperature to 350°F (180°C).
Salt and pepper the fish fillets and place them on top of the potatoes
and onions. Drizzle with olive oil and bake for 10 minutes.
Serve the fish with mâche salad.

400

Tub Gurnard
with Black-Eyed Peas

Note *Tub gurnard, or tub fish, is called* gallinella di mare *in Italian.*

Preparation time 20 minutes
Cooking time 20 minutes
Wine *Verdicchio dei Castelli di Josi*

BLACK-EYED PEAS
7 oz (200 g) black-eyed peas
2 garlic cloves
thyme
1 tomato, chopped
salt and pepper
1/2 chilli pepper, deseeded
 and chopped
6-7 cherry tomatoes, halved
6 tbsps extra-virgin olive oil
parsley

FISH
3.5 oz (100 g) sliced almonds
14 oz (400 g) tub gurnard fillets
2 tbsps extra-virgin olive oil
salt and pepper

Soak the black-eyed peas for 8 hours. Boil the beans with 1 garlic clove, thyme and tomato. Season with salt and pepper.
Toast the almonds for a few minutes and let cool completely.
Smash the remaining garlic clove. Heat olive oil in a frying pan. Sauté the garlic, chilli and parsley. Add the black-eyed peas and cook for 2 minutes. Add the tomatoes and season with salt and pepper.
Season the fish with salt and pepper and cover with almonds. Heat 2 tablespoons of olive oil in a non-stick pan and sauté the fillets. Serve the fish with the black-eyed peas.

Mullet-Stuffed Endive with Tomato Sauce

Preparation time 35 minutes
Cooking time 40 minutes
Wine *Colli Piacentini Ortrugo*

parsley
7 tbsps heavy cream
paprika
curry powder
salt and pepper

ENDIVE
juice of 1 lemon
1/2 cup (1.7 oz or 50 g)
 plain flour
14 oz (400 g) endive

FILLING
3.5 oz (100 g) red mullet fillets
1 egg

TOMATO SAUCE
2 tbsps extra-virgin olive oil
1 garlic clove
2 basil leaves
7 oz (200 g) canned crushed
 tomatoes
salt and pepper

402

Preheat oven to 230°F (110°C).
Bring a large pot of water to a boil. Add lemon juice and flour. Add the endive and boil for 20-25 minutes. Drain and pat dry.
Wash, dry and finely chop the mullet fillets. Add the egg, parsley and cream and mix well. Season with paprika, curry, salt and pepper. Puree the mixture.
Line 4 round cookie cutters with endive leaves. Dice the remaining endive and add to the fish filling. Place a spoonful of filling on the endive leaves and then fold them over to form a closed dumpling. Place the dumplings on a baking sheet and bake for 10 minutes.
Heat the oil in a saucepan. Add the garlic clove and basil then add the crushed tomatoes and simmer for 10 minutes. Puree and season with salt and pepper.
Place a spoonful of sauce on each serving plate and top with 1 dumpling. Serve immediately.

Drunken Octopus with Potatoes

Preparation time 20 minutes
Cooking time 35 minutes
Wine *Friuli Collio Cabernet*

12 cups (3 l) water
1½ cups (350 ml)
 Cabernet Sauvignon
2 garlic cloves
2 chilli peppers
2 celery stalks
1 medium octopus
5-6 potatoes
3 tbsps extra-virgin olive oil
salt and pepper
3 onions, peeled and quartered

Preheat oven to 400°F (200°C)
Bring water, wine, garlic, chilli
peppers and celery to a boil. Add
the whole octopus and boil for
35 minutes. Let the octopus cool
in the cooking liquid.
Chop the potatoes, place them
in a baking dish, drizzle with oil
and season with salt and pepper.
Roast until tender.
Boil the onions in lightly salted
water until transparent. Drain and
cool, drizzle with olive oil and
season with salt and pepper.
Chop the octopus and mix it with
the potatoes and onions. Serve
warm.

Herbed Trout Fillets

Preparation time 10 minutes
Cooking time 10 minutes
Wine *Trentino Müller Thurgau*

1.3 lb (600 g) trout fillets
rosemary, sage, thyme, parsley
juice of 1 lemon
salt and pepper
4 tbsps extra-virgin olive oil
1 garlic clove, smashed

Preheat the grill.
Wash the trout fillets and pat
them dry with a paper towel.
Mince the rosemary, sage,
thyme and parsley together.
Brush the fish with olive oil,
season with salt and pepper
and sprinkle with two-thirds of
the minced herbs. Grill the trout
fillets for 3-4 minutes per side.
In a small bowl mix the lemon
juice with a pinch of salt and
pepper. Whisk in the remaining
olive oil to emulsify the dressing.
Add remaining herbs and garlic
clove.
Serve the fish immediately with
the herb vinaigrette.

403

Steamed Sea Bream with Porcini

Nota *Some believe that the name polenta comes from the Latin* pollen, *meaning flower of flour, while others believe that it derives from* puls, *meaning spelt soaked in water. Regardless of the origins of the name, polenta has been an important food staple since medieval times.*

Preparation time 20 minutes
Cooking time 20 minutes
Wine *Bardolino Chiaretto*

4 sea bream fillets
3 tbsps extra-virgin olive oil
parsley, minced
salt and pepper
5 fresh porcini mushrooms
1 garlic clove
2 cups (500 ml) water
1/2 cup (2.5 oz or 70 g) instant
 polenta cornmeal

404

Preheat oven to 340°F (170°C).
Cut the sea bream fillets into diamond-shaped pieces. Place in a baking dish and drizzle with 1 tablespoon olive oil. Season with parsley, salt and pepper. Cover and refrigerate.
Clean and thickly slice the porcini mushrooms.
Heat remaining olive oil in a frying pan and add the garlic clove. Add mushrooms and sauté over high heat for a few minutes. Season with salt and pepper.
Salt the water and bring to a boil. Whisk in the cornmeal and cook until the polenta is creamy. Remove from heat.
Line a baking sheet with parchment paper. Spread the polenta on the parchment paper to form small rounds. Bake in the oven for 13-14 minutes.
Meanwhile, steam the sea bream until tender.
Compose plates by alternating layers of polenta rounds with fish and mushrooms.

Lobster in Saffron Vegetable Stew

Preparation time 20 minutes
Cooking time 30 minutes
Wine *Metodo Classico*
Franciacorta Rosé

♟ ♟

2 fennel bulbs
4 tbsps extra-virgin olive oil
0.2 oz (5 g) saffron
1/2 cup (120 ml) white wine
2 cups (500 ml) fish broth
2 tomatoes
1 tsp corn flour
2 tbsps Pernod
1 knob of butter
salt and pepper
6 cups (1.5 l) court bouillon
 or vegetable broth
4 small lobsters

Wash the fennel bulbs and thinly slice them using a mandoline,
reserving the leaves.
Heat the olive oil in a saucepan and add the fennel. Cook the fennel
over low heat for a few minutes and then add the saffron, wine and
fish broth. Bring to a boil and reduce to a third of the original liquid.
Blanch the tomatoes for 1 minute. Peel and dice them.
Chop the fennel leaves.
Dissolve the corn flour in the Pernod and pour into the saucepan.
Cook for another 2 minutes until the sauce thickens. Whisk in the
cold butter, tomatoes and fennel leaves. Season with salt and
pepper and keep warm.
Bring the court bouillon to a boil and add lobsters. Boil for
10-12 minutes.
Remove the lobsters from the broth. Remove the head using a knife
and pull the tail out of the shell.
Pour the fennel stew into shallow bowls and top with lobster meat.
Garnish with fennel leaves and serve immediately.

Cod-Stuffed Cabbage Rolls

12 Savoy cabbage leaves
salt
juice of 1 lemon
4 tbsps extra-virgin olive oil
1 garlic clove
12.5 oz (350 g) cod, chopped
1/2 cup (120 ml) white wine
thyme
white pepper
2 shallots, minced
2 carrots, peeled and julienned
2 zucchini, green part only,
 julienned
5 tbsps breadcrumbs
3 tbsps extra-virgin olive oil
sea salt

406

Preparation time 25 minutes
Cooking time 20 minutes
Wine *Chardonnay del Piave*

Blanch the cabbage leaves in salted water with lemon juice. Remove from heat and dry on a kitchen towel. Cut away the centre stalk leaving the leaf intact.

Heat half the oil in a frying pan with the garlic. Add the cod and sauté for a few minutes. Add the wine. Remove from heat and let cool.

Mince the cod and season with thyme and white pepper. Spread the mixture over the cabbage leaves.

Cook the shallots in a frying pan with a little water and salt until soft. Place a few slices of carrots and zucchini on each cabbage leaf and top with a small spoonful of shallots. Roll up the cabbage leaves and place in an oiled baking dish.

Sprinkle with sea salt and breadcrumbs and drizzle with remaining 3 tablespoons of oil.

Broil for 10 minutes or until golden-brown. Serve immediately.

Swordfish Fillets with Pink Grapefruit

Note *Grapefruit is native to India and was introduced to Italy by way of the United States. Grapefruit can be used in both sweet and savoury foods.*

Preparation time 5 minutes
Cooking time 15 minutes
Wine *Friuli Collio Sauvignon*
♟

1 lb (450 g) swordfish fillets
lemon thyme, minced
salt
white pepper
3 tbsps extra-virgin olive oil
1 pink grapefruit
2 garlic cloves, smashed
black pepper

Preheat oven to 400°F (200°C).
Season the fish with lemon thyme, salt, white pepper and olive oil. Refrigerate.
Peel the grapefruit and remove pith and membranes to create segments.
Place the smashed garlic cloves in the bottom of an oiled baking dish. Carefully place the fish fillets in the baking dish and then top with the grapefruit segments. Drizzle with olive oil and season with ground black pepper. Cover with aluminum foil and cut out small holes in the top of the foil.
Bake for 15 minutes. Serve immediately.

Sautéed Salmon in Pinot Bianco

Preparation time 20 minutes
Cooking time 20 minutes
Wine *Alto Adige Pinot Bianco
Riserva*

1.25 lb (550 g) salmon fillet
salt and pepper
dill
1 tsp pink peppercorns
4 fennel bulbs
juice of 1 lemon
3/4 cup (4 oz or 120 g)
 breadcrumbs
1 egg
2 tbsps extra-virgin olive oil
1 tbsp plain flour
3 tbsps butter
3/4 cup (180 ml) Pinot Bianco

Preheat oven to 400°F (200°C).
Wash the salmon and cut it into 4 pieces. Season with salt, pepper, dill and pink peppercorns. Cover and refrigerate.
Quarter the fennel bulbs and steam them over water with lemon juice. Remove from heat when tender, and let cool.
Mix the breadcrumbs and egg. Coat the fennel with the breadcrumb mixture and season with salt. Place the fennel in a baking dish and drizzle with olive oil. Bake for 10 minutes.
Meanwhile, dust the salmon with flour. Heat the butter in a frying pan and add the salmon. Sauté for a few minutes and then add the wine. Cook over low heat until the salmon is cooked and the wine reduced. Serve with the gratinéed fennel.

Calamaretti with Black-Eyed Peas

Preparation time 15 minutes
Cooking time 35 minutes
Wine *Ribolla Gialla*

1 cup (7 oz or 200 g) black-eyed
 peas
2 garlic cloves
1 rosemary sprig
4.5 oz (130 g) very small squid
4 tbsps extra-virgin olive oil
6 cherry tomatoes, halved
salt and pepper
mixed herbs for fish

Boil the black-eyed peas with
1 garlic clove and rosemary
sprig until tender. Drain and set
aside.
Wash the squid and remove the
eye and internal bone.
Heat oil in a frying pan and add
1 garlic clove. Add tomatoes
and season with salt and
pepper. Sauté for a few minutes
and then add the black-eyed
peas and a little hot water.
Transfer to 4 serving bowls.
Season the squid with salt and
herbs. Sauté in a non-stick
frying pan for a few seconds.
Drizzle with olive oil and serve
immediately.

Salmon and Lettuce Parcels

Preparation time 20 minutes
Cooking time 15 minutes
Wine *Etna Bianco*

1 lb (500 g) salmon fillet
1 head butter lettuce
7 oz (200 g) rice tagliolini
 or vermicelli
2 tbsps extra-virgin olive oil
zest of 1 lemon
salt and pepper

Preheat oven to 375°F (190°C).
Wash the salmon and cut it into
4 pieces.
Blanch the lettuce leaves.
Boil the rice tagliolini until al dente
and drain. Rinse with cold water.
Brush the salmon with oil and
season with lemon zest, salt and
pepper. Wrap each salmon piece
in 1 lettuce leaf to make a closed
package.
Divide the tagliolini into
4 portions. Lay the tagliolini out
to form 4 rectangular sheets.
Wrap each salmon package in
the tagliolini and cut away the
excess pasta. Place on a baking
sheet and bake for 15 minutes.
Serve immediately.

Egg Steamers with Squash

Preparation time 15 minutes
Cooking time 10 minutes
Wine *Castel del Monte Rosato*

**4 tbsps extra-virgin olive oil
1 shallot, minced
1 sprig rosemary
1/4 Kabocha squash, cubed
1/2 cup (120 ml) vegetable broth
salt and pepper
4 eggs
chives, minced**

410

Heat 2 tablespoons oil in a saucepan and sauté the shallot. Add the rosemary. Add squash and broth and cook, covered, for 15 minutes. Season with salt and pepper
Use the rest of the oil to oil 4 coffee cups. Break 1 egg into each one. Cover with plastic wrap and steam in a steaming basket for 7 minutes.
When cooked, run a knife around the edge to loosen and serve with the squash, garnished with chives.

Doge's Omelette

Preparation time 10 minutes
Cooking time 10 minutes
Wine *San Severo Bianco*

3½ tbsps butter
1 large leek, trimmed and thinly
 sliced
3 cups (3.5 oz or 100 g) spinach,
 shredded
3.5 oz (100 g) winter squash,
 thinly sliced
salt and pepper
4 eggs
3.5 oz (100 g) Parmesan, shaved

411

Heat the butter in a frying pan and sauté the leek. Add the spinach
and squash and cook for a few minutes, seasoning with salt and
pepper.
Break the eggs in a bowl and beat lightly with a little salt and
pepper, then add to the pan with the vegetables and stir.
Add the Parmesan, and when the omelette starts to firm, take a
fork and gently separate it from the edge of the pan. Then fold the
omelette over in half.
Serve immediately on a serving plate and divide into 4 portions at
the table.

Polenta Pizza with Greens
(Molise)

Note *In Abruzzo this dish is known as* pizza e fuje, *pizza and leaves in the local dialect. Traditionally it is cooked on a grill over an open fire, though it can also be prepared in the oven.*

Preparation time 15 minutes
Cooking time 1 hour
Wine *Trebbiano del Molise*

salt
1¼ cup (7 oz or 200 g) polenta cornmeal
7 oz (200 g) mixed wild greens (chicory, chard, dandelion, borage)
3 tbsps extra-virgin olive oil
1 garlic clove, minced

412

Prepare a grill or barbecue.
Bring a pot of salted water to the boil and slowly whisk in the cornmeal, stirring continuously to avoid lumps forming. Cook for around 40 minutes, stirring often, then pour into a baking dish and spread to make an even layer. Let cool.
Remove the polenta from the dish and grill on the barbecue for around 45 minutes.
Meanwhile boil the greens in lightly salted water. Heat the oil in a large frying pan and sauté the garlic, and when the greens are tender, drain with a slotted spoon directly into the pan. Stir and cook for a couple of minutes.
Remove the polenta from the heat, and top with the greens. Slice and serve hot.

Valle d'Aosta-Style Polenta

Preparation time 20 minutes
Cooking time 45 minutes
Wine *Valle d'Aosta Arnad-Montjovet*

4 cups (1 l) water
salt
3 cups (1 lb or 500 g)
 polenta cornmeal
3/4 cup (7 oz or 200 g) butter,
 melted
10.5 oz (300 g) fontina cheese

Preheat oven to 400°F (200°C).
Bring the water to a boil with
a little salt, then whisk in the
polenta, stirring with a wooden
spoon. Continue cooking,
stirring constantly, until the
polenta pulls away from the
sides of the pot. The polenta
should not be too dry; add
more water if necessary.
Butter a baking dish and pour
in half of the polenta. Lay slices
of fontina on top, cover with
the rest of the polenta then
pour over the melted butter. If
desired, top with a few more
slices of fontina.
Bake for a few minutes until the
cheese melts and serve hot.

Fonduta
(VALLE D'AOSTA)

Preparation time 10 minutes
Cooking time 40 minutes
Wine *Valle d'Aosta Chambave Rosso*

14 oz (400 g) fontina cheese
1 garlic clove, smashed
3/4 cup (180 ml) milk
1 knob of butter
4 egg yolks
salt
crusty bread

Remove any rind from the
cheese and cut into cubes.
Place in a saucepan with the
garlic and milk. Let sit for 2
hours in a cool, dry place
(not the refrigerator).
Drain the cheese from the milk
and discard the garlic. Place in
a saucepan with the butter and
cook over a low flame, stirring
constantly. As soon as it starts
to melt, add the egg yolks
one at a time, stirring quickly.
Season with salt. When the
mixture is smooth and creamy,
pour into serving plates and
serve with the bread, toasted.

Ricotta Flan
with Radicchio Sauce

Preparation time 15 minutes
Cooking time 1 hour 15 minutes
Wine *Greco di Tufo*

FLAN
1 medium potato
 (around 7 oz or 200 g)
10.5 oz (300 g) ricotta
2 eggs
2 egg whites
salt and pepper
nutmeg, grated
1 knob of butter
3 tbsps breadcrumbs

SAUCE
2 heads Treviso radicchio
2 tbsps extra-virgin olive oil
1 tbsp plain flour
1¼ cups (300 ml) vegetable broth
salt and pepper

414

Preheat oven to 350°F (180°C).
Boil the potato, drain, peel and pass through a food mill together
with the ricotta. Place in a bowl and mix in the eggs. Beat the egg
whites to soft peaks and fold into the potato mixture. Season with
salt, pepper and nutmeg.
Butter 6 individual aluminum moulds and coat with breadcrumbs.
Fill with the potato mixture and bake for 20 minutes.
Cut the radicchio into strips. Heat the oil in a saucepan and sauté
the radicchio for 2-3 minutes. Sprinkle with flour, stir, add the
broth, salt and pepper and cook for 10 minutes. Puree the sauce
with an immersion blender and adjust the seasoning.
Serve the flan very hot together with the radicchio sauce.
If desired, garnish with radicchio leaves whole or cut into strips.

Sausage and Greens Pizza

Preparation time 20 minutes
Cooking time 25 minutes
Beer *English Pale Ale*

🍳

1 bunch bitter greens
 (turnip tops, broccoli rabe)
2 Neapolitan sausages
3 tbsps extra-virgin olive oil
2 garlic cloves, crushed
1/2 dried red chilli pepper,
 crumbled
salt and pepper
10.5 oz (300 g) pizza dough
 (see p. 1093)

415

Preheat oven to 400°F (200°C).
Remove the tough stalks from the greens. Wash the leaves well,
drain without drying completely, and set aside.
Heat a frying pan with a little water and boil the sausages, pricked
with a fork, for around 5 minutes to remove some of the fat.
Heat the oil in another frying pan and sauté the garlic and chilli.
Add the wet greens and cover. Cook for 5 minutes, stirring a
couple of times.
Cut the sausages in half lengthwise and place in the middle
of the greens. Season with salt and pepper and cook for another
8 minutes.
Roll the dough out thickly. Top with the greens and crumble the
sausage meat over them. Bake for around 12 minutes and serve
hot.

Polenta with Fontina

Preparation time 30 minutes
Cooking time 30 minutes
Wine *Trentino Marzemino*

5 cups (1.25 l) water
salt
2 cups (12.5 oz or 350 g)
polenta cornmeal
7 oz (200 g) fontina cheese,
 sliced
4 tbsps grated Parmesan
4-5 basil leaves

Preheat oven to 425° F (220°C).
Bring the water to a boil in a saucepan with some salt. Whisk in
the polenta, stirring constantly to avoid lumps forming. Cook for
around 20 minutes.
Pour the polenta onto a dampened wooden board and smooth out
the surface with a spatula until the polenta layer is 1/3 inch
(1 cm) thick. Use a cookie cutter to cut out polenta circles, then
cut each circle in half.
Alternate layers of polenta and fontina in a buttered baking dish
and press down slightly to compact them. Top with Parmesan.
Bake for around 15 minutes.
Finish on broil for a few minutes to brown.
Sprinkle with basil leaves and serve hot.

416

Potato and Chicory Bakes

Preparation time 20 minutes
Cooking time 30 minutes
Wine *Greco di Tufo*

3 yellow-fleshed potatoes
1 bunch catalogna chicory
2 tbsps extra-virgin olive oil
1/2 yellow onion, sliced
7 oz (200 g) mozzarella, cubed
2 tbsps breadcrumbs
1 tbsp gomasio (sesame salt)

Preheat oven to 400°F (200°C).
Boil the potatoes, unpeeled.
Blanch the catalogna for a few
minutes in boiling water. Drain,
squeeze out excess water and
chop finely.
Heat the oil and sauté the onion
for 5 minutes.
Peel the potatoes and mash
them with a fork, then add the
onion and catalogna. Mix in the
mozzarella.
Mix together the breadcrumbs
and gomasio and coat paper
baking cups with the mixture.
Pour in the vegetable mixture,
sprinkle with breadcrumbs and
bake for 15 minutes. Serve
warm.

Tomini with Almonds

Preparation time 10 minutes
Cooking time 20 minutes
Wine *Ribolla Gialla*

2 tbsps extra-virgin olive oil
1 shallot, minced
1/4 Savoy cabbage, julienned
salt and pepper
4 fresh tomini cheeses
2 tbsps sliced almonds

Preheat a grill or broiler.
Heat the oil in a frying pan,
sauté the shallot briefly then add
the cabbage and cook for 20
minutes over moderate heat.
Season with salt and pepper.
Grill or broil the tomini until they
are hot through and slightly
browned.
Toast the almonds in a non-stick
pan for a few minutes.
Serve the tomini over the
sautéed cabbage, topped with
the toasted almonds.

Fennel with Chickpea Puree

Preparation time 35 minutes
Cooking time 2 hours
Wine *Terlaner*

1 cup (7 oz or 200 g)
 dried chickpeas
1 bay leaf
2 garlic cloves
6 fennel bulbs
1 tbsp tahini
salt and pepper
thyme
4 tbsps extra-virgin olive oil
2½ tbsps sesame seeds

418

Soak the chickpeas overnight, then boil in water with the bay leaf
and 1 garlic clove for 50 minutes.
Preheat oven to 350°F (180°C).
Puree the chickpeas in a food processor, using some of the
cooking water, to obtain a thick cream. Add tahini, salt and
pepper.
Cut the fennel bulbs in half and remove and reserve the green
leaves. Boil the bulbs until tender then set to dry on a clean
kitchen towel. Carefully scoop out the inside using a teaspoon.
Finely chop the scooped-out fennel and mix with the chickpea
puree. Use this mixture to fill the hollow fennel halves. Place in
an oiled baking dish and surround with thyme, fennel leaves, the
remaining garlic clove and a drizzle of oil. Sprinkle with sesame
seeds and bake for 10-15 minutes. Serve hot or warm.

Cardoon Gratin

Preparation time 20 minutes
Cooking time 2 hours 30 minutes
Wine *Trebbiano d'Abruzzo*

1 cardoon
1 lemon
2 tbsps plain flour
salt
4 cups (1 l) water
2 tbsps extra-virgin olive oil
1½ cups (350 ml) milk
3 tbsps grated Parmesan
3 tbsps butter

Clean the cardoon, removing the tough end of the stalks and the fibers. Cut into pieces and rub with 1/2 the lemon to stop discolouring.
Mix the flour with a little water in a saucepan, add the juice of the remaining lemon, a pinch of salt, the water and the cardoon pieces. Cook, covered, over low heat for around 2 hours. Preheat oven to 350°F (180°C). Oil a baking dish. Drain the cardoons and place in the dish. Add milk, Parmesan and pieces of butter. Bake for around 30 minutes, until the surface is well-browned.

Broccoli with Anchovies

Preparation time 10 minutes
Cooking time 15 minutes
Wine *Bianco dei Castelli Romani*

1 head romanesco broccoli
 (around 1.3 lb or 600 g)
salt and pepper
4 tbsps extra-virgin olive oil
2 garlic cloves, smashed
4 anchovy fillets in oil
1 tbsp minced parsley
3/4 cup (3.5 oz or 100 g)
 pitted black olives

Cut the broccoli into florets and boil in salted water until al dente. Drain and place in a bowl.
Heat the oil in a saucepan with the garlic and anchovies, stirring to dissolve them. Add parsley and olives. Remove garlic, sprinkle with pepper and continue cooking, stirring constantly.
Toss the broccoli with the olives, adjust the salt and let sit a few minutes before serving.

Cannellini Beans with Sautéed Greens

Note *Radicchio is a kind of chicory, with red, white-veined leaves. The most common variety is round, with tightly packed leaves, while the Treviso variety is elongated and resembles a head of endive.*

420

Preparation time 40 minutes
Cooking time 2 hours 20 minutes
Wine *Bardolino Chiaretto*

1 cup (7 oz or 200 g)
 dried cannellini beans
salt and pepper
1 bay leaf
1 garlic clove
1 celery stalk
4 tbsps extra-virgin olive oil
1 shallot, minced
1/2 head lettuce, shredded
1 head endive, shredded
1 head Treviso radicchio, shredded
2 bunches arugula, shredded
2 tbsps balsamic vinegar

Soak the beans for 12 hours. Boil until tender in lightly salted water with the bay leaf and garlic clove.
Remove the fibers from the celery and cut into 1-inch (2½ cm) pieces. Blanch in boiling salted water for 3-4 minutes, drain and set aside.
Heat 2 tablespoons oil in a non-stick pan with the shallot. Add the lettuce, endive, radicchio and arugula and sauté over high heat. Season with salt and pepper. Add the beans and celery. Let cook for a few minutes, then add the balsamic vinegar and some pepper. Serve hot, drizzled with the remaining oil.

Roasted Pepper
and Potato Tartlets

Preparation time 15 minutes
Cooking time 30 minutes
Wine *Sicilia Chardonnay*

2 small yellow-fleshed potatoes
1 red bell pepper
3 tbsps extra-virgin olive oil
salt and pepper
thyme
2 sheets phyllo dough
2 tbsps butter, melted

Preheat oven to 400°F (200°C).

Boil the potatoes, unpeeled, until the center is tender. Drain and let cool.

Meanwhile cut the pepper in half, remove the seeds and white parts, brush with a little oil and roast in the oven for 5 minutes on each side. Seal in a plastic bag and let steam for about 10 minutes, then peel.

Peel the potatoes and place in a food processor with the peppers, salt, pepper and thyme leaves. Add the remaining oil and blend to a smooth cream.

Roll out the phyllo dough, place 1 sheet on top of the other, brush with melted butter and sprinkle with a little salt. Cut out circles and place them in 8 individual aluminium or stainless steel moulds. Bake for about 5 minutes then let cool. Unmould and fill with the potato and pepper cream. Garnish as desired and serve.

Cauliflower Rissoles

Preparation time 10 minutes
Cooking time 1 hour
Wine *Alto Adige Pinot Bianco*

**1 cauliflower
salt and pepper
1 egg
4 tbsps grated Parmesan
parsley, minced
breadcrumbs
extra-virgin olive oil**

422

Preheat oven to 400°F (200°C).
Cut the cauliflower into florets, discarding the hard stalk. Boil in
salted water for 10 minutes. Place in a bowl and mash with a fork.
Stir in egg, Parmesan and parsley and enough breadcrumbs to
make a fairly dry mixture. Season with salt and pepper.
Oil a baking sheet and sprinkle with breadcrumbs. Form balls
with the cauliflower mixture, set on the baking sheet and bake for
around 35 minutes until they are golden. Serve hot, with a mixed
salad if desired.

Note *Choose a cauliflower wich is firm, which compact florets
and green (not yellow) leaves. Cauliflower is high in fiber, vitamins
(particularly C) and minerals and also contains antioxidants.*

Mixed Vegetables with Curry

Preparation time 10 minutes
Cooking time 20 minutes
Wine *Prosecco di Conegliano Brut*

2 potatoes, cubed
3 carrots, sliced
4 asparagus spears, sliced
2 tbsps extra-virgin olive oil
1 shallot, minced
3 zucchini, sliced
4-5 mushrooms, sliced
1/2 cup (120 ml) vegetable broth
salt and pepper
1 tsp curry powder

Blanch the potatoes, carrots and asparagus for 4 minutes in boiling water.
Heat the oil in a saucepan and sauté the minced shallot until soft. Add the blanched potatoes, carrots and asparagus and the zucchini and mushrooms and sauté briefly. Add broth and adjust salt and pepper. Add curry and continue cooking until vegetables are tender. Serve hot, accompanied with pilaf rice if desired.

Brussels Sprout Gratin

Preparation time 15 minutes
Cooking time 18 minutes
Wine *Breganze Pinot Grigio*

10.5 oz (300 g) Brussels sprouts
2 tbsps extra virgin olive oil
4 tbsps grated Parmesan
salt and pepper
3.5 oz (100 g) fontina cheese, thinly sliced
1/3 cup (1 oz or 30 g) walnuts, coarsely chopped

Preheat oven to 350°F (180°C). Boil the Brussels sprouts for 7-8 minutes, drain and toss with oil, Parmesan and a little salt and pepper. Place in a ceramic baking dish. Top with slices of fontina and sprinkle with walnuts
Switch to the broiler setting and bake for around 10 minutes, until the fontina melts. Serve immediately.

Note *Brussels sprouts are a member of the cabbage family and are high in vitamins A and C and a good source of iron.*

423

Cardoons alla Parmigana

Preparation time 15 minutes
Cooking time 25 minutes
Wine *Marino Superiore*

424

1.75 lb (800 g) cardoons, cut into
 large pieces
2 tbsps plain flour
8 tbsps extra-virgin olive oil
juice of ½ lemon
salt and pepper
1 egg, beaten
sunflower oil
1¼ cups (300 ml) tomato sauce
 (see p. 1099)
3 tbsps butter, melted
1 cup (3.5 oz or 100 g)
 grated Parmesan
7 oz (200 g) mozzarella, sliced

Preheat oven to 350°F (180°C).
Place the cardoons in a saucepan with 1 tablespoon flour, a drizzle
of oil, the lemon juice and a pinch of salt and cover with cold
water. Bring to a boil and cook until tender. Drain, dry, dust with
flour and dip in beaten egg.
Heat the sunflower oil in a frying pan and fry the cardoons.
Mix the tomato sauce with melted butter and adjust salt and
pepper.
Lay a layer of cardoons in a baking dish, top with half of the
tomato sauce, half of the Parmesan and all the mozzarella. Top
with the rest of cardoons and finish with tomato and Parmesan.
Bake for around 20 minutes until golden on top.

Green Bean and Carrot Flan

Preparation time 20 minutes
Cooking time 1 hour
Wine *Alto Adige Pinot Bianco*

5 tbsps butter
6½ tbsps plain flour
1¾ cups (400 ml) milk
salt and pepper
1.5 lb (700 g) green beans,
 chopped
3 large carrots, chopped
4 eggs, separated
5.5 oz (150 g) Castelmagno
cheese, grated

425

Preheat oven to 350°F (180°C).
Melt 3 tablespoons of butter in a saucepan. Stir in the flour. As
soon the mixture starts to bubble add the milk and little salt and
continue cooking, whisking constantly, until thickened. Remove the
béchamel from the heat and let cool.
Boil the beans and carrots until al dente. Drain and reserve 2
handfuls of beans. Lay the rest of the beans in a ring mould. Puree
the reserved beans and carrots and sauté the puree in a frying
pan with the remaining butter for 5 minutes. Season with salt and
pepper.
Mix the egg yolks into the béchamel. Beat the egg whites into soft
peaks. Mix the vegetable puree and cheese into the béchamel and
fold in the egg whites. Pour into the ring mould, place in a baking
dish half-full of water and bake for 45 minutes. Serve warm.

Potato Skewers
with Gorgonzola Sauce

Preparation time 10 minutes
Cooking time 20 minutes
Wine *Alto Adige Terlaner*

20 new potatoes
salt and pepper
1 onion
3 tbsps milk
5.5 oz (150 g) strong Gorgonzola,
 chopped
nutmeg, grated
1 knob of butter

Boil the potatoes in salted water and drain as soon as the center
is tender, but still firm. Cool in ice water.
Quarter the onion and separate the layers. Blanch for 1 minute,
drain and dry.
Thread the potatoes on wooden skewers, alternating with onion
pieces. Grill for 5 minutes on each side on a cast-iron grill pan over
moderate heat, season with salt and pepper and place on serving
plates.
Meanwhile heat the milk until warm, add Gorgonzola and nutmeg
and remove from the heat. Stir with a fork until the cheese has
melted. Blend in a blender with the butter and pour over the
skewers.

426

Steamed Vegetables

Preparation time 10 minutes
Cooking time 20 minutes
Wine *Alto Adige Sauvignon*

♟

12.5 oz (350 g) winter squash,
 cubed
7 oz (200 g) Brussels sprouts
4 tbsps extra-virgin olive oil
2 fennel bulbs, cut into wedges
2 leeks, cut into 1½-inch
 (3-4 cm) pieces
2 carrots, cut into sticks
juice of 1 lemon
chives, chopped
salt and pepper

Place all the vegetables in a
large steaming basket and
steam, removing the vegetables
as they become tender.
Whisk the lemon juice with the
oil, pinches of salt and pepper
and the chives. Drizzle the
vegetables with the dressing
and serve hot.

Prawn and White Bean Salad

Preparation time 25 minutes
Cooking time 3 minutes
Wine *Roero Arneis*

♟

14 oz (400 g) shelled prawns
8 tbsps extra-virgin olive oil
salt and freshly ground pepper
1⅓ cups (9 oz or 250 g)
 large white beans, cooked
2 bunches arugula
3 spring onions, sliced
2 tbsps balsamic vinegar

427

Toss the prawns with a little oil,
salt and pepper. Heat a
non-stick frying pan and sauté
the prawns for 2-3 minutes.
Add the beans and adjust salt
and pepper to taste.
Tear the arugula into pieces
and arrange on serving plates.
Top with prawns and beans,
spring onion, drizzles of oil and
vinegar, salt and freshly ground
pepper.

Lettuce Soufflés
with Crescenza Sauce

Preparation time 20 minutes
Cooking time 40 minutes
Wine *Colli Piacentini*
Pinot Grigio

SOUFFLÉS
1 head lettuce
3 eggs, separated
1 tbsp grated Parmesan
9 oz (250 g) béchamel
 (see p. 1096)
1 knob of butter
breadcrumbs

SAUCE
2 tbsps milk
7 oz (200 g) crescenza cheese,
 chopped
2 oz (50 g) taleggio cheese,
 chopped
salt and white pepper

GARNISH
lettuce leaves

428

Preheat oven to 350°F (180°C).
Boil the lettuce for 10 minutes, drain and cool. Squeeze out excess water and blend in a food processor with the egg yolks. Pour into a bowl and add Parmesan and béchamel.
Beat the egg whites into stiff peaks and fold into the lettuce mixture.
Butter individual moulds, sprinkle with breadcrumbs and pour in the batter. Place in a baking dish half-filled with water and bake for 30 minutes.
Place the milk and cheeses in a saucepan with salt and pepper and cook over medium heat for 5 minutes, stirring constantly, until the cheese melts.
Remove the soufflés from the oven and serve with the cheese sauce. Garnish with lettuce leaves.

Truffled Artichoke Flan

Preparation time 30 minutes
Cooking time 40 minutes
Wine *Frascati*

FLAN
6 baby artichokes
juice of 1 lemon
1 knob of butter
1 garlic clove
salt and pepper
3 eggs
4 tbsps grated Parmesan
3/4 cup plus 1 tbsp (200 ml) milk

7 tbsps heavy cream
2 oz (50 g) truffle cream
nutmeg, grated
parsley and marjoram, chopped

SAUCE
4 tbsps extra-virgin olive oil
1 shallot, sliced
2 potatoes, diced
2 tbsps grated Parmesan
salt and pepper
4-5 drops truffle oil

429

Preheat oven to 350°F (180°C).
Trim and slice the artichokes and immerse in a bowl of water and lemon juice.
Melt the butter with the garlic clove, add the drained artichoke slices and salt and sauté for a few minutes. Add a little water and cook for 10-15 minutes. Remove the garlic and puree the artichokes. Sieve the puree into a bowl and add the eggs, Parmesan, milk, cream, truffle cream, salt, pepper and nutmeg. Add parsley and marjoram and pour the mixture into a rectangular mould. Bake for 35-40 minutes.
Heat the oil in a saucepan and sauté the shallot and potatoes briefly. Cover with water, season with salt and cook, covered, until potatoes are tender. Drain and puree with the Parmesan, salt, pepper and truffle oil, adding a little cooking water if necessary. Serve the flan hot with the potato sauce.

Spinach-Stuffed Onions

Preparation time 20 minutes
Cooking time 20 minutes
Wine *Lambrusco di Sorbara*

1.3 lb (600 g) onions
salt and pepper
2 tbsps extra-virgin olive oil
2 oz (60 g) pancetta,
  cut into strips
9 oz (250 g) baby spinach,
  chopped
3 tbsps butter
5 tbsps grated Parmesan

Preheat oven to 350°F (180°C).
Peel the onions, cut in half and boil in lightly salted water until al dente. Drain and set aside.
Brown the pancetta in a frying pan with the oil. Add the spinach and season with a little salt and pepper. Cook for 3-4 minutes.
Scoop out some of the insides of the onion halves. Butter a baking sheet with half of the butter and lay the onion halves on it. Fill them with the spinach and top with Parmesan and some pieces of butter.
Bake for 5-10 minutes. Serve immediately.

Bitter Greens with Fonduta

Preparation time 25 minutes
Cooking time 15 minutes
Wine *Lagrein Rosato*

1.3 lb (600 g) broccoli rabe
 or turnip tops
2/3 cup (150 ml) milk
4 oz (120 g) Gruyère cheese,
 grated
4 oz (120 g) Emmenthal cheese,
 grated
salt
ground cinnamon

Steam the greens until tender.
Heat the milk in a non-stick pan
and add the cheeses, stirring
constantly, until the sauce
is smooth. Add extra milk if
necessary.
Lightly salt the greens and
arrange on a serving plate. Just
before serving pour over the
cheese sauce, sprinkle with
cinnamon and serve.

Chard Flan with Pine Nuts

Preparation time 10 minutes
Cooking time 40 minutes
Wine *Cirò Rosato*

1.75 lb (800 g) Swiss chard
nutmeg, grated
salt and pepper
3/4 cup (2.5 oz or 70 g)
 grated Parmesan
2 eggs
2 tbsps butter
1/2 cup (3 oz or 80 g) pine nuts

Preheat oven to 350°F (180°C).
Blanch the chard in a little
boiling water, with no salt.
Drain, squeeze out excess
water and puree. Mix with
Parmesan, puree again, and
season to taste with nutmeg,
salt and pepper. Mix in the
eggs.
Butter a mould and sprinkle the
bottom with pine nuts. Pour in
the chard mixture and smooth
the surface with a spoon. Bake
for 15 minutes, turning a few
times so it cooks evenly. Serve
warm.

New Potatoes with Herb Salt

Preparation time 10 minutes
Cooking time 20 minutes
Wine *Alto Adige Santa Maddalena*

sunflower oil
1 lb (500 g) new potatoes
2 sprigs rosemary
2 sprigs sage
2 sprigs thyme
coarse salt
freshly ground pepper

Preheat oven to 400°F (200°C). Heat the sunflower oil in a wide frying pan and fry the potatoes until they are crunchy outside. Drain and place in a baking dish.
Mince the rosemary, sage and thyme together and mix with 2 handfuls coarse salt. Sprinkle over the potatoes and bake for 10 minutes.
Serve the potatoes hot with a sprinkling of freshly ground pepper.

Mini Potato and Spinach Soufflés

Preparation time 30 minutes
Cooking time 25 minutes
Wine *Alto Adige Schiava*

2 small potatoes (10.5 oz 300 g)
7 oz (200 g) spinach
2 tbsps butter
3 eggs, separated
salt and pepper
nutmeg, grated
2 oz (50 g) Gruyère cheese, diced

Preheat oven to 350°F (180°C). Boil the potatoes, peel and mash them.
Blanch the spinach in a little water. Drain, squeeze out excess water, chop finely and stir into the mashed potatoes. Add butter, egg yolks, salt, pepper, a little nutmeg and the cheese. Beat 2 egg whites to stiff peaks and fold into the mixture.
Fill individual moulds 2/3-full and bake for 20-25 minutes.

432

Potato, Squash and Cabbage Roll with Walnut-Herb Sauce

Preparation time 20 minutes
Cooking time 2 hours
Wine *Gambellara*

9 oz (250 g) winter squash, sliced
2 small (10.5 oz or 300 g) starchy potatoes
5-6 Savoy cabbage leaves
2 eggs
4 tbsps plain flour
2 tbsps grated Parmesan
salt and pepper
ground cinnamon
parsley, marjoram and thyme, chopped
4 tbsps extra-virgin olive oil
1/3 cup (1 oz or 30 g) walnuts

Preheat oven to 350°F (180°C).
Lay the squash on a baking sheet and cover with aluminum foil. Bake for 25 minutes. Pass half through a food mill and cut the rest into cubes.
Boil, peel and mash the potatoes.
Blanch the cabbage leaves for a few minutes and let dry on a clean kitchen towel.
Mix the mashed potatoes and pureed squash together with the eggs, flour, Parmesan, salt, pepper and a pinch of cinnamon. Stir in the squash cubes.
Lay the cabbage leaves in a single layer on a sheet of parchment paper. Spread the potato and squash mixture over them and roll up the paper. Seal the ends and tie the whole roll with kitchen string. Bake for 40 minutes.
Meanwhile puree the herbs with the oil, walnuts, salt and a little cold water.
Remove the roll from the oven and let cool. Slice and serve with walnut-herb sauce.

Smoked Herring and Potato Salad

Preparation time 10 minutes
Cooking time 20 minutes
Wine *Alto Adige Terlaner*

3 yellow-fleshed potatoes
salt and pepper
20 green beans
2 carrots, peeled and sliced
5 snow peas
1 tbsp vinegar
2 tbsps extra-virgin olive oil
1 tbsp tahini
parsley, minced
1 red onion, thinly sliced
2 smoked herring fillets
   (around 7 oz or 200 g), chopped

434

Place the potatoes in cold, salted water and bring to a boil. Cook until tender in the center then drain and cool.

Meanwhile boil the green beans, snow peas and carrots. Drain and immerse in ice water to stop the cooking and keep the colours bright.

Whisk the vinegar with the oil, tahini and parsley.

Peel the potatoes and cut into cubes.

Arrange the potatoes, green beans, snow peas, carrots and onion with the herring on serving plates and drizzle with sesame dressing.

Baked Winter Vegetables with Foie Gras

Preparation time 20 minutes
Cooking time 25 minutes
Wine *Friuli Collio Sauvignon*
♟

4 tbsps extra-virgin olive oil
1 onion, julienned
1 garlic clove
2 carrots, peeled and diced
2 new potatoes, peeled and diced
1/4 green-skinned winter
 squash, diced
salt and pepper
1/4 cauliflower, cut into florets
1 head broccoli, cut into florets
1 egg
1 tbsp breadcrumbs
1.5 oz (40 g) foie gras terrine
4 cumin crackers

435

Preheat oven to 350°F (180°C).
Heat the oil in a saucepan and sauté the onion and unpeeled garlic. Add carrots and potatoes and cook for 3-4 minutes. Add squash and season with salt and pepper.
Blanch the cauliflower and broccoli in salted water until al dente. As soon as the squash is cooked, add the cauliflower and broccoli to the rest of the vegetables. Let cool, then stir in the egg and breadcrumbs.
In a rectangular mould in layer the vegetables to a height of 1 inch (2 centimeters). Bake for 15 minutes and cut into squares. Serve with squares of foie gras and crackers.

Mediterranean Cauliflower Salad

Preparation time 15 minutes
Cooking time 6 minutes
Wine *Vermentino di Gallura*

1 cauliflower, cut into florets
2 tomatoes, peeled
10 spicy green olives, pitted
 and chopped
juice of 1 lemon
salt
parsley, minced
3 tbsps extra-virgin olive oil
8 anchovy fillets in vinegar

Steam the cauliflower florets
for 6 minutes. Blanch the
tomatoes in boiling water. Drain
and immerse in cold water.
Drain, peel, deseed and cut into
strips.
Mix the steamed cauliflower
florets, tomato strips and
chopped olives.
Emulsify the lemon juice, salt,
parsley and oil and pour over
cauliflower mixture. Stir well and
let sit for 30 minutes.
Serve topped with anchovy
fillets.

Brussels Sprouts with Apples

Preparation time 10 minutes
Cooking time 10 minutes
Wine *Alto Adige Gewürztraminer*

12.5 oz (350 g) Brussels sprouts
salt and pepper
2 apples
1 organic lemon
1 tbsp extra-virgin olive oil
1 bay leaf
1 tsp plain flour
1/2 cup (120 ml) white wine
1 tbsp ground cinnamon
1/4 cup (1 oz or 30 g) slivered
 almonds, toasted

Boil the Brussels sprouts in
salted water until tender.
Peel and slice the apples,
sprinkle with lemon juice, and
brown in a frying pan with the
oil and bay leaf. Dissolve the
flour in 1/2 cup (120 ml) water
and add to the apples with the
wine and pinches of salt and
pepper.
Grate the zest of half the
lemon, add to the apples
and cook for 5 minutes. Add
Brussels sprouts and cook for
a few more minutes. Serve
sprinkled with cinnamon and
toasted almonds.

436

Potato and Mushroom Bake

Preparation time 15 minutes
Cooking time 45 minutes
Wine *Friuli Collio Merlot*

4 yellow-fleshed potatoes
3 tbsps extra-virgin olive oil
rosemary
1 garlic clove, smashed
3½ cups (9 oz or 250 g)
 chopped mushrooms
salt and pepper
9 oz (250 g) mozzarella,
chopped

Preheat oven to 400°F (200°C).
Boil the potatoes and drain as
soon as the center is tender.
Cool and chop.
Heat the oil and rosemary in
a non-stick frying pan and
sauté the garlic until golden.
Add the mushrooms and
sauté, seasoning with salt and
pepper. Remove the garlic and
rosemary and add potatoes.
Pour the mushroom and potato
mixture into a baking dish and
cover with mozzarella. Bake for
15 minutes and serve.

Stuffed New Potatoes

Preparation time 20 minutes
Cooking time 25 minutes
Wine *Trentino Müller Thurgau*

20 new potatoes
salt and pepper
2 tbsps extra-virgin olive oil
5 cups (5.5 oz or 150 g) spinach
1 garlic clove, unpeeled
2 fresh porcini mushrooms
parsley and mint, minced

Preheat oven to 400°F (200°C).
Peel the potatoes and, using a
sharp paring knife, carve them
into little boat shapes, with a
cavity in the middle. Blanch in
boiling salted water for 8-10
minutes.
Heat a little oil in a frying pan and
sauté the spinach with a little salt
for 2 minutes.
Heat the rest of the oil in another
frying pan and sauté the garlic
with the mushrooms, parsley
and mint over high heat. Add the
spinach to the mushrooms and
adjust salt and pepper.
Fill the potatoes with the mixture
and bake for 10 minutes, then
broil for a few minutes.
Serve hot.

Cabbage Involtini with Emmenthal

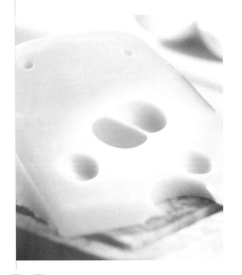

438

Preparation time 20 minutes
Cooking time 15 minutes
Wine *Lamezia Greco*

9 oz (250 g) Savoy cabbage
 leaves
salt and pepper
2 large carrots, cut into matchsticks
4 tbsps extra-virgin olive oil
1 large zucchini, julienned
3.5 oz (100 g) Emmenthal cheese
1 garlic clove
1 spring onion, sliced
2 cup (10.5 oz or 300 g) cherry
 tomatoes, quartered

Blanch the cabbage leaves in boiling salted water for 3-4 minutes and lay on a tray.
Blanch the carrot sticks in the same water as the cabbage for a couple of minutes.
Heat half the oil in a frying pan and add the zucchini, carrots, salt and pepper and sauté for 3-4 minutes.
Place a little pile of carrots and zucchini in the center of every cabbage leaf. Add 1 slice Emmenthal and roll up the leaves, fixing closed with toothpicks.
Heat the remaining oil in a saucepan and brown the garlic and spring onion. Add tomatoes, adjust salt and pepper, cook for 4-5 minutes then add the involtini. Lower the heat, cover, and cook for 10 minutes. Serve hot.

Roast Onion and Carrot Salad

Preparation time 25 minutes
Cooking time 12 minutes
Wine *Gambellara*

15 pearl onions
salt and pepper
1 tsp sugar
5 tbsps extra-virgin olive oil
2 carrots, peeled and cut into
 sticks
1 head iceberg lettuce, shredded
2 tbsps Taggiasca olives
2 tbsps preserved mushrooms
 in oil

Preheat oven to 400°F (200°C).
Blanch the onions in boiling
salted water for 3 minutes.
Drain and toss with sugar, salt
and 3 tablespoons oil. Roast
for 7-8 minutes until they start
to colour. Remove from the
oven and halve.
Soak the carrot sticks in ice
water for 5 minutes to make
them crunchy.
Compose the salad, starting
with a bed of lettuce, then
adding the roasted onions,
crunchy carrots, olives and
mushrooms. Season with
salt, pepper and oil and serve
immediately.

Potato and Fontina Strata

Preparation time 20 minutes
Cooking time 30 minutes
Wine *Valdadige Rosso*

1 lb (500 g) yellow-fleshed potatoes
salt and pepper
1 cup (250 ml) milk
7 oz (200 g) fontina cheese, sliced
1/2 cup (3.5 oz or 100 g) butter
nutmeg, grated

Preheat oven to 350°F (180°C).
Cook the potatoes for 10
minutes in boiling salted water.
Peel and slice into 1/5-inch
(1/2 cm) thick slices.
Pour a little milk into a baking
dish, then make a layer of
potatoes and a layer of cheese
slices and top with some
pieces of butter. Season with
salt, pepper and nutmeg and
continue making layers until the
ingredients have been used up.
Finish with the remaining milk.
Bake for around 20 minutes.
Serve hot.

439

Potato Croquettes with Artichokes

Preparation time 20 minutes
Cooking time 10 minutes
Wine *Bianco Valdichiana*

440

1 lb (500 g) potatoes
1 egg
5 tbsps breadcrumbs
1 cup (3.5 oz or 100 g)
 grated Parmesan
parsley, minced
salt and pepper
3 tbsps plain flour
6 tbsps extra-virgin olive oil
2 tbsps butter
2 garlic cloves, crushed
1 lb (450 g) baby artichokes
sunflower oil

Boil the potatoes and mash them. Stir in the egg, breadcrumbs,
Parmesan, parsley, salt and pepper and mix until uniform. Form
into little balls and squash slightly until they are about 1/2 inch
(1 cm) thick. Dust with flour on both sides.
Trim the hard, external leaves from the artichokes and slice thinly.
Heat the oil and butter in a frying pan and sauté the garlic. Add
the artichokes and remove the garlic. Season with salt and pepper
and sauté over medium heat for 4 minutes. Sprinkle with parsley
and remove from the heat.
Heat the sunflower oil in a frying pan and fry the potato croquettes
for 1-2 minutes, until golden. Drain on paper towels. Serve, topped
with the artichokes.

Potato and Roast Pepper Cream

Preparation time 20 minutes
Cooking time 35 minutes
Wine *Alto Adige Pinot Bianco*

2 small yellow-fleshed potatoes
2 broccoli spears
4 tbsps extra-virgin olive oil
1 spring onion, sliced
1 red bell pepper
salt and pepper
lemon thyme
4 thin slices mild provola cheese

441

Preheat oven to 425° F (220°C).
Boil the potatoes and steam the broccoli until al dente.
Heat 1 tablespoon olive oil in a saucepan and sauté the spring
onion until soft. Add the broccoli and sauté, seasoning with salt
and pepper. Blend to a puree and set aside.
Roast the pepper in the oven, under the broiler or over an open
flame, close in a plastic bag for a few minutes, then peel and
deseed.
Place the pepper, boiled potatoes, salt, pepper, remaining oil and
lemon thyme in a food processor and blend to a smooth cream.
Refrigerate.
Line a baking sheet with parchment paper and lay the provola
slices on it. Bake for about 7 minutes then remove from the oven
and cool over a rolling pin or teacup so they harden in the shape
of an arc.
Make circles of broccoli puree with a cookie cutter in the center of
serving plates, top with the provola wafer then top with potato and
pepper puree.

Carrot and Potato Rösti

Note *Carrots, the bright-orange roots of a member of the parsley family, have long been renowned for their healthiness. They are very high in vitamin A. Carrots have been part of the Mediterranean diet since the time of the Ancient Greeks, but are not so common in contemporary Italian cuisine.*

Preparation time 25 minutes
Cooking time 15 minutes
Wine *Valle d'Aosta Nus Malvoisie*

4 tbsps butter
4 small carrots, peeled and
 julienned
2 potatoes, peeled and
 julienned
salt

442

Melt a knob of butter in a non-stick frying pan.
Mix together the carrots and potatoes, take a handful of them and spread out in the pan. Let cook for 2-3 minutes each side and remove from the pan when well browned.
Repeat, always adding another knob of butter, until all the vegetables have been used up.
Salt the rösti and serve.

Sweet-and-Sour Onions

Preparation time 15 minutes
Cooking time 10 minutes
Wine *Trebbiano d'Abruzzo*

3½ tbsps butter
2 white onions, sliced
1 tbsp raisins
1 tbsp vin santo or other sweet
 wine
1 tbsp pine nuts
1 tsp white wine vinegar
salt and pepper
2 handfuls fresh spinach

Heat the butter in a frying pan
and sauté the onion over low
heat.
Soak the raisins in vin santo
and a little hot water. Drain and
add to the onions together with
the pine nuts. Add vinegar,
let evaporate then add a little
water, salt and pepper, and let
cook slowly until onions are
very soft.
Meanwhile steam the spinach
and squeeze out any excess
water. On 4 serving plates
make 4 circles of spinach with
a cookie cutter as a stencil,
then top with the onions and
serve immediately.

Fried Potato and Cabbage Skewers

Preparation time 20 minutes
Cooking time 40 minutes
Wine *Metodo Classico
Franciacorta Brut*

2 potatoes
3 tbsps extra-virgin olive oil
1 garlic clove
1/4 Savoy cabbage, julienned
salt and pepper
3 tbsps finely chopped cashews
poppy seeds
sunflower oil

443

Boil the potatoes for around 20
minutes. Drain, cool, peel and
mash.
Heat the olive oil in a saucepan
and sauté the garlic, then add
the cabbage and sauté. Add a
little water and cook until tender
but still al dente, and season
with salt and pepper to taste.
Mix the potatoes and cabbage
with the cashews, then form
little balls and thread them on
small wooden skewers. Dip
in poppy seeds and fry in hot
sunflower oil. Serve hot.

Endive and Ham Involtini with Pistachios

Preparation time 20 minutes
Cooking time 15 minutes
Wine *Roero Arneis*

1¾ cups (400 ml) vegetable broth
5 tbsps butter
1 shallot, minced
1 tbsp sugar
4 Belgian endives, halved
 lengthwise
salt and pepper
juice of 1 lemon
5 tbsps white wine
8 slices ham
8 slices mild cheese
1/4 cup (1 oz or 30 g) pistachios,
 toasted and coarsely chopped

444

Preheat oven to 350°F (180°C).
Cook the broth down until reduced to half its original volume.
Melt 2 tablespoons of butter in a frying pan and sauté the shallot,
sprinkling it with sugar. Add the endive halves, season with salt
and pepper and add lemon juice and wine. Let evaporate, then
add the reduced broth and 2 tablespoons butter and cook,
covered, over low heat for 10 minutes.
Lay the ham slices on a cutting board and top each one with
a slice of cheese and 1 endive half then roll up and place in a
buttered baking dish. Sprinkle with pistachios and drizzle over the
endive cooking liquid. Bake for 5 minutes and serve immediately.

Green Beans with Red Cabbage

Preparation time 20 minutes
Cooking time 30 minutes
Wine *Soave*

3 tbsps extra-virgin olive oil
1 garlic clove, smashed
1 large yellow-fleshed potato, diced
1/2 red cabbage, thinly sliced
vegetable broth
2 cups (7 oz or 200 g) green beans
salt

Heat the oil in a saucepan with the garlic. Remove when golden and add the potatoes and cabbage. Brown for 5 minutes then add a little broth and some salt and cook for another 20 minutes.
Steam the trimmed green beans until al dente. Cool then cut into bite-sized pieces and toss with oil and salt.
Puree the potato and cabbage, salt to taste and place in a pastry bag. Serve the beans accompanied by the puree, piped onto the plates.

Cauliflower-Filled Zucchini Rolls

Preparation time 15 minutes
Cooking time 15 minutes
Wine *Gavi*

4 large zucchini, sliced lengthways
1/2 cauliflower
salt
1 tbsp white wine vinegar
1 tsp capers, chopped
2 tbsps extra-virgin olive oil
thyme

Grill the zucchini slices on a ridged cast-iron grill pan.
Blanch the cauliflower in salted water with the vinegar until soft. Drain and puree, then stir in capers, oil and thyme.
Place a spoonful of cauliflower puree on each zucchini slice and roll up, securing with a toothpick. Grill for 1 minute. Serve warm.

445

Bean Rissoles with Spring Onions

446

Preparation time 20 minutes
Cooking time 25 minutes
Wine *Lago di Caldaro*

1 cup (7 oz or 200 g) dried
 borlotti beans
1 bay leaf
salt and pepper
3 tbsps extra-virgin olive oil
1 zucchini, minced
1 carrot, minced
1 celery stalk, minced
1/2 onion, minced
1 cup (9 oz or 250 g)
 crushed tomatoes
1 egg
3 tbsps grated Parmesan
1 tbsp minced parsley
2 spring onions, thinly sliced

Preheat oven to 350°F (180°C).
Soak the beans in cold water overnight. Boil with the bay leaf and
a pinch of salt until tender, then drain and set aside to cool.
Meanwhile heat 2 tablespoons oil and sauté the zucchini, carrot,
celery and onion for a few minutes, add the tomato, salt and
pepper and cook for 10-12 minutes.
Roughly mash the beans with the back of a fork and stir in the
egg, Parmesan and parsley. Salt and pepper to taste then form
little balls and lay on an oiled baking sheet. Bake for 15 minutes.
Soak the spring onion in cold water for 5 minutes, drain and toss
with oil and salt. Divide between the serving plates, then top with
the hot rissoles. Drizzle over the tomato sauce and serve.

Leek Gratin with Béchamel

Preparation time 15 minutes
Cooking time 40 minutes
Wine *Fiano di Avellino*

LEEKS
4 short, fat leeks
salt
1 tbsp sesame oil
5 tbsps breadcrumbs

BÉCHAMEL
2 tbsps corn oil
6½ tbsps plain flour
1¾ cups (400 ml) hot soy milk
salt
nutmeg, grated

Preheat oven to 350°F (180°C).
Trim the leeks and blanch in boiling salted water for 7-8 minutes.
Halve them lengthways.
Brush a baking dish with sesame oil and sprinkle in half the
breadcrumbs, then arrange the leek halves.
Heat the corn oil, add the flour and cook, stirring constantly, over
low heat. Remove from the heat and slowly pour in the hot soy
milk, whisking constantly. Season with salt and nutmeg and return
to the heat, cooking for 15 minutes, whisking constantly.
Pour the béchamel over the leeks, sprinkle with the remaining
breadcrumbs and bake for 15-20 minutes.

Artichoke Quiche

Preparation time 25 minutes
Cooking time 40 minutes
Wine *Bardolino Chiaretto*

448

6 medium artichokes
4 tbsps extra-virgin olive oil
1 small onion, thinly sliced
1 garlic clove, smashed
salt and pepper
parsley, minced
3 eggs
5.5 oz (150 g) fontina cheese,
 diced
1 cup (3.5 oz or 100 g) grated
 Parmesan
9 oz (250 g) puff pastry
butter

Preheat oven to 350°F (180°C).
Trim the artichokes, removing the hard outer leaves and any
choke, and slice thinly.
Heat the oil in a frying pan and sauté the onion and garlic. Add the
artichoke slices, lightly salt and pepper them, and cook for 8-10
minutes over medium heat. Stir in the parsley.
Place the artichokes in a bowl and stir in 2 eggs, fontina and
Parmesan. Season with salt and pepper and mix well.
Roll the puff pastry out to 1/5 inch (1/2 cm) thick and line a lightly
buttered pie dish. Pour in the artichoke mixture and fold the edges
of the dough towards the center. Cut the leftover dough into
1/2-inch (1 cm) wide strips and lay them diagonally across the
quiche. Beat the remaining egg and use it to brush the top of the
quiche. Bake for 30 minutes. Serve hot or warm.

Winter Vegetable Sauté

Preparation time 20 minutes
Cooking time 30 minutes
Wine *Lagrein Rosato*

2 small artichokes
1/2 cauliflower, cut into florets
salt and pepper
2 tbsps extra virgin olive oil
1 onion, minced
2 carrots, chopped
1 potato, chopped
2 fennel bulbs, cut into thin
 wedges
vegetable broth
parsley, minced

449

Trim the artichokes, removing the hard outer leaves, the stalk and
the choke, and cut into wedges.
Blanch the cauliflower in boiling salted water for a few minutes.
Heat the oil in a wide frying pan and sauté the onion. Add the
carrots and potatoes and cook for 10 minutes. Add the artichokes,
cook for 10 minutes, then add the fennel and cauliflower. Continue
cooking, adding a little broth, salt and pepper, until all the
vegetables are tender. Sprinkle with parsley, adjust salt and pepper
if necessary, and serve hot.

Endive and Leek Tart

Preparation time 45 minutes
Cooking time 45 minutes
Wine *Colli Piacentini Sauvignon*

2 tbsps butter
4 tbsps plain flour
1 cup (250 ml) hot milk
salt and pepper
3 tbsps extra-virgin olive oil
1 large leek, sliced
1 Belgian endive, sliced
1 egg
5 tbsps grated Parmesan
chives, minced
9 oz (250 g) pie crust dough
(see p. 1093)

450

Preheat oven to 350°F (180°C).
Melt the butter in a saucepan, add the flour and cook, stirring, for a few minutes. Add the hot milk and a pinch of salt and continue cooking until the béchamel becomes thick.
Heat the oil in a frying pan and brown the leek. Add the endive and sauté for 4-5 minutes. Season with salt and pepper and cook for another 10 minutes. Remove from the heat and cool slightly, then mix in the egg, Parmesan and chives. Stir in the béchamel, using a wooden spoon.
Divide the dough in 2 parts and roll them both out to a thickness of around 1/5 inch (1/2 cm). Butter and flour a pie pan and line with the dough. Fill with the endive mixture then cover with the second sheet of dough. Bake for 30 minutes. Serve hot or warm.

Mediterranean Potato Pie

Preparation time 25 minutes
Cooking time 15 minutes
Wine *Alto Adige Sylvaner*

1 lb (500 g) potatoes
4 tbsps extra-virgin olive oil
2½ tbsps minced onion
1 tbsp oregano
1/2 cup (120 ml) white wine
7 tbsps tomato puree
2 eggs
6 tbsps grated Parmesan
1/3 cup (2 oz or 50 g)
 pitted olives, sliced
salt
1 knob of butter
3 oz (80 g) scamorza cheese,
 thinly sliced

451

Preheat oven to 350°F (180°C).

Boil the potatoes, then drain, peel and mash them.

Heat the oil in a saucepan and sauté the onion. Add oregano and white wine and let evaporate. Add the tomato and cook for 3-4 minutes.

Mix the mashed potato, eggs, Parmesan, tomatoes, olives and a pinch of salt.

Butter a baking dish and pour in half the potato mixture. Spread out with a spoon. Cover with slices of scamorza and then spread over the rest of the potatoes. Sprinkle with Parmesan and pieces of butter.

Bake for around 30 minutes. Serve warm.

Cabbage and Potato Cakes

Preparation time 25 minutes
Cooking time 15 minutes
Wine *Friuli Collio Merlot*

2 yellow-fleshed potatoes
salt and pepper
1 knob of butter
1 shallot, minced
2 carrots, peeled and chopped
2 tbsps extra-virgin olive oil
1 garlic clove, unpeeled and
 smashed
1/4 Savoy cabbage, julienned
1 egg
1 tbsp grated Parmesan
1 tbsp breadcrumbs
1/2 tbsp mayonnaise
1/2 tbsp yogurt
dill, chopped

452

Boil the potatoes in salted water, and drain as soon as they are tender in the center. Peel and mash.

Melt the butter in a frying pan and sauté the shallot. Add the carrots and cook for 5 minutes, adding a little hot water and seasoning with salt and pepper.

Heat the oil in a non-stick frying pan and brown the garlic, then add the cabbage and sauté until crispy (5-6 minutes).

Add the carrots and cabbage to the mashed potatoes and mix together with the egg, Parmesan and breadcrumbs.

Using a cookie cutter form small rounds and chill in the refrigerator. Grill for 2 minutes on each side on a barbecue or a cast-iron grill pan.

Mix the mayonnaise and yogurt with the dill and serve with the potato cakes.

Cardoon Flans with Bagna Caoda Sauce

Preparation time 25 minutes
Cooking time 2 hours 20 minutes
Wine *Colli del Trasimeno Bianco*
♟ ♟

FLANS
1 lb (500 g) cardoons, cut into
 pieces
3/4 cup (200 ml) milk
6 tbsps béchamel (see p. 1096)
3 eggs, separated
1 cup (3.5 oz or 100 g) grated
 Parmesan
salt and pepper
butter
breadcrumbs

SAUCE
6 anchovies in salt
5 garlic cloves, sliced
3-4 tbsps extra-virgin olive oil
1/3 cup (80 ml) heavy
 cream

453

Boil the cardoons for 30 minutes in a mixture of water and the milk. Drain and puree in a food processor.
Preheat oven to 350°F (180°C).
Mix the béchamel, egg yolks, Parmesan and cardoons in a bowl.
Beat the egg whites into stiff peaks and fold into the béchamel mixture. Season with salt and pepper.
Butter individual moulds and sprinkle with breadcrumbs. Fill with the batter and place the moulds in a baking dish half-filled with water. Bake for 1 hour 30 minutes.
Soak the anchovies in water for 10 minutes to remove the salt. Drain and place in a small terracotta pot with the garlic and cover with oil. Cook over low heat for around 20 minutes until the mixture is creamy. Add the cream and cook for a few more minutes, stirring constantly.
Remove the cardoon flans from the oven, invert on plates and top with bagna caoda sauce. Serve immediately.

Artichokes alla Romana
(LAZIO)

Note *This dish can be enriched by adding some crumbled sausage meat to the artichoke stuffing, or some finely minced anchovies.*

Preparation time 30 minutes
Cooking time 20 minutes
Wine *Bianco Capena*

8 small globe artichokes
juice 1 lemon
1 bunch parsley
1 garlic clove
mint
salt and pepper
extra-virgin olive oil
lemon slices

454

Cut the stalks off the artichokes and trim them, removing the hard external leaves and the choke. Soak for a few minutes in water and the lemon juice.
Meanwhile mince together the parsley, garlic and a little mint. Drain the artichokes, dry and fill the insides with the parsley mixture. Close the petals and season with salt and pepper. Arrange the artichokes in a large pan and cover with a mixture of oil and water. Cook, covered, over a low heat until tender. Drain and serve cooled, garnished with mint leaves and lemon slices.

Artichokes alla Giudia
(LAZIO)

Preparation time 20 minutes
Cooking time 20 minutes
Wine *Cerveteri Bianco*

8 small globe artichokes
juice of 1 lemon
salt and pepper
extra-virgin olive oil

Cut the stalks off the artichokes and trim them, removing the hard external leaves and the choke. Soak for a few minutes in water and the lemon juice. Drain, dry and open out the petals. Season with salt and pepper.
Heat abundant oil in a large saucepan and cook the artichokes, covered, for around 20 minutes over a low heat, turning halfway through. Increase the heat, uncover the pan and fry the artichokes until crispy outside and tender inside. Drain and dry on paper towels. Serve hot.

455

New Potatoes
with Two Cheeses

Note *New potatoes
are just young, small
potatoes of any variety.
They have thin skin and
crisp-textured flesh, and
are usually cooked whole
because of their small
size.*

Preparation time 15 minutes
Cooking time 13 minutes
Wine *Friuli Collio Merlot*

**8 new potatoes
7 oz (200 g) mozzarella, diced
5.5 oz (150 g) Cheddar, diced
nutmeg, grated
salt and pepper**

456

Steam the potatoes for 8 minutes.
Cut in half and scoop out a little of the interior.
Squeeze the mozzarella to remove any excess liquid.
Mix with the Cheddar, a little nutmeg and pinches of salt
and pepper.
Fill the potato halves with the cheeses and brown for 5 minutes
under the broiler. Serve immediately.

Steamed Crème Brûlée

Preparation time 20 minutes
Cooking time 10 minutes
Wine *Gewürztraminer Passito*

Serves 6

17 fl oz (500 ml) whipping cream
1/2 vanilla bean
6 egg yolks
1/4 cup (1.9 oz or 55 g) sugar
2 tbsps Grand Marnier
salt
1/2 cup (100 g) raw sugar

Preheat the broiler.
Heat the cream and vanilla bean and infuse for 20 minutes.
Remove vanilla bean.
Beat the egg yolks with the sugar and a pinch of salt until they become thick and pale yellow.
Slowly whisk the cream into the egg yolks and continue whisking until the mixture is cool.
Add the Grand Marnier and pour the mixture into 6 ramequins. Cover with plastic wrap.
Steam the crème brulée for 12 minutes, remove the plastic wrap and transfer to the refrigerator.
When completely cool, sprinkle the crème brulée with the raw sugar and place on a baking sheet. Broil until the sugar caramelizes and transfer the ramequins to a baking dish. Fill half-full with ice water. Cool slightly and serve.

Dark Chocolate and Coffee Charlotte

Note *Chocolate originated in Mexico, where was used by the Aztecs. They mixed toasted smashed chocolate beans, pepper, chilli and vanilla together with water to make an after-dinner drink.*

Preparation time 40 minutes
Cooking time 10 minutes
Wine *Moscato Passito di Pantelleria*
♟ ♟

3.5 oz (100 g) dark chocolate
3.4 fl oz (100 ml) whipping cream
3 egg whites
salt
2 gelatin sheets
2 fl oz (60 ml) espresso
1 egg yolk
5.2 oz (150 g) lady fingers

460

Melt the chocolate in a double boiler with 3 tablespoons of cream.
Beat the egg whites and a pinch of salt into stiff peaks.
Whip the remaining cream.
Soak the gelatin in cold water for a few minutes. Drain and squeeze out the excess water. Dissolve the gelatin in a little espresso.
Add 1 egg yolk and the gelatin to the chocolate mixture. Fold in the egg whites and then the whipped cream.
Soak the lady fingers in the remaining espresso and line a baking dish with them. Add the chocolate mousse and let chill for 4 hours. Slide a thin, dampened knife around the pan. Quickly invert the charlotte onto a serving plate. If desired, decorate the charlotte with whipped cream and shaved chocolate.

Chocolate Bavarian Cream

Preparation time 25 minutes
Cooking time 5 minutes
Wine *Banyuls*

8.4 fl oz (250 ml) milk
zest of 1 orange
4 gelatin sheets
2.8 oz (80 g) dark chocolate,
 chopped
2 egg yolks
1/2 cup (3.5 oz or 100 g) sugar
8.4 fl oz (250 ml) whipping cream
1/2 cup (125 ml) Grand Marnier

Simmer the milk and orange zest.
Soak the gelatin in cold water
for a few minutes. Drain and
squeeze out the excess water.
Transfer half of the milk to a bowl
and stir in chocolate.
Beat the egg yolks and the sugar
together and add the chocolate
milk. Return to the saucepan
and cook over low heat. Add the
gelatin and mix until the mixture
starts to thicken. Remove from
heat, strain and let cool.
Whip the cream and fold into the
cooled chocolate mixture.
Coat 4 ramequins with Grand
Marnier. Pour the chocolate
cream into the ramequins and
refrigerate for 3 hours.

Chocolate Crème Brûlée

Preparation time 25 minutes
Cooking time 15 minutes
Wine *Barolo Chinato*

6.7 fl oz (200 ml) whipping cream
3.4 fl oz (100 ml) milk
2 egg yolks
3 tbsps sugar
1 tsp corn flour
2 drops hazelnut extract
2.8 oz (80 g) extra-dark chocolate,
 chopped
1 tbsp raw sugar

461

Heat the cream and milk in a
saucepan without boiling.
Beat the egg yolks and the
sugar in a mixing bowl. Add the
corn flour and hazelnut extract.
Slowly whisk the warm milk
mixture into the eggs. Transfer
to a double boiler and make
sure that the water never comes
to a boil. Cook the cream until
it coats the back of a spoon.
Add the chopped chocolate and
stir to combine. Remove from
heat and pour into 4 ramequins.
Refrigerate until ready to serve.
Sprinkle the crème brûlées
with raw sugar and broil under
a hot broiler until the sugar
caramelizes. Serve immediately.

Nut Semifreddo with Moscato and Chocolate Sauce

Note *In Italian, the term frutta secca, dried fruit, refers to both dried fruit and nuts. They are categorized together because both have a very low water content allowing for lengthy preservation.*

Preparation time 3 hours
Cooking time 40 minutes
Wine *Moscato di Trani*

SEMIFREDDO
4 egg yolks
1¼ cups (8.8 oz or 250 g) raw sugar
2 fl oz (60 ml) Moscato wine
2½ tbsps honey
1 cup (5.2 oz or 150 g) chopped mixed nuts (hazelnuts, almonds, pistachios and walnuts)
13.5 fl oz (400 ml) whipping cream
1/3 cup (1 oz or 30 g) cocoa powder

CHOCOLATE SAUCE
5.2 oz (150 g) dark chocolate
8.4 fl oz (250 ml) whipping cream

Beat the egg yolks and sugar together with the Moscato and honey. Add the nuts.
Whip the cream and fold into the nut mixture.
Sprinkle a rectangular terrine or loaf pan with cocoa and pour in the cream. Refrigerate for 3 hours.
Melt the chocolate and cream in a small saucepan over low heat.
Remove the semifreddo from the refrigerator and slice. Top with chocolate sauce.

Vin Santo Bavarian Cream with Caramel Sauce

Preparation time 25 minutes
Cooking time 15 minutes
Wine *Vin Santo*
♟ ♟

5 fl oz (150 ml) vin santo
10 fl oz (300 ml) whipping cream
12 cape gooseberries (physalis)
1.8 oz (50 g) dark chocolate

BAVARIAN CREAM
8.4 fl oz (250 ml) milk
1 vanilla bean
3 gelatin sheets
4 eggs, separated
2/3 cups (4.4 oz or 125 g) sugar

CARAMEL SAUCE
1/2 cup (3.5 oz or 100 g) sugar
3 tbsps water
1 tsp lemon juice
6.8 fl oz (200 ml) whipping cream

Simmer the milk with the vanilla bean and then remove the vanilla bean. Soak the gelatin in cold water for a few minutes. Drain and squeeze out the excess water.
Beat the egg yolks and the sugar. Slowly whisk in the hot milk and then the vin santo and gelatin. Continue stirring until the gelatin has dissolved.
Strain the milk mixture into a bowl. Place the bowl in a cold water bath for 30 minutes.
Whip the whipping cream to stiff peaks and fold it into the milk mixture.
Pour the cream into a mould and refrigerate for 3 hours.
Melt the chocolate in a double boiler and dip the cape gooseberries in the melted chocolate. Let cool.
Dissolve the sugar for the sauce in the water and the lemon juice in a saucepan. Cook until the syrup turns a light brown colour. Add the cream and boil for 10 minutes.
Invert the Bavarian cream onto a serving plate and pour the caramel sauce over the top. Decorate with the chocolate-dipped cape gooseberries.

Brachetto Mousse

Preparation time 30 minutes
Cooking time 15 minutes
Wine *Brachetto*

10 fl oz (300 ml) Brachetto wine
2 tbsps sugar
1½ gelatin sheets
5 fl oz (150 ml) whipping cream
10.5 oz (300 g) puff pastry
2 tbsps butter, melted
1 tbsp icing sugar

464

Boil the wine and sugar and reduce to 1/3 of the original volume. Soak the gelatin in cold water for a few minutes. Drain and squeeze out the excess water.
Set 2 tablespoons of the wine reduction aside and dissolve the gelatin in the remaining reduction. Let cool.
Whip the whipping cream and then carefully mix the wine reduction into the whipped cream. Pour the wine cream into 4 ramequins and refrigerate for 1 hour.
Preheat the oven to 375°F (190°C).
Roll out the puff pastry and make diagonal incisions along the surface. Brush the pastry with melted butter and sprinkle with sugar. Cut the pastry into 2-inch (5 cm) by 1/2-inch (1 cm) rectangles. Bake until golden-brown, remove from the oven and let cool.
Invert the ramequins onto serving plates and decorate with puff pastry wafers. Drizzle the reserved wine reduction over the top of the mousse.

Chocolate Cake
with Coffee Icing

CAKE
2 eggs
salt
1¼ cups (8.8 oz or 250 g)
 sugar
1¾ cups (7 oz or 200 g)
 plain flour
1 cup (3.5 oz or 100 g)
 cocoa powder
8.4 fl oz (250 ml) milk
2 tsps baking powder

ICING
14 tbsps (7 oz or 200 g) butter
1⅔ cups (7 oz or 200 g)
 icing sugar
2 egg yolks
4 fl oz (120 ml) espresso

Preparation time 30 minutes
Cooking time 1 hour
Wine *Moscadello di Montalcino*

465

Preheat oven to 350°F (180°C).
Beat the eggs with a pinch of salt and then add the sugar, flour and
cocoa powder. Beat in the milk and then add the baking powder.
Butter and flour a cake pan and pour in the batter. Bake for 1 hour.
Cream the butter, sugar and egg yolks together until the mixture has
a smooth consistency. Add the espresso, mixing to obtain a smooth
and slightly thinner consistency.
Remove the sponge cake from the oven. Let cool and then slice in
half horizontally to form 2 rounds. Spread the icing over the bottom
round and cover with the second round. Fill a pastry bag with the
remaining icing and decorate the top of the cake. Refrigerate for 1
hour before serving.

Italian Trifle with Chocolate

Note *Alchermes is a sweet red liqueur frequently used in baking. It was initially made by Florentine monks who infused alcohol with herbs, spices and sugar. The infusion was then coloured using cochineal.*

Preparation time 35 minutes
Cooking time 10 minutes
Wine *Zibibbo*

2 egg yolks
2/3 cup plus 2 tbsps
 (4.9 oz or 140 g) sugar
1 tsp vanilla extract
1/4 cup (1 oz or 30 g)
 plain flour
8.4 fl oz (250 ml) milk
6.7 fl oz (200 ml) hot water
4 tbsps Alchermes liqueur
10.5 oz (300 g) sponge cake
2.4 oz (70 g) dark chocolate

466

Beat the egg yolks and 1/3 cup (2.1 oz or 60 g) sugar together until thick and creamy. Add the vanilla extract and flour.
Heat the milk in a saucepan. Whisk the hot milk into the egg mixture. Return to the saucepan and cook over low heat for at least 5 minutes.
Dissolve the remaining sugar in the hot water, add the Alchermes and let cool. Brush the sponge cake rounds with the Alchermes syrup.
Melt the chocolate in a double boiler.
Make the trifle by layering the pastry cream, sponge cake and chocolate in a trifle bowl. Refrigerate for 2 hours before serving.

Pastry Cream with Almond Brittle

Preparation time 15 minutes
Cooking time 15 minutes
Wine *Malvasia delle Lipari*

ALMOND BRITTLE
1 cup (4.2 oz or 120 g)
 slivered almonds
2/3 cups (4.2 oz or 120 g) sugar
4 tbsps water

PASTRY CREAM
17 fl oz (500 ml) milk
4 egg yolks
1/3 cup plus 2 tbsps
 (2.8 oz or 80 g) sugar
1/4 cup (1 oz or 30 g)
 plain flour
1 tbsp corn flour

467

Preheat oven to 400°F (200°C).
Toast the slivered almonds in the oven for 5 minutes.
Line a baking sheet with parchment paper.
Let the sugar and water caramelize over medium heat. Add the almonds and pour the mixture onto the baking sheet. Smooth the brittle into a thin layer using a buttered spatula. Let cool.
Bring the milk to a simmer in a saucepan.
Beat the egg yolks with the sugar. Add the flour and corn flour. Whisk in the hot milk and then return to the saucepan. Cook over low heat, stirring constantly, until the cream thickens. Let cool.
Pour the pastry cream into small serving bowls and refrigerate.
Garnish the cooled pastry cream with almond brittle.

Amaretto Rum Mousse

Note *Rum is a spirit made from sugar cane, typical of the Caribbean. Legend says that rum was the drink of choice of the pirates that roamed the Caribbean Sea and that the name rum comes from the word* rumbullion, *the ruckus made by celebratory pirates.*

468

Preparation time 15 minutes
Cooking time 10 minutes
Wine *Oltrepò Pavese Malvasia*

10 fl oz (300 ml) milk
zest of 1 lemon
2 egg yolks
1/2 cup (3.5 oz or 100 g) sugar
1 tsp vanilla extract
3 tbsps dark rum
1/4 cup (1.2 oz or 35 g)
 plain flour
1.7 oz (50 g) amaretto cookies
8.4 fl oz (250 ml) whipping cream

Bring the milk and lemon zest to a boil.
Meanwhile, beat the egg yolks with the sugar, vanilla extract and rum. Whisk in the flour and continue mixing until pale yellow and fluffy.
Slowly whisk the boiling milk into the egg mixture. Transfer back to the saucepan and bring to a simmer, stirring constantly.
Remove the pastry cream from the stove and let cool slightly.
Crumble the amaretto cookies into the pastry cream.
Whip the whipping cream and fold into the pastry cream.
Transfer the mousse into individual serving bowls and refrigerate for at least 1 hour.

Brown Rice Pudding
with Apples and Chocolate

Note *Rice originated in Indonesia around 7000 BC and subsequently spread throughout the surrounding areas: China, Southeast Asia and India. The Mesopotamians used rice as a staple food whereas the Greeks and Romans knew only of its medicinal properties.*

Preparation time 30 minutes
Cooking time 45 minutes
Wine *Asti Moscato Spumante*

2 Golden Delicious apples
2 tbsps raw sugar
1/2 cup (3.5 oz or 100 g) brown rioc
17 fl oz (500 ml) milk
2 tbsps sugar
1 tbsp honey
2 tbsps whipping cream
2.4 oz (70 g) dark chocolate
1 banana

469

Preheat oven to 350°F (180°C).
Peel, core and thinly slice the apples.
Line a baking sheet with parchment paper. Place the apple slices on the tray and sprinkle them with the raw sugar. Bake for 20 minutes.
Blend the uncooked rice in a food processor until it resembles a coarse meal.
In a small saucepan bring the ground rice, milk and sugar to a simmer and cook for about 20 minutes, adding water if necessary.
Puree the cooked rice with the honey and let cool.
Heat the cream and add the chocolate, stirring until the mixture is smooth.
Slice the banana and cut the cooked apple into pieces.
Layer the fruit, rice pudding and chocolate sauce in individual serving bowls. Refrigerate for 30 minutes and serve.

Cocoa-Rum Cookies

Preparation time 20 minutes
Cooking time 15 minutes
Wine *Vin Santo*

2/3 cups (3.1 oz or 90 g) hazelnuts
1/2 cup (3.5 oz or 100 g) sugar
5½ tbsps cocoa powder
3/4 cups (3.5 oz or 100 g)
 plain flour
6 tbsps butter, cut into
 small pieces
1 tbsp dark rum
1 pinch of salt

In a food processor, blend the
hazelnuts with the sugar. Place
in a bowl, sift in the cocoa
powder, then add the flour
and butter. Add rum and salt
and stir until combined. Form
a ball, cover with plastic wrap
and let rest in a cool place
for 20 minutes.
Preheat oven to 350°F (180°C).
Unwrap the dough and form
walnut-sized balls, then shape
each ball into a small dome.
Line a baking sheet with
parchment paper and place
the cookies on the baking sheet.
Bake for 15 minutes. Remove
from heat and cool completely
before serving.

Flourless Chocolate Cake

Preparation time 15 minutes
Cooking time 30 minutes
Wine *Banyuls*

8.8 oz (250 g) dark chocolate
14 tbsps (7 oz or 200 g)
 butter
1 cup (3.5 oz or 100 g)
 icing sugar
4 eggs

Preheat oven to 350°F (180°C).
Break the chocolate up into
pieces and place them
in a double boiler. Melt the
chocolate over low heat and
then add the butter, stirring
constantly. Add the icing sugar
and stir until smooth. Add the
eggs one by one and mix well.
Butter and flour a loaf pan and
pour the batter into the pan.
Bake for 25-30 minutes.
Let the cake cool and then
invert it onto a serving plate.

Note *For a spiced variation, try
sifting a little cinnamon with the
icing sugar into the cake batter.*

470

Individual Rice Puddings with Apples

Preparation time 20 minutes
Cooking time 40 minutes
Wine *Porto Ruby*

25.3 fl oz (750 ml) milk
3/4 cups (5.2 oz or 150 g) sugar
2 tbsps butter
1¼ cups (8.8 oz or 250 g)
 Originario rice
1½ tbsps rum
1 lb (500 g) Golden Delicious apples
1 oz (30 g) candied citron peel,
 diced
1/3 cup (1.4 oz or 40 g)
 chopped walnuts
4 egg whites
plain flour

471

Preheat oven to 350°F (180°C).
Bring the milk and half the sugar to a boil.
In another saucepan melt 1 tablespoon butter and add the rice.
Toast the rice for a few minutes and then add the rum and let the alcohol evaporate. Add the hot milk and cook until the rice is soft.
Peel, core and chop the apples.
Add the apples, citron and chopped walnuts to the rice.
Beat the egg whites. When they become frothy sprinkle in the remaining sugar and beat into stiff peaks. Fold the egg whites into the rice.
Butter and flour 4 ramequins and fill them with the rice mixture.
Bake for 20 minutes, let cool slightly and serve.

Double Chocolate Cake

Preparation time 25 minutes
Cooking time 30 minutes
Wine *Trentino Moscato Rosa*

♟ ♟

CAKE
7 oz (200 g) gianduia chocolate
5 eggs, separated
1/2 cup (3.5 oz or 100 g) sugar
1/3 cup (1.7 oz or 50 g)
  toasted almonds, chopped
1/3 cup (1.4 oz or 40 g)
  plain flour
salt
1 knob of butter

GLACÉ
7 oz (200 g) dark chocolate
3 tbsps butter

472

Preheat oven to 320°F (160°C).
Melt the chocolate in a double boiler. Beat the egg yolks with
the sugar until creamy. Whisk in the melted chocolate. Add the
almonds, candied orange and flour and mix well.
Beat the egg whites and a pinch of salt to stiff peaks. Carefully fold
into the chocolate mixture using a wooden spoon.
Butter and flour a 8-inch (22 cm) spring-form pan. Pour in the
batter and bake for 30 minutes.
Remove the cake from the oven and cool slightly. Invert the cake
onto a work surface. Cut out 4 hearts using a cookie cutter or a
stencil.
Melt the chocolate and butter together and pour the glacé over the
4 cakes. Let cool completely and serve.

Red Grape Cake

Preparation time 20 minutes
Cooking time 25 minutes
Wine *Moscato Spumante*

1 knob of butter
3 tbsps honey
1 tbsp water
1 bunch red grapes, halved
 and deseeded
8.5 oz (240 g) ricotta
2 eggs
3 egg whites
salt
ground cinnamon

473

Preheat oven to 350°F (180°C).
Dampen and wring out a piece of parchment paper. Butter the
damp paper and use it to line a dome shaped baking pan.
Heat the honey and 1 tablespoon water in a saucepan and then
add the grapes. Sauté for a few minutes over high heat. Remove
from heat, drain half of the grapes and reserve.
Whip the ricotta until creamy and add the eggs, a pinch of
cinnamon and the drained grapes.
Beat the egg whites and a pinch of salt to stiff peaks. Fold the egg
whites into the ricotta.
Pour the batter into the lined dome pan and bake in a water bath
for 20 minutes.
Remove from the oven and let cool slightly. Transfer to the
refrigerator briefly.
Invert the cake onto a serving dish. Sprinkle with cinnamon and
serve warm with the remaining grapes.

Red Wine Cake with Nuts

Preparation time 25 minutes
Cooking time 15 minutes
Wine *Sicilia Cabernet-Sauvignon*

3 tbsps raisins
4 fl oz (120 ml) Cabernet
 Sauvignon wine
4 tbsps chopped mixed nuts
 (almonds, walnuts and hazelnuts)
1/3 cup (2.1 oz or 60 g) sugar
17 fl oz (500 ml) extra-virgin
 olive oil
2 tbsps pine nuts
4 fl oz (120 ml) Alchermes liqueur
1 cup (4.4 oz or 125 g)
 plain flour
2 tsps baking powder
1 knob of butter
icing sugar

Preheat oven to 350°F (180°C).
Soak the raisins in the wine for
5 minutes. Add the raisins and
wine to the nuts and mix well.
Add the sugar, oil, pine nuts and
Alchermes and mix well. Sift the
flour and baking powder into the
batter and mix well.
Butter and flour 4 ramequins
and pour in the batter. Bake for
30 minutes. Remove from the
oven, sprinkle with icing sugar
and serve.

Chocolate Ricotta Cake

Preparation time 15 minutes
Cooking time 30 minutes
Wine *Aleatico*

2 egg yolks
1 cup (7 oz or 200 g) sugar
3 egg whites
salt
1 lb (17.3 oz or 500 g) ricotta,
 strained sieved
3.5 oz (100 g) dark chocolate,
 chopped
3 tbsps raisins
4 tbsps rum
corn flour

Preheat oven to 350°F (180°C).
Beat the egg yolks with the
sugar.
Whip the egg whites and a
pinch of salt to stiff peaks.
Mix the ricotta and the
chocolate into the egg yolks
and fold in the egg whites.
Soak the raisins in the rum and
add them to the mixture.
Line a cake pan with parchment
paper and pour in the batter.
Sprinkle the top of the cake
with corn flour and bake for
25-30 minutes.

474

Cinnamon Cookies

Preparation time 20 minutes
Cooking time 10 minutes

10 tbsps (5.2 oz or 150 g) butter
1/3 cup plus 2 tbsps
 (2.8 oz or 80 g) raw sugar
1 egg
1 tsp ground cinnamon
1 pinch of salt
3/4 cup (3.5 oz or 100 g)
 plain flour
1/2 tsp baking powder
8 oz (250 g) cornflakes
butter
icing sugar

Preheat oven to 350°F (180°C).
Cream the butter and sugar. Add
egg, cinnamon, and salt. Sift in
flour and baking powder and mix
well. Add the cornflakes and mix.
Place 2 sheets of parchment
paper on a work surface. Pour
the dough onto one and place
the other over the top. Roll out
the dough into a 1/5-inch (1/2
cm) sheet. Remove the top sheet
and cut out rounds.
Place the cookies on a buttered
and floured baking sheet and
bake for 10 minutes. Sprinkle
with icing sugar and serve.

Blueberry and Chocolate Pastries

Preparation time 25 minutes
Cooking time 10 minutes
Wine *Trentino Moscato Rosa*

2 eggs
3 tbsps grappa
1/3 cup (2.6 oz or 75 g) sugar
3 tbsps melted butter
salt
2⅓ cups (10.5 oz or 300 g)
 plain flour
1 basket of blueberries
2.1 oz (60 g) dark chocolate,
 chopped
sunflower oil
icing sugar

475

Mix the eggs, grappa, sugar,
butter and salt. Whisk in the
flour. Mix to form a smooth and
elastic dough. Cover with plastic
wrap and refrigerate for 30
minutes.
Roll out the dough into a thin
sheet and cut out circles. Place
2 blueberries on each round and
sprinkle with chocolate. Fold
each in half and press down
on the edges to seal. Heat the
sunflower oil in a saucepan and
fry the pastries. Drain on paper
towels and sprinkle with icing
sugar.

Fruit Cake

1 tsp dry active yeast
1.6 fl oz (50 ml) warm water
4 tbsps corn malt
3.4 fl oz (100 ml) hot rice milk
1¼ cups (5.2 oz or 150 g)
 kamut flour
1¼ cups (5.2 oz or 150 g)
 plain flour
salt
2 tbsps raisins
1 tbsp grappa
1/2 cup (1.7 oz or 50 g) hazelnuts,
 chopped
2 dried figs, chopped
4 pitted prunes, chopped
3 tbsps coconut flakes,
 plus extra for garnish
ground cinnamon

476

Preparation time 30 minutes
Cooking time 45 minutes
Wine *Gewürztraminer
Vendemmia Tardiva*

👨‍🍳 👨‍🍳

Dissolve the yeast in the water with 3 tablespoons of corn malt. Add
the hot rice milk and let sit for 10 minutes. Sift the 2 flours together
and mix in a little of the yeast mixture with a fork. Add some more
liquid and pinch of salt. Mix in the remaining liquid. Let rise for 2
hours.
Soak the raisins in the grappa. Add the nuts, raisins, dried fruit,
coconut and cinnamon to the dough and mix well. Cover and let rise
for another 2 hours. Meanwhile, preheat oven to 300°F (150°C).
Place the bread in a loaf pan and bake for 10 minutes. Raise the oven
temperature to 325°F (170°C) and bake for another 35 minutes.
Dissolve remaining corn malt in 1 tablespoon of warm water.
Remove the cake from the oven and brush with malt syrup. Decorate
with coconut flakes.

Pear and Cinnamon Cake

Preparation time 45 minutes
Cooking time 40 minutes
Wine *Sicilia Moscato Spumante*

1 tsp (12 g) dry active yeast
3.4 fl oz (100 ml) warm water
4 cups (17 oz or 500 g)
 plain flour
6 eggs
1⅓ cups (9.5 oz or 270 g) sugar
10 tbsps (5.2 oz or 150 g) butter,
 melted
2 tbsps ground cinnamon
2 Decana pears

Dissolve the yeast in warm water. Mix half of the flour with the yeast
and water and knead to form a smooth dough. Let rest for 20
minutes.
Meanwhile, beat 5 eggs and the sugar in a mixing bowl.
Pour the remaining flour onto a work surface and make a well in
the centre. Place the risen dough in the well and add the eggs and
butter. Mix the dough, sprinkling in the cinnamon. When the dough
comes together, continue to knead until smooth and elastic.
Butter and flour an 8-inch (22 cm) spring-form pan. Pour the dough
into the pan and let rise for 20 minutes in a warm, dry place.
Preheat the oven to 350°F (180°C).
Meanwhile, peel, core and dice the pears.
When the dough has risen for the last time, sprinkle the pear pieces
over the top and brush with the remaining egg. Bake for 40 minutes
and serve.

Fresh Fruit Tart

Note *This pâte sablée recipe will make two large tarts. Leftover dough may be frozen for up to 2 months.*

Preparation time 45 minutes
Cooking time 40 minutes
Wine *Colli di Parma Malvasia Dolce*
🍴 🍴

Serves 6

PÂTE SABLÉE
2 cups (14 oz or 400 g) sugar
2 cup plus 3 tbsps (17 oz or 500 g)
 butter
6 egg yolks
zest of 1 lemon
salt
8 cups (2.2 lbs or 1 kg)
 plain flour

FILLING
2 mandarin oranges
1 apple
1 pear
1 banana
2 kiwis
1 orange
Chantilly cream (see p. 1101)
fruit jelly

Mix the sugar, butter, egg yolks, lemon zest and salt and then add the flour. Mix well to form a smooth dough. Cover with plastic wrap and refrigerate for 30 minutes.
Preheat the oven to 320°F (160°C).
Divide the dough in half. Reserve half for later use. Roll out the remaining dough into a large circle. Line a tart tin with the dough and pierce the surface with a fork. Cover with foil and fill the tart with pie weights or dried beans.
Bake for 15 minutes. Remove the crust from the oven and let cool. Meanwhile, peel and slice the fruit.
Fill the tart shell with Chantilly cream and arrange the sliced fruit over the cream. Top with fruit jelly.

Chocolate Blackcurrant Cakes

Preparation time 20 minutes
Cooking time 15 minutes
Wine *Trentino Moscato Rosa*

1.7 oz (50 g) milk chocolate
1 tbsp whipping cream
1/2 cup (3.5 oz or 100 g)
 blackcurrant jam
3.5 oz (100 g) dark chocolate
6 tbsps (2.8 oz or 80 g) butter
2 eggs
1/3 cup (2.4 oz or 70 g) sugar
3 tbsps plain flour
icing sugar
fresh blackcurrants

Melt the milk chocolate with the cream and stir in the currant jam.
Pour the mixture into an aluminum pie pan and freeze for 2 hours.
Preheat the oven to 400°F (200°C).
Melt the dark chocolate and butter in a double boiler.
Beat the eggs and sugar and whisk in the flour a little at a time.
Carefully add the chocolate to the egg mixture. Transfer half of
the mixture into 4 buttered ramequins or 1 soufflé dish. Each
dish should be only half full. Then add spoonfuls of the frozen
blackcurrant-chocolate mixture to the ramequins. Top with
remaining chocolate mixture.
Bake the cakes for 12 minutes. Remove from the oven and cool
slightly. Invert the cakes and decorate them with icing sugar and
fresh currants.

479

Blueberry Tartlets

Preparation time 30 minutes
Cooking time 20 minutes
Wine *Alto Adige Moscato Rosa*
♟ ♟

480

PÂTE SABLÉE
7 tbsps (3.5 oz or 100 g) butter
1/3 cup (2.8 oz or 80 g) sugar
2 egg yolks
salt
zest of 1/2 lemon
1⅔ cups (7 oz or 200 g)
 plain flour

FILLING
8.4 fl oz (250 ml) milk
1/3 cup (2.1 oz or 60 g) sugar
1½-inch (4 cm) piece of vanilla
 bean
2 egg yolks
1/4 cup (1 oz or 30 g)
 plain flour
1¼ cups (7 oz or 200 g) blueberries

Preheat oven to 350°F (180°C).
Mix the butter, sugar, egg yolks, salt, lemon zest and flour to form a
smooth dough. Refrigerate until ready to use.
For the filling, bring the milk, half of the sugar and vanilla bean to a
boil.
Beat the egg yolks and remaining sugar until thick and foamy. Add
the flour and then the hot milk, return to the saucepan and cook over
medium heat for 3-4 minutes. Remove the vanilla bean and let cool.
Roll out the pâte sablée into a sheet 1/5-inch (1/2 cm) thick.
Butter and flour 4 round tart tins. Line the tins with the dough.
Bake the pastry shells for 15 minutes. Remove from heat and let
cool completely.
Unmould the pastry shells. Pour the pastry cream into the 4 pastry
shells and top with blueberries.

Cream Puffs

Preparation time 30 minutes
Cooking time 40 minutes
Wine *Malvasia delle Lipari*
♟ ♟ ♟

8.4 fl oz (250 ml) water
1 knob of butter
salt
1 cup plus 3 tbsps (5.3 oz or 150 g)
 plain flour
2 eggs
10 fl oz (300 ml) milk
zest of 1 lemon
1 tsp vanilla
1 egg yolk
1/3 cup plus 2 tbsps
 (2.8 oz or 80 g) sugar
6.7 fl oz (200 ml) whipping cream
icing sugar

481

Preheat the oven to 350°F (180°C).
Pour the water into a saucepan. Add the butter and a pinch of salt
and bring to a boil. Once boiling add two-thirds of the flour and
mix with a wooden spoon until smooth. Remove from heat and let
the mixture cool slightly. Add the eggs one at a time and mix to
form a dense, shiny dough.
Butter and flour a baking sheet.
Fill a pastry bag with the dough and make 4-inch (10 cm) puffs.
Bake for 30 minutes. Remove from the oven and set aside.
Bring the milk, lemon zest and vanilla extract to a boil. In a mixing
bowl beat the egg yolk, sugar and remaining flour. When the milk
boils, whisk it into the egg yolk mixture. Return to the saucepan
and bring to a boil, stirring constantly. Remove from heat and let
the cream cool.
Whip the whipping cream and fold into the cooled cream mixture.
Cut the puffs in half and fill with the cream. Sprinkle with icing
sugar and serve.

Chocolate Almond Fritters

Note *Almonds have been used in confectionery for many centuries. It has been documented that almonds were used in primitive sweets made with honey, milk and fresh or dried fruit.*

FRITTERS
5.2 oz (150 g) dark chocolate
1.6 fl oz (50 ml) skim milk
1.6 fl oz (50 ml) whipping cream
1 tbsp truffle oil
1 cup (3.5 oz or 100 g)
 cocoa powder
2 eggs, beaten
2/3 cup (3.5 oz or 100 g)
 almonds, finely chopped
17 fl oz (500 ml) sunflower oil

SAUCE
1¾ cups (5.6 oz or 160g)
 cocoa powder
8.4 fl oz (250 ml) hot water
2 fl oz (60 ml) espresso coffee
2/3 cup (4.5 oz or 130 g) sugar

482

Preparation time 20 minutes
Cooking time 10 minutes
Wine *Malvasia delle Lipari*

Melt the chocolate in a double boiler. Mix the milk and cream with the truffle oil in a saucepan and bring to a boil. Add the melted chocolate and mix. Let cool completely. Once cool, roll the mixture into balls and then roll the balls in the cocoa powder. Freeze the chocolate balls for 2 hours.
Remove the chocolate balls from the freezer. Dip the croquettes in the egg and then roll in the almonds to coat.
Heat the sunflower oil. Fry the fritters and drain on paper towels. Mix the cocoa powder with the hot water. Add the coffee and sugar and mix well. Serve the fritters with the chocolate sauce.

Ricotta and Gianduia Tart

Note *Ricotta is a milk product made from the curd that is leftover after cheesemaking a little milk is added to the curds to soften the consistency of the ricotta.*

Preparation time 40 minutes
Cooking time 40 minutes
Wine *Asti Moscato Spumante*
♟

17 fl oz (500 ml) milk
4 egg yolks
2/3 cup (4.4 oz or 125 g) sugar
1/3 cup (1.7 oz or 50 g)
 plain flour
3 drops hazelnut extract
2.8 oz (80 g) gianduia chocolate,
 chopped
3.5 g (100 g) ricotta
8.8 oz (250 g) pâte sablée
 (see p. 1092)

483

Preheat oven to 350°F (180°C).
Bring milk to a boil in a saucepan.
Beat the egg yolks with the sugar. Add the flour and hazelnut extract. Whisk in the boiling milk and then transfer back to the saucepan. Cook until the cream begins to thicken, whisking constantly.
Pour the egg and milk mixture into a bowl and add the chocolate. Mix until the chocolate melts. Let cool and then add the ricotta. Roll out three-quarters of the pâte sablée. Line a pie pan with the dough and pierce the surface with a fork. Fill with the ricotta cream. Roll out the remaining pâte sablée and cut into long strips. Place the strips across the top of the tart to form a lattice. Brush the tart surface with milk and bake for 30 minutes. Let cool and then refrigerate for 1 hour before serving.

Vanilla and Orange Infused Pineapple with Sorbet

Note *When choosing a pineapple, make sure to check the colour of the skin below the outer thorns. A ripe pineapple will be several shades of orange. An under-ripe pineapple will be green and over-ripe fruit will be brown.*

Preparation time 10 minutes
Cooking time 15 minutes

2 oranges
3 vanilla beans
1 tbsp acacia honey
1 large pineapple,
  peeled and cored
7 oz (200 g) orange sorbet

484

Place the juice and peels of the oranges with a little water in a saucepan and bring to a boil.

Slice 1 vanilla bean in half lengthwise and remove the seeds with the tip of a knife. Add the vanilla seeds to the honey and dilute with a little orange juice. Brush the pineapple with the honey mixture.

Add the remaining vanilla bean halves to the hot orange juice. Place the pineapple in a steamer basket and place the basket in the pan with the orange juice, make sure the pineapple is not immersed in the water. Steam the pineapple for 6 minutes and transfer to a serving dish. Refrigerate until completely cool.

Fill the centre of the pineapple with the orange sorbet and freeze for 1 hour.

Meanwhile, reduce the steaming liquid.

Thickly slice the pineapple and pour the reduction over the top. Decorate with the remaining vanilla beans.

Citrus-Glazed Baby Apples

Note *Oranges were grown in ancient China and Japan. The fruit arrived in Europe around the 12th century. Oranges came to be an important crop in Italy (especially in the regions of Sicily and Campania) in the 14th and 15th centuries.*

Preparation time 25 minutes
Cooking time 40 minutes
♟ ♟

6.7 fl oz (200 ml) water
1 tsp whole cloves
1 cinnamon stick
1/2 cup (3.5 oz or 100 g) sugar
juice of 2 oranges
juice of 1/2 lemon
2 tbsps Grand Marnier
2 tbsps acacia honey
16 baby apples
1 tbsp whipping cream
2 tbsps grated candied
 orange peel
dark chocolate, shaved

485

Place the water, cloves, cinnamon, sugar, orange and lemon juice and Grand Marnier in a saucepan and boil for 5 minutes.
Add the honey and the whole apples.
Cook for 30 minutes over low heat. Remove from the stove and let the apples cool in their syrup.
Preheat the oven to 375°F (190°C).
Line a baking sheet with wax paper and place the apples on the baking sheet.
Reduce cooking liquid by 1/3 and then glaze the apples with the reduction.
Bake for 10 minutes, basting the apples with the syrup every few minutes.
Serve the apples warm with a little cream, candied orange zest and shaved chocolate.

Prato-Style Biscotti (Tuscany)

Preparation time 20 minutes
Cooking time 20 minutes
Wine *Vin Santo*

1 cup (4.5 oz or 130 g) almonds
4 cups (1 lb or 500 g)
 plain flour
4 eggs
2½ cups (1 lb or 500 g) sugar
1 tsp baking soda
1 pinch of salt

Preheat oven to 300°F (150°C). Toast the almonds for 10 minutes. Chop three-quarters and keep the rest whole. Pour the flour onto a work surface and make a well in the centre. Add the eggs, sugar, baking soda and salt to the centre of the well. Mix well until uniform. Mix all the almonds into the dough.
Line a baking sheet with wax paper. Form 2 long thin loaves with the dough. Place them on the baking sheet and bake for 10 minutes.
Remove from the oven and slice the hot loaves on the diagonal to form biscotti. Place the biscotti on the baking sheet and return to the oven until lightly brown.

Almond Meringues (Emilia Romagna)

Preparation time 30 minutes
Cooking time 30 minutes
Wine *Albana di Romagna Passito*

1 cup plus 1 tbsp (3.5 oz or 150 g)
 peeled almonds
1/3 cup (3.8 oz or 110 g) honey
4 cups (1 lb or 500 g) plain
 flour
5 egg whites
salt
1¾ cups (12.3 oz or 350 g) sugar
milk
1 knob of butter

Preheat oven to 350°F (180°C). Toast the almonds for 1 minute in the oven and then coarsely chop.
Mix the honey and almonds and then add the flour.
Beat the egg whites with a pinch of salt. When frothy add the granulated sugar and beat to stiff peaks. Fold the egg whites into the almond mixture. If the mixture is too thick add a few drops of milk.
Butter a baking sheet and drop the dough onto the baking sheet with a teaspoon.
Bake for 30 minutes. Let cool completely and then serve.

486

Brutti ma Buoni (TUSCANY)

Preparation time 30 minutes
Cooking time 40 minutes
Wine *Vin Santo*

2/3 cup (3.5 oz or 100 g) almonds
3/4 cup (2.8 oz or 80 g)
 icing sugar
1 egg white
salt
5 tsps granulated sugar
1 knob of butter

Preheat oven to 250°F (130°C). Finely chop the almonds and then toast for a few minutes. Add the icing sugar to the almonds.
Beat the egg white and a pinch of salt. When frothy add the granulated sugar and beat to stiff peaks. Fold the almond mixture into the egg whites.
Butter a baking sheet. Using a teaspoon, drop the batter onto the baking sheet to form irregular shaped cookies.
Bake for 40 minutes until golden-brown.

Castagnole Cookies (LAZIO)

Preparation time 30 minutes
Cooking time 20 minutes
Wine *Aleatico di Gradoli*

Serves 8

7 tbsps (3.5 oz or 100 g) butter
3¼ cups (14 oz or 400 g)
 plain flour
1/4 cup (1.7 oz or 50 g) sugar
4 eggs
2 fl oz (60 ml) rum
zest of 1 lemon
salt
sunflower oil
icing sugar

Clarify the butter in a double boiler and then transfer to a bowl. Sift the flour into the butter and then add the sugar, eggs, rum, lemon zest and a pinch of salt. Mix well.
Roll the dough into chestnut-sized balls.
Heat the sunflower oil. Fry the cookies until they puff up. Drain on paper towels and sprinkle with icing sugar.

487

Sabayon Pears with Whipped Cream

Preparation time 15 minutes
Cooking time 20 minutes
Wine *Passito di Pantelleria*

1 pear
4 egg yolks
2/3 cups (4.2 oz or 120 g) sugar
2 tbsps dry Marsala wine
4 ladyfingers
5 fl oz (150 ml) whipping cream
2.8 oz (80 g) dark chocolate

488

Peel the pear and cook it in a covered saucepan for a few minutes with 1 tablespoon of water.
Reserve the cooking liquid and quarter the pear. Remove the core.
Beat the egg yolks and sugar and add 2 tablespoons of Marsala wine. Place the mixture in a double boiler and cook, whisking constantly, until the sauce becomes foamy and doubles in volume. Make sure that the sauce does not boil.
Remove from heat and immerse the pan in a cold water bath. Continue stirring until the sauce has cooled slightly. Let the sauce cool completely in the water bath, stirring occasionally.
Brush the ladyfingers with the reserved pear cooking liquid and line the bottom of 4 individual ramequins with the ladyfingers. Place 1 pear quarter in each ramequin and then top with the sabayon sauce. Decorate with chocolate shavings and whipped cream.

Walnut and Pistachio Cake

Preparation time 20 minutes
Cooking time 45 minutes
Wine *Verduzzo di Ramandolo*
♟♟

1/4 cup (1.4 oz or 40 g)
 granulated sugar
1/2 tbsp water
6 tbsps (3.1 oz or 90 g) butter
1/4 cup (1.4 oz or 40 g) raw sugar
1 egg
3/4 cup (3.5 oz or 100 g)
 self-rising flour
salt
1/3 cup (1 oz or 30 g) walnuts,
 chopped
3/4 cup (3.5 oz or 100 g)
 pistachios
icing sugar

Preheat the oven to 350°F (180°C).
Heat the sugar until it caramelizes and turns golden-brown.
Remove from heat and add the water.
Cream the butter and raw sugar. Add the egg and then the
caramel. Slowly sift in the flour and a pinch of salt. Add the
walnuts and whole pistachios. Pour the batter into a rectangular
baking dish and bake for 40-45 minutes.
Invert the cake onto a serving dish and sprinkle with icing sugar.

Panpepato
(UMBRIA)

Preparation time 10 minutes
Cooking time 20 minutes
Wine *Sagrantino di Montefalco Passito*

Serves 6-8

2/3 cup (3.5 oz or 100 g) raisins
1 cup (3.5 oz or 100 g) walnuts
3/4 cup (3.5 oz or 100 g) hazelnuts
2/3 cup (3.5 oz or 100 g) peeled
 almonds
5 oz (150 g) dark chocolate
3.5 oz (100 g) candied fruit
nutmeg, grated
pepper
2 tsps ground cinnamon
6.7 fl oz (200 ml) honey
plain flour

490

Preheat the oven to 350°F (180°C).
Soak the raisins in warm water for a few minutes. Drain and
squeeze out the excess water.
Finely chop the walnuts, hazelnuts, almonds, chocolate and
candied fruit and mix together. Add pinches of nutmeg and
pepper, and then the cinnamon and raisins.
Heat the honey and a little water in a saucepan and bring to a boil.
Pour the boiling honey over the nut mixture. Mix until the chocolate
melts and then sift in enough flour to combine the dough.
Form 6 rounds and place them on a parchment paper-lined baking
sheet.
Bake for 10 minutes. Remove from the oven and cool completely
before serving. The panpepato may be stored for up to 2 weeks in
an air-tight container.

D E S S E R T S

spring

Greet the return of spring with
fresh new dishes: first courses
of vegetables and fish, light
mains featuring brightly
coloured spring vegetables
and delicate desserts
based on fruit, all using
the season's delicious
new produce.

Caponata in Puff Pastry

Preparation time 20 minutes
Cooking time 40 minutes
Wine *Montecarlo Bianco*

8 tbsps extra-virgin olive oil
1 garlic clove
1/2 white onion, roughly
 chopped
1¾ cups (7 oz or 200 g) cubed
 pumpkin
1/2 yellow bell pepper, diced
1/2 red bell pepper, diced
salt and pepper
12 small zucchini, diced
8 cherry tomatoes, diced
oregano
1 roll (9 oz or 250 g) puff pastry

Preheat oven to 400°F (200°C).
Heat the oil in a frying pan with the unpeeled garlic clove and
add the chopped onion. Sauté for 3 minutes.
Add the pumpkin cubes, sauté briefly, then add the diced bell
peppers. Lightly salt to taste and cook for 6-7 minutes, adding a
little water if necessary.
Add the diced zucchini and tomatoes, sprinkle with oregano and
a little pepper and continue cooking until all the vegetables are
tender.
Meanwhile cut out 4 circles from the puff pastry, 2½-inches
(6 cm) in diameter. Place the circles on 4 upside-down, oven-proof
teacups or other hemispherical moulds to create baskets. Bake for
10 minutes.
Remove the baskets from the oven and fill with the hot vegetable
caponata.

Salt Cod and Potato Croquettes

496

Preparation time 35 minutes
Cooking time 40 minutes
Wine *Malvasia Istriana*

3 potatoes
2½ cups (600 ml) water
1¾ cups (400 ml) milk
2 shallots, sliced
parsley
9 oz (250 g) soaked salt cod
1 tbsp grated Parmesan
2 tbsps heavy cream
salt and pepper
6¼ tbsps plain flour
2 eggs, beaten
3/4 cup (3.5 oz or 100 g)
 breadcrumbs
sunflower oil

Peel the potatoes and cut into 1/5-inch (1/2 cm) thick slices.
Heat the water and milk with the shallots and parsley. Add
potatoes and salt cod. Simmer for 20 minutes then leave to cool.
Drain potatoes and salt cod. Remove any bones from the cod then
puree in a food processor. Stir in Parmesan and cream. Season
with salt and pepper to taste then let cool completely.
Form croquettes with dampened hands and dip them in flour,
then eggs, then breadcrumbs. Heat the sunflower oil and fry the
croquettes. Drain on paper towels and serve hot.

Rice and Provola Arancini

Preparation time 20 minutes
Cooking time 25 minutes
Wine *Greco di Tufo*

2 tbsps extra-virgin olive oil
1/2 yellow onion, minced
3/4 cup (5.5 oz or 150 g)
 Carnaroli or Roma rice
4 cups (1 l) vegetable broth
basil, minced
salt and pepper
4 oz (120 g) mild provola cheese
1 egg, beaten
3/4 cup (3.5 oz or 100 g)
 breadcrumbs
sunflower oil for frying

Heat the oil in a saucepan and sauté the onion until soft. Add the rice and continue cooking, adding broth little by little until rice is al dente.
Add the basil to the rice and season with salt and pepper. Transfer to a bowl and let cool. Cut the provola into cubes and mix into the cooled rice. Form small balls of the rice mixture. Dip the balls in egg then roll in breadcrumbs. Let sit for 20 minutes. Fry in sunflower oil and serve hot.

Zucchini and Prawn Toasts

Preparation time 15 minutes
Cooking time 8 minutes
Wine *Lagrein Rosato*

2 tbsps extra-virgin olive oil
1 garlic clove, smashed
7 oz (200 g) shelled prawns,
 chopped
salt and pepper
2 zucchini, diced
2 tbsps vegetable broth
1/2 baguette

Heat a non-stick pan with the oil and garlic and sauté until golden. Add the zucchini and sauté over high heat for 2 minutes. Add prawns and cook for another 2 minutes, seasoning with salt and pepper. Stir in vegetable broth and keep warm.
Slice the baguette and toast it in the oven or under the broiler. Top with the zucchini and prawn mixture and serve hot.

497

Phyllo Triangles with Ricotta and Tomatoes

Note *Phyllo dough can be replaced by a lighter dough made from 3/4 cup (3.5 oz or 100 g) plain flour and 3/4 cup (3.5 oz or 100 g) farro (emmer wheat) flour. Add a pinch of salt and pepper, 1 tbsp extra-virgin olive oil and warm water. Let the dough rest then roll out very thinly and continue with the recipe.*

498

Preparation time 20 minutes
Cooking time 5 minutes
Wine *Bianco d'Alcamo*

7 oz (200 g) sheep's milk ricotta
1 tbsp grated Pecorino Romano cheese
1 sprig thyme
freshly ground pepper
4 sheets phyllo dough
2 San Marzano or plum tomatoes, diced
1 garlic clove
2 tbsps extra-virgin olive oil
salt and pepper
sunflower oil

Beat the ricotta with pecorino and thyme leaves until creamy and season with freshly ground pepper.
Cut the phyllo dough into 3-inch (8 cm) wide strips. Place 1 teaspoon of ricotta filling on the top part of each strip. Starting at the top corner, fold the dough over to form a triangle and then fold 2 more times to create a triangular parcel like a samosa. Continue until all the filling is used.
Toss tomatoes with garlic, oil, salt and pepper. Let sit for 10 minutes.
Meanwhile heat the sunflower oil and fry the parcels. Serve very hot, over the tomato salad.

Lettuce and Grouper Rolls

Preparation time 20 minutes
Cooking time 5 minutes
Wine *Colli di Parma Malvasia*

10.5 oz (300 g) grouper fillet
1 orange
3 tbsps extra-virgin olive oil
1 garlic clove, smashed
5-6 black olives, pitted and
 roughly chopped
salt and pepper
parsley, minced
1 head lettuce
2 red tomatoes
extra-virgin olive oil
salt and pepper
4 slices white sandwich bread
butter

499

Remove any bones from the fish and cut into pieces.
Squeeze the orange and strain the juice.
Heat the oil and garlic in a frying pan and brown the fish for
2 minutes. Add the orange juice, let reduce, then add the olives.
Season with salt, pepper and a little parsley.
Separate the lettuce leaves, keeping them whole, and blanch in
boiling water for 3 seconds. Immerse in ice water then dry on a
clean kitchen towel. Place a small amount of grouper in the middle
of each leaf, fold in the outside edges and wrap into rolls.
Chop the tomatoes, removing the seeds, and toss the fish with oil,
salt and pepper.
Toast the bread and spread with butter.
Serve the lettuce rolls on the toast, topped with a few pieces
of tomato.

Eggplant Bruschetta

Preparation time 20 minutes
Cooking time 15 minutes
Wine *Alto Adige Pinot Bianco*

4 tbsps extra-virgin olive oil
1 shallot, minced
2 eggplant, diced
salt and pepper
2 thyme sprigs
7 oz (200 g) robiola cheese
8 slices bread

Heat 3 tablespoons oil in a
non-stick frying pan and gently
sauté the shallot. Add the
eggplant and cook for
10-12 minutes, seasoning with
salt and the thyme leaves.
As soon as the eggplant tender,
puree it in a food processor
with the robiola. Adjust salt and
pepper and let cool.
Drizzle the bread with oil and
toast in the oven or under the
broiler.
Serve the cooled eggplant
puree, formed into quenelles,
on top of the hot toast.

Bresaola Involtini

Preparation time 15 minutes
Wine *Verduzzo di Ramandolo*

5.5 oz (150 g) ricotta
7 oz (200 g) goat's cheese
1 bunch chives, minced
1 teaspoon orange-blossom
 honey
salt and pepper
16 slices bresaola

Sieve the ricotta and mix in a
bowl with the goat's cheese.
Add 1/2 of the minced chives
and honey and season to taste
with salt and pepper. Beat
the mixture until creamy and
transfer to a pastry bag with
a smooth tip. Pipe the ricotta
mixture onto the bresaola
slices and roll them up. Dip the
ends in the remaining chives,
pressing down to adhere.
Serve the bresaola rolls
immediately.

Note *Bresaola is an air-dried
salted beef, from the Valtellina
area of Lombardy.*

500

Herb and Cheese Crostini

Preparation time 15 minutes
Wine *Rosso di Montalcino*

3.5 oz (100 g) sheep's milk
 ricotta
5.3 oz (150 g) mild goat's cheese
3.5 oz (100 g) fresh soft cheese
1 tbsp minced aromatic herbs
 (thyme, basil, chives, rosemary)
1 tbsp extra-virgin olive oil
salt and freshly ground pepper
1 baguette

Sieve the ricotta and mix
together with the goat's cheese
and fresh soft cheese. Stir in
the herbs and oil and then
season with a pinch of salt
and freshly ground pepper.
Refrigerate for 1 hour or until
the cheese mixture is firm.
Slice the baguette and toast
under the broiler. Spread the
cheese and herb mixture
on the toasts and serve, if
desired, with a selection of raw
vegetable crudités.

Creamed Pea Crostini

Preparation time 10 minutes
Cooking time 12 minutes
Wine *Prosecco di Conegliano
e Valdobbiadene Brut*

2 tbsps extra-virgin olive oil
1 shallot, minced
1½ cups (7 oz or 200 g)
 new peas
3/4 cup (200 ml) vegetable broth
salt and pepper
8 slices sandwich bread
2.5 oz (70 g) sliced prosciutto
1.5 oz (40 g) Parmesan, shaved

501

Heat the oil in a saucepan and
sauté the shallot. As soon as
it is transparent, add the peas
and broth. Season to taste with
salt and pepper. Cook for
12 minutes.
Puree the peas into a cream
and let cool.
Cut the bread into circles and
toast until the broiler or grill.
Slice the prosciutto into thin
strips and roll into curls.
Spread the pea cream on the
bread. Top each slice with
1 Parmesan shaving and
1 prosciutto curl.

Eggplant Rounds with Chickpea Pâté

Note *Chickpeas can be found already cooked in cans or glass jars; dried, to be soaked for 10-12 hours and then boiled; or toasted and salted to be nibbled on with drinks. Chickpeas are also ground into flour, sometimes known as gram or besan, which is commonly used in Liguria to make focaccia and farinata.*

502

Preparation time 15 minutes
Cooking time 45 minutes
Wine *Alto Adige Pinot Bianco*

1 cup (7 oz or 200 g) dried chickpeas
2 tbsps extra-virgin olive oil
2 garlic cloves, smashed
rosemary
2 tbsps heavy cream
salt and pepper
2 small, long eggplants
8 tbsps sunflower oil

Soak the chickpeas overnight then boil for 40-45 minutes.
Heat the olive oil and sauté the garlic and rosemary.
Add chickpeas and cook for a few minutes, then remove the garlic and rosemary. Puree the chickpeas with the cream and adjust salt and pepper.
Cut the eggplant into 1-inch (2 cm) thick slices and salt them.
Heat the sunflower oil in a frying pan and cook the eggplant until soft and golden-brown. Drain on paper towels.
Preheat the broiler.
Line a baking tray with parchment paper and place the eggplant slices in 1 layer on it. Top each slice with a little chickpea puree.
Heat for a few minutes under the broiler and serve.

APPETIZER

Potato, Asiago and Pancetta Tart

Preparation time 10 minutes
Cooking time 45 minutes
Wine *Bardolino Chiaretto*

2 small yellow-fleshed potatoes
salt and pepper
1/3 cup (2 oz or 50 g) fava beans
2.5 oz (70 g) pancetta, diced
6.5 oz (180 g) Asiago cheese,
 diced
2 eggs, beaten

Preheat oven to 375° F (190°C).
Place the potatoes in cold
salted water, bring to a boil and
cook until tender. Drain, peel
and mash in a bowl.
Blanch the favas in boiling
water, immerse in ice water
then remove the external skin.
Brown the pancetta in a small
frying pan.
Mix the Asiago, favas, pancetta,
eggs, salt and pepper with
the potatoes. Fill 4-6 round,
buttered moulds with the
mixture and bake for 20
minutes. Serve hot.

Anchovy Frittata

Preparation time 20 minutes
Cooking time 30 minutes
Wine *Fiano d'Avellino*

2 lb (1 kg) fresh anchovies
salt
parsley, minced
5 tbsps grated pecorino cheese
4 eggs, beaten
I tbsp breadcrumbs
4 tbsps extra-virgin olive oil
basil

Preheat oven to 400°F (200°C).
Remove the heads and
backbones from the anchovies,
wash them and dry on a clean
kitchen towel. Lay them in an
oiled baking dish and sprinkle
each one with salt, parsley and
pecorino. Pour over the eggs,
sprinkle with breadcrumbs and
drizzle with oil.
Bake for 25-30 minutes.
Serve garnished with basil and
parsley.

503

Rosemary and Cheese Crackers

Note *These crackers work well as a snack with drinks and will keep for a week in an air-tight container. They can be topped with a mixture of ricotta with minced dill and minced gherkins.*

Preparation time 10 minutes
Cooking time 15 minutes
Wine *Alto Adige Gewürztraminer*

1/2 cup (3.5 oz or 100 g) cold butter, diced
2 oz (50 g) Emmenthal cheese
5 tbsps grated Parmesan
1 cup (4 oz or 120 g) plain flour
salt and pepper
2 tbsps rosemary flowers
rosemary sprigs

504

Quickly mix together the butter, Emmenthal, Parmesan and flour to form a dough. Season with salt and pepper and mix in the rosemary flowers. Roll the dough in a sheet of parchment paper, forming a 1½-inch (4 cm) diameter cylinder. Refrigerate for at least 30 minutes.
Preheat oven to 350°F (180°C).
Remove the paper and cut the roll into 1/3-inch (1 cm) thick slices. Lay on a baking tray and bake for around 15 minutes.
Let cool and serve garnished with rosemary sprigs.

Spinach Cascioni
(MARCHE)

Preparation time 40 minutes
Cooking time 30 minutes
Wine *Verdicchio dei Castelli di Jesi Spumante*

4 cups (1 lb or 500 g) plain flour
5 tbsps extra-virgin olive oil
7 tbsps warm milk
salt
2½ tsps dry active yeast
1 knob of butter
1 lb (500 g) spinach, chopped
3.5 oz (100 g) caciotta cheese, chopped
2 tbsps extra-virgin olive oil

Mound the flour on a work surface and mix in the oil, warm milk, a pinch of salt and yeast. Knead vigorously to obtain a smooth, uniform dough. Let the dough rest for 30 minutes, covered with a clean kitchen towel.
Divide the dough into small portions and roll out into flat, tortilla-like circles.
Melt the butter in a frying pan and sauté the chopped spinach until wilted.
Place a little sautéed spinach in the middle of each dough circle and top with some pieces of cheese. Fold over the dough to create half-moons and press down firmly around the edges to seal well.
Heat the oil in a frying pan and cook the cascioni on both sides until golden-brown. Serve hot.

505

Eggplant Napoletana

Preparation time 30 minutes
Cooking time 1 hour 10 minutes
Wine *Greco di Tufo*
♟ ♟

**1.75 lb (800 g) San Marzano
  or plum tomatoes, chopped
1 spring onion, chopped
1 bunch Neapolitan basil
salt and freshly ground black
  pepper
6 small eggplant, sliced
2 cups (500 ml) extra-virgin
  olive oil
2 eggs
7 tbsps grated Parmesan
10.5 oz (300 g) mozzarella,
  cut into strips**

506

Place the tomatoes, spring onion and a few leaves of basil in a
saucepan and cook until they soften. Pass through a food mill and
return to the heat for 10 minutes. Season with salt and pepper.
Sprinkle the eggplant slices with salt and place in colander. Leave
to drain for 1 hour, then rinse and dry. Heat the oil until very hot
and fry the eggplant slices. Dry on paper towels.
Beat the eggs and the tomato sauce for a few minutes.
Spread 3 tablespoons tomato sauce in a baking dish, then top
with a layer of eggplant. Sprinkle over 1 tablespoon Parmesan, the
remaining basil and 2-3 tablespoons tomato sauce then cover with
half of the mozzarella. Make another layer identical to the first and
top with the remaining Parmesan. Bake for about 1 hour. Serve
warm.

Sea Bass Carpaccio

Preparation time 15 minutes
Wine *Fiano di Avellino*
♟

7 oz (200 g) sea bass fillets
thyme and parsley, minced
coriander seeds, crushed
juice of 1 lemon
3 tbsps light extra-virgin olive oil
1 head lettuce
salt

Slice the sea bass fillets
into very thin slices. Cover
with plastic wrap and gently
pound them out with a meat
tenderizer until thin and almost
transparent.
Arrange the sea bass slices
on a serving plate and sprinkle
over the thyme, parsley,
crushed coriander seeds, lemon
juice (reserving 1 tablespoon)
and 1 tablespoon oil. Let sit to
marinate for about 8 minutes.
Tear the lettuce leaves into
pieces and dress with the
remaining oil, lemon juice and
salt to taste.
Serve the sea bass carpaccio
with the salad.

Spinach-Tomato Canapés

Preparation time 15 minutes
Cooking time 5 minutes
Wine *Gambellara*
♟

6 cups (6.5 oz or 180 g) spinach
5.5 oz (150 g) ricotta
2 tbsps extra-virgin olive oil
nutmeg, grated
salt and pepper
6 slices white sandwich bread
4 Camone tomatoes, thinly
 sliced
oregano

507

Blanch the spinach in boiling
water, drain, cool and squeeze
out excess water. Blend in a
food processor with the ricotta,
oil and nutmeg and adjust salt
and pepper.
Spread the spinach cream on
3 slices of bread, top with the
remaining 3 slices and press
down. Place the tomato slices
on the bread, overlapping
slightly, and season with a little
salt and oregano. Arrange on
a tray, cut into quarters and
serve.

Buffalo Mozzarella and Black Olive Panzerotti

Preparation time 30 minutes
Cooking time 5 minutes
Wine *Greco di Tufo*

508

2 tsps active dry yeast
salt and pepper
7 tbsps warm water
1 tsp lard
1½ cups (7 oz or 200 g)
 plain flour
1 buffalo mozzarella
 (9 oz or 250 g)
2 red, ripe tomatoes, chopped
thyme and basil, minced
fennel seeds
3 tbsps extra-virgin olive oil
2 tbsps pitted black olives,
 chopped
sunflower oil

Mix the yeast and salt in the warm water, add the lard and mix
with the flour to make a dough. Let rest for 1 hour, making an
x-shaped incision on the surface to allow rising.
Meanwhile cut the mozzarella into cubes and place in a colander
to drain.
Toss the tomatoes with herbs, fennel seeds, oil, salt and pepper.
Roll out the dough and cut out circles with a cookie cutter. Fill with
mozzarella and olives and close over to make half-moons.
Heat the sunflower oil until very hot and fry the panzerotti. Drain
on paper towels and serve with the tomatoes.

Truffled Leek Panzerotti

Preparation time 25 minutes
Cooking time 15 minutes
Wine *Dolcetto d'Alba*
👨‍🍳 👨‍🍳

1 cup (5.5 oz or 150 g)
 plain flour
3 tbsps extra-virgin olive oil
salt
3 tbsps water
1 tsp lard
1 knob of butter
1 leek, thinly sliced
3.5 oz (100 g) whole-wheat
 bread
3/4 cup (200 ml) milk
1 tbsp truffle oil
1/2 white truffle, minced
sunflower oil

Place the flour in a bowl and add oil, salt, water and lard. Mix
vigorously then transfer to a floured work surface and continue
kneading until a smooth and elastic dough is obtained. Form into
a ball, wrap in plastic wrap and refrigerate.
Melt the butter in a saucepan and sauté the leeks with a little
water until transparent.
Slice the bread and soak in milk until soft, then squeeze out
excess milk. Add to the leeks together with truffle oil. Let cool,
then stir in the truffle.
Roll out the dough and form large round ravioli stuffed with the
leek mixture. Seal the edges well. Heat the sunflower oil until very
hot and fry the panzerotti. Serve hot.

Amaranth with Vegetables and Almonds

Preparation time 25 minutes
Cooking time 25 minutes
Wine *Lago di Caldaro Rosato*

510

2 tbsps extra-virgin olive oil
2 spring onions, minced
3/4 cup (5.5 oz or 150 g)
 amaranth seeds
1/2 tsp turmeric
1 carrot, diced
1 zucchini, diced
1/2 tsp ground cumin
salt and pepper
1/4 cup (1 oz or 30 g) slivered
 almonds

Heat 1 tablespoon oil in a frying pan and sauté 1 minced spring
onion until soft.
Add the amaranth to the pan and toast, stirring constantly, then
add some water and the turmeric and continue cooking for
20 minutes. Set aside.
Heat 1 tablespoon oil in another frying pan and sauté the
remaining spring onion with a little water. Add the diced carrot
and zucchini and season with cumin and salt and pepper to taste.
Cook for 2 minutes.
Toast the almonds in a non-stick pan for a few minutes until
golden-brown, taking care not to burn them.
Toss the amaranth with the vegetables and serve hot, topped
with the almonds.

APPETIZER

Beef Carpaccio Skewers

Preparation time 20 minutes
Wine *Lagrein Rosato*

7 oz (200 g) top-quality beef
 tenderloin, thinly sliced
2 tbsps extra-virgin olive oil
salt and pepper
8 slices white sandwich bread
2 tbsps black olive tapenade
7 oz (200 g) mozzarella,
 thinly sliced
1 bunch arugula, finely chopped

Brush a little oil on the meat, or rub in with fingertips, and season with salt and pepper to taste.

Remove the crusts from the bread slices.

Create a very tall sandwich of bread, starting with 1 bread slice, then a layer of tapenade, a layer of mozzarella slices, another bread slice, a layer of chopped arugula, a layer of beef slices, another bread slice and so on, finishing with a layer of bread. Press down well to compact, wrap the entire sandwich in plastic wrap and refrigerate for 20 minutes.

Remove from the refrigerator, carefully unwrap and cut into quarters. Thread each quarter onto a wooden skewer so it stays intact. Serve immediately.

Nettle Croquettes
(PIEDMONT)

Note *For this recipe use only the smallest, youngest, most tender nettles.*

Preparation time 15 minutes
Cooking time 5 minutes
Wine *Erbaluce di Caluso Spumante Brut*

512

salt
1 lb (500 g) young nettle tips
2 eggs
4 tbsps grated Parmesan
1 tbsp breadcrumbs
3 tbsps plain flour
extra-virgin olive oil

Bring a large pot of salted water to a boil and boil the nettles until tender. Drain, squeeze out excess water and dry well.
Roughly chop the nettle leaves and place them in a bowl. Mix in the eggs, grated Parmesan, breadcrumbs and a pinch of salt. Mix until smooth and semi-firm.
Form the nettle mixture into medium-sized balls and dust with flour.
Heat the olive oil in a large frying pan and fry the nettle croquettes. Drain, dry on paper towels and serve hot.

Calabrian-Style Onion Rings
(CALABRIA)

Preparation time 10 minutes
Cooking time 10 minutes
Wine *Arghilla*

8 Tropea or other sweet red onions
3/4 cup (3.5 oz or 100 g)
 plain flour
2 eggs
salt
5 tbsps breadcrumbs
5 tbsps grated pecorino cheese
sunflower oil for frying

Peel the onions and cut into 1/5-inch (1/2 cm) thick rings. Wash under cold running water, then leave to dry on a clean kitchen towel for a few minutes.
Mound the flour on a work surface. Beat the eggs with a little salt. Mix the breadcrumbs with the pecorino in a large bowl.
Dip the onions first in the flour, then the eggs and then the breadcrumbs.
Heat the sunflower oil and fry the breaded onion rings. Drain with a slotted spoon as soon as they are golden, dry on paper towels and serve immediately.

513

Pea Crêpes

Note *Emmer, known in Italian as farro, is a type of wheat rich in protein, minerals, vitamins and fiber. It is enjoying a renaissance in Mediterranean cooking, but has been used since ancient times. The Etruscans made little breads with farro flour and ate them with vegetables and beans.*

514

Preparation time 15 minutes
Cooking time 30 minutes
Wine *Malvasia Istriana*

2 eggs
2 cups (500 ml) milk
3.5 oz (100 g) emmer flour
3/4 cup (3.5 oz or 100 g)
 plain flour
salt and white pepper
2 tbsps extra-virgin olive oil
1 shallot, minced
2¾ cups (12 oz or 350 g) peas
1/2 cup (120 ml) vegetable broth
2 tbsps heavy cream
2 oz (60 g) mimolette cheese
 (or other aged, hard cheese),
 grated

Preheat oven to 400°F (200°C).
Mix the eggs and milk in a bowl and sift in the flours. Mix a batter, season with salt and pepper and let rest for 20 minutes. Pass the batter through a sieve.
Heat the oil in a frying pan and sauté the shallot. Add peas and cover with broth. Cook over low heat for 15 minutes, then puree in a food processor with the cream. The puree should be quite thick.
Heat a non-stick pan with a little oil then make crêpes, using 1 ladleful of batter at a time.
Let them cool, then spread 1 tablespoon of pea puree on each one and roll up. Place in a baking dish and cover with aluminum foil. Bake for 5 minutes, then slice and serve with grated cheese.

Prosciutto and Arugula Roll

Preparation time 10 minutes
Wine *Ortrugo dei Colli Piacentini*
♟

7 oz (200 g) arugula
5.5 oz (150 g) squacquerone
 or other soft cheese
2 oz (50 g) mascarpone
3 tbsps grated Parmesan
salt and pepper
7 oz (200 g) prosciutto, sliced

Coarsely chop the arugula.
Mix the squacquerone,
mascarpone and Parmesan in a
bowl and season with salt and
pepper.
Lay out the prosciutto slices,
on a sheet of wax-paper
paper and spread them with
the cheese mixture. Top with
arugula. Roll the prosciutto
roll up tightly in the paper and
refrigerate for at least 1 hour.
Remove from the refrigerator
and slice. Serve at room
temperature.

Eggplant and Zucchini Strudel

Preparation time 25 minutes
Cooking time 35 minutes
Wine *Refosco dal Peduncolo
Rosso*
♟ ♟

1 small eggplant
6 tbsps extra-virgin olive oil
1 garlic clove
3 small zucchini
salt and pepper
5.5 oz (150 g) Calabrian coppa
9 oz (250 g) puff pastry
poppy seeds

515

Preheat oven to 375° F (190°C).
Cut the eggplant into wedges,
cut out the seeds, and dice the
rest. Heat 5 tablespoons oil
in a frying pan with the garlic
and sauté the eggplant. Cut
the zucchini into thick rounds
and add to the pan. Continue
cooking for a few minutes, but
leave the vegetables al dente.
Season with salt and pepper.
Cut the coppa into strips and
add to the vegetables. Spread
the mixture onto the sheet of
pastry and close like a calzone.
Brush the pastry with remaining
olive oil and sprinkle with poppy
seeds and a little salt. Bake for
25 minutes.

Parmesan Flan with Arugula and Tomatoes

Preparation time 20 minutes
Cooking time 30 minutes
Wine *Bolgheri Bianco*

2 eggs
1 cup (3.5 oz or 100 g) grated Parmesan
1/2 cup (120 ml) heavy cream
1/2 cup (120 ml) milk
salt and pepper
nutmeg, grated
butter
4 tomatoes
2 tbsps extra-virgin olive oil
2 bunches arugula

516

Preheat oven to 275° F (140°C).
Beat the eggs with a fork; add the Parmesan, cream, milk, salt, pepper and a grating of nutmeg.
Place a baking dish half-filled with water in the oven to use as a bain-marie.
Butter individual moulds and pour in the egg mixture. Place in the bain-marie and bake for 30 minutes.
Meanwhile blanch the tomatoes, drain and cool in ice water. Cut in half, remove seeds, and roughly chop the flesh. Toss with salt, pepper and olive oil.
Remove the flans from the oven and let cool.
Tear the arugula by hand into small pieces. Arrange on serving plates, unmould the flans on top and garnish with 2 tablespoons of tomatoes.

Devilled Eggs with Smoked Salmon

Note *Tender chives with the most delicate flavour can be found in the spring, before the plants have flowered.*

Preparation time 10 minutes
Cooking time 10 minutes
Wine *Cinque Terre*

6 eggs
3 tbsps mayonnaise
1 bunch chives
salt and pepper
3.5 oz (100 g) smoked salmon

Boil the eggs for 5-6 minutes. Cool, remove the shells and cut
the eggs in half horizontally.
Remove the yolks and place in a bowl with the mayonnaise,
some minced chives, salt and pepper and mix well until smooth.
Fill the egg halves with the mixture, and serve with slices
of smoked salmon, garnished with whole chives.

517

Greek Yogurt Vol-au-Vents

Preparation time 5 minutes
Wine *Prosecco di Conegliano e Valdobbiadene Brut*
👨‍🍳

3 gherkins
10 black olives, pitted
17 mint leaves
5.5 oz (150 g) Greek yogurt
salt and pepper
1 tbsp extra-virgin olive oil
12 prepared vol-au-vents

Rinse the gherkins and chop roughly. Mince half of the olives and 5 mint leaves. Mix chopped gherkins, olives and mint into the yogurt with salt, pepper and oil. Slice the remaining olives. Fill the vol-au-vents with the yogurt mixture and top with 1 olive slice and 1 mint leaf.

Note *Yogurt is packed with minerals, particularly calcium and phosphorous, and vitamins, particularly from the B group.*

Mediterranean Crostini

Preparation time 25 minutes
Wine *Etna Bianco*
👨‍🍳

5-6 capers in salt
2 tomatoes
3 tbsps extra-virgin olive oil
1/2 garlic clove
7-8 basil leaves
salt and pepper
8 slices crusty bread

Rinse the capers.
Blanch the tomatoes for 20 seconds in boiling water. Immerse in ice water, then peel. Cut into wedges and place in a blender or food processor with oil, garlic, basil and capers. Season with salt and pepper and puree.
Toast the bread slices and serve topped with the cold tomato puree.

518

Octopus and Potato Salad

Preparation time 15 minutes
Cooking time 45 minutes
Wine *Elba Bianco*

4 garlic cloves
1 dried red chilli pepper
14 oz (400 g) octopus
3 yellow-fleshed potatoes
1 spring onion, minced
10 cherry tomatoes, halved
parsley, minced
10 Taggiasca or other black
 olives in oil
3 tbsps extra-virgin olive oil
salt and pepper

Bring to a large pot of water to a boil with the garlic and chilli. When it boils, add the octopus and cook for 35 minutes. Let cool in the water for 2 hours. Drain and cut into small chunks. Place in a bowl. Boil the potatoes until tender, then drain, peel, cut into cubes and add to the octopus. Stir in spring onion, tomatoes, parsley, olives and extra-virgin olive oil and season with salt and pepper.

Langoustine Carpaccio

Preparation time 10 minutes
Cooking time 10 minutes
Wine *Metodo Classico Franciacorta Saten*

lemon verbena, chopped
4 tbsps extra-virgin olive oil
12 large langoustines
3/4 cup (180 ml) Metodo
 Classico Franciacorta wine
6 peppercorns
salt and pepper
dill, marjoram, chervil
 and tarragon, minced
toasted bread

Place the lemon verbena in a saucepan with a little oil and the langoustine heads. Sauté until browned and add the wine and peppercorns. Reduce to 1/3 of the original volume. Strain, adjust salt and pepper and let cool. Shell and devein the langoustines. Slice and toss with minced herbs, a little oil and salt. Arrange on a plate and squash with the back of a fork. Pour over the wine sauce and serve with toast.

519

Polenta with Pea Cream

Preparation time 20 minutes
Cooking time 55 minutes
Wine *Gutturnio Classico*

1/2 cup (120 ml) water
coarse salt
1/2 cup (3.5 oz or 100 g) instant
 polenta cornmeal
2 tbsps extra-virgin olive oil
1 shallot, minced
1/2 red chilli pepper
1/2 cup (120 ml) vegetable broth
1½ cups (7 oz or 200 g) peas
salt and pepper
chives, minced
sunflower oil

Bring the water to a boil with
the coarse salt and whisk in
the polenta, stirring constantly.
Cook until thick, then pour into
a baking dish and cool.
Heat the olive oil and sauté the
shallot with the chilli. Add broth
and peas and cook until tender.
Season with salt and pepper
and puree. Add chives.
Cut the polenta into cubes and
fry in hot sunflower oil. Serve
with the pea puree.

Bacon-Wrapped Prunes

Preparation time 15 minutes
Cooking time 5 minutes
Wine *Prosecco di Conegliano
e Valdobbiadene Brut*

16 prunes, pitted
lemon thyme
8 thin slices bacon

Preheat oven to 400°F (200°C).
Open the prunes and stuff with
2 lemon thyme leaves each.
Cut the bacon slices in half and
roll each prune tightly in bacon.
Close with a toothpick.
Bake for a few minutes. Serve
warm.

Note *Prunes are dried plums,
high in antioxidants and rich
dietary fiber. In the United
States, this appetizer is known
as Devils on Horseback. Here it
is enlivened with the addition
of fragrant lemon thyme.*

520

Smoked Salmon Canapés

Preparation time 15 minutes
Wine *Metodo Classico Franciacorta Brut*

1/2 head lettuce
2 tbsps extra-virgin olive oil
1 garlic clove, smashed
salt and pepper
8 slices whole-grain bread
9 oz (250 g) smoked salmon,
 cut into strips
10 black olives,
 pitted and halved
1 lime, peeled, segmented
 and chopped

Wash the lettuce and leave some water on the leaves.
Heat the oil in a saucepan with the garlic and add the lettuce. Sauté briefly then season with salt and pepper and puree.
Cut the bread slices into little squares. Spread with lettuce puree and top each one with a rolled strip of smoked salmon, a piece of lime pulp and 1/2of a black olive.

Note *Smoked salmon can be found from Scotland, Norway, Denmark, France, the Netherlands and Canada.*

Tuna with Roast Pepper Sauce

Preparation time 20 minutes
Cooking time 20 minutes
Wine *Cirò Bianco*

2 red bell peppers
14 oz (400 g) fresh tuna fillet
3 tbsps extra-virgin olive oil
1 garlic clove
thyme
salt and pepper
15 olives, pitted

Roast the peppers over an open flame. Close in a plastic bag to steam.
Slice the tuna. Heat a frying pan with the oil, garlic and thyme. Brown the tuna slices on both sides. Season with a little pepper and remove from the heat as soon as the tuna is browned on the outside.
Puree the olives in a food processor and spread on the tuna slices.
Peel the peppers, remove the seeds and chop finely to obtain a sauce. Season with salt and pepper.
Serve the tuna slices with pepper sauce.

521

Genoa-Style Focaccia
(LIGURIA)

Note *Italy is full of focaccia. Traveling through the country one can taste every possible kind of focaccia, seasoned with pork cracklings, herbs or spices, baked in the oven or grilled over charcoal. However the true homeland of focaccia is Liguria, where it is often filled with cheese or topped with potatoes and other vegetables.*

Preparation time 30 minutes
Cooking time 30 minutes
Beer *Light Ale*

2 potatoes
5 tsps (0.7 oz or 20 g) active dry yeast
3/4 cup (180 ml) warm milk
3 cups plus 3 tbsps (14 oz or 400 g) plain flour
salt
6 tbsps extra-virgin olive oil
coarse salt

522

Peel the potatoes, boil under tender and mash into a puree.
Dissolve the yeast in the warm milk.
Mound the flour on a work surface. Mix in the yeast and milk, regular salt, potato puree and 2 tablespoons olive oil. Knead the ingredients well to obtain a soft and smooth dough, adding warm water if necessary. Cover with a clean kitchen towel and let rest for at least 45 minutes.
Preheat oven to 400°F (200°C).
Roll the dough out on a lightly oiled baking tray. Form deep dimples in the dough with fingertips. Sprinkle over coarse salt, drizzle with oil and bake until surface is golden-brown.
Serve sliced, accompanied by cheeses and cured meats if desired.

APPETIZER

Spicy Crostini
(CALABRIA)

Preparation time 10 minutes
Cooking time 10 minutes
Wine *Melissa Bianco*

extra-virgin olive oil
1 red chilli pepper, minced
2 garlic cloves, peeled
1 cup (7 oz or 200 g)
 peeled tomatoes
oregano
salt and pepper
crusty bread

Heat the oil in a frying pan with the chilli and garlic. Add tomatoes and chop them with a knife in the pan. Add a pinch of oregano and adjust salt and pepper to taste. Cook until reduced and thickened. Meanwhile cut the bread into thick slices and toast in a non-stick frying pan or under the broiler.
Let the sauce cool then spread over the hot toast. Serve immediately.

Cecina
(TUSCANY)

Preparation time 5 minutes
Cooking time 30 minutes
Wine *Bianco Vergine della Valdichiana*

6 cups (1.5 l) water
3¼ cups (10.5 oz or 300 g)
 chickpea flour
7 tbsps extra-virgin olive oil
1 tsp salt
freshly ground pepper

Place the water in a bowl and sprinkle in the chickpea flour little by little, whisking constantly to avoid lumps forming. Add 6 tablespoons oil and salt and mix to obtain a smooth batter. Let rest for 30 minutes.
Oil a baking sheet and pour in the batter. Bake until a crust forms on the surface. Serve hot, topped with a sprinkling of freshly ground pepper.

523

Marinated Swordfish

Note *Potatoes can be categorized by the qualities of their flesh: yellow ones are firmer, while white ones have a higher starch content. Potatoes can be grown in many different environments and the tubers can be harvested during a long period from April to December.*

524

Preparation time 30 minutes
Cooking time 30 minutes
Wine *Metodo Classico*
Franciacorta Rosé

1 swordfish fillet
 (around 7 oz or 200 g)
1 lemon
salt
6 tbsps fruity extra-virgin olive oil
pink peppercorns
wild fennel leaves or dill, minced
1 yellow-fleshed potato
thyme and parsley, minced
2 carrots
1 head broccoli
1/2 celery root (celeriac)

Remove the skin from the fish and cut into small diamond-shapes. Squeeze most of the lemon juice into a bowl and dissolve a little salt in it. Add 2 tablespoons oil, pink pepper and fennel leaves and emulsify with an immersion blender. Add the swordfish, cover with plastic wrap and refrigerate for 2 hours.
Meanwhile boil the potato, peel and slice. Toss with parsley, 1 tablespoon oil and salt.
Slice the carrots into rounds, cut the broccoli into florets, slice the celeriac and blanch all the vegetables separately, until al dente.
Toss broccoli with salt, 1 tablespoon oil and remaining lemon juice; carrots with 1 tablespoon oil and thyme; and celeriac with 1 tablespoon oil and salt.
Arrange the vegetables on serving plates and top with pieces of marinated swordfish.

A P P E T I Z E R

Pea Flan with Spinach Sauce

Preparation time 15 minutes
Cooking time 1 hour
Wine *Alto Adige Pinot Bianco*

FLAN
2 tbsps extra-virgin olive oil
1/2 onion, minced
2⅓ cups (10.5 oz or 300 g)
 peas
salt and pepper
3/4 cup (180 ml) water
7 oz (200 g) ricotta
3 tbsps grated Parmesan
3 eggs
3 tbsps heavy cream
butter

SPINACH SAUCE
10.5 oz (300 g) spinach
1 shallot, minced
2 tbsps extra-virgin olive oil
nutmeg, grated
salt

525

Preheat oven to 350°F (180°C).
Heat 2 tablespoons oil and sauté the onion for few minutes.
Add the peas, salt and water and cook, covered, for 20 minutes.
Mix the ricotta, Parmesan, eggs, cream, salt and pepper in a bowl.
Blend the peas into a puree with a little water and add to the
ricotta mixture.
Butter a loaf pan and pour in the mixture. Bake in a bain-marie for
35-40 minutes.
Meanwhile wash the spinach and leave some water on the leaves.
Sauté the shallot in 2 tablespoons oil and add the spinach. Cook,
covered, for 5 minutes, then blend into a puree. Season with
nutmeg and salt to taste.
Unmould the flan and serve sliced with the spinach sauce.

Tomatoes Stuffed with Cod and Peas

Preparation time 15 minutes
Cooking time 20 minutes
Wine *Friuli Collio Sauvignon*

4 tomatoes
salt and pepper
1¼ cup (5.5 oz or 150 g) peas
3 tbsps extra-virgin olive oil
1 shallot, minced
7 oz (200 g) cod fillet, chopped
1/2 cup (120 ml) vegetable broth
parsley, coarsely chopped

526

Slice the top off the tomatoes and remove the seeds. Salt the inside and turn upside-down in a colander to drain.
Boil the peas in salted water until tender.
Heat the oil in a saucepan and sauté the shallot. Add the cod and cook for a few minutes. Add the cooked peas and a little broth. Season with salt and pepper, mix in some parsley and fill the tomatoes with the mixture.
The tomatoes can be served raw or gratinéed in the oven then cooled before serving.

Baked Anchovies
(PUGLIA)

Preparation time 10 minutes
Cooking time 20 minutes
Wine *Locorotondo Spumante*

5 tbsps capers in salt
1 garlic clove
4-5 mint leaves
oregano
2.2 lb (1 kg) anchovies
1⅔ cups (7 oz or 200 g)
 breadcrumbs
3 tbsps extra-virgin olive oil
vinegar
salt

Preheat oven to 350°F (180°C).
Wash the capers under running water and dry. Mince them
together with the garlic, mint leaves and oregano.
Debone and wash the anchovies, then layer them in a baking
dish (ideally made of terracotta) interspersed with layers of
breadcrumbs and the garlic-herb mixture. Drizzle with oil and
sprinkle over some vinegar. Bake for around 20 minutes until the
fish are cooked through.
Serve hot or warm, adjusting salt if necessary.

Spinach Croquettes

Preparation time 15 minutes
Cooking time 6 minutes
Wine *Prosecco di Conegliano
e Valdobbiadene Brut*

10.5 oz (300 g) spinach
9 oz (250 g) ricotta
salt and pepper
nutmeg, grated
1 egg
2 tbsps grated Parmesan
1 tbsp breadcrumbs
1/3 cup (2 oz or 50 g)
 finely chopped cashews

Boil the spinach, squeeze
out excess water and let
cool. Coarsely chop and mix
with ricotta. Season with
salt, pepper and a grating of
nutmeg. Mix well and add egg,
Parmesan and breadcrumbs.
Form croquettes, flatten slightly
and roll in the cashews.
Cook on a grill or cast-iron
pan for 3 minutes each side,
until the outside is crunchy
and the inside still soft. Serve
immediately.

Prawns and White Beans

Preparation time 15 minutes
Cooking time 40 minutes
Wine *Falanghina del Sannio*

4 tbsps extra-virgin olive oil
1 large shallot, minced
1 dried chilli pepper, deseeded
 and crumbled
1½ cups (9 oz or 250 g) cooked
 cannellini beans
10.5 oz (300 g) shelled prawns
 parsley, minced
10 cherry tomatoes, quartered
salt and white pepper
1/2 cup (120 ml) hot fish broth
 (made with prawn heads)

Heat the oil in a saucepan and
sauté the shallot and chilli. Add
beans, cook for a few minutes
then add prawns and parsley.
Stir and add tomatoes, salt
and pepper. Add broth and
simmer for 10 minutes. Season
with salt and serve topped with
a drizzle of olive oil and hot
toasts, if desired.

530

Prosciutto Involtini

Preparation time 20 minutes
Cooking time 10 minutes
Wine *Prosecco di Conegliano e Valdobbiadene Brut*
♟

2 small eggplants
salt and pepper
extra-virgin olive oil
2 whole mozzarellas
5.5 oz (150 g) prosciutto, sliced

Thinly slice the eggplants, salt the slices and place them in colander to drain for 30 minutes. Pat dry the eggplant slices and grill them for a few minutes on each side. Sprinkle with oil and season with salt and pepper to taste.

Cut the mozzarella into thick strips.

Lay out the prosciutto slices on a work surface and place 1 eggplant slice and a few mozzarella strips on each one, then roll up each slice and fix with a toothpick.

Let the involtini rest briefly so the flavours blend. Serve at room temperature.

Prawns with Mirto

Preparation time 10 minutes
Cooking time 4 minutes
Wine *Vermentino di Gallura*
♟

16 large prawns
2 tbsps extra-virgin olive oil
1 garlic clove, smashed
1 sprig myrtle (optional)
1 tbsps mirto liqueur
1 tbsp rice flour
1/2 cup (120 ml) Vermentino di Gallura wine
salt and pepper

Remove the heads and shell the prawns, then devein with a toothpick.

Heat the oil in a non-stick frying pan and sauté the garlic and myrtle sprig, if using. Add liqueur and let evaporate over high heat.

Dust the prawns with rice flour and add to the pan. Pour over the wine and season with salt and pepper. Cook until wine has reduced and prawns are cooked through. Serve immediately.

Note *Mirto is a liqueur made in Sardinia from myrtle berries and leaves.*

Ginger-Lime Scallops

Note *Spinach is a very popular vegetable not just for its taste but also because nutritional qualities (rich in iron and vitamins A and C) have been much lauded by the scientific community. Spinach is also widely used because it freezes well.*

532

Preparation time 25 minutes
Cooking time 15 minutes
Wine *Sicilia Chardonnay*

salt and pepper
2½ cups (9 oz or 250 g) white mushrooms
1 tbsp plain flour
juice of 1 lemon
5 tbsps extra-virgin olive oil
3 tbsps grated ginger
1 organic lime
20 cleaned scallops
4 slices crusty bread
10.5 oz (300 g) baby spinach

Bring a small pan of salted water to a boil. Add mushrooms, flour and half the lemon juice and cook for around 5 minutes. Drain and toss with 2 tablespoons olive oil, a pinch of salt and pepper to taste.
Preheat the broiler to the maximum setting.
Mix the ginger with 2 tablespoons oil and the grated zest of the lime. Arrange the scallops on a baking dish. Pour over the ginger-lime mixture and let sit for 5 minutes.
Broil the scallops for 2 minutes.
Toast the bread under the broiler and place 1 slice on each serving plate.
Toss the spinach with salt and remaining oil and lemon juice, then divide between the toasts. Top with mushrooms and scallops. Garnish with lime slices.

Warm Snow Pea and Lobster Salad with Balsamic Reduction

Note *Snow peas, also known as mangetout, are a kind of pea with a large, flat, edible pod.*

Preparation time 20 minutes
Cooking time 35 minutes
Wine *Friuli Collio Sauvignon*
♙ ♙

1⅔ cups (7 oz or 200 g)
 minced celery, carrot and onion
peppercorns
1/2 (120 ml) cup white wine
salt and white pepper
1 small lobster
10.5 oz (300 g) snow peas
4 tbsps extra-virgin olive oil
1 tsp toasted sesame seeds
6 tbsps balsamic vinegar
1.5 oz (40 g) caviar
parsley, minced
4 thin breadsticks

533

Place the minced celery, carrot and onion with the peppercorns, wine and a little salt in a saucepan with water and bring to a boil to make court bouillon.

Meanwhile make a splint for the lobster by tying it to a thin piece of wood. Immerse in the court bouillon and cook for 10 minutes. Drain and let cool.

Steam the snow peas until al dente then cut diagonally into diamond shapes and toss with oil, salt and sesame seeds.

Cook the balsamic vinegar in a small saucepan until reduced to 1/3 of the original volume, then cool.

Remove the shell from the lobster and slice the meat. Serve it on top of the warm snow peas, drizzled with the balsamic reduction. Top with a small quenelle of caviar, a sprinkling of parsley and a breadstick.

Steamed Grouper and Zucchini Timbales

Note *Grouper is a very adaptable fish, and can be cooked on the grill, wrapped in parchment paper, poached in court bouillon or roasted.*

Preparation time 10 minutes
Cooking time 35 minutes
Wine *Torbato d'Alghero*
♟

2 firm zucchini
9 oz (250 g) grouper fillet
1 small potato
2 tbsps extra-virgin olive oil
1 shallot, finely minced
parsley, minced
1/2 organic lemon
salt and pepper
2 tbsps pesto

534

Slice the zucchini lengthwise and grill briefly on a very hot cast-iron grill pan.
Remove any bones from the fish and cut into chunks.
Boil the potato and cut into chunks.
Heat the oil in a frying pan and sauté the shallot. Add the potato, then the grouper. Remove immediately from the heat and sprinkle with parsley (the grouper should not cook in the pan).
Blend the potato-grouper mixture in a food processor, season with salt and pepper and add a little lemon juice and grated lemon zest.
Line 4 individual moulds with plastic wrap, then with zucchini slices, and fill with the puree. Fold down the zucchini sticking up over the edge and press down well with the back of a spoon.
Steam for around 10 minutes. Serve garnished with a few drops of pesto.

A P P E T I Z E R

Lemon-Steamed Salmon and Zucchini Rolls

Preparation time 15 minutes
Cooking time 8 minutes
Wine *Alto Adige Pinot Bianco*

10.5 oz (300 g) salmon fillet
3 firm zucchini
3/4 cup (180 ml) water
2 lemons
1 tbsp yogurt
salt and pepper
1 tbsp mayonnaise

Remove any bones and the skin from the salmon. Cut the fillet into very thin slices and lay them out on a tray.
Cut the zucchini into 1½-inch (4 cm) long chunks and cut each chunk lengthwise into 4 wedges. Remove the central seeds.
Roll each piece of zucchini in a slice of salmon and place the rolls in a steamer basket.
Place the water in a saucepan. Halve the lemons, squeeze the lemon juice into the water and also add the squeezed lemon halves.
Place the steamer basket over the lemon infusion, bring to a boil and steam the rolls, covered, for around 8 minutes.
Meanwhile mix the yogurt and mayonnaise together.
Once cooked season the salmon rolls with salt and pepper and serve immediately, accompanied with the yogurt mayonnaise.

535

Grilled Mozzarella in Carrozza

Note *Mozzarella in carrozza means mozzarella in a carriage, referring to the bread which encases it.*

Preparation time 15 minutes
Cooking time 5 minutes
Wine *Lacryma Christi del Vesuvio*

536

6 slices white sandwich bread
2 tbsps milk
2 cow's milk mozzarellas
 (5 oz or 125 g each), thinly sliced
4 anchovy fillets in oil, drained
 and chopped
1 egg
salt and pepper
3 tbsps breadcrumbs
3 tbsps extra-virgin olive oil
1 garlic clove, smashed
2 zucchini, julienned
5 squash blossoms, chopped
1 tomato, diced

Cut the crust off the bread and moisten with a little milk. Make
3 sandwiches with the mozzarella and anchovies. Cut each into
quarters and press down firmly on each one.
Beat the egg with a little salt. Dip the little sandwiches into the
egg, shake off excess, then coat in breadcrumbs. Cook in a very
hot cast-iron pan until golden on both sides.
Heat the olive oil with the garlic in a non-stick frying pan and sauté
the zucchini, then add the blossoms. Season with salt and pepper
and divide between serving plates. Set the mozzarella in carrozza
around the zucchini and garnish with pieces of tomato.

Prawn and Sesame Toasts

Preparation time 15 minutes
Cooking time 5 minutes
Wine *Prosecco di Conegliano e Valdobbiadene Brut*
♟

4 slices sandwich bread
3.5 oz (100 g) small shelled
 prawns, minced
2 oz (60 g) sole fillet, minced
2 eggs, beaten
salt and pepper
3/4 cup (3.5 oz or 100 g)
 breadcrumbs
5 tbsps sesame seeds
sunflower oil

Toast the slices of bread and
cut into quarters.
Mix together the prawns, sole,
1 tablespoon beaten egg, salt
and pepper.
Mix the breadcrumbs and
sesame seeds together.
Spread a layer of prawn mixture
on each piece of toast, dip into
beaten egg and then sesame
breadcrumbs.
Heat the sunflower oil in a frying
pan and fry the prawn toasts
for a few minutes until golden.
Drain and dry on paper towels.
Serve hot.

Ham and Speck Ham Strudels

Preparation time 20 minutes
Cooking time 15 minutes
Wine *Metodo Trento Talento Brut*
♟

9 oz (250 g) puff pastry
1 egg, separated
3.5 oz (100 g) ham, sliced
3.5 oz (100 g) mild provolone,
 cubed
3.5 oz (100 g) speck ham, sliced
3.5 oz (100 g) Brie, sliced
poppy seeds
sesame seeds

537

Preheat oven to 350°F (180°C).
Roll the puff pastry out with a
rolling pin and cut 4-inch
(10 cm) squares. Brush the edges
of each square with egg white.
Place 1 slice of ham and some
pieces of provolone on half the
squares, then fold in half, sealing
the edges to close. Stuff the
remaining squares with slices of
speck ham and Brie, fold in half
and seal.
Brush the top of the strudels'
surfaces with egg white and
sprinkle the ham strudels with
poppy seeds and the speck ham
strudels with sesame seeds. Bake
for 15 minutes and serve hot.

Garlic Strichetti
(Emilia-Romagna)

Note *A surplus of parsley can be conserved for the winter in various ways: dried, frozen, cooked in a sauce or canned. The best way is to freeze it in little bags or immersed in water in ice-cube trays.*

Preparation time 30 minutes
Cooking time 30 minutes
Wine *Colli Bolognesi Riesling Italico*
♟ ♟

2⅓ cups (10.5 oz or 300 g) plain flour
3 eggs
14 oz (400 g) tomatoes
4 tbsps extra-virgin olive oil
8 garlic cloves, finely minced
parsley, finely minced
salt and pepper
6 tbsps grated Parmesan

538

Mound the flour on a work surface and break the eggs into the centre. Mix by hand, working vigorously to obtain a smooth, uniform and quite elastic consistency. Roll the dough out with a rolling pin and cut 1½-inches (4 cm) and 2⅓-inches (6 cm) long rectangles using a rolling pasta-cutter. Using thumb and index finger pinch the centre of each one to obtain a butterfly shape.
Blanch the tomatoes, drain and peel.
Heat the oil in a large frying pan and sauté a garlic and parsley for a few minutes. Add tomatoes, season with salt and pepper and cook over high heat for 10 minutes.
Bring a large pot of salted water to the boil and cook the pasta shapes. Drain and toss with the tomatoes. Serve hot with a generous sprinkling of Parmesan.

Langoustines with Carrot Puree

Preparation time 20 minutes
Cooking time 25 minutes
Wine *Alto Adige Pinot Bianco*

3 tbsps butter
1/2 onion, minced
5-6 large carrots, peeled and
  sliced
1 potato, peeled and sliced
thyme
salt and pepper
1 tbsp extra-virgin olive oil
1 garlic clove
16 shelled langoustine tails

Melt the butter in a saucepan
and sauté the onion until soft.
Add carrots and potato, brown
for 5 minutes then cover with
hot water. Cook over medium
heat until soft then puree.
Season with thyme, salt and
pepper.
Heat the oil in a frying pan with
the garlic clove and sauté the
langoustines, adding salt and
pepper to taste. Serve the
carrot cream topped with the
langoustines.

Vegetable Soup with Pasta

Preparation time 10 minutes
Cooking time 25 minutes
Wine *Bolgheri Bianco*

4 tbsps extra-virgin olive oil
1 onion, sliced
2 carrots, diced
1 celery stalk, diced
salt
3/4 cup (3.5 oz or 100 g) peas
2/3 cup (3.5 oz or 100 g) fava beans
1 tsp tomato paste
4 cups (1 l) water
3 cups (3.5 oz or 100 g) shredded
  Swiss chard
4 oz (120 g) thin rye tagliatelle
basil, julienned

539

Heat 2 tablespoons oil in a
saucepan and sauté the onion,
carrot and celery with salt. Add
peas, favas, tomato paste and
cover with water. Adjust salt,
bring to a boil and cook for
10-15 minutes over moderate
heat. Add chard, bring to a boil
and add tagliatelle. Continue
cooking until pasta is done then
remove from heat. Serve with
basil and a drizzle of oil.

Creamed Zucchini and Salt Cod with Mint

Note *Salt cod must be desalted before use. Immerse in cold water and scrub to remove external salt. Let soak for at least 2 days, changing the water frequently. For the first 24 hours the cod should be kept under cold running water, and then it can be changed every 6-8 hours.*

Preparation time 15 minutes
Cooking time 25 minutes
Wine *Colli Piacentini Chardonnay*
♟

6 tbsps extra-virgin olive oil
1/2 onion, thinly sliced
1 garlic clove
1 lb (500 g) soaked salt cod
3 pale zucchini, diced
2/3 cup (150 ml) heavy cream
4 cups (1 l) vegetable broth
5-6 mint leaves
salt and pepper

540

Heat 2 tbsps oil in a saucepan and sauté the onion and garlic.
Remove the skin and any bones from the salt cod and chop.
Reserve a few pieces for garnish and add the rest to the onions.
Add 2 zucchini and cream, cover with broth and cook for about 20 minutes.
Puree the mixture with the mint and 2 tablespoons oil, and season with salt and pepper.
Heat 1 tablespoon oil in a frying pan and sauté the remaining zucchini.
Place the puree in shallow bowls, top with reserved salt cod and zucchini and drizzle with oil.

Zucchini Velouté
with Parmesan Croutons

Note *A velouté can be thickened with potatoes, potato flakes (used for mashed potatoes) or rice flour, which needs only a very short cooking time.*

Preparation time 20 minutes
Cooking time 40 minutes
Wine *Vermentino di Gallura*
♟

4 tbsps extra-virgin olive oil
1/2 onion, thinly sliced
1 tbsp Carnaroli rice
3 medium zucchini, sliced
vegetable broth
2 slices crusty bread
1 tbsp grated Parmesan
1 sprig thyme
salt and pepper
sunflower oil for frying
1/2 leek, very thinly sliced
1 tbsp plain flour

541

Preheat oven to 350°F (180°C).
Heat 2 tablespoons oil in a saucepan and sauté the onion. Add the rice and toast. Add zucchini and some vegetable broth and cook for about 20 minutes.
Meanwhile cut the bread into cubes, drizzle with remaining oil and toast in the oven for 5 minutes. Just before removing from the oven, sprinkle over the Parmesan.
Puree the zucchini mixture and season with thyme, salt and pepper.
Heat the sunflower oil. Dust the leek slices with flour and fry until crispy.
Serve the zucchini velouté with the croutons and fried leeks.

Spicy Cuttlefish and Chard Soup

Note *Swiss chard is a herbaceous plant, closely related to sugar beets. It is low in calories and rich in vitamin A and iron like spinach.*

Preparation time 15 minutes
Cooking time 25 minutes
Wine *Cinque Terre*

10.5 oz (300 g) baby cuttlefish
1 garlic clove
3 tbsps extra-virgin olive oil
1 dried red chille pepper, deseeded
parsley, minced
3 tbsps white wine
salt and pepper
3 tbsps tomato sauce
7 Swiss chard leaves, shredded

Wash the cuttlefish and remove the hardest fins and the black eye. Cut the rest into pieces.
Remove the green shoot from the garlic and chop finely.
Heat the oil in a saucepan and sauté the garlic. Crumble in the chille pepper and then add the cuttlefish. Cook for 5 minutes, sprinkling with parsley and white wine. Lightly salt to taste and add tomato sauce. Cook for another 7-8 minutes, with the lid halfway on. Add the chard and a little hot water. Let cook down and thicken then adjust salt and pepper.
Serve soup with garlic croutons, if desired.

Tomato and Thyme Soup with Tuna

543

Note *The fresh tuna could be replaced by steamed and shelled prawns, or sautéed and shelled mussels. A fresh, deseeded chille pepper could be used instead of the driedflakes.*

Preparation time 15 minutes
Cooking time 20 minutes
Wine *Lugana*

4 ripe tomatoes
1 red bell pepper
2 sprigs thyme
4 tbsps extra-virgin olive oil
2 garlic cloves, crushed
dried red chille flakes
salt and pepper
1/2 cup (120 ml) vegetable broth
10.5 oz (300 g) fresh tuna

Cut an X in the bottom of the tomatoes, blanch in boiling water, peel, remove the seeds and chop roughly.
Roast the pepper directly on the gas burner or on a grill. Close in a plastic bag for a few minutes, then peel and chop roughly.
Toss the tomatoes and pepper with the thyme leaves.
Heat a saucepan with 2 tablespoons oil and the garlic. Add tomatoes and peppers and brown together with salt, pepper and a pinch of chille. Add a little broth, and puree in a blender.
Cut the tuna into bite-sized chunks. Heat 2 tablespoons oil in a non-stick pan and brown the tuna, turning once.
Divide the tuna between shallow soup bowls and pour over the tomato soup.

Octopus Soup

Preparation time 15 minutes
Cooking time 1 hour
Wine *Fiano di Avellino*

1¼ cups (9 oz or 250 g) pearled
  emmer wheat (farro)
3 cups (750 ml) water
1 small octopus
 (around 1 lb or 450 g)
6 tbsps extra-virgin olive oil
2 garlic cloves, crushed
1/2 red chille pepper, minced
1 tomato, chopped
parsley, minced
salt and white pepper

Boil the emmer wheat with
water for 50 minutes and let
rest for 10 minutes.
Meanwhile cut the octopus into
small pieces.
Heat the oil in a saucepan
and sauté the garlic, chille and
tomato. Add octopus and cook
for 5 minutes over medium
heat, adding parsley.
Add octopus mixture to the
emmer, adjust salt and pepper
and serve hot.

Asparagus and Saffron Farfalle

Preparation time 15 minutes
Cooking time 25 minutes
Wine *Alto Adige Pinot Bianco*

10 asparagus spears
3 tbsps extra-virgin olive oil
1 shallot, minced
1/2 cup (120 ml) vegetable broth
salt
1 pinch saffron
12.5 oz (350 g) farfalle
2 boiled eggs, yolks only
parsley, minced

Peel the bottoms of the
aspargus spears and slice the
spears into rounds.
Heat the oil in a saucepan and
sauté the shallot. Add aspargus
and broth and cook over low
heat for 5 minutes.
Bring a large pot of salted
water to the boil, add the
saffron and cook the farfalle
until al dente. Drain, rinse
with cold water, and toss with
the asparagus. Crumble the
egg yolks over the pasta and
sprinkle with parsley.

544

Robiola and Arugula Linguine

Preparation time 15 minutes
Cooking time 10 minutes
Wine *Roero Arneis*

2 bunches arugula
1 garlic clove, peeled
6 tbsps grated Parmesan
salt
6 tbsps extra-virgin olive oil
4.5 oz (125 g) robiola cheese
dried red chille flakes
12.5 oz (350 g) linguine
Parmesan shavings

Puree the arugula (reserving some leaves for garnish), garlic, grated Parmesan and 1/2 teaspoon salt, pouring in a thin stream of oil. Add robiola, a pinch of chille and continue blending for a few seconds. Bring a large pot of salted water to a boil and cook the linguine until al dente. Drain, reserving some cooking water. Toss with the arugula puree adding a little cooking water if necessary and top with arugula leaves and Parmesan shavings.

Spinach and Salmon Fusilli

Preparation time 20 minutes
Cooking time 10 minutes
Wine *Bianco dei Castelli Romani*

3 tbsps extra-virgin olive oil
2⅔ cups (7 oz or 200 g) sliced mushrooms
salt and pepper
7 oz (200 g) salmon fillet, diced
10.5 oz (300 g) spinach, chopped
2 tbsps heavy cream
12.5 oz (350 g) fusilli

Heat the oil in a large frying pan, add the mushrooms and sauté for 3-4 minutes. Season with salt, add salmon and spinach and cook for a couple of minutes. Stir in the cream and remove from heat. Bring a large pot of salted water to a boil and cook the fusilli until al dente. Drain and toss with the sauce in the frying pan. Return to the heat and cook for 2 minutes. Sprinkle with pepper and serve hot.

Valtellina-Style Buckwheat Pasta (LOMBARDY)

Note *This traditional pasta from the north of Italy is known as* pizzoccheri. *In the summer it is served with Swiss chard, and in the winter with Savoy cabbage.*

Preparation time 20 minutes
Cooking time 20 minutes
Wine *Valtellina Superiore Valgella*

3 cups (9 oz or 350 g) black
 buckwheat flour
3/4 cup (3.5 oz or 100 g)
 plain flour
salt
1 lb (500 g) Swiss chard, chopped
9 tbsps grated Grana Padano
 cheese
14 oz (400 g) unaged
 Valtellina Casera cheese, sliced
3 tbsps butter
3 garlic cloves, crushed

546

Mix the 2 flours and mound on a work surface. Form a well in the centre and pour in enough water to obtain a smooth dough. Mix well, let rest for a few minutes then roll out a thin sheet. Cut first into rectangles 2¾-inches (7 cm) wide and then into 1/5-inch (½ cm) thick tagliatelle.
Bring a pot of salted water to a boil. Add the chard, and 7 minutes before it is done cooking, add the pasta. When it is cooked, use a slotted spoon to drain some of the pasta and chard and place in a baking dish. Top with a layer of grated Grana and Casera cheese, then add some more pasta and chard and continue making layers, finishing with a thin layer of cheese.
Melt the butter with the garlic cloves, remove the garlic and pour the butter over the pasta. Serve hot.

Ricotta and Swiss Chard Dumplings (PIEDMONT)

Note *This dish is called* rabatòn, *from the Piedmontese dialect* rabatare, *meaning to roll, refering to the motion of rolling the dumplings in flour giving them an elongated shape.*

Preparation time 25 minutes
Cooking time 20 minutes
Wine *Roero Arneis*

10.5 oz (300 g) Swiss chard
1 lb (500 g) ricotta
1½ cups (5.5 oz or 150 g) grated
 Parmesan plus extra
 for topping
2/3 cup (2.5 oz or 75 g)
 breadcrumbs
3 eggs
salt and pepper
nutmeg, grated
plain flour
butter

Preheat oven to 350°F (180°C).
Blanch the Swiss chard for a few minutes in abundant water, drain, dry and chop finely. Place in a bowl and sieve in the ricotta, then add the Parmesan, breadcrumbs, eggs, pinches of salt and pepper and some nutmeg. Mix well; the consistency should be fairly dense. If it is too soft, add some flour.
Form walnut-sized balls in the palm of the hand, then roll on a floured work surface to obtain a more elongated shape.
Bring a large pot of salted water to a boil and boil the dumplings for 5 minutes. Drain with a slotted spoon and arrange in a baking dish. Top with grated Parmesan and pieces of butter. Bake for a few minutes to brown the top and serve hot.

548

Prawn and Artichoke Penne

Preparation time 20 minutes
Cooking time 10 minutes
Wine *Colline Lucchesi Bianco*

3 baby artichokes
2 tbsps extra-virgin olive oil
parsley, minced
1 garlic clove, minced
2 oz (50 g) pancetta, julienned
5.5 oz (150 g) shelled prawns
3/4 cup (180 ml) white wine
salt and pepper
12.5 oz (350 g) penne
1 oz (30 g) mild pecorino, shaved

Remove the tough external
leaves from the artichokes, cut
in 1/2 and then slice.
Heat the oil in a frying pan
and sauté the parsley, garlic
and pancetta. When they start
to brown add the prawns,
sauté for a few minutes then
add wine and artichokes and
season with salt and pepper.
Bring a large pot of salted
water to a boil and cook the
penne until al dente. Add to
the sauce together with 1
tablespoon cooking water.
Toss, sprinkle with pecorino
and serve.

Pasta with Peas and Carrots

Preparation time 10 minutes
Cooking time 20 minutes
Wine *Lugana*

1 knob of butter
1 shallot, minced
1½ cups (7 oz or 200 g) peas
salt and pepper
4 cups (1 l) hot vegetable broth
1 tsp fresh goat's cheese
3 tbsps extra-virgin olive oil
12.5 oz (350 g) pipe, lumache
 or conchiglie pasta
2 carrots, diced
1 tbsp grated Parmesan

Melt the butter in a saucepan
and sauté the shallot. Add
peas and cook for 5 minutes,
seasoning with salt and pepper.
Cover with hot broth and cook
until peas are tender. Puree
with goat's cheese and 2
tablespoons oil.
Bring a large pot of salted to
a boil and cook the pipe until
al dente. Heat 1 tablespoon oil
in a frying pan and sauté the
carrots.
Drain the pasta and toss with
pea puree.
Stir Parmesan into pasta and
serve with carrot cubes.

Dumplings with Vegetable Caponatina

Note *If you do not have a spaetzle press, the dough can also be formed into little gnocchi by hand, using the back of a fork to slightly squash them.*

Preparation time 30 minutes
Cooking time 12 minutes
Wine *Lagrein Rosato*

DUMPLINGS
2 cups (9 oz or 250 g)
 plain flour
1/2 cup (120 ml) milk
2 eggs
nutmeg, grated
salt and pepper
extra-virgin olive oil

CAPONATINA
1 zucchini, diced
1/2 yellow bell pepper, diced
2 vine-ripened tomatoes
2 tbsps extra-virgin olive oil
2½ tbsps pine nuts
4 tbsps pitted black olives,
 chopped
2½ tbsps capers, rinsed
 and squeezed out
3 basil leaves, chopped
dried red chille flakes

549

Mix all the dumpling ingredients except for the oil together in a bowl, whisking to obtain a thick batter.
Bring a pot of salted water to a boil. Using a spaezle press or potato ricer form the dumplings directly into the water. Cook for 3-4 minutes, drain and rinse with cold water. Toss with a little olive oil.
Blanch the zucchini and pepper in boiling water for 2 minutes. Blanch the tomatoes, peel, remove the seeds and dice the pulp. Heat the oil in a frying pan and lightly toast the pine nuts. Stir in the vegetables, olives, capers and basil. Add the dumplings to the mixture and briefly sauté over high heat. Sprinkle with a pinch of chille and serve immediately.

Asparagus and Scamorza Lasagna

2 lb (1 kg) asparagus
1 shallot
1 ladleful vegetable broth
1¾ cups (400 ml) béchamel
 (see p. 1096)
salt and pepper
7 oz (200 g) fresh egg pasta
 dough (see p. 1094)
3.5 oz (100 g) smoked scamorza
 cheese, sliced
1 cup (3.5 oz or 100 g) grated
 Parmesan
3½ tbsps (1.8 oz or 50 g) melted
 butter

550

Preparation time 45 minutes
Cooking time 30 minutes
Wine *Alto Adige Terlaner Riserva*

Preheat oven to 350°F (180°C).
Cut off the asparagus tips, and slice the stalks into rounds. Boil the
tips for 3-4 minutes.
Soften the shallot with a little water in a saucepan, add the
asparagus stalks and cook over low heat for a few minutes. Add
vegetable broth and cook for another 10 minutes. Puree the
asparagus, stir in the béchamel and season with salt and pepper.
Roll out the pasta dough and cut out rectangles. Blanch in boiling salted
water for a couple of minutes and let cool on a clean kitchen towel.
Butter a baking dish. Start with a layer of pasta pieces, 1 ladleful
of asparagus béchamel, slices of scamorza, grated Parmesan and
asparagus tips and repeat the layers, finishing with a layer of pasta.
Brush with melted butter and top with a sprinkling of Parmesan. Bake
for 15 minutes. Serve hot.

Spinach Rice

Preparation time 20 minutes
Cooking time 20 minutes
Wine *Val d'Aosta Pinot Grigio*

1 cup (7 oz or 200 g) Basmati rice
2 tbsps extra-virgin olive oil
1 spring onion, minced
2½ cups (600 ml) vegetable broth
12.5 oz (350 g) spinach, chopped
salt and pepper
2 tbsps heavy cream
5.5 oz (150 g) sheep's milk ricotta
thyme, tarragon and chives, minced

Rinse the rice. Heat oil, sauté the spring onion then add rice and toast. Add broth and let cook for 20 minutes over medium heat, adding half the spinach after 10 minutes and the rest at the end of cooking. Season with salt and pepper and let sit 10 minutes. Stir in the cream and let sit 10 minutes. Mix together ricotta and herbs and serve the rice with quenelles made from the ricotta mixture.

Artichoke and Saffron Risotto

Preparation time 15 minutes
Cooking time 20 minutes
Wine *Etna Bianco*

4 baby artichokes
juice and zest of 1 lemon
2 tbsps extra-virgin olive oil
1 knob of butter
1 shallot, minced
1½ cups (10.5 oz or 300 g) Vialone Nano rice
4 cups (1 l) vegetable broth
1 pinch saffron
1 tbsp grated Parmesan
salt and pepper

Remove the tough external leaves and inner choke from the artichokes and immerse in water with lemon juice. Slice 2 of the artichokes.
Heat the oil and butter in a frying pan and sauté the shallot. Add the artichoke slices and sauté briefly, then add rice, toast, and add broth. Finely chop the remaining artichokes and add them halfway through cooking with the saffron.
When the rice is cooked stir in Parmesan and grated lemon zest and adjust salt and pepper before serving.

551

Saffron Garganelli with Tomatoes and Favas

Preparation time 30 minutes
Cooking time 15 minutes
Wine *Vermentino di Gallura*

3/4 cup (5.3 oz or 150 g) semolina flour
3/4 cup (3.5 oz or 100 g) plain flour
2 eggs
5 tbsps extra-virgin olive oil
salt and pepper
1 pinch saffron
10.5 oz (300 g) vine-ripened tomatoes
1⅓ cup (7 oz or 200 g) fresh fava beans
2 garlic cloves, crushed
basil
2 tbsps grated pecorino

552

Mix together the two flours, eggs, 2 tablespoons oil, a pinch of salt and the saffron dissolved in a little water to make a smooth and elastic dough. Form a ball, wrap in plastic wrap and let rest for 20 minutes.
Blanch the tomatoes in boiling water for 30 seconds, drain and reserve the water, remove the skin and seeds and dice.
Blanch the favas in the same water, drain and remove the outer skin.
Heat the oil with the garlic in a frying pan, sauté briefly and add tomatoes and favas. Salt to taste and cook for a few minutes then set aside.
Roll the dough out into a not-too-thin sheet and cut into 3/4-inch (2 cm) squares. Roll each square up starting from one corner.
Bring a large pot of salted water to a boil and cook the garganelli until al dente. Drain and toss with the tomato and fava sauce.
Sauté for a few minutes to amalgamate and add basil, pecorino and a pinch of pepper.

Corn Fusilli with Green Beans and Squash

Preparation time 20 minutes
Cooking time 20 minutes
Wine *Colli di Luni Bianco*

3 tbsps extra-virgin olive oil
1/2 shallot, minced
1 garlic clove, halved
1/4 leek, finely sliced
1/2 dried red chille pepper,
 deseeded
2 cups (9 oz or 250 g) diced
 summer squash
salt and pepper
2 cups (7 oz or 200 g) green beans
1/2 cup (120 ml) hot vegetable broth
1 firm red tomato
14 oz (400 g) corn fusilli

553

Heat the oil, sauté the shallot, garlic and leek and crumble in the chille. As soon as the shallot is transparent remove the garlic and add the summer squash. Season with salt and pepper and continue cooking.

Meanwhile top and tail the green beans, blanch for 3 minutes in salted water and immerse immediately in ice water. Cut into bite-sized pieces and add to the squash together with a little hot broth and continue cooking.

Remove the seeds from the tomato and cut the flesh into strips. Add to the pan and season with salt and pepper.

Bring a large pot of salted water to a boil and cook the fusilli until still very al dente. Drain and toss with the vegetables and broth until cooked through.

Artichoke Risotto

Preparation time 15 minutes
Cooking time 20 minutes
Wine *Trentino Nosiola*

2 tbsps butter
1 shallot, minced
vegetable broth
1½ cups (10 oz or 280 g)
 Vialone Nano rice
4 artichokes
thyme
grated zest of 1/2 organic lemon
1 tbsp grated Parmesan
3.5 oz (100 g) crescenza cheese
salt and pepper

Melt the butter and sauté the shallot with a little broth. Add rice, toast over high heat then add broth little by little, stirring frequently.
Remove the external leaves and choke from the artichoke and finely chop the heart. Add to the risotto as it cooks.
Mince together the thyme and grated lemon zest and add to the rice.
When the rice is cooked, stir in Parmesan and crescenza. Adjust salt and pepper and serve immediately.

Strawberry and Champagne Risotto

Preparation time 25 minutes
Cooking time 20 minutes
Wine *Sicilia Chardonnay*

3½ tbsps butter
1/2 spring onion, minced
1¼ cups (9 oz or 250 g)
 Vialone Nano rice
3/4 cup (180 ml) Chardonnay wine
10 strawberries, diced
grated zest of 1 organic lemon
2 oz (50 g) robiola cheese
salt and white pepper

Melt the butter and sauté the spring onion. Add rice and toast over high heat, stirring continuously. Add wine and let evaporate. Add 1/3 strawberries and start adding hot water, little by little. Continue cooking, adding a little more hot water whenever the rice dries out. When the rice is cooked stir in the lemon zest, remaining strawberries and robiola. Adjust salt and pepper and serve.

554

Orzotto
in Parmesan Baskets

Note *Orzotto is like risotto, but made with pearled barley (orzo in Italian) instead of rice.*

Preparation time 20 minutes
Cooking time 20 minutes
Wine *Cabernet*
👨‍🍳👨‍🍳

4 tbsps extra-virgin olive oil
1 garlic clove, peeeld
1 medium potato, diced
2 large carrots, diced
1 medium zucchini, diced
3/4 cup (3.5 oz or 100 g) peas
1 bay leaf
2 sage leaves
1 knob of butter
4 tbsps minced onion
1½ cups (10.5 oz or 300 g)
 pearled barley
1/2 cup (120 ml) white wine
2½ cups (600 ml) vegetable broth
3 tbsps grated Parmesan
chives, minced
salt and pepper

555

Preheat oven to 350°F (180°C).
Heat the oil and garlic in a frying pan and brown the potato, carrots and zucchini. Add peas, bay, sage, salt and pepper and continue cooking over high heat for a few minutes.
Melt the butter in a saucepan and sauté the onion. Add barley and toast, add wine and let evaporate, then add broth. Cook, stirring frequently, for 15 minutes.
Oil a baking sheet and place a round, 4-inch (10 cm) diameter cookie cutter in the middle. Sprinkle a thin layer of Parmesan inside it and bake for around 5 minutes. Place over an upside-down cup and remove the cookie cutter, creating a basket. Repeat these steps to obtain 6 Parmesan baskets and let cool and harden.
When the barley is almost cooked, add the vegetables (discarding bay and sage), season with salt and sprinkle with chives. Serve the barley in the Parmesan baskets, sprinkled with more Parmesan.

First of May Maltagliati

Note *Fava beans can be found in Italy fresh or dried. Fresh they can be eaten raw, with cheese or bread, or cooked in soups. Dried favas, if peeled, can be boiled without pre-soaking.*

Preparation time 30 minutes
Cooking time 10 minutes
Wine *Bardolino Chiaretto*
♟

1½ cups (7 oz or 200 g)
 plain flour
2 eggs
salt and pepper
2 tbsps raisins
1 tbsp vin santo or other sweet wine
2 oz (60 g) pancetta
2 tbsps extra-virgin olive oil
1 garlic clove, unpeeled and halved
5-6 fava bean pods
5 tbsps grated aged pecorino cheese

556

Mix the flour with the eggs and a pinch of salt to obtain a smooth and elastic dough. Wrap in plastic wrap and refrigerate for 30 minutes.
Soak the raisins in vin santo and a little warm water.
Cut the pancetta into strips and brown in a non-stick pan with oil and garlic. Shell the favas and remove the external skin, then add to the pancetta. Add 2 tablespoons water and pepper. Drain and squeeze excess moisture out of raisins then add to the pan.
Roll out the dough with a pasta machine, then cut into irregular rectangles. Bring a large pot of salted water to a boil and cook the pasta. Drain directly into the frying pan and toss with sauce and pecorino. Serve immediately.

Gnocchetti in Zucchini Cream

Preparation time 20 minutes
Cooking time 15 minutes
Wine *Torbato di Alghero*
℘

2 tbsps extra-virgin olive oil
1 garlic clove, smashed
3 young zucchini, thickly sliced
salt and pepper
1/2 cup (120 ml) vegetable broth
12.5 oz (350 g) gnocchetti
 (small gnocchi)
3-4 basil leaves
7-8 cherry tomatoes, quartered
1 tbsp toasted pine nuts, minced

557

Heat the oil and garlic in a frying pan and sauté the zucchini.
Season with salt and pepper. As soon as the zucchini start to
brown, add the broth and cook, covered, until tender.
Meanwhile boil the gnocchetti until al dente, drain and cool under
cold running water.
Let the zucchini cool, remove the garlic and puree with the basil in
a food processor. Mix with the gnocchetti, tomatoes and pine nuts
and serve.

Cold Orecchiette with Vegetable Caponata

Preparation time 20 minutes
Cooking time 20 minutes
Wine *Bianco d'Alcamo*

3 tbsps extra-virgin olive oil
1 yellow onion, minced
1 garlic clove, smashed
1/2 eggplant, deseeded
 and diced
5-6 aspargus spears,
 sliced
2 carrots, diced
salt and pepper
2 zucchini, green part only,
 diced
hot vegetable broth (optional)
3 basil leaves
12.5 oz (350 g) orecchiette
1 tomato, deseeded and diced

558

Heat the olive oil and sauté the onion until golden. Add garlic
and eggplant, then the asparagus. Cook for 3 minutes then add
carrots. Season with salt and pepper. Add the zucchini together
with a little broth or hot water and basil.
Bring a pot of salted water to a boil and add orecchiette. As soon
as they are al dente drain and cool under cold running water.
Once the vegetables are cooked, remove from the heat and let
cool. Add tomatoes and pasta, let rest 20 minutes then serve.

Farro and Fava Salad

Preparation time 30 minutes
Cooking time 30 minutes
Wine *Prosecco di Conegliano e Valdobbiadene Brut*
🍳

1⅓ cups (7 oz or 200 g)
 fava beans
salt and pepper
2 tbsps extra-virgin olive oil
1 shallot, minced
1/2 red chille pepper
1¼ cups (9 oz or 250 g)
 pearled farro (emmer wheat)
4 cups (1 l) vegetable broth
5 mint leaves
sunflower seeds (optional)

Blanch the favas in lightly salted boiling water for 2 minutes and cool under cold water. Remove the external skin.
Heat the oil and sauté the shallot. Add chille pepper.
Add the favas, sauté and add the farro. Cover with broth and cook for 25 minutes over medium heat. Let rest for 10 minutes. Add mint and season with salt and pepper. Serve topped with sunflower seeds toasted in the oven, if desired.

Warm Chicken-Zucchini Salad

Preparation time 15 minutes
Cooking time 25 minutes
Wine *Alto Adige Chardonnay*
🍳

1½ cups (10.5 oz or 300 g)
 wheat berries
salt and pepper
1/4 roast chicken
2 zucchini
2 spring onions, finely sliced
thyme
6 tbsps extra-virgin olive oil

Boil the wheat berries in salted water for around 15 minutes. Cool under cold running water, drain and place in a bowl. Remove the chicken meat from the bones and crumble it by hand into the wheat berries. Cut each zucchini into 6 wedges, then into sticks, and grill on a ridged cast-iron grill pan for 3 minutes. Season with salt. Toss with the chicken and wheat berries, spring onion, thyme, oil, salt and a little pepper.

559

Artichoke Crêpes

Preparation time 50 minutes
Cooking time 30 minutes
Wine *Alto Adige Gewürztraminer*
♟ ♟

CRÊPES
1 cup (4.5 oz or 125 g)
 plain flour
1 cup (250 ml) milk
2 eggs
salt
1 tbsp extra-virgin olive oil

FILLING
4 baby artichokes
4 tbsps extra-virgin olive oil
1/2 carrot, minced
1/2 onion, minced
1 celery stalk, minced
salt and pepper
14 oz (400 g) sheep's milk ricotta
1 egg
8 tbsps grated Parmesan
1 cup (250 ml) béchamel
 (see p. 1096)

560

Preheat oven to 400°F (200°C).
Mix all the crêpe ingredients into a batter.
Trim the artichokes of tough external leaves, remove the choke
and slice.
Heat oil in a frying pan and sauté the carrot, onion and celery. Add
artichokes and brown for 5 minutes then season with salt and
pepper. Finely chop 2/3 artichokes and reserve the rest.
Heat a non-stick frying pan and add a little oil. Pour in 1 ladleful of
crêpe batter and cook over medium heat, flipping once. Continue
until batter is used up, making about 12 crêpes.
Mix the minced artichokes with the ricotta, egg, half the Parmesan
and a little salt. Fill the crêpes and roll up.
Spread a layer of béchamel in a buttered baking dish, arrange the
crêpes on top and cover with the rest of the béchamel. Sprinkle
with remaining Parmesan and reserved artichoke slices. Bake for
15 minutes, until the top is golden-brown. Serve immediately.

Green and Yellow Maltagliati

Note *Adding the boiled egg yolk gives a creaminess and colours the asparagus cooking liquid, and makes the pasta creamier.*

Preparation time 30 minutes
Cooking time 15 minutes
Wine *Lugana*
♟

MALTAGLIATI
2 cups (8.8 oz or 250 g) plain flour
1/2 cup (120 ml) water
2 eggs
salt

SAUCE
2 tbsps extra-virgin olive oil
1 knob of butter
1 shallot, minced
6 asparagus spears, peeled and thinly sliced
2 zucchini, deseeded and diced
1/2 cup (120 ml) hot vegetable broth
salt and pepper
2 boiled eggs, yolks only

Mix the flour, water, eggs and a little salt to obtain a smooth dough. Let rest for 30 minutes.
Roll out the dough and cut into strips of around 5-inches (12 cm).
Heat the oil and butter in a saucepan and sauté the shallot. Add asparagus, then zucchini and sauté for 2 minutes. Add hot broth and continue cooking until vegetables are tender, seasoning with salt and pepper. Crumble the yolks into the pan.
Bring a large pot of salted water to the boil and cook the pasta. Drain and toss with the sauce. Serve immediately.

Trenette with Mint Pesto and Pecorino

Preparation time 10 minutes
Cooking time 15 minutes
Wine *Riviera Ligure di Ponente Pigato*

562

5 tbsps extra-virgin olive oil
1 spring onion, sliced
2 cups (10.5 oz or 300 g) cherry
 tomatoes, quartered
1 bunch mint
1/2 garlic clove
1/4 cup (1 oz or 30 g) almonds
4 tbsps grated Parmesan
salt
11.5 oz (320 g) trenette or linguine
4 oz (120 g) aged Pecorino
 Sardo cheese, shaved

Heat 2 tablespoons oil in a frying pan and sauté the spring onion.
Add the tomatoes and cook over high heat for 5 minutes.
Puree the mint (reserving a few leaves for garnish), remaining oil
and garlic in a food processor. Add almonds, Parmesan and a little
cold water. Puree until a smooth sauce is obtained.
Bring a large pot of salted water to a boil and cook the trenette
until al dente. Add to the tomatoes, mix in the pesto and pecorino
shavings, stir quickly and serve topped with a few mint leaves.

Rice and Ham Timbale

Note *To select the freshest zucchini, choose ones with firm flesh, a shiny skin and no marks. They can be kept refrigerated in the vegetable crisper for around 3 days.*

Preparation time 15 minutes
Cooking time 35 minutes
Wine *Gambellara*

3 tbsps extra-virgin olive oil
1 garlic clove
2 medium zucchini, sliced
salt and pepper
1½ cups (10.5 oz or 300 g)
 Vialone Nano rice
3½ tbsps butter
1¼ cup (4 oz or 120 g)
 grated Parmesan
4 oz (120 g) ham, sliced
4 tbsps breadcrumbs

Preheat oven to 375° F (190°C).
Heat the oil and garlic in a frying pan and sauté the zucchini. Season with salt and pepper and continue cooking until lightly coloured.
Meanwhile boil the rice for about 10 minutes, drain and mix with 1 knob of butter and Parmesan.
Butter a baking dish. Spread a layer of rice in the bottom and top with a layer of zucchini and a layer of ham. Repeat, finishing with a layer of rice. Sprinkle over the breadcrumbs and bake for about 15 minutes, until the top is golden. Serve hot.

Asparagus and Robiola Risotto

Note *Enrich the colour and flavour of the risotto with a pinch of saffron dissolved in some broth. Or give an exotic touch with a little mild curry powder.*

Preparation time 10 minutes
Cooking time 20 minutes
Wine *Lugana*

564

3½ tbsps butter
1 onion, minced
1 bunch asparagus, peeled, trimmed and sliced
1¾ cups (12.5 oz or 360 g) Carnaroli rice
1/2 cup (120 ml) white wine
hot vegetable broth
5.5 oz (150 g) robiola
1 tbsp grated Parmesan
nutmeg, grated

Melt the butter in a saucepan and sauté the onion. Add the asparagus, reserving a few tips for garnish. Cook for a few minutes then add the rice. Toast over high heat, add wine and let evaporate, then add hot broth little by little, stirring frequently, until rice is al dente.
Stir the robiola, Parmesan and nutmeg into the cooked rice. Serve hot, garnished with reserved asparagus tips.

Trofiette with Favas

Preparation time 20 minutes
Cooking time 1 hour 10 minutes
Wine *Cinque Terre*

9 oz (250 g) fava bean pods
3 tbsps extra-virgin olive oil
1 large spring onion, minced
1 garlic clove
1 red chille pepper, julienned
7 oz (200 g) soft salami meat
 or ground pork
1/2 cup (120 ml) white wine
7 oz (200 g) cherry tomatoes,
 quartered
1/2 cup (3.5 oz or 100 g)
 cooked chickpeas
salt
9 oz (250 g) trofiette or fusilli
basil, shredded
parsley, minced
6 tbsps grated Parmesan
3.5 oz (100 g) aged caciotta
 cheese, diced

565

Shell the favas, remove the external skin from the beans and place
them in a bowl.
Heat the oil and sauté the spring onion with the garlic, chille and
the soft salami, crumbled with a fork. When the meat is well-
browned, add white wine and let evaporate. Add the tomatoes.
Add the chickpeas and cook for 10 minutes.
Bring a large pot of salted water to a boil and cook the trofiette
until al dente. Drain and add to the pan with the sauce together
with the basil, parsley, Parmesan and caciottta. Stir well and serve
immediately.

Buckwheat Tagliatelle with Favas

Preparation time 25 minutes
Cooking time 20 minutes
Wine *Alto Adige Santa Maddalena*

1½ cups (7 oz or 200 g)
 plain flour
3/4 cup plus 1 tbsp (3.5 oz or 100 g)
 buckwheat flour
3 eggs
salt
2 tbsps extra-virgin olive oil
2 garlic cloves, smashed
1/2 red chille pepper
9 oz (250 g) fava bean pods
3/4 cup (200 ml) vegetable broth
6 tbsps grated semiaged pecorino
 cheese
pecorino shavings

566

Sift the 2 flours together and mound on a work surface. Make a well in the centre and break in the eggs. Add a pinch of salt and work well to obtain a smooth dough. Wrap in plastic wrap and let rest for 20 minutes.
Using a pasta machine, roll out the dough and cut tagliatelle.
Shell and peel the fava beans.
Heat the oil in a frying pan, sauté the garlic and chille then add the favas and broth and cook for 10 minutes over medium heat. Remove the garlic and chille and stir in the grated pecorino.
Bring a pot of salted water to the a boil and cook the tagliatelle for 2 minutes. Drain and add to the pan with the sauce and continue cooking until al dente. Sprinkle the pasta with pecorino shavings and serve immediately.

Penne with Green Bean Pesto

Preparation time 25 minutes
Cooking time 35 minutes
Wine *Vermentino Riviera Ligure di Ponente*
♟

3 cups (12.5 oz or 350 g) green beans
4 tbsps extra-virgin olive oil
1 garlic clove, minced
1 small onion, minced
salt and pepper
6 basil leaves
12.5 oz (350 g) smooth penne
2½ tbsps toasted pine nuts

567

Boil the green beans for about 10 minutes. Drain, reserving the cooking liquid and keeping it warm.
Heat the oil and sauté the garlic and onion. Add the green beans, 1/2 cup (120 ml) of the cooking liquid and a pinch of salt. Cook for another 10-15 minutes then let cool.
Puree the beans with the basil and a little cooking liquid to obtain a smooth sauce. Season with salt and pepper and keep warm.
Cook the pasta until al dente using the green bean cooking liquid, drain and toss with the pesto. Drizzle with oil, sprinkle with pepper and top with pine nuts.

Fish Brodetto
(Abruzzo)

Preparation time 30 minutes
Cooking time 30 minutes
Wine *Trebbiano d'Abruzzo*

Serves 6

2 lb (1 kg) mixed fish for soup
 (cod, monkfish, dogfish, skate,
 squid, cuttlefish, prawns)
7 tbsps extra-virgin olive oil
2 garlic cloves, peeled
1/2 hot chille pepper, minced
1.75 lb (800 g) tomatoes, chopped
salt
parsley, minced

568

Clean the fish under cold
running water, shell the
mollusks and fillet the fish.
Heat the oil in a saucepan and
sauté the garlic and chille. Add
the tomato and cook down until
thickened.
Add the fish in order of
cooking time, starting with the
crustaceans and mollusks and
finishing with the fish, leaving
cod, mullet and prawns for last.
Cook, covered, for 15 minutes,
adjust salt, sprinkle with parsley
and serve.

Trentino-Style Gnocchetti

Preparation time 15 minutes
Cooking time 20 minutes
Wine *Trentino Müller Thurgau*

2 cups (500 ml) milk
3/4 cup (5.3 oz or 150 g)
 semolina flour
2 tbsps extra-virgin olive oil
beef broth

Bring the milk to a boil in a
large saucepan. Sprinkle in
the semolina and cook for 15
minutes, whisking continuously
to avoid lumps forming.
Oil a baking dish and pour in
the semolina, spreading out to
make an even layer. Let cool
then use a teaspoon to form
gnocchetti a little bigger than a
hazelnut.
Heat abundant beef broth
and boil the gnocchetti for 5
minutes. Serve in hot broth.

Note *This simple recipe may be
enriched by adding diced speck
ham to the semolina mixture.*

Pane Carasau with Eggs (SARDINIA)

Preparation time 5 minutes
Cooking time 20 minutes
Wine *Carignano del Sulcis Rosato*

4 cups (1 l) vegetable broth
8 sheets Sardinian pane carasau
1¾ cups (400 ml) tomato sauce
salt
5.5 oz (150 g) aged pecorino
 cheese, grated
4 eggs

Divide the broth between 2
large saucepans and heat.
In one, immerse the sheets
of pane carasau for a few
seconds, drain and place on a
serving plate, layered with a few
spoonfuls of tomato sauce, a
pinch of salt and some grated
pecorino between each sheet.
In the other pan, poach the
eggs one at a time. Lay on
top of the pane carasau and
sprinkle with pecorino. Serve
immediately.

Penne all'Arrabbiata (LAZIO)

Preparation time 20 minutes
Cooking time 40 minutes
Wine *Velletri Rosso*

1 lb (500 g) tomatoes
3 tbsps extra-virgin olive oil
2 garlic cloves, crushed
1 hot red chille pepper, minced
salt
14 oz (400 g) penne
parsley, minced

Blanch the tomatoes in boiling
water for a few minutes, drain,
peel and chop the flesh.
Heat the oil in a frying pan and
sauté garlic and chille. Add
tomatoes. Season with salt and
continue cooking for around 30
minutes.
Bring a large pot of salted
water to a boil and cook the
penne until al dente. Drain
and toss in the frying pan with
the tomato sauce. Serve hot,
sprinkled with parsley.

569

Pappardelle with Vegetable Ragù

Preparation time 25 minutes
Cooking time 30 minutes
Wine *Cinque Terre*

2 small artichokes
juice of 1 lemon
4 tbsps extra-virgin olive oil
1 large leek, diced
2 garlic cloves, smashed
1 small eggplant, peeled and diced
2 zucchini, diced
6 basil leaves, chopped
10 black olives in oil, pitted
salt and pepper
10.5 oz (300 g) dried egg
  pappardelle

570

Clean the artichokes, removing the tough outer leaves and the
choke. Dice and immerse in water and lemon juice.
Heat half the oil in a frying pan and sauté the leek. Add artichokes
and sauté over high heat for a few minutes. Add a little water and
cook, covered, for 15 minutes.
In another frying pan heat the remaining oil and garlic. Sauté first
the eggplant, with a pinch of salt, until tender, then remove from
the pan and sauté the zucchini with a pinch of salt. Add eggplant
and zucchini to artichokes and cook for 5 minutes. Add the basil,
olives and a pinch of pepper.
Bring a large pot of salted water to a boil and cook the
pappardelle until al dente. Drain, reserving a little cooking water,
and toss with the sauce together with a little of the cooking water.
Serve immediately.

Vegetable Farro with Prawns

Preparation time 30 minutes
Cooking time 45 minutes
Wine *Alto Adige Sylvaner*
♟

1 cup (7 oz or 200 g) pearled
 farro (emmer wheat)
8 prawns
herb oil
4 tbsps extra-virgin olive oil
3/4 cup (3.5 oz or 100 g) minced
 celery, carrot and onion

1/2 cup (120 ml) white wine
2 tomatoes, chopped
parsley
1 shallot, minced
1 garlic clove, smashed
1/2 eggplant, diced
1 celery stalk, diced
1 carrot, diced
1 zucchini, diced
thyme
salt and pepper

571

Wash the farro in cold water and boil until tender.
Shell the prawns, removing and reserving the head and shell. Toss
the prawns with a little herb oil and set aside.
Heat half the oil in a saucepan and sauté the minced celery, carrot
and onion. Add prawns shells and heads, cook for a few minutes,
then add wine. Cover with cold water and bring to a boil. Add
tomatoes and parsley and cook for 25 minutes, crushing the
prawns heads against the pan with a wooden spoon.
Heat the remaining oil and sauté the shallot and garlic. Add
eggplant and celery, sauté, then add carrot and zucchini. Add
some thyme and cook until vegetables are tender. Remove the
garlic and season with salt and pepper.
Pass the prawns broth through a food mill, then cook down until
reduced.
Sauté the prawns in a frying pan until cooked through.
Mix the farro and vegetables and serve topped with prawns and a
little reduced prawns broth.

Chickpea Gnocchetti with Mussels

Preparation time 45 minutes
Cooking time 1 hour 20 minutes
Wine *Elba Bianco*

2 cups (14 oz or 400 g) chickpeas
2 small potatoes (12.5 oz or 350 g)
1 egg
1 cup plus 3 tbsps (5.3 oz or 150 g)
 plain flour
salt and pepper
2 lb (1 kg) mussels
4 tbsps extra-virgin olive oil
1 garlic clove
1/2 red chille pepper
2¼ cups (12.3 oz or 350 g) cherry
 tomatoes, quartered
1/2 cup (100 ml) tomato sauce
parsley, minced

572

If the chickpeas are dried, soak them overnight then boil until
tender. Puree in a food processor or pass through a food mill.
Boil, peel and mash the potatoes. Mix in the chickpea puree,
add egg, flour and a pinch of salt and mix until smooth. Form
gnocchetti and roll out slightly on a floured tray.
Debeard the mussels and wash under running water.
Heat the oil in a frying pan and sauté the garlic and chille. Add
tomatoes and tomato sauce and cook for 5 minutes. Add mussels
and continue to cook over high heat until they are all opened.
Remove garlic and chille and sprinkle with parsley.
Bring a pot of salted water to a boil and cook the gnocchetti.
When they rise to the surface, drain and toss with the sauce.
Adjust salt and pepper and serve.

Cuttlefish Caramelle

Preparation time 40 minutes
Cooking time 15 minutes
Wine *Malvasia Istriana*
♟ ♟

PASTA
2 cups (8.8 oz or 250 g)
 plain flour
3 tbsps extra-virgin olive oil
2 eggs
1 egg yolk
1 pinch saffron
thyme leaves
salt

FILLING
2 slices sandwich bread
1/2 cup (120 ml) milk
3 tbsps extra-virgin olive oil
1 garlic clove
3 cuttlefish, roughly chopped
salt and pepper

SAUCE
1/2 cup (120 ml) white wine
1/2 cup (120 ml) fish broth
1 knob of butter
2 zucchini, deseeded and
 julienned

573

Mix together the pasta ingredients to obtain a smooth dough. Wrap in plastic wrap and refrigerate for 20 minutes.
Soak the bread in the milk until soft, drain and squeeze out excess milk.
Meanwhile heat the oil in a frying pan with the garlic. Add the cuttlefish and sauté for 3 minutes. Remove garlic. Add soaked bread and puree in a food processor, adjust salt and pepper then set aside.
Using the same frying pan, heat the wine and fish broth and cook down to reduce by half over low heat.
Roll out the dough into a thin sheet. Cut out rectangles and place a spoonful of the cuttlefish mixture in the centre. Fold the rectangle in half and twist the ends so they look like wrapped candies.
Melt the butter in a frying pan, sauté the zucchini for a few minutes then add the wine and broth reduction.
Bring a pot of salted water to a boil and cook the caramelle for 4 minutes. Toss with the sauce and serve hot.

Monk's Risotto

(LOMBARDY)

Note *This dish was supposedly invented by the monks of the Charterhouse of Pavia, a famous monastery complex in Lombardy.*

Preparation time 30 minutes
Cooking time 50 minutes
Wine *Oltrepò Pavese Cortese*
🍷 🍷

574

salt
1 celery stalk
1 carrot
2 onions (1 whole and 1 minced)
1 bay leaf
10.5 oz (300 g) small prawns
10.5 oz (300 g) frog legs
fennel seeds
2 cups (9 oz or 250 g) peas
2 tbsps extra-virgin olive oil
3/4 cup (180 ml) white wine
5 tbsps butter
1½ cups (10.5 oz or 300 g) Carnaroli rice

Bring a large pot of salted water to a boil and add the celery, carrot, whole onion, bay, prawns, frog legs and a few fennel seeds. Cook for 5 minutes and remove the prawns and frog legs, reserving the water with the vegetables.
Separately boil the peas in a little water for 10 minutes, then drain. Remove the frog meat from the bones and shell the prawns. Put the prawns shells in the cooking water with the vegetables and cook for 15 minutes, then strain.
Heat the oil in a saucepan and sauté half the minced onion until golden. Add the prawns and frog meat and continue cooking over high heat, stirring with a wooden spoon. Add the wine and let evaporate, then add the boiled peas and salt and cook for about 5 minutes, adding a little of the broth.
In another saucepan melt 3 tablespoons butter and sauté the remaining onion until golden. Add the rice and toast, then continue cooking adding ladlefuls of broth little by little until rice is done. Stir in remaining butter.
Serve the risotto hot, topped with the frog legs, peas and prawns.

Linguine with Pesto
(LIGURIA)

Note *Other types of pasta shapes can be used for this recipe, like trenette.*
More flavur can be added by sprinkling over some grated pecorino cheese or a mixture of grated pecorino and Parmesan.

Preparation time 30 minutes
Cooking time 25 minutes
Wine *Riviera Ligure di Ponente Pigato*

PASTA
salt
2 potatoes, cut into small cubes
1 cup (3.5 oz or 100 g) green beans, cut into 1/2 -inch (1 cm) pieces
1 lb (450 g) linguine

PESTO
40 basil leaves
1 tbsp grated pecorino cheese
4 tbsps grated Parmesan
2 tbsps pine nuts
5 tbsps extra-virgin olive oil
1 garlic clove
salt

575

Bring a large pot of salted water to a boil and add the potatoes and green beans. Return to a boil then add the linguine and cook until al dente.
Meanwhile, prepare the pesto using the ingredients listed, following the recipe on p. 1098.
Drain the linguine and vegetables into a serving bowl, using a slotted spoon.
Dilute 5 tablespoons pesto with 1 tablespoon of the pasta cooking water and add to the linguine, mixing well. Serve hot, sprinkled with grated Parmesan if desired.

Pennette with Langoustines, Favas and Wild Fennel

Preparation time 25 minutes
Cooking time 20 minutes
Wine *Ostuni Bianco*

4 tbsps extra-virgin olive oil
1 large spring onion, sliced
1 lb (500 g) fava bean pods
 shelled and peeled
salt
2 tbsps minced parsley
1 garlic clove, smashed
1 chille pepper, thinly sliced
2 lb (1 kg) langoustines
1/2 cup (120 ml) white wine
3 sprigs wild fennel or dill,
 2 whole and 1 minced
12.5 oz (350 g) pennette

Heat 1 tablespoon oil in a frying pan and sauté the spring onion.
Add the favas and a little salt, cook for 3-4 minutes and sprinkle
with 1 tablespoon parsley.
Heat the rest of the oil in a frying pan with the garlic and chille.
Add the langoustines with a little salt and sauté over high heat for
a couple of minutes, then add the white wine. Cover the pan and
continue cooking for 5-10 minutes, until langoustines are cooked
through.
Bring a large pot of salted water to the boil with 2 sprigs wild
fennel, and boil the pennette until al dente.
Meanwhile, reserve a few whole langoustines for garnish, shell
the rest and return to the pan with the favas. Drain the pennette
into the pan and toss with the favas, shelled langoustines and
remaining parsley and wild fennel. Garnish with whole langoustines
and serve.

Prawn and Potato Ravioli
with Pea Sauce

Preparation time 45 minutes
Cooking time 30 minutes
Wine *Friuli Annia Chardonnay*
♟ ♟

1½ cups (7 oz or 200 g)
 plain flour
7 tbsps room-temperature
 milk
3 potatoes
8 prawns
1 tbsp extra-virgin olive oil
1 celery stalk, minced
1 small carrot, minced
1 shallot, minced
1/2 cup (120 ml) white wine
parsley, minced
salt and pepper
1 cup (4.5 oz or 130 g) peas

577

Mix together the flour and milk to make a dough, wrap in a clean
cloth napkin and let rest for 20 minutes.
Boil, peel and mash the potatoes.
Detach the heads of the prawns from the tails, blanch the tails in
boiling water for 2 minutes and shell.
Heat the oil and sauté celery, carrot and shallot. Add the prawns
heads and sauté over high heat for a few minutes, then add wine.
Cover with warm water and cook for 20 minutes.
Chop the prawns tails and then mix with the potatoes and some
parsley and season with salt and pepper. Let sit for 10 minutes.
Roll the dough out thinly and make ravioli filled with the potato-
prawn mixture.
Pass the broth through a food mill and return to the heat to
reduce. Add the peas and cook for 10 minutes, then puree in a
food processor or blender.
Bring a large pot of salted water to a boil and cook the ravioli.
Drain and serve with the pea sauce.

Venere Rice with Prawns and Asparagus

Preparation time 15 minutes
Cooking time 20 minutes
Wine *Trentino Müller Thurgau*

1 knob of butter
1 shallot, minced
1 cup (7 oz or 200 g)
 black Venere rice
8 asparagus spears
2 tbsps extra-virgin olive oil
1 garlic clove, smashed
salt and pepper
1/2 cup (120 ml) vegetable broth
1 pinch saffron
12.5 oz (350 g) prawns, shelled
parsley, minced

578

Melt the butter in a saucepan and sauté the shallot. Add the rice and toast briefly over high heat, then add hot water little by little, stirring frequently, until rice is cooked.

Meanwhile peel the asparagus with a vegetable peeler to remove the tough outer skin and break off the hard part of the stalk. Cut into bite-sized pieces.

Heat the oil in a frying pan with the garlic, add asparagus, salt and pepper and sauté. Add a little broth and continue cooking for 2 minutes. Dissolve the saffron in the remaining broth and add to the pan together with the prawns. Continue cooking until prawns are cooked through, then add parsley, salt and pepper.

Serve the rice in the centre of a serving plate, shaped into a circle using a round cookie cutter. Top with prawns and asparagus and serve immediately.

Fresh Trofie with Clams and Broccoli Rabe

Preparation time 10 minutes
Cooking time 20 minutes
Wine *Vermentino della Riviera*
Ligure di Ponente

1 lb (500 g) clams
coarse salt
1¾ cups (8 oz or 230 g)
 plain flour
salt
3 tbsps extra-virgin olive oil
2 garlic cloves, 1 minced
 and 1 smashed
1 bunch broccoli rabe or turnip tops,
 roughly chopped
1/2 red chille pepper
parsley, minced

579

Wash the clams and place in a basin with water and a handful of coarse salt to purge them for 30 minutes.
Mound the flour on a work surface and add a pinch of salt and enough water to make a firm dough. Break off pieces the size of a chickpea and roll on a wooden board with the palm of the hand to make long, twisted shapes, fatter in the middle and pointed at the ends.
Heat 1 tablespoon oil with the minced garlic and sauté the broccoli rabe for 3 minutes.
Rinse the clams and put them in a frying pan with the remaining oil, smashed garlic and chille. As soon as they open, transfer to a plate and keep warm. Remove the garlic and chille from the clam cooking liquid.
Bring a pot of salted water to the boil and cook the trofie. Drain and toss in the clam cooking liquid. Add the broccoli rabe, cook for 2 minutes, then add the clams. Stir well and serve hot, sprinkled with parsley.

Corzetti with Genoan-Style Sauce
(LIGURIA)

Preparation time 50 minutes
Cooking time 10 minutes
Wine *Cinque Terre*

CORZETTI
4 cups (1 lb or 500 g)
 semolina flour
2 egg yolks
salt

SAUCE
1 bread roll, crust removed
4 tbsps vinegar
5 pitted olives, minced

1 garlic clove, minced
1 salted anchovy, rinsed,
 deboned and minced
1 egg yolk
3½ tbsps brined
 capers, minced
2 bunches parsley, minced
salt and pepper
3 tbsps extra-virgin olive oil
juice of 1/2 lemon

580

Mound the flour on a work surface, make a well in the centre and
add the egg yolks. Work by hand to obtain a smooth and uniform
dough, adding another egg yolk if the dough is too hard. Divide
the dough into small portions the size of a bean. With index fingers
flatten each piece into an oval shape. Spread the corzetti out on a
floured surface and let dry.
Meanwhile make the sauce. Soak the soft part of the bread in
the vinegar until soft, then drain and squeeze out excess liquid.
Mix with the olives, garlic, anchovy, egg yolk, capers and parsley,
season with salt and pepper and pound with a mortar and pestle
to obtain a smooth consistency, then blend in olive oil and lemon
juice.
Bring a pot of salted water to a boil and cook the corzetti. Drain
with a slotted spoon into a serving bowl and toss with the sauce.
Serve hot, sprinkled with grated Parmesan if desired.

Spoleto-Style Strangozzi
(Umbria)

Note *Strangozzi or stringozzi, thick and rough tagliatelle, get their name from* stringhe, *shoelaces, and in Spoleto, a medieval hill-town in the heart of Umbria, they are often served with this flavoursome tomato sauce.*

Preparation time 25 minutes
Cooking time 35 minutes
Wine *Orvieto Classico*

STRANGOZZI
3 cups plus 3 tbsps
 (14 oz or 400 g) plain flour
1¾ cups (400 ml) water
salt

SAUCE
2 tbsps extra-virgin olive oil
2 garlic cloves, smashed
1 bunch parsley, roughly chopped
2 dried red chille peppers
1 lb (500 g) tomatoes,
 roughly chopped
salt and pepper

581

Mix the flour, water and a little salt to form a smooth dough. Roll out into a thick sheet and let dry slightly then cut into irregular strips.
Heat the oil in a frying pan with the garlic, parsley and chille. Add tomatoes, season with salt and pepper and cook for about 30 minutes to obtain a thick sauce.
Bring a pot of salted water to the boil and cook the strangozzi until they rise to the surface of the water. Drain with a slotted spoon and toss carefully with the sauce, then serve hot.

Semolina Gnocchi with Asparagus and Langoustines

Preparation time 30 minutes
Cooking time 10 minutes
Wine *Greco di Tufo*

582

2 cups (500 ml) low-fat milk
salt and pepper
nutmeg, grated
1 cup (6.5 oz or 180 g) semolina
  flour
1 egg yolk
5 tbsps grated Parmesan
1 tbsp extra-virgin olive oil
14 oz (400 g) asparagus
2 tbsps butter
1 shallot, minced
10.5 oz (300 g) shelled
  langoustines, roughly chopped
1/2 cup (120 ml) dry white wine

Bring the milk to a boil with a pinch of salt and nutmeg. Sprinkle in the semolina flour and cook for 7-8 minutes, whisking constantly. Remove from the heat and add the yolk and half the grated Parmesan, stirring vigorously.

Oil a smooth surface and pour out the semolina mixture. Spread out into a 1/2-inch (1 cm) thick layer and cool.

Meanwhile boil the asparagus until tender. Remove and set aside the tips and puree the stalks with salt and pepper.

Melt 1 tablespoon butter in a frying pan and sauté the shallot until golden. Add the langoustines and asparagus tips and sauté briefly, then add white wine and let evaporate. Season with salt and pepper.

Cut circles of 1½-inches (3-4 centimeters) in diameter out of the semolina layer with a small cup or shot glass, dipping the edge in water. Arrange the gnocchi in a buttered, round baking dish, leaving a space in the centre. Sprinkle with remaining Parmesan and some pieces of butter and broil or bake until golden on top.

Remove the gnocchi from the oven, pour the asparagus puree into the middle and top with the langoustines and asparagus tips.

Pea and Prawn Risotto

Note *Vialone Nano is one of the varieties of short-grain rice most suitable for risotto, along with others like Carnaroli and Arborio.*

Preparation time 25 minutes
Cooking time 20 minutes
Wine *Marino Superiore*

1 onion, sliced
1½ cups (7 oz or 200 g) peas
6 cups (1.5 l) hot vegetable broth
2 tbsps extra-virgin olive oil
3 tbsps butter
1½ cups (10.5 oz or 300 g)
 Vialone Nano rice
1/2 cup (120 ml) white wine
1 lb (450 g) prawns
1 tbsp minced mixed herbs
 (parsley, rosemary, marjoram)
2 tomatoes, blanched, peeled
 and diced
3 tbsps grated Parmesan

583

Put half the onion in a small saucepan with the peas and 1 ladleful of broth. Cook until tender then puree 3/4 of the peas.

Heat the oil and half the butter in a saucepan and sauté remaining onion until soft. Add the rice and toast for a few minutes, stirring, then add wine and let evaporate. Cover with hot broth and stir, then continue cooking, adding alternately the broth and the pea puree, little by little, and stirring frequently.

Remove the heads from the prawns and shell most of them, reserving a few whole for garnish.

Just before the rice is done, add the shelled prawns, whole peas, mixed herbs, tomatoes, Parmesan and remaining butter. Continue cooking until rice is done.

Meanwhile sauté the whole prawns tails in a non-stick frying pan until cooked through.

Serve the risotto topped with the prawns.

Spaghetti with Prawns and Squash Blossoms

Note *When buying squash blossoms make sure the colour is bright, the flowers are open and the petals are firm and not curled. Squash blossom, easily digestible and rich in vitamin A.*

584

Preparation time 15 minutes
Cooking time 15 minutes
Wine *Roero Arneis*

1½ cups (6.5 oz or 180 g) green beans
12 jumbo prawns
2 tbsps extra-virgin olive oil
1 garlic clove, minced
1/2 red chille pepper, minced
parsley, minced
salt
1/2 cup (120 ml) white wine
8 large squash blossoms, sliced
1 tomato, deseeded and chopped.
14 oz (400 g) spaghetti alla chitarra

Trim the green beans and blanch in boiling salted water for 4 minutes.
Remove the heads from the prawns and halve lengthways, removing the legs but leaving the shell.
Heat the oil in a frying pan and sauté the garlic, chille and parsley.
Add prawns and sauté, season with salt then add wine. As soon as it has evaporated, add the green beans and squash blossoms.
Add a little water and continue cooking for a few minutes, covered, to blend all the flavours, then stir in the tomatoes.
Bring a large pot of salted water to a boil and cook the spaghetti until al dente. Drain and toss with the sauce, adding a little of the cooking water.

Broccoli Ravioli with Seafood

Preparation time 30 minutes
Cooking time 20 minutes
Wine *Greco di Tufo*
♟ ♟

SAUCE
10.5 oz (300 g) clams
salt
2 tbsps extra-virgin olivo oil
1 garlic clove, minced
1/2 dried red chille pepper
10.5 oz (300 g) mussels, cleaned
 and debearded
2 thin slices lardo, minced
8 jumbo prawns, shelled
parsley, minced

RAVIOLI
2⅓ cups (10.5 oz or 300 g)
 plain flour
2/3 cup (150 ml) warm milk
salt

FILLING
1 head broccoli
salt and pepper
extra-virgin olive oil

Soak the clams in a bowl of salted water for 30 minutes to purge them.
Mix the flour with the warm milk and a little salt to make an elastic dough.
Break the broccoli into florets and boil until al dente. Drain and cool in ice water, then squeeze out excess liquid and chop finely. Mix with salt, pepper and oil.
Heat the oil in a frying pan with garlic and chille then add the mussels and clams. Cook, covered, until they open.
Roll out the pasta and make ravioli with the broccoli filling.
Shell the mussels and clams and strain their cooking liquid.
Heat the lardo in another frying pan, add the prawns and sauté briefly. Add the mussel and clam cooking liquid and continue cooking until done, then add mussels and clams.
Bring a pot of salted water to a boil and cook the ravioli for 30 seconds. Drain and add to the pan. Sprinkle with parsley and serve.

Bigoli with Tench and Rucola

Preparation time 30 minutes
Cooking time 35 minutes
Wine *Garganega del Garda*

1 tench (about 1 lb or 500 g)
1 large carrot
1/2 onion
1 celery stalk
7 tbsps extra-virgin olive oil
3/4 cup (180 ml) white wine
5 cups (3.5 oz or 100 g) arugula,
   chopped
2 tomatoes, diced
salt and pepper
10.5 oz (300 g) fresh bigoli
   or spaghetti

Clean and gut the tench and rinse with cold water. Boil for 10
minutes, drain and let cool. Remove the meat from the bones and
roughly chop.
Finely chop the carrot, onion and celery in a food processor.
Heat the oil and sauté carrot, onion and celery for 2-3 minutes.
Add the tench meat and brown over high heat for 3 minutes. Add
white wine and let evaporate over medium heat. Add the arugula
and tomatoes and continue cooking for around 20 minutes.
Season with salt and pepper
Meanwhile bring a pot of salted water to a boil and cook the bigoli
until al dente. Drain and toss with the sauce over high heat. Serve
immediately.

Tagliolini and Scallops with Pinot Bianco

Note *Asparagus can be kept in the refrigerator, wrapped in a damp cloth, for 3-4 days. Remove the tough, fibrous part of the stalk before cooking, and cook the asparagus spears tied together in a bunch.*

Preparation time 20 minutes
Cooking time 20 minutes
Wine *Alto Adige Pinot Bianco*

6 tbsps extra-virgin olive oil
1 shallot, minced
9 oz (250 g) shelled scallops, diced
7 tbsps Pinot Bianco wine
1 knob of butter
1 cup (5.5 oz or 150 g) asparagus tips
4 small zucchini, julienned
4 zucchini flowers, chopped
salt
fresh ginger
14 oz (400 g) fresh egg tagliolini or other long, thin pasta

587

Heat the oil and sauté half the shallot. Add the scallops, sauté briefly, then add wine. Transfer to a covered container and keep warm.

In the same pan melt the butter and sauté the remaining shallot. Add asparagus and zucchini, cover and cook for 10 minutes, adding a little hot water if necessary. Just before they are done, add the zucchini flowers.

Add the scallops to the vegetables, season with salt and add a little grated ginger.

Bring a pot of salted water to a boil and cook the tagliolini, then toss with the sauce in the frying pan. Serve hot.

Barley with Mussels and Spinach

Preparation time 20 minutes
Cooking time 30 minutes
Wine *Trentino Nosiola*

6 tbsps extra-virgin olive oil
1 garlic clove, smashed
1/2 red chille pepper
parsley, minced
1 lb (500 g) mussels, washed
 and debearded
1 shallot, minced
1½ cups (10 oz or 280 g) pearled
 barley
5 cups (5.5 oz or 150 g) spinach
salt and pepper

588

Heat 1 tablespoon oil in a saucepan with the garlic, chille and a little parsley. Add the mussels and cook over high heat until they open. Strain the cooking liquid. Shell the mussels and pour over a little of the cooking liquid to keep moist.
Heat 4 tablespoons oil in another saucepan and sauté the shallot with a little hot water. Add the barley and toast well then add a little hot water and continue cooking like a risotto, adding the remaining mussel cooking liquid and water little by little and stirring frequently.
Meanwhile blanch the spinach and squeeze out most of the water. Puree in a food processor, adding 1 tablespoon oil.
Just before the barley is cooked, add the spinach and mussels and season with salt and pepper. Mix well and continue cooking until barley is tender, then serve immediately.

Imola-Style Garganelli
(EMILIA-ROMAGNA)

Note *This recipe comes from the town of Imola, not for from Bologna. The region of Emilia-Romagna is know for rich dishes like this, using butter, cream, prosciutto and egg pasta.*

Preparation time 15 minutes
Cooking time 20 minutes
Wine *Montuni del Reno*

1/2 cup (2.5 oz or 70 g) peas
2 tbsps butter
2.5 oz (70 g) prosciutto, diced
1 cup (250 ml) heavy cream
3 red bell peppers, diced
salt and pepper
10.5 oz (300 g) egg garganelli
 or penne
1 cup (3.5 oz or 100 g)
 grated Parmesan

589

Boil the peas in abundant water until tender, then drain and rinse under cold running water.
Melt the butter in a frying pan and brown the prosciutto for a few minutes. Add the cream, peas and peppers and bring to a boil over medium heat. Season with salt and pepper.
Bring a pot of salted water to a boil and cook the garganelli until al dente. Toss with the sauce, stirring well, and serve hot, topped with grated Parmesan.

Calcioni with Ragù
(MARCHE)

Preparation time 30 minutes
Cooking time 50 minutes
Wine *Rosso Conero*

Serves 6-8

1½ cups (7 oz or 200 g)
 plain flour
4 egg yolks
2 lb (1 kg) sheep's milk ricotta
5 tbsps grated Parmesan
2 eggs
nutmeg, grated
salt

2 tbsps extra-virgin olive oil
1 onion, minced
1 carrot, minced
1 celery stalk, minced
14 oz (400 g) ground beef
1 cartilaginous beef bone
2 lb (1 kg) peeled tomatoes
1 tbsp tomato paste
marjoram

Mix the flour and egg yolks to obtain a smooth, uniform dough.
Roll out into a thin sheet and cut out 3-inch (8 cm) diameter disks
using a cookie cutter.
Sieve the ricotta into a bowl and mix with the Parmesan, eggs, a
pinch of nutmeg and salt.
Place 1 tablespoon of filling in the centre of each circle and fold in
half, pressing around the edges with the tines of a fork to seal.
Heat the oil in a frying pan and sauté the onion, carrot and celery.
Add the beef and the bone and brown for a few minutes, then add
the tomatoes, concentrate and a little marjoram. Season with salt
and cook for 40 minutes, then remove from the heat and discard
the bone.
Bring a pot of salted water to a boil, cook the calcioni, drain and
toss in the pan with the ragù. Sprinkle with Parmesan and serve.

Spiced Risotto with Chicken Ragù
(MARCHE)

Note *To prepare the chicken ragù, brown 1.4 oz (40 g) diced pancetta in a saucepan with 1 garlic clove and 1 rosemary sprig, then add 7 oz (200 g) minced chicken giblets. Add ½ cup (120 ml) white wine, let evaporate, then add 1 ladleful tomato sauce, a pinch of cinnamon, grated nutmeg, grated lemon zest, salt and pepper. Cook, covered, for around 30 minutes.*

Preparation time 10 minutes
Cooking time 25 minutes
Wine *Rosso Piceno*

Serves 4-6

5½ tbsps butter
1 onion, minced
2½ cups (1 lb or 500 g) Carnaroli rice
4 cups (1 l) water
5 tbsps grated pecorino cheese
ground cinnamon
chicken ragù (see note)
grated zest of 1 organic lemon

Preheat oven to 350°F (180°C).
Melt 4 tablespoons butter in a saucepan and sauté the onion. Add the rice and toast for 1 minute then add 1 ladleful water. Continue cooking, adding water little by little, stirring frequently with a wooden spoon.
After 10 minutes stir in 3 tablespoons pecorino and a pinch of cinnamon, then 5 minutes later stir in 2 tablespoons chicken ragù. Continue cooking until the rice is al dente.
Sprinkle the remaining pecorino and grated lemon zest around a baking dish or ring mould, then add a layer of rice. Cover with 1 spoonful of chicken ragù and repeat until all the rice has been used up. Top with pieces of the remaining butter and bake for about 5 minutes. Serve hot.

Gnocchi with Salmon and Fennel

Note *Gnocchi, little dumplings, are usually made from potato dough (in the north of Italy) or semolina (in the south). They can be boiled in broth or water, or baked.*

Preparation time 15 minutes
Cooking time 20 minutes
Wine *Bolgheri Bianco*

salt and pepper
14 oz (400 g) semolina gnocchi
1 fennel bulb
juice of ½ lemon
2 young zucchini with flowers
 attached, thinly sliced
7 oz (200 g) smoked salmon,
 cut into strips
1 bunch wild fennel or dill, minced
3 tbsps extra-virgin olive oil

592

Bring a pot of salted water to a boil and cook the gnocchi until al dente. Drain and cool under running water.
Boil the fennel in water and lemon juice until tender. Drain, cool and slice thinly. Mix with zucchini, salmon, wild fennel and oil and season with salt and pepper.
Toss the gnocchi with the sauce, let sit for a few minutes then serve.

Meatballs with Salad

Preparation time 15 minutes
Cooking time 10 minutes
Wine *Refosco dal Peduncolo Rosso*

10.5 oz (300 g) lean ground beef
1 egg
salt and pepper
sunflower oil
2 bunches mixed salad leaves
10 cherry tomatoes, halved
 or quartered
1/2 cup (5.5 oz or 150 g) canned
 sweet corn, drained and rinsed
4 tbsps extra-virgin olive oil

Mix the ground beef with the egg, salt and pepper to obtain a soft, uniform mixture. With dampened hands, form cherry-sized meatballs and lay them on a plate.
Heat the sunflower oil in a frying pan and fry the meatballs until golden. Drain on paper towels.
Compose the salad, mixing the salad leaves, tomatoes and sweet corn with the meatballs and dressing it with salt, pepper and a drizzle of olive oil.

595

Spring Lamb Stew

Note *The lamb can be replaced by veal or beef.*

Preparation time 30 minutes
Cooking time 45 minutes
Wine *Refosco dal Peduncolo Rosso*

3 tbsps lard
extra-virgin olive oil
2⅓ cups (10.5 oz or 300 g) peas
salt and pepper
1 onion, finely sliced
2 lb (1 kg) lamb for stew,
 cut into pieces
1/2 cup (120 ml) white wine
3 eggs, beaten
5 tbsps grated Parmesan
parsley, minced

Heat 1 tablespoon lard and some olive oil in a frying pan.
Add peas and salt, cover and cook, adding a little water, until tender.
Heat the rest of the lard and some olive oil in saucepan and sauté the onion for a few minutes. Add the meat and increase the heat. Cook, stirring often, until the meat is browned on all sides. Add the white wine and let evaporate slowly, lowering the heat. Season with a little salt and continue cooking.
After 30 minutes add the peas, eggs, Parmesan, parsley, a pinch of pepper and a little salt and stir until the eggs are firm. Remove from the heat and serve immediately.

Chicken with Favas

Preparation time 20 minutes
Cooking time 15 minutes
Wine *Alto Adige Santa Maddalena*
♟

8 chicken thighs
4 tbsps extra-virgin olive oil
salt and pepper
rosemary
12.5 oz (350 g) fava bean pods
1 shallot, minced
1/2 red chilli pepper, deseeded
2 oz (50 g) pancetta, julienned
2 garlic cloves, unpeeled
 and halved

Preheat oven to 400°F (200°C).
Marinate the chicken in 2
tablespoons oil, salt, pepper
and rosemary for 10 minutes.
Shell and blanch the favas.
Cool and remove tough outer
skin. Heat the remaining oil in a
saucepan and sauté the shallot
until soft with the chilli. Add the
pancetta and favas, cover and
cook for around 7 minutes.
Set the chicken in a baking dish
with the garlic cloves and bake for
around 15 minutes, until cooked
through. Serve the chicken thighs
on a bed of fava beans.

Lamb with Pinot Noir

Preparation time 20 minutes
Cooking time 1 hour
Wine *Alto Adige Pinot Nero Riserva*
♟ ♟

1 lb (500 g) lamb loin
4½ tbsps lard
salt
1¼ cups (300 ml) Pinot Noir wine
1/2 shallot, quartered
1 tsp chestnut honey
1 tsp peppercorns

597

Cut the lamb into 4 pieces and
place in a pan with the lard,
cook on the stove over a very
low heat, so the meat stays
tender and succulent.
As soon as the meat, gives
off rosy juices instead of red
blood, when pierced with
a toothpick, remove from
the heat.
Drain away the cooking fat
and season the meat with salt.
Meanwhile, place the wine in
a saucepan with the shallot,
honey and peppercorns and
cook down until thickened,
then strain.
Slice the meat and glaze
with the wine reduction.

Valdostana Veal Cutlets
(VALLE D'AOSTA)

Preparation time 15 minutes
Cooking time 20 minutes
Wine *Valle d'Aosta Donnas*

4 veal cutlets
(about 7 oz or 200 g each)
3.5 oz (100 g) fontina cheese,
sliced
salt and pepper
1 egg
3 tbsps plain flour
3 tbsps breadcrumbs
1/2 cup (3.5 oz or 100 g) butter

598

Slice into the cutlets horizontally with a sharp knife, creating a kind
of pocket. Fill with fontina and close, pounding the edges with
a meat tenderizer to seal. Season with salt and pepper.
Beat the egg in a bowl and place the flour and breadcrumbs
in separate bowls. Dip the cutlets in the flour, the egg, and then
the breadcrumbs, and press down with the palm of the hand so
they stick.
Melt the butter in a wide saucepan over high heat and sauté the
cutlets, browning well on both sides. Lower the heat and continue
cooking until the cheese melts and the meat is done.
Serve hot, with shavings of truffle, if desired.

Poached Chicken with Myrtle
(SARDINIA)

Note *Myrtle is an evergreen shrub or small tree whose leaves contain a fragrant essential oil. In Sardinia myrtle leaves and berries are used to make mirto liqueur.*

Preparation time 20 minutes
Cooking time 2 hours
Wine *Monica di Cagliari*

Serves 6-8

1 chicken (4.5 lb or 2 kg)
myrtle leaves
1 carrot
1 onion
1 celery stalk
salt and pepper

599

Stuff the cleaned chicken with some myrtle leaves and tie with kitchen string. Place in a large pan with the carrot, onion, celery, a few more myrtle leaves and salt and pepper. Cover with water and boil for around 2 hours over medium heat.
Serve hot, accompanied by a green salad if desired.

Pork Ribs with Capers and Anchovies

600

Preparation time 10 minutes
Cooking time 30 minutes
Wine *Nero d'Avola*

1.5 lb (700 g) pork ribs
salt and pepper
2 tbsps plain flour
4 tbsps extra-virgin olive oil
1 garlic clove
2 lemons
1/2 cup (120 ml) white wine
2 tbsps capers
5 anchovy fillets
1 bay leaf
vegetable broth
5 cups (3.5 oz or 100 g) mesclun
2/3 cup (3.5 oz or 100 g)
 cherry tomatoes

Cut the pork ribs in half, season with salt and pepper and dust with flour.

Heat the oil and brown the garlic clove. Add the ribs, the juice of 1 lemon, wine, capers, anchovies and bay leaf. Cook briefly over high heat then cover and turn the heat down to medium. Cook for 30 minutes. If the liquid dries up, add a little vegetable broth. Meanwhile thinly slice the remaining lemon and toss the mesclun and tomatoes together.

Serve the pork ribs garnished with lemon slices and salad.

Lamb with Pea and Potato Purees

PUREES
3 tbsps extra-virgin olive oil
1/2 yellow onion, minced
1 chilli pepper, minced
2 potatoes, diced
vegetable broth
salt
1 knob of butter
1 shallot, minced
1½ cups (7 oz or 200 g) peas
7 tbsps heavy cream

LAMB
13.5 oz (380 g) lamb
2 tbsps plain flour
4 tbsps extra-virgin olive oil
1 garlic clove, smashed
1 bay leaf
1/2 cup (120 ml) red wine
salt and pepper

601

Preparation time 20 minutes
Cooking time 35 minutes
Wine *Montepulciano d'Abruzzo*

Preheat oven to 375° F (190°C).
Heat the oil for the purees and sauté onion and chilli until onion is golden. Add the potatoes and brown slightly, then add a little broth and salt and cook until falling apart. Puree.
Melt the butter and sauté the shallot, then add the peas and a little broth. When tender season with salt, add cream and puree.
Cut the lamb into bite-sized pieces and lightly dust with flour.
Heat oil for the lamb with the garlic and bay in an oven-proof frying pan. Brown the lamb pieces. Add wine, let reduce and season with salt and pepper. Finish cooking in the oven for 10 minutes.
Remove from the oven and drain the pan juices. Strain and reduce.
Serve the lamb over the purees with the reduced pan juices.

Lamb Chops with Nero d'Avola

Note *Nero d'Avola has been called the prince of Sicilian wines, and it's the most common grape variety on the island. It produces fruit with a high sugar content, so the wine can easily arrive at an alcohol level as high as 15%. Modern winemaking technology has found ways to lower the sugar content and increase the acidity, so now even 100% Nero d'Avola wines can be made with great structure, and rank among some of the best Italian reds.*

Preparation time 15 minutes
Cooking time 25 minutes
Wine *Nero d'Avola*

extra-virgin olive oil
4 lamb loin chops
2 oz (50 g) black-olive tapenade
1¼ cups (5.5 oz or 150 g)
 breadcrumbs
1 artichoke, trimmed and sliced
5 large asparagus spears, sliced
1½ cups (3.5 oz or 100 g) snow
 peas
1 cup (3.5 oz or 100 g) green beans
salt
Nero d'Avola wine
beef broth

Preheat oven to 350°F (180°C).
Heat some oil until very hot, and brown the lamb chops on both sides. Arrange on a baking sheet and top with tapenade, breadcrumbs and a drizzle of oil. Bake for 10 minutes.
Blanch the vegetables individually until just al dente. Heat 1 tablespoon oil in a saucepan and briefly sauté the vegetables together, seasoning with salt to taste.
Mix the wine and broth together in a saucepan and cook down until reduced and thickened.
Serve the lamb chops with the red wine sauce and the vegetables.

Chicken with Pistachios

Preparation time 10 minutes
Cooking time 15 minutes
Wine *Bardolino Chiaretto*

2 chicken breasts
juice of 1/2 lemon
salt and pepper
extra-virgin olive oil
1 garlic clove, smashed
2 spring onions, sliced
white wine
4 large zucchini, sliced diagonally
1 tsp curry powder
3 tbsps pistachios

Rinse the chicken and cut into bite-sized pieces. Toss with lemon juice and a little salt. Heat some oil in a wok and sauté the garlic until golden. Add the spring onions and sauté for 3 minutes, then add the chicken. Add a little wine, let reduce, then add the zucchini. Season with salt and pepper. Add the pistachios and curry and continue cooking over medium heat until the chicken is cooked through and the zucchini is tender. Serve hot.

Chicken in Creamy Curry

Preparation time 10 minutes
Cooking time 40 minutes
Wine *Alto Adige Santa Maddalena*

1 tbsp extra-virgin olive oil
1 garlic clove, minced
1 onion, minced
1 chicken (about 2 lb or 1 kg), cut into pieces, skin removed
salt and pepper
1 tsp curry powder
hot vegetable broth
3/4 cup (200 ml) béchamel (see p. 1096)
1 apple, peeled and chopped

Heat some oil in a non-stick frying pan and sauté the garlic and onion. Add the chicken, season with salt and pepper, and sauté, stirring often. After a few minutes sprinkle over the curry and a little hot broth. When the chicken is cooked through remove from the cooking liquid. Add the béchamel and apple and cook until tender then pass through a sieve.
Serve the chicken with the sauce.

Stuffed Rabbit

Preparation time 1 hour
Cooking time 1 hour 10 minutes
Wine *Capriano del Colle Rosso*
♟ ♟

3 eggs
1 cup (3.5 oz or 100 g) grated
 Parmesan
salt and pepper
3 rosemary sprigs
1 rabbit, deboned
5.5 oz (150 g) ham, sliced
1 pork tenderloin
4 tbsps butter
6 tbsps extra-virgin olive oil
3 garlic cloves, smashed
1½ cups (350 ml) white wine

Beat the eggs with the Parmesan, salt and pepper.
Melt half the butter in a frying pan, add the eggs and make an
omelette, leaving the inside quite soft.
Mince 1 rosemary sprig and sprinkle over the rabbit with salt and
pepper. Stuff the rabbit with the ham, omelette, pork and a little
salt, and tie closed tightly with kitchen string.
Heat the rest of the butter and the oil in large oven-proof saucepan
and sauté the garlic with the rest of the rosemary until golden. Add
the rabbit and brown evenly on all sides. Pour over half the wine.
Bake in the oven for about 1 hour, basting with the rest of the wine
during the cooking and adding a little water if necessary.
Remove from the oven and let cool slightly. Cut into thick slices
and serve with the pan juices drizzled over.

Lamb Chops with Artichokes, Pistachios and Mint

Preparation time 20 minutes
Cooking time 10 minutes
Wine *Oltrepò Pavese Pinot Nero*

1⅓ lb (600 g) lamb chops
3 tbsps plain flour
2-3 small artichokes
4 tbsps extra-virgin olive oil
1 garlic clove
salt and pepper
2 spring onions, thinly sliced
1/2 cup (2 oz or 60 g) pistachios,
 shelled and halved
1/2 cup (120 ml) white wine
5-6 mint leaves, minced

605

Trim the lamb chops of excess fat and scrape the bones clean.
Dust lightly with flour on both sides.
Trim the artichokes, removing the choke and hard outer leaves,
and slice thinly.
Heat the oil over high heat and sauté the garlic until golden. Add
the lamb and brown on both sides for 3-4 minutes. Season with
salt and pepper.
Add the artichokes and spring onions and then the pistachios.
Cook for 2-3 minutes then add white wine, let reduce and cook
for 3-4 minutes. Just before removing from the heat stir in half the
mint. Arrange on a serving plate and top with the rest of the mint.
Serve immediately.

Prato-Style Stuffed Celery
(TUSCANY)

Note *If there is any filling left over it can be used to make flavoursome meatballs, which can be poached in boiling beef or vegetable broth.*

Preparation time 40 minutes
Cooking time 30 minutes
Wine *Morellino di Scansano*

4 large celery stalks
salt and pepper
10.5 oz (300 g) ground veal
 or beef
5.5 oz (150 g) mortadella,
 finely chopped
5 eggs
5 tbsps grated Parmesan
1/2 garlic clove, minced
nutmeg, grated
parsley, minced
6½ tbsps plain flour
olive oil
14 oz (400 g) beef ragù
 (see p. 1099)

Remove the largest fibers from the celery stalks. Cut celery into lengths of around 3-inches (8 cm). Boil in abundant salted water until tender, drain and wrap in a clean kitchen towel to cool and dry.
Meanwhile make the filling: Mix the ground veal, mortadella, 2 eggs, Parmesan, garlic, nutmeg, parsley, salt and pepper.
When dry, fill half of the celery pieces with the filling and cover with the others. Secure with toothpicks or tie with kitchen string.
Beat 3 eggs in a bowl. Dip the stuffed celery first in the flour, then the egg.
Heat the olive oil until very hot and fry the celery pieces. Drain and dry on paper towels.
Heat the beef ragù and as soon as it starts to simmer add the celery pieces and cook briefly before serving.

Chicken in Porchetta (UMBRIA)

Preparation time 30 minutes
Cooking time 1 hour
Wine *Colli Altotiberini Rosso*

3.5 oz (100 g) pancetta
3.5 oz (100 g) chicken livers
1 bunch wild fennel or dill
1 sprig rosemary
1 garlic clove
1 chicken (about 2 lb or 1 kg)
2 tbsps extra-virgin olive oil
salt and pepper

Preheat oven to 350°F (180°C).
Mince together the pancetta,
livers, fennel, a little rosemary
and the garlic. Stuff the chicken
with the mixture, season
with salt and pepper and tie
with kitchen string. Place in
a roasting pan with oil and
remaining rosemary and roast
for around 1 hour.
Serve hot.

Note *Other aromatic herbs, like
marjoram or thyme, can be used
instead of wild fennel.*

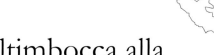

Saltimbocca alla Romana (LAZIO)

Preparation time 20 minutes
Cooking time 10 minutes
Wine *Cesanese di Olevano
Romano*

8 thinly sliced veal steaks
8 slices prosciutto
 (about 5.5 oz or 150 g)
8 sage leaves
3 tbsps butter
salt
1/2 cup (120 ml) white wine

Pound out the veal slices until
very thin. Lay 1 slice prosciutto
and 1 sage leaf on each
one and roll up, fixing with a
toothpick so the filling cannot
fall out.
Melt the butter in a frying pan
and sauté the veal rolls until
evenly browned. Season with
salt, add the wine and let
reduce, cooking over medium
heat for around 5 minutes, and
turning halfway through.
Serve hot with the cooking
liquid.

Lamb with Mint and Ginger

Preparation time 15 minutes
Cooking time 20 minutes
Wine *Rosso Conero Riserva*

10 mint leaves, roughly chopped
1 rosemary sprig, stem removed
 and leaves chopped
parsley, coarsely chopped
6 tbsps extra-virgin olive oil
1 garlic clove, sliced
1 piece fresh ginger, grated
salt and pepper
12 lamb chops

Mix the mint, rosemary, parsley, oil, garlic, ginger, salt and pepper in a bowl and beat with a fork to emulsify. Brush the lamb chops with the mixture and refrigerate for 10 minutes. Heat a cast-iron grill pan or a barbecue and grill the lamb chops. Season to taste and serve with a green salad or vegetables if desired.

Hamburgers with Provola

Preparation time 15 minutes
Cooking time 20 minutes
Wine *Enfer d'Arvier*

10.5 oz (300 g) ground beef
salt and pepper
2 tbsps extra-virgin olive oil
1/2 garlic clove, minced
2 large zucchini, sliced
2 slices crusty bread
4 slices mild provola cheese

Mix the ground beef with salt, pepper, oil and garlic.
Grill the zucchini slices on a cast-iron grill pan.
Cut out circles of bread with a cookie cutter and grill.
Using the same cookie cutter cut out disks of meat.
Cut the provola into circles a little smaller than the meat.
Cook the hamburgers in a cast-iron pan, and as soon as they are flipped over, place the cheese on top.
Place 1 slice of zucchini on each piece of bread and top with the hamburger.

608

Beef Fillet with Red-Wine Sauce

Preparation time 20 minutes
Cooking time 20 minutes
Wine *Salice Salentino*
♟ ♟

BEEF
2 tbsps butter
3 tbsps sunflower oil
4 beef fillets
 (around 7 oz or 200 g each)
salt and white pepper
9 oz (250 g) beef marrow
2 tbsps minced shallot
5 tbsps minced parsley
2 slices sandwich bread, diced

SAUCE
3 tbsps butter
1 shallot, minced
1½ cups (350 ml) young red wine
thyme sprigs, bay leaf
salt and white pepper

Heat 1 tablespoon butter and the sunflower oil. Salt and pepper
the beef and brown for 4 minutes on each side, then hold upright
with tongs and brown the edges also.
Pass the marrow through a sieve and mix in a bowl with the
minced shallot and parsley.
Melt 1 tablespoon butter in a frying pan and brown the bread.
Add the marrow mixture.
Spread the bread and marrow mixture on the beef fillets and
brown under the broiler for 5 minutes.
Meanwhile make the sauce: Melt 1 tablespoon butter and sauté
the shallot. Add the wine, thyme and bay and cook until reduced
to 1/3 the original volume. Salt and pepper to taste. Stir in the
remaining butter then strain the sauce.
Pour the sauce on the serving plates, place the beef on top and
serve immediately.

Turkey Involtini with Vin Santo

Note *Vin santo is a historic, amber-coloured dessert wine, typically Tuscan, made from grapes which are first dried to concentrate the sugars.*

Preparation time 15 minutes
Cooking 20 minutes
Wine *Grignolino d'Asti*
♟

8 slices turkey breast
10 cherry tomatoes, chopped
3 oz (80 g) mozzarella,
 cut into strips
16 black olives, pitted
 and chopped
salt
16 basil leaves, julienned
2 tbsps plain flour
extra-virgin olive oil
1 garlic clove
rosemary
1/2 cup (120 ml) vin santo

610

Lay the turkey slices on a cutting board and pound out lightly. Place the tomatoes, mozzarella and olives on paper towels to dry any excess moisture.
Salt the turkey on one side and lay a little of the tomatoes, mozzarella, olives and basil on each one. Roll up and tie with kitchen string lengthwise and in the middle, then dust with flour. Heat the oil with the garlic and rosemary and brown the involtini for a few minutes, turning every so often and seasoning with salt. Pour in the vin santo, let reduce slightly then cover, reduce the heat and cook for 15 minutes.
Serve the involtini hot with the pan juices.

Herbed Veal Shank with Beer

Note *Tarragon smells a little like mint and parsley, and pairs well with eggs, meat and fish. It is used to flavour mustards and vinegars.*

Preparation time 15 minutes
Cooking time 25 minutes
Wine *Alto Adige Pinot Nero*
♟

1 beef shank
1 egg white
salt and pepper
mixed aromatic herbs
 (tarragon, rosemary, sage,
 coriander), minced
3 tbsps extra-virgin olive oil
3 garlic cloves
3/4 cup (200 ml) double-malt beer

611

Debone the veal shank with a strong, sharp knife. Trim away excess fat. Beat the egg white with salt and pepper and brush the meat with it.
Roll the meat in the herbs and press so they stick to it. Wrap tightly in plastic wrap. Let rest in the lower half of the refrigerator for 15 minutes.
Preheat oven to 400°F (200°C).
Oil a roasting pan and lay the garlic cloves, unpeeled, on it. Unwrap the meat and place on the baking sheet, and roast for around 40 minutes. Halfway through add the beer and let evaporate with the oven door ajar.
Serve the veal shank with the pan juices.

Milanese-Style Veal Cutlets
(Lombardy)

Preparation time 15 minutes
Cooking time 20 minutes
Wine *San Colombano*

4 veal cutlets
3 tbsps breadcrumbs
2 eggs
salt
nutmeg, grated (optional)
3 tbsps butter

Pound out the cutlets with a meat tenderizer until thin and make
small cuts around the edges with a sharp knife.
Spread the breadcrumbs on a work surface.
Beat the eggs in a bowl with salt and a pinch of nutmeg,
if desired.
Dip the cutlets in the egg mixture and then the breadcrumbs,
coating well on both sides.
Melt the butter in a frying pan and fry the breaded cutlets, turning
often so they cook evenly and brown on both sides. Remove from
the pan and dry on paper towels. Serve hot, seasoned with a
pinch of salt, and accompanied by fried potatoes, if desired.

612

Ischia-Style Rabbit
(CAMPANIA)

Preparation time 20 minutes
Cooking time 30 minutes
Wine *Vesuvio Rosato*

1 rabbit (about 3.3 lb or 1.5 kg)
2 tbsps extra-virgin olive oil
3/4 cup (180 ml) white wine
1 lb (500 g) ripe tomatoes,
 chopped
rosemary leaves
salt and pepper
basil leaves, torn

Cut the rabbit into pieces, wash and dry. Reserve the liver.
Heat the oil in a frying pan and brown the rabbit pieces. Add the
white wine and let evaporate.
Add tomatoes, rosemary, salt and pepper. Cover and lower the
heat and continue cooking until the rabbit is cooked through,
adding a little water if necessary.
10 minutes before the end of cooking add the liver.
Serve hot, garnished with basil.

613

Steaks with Mushrooms and Potatoes

Preparation time 30 minutes
Cooking time 25 minutes
Wine *Velletri Rosso*

2 cups (5.5 oz or 150 g)
 sliced mushrooms
salt
basil, minced

POTATOES
1¼ cups (300 ml) sunflower oil
1 garlic clove
1 lb (450 g) potatoes,
 cut into matchsticks
salt

MUSHROOMS
3 tbsps extra-virgin olive oil
5 spring onions, sliced
1/2 cup (2 oz or 50 g) walnuts,
 finely chopped

STEAK
2 garlic cloves
rosemary sprig
sage leaves
4 tbsps extra-virgin olive oil
2 beef entrecôtes
 (around 2 lb or 900 g)
1/2 cup (120 ml) white wine
salt

614

Make the potatoes: Heat the oil and sauté the garlic until golden-brown, then remove. Fry the potatoes for 5 minutes. Drain, dry on paper towels and lightly salt.
Make the mushrooms: Heat the oil and sauté the spring onions until golden. Add the walnuts and mushrooms, salt to taste and sauté over high heat for 5 minutes, then stir in the basil.
Make the steaks: Brown the garlic, rosemary and sage with the oil, then add the beef and brown for about 2 minutes on all sides. Add the wine and salt to taste. After 1 minute add the mushroom mixture and cook for another 2 minutes. Remove the meat from the pan, debone and cut into thick slices. Serve with the potatoes, mushrooms and pan juices.

Crispy Duck Breast with Marsala and Pink Pepper

Note *Pink peppercorns are the berries of a South American shrub. They have a similar fragance to black pepper, but are much lighter and less fruity.*

Preparation time 15 minutes
Cooking time 15 minutes
Wine *Capri Bianco*

2 duck breasts (about 1 lb or 450 g)
2 tbsps plain flour
4 tbsps extra-virgin olive oil
1 garlic clove, peeled
2 rosemary sprigs
4-5 sage leaves
salt and pepper
3/4 cup (180 ml) Marsala wine
2 tsps pink peppercorns
1/2 cup (120 ml) vegetable broth

Dust the duck breasts with flour.
Heat the oil in a frying pan and brown the garlic. Place the duck in the pan with the rosemary and sage and brown on all sides for no more than 4 minutes. Season with salt and pepper, add the wine and let reduce. Add pink peppercorns and broth, salt to taste and cook for another 5 minutes on medium heat.
Remove the duck from the pan and slice into very thin slices along the diagonal. Serve hot, drizzled with the pan juices and a mixed salad, if desired.

Marinated Turkey with Tomatoes

Note *This recipe can be varied by replacing the tomatoes with 2 red peppers. Roast in a hot oven, close in a plastic bag then peel. Deseed and roughly chop, toss with extra-virgin olive oil and minced garlic and parsley, and serve with the turkey and salad.*

Preparation time 15 minutes
Cooking time 15 minutes
Wine *Soave Superiore*

TURKEY
14 oz (400 g) turkey breast
salt and pepper
2 rosemary sprigs, minced
extra-virgin olive oil

GARNISH
3/4 cup (3.5 oz or 100 g)
 breadcrumbs
parsley, minced
2 tbsps garlic-flavoured oil
2 tomatoes, thickly sliced
salt
1 bunch mixed salad leaves
3 tbsps extra-virgin olive oil

Slice the turkey breast and place in a bowl with salt, pepper, rosemary and oil. Stir, cover with plastic wrap and refrigerate for 15 minutes. Mix the breadcrumbs with the parsley and garlic oil. Salt the tomato slices and dip in the seasoned breadcrumbs. Toss the torn salad leaves with salt and a little oil and divide between the plates.
Grill the turkey slices and tomatoes on a ridged cast-iron grill pan. Serve over the salad.

Beer-Braised Chicken with Mushrooms

Preparation time 20 minutes
Cooking time 35 minutes
Wine *Marino Superiore*

8 tbsps extra-virgin olive oil
1 garlic clove, minced
1 bunch parsley, minced
1 small onion, minced
salt and pepper
1 chicken, cut into pieces
2 tbsps semolina flour
4 cups (10.5 oz or 300 g)
 quartered mushrooms
3/4 cup (180 ml) light ale or lager

617

Mix half the oil with the garlic, most of the parsley, the onion, salt
and pepper and pour over the chicken in a bowl. Marinate for
1 hour.
Heat the rest of the oil in a saucepan. Drain and flour the
chicken pieces then brown for 4-5 minutes on all sides. Add the
mushrooms, adjust the salt, cover and cook until the mushrooms
have given off all their liquid.
Add the beer and cook for another 15 minutes, until the chicken
is cooked through.
Adjust salt and pepper if necessary, sprinkle with more parsley
and serve.

Warm Rabbit and Chickpea Salad

Note *Capers are the closed flower buds of the caper plant, preserved in salt, vinegar or brine. They can be used to flavour all kinds of savoury dishes like pastas, sauces and salads.*

Preparation time 20 minutes
Cooking time 15 minutes
Wine *Lagrein Rosato*

2 saddles of rabbit
4 tbsps extra-virgin olive oil
2 sage leaves
2 garlic cloves, smashed
1 tbsp balsamic vinegar
1 cup (200 g or 7 oz) dried chickpeas, soaked and boiled
salt and pepper
1/2 cup (120 ml) Lagrein Rosato wine
15 salted capers, rinsed and chopped

Detach the loins from the rabbit saddles and remove the lower part attached to the stomach. Cut this part into strips. Heat half the oil, sage and 1 garlic clove in a frying pan and sauté these strips. Add the balsamic vinegar and the chickpeas, and stir well. Season with salt and pepper to taste.

In another frying pan, heat the remaining oil with the other garlic clove. Brown the 4 rabbit loins over high heat. Season with salt and pepper and pour over the wine. Stir so anything stuck to the bottom of the pan dissolves in the wine. Remove the meat from the pan and cut into thick slices.

Divide the chickpea mixture between 4 shallow bowls, add the capers and divide the loin slices between each bowl. Pour over the pan juices and serve.

Asparagus Involtini

Preparation time 20 minutes
Cooking time 30 minutes
Wine *Alto Adige Sauvignon Riserva*

INVOLTINI
12.5 oz (350 g) pencil asparagus
8 beef sirloin tip steaks
 (around 14 oz or 400 g)
salt and pepper
1/2 cup (2 oz or 50 g)
 grated Parmesan
1 tbsp extra-virgin olive oil

GARNISH
1¼ cups (7 oz or 200 g)
 chopped tomatoes
salt and pepper
1 tsp balsamic vinegar
1 tbsp extra-virgin olive oil

619

Trim the asparagus, removing the woody part of the stalk. Divide
into 8 bunches, tie with kitchen string, and boil until still very al
dente. Drain and dry on a clean kitchen towel.
Meanwhile pound out the beef steaks. Season with salt and
pepper and sprinkle one side with Parmesan, pressing down so it
sticks.
Untie the asparagus and place 1 bundle on each slice of beef. Roll
up and close with a toothpick or more string.
Heat the oil in a frying pan and brown the involtini on all sides.
Cover and cook for a few minutes.
Dress the tomatoes with salt, pepper, balsamic vinegar and olive oil.
Serve the involtini, with the toothpick or string removed, with the
tomato salad.

Salmon in Curry Sauce

Preparation time 20 minutes
Cooking time 10 minutes
Wine *Alto Adige Sauvignon*

SALMON
20 asparagus spears
1 knob of butter
4 salmon fillets
 (4.5 oz or 130 g each)
salt and pepper
1 lemon, sliced

SAUCE
7 tbsps vegetable broth
1 tsp mild curry powder
salt and pepper
2 tbsps heavy cream
corn flour

620

Snap off and discard the woody part of the asparagus stalks and
steam them for 5 minutes. Melt the butter in a frying pan and
sauté the asparagus until tender.
Cut the fillets in half, season with salt and pepper and place in a
steaming basket with the lemon slices.
Place the broth, curry, salt and pepper in a saucepan and bring
to a boil. Cook until slightly reduced then whisk in the cream and
corn flour to thicken. Keep warm.
Steam the salmon for 10 minutes then serve with the asparagus
and curry sauce.

Grilled Stuffed Sardines

Preparation time 15 minutes
Cooking time 10 minutes
Wine *Bianchello del Metauro*

16 sardines
3/4 cup (180 ml) white wine
1 tbsp raisins
3 tbsps extra-virgin olive oil
2 garlic cloves, smashed
1 tbsp pine nuts
1 slice white bread
3/4 cup (3.5 oz or 100 g)
 breadcrumbs
parsley, minced
salt

621

Open the sardines like a book, leaving them attached along the
back. Remove the head and backbone. Wash and place in a bowl,
covered with wine, for 10 minutes.
Soak the raisins in warm water.
Heat the oil and garlic in a non-stick frying pan. Add the pine nuts
and toast, then add the raisins with just a little of their soaking
water. Crumble in the bread and add a few breadcrumbs. Cook
for a few minutes and stir in the parsley.
Drain and dry the sardines and stuff with the bread mixture. Roll
them up, securing with a toothpick if necessary, and dip in the
remaining breadcrumbs. Grill briefly. Serve immediately with a
drizzle of oil and a light sprinkling of salt.

Seared Salmon and Sea Bass

Note *Lemon thyme has a slightly citrus aroma, and is often used to flavour vegetables, salads and fish.*

Preparation time 15 minutes
Cooking time 5 minutes
Wine *Greco di Tufo*

9 oz (250 g) sea bass fillet
9 oz (250 g) salmon fillet
salt
4 tbsps extra-virgin olive oil
juice of 1 lemon
1 spring onion, thinly sliced
frisée lettuce
1 sprig lemon thyme

622

Remove any bones and the skin from the fish. Place in a bowl and sprinkle over salt and a little oil.
Dissolve a little salt in 1/2 the lemon juice and wisk with the oil. Pour over the fish and add the spring onion. Cover with plastic wrap and refrigerate for 20 minutes.
Remove the fish from the marinade and cut into squares.
Tear up the frisée and dress with a little salt, oil and remaining lemon juice. Divide between serving plates.
Heat a cast-iron pan and cook the fish on just 1 side until crispy, leaving the other side soft and almost raw.
Adjust the seasoning and place on the salad leaves. Sprinkle with lemon thyme leaves.

Marinated Anchovy Salad

Preparation time 20 minutes
Cooking time 45 minutes
Wine *Bianco d'Alcamo*

20 anchovies
5 tbsps white wine vinegar
1 garlic clove, sliced
oregano
4 tbsps extra-virgin olive oil
1/3 cup (2.5 oz or 70 g) red lentils
salt
2 cups (7 oz or 200 g)
 cooked green beans
1 spring onion, thinly sliced

Open the anchovies like a book, removing the head and backbone. Wash and soak for 15 minutes in vinegar. Drain and place in a bowl with the garlic and oregano and cover with oil. Marinate at least overnight.
Boil the lentils in salted water for 40 minutes.
Arrange the green beans on serving plates and top with anchovies, spring onions and lentils. Serve immediately.

Salmon with Leeks and Eggplant

Preparation time 20 minutes
Cooking time 25 minutes
Wine *Trentino Nosiola*

4 salmon fillet steaks
 (5.5 oz or 150 g each)
6 tbsps extra-virgin olive oil
thyme
1 leek, sliced
1 eggplant, diced
salt and pepper

Marinate the salmon in 4 tablespoons oil with some thyme leaves for 10 minutes. Meanwhile heat 1 tablespoon oil in a small saucepan and sauté the leek.
Heat another non-stick frying pan with 1 tablespoon oil and sauté the eggplant with a little salt and pepper.
Heat a cast-iron pan until very hot and sear the salmon for 2 minutes on each side, starting with the skin side first. Adjust salt and pepper and serve with leeks and sautéed eggplant.

623

Fried Pecorino-Stuffed Anchovies

Note *Anchovies are popular preserved in salt or oil, but they are often eaten fresh in Italy, particularly along the coast and in the spring, when they are at their tastiest.*

624

Preparation time 20 minutes
Cooking time 15 minutes
Wine *Albana di Romagna*
♟

2 lb (1 kg) fresh anchovies
salt
3-4 anchovies in salt
8 tbsps breadcrumbs
1 egg yolk
1 garlic clove, minced
5 tbsps grated pecorino cheese
oregano
milk
1 egg
4 cups (1 l) sunflower oil

Carefully remove the head and backbone the anchovies. Wash under running water and lay in a colander to drain, sprinkled with a little salt.
Rinse the preserved anchovies, chop and mix with the breadcrumbs, egg yolk, garlic, pecorino and a pinch of oregano. Add a little milk if too dry.
Open an anchovy like a book and place some filling on top. Place another opened anchovy on top and press down. Continue with the rest of the anchovies.
Beat the egg with a little salt. Dip the anchovies in the egg and then the breadcrumbs.
Heat the sunflower oil until very hot and fry the anchovies.
Drain on paper towels and serve hot.

Gratinéed Scallops with Ginger

Preparation time 40 minutes
Cooking time 25 minutes
Wine *Colli Piacentini Chardonnay*

12 scallops, with shells
1/2 cup (120 ml) white wine
3/4 cup (200 ml) vegetable broth
7 tbsps heavy cream
2 oz (60 g) fresh ginger, sliced
salt and pepper
4 tbsps extra-virgin olive oil
1 garlic clove
3 small zucchini, diced
2 slices sandwich bread
parsley

Preheat oven to 400°F (200°C).
Wash the scallops and shells well.
Place the white wine, broth, cream and ginger in a saucepan.
Bring to a boil, lower the heat and cook until reduced by 1/2.
Strain and adjust salt and pepper to taste.
Heat a non-stick frying pan with 2 tablespoons oil and the garlic
clove. Sauté the zucchini until tender. Season with salt and pepper.
Place 1 tablespoon of zucchini in each empty scallop shell.
Use the same frying pan to sear the scallops for 1 minute on each
side, then place on top of the zucchini.
Blend the bread with the parsley and 2 tablespoons oil in a food
processor.
Spoon some ginger-cream sauce over each scallop, then top with
the breadcrumbs. Bake for 10 minutes then serve immediately.

625

Steamed Salt Cod with Red Onions

Preparation time 15 minutes
Cooking time 10 minutes
Wine *Malvasia Istriana*

SALT COD AND ONIONS
14 oz (400 g) desalted salt cod
 (see p. 540)
1½ cups (350 ml) water
10 basil leaves
1 rosemary sprig
4 sage leaves
1 garlic clove, unpeeled
1 red onion, thinly sliced
1 tbsp white wine vinegar
3 tbsps extra-virgin olive oil
salt and pepper

GARNISH
extra-virgin olive oil
pepper
4 basil leaves, thinly sliced
1 organic lemon, sliced

626

Remove any bones from the salt cod and cut into equal-sized pieces. Lay them in a steaming basket.
Heat the water, herbs and garlic in a saucepan and set the steaming basket over the water. Cover with the lid or aluminum foil and steam until tender.
Toss the onion slices with vinegar, oil, salt and pepper and let sit for 10 minutes.
Break up the cod pieces and arrange on plates, topped with the onion slices and drizzled with a little oil and sprinkled with pepper, garnished with basil leaves and lemon slices.

Breaded Squid Skewer

Preparation time 15 minutes
Cooking time 15 minutes
Wine *Biferno Bianco*

5 large squid
 (around 1 lb or 500 g)
5 tbsps extra-virgin olive oil
2 garlic cloves, smashed
3 sage leaves
1/2 dried red chilli pepper
1¼ cup (5.5 oz or 150 g)
 breadcrumbs
1 tbsp salted peanuts, minced
parsley, minced
salt and pepper

Wash and peel the squid and cut into pieces.
Heat the oil in a frying pan and sauté the garlic, sage and chilli.
Remove them and add the breadcrumbs, stirring with a spoon, so
they absorb the oil evenly. Pour into a bowl and let cool.
Stir the peanuts and parsley into the breadcrumbs.
Bread the squid pieces with the mixture and thread onto wooden
skewers. Grill on a barbecue, not too close to the heat, or on a
cast-iron pan, over low heat.
Adjust salt and pepper and serve with a salad, if desired.

629

Sesame Tempura Squid with Salad

Note *Sesame seeds are much used as a seasoning in southern Italian cooking, and they are also at the base of many Middle Eastern dishes, sometimes in the form of tahini, sesame seed paste. They are rich in minerals and can be used both as a flavouring or to coat ingredients, as in this recipe.*

Preparation time 15 minutes
Cooking time 10 minutes
Wine *Ribolla Gialla*

SQUID
14 oz (400 g) small squid
1 tbsp sesame seeds
6 tbsps plain flour
3 tbsps rice flour
2 tbsps semolina flour
salt and pepper
sparkling water
sunflower oil

SALAD
2 tbsps extra-virgin olive oil
juice of 1 lemon
salt
1 bunch mixed lettuce leaves

Clean and gut the squid, removing the central bone and the eye. Wash and dry, then cut into rings, reserving the head.
Toast the sesame seeds in a non-stick frying pan.
Mix the flours with a little salt, pepper and the sesame seeds. Whisk in enough sparkling water to make a fluid batter, and whisk until smooth.
Heat the sunflower oil.
Dip the squid in the batter, drain off excess, then fry in the hot oil for around 30 seconds, working in batches. Drain and dry on paper towels and sprinkle with a little salt.
Whisk together the oil, lemon juice and salt and dress the salad leaves. Serve with the squid.

Sautéed Cod with Lemon

Preparation time 15 minutes
Cooking time 15 minutes
Wine *Sicilia Chardonnay*

1 lb (500 g) cod fillet
2 tbsp plain flour
1 tbsps ground crackers
salt and pepper
3 tbsps extra-virgin olive oil
2 garlic cloves, smashed
3/4 cup (180 ml) Chardonnay wine
10 green olives, chopped
juice and zest of 1 lemon

Remove any bones from the cod and cut into bite-sized pieces.
Mix the flour, ground crackers and a little salt. Dip the cod pieces into the mixture.
Heat the oil and sauté the garlic. Add the cod and brown slightly. Add the wine, and as soon it has evaporated, add the olives, lemon juice and a little zest. Season with salt and pepper. As soon as the fish is cooked through, transfer to plates and serve.

Monkfish with Eggplant

Preparation time 10 minutes
Cooking time 25 minutes
Wine *Friuli Isonzo Pinot Grigio*

3 tbsps extra-virgin olive oil
1 shallot, minced
1 eggplant, deseeded and diced
1.25 lb (550 g) monkfish,
 cut into bite-sized pieces
1/2 cup (120 ml) white wine
1 tbsp capers
salt and white pepper
lemon thyme, minced

631

Heat the oil and sauté the shallot until soft. Add the eggplant and cook for 2 minutes. Move the eggplant to the edges of the pan and add the monkfish to the middle. Cook for 7-8 minutes, adding the wine and capers. Season with salt and white pepper and sprinkle over the lemon thyme. Serve hot.

Turbot with Sweet and Sour Caponata

Preparation time 20 minutes
Cooking time 25 minutes
Wine *Verduzzo del Piave*

CAPONATA
4 tbsps extra-virgin olive oil
1 small eggplant, diced
1 zucchini, diced
4 ripe tomatoes
1 onion, sliced
1 celery stalk, diced
2 tbsps white wine vinegar
1 tsp sugar
1/2 cup (120 ml) water
salt and pepper

TURBOT
1 lb (500 g) turbot fillets
extra-virgin olive oil
salt and pepper
thyme, marjoram and chives,
 minced
2 garlic cloves, smashed
1/2 cup (120 ml) white wine

632

Preheat oven to 350°F (180°C).
Heat 1 tablespoon oil in a frying pan and sauté the eggplant until tender. Remove from the pan, add another tablespoon of oil, and sauté the zucchini. Remove and set aside.
Blanch the tomatoes in boiling water for 30 seconds, peel, deseed and chop.
Heat the remaining oil and sauté the onion. Add the celery and sauté for a few minutes. Add the eggplant, zucchini, tomatoes, vinegar, sugar and water and cook for 10 minutes over low heat. Salt and pepper to taste and keep warm.
Lay the turbot fillets on an oiled baking sheet and season with salt and pepper. Sprinkle over the herbs, garlic and white wine and bake for 10-12 minutes. Serve with the caponata.

Almond Trout Fillets with Asparagus

Preparation time 15 minutes
Cooking time 15 minutes
Wine *Metodo Classico*
Franciacorta Rosé

1 bunch asparagus
 (12.5 oz or 350 g)
salt and pepper
5 slices sandwich bread
1 bunch parsley
1 cup (3.5 oz or 100 g)
 slivered almonds
2 egg whites
4 fillets of salmon trout
4 tbsps extra-virgin olive oil
2 tbsps butter
1 oz (30 g) fresh ginger, grated
chervil

Snap off the woody end of the asparagus spears and peel the ends with a vegetable peeler. Cook in boiling salted water for 6-7 minutes, drain and set aside.
Blend the bread with the parsley leaves in a food processor and mix with the almonds.
Beat the egg whites with a fork. Dip the trout fillets in the egg whites and then in the breadcrumb mixture. Press lightly so it sticks.
Heat the oil in a wide frying pan and sauté the fillets until golden on both sides.
In another frying pan melt the butter and sauté the asparagus with ginger, salt and pepper.
Make a base of asparagus on every plate and top with a trout fillet. Garnish with chervil leaves and serve.

Trieste-Style Fish Soup
(Friuli-Venezia Giulia)

Preparation time 15 minutes
Cooking time 30 minutes
Wine *Colli Orientali del Friuli
Ribolla Gialla*

3.3 lb (1.5 kg) mixed fish
 for soup
plain flour
sunflower oil
extra-virgin olive oil
1 onion, minced
1 garlic clove, minced
1 tbsp tomato sauce
4 cuttlefish, cleaned
 and chopped
3/4 cup (180 ml) white wine
4 langoustines, shelled
salt and pepper
parsley, minced

634

Clean the fish and cut into fillets. Dip in flour and fry in hot
sunflower oil. Drain and dry on paper towels.
Heat a splash of olive oil in a saucepan and sauté the onion and
garlic until soft. Add the tomato sauce and cuttlefish. Add the wine
and let evaporate. Continue cooking until cuttlefish is done. Add
the langoustines and fried fish fillets. Season with salt and pepper
and sprinkle with parsley. Turn off the heat and cover.
Let sit for 1 hour before serving.

Fried Mussels
(Puglia)

Preparation time 10 minutes
Cooking time 20 minutes
Wine *Gioia del Colle Bianco*

Serves 6

2.2 lb (1 kg) mussels
3/4 cup (3.5 oz or 100 g)
 plain flour
2 egg yolks
salt
sunflower oil

Wash the mussels under running water and place in a saucepan.
Cover and cook over low heat, stirring every so often, until they
open. Remove from the pan and take the mussels out of their
shells.
Place the flour on a plate and beat the egg yolks with a pinch of salt
in a bowl. Dip the mussels in the flour and then the yolks.
Heat abundant sunflower oil in a large frying pan, and just before it
starts to smoke, fry the mussels for about 10 minutes or until they
are golden. Drain with a slotted spoon and dry on paper towels.
Serve hot.

Mediterranean-Style John Dory

Preparation time 15 minutes
Cooking time 20 minutes
Wine *Riviera Ligure di Ponente Pigato*

2⅔ cups (14 oz or 400 g) miniature plum tomatoes
3 tbsps extra-virgin olive oil
1.3 lb (600 g) John Dory fillets
salt and pepper
1 tbsp capers
2 anchovies in salt
1 garlic clove, sliced
10 black olives
1 tbsp mixed aromatic herbs

Preheat oven to 425° F (220°C).
Blanch the tomatoes, peel, deseed and cut into strips.
Oil a baking dish and lay the fish fillets on it. Season with salt and pepper and top with tomatoes, capers, crumbled anchovies, garlic, olives and 1/2 the herbs. Cover with aluminium foil and bake for 20 minutes, turning halfway through.
Remove from the oven, drizzle with oil, sprinkle with remaining herbs and serve immediately.

636

Tub Gurnard all'Acquapazza

Note *Gurnard can be stewed or boiled, and is commonly used in Italy in fish soups.*

Preparation time 20 minutes
Cooking time 20 minutes
Wine *Greco di Tufo*

1 tub gurnard
(around 1.5 lb or 700 g),
cleaned and gutted
3 tbsps extra-virgin olive oil
1 carrot, peeled and diced
1 celery stalk, diced
2 garlic cloves
3/4 cup (180 ml) Greco di Tufo wine
oregano
8 cherry tomatoes, halved
salt and pepper

Cut a shallow incision down both sides of the fish, from the head to the tail.
Heat the oil in a frying pan and brown the carrot and celery with the garlic until soft. Add 1 ladleful of water, bring to a boil, add the wine and a pinch of oregano, let the alcohol cook off, then add the tub gurnard. The water should come halfway up the fish. Add the tomatoes, season with salt and pepper and cook, covered, over medium heat for 20 minutes, frequently basting the fish with the cooking liquid.
Let rest for 15 minutes, then fillet and serve the fish with the cooking liquid.

Marche-Style Fried Fish
(MARCHE)

Note *This dish is called as* paranzola, *referring to all the catch from boats called* paranza, *which have been used in the Adriatic since the 1950s.*

Preparation time 15 minutes
Cooking time 2 minutes
Wine *Verdicchio dei Castelli di Jesi Spumante*

14 oz (400 g) tiny mixed fish (whitebait)
1½ cups (7 oz or 200 g) plain flour
sunflower oil
salt

638

Rinse the fish in cold running water, drain and dry carefully using a clean kitchen towel.
Coat the fish with the flour and shake off any excess.
Heat a large frying pan with the sunflower oil then fry the fish for 2 minutes, until a light-brown crust forms Drain with a slotted spoon and dry on paper towels. Lightly salt and serve immediately, with a green salad if desired.

MAIN COURSES

Beccafico Sardines
(SICILY)

Preparation time 30 minutes
Cooking time 20 minutes
Wine *Corvo di Casteldaccia Bianco*

SARDINES
2.2 lb (1 kg) fresh sardines
extra-virgin olive oil

FILLING
2 tbsps grated pecorino cheese
1 tbsp breadcrumbs
2 garlic cloves, minced
1 bunch parsley, minced
salt and pepper
2 eggs

GARNISH
lemon wedges
oregano

639

Remove the heads from the sardines, open them and remove the guts and bones. Wash and dry with paper towels.
Mix the pecorino, breadcrumbs, garlic, parsley, salt and pepper in a bowl. Add 1 egg and mix well.
Beat the remaining egg. Fill each sardine with a little of the filling and brush along the edges with the beaten egg, then roll up.
Secure with a toothpick if necessary.
Heat the oil in a frying pan, and when hot add the stuffed sardines. Fry, turning when they become golden on one side. Drain from the oil, dry on paper towels and place on a serving plate.
Serve with lemon wedges and a sprinkling of oregano.

Roast Tub Gurnard with Escarole, Olives and Potatoes

Preparation time 15 minutes
Cooking time 20 minutes
Wine *Riesling Renano*

1 tub gurnard
 (about 1.3 lb or 600 g)
salt and pepper
2 garlic cloves
1 sprig of thyme
5 tbsps extra-virgin olive oil
1/2 cup (120 ml) white wine
1 head escarole, chopped
2 tbsps black olives
1 large potato, peeled and diced

640

Preheat oven to 375° F (190°C).
Gut the gurnard and wash it carefully, removing any internal
fibers. Season with salt and pepper and place 1 chopped
garlic clove and the thyme leaves inside. Place in a parchment
paper- lined baking dish, drizzle with 2 tablespoons oil and roast
for 20 minutes. Pour the wine over the fish after 12 minutes.
Heat 2 tablespoons oil in a saucepan with 1 smashed garlic clove.
Add the escarole and olives. Cook, covered, for 5 minutes,
stirring frequently. Salt to taste.
Heat 1 tablespoon oil in a non-stick frying pan and sauté the
potato, seasoning with salt and pepper.
Fillet the fish and serve on a bed of escarole, olives and potato.

Giant Prawns with Favas

Preparation time 20 minutes
Cooking time 20 minutes
Wine *Carso Sauvignon*

9 oz (250 g) fava bean pods
5 tbsps extra-virgin olive oil
1 garlic clove, minced
1 bunch parsley, destemmed
 and minced
1 cup (7 oz or 200 g) crushed
 tomatoes
salt and pepper
1 lb (500 kg) jumbo prawns,
 heads attached
3/4 cup (180 ml) white wine
zest of 1 organic lemon,
 thinly sliced

Shell the favas and remove the skin from the beans.
Heat the oil and sauté the garlic and parsley. Add the favas and stir. Add the tomatoes, salt and pepper to taste, and cook for 10 minutes.
Shell the prawns, leaving the heads attached. Rinse under running water then add to the tomatoes. Add the wine, adjust salt and pepper and cook for another 10 minutes.
Just before serving, top with thin strips of lemon zest.

Pepper-Stuffed Sardines

Preparation time 20 minutes
Wine *Sicilia Chardonnay*

1.3 lb (600 g) sardines
1/2 red bell pepper, julienned
1/2 yellow bell pepper, julienned
1/2 green bell pepper, julienned
1 bunch chives
juice of 5 lemons
extra-virgin olive oil
salt

Clean the sardines, removing the head and opening them like a book to remove the bones. Wash, dry and sprinkle with salt.
Mix the peppers together. Lay out the sardines and place a few pepper strips on each one, then roll up and tie with a chive. Place in a glass container, cover with lemon juice and let marinate for 2 hours. Transfer to a serving plate, drizzle with oil and serve.

Note *Fresh sardines and anchovies can be easily confused. However the anchovy has an upper jaw much longer than the lower one, while the sardine has the opposite.*

641

Cuttlefish and Roast Pepper Kebabs

Preparation time 30 minutes
Cooking time 25 minutes
Wine *Verduzzo del Piave*

KEBABS
1.3 lb (600 g) baby cuttlefish
3/4 cup (180 ml) white wine
1/2 lemon
salt and pepper
1 bay leaf
1 red bell pepper
1 yellow bell pepper
1/2 cup (2 oz or 60 g)
 breadcrumbs
parsley and oregano, minced
4 tbsps extra-virgin olive oil

GARNISH
mixed lettuce leaves
juice of 1 lemon
extra-virgin olive oil

642

Preheat oven to 400°F (200°C).
Clean the cuttlefish, removing the head from the sac and rinsing for a long time under running water.
Bring abundant water to a boil in a saucepan with the white wine, 1/2 lemon, salt and bay, and boil the cuttlefish for 2-3 minutes. Drain and set aside.
Roast the peppers over an open flame or under the broiler, close in a plastic bag for 10 minutes to steam, then peel and deseed. Cut into strips ¾-inch (2 cm) wide.
Mix the breadcrumbs with parsley, oregano, pepper and the oil. Dip the cuttlefish in the breadcrumbs and thread them onto wooden skewers, alternating with pepper strips. Lay the skewers on a parchment paper-lined baking sheet. Bake for 10 minutes, turning at least once.
Toss the lettuce leaves with oil and lemon juice. Serve the kebabs with the salad.

Sea Bass with Saffron-Chardonnay Sauce

Preparation time 30 minutes
Cooking time 20 minutes
Wine *Chardonnay*

7 tbsps tomato sauce
1 tsp white wine vinegar
1/2 tsp sugar
2 basil leaves
salt and pepper
14 oz (400 g) sea bass fillets
2 tbsps sesame seeds
3 tbsps extra-virgin olive oil
3/4 cup (3.5 oz or 100 g)
 minced celery, carrot and onion
3/4 cup (180 ml) Chardonnay wine
1 pinch saffron
corn flour
1 knob of cold butter
7-8 Taggiasca or other black
 olives, pitted and chopped

643

Place the tomato sauce, vinegar, sugar, basil leaves and a pinch of salt in a small saucepan and cook over low heat until reduced and thickened.

Meanwhile debone, scale and trim the fish fillets, reserving the scraps. Cut the fillets into squares and make little cuts on the skin side so it doesn't curl up during cooking. Season with salt and pepper and dip the side without skin in the sesame seeds.

Heat 2 tablespoons oil in a saucepan and brown the fish scraps, celery, carrot and onion. Add the wine and a little water and let reduce. Strain and add the saffron and cook down further. Mix a pinch of corn flour with the butter then whisk into the sauce to thicken.

Heat 1 tablespoon oil in a frying pan and brown the fish pieces, seasoning with salt to taste.

Serve the sea bass with drizzles of the tomato and saffron sauces, topped with chopped olives.

Marinated Prawns with Balsamic Onions

Note *The marinated prawns can be used to make kebabs, alternated with slices of zucchini, onion layers, bell pepper strips, pieces of tomato and pieces of squid. Lay the skewers in a baking dish, sprinkle with salt and minced rosemary, drizzle with oil and bake at 350°F (180°C) for 20 minutes. Serve immediately.*

644

Preparation time 10 minutes
Cooking time 30 minutes
Wine *Metodo Classico Franciacorta Rosé*

PRAWNS
20 jumbo prawns
10 cherry tomatoes, quartered
3 tbsps extra-virgin olive oil
juice of 1/2 lemon
2 garlic cloves, sliced
parsley, minced
thyme leaves
salt and pepper

ONIONS
3 tbsps extra-virgin olive oil
15 pearl onions, peeled
1 tbsp balsamic vinegar
1 tsp sugar

Place the prawns in a baking dish with the tomatoes and toss with oil, lemon juice, garlic, parsley, thyme, salt and pepper. Refrigerate for 2 hours.
Preheat oven to 400°F (200°C).
Meanwhile heat the 3 tablespoons oil for the onions in a saucepan and sauté the onions for 5 minutes. Add the balsamic vinegar, a little water and the sugar. Cover and cook for 10 minutes over low heat, until the onions are tender.
Roast the prawns for 12 minutes and serve directly from the baking dish, with the onions.

Plaice Cakes with Tomato Sauce

Preparation time 10 minutes
Cooking time 10 minutes
Wine *Elba Bianco*
♟

14 oz (400 g) plaice fillets
1/4 cup (60 ml) béchamel
 (see p. 1096)
1/3 cup (2 oz or 50 g) pitted
 black olives, minced
1 tomato, peeled, deseeded
 and diced
parsley, minced
salt and pepper
breadcrumbs
extra-virgin olive oil
1 garlic clove
1/2 cup (3.5 oz or 100 g)
 tomato puree

645

Puree the plaice fillets in a food processor. Place in a bowl and
mix with bechamel, olives, tomato, and parsley and season with
salt and pepper to taste. Mix in enough breadcrumbs to bind the
mixture.
Form the mixture into balls and place in an oiled, microwave-proof
dish. Microwave at the maximum setting for 4 minutes.
Heat 2 tablespoons oil in a small saucepan with the garlic.
Add the tomato, adjust salt and pepper and bring to a simmer.
Pour the hot tomato sauce over the fish cakes and serve
immediately.

Salt Cod and Potato Gratin

14 oz (400 g) salt cod
1 garlic clove, smashed
1 onion, sliced
2 medium potatoes, 1 diced
 and 1 sliced
3/4 cup (180 ml) white wine
2 cups (500 ml) milk
7 tbsps heavy cream
salt and pepper
thyme and marjoram
5.5 oz (150 g) fava bean pods
1 knob of butter
4 tbsps extra-virgin olive oil
4 tomatoes, peeled and diced

646

Preparation time 20 minutes
Cooking time 1 hour
Wine *Bianco d'Alcamo*

Desalt the cod by soaking in cold water for 2 days, changing the
water often. Remove the skin and cut into chunks.
Heat 2 tablespoons oil and sauté the onion. Brown the cod and
the diced potato. Cook for a few minutes, then add wine and let
evaporate. Add the milk and cook for 20 minutes.
Add the cream, adjust salt and pepper to taste, sprinkle with thyme
and marjoram and continue cooking for another 20 minutes.
Shell the fava beans, blanch and remove the outer skin.
Boil the potato slices in salted water until tender.
Butter individual moulds and layer with potato slices and the cod
mixture. Broil until golden on top.
Meanwhile heat the remaining 2 tablespoons oil with the garlic,
thyme and marjoram and sauté the tomatoes briefly.
Serve the cod and potatoes with the favas and tomatoes.

Salmon and Aspargus Terrine

Preparation time 20 minutes
Cooking time 25 minutes
Wine *Friuli Isonzo Chardonnay*

10.5 oz (300 g) salmon fillet
salt and pepper
juice of 1 lemon
1/2 bunch pencil asparagus
2 large zucchini, thinly sliced
 lengthwise
1 knob of butter
1 shallot, julienned
2-3 sheets gelatin
2-3 tbsps heavy cream
chives, minced
lemon thyme, minced

647

Boil the salmon fillet in salted water with 1/2 the lemon juice until
just cooked through. Cool, remove bones and skin and puree in
a food processor.
Boil asparagus in salted water with the remaining lemon juice until
just al dente.
Heat a ridged cast-iron grill pan and grill the zucchini slices for
30 seconds on each side.
Line a triangular terrine mould with plastic wrap and then with the
slices of zucchini, overlapping them slightly.
Melt the butter and sauté the shallot with a little water.
Dissolve the gelatin in a little water and mix with the pureed salmon,
cream, shallot, chives, lemon thyme and salt and pepper to taste.
Fill the mould halfway with the mixture. Lay in the aspargaus and
pour over the rest of the salmon mixture. Level off the top and
refrigerate until firm. Unmould the terrine and serve sliced.

Alghero-Style Tuna
(Sardinia)

Preparation time 20 minutes
Cooking time 30 minutes
Wine *Torbato di Alghero*

1.75 lb (800 g) fresh tuna
juice of 1/2 lemon
3 tbsps extra-virgin olive oil
1/2 onion, minced
1 celery stalk, minced
3 bay leaves
7 tbsps white wine
1/4 cup (1 oz or 30 g) pitted
 black olives
salt

648

Place the tuna in a bowl, cover with water and lemon juice and let soak for 2 hours.
Meanwhile heat the oil in a frying pan and sauté the onion, celery and bay.
Drain the tuna and add to the frying pan. Cook over low heat for 20 minutes, turning carefully every so often.
Add the white wine, let evaporate, and add the olives. Season with salt to taste, cover and cook until the tuna is done.
Serve the tuna hot, sliced, with the olives and pan juices.

Sautéed Clams and Mussels with Garlic and Parsley (Sardinia)

Note *The clams and mussels can be served in shallow soup bowls, with a slice of toasted bread rubbed with garlic on the side.*

Preparation time 20 minutes
Cooking time 10 minutes
Wine *Vermentino di Gallura*

1.3 lb (600 g) clams
1.3 lb (600 g) mussels
2 tbsps extra-virgin olive oil
2 garlic cloves, minced
parsley, minced
salt

Wash the clams and mussels well. Place in a large frying pan and cook over high heat until they open and give off their liquid. Remove from the heat and set aside.
Meanwhile heat the oil in another frying pan and sauté the garlic and parsley. Add the clams and mussels, still in their shells, together with their liquid.
Cook for around 10 minutes, adding salt to taste.
Serve hot.

Eggplant and Sesame Tart

Preparation time 20 minutes
Cooking time 50 minutes
Wine *Friuli Collio Sauvignon*

CRUST
1¾ cups (7.8 oz or 220 g)
 plain flour
1 tsp baking powder
salt
1 tbsp sesame oil
2 tbsps toasted sesame seeds

FILLING
3 tbsps extra-virgin olive oil
2 spring onions, minced
1 large eggplant, diced
salt and pepper
4 large zucchini, sliced
lemon thyme
1/2 cup (120 ml)
 hot vegetable broth
1 egg white
2 tbsps grated Parmesan

650

Preheat oven to 400°F (200°C).
Mix the flour with the baking powder, a pinch of salt, sesame oil,
sesame seeds and a little warm water to make a smooth dough.
Wrap in plastic wrap and refrigerate.
Heat the olive oil in a saucepan and sauté the spring onions until soft.
Add the eggplant and a little salt and cook, covered, for 5-6 minutes.
Add the zucchini to the pan with the thyme leaves and brown briefly.
Add the hot broth and continue cooking until the vegetables are soft,
then puree in a blender or food processor. Let cool.
Beat the egg white with a pinch of salt until it just starts to thicken,
then stir into the cooled vegetables with the Parmesan. Adjust salt
and pepper to taste.
Roll out the dough and line a floured pie dish. Pierce the dough with
a fork and fill with the vegetable mixture. Bake for 35 minutes. Serve
hot or warm.

Eggplant and Goat's Cheese with Honey Vinegar

Preparation time 20 minutes
Cooking time 10 minutes
Wine *Falerio dei Colli Asolani*

EGGPLANT
4 cups (1 l) sunflower oil
2 eggplants, thinly sliced
2 tbsps plain flour
salt and pepper

SAUCE
7 tbsps white wine vinegar
dried chilli pepper flakes
1 tbsp acacia honey
salt
3 tbsps extra-virgin olive oil

GARNISH
2 aged goat's cheeses, sliced
freshly ground pepper
marjoram

651

Heat the oil in a saucepan or frying pan until very hot. Dip the eggplant slices in flour and fry in the hot oil until golden-brown. Drain and dry on paper towels. Lay out on a tray and sprinkle with salt.
Heat the vinegar and a pinch of chilli flakes in a small saucepan for a few minutes. Remove from the heat and add the honey and 1/2 teaspoon salt and let cool. Stir in the olive oil and pour over the eggplant. Let sit for 10 minutes.
Top each eggplant slice with a slice of goat's cheese. Sprinkle with pepper and marjoram leaves.

Stuffed Mozzarella

Preparation time 10 minutes
Cooking time 10 minutes
Wine *Ortrugo*

4 whole cow's milk mozzarellas
3/4 cup (3.5 oz or 100 g) peas
salt and pepper
3 tbsps extra-virgin olive oil
1 shallot, minced
3.5 oz (100 g) ham, diced
2 tbsps grated Parmesan
3-4 basil leaves, torn
2 tbsps tomato sauce
1 egg
3/4 cup (3.5 oz or 100 g)
  breadcrumbs
2 cups (500 ml) sunflower oil

652

Dry the mozzarellas on paper towels. Slice a lid off the top, and
scoop out the inside reserving it for another use.
Boil the peas in salted water for 5 minutes. Heat 1 tablespoon oil
in a frying pan with the minced shallot, then drain the peas and
add to the pan. Sauté for a few minutes then place in a bowl
and add the ham, Parmesan, basil, tomato sauce, 2 tablespoons
oil, salt and pepper. Mix well then stuff the mozzarellas with the
mixture and close with the lid.
Beat the egg in a bowl and pour the breadcrumbs into another
bowl. Dip each mozzarella in egg and then in breadcrumbs, then in
egg and then breadcrumbs again.
Heat the sunflower oil until very hot and fry the mozzarellas until
golden. Drain on paper towels and serve hot, with a lettuce and
tomato salad if desired.

Mini Mozzarella in Carrozza

Preparation time 15 minutes
Cooking time 10 minutes
Wine *Prosecco di Conegliano
e Valdobbiadene Brut*

653

10 slices sandwich bread,
 crusts removed
sunflower oil
10-12 small cow's milk
 mozzarella balls (bocconcini),
 halved
7-8 anchovy fillets in oil,
 drained and chopped
2 eggs, beaten
1¼ cups (5.5 oz or 150 g)
 breadcrumbs
salt

Cut the bread slices into squares a little larger than the mozzarella
balls.
Heat a saucepan with abundant sunflower oil.
Place 1/2 mozzarella ball on each bread square and top with
a small amount of anchovy. Brush the edges of the bread with
beaten egg and cover with a second bread square, pressing down
on the edges to seal.
Continue making the miniature sandwiches until the ingredients
have been used up.
Dip each one in beaten egg and then in breadcrumbs, pressing
the breadcrumbs on.
Fry the sandwiches in the very hot oil and drain on paper towels.
Lightly salt and serve immediately.

Schiacciata with Oregano and Tomatoes

Note *Schiacciata is a flatbread similar to focaccia. To give a richer flavour to the bread try adding slices of sun-dried tomatoes in oil to the topping.*

Preparation time 10 minutes
Cooking time 20 minutes
Wine *Vermentino della Riviera Ligure di Ponente*

14 oz (400 g) focaccia dough
 (see recipe p. 1093)
plain flour
salt and pepper
4 tbsps extra-virgin olive oil
2 tomatoes
1 tsp dried oregano

Roll the dough out on a floured work surface and lay on an oiled baking sheet. Sprinkle with a little salt and pepper, drizzle with the remaining oil and let rise in a warm place for 25 minutes.
Preheat oven to 450° F (230°C).
Thinly slice the tomatoes with a serrated knife. Lay the tomato slices on top of the dough, leaving 1/2 inch (1 cm) between each slice. Sprinkle with oregano and a little more salt. Bake for about 20 minutes and let cool.
Serve warm, accompanied by cured meats and cheeses if desired. It also makes an ideal mid-afternoon snack.

Scrambled Eggs with Green Beans and Ham

Note *Green beans are called* fagiolini *in Italian, meaning little bean. They are a popular vegetable in Italian cuisine, whether boiled in salted water, sautéed in butter or steamed as in this recipe.*

Preparation time 15 minutes
Cooking time 15 minutes
Wine *Lagrein Rosato*

2 handfuls green beans
3 eggs
7 oz (200 g) cow's milk mozzarella
2 thick slices ham
1 knob of butter
salt and pepper

Top and tail the green beans, place in a steaming basket and steam for around 7 minutes.
Meanwhile beat the eggs in a bowl.
Cut the mozzarella into thin strips, squeeze out excess moisture and pat dry with paper towels.
Cut the ham into thin strips.
Melt the butter in a non-stick frying pan and pour in the eggs. Start stirring with a wooden spoon immediately. Stir in the mozzarella, and continue stirring constantly. Season with salt and pepper to taste.
Serve the eggs with the steamed green beans and ham strips.

655

Casatiello

(CAMPANIA)

Note *This typical Neapolitan bread is an Easter classic. Instead of a Bundt pan, this bread can also be baked in a flat, round baking pan, placing an oven-proof cup in the middle to maintain the ring shape during cooking.*

Preparation time 30 minutes
Cooking time 45 minutes
Wine *Falanghina*

Serves 6-8

2½ tbsps (1 oz or 30 g)
 dry active yeast
4¾ cups (1.3 lb or 600 g)
 plain flour
3 tbsps lard
salt
4 eggs

656

Dissolve the yeast in a little warm water.
Mound the flour on a work surface and make a well in the middle. Add the yeast mixture, 2 tablespoons lard and a pinch of salt to the well. Mix to form a smooth and uniform dough with a fairly soft consistency, adding water as necessary. Form a ball and cover with a clean kitchen towel. Leave to rise for around 3 hours, until doubled in volume.
Knead the dough for a few more minutes. Grease a Bundt pan with the remaining teaspoon of lard. Form the dough into a doughnut shape and place in the pan. Bury the whole eggs in the dough and bake for around 45 minutes. Remove from the oven and cool before serving.

Cheese Bread
(UMBRIA)

Note *This is also a traditional Easter bread.*

Preparation time 20 minutes
Cooking time 50 minutes
Wine *Orvieto Classico*

4 eggs
4 cups (1 lb or 500 g)
 plain flour
6 tbsps extra-virgin olive oil
1½ cups (5.5 oz or 150 g)
 grated Parmesan
1¼ cups (4.5 oz or 125 g)
 grated pecorino cheese
3¾ tsp (0.5 oz or 15 g)
 dry active yeast
3/4 cup (180 ml) milk
salt and pepper
4.5 oz (125 g) pecorino cheese,
 cut into matchsticks

Break the eggs into a bowl and stir in the flour, oil, Parmesan and 1/2 the pecorino with a wooden spoon. Dissolve the yeast in the milk and add to the mixture. Season with salt and pepper to taste. Knead to obtain a smooth and uniform dough.
Spread the dough into a high-edged, narrow baking tin. It should come halfway up the sides. Insert the pecorino sticks vertically into the dough. Cover with a clean kitchen towel and let rise for 2 hours in a warm, dry place.
Preheat oven to 375° F (190°C).
When the dough has doubled in volume, bake until the surface is golden. Serve warm or at room temperature.

Ricotta and Fava Terrine

Note *When choosing fava beans, make sure the pods are crisp and have no marks or cracks. If not consumed immediately, the beans can be blanched for 3 minutes and then frozen. Favas are among the beans with the fewest calories, and they are high in protein, fiber, vitamins and minerals.*

Preparation time 10 minutes
Cooking time 40 minutes
Wine *Alto Adige Sylvaner*

TERRINE
1.3 lb (600 g) fava bean pods
14 oz (400 g) ricotta
1 cup (3.5 oz or 100 g)
 grated Parmesan
salt and pepper
3 egg whites
1 knob of butter

GARNISH
1 head lettuce
2 tbsps extra-virgin olive oil
juice of 1 lemon
salt

658

Preheat oven to 320° F (160°C).
Shell the favas and blanch the beans in boiling water for 2 minutes. Cool in cold water and remove the outer skin.
Mix the ricotta with the Parmesan, add salt and pepper to taste, and mix in 3/4 of the favas. Beat the egg whites into peaks and fold into the ricotta.
Pour the mixture into a buttered mould, cover with aluminum foil and bake in a bain-marie for 40 minutes.
Remove from the oven and cool, then unmould. Serve the terrine cold, in slices, accompanied by a salad of lettuce and the remaining favas, dressed with oil, lemon juice and salt.

Mediterranean Vegetable Pizza

Note *Peppers are rich in vitamin C and low in calories. The sweeter varieties, like bell peppers, are more digestible, while the spicy ones like chillis should be used with care.*

Preparation time 20 minutes
Cooking time 30 minutes
Beer *Belgian Wheat Beer*

DOUGH
2 tbsps (0.9 oz or 25 g) dry active yeast
1/2 tsp sugar
3/4 cup (200 ml) warm water
1½ cups (7 oz or 200 g) whole-wheat flour
1½ cups (7 oz or 200 g) plain flour
4 tbsps extra-virgin olive oil

TOPPING
1 red onion, sliced
1 zucchini, thinly sliced
1/2 yellow bell pepper, cut into strips
1/2 red bell pepper, cut into strips
extra-virgin olive oil
salt and pepper

659

Dissolve the yeast and sugar in the warm water and mix it with the flours and oil to obtain a smooth dough, adding more water if necessary. Let rest for 2 hours.
Roll out the dough into a thick layer. Arrange the vegetables on the dough, drizzle with olive oil and sprinkle with salt and pepper. Let rest for another hour.
Preheat oven to 375° F (190°C).
Bake the pizza for 20 minutes and serve hot.

Ricotta, Chard and Hazelnut Rissoles

Note *Gomasio (sesame salt) can be made at home. Rinse 1 lb (500 g) sesame seeds with cold water and leave to dry. Toast them in a frying pan over medium-low heat until they start to pop, and when pressed between the fingers they crush easily. Remove from the pan and toast 1.2 oz (35 g) sea salt in the same pan. Mix with the sesame seeds and pound in a mortar and pestle. The gomasio can be stored in glass jars.*

Preparation time 15 minutes
Cooking time 15 minutes
Wine *Prosecco di Valdobbiadene Extra Dry*

1 bunch Swiss chard
salt and pepper
7 oz (200 g) ricotta
2 eggs
4 tbsps (finely chopped) hazelnuts, nutmeg, grated
1 cup (4 oz or 120 g) breadcrumbs
2 tbsps gomasio (see note)
sunflower oil

660

Blanch the Swiss chard in lightly salted water for a few minutes. Drain and puree in a food processor with the ricotta and eggs. Season with salt and pepper to taste. Stir in the hazelnuts and nutmeg.
Form the mixture into balls.
Mix the breadcrumbs and gomasio together and dip the balls in the mixture.
Heat the oil until very hot and fry the rissoles. Dry on paper towels and serve hot.

Artichoke and Sun-Dried Tomato Pizza

Note *To reconstitute dried cherry tomatoes, wash well and soak for about 1 hour in water. Drain, dry and steam for 10 minutes. Dry on a clean kitchen towel overnight. Fill a jar with layers of tomatoes with garlic slices, bay leaves and thyme sprigs, and cover with extra-virgin olive oil.*

Preparation time 15 minutes
Cooking time 20 minutes
Beer *Irish Stout*

DOUGH
2 tbsps (0.9 oz or 25 g)
 dry active yeast
4 cups (1 lb or 500 g)
 whole-wheat flour
2 tbsps extra-virgin olive oil
salt

TOPPING
7 oz (200 g) cow's milk mozzarella,
 cubed
10.5 oz (300 g) baby artichokes
 preserved in oil, drained
 and quartered
1 oregano sprig
pepper
3 tbsps extra-virgin olive oil
20 sun-dried cherry tomatoes in oil

661

Dissolve the yeast in a little warm water. Add it to the flour together with the oil, a pinch of salt and enough water needed to obtain a smooth dough which comes away easily from the work surface.
Form into a ball and let rise in a warm place for 1 hour 30 minutes.
Preheat oven to 400°F (200°C).
Roll the dough out with a rolling pin. Form 2 disks, 1/5 inch (1/2 cm) thick, and lay them on 2 baking sheets.
Dry the mozzarella on paper towels and scatter over the pizzas together with the artichoke wedges, oregano leaves, a sprinkling of pepper and a drizzle of oil. Bake for 15 minutes, scatter the cherry tomatoes over the top, then bake for about another 5 minutes.

Rice-Stuffed Zucchini

Preparation time 20 minutes
Cooking time 30 minutes
Wine *Val d'Adige Pinot Grigio*

3½ tbsps butter
1 shallot, minced
1/2 cup (3.5 oz or 100 g)
 Vialone Nano rice
hot vegetable broth
1 tsp ground saffron
salt and pepper
3.5 oz (100 g) Pecorino Romano
 cheese, grated
8 large zucchini
1 tbsp extra-virgin olive oil

662

Heat the butter in a saucepan and add the shallot. Sauté until transparent and add the rice. Toast over high heat for 1 minute until the rice smells nutty, then add a little hot broth. Continue adding the broth as it is absorbed by the rice. After 5 minutes add the ground saffron and season to taste with salt and pepper. Continue cooking the risotto, adding more broth as necessary, until the rice is al dente, about 10 more minutes. Remove the rice from heat and stir in the grated cheese.
Cut the zucchini lengthwise in half. Scoop out the flesh with a paring knife or a spoon. Blanch the zucchini for 3 minutes in boiling water or steam for 5 minutes. Remove from heat and let cool slightly. Fill each zucchini half with rice and set aside to cool completely.
Heat a cast-iron grill pan. Grill each stuffed zucchini half for 3-4 minutes, making sure that the rice filling is hot as well. Transfer to a serving plate and drizzle with olive oil. Serve immediately.

Asparagus Rice with Sabayon

Preparation time 15 minutes
Cooking time 20 minutes
Wine *Friuli Isonzo Sauvignon*

ASPARAGUS
1 cup (7 oz or 200 g) Basmati rice
salt and pepper
20 asparagus spears

SABAYON
2 egg yolks
3 tbsps vegetable broth
juice of 1/2 lemon
1 tsp corn flour

Rinse the rice and place in a saucepan. Cover with 3 inches (6 cm) of lightly salted water and cook for 20 minutes. Set aside. Trim the asparagus and steam for 7 minutes.
Mound the rice on serving plates and top with asparagus. Season with salt and pepper.
Beat the egg yolks, broth and lemon juice in a double boiler. Whisk in the corn flour and cook the sauce over low heat, whisking constantly, until it thickens. Pour the sauce over the rice and asparagus and serve.

Endive with Hazelnut Oil

Preparation time 20 minutes
Cooking time 10 minutes
Wine *Cirò Rosato*

3 heads Belgian endive
5 carrots, diced
1 knob of butter
salt and pepper
10 hazelnuts
4 tbsps extra virgin olive oil

Remove 2 outer leaves from the endive and slice into 6 wedges. Blanch the endive wedges for 1 minute and drain. Pat dry.
Heat a cast-iron grill pan and grill the endive wedges.
Meanwhile, boil the carrots until tender and drain. Melt the butter in a saucepan and sauté the carrots briefly. Season with salt and pepper and set aside.
Toast the hazelnuts briefly in a non-stick pan. Mash them with olive oil in a mortar and pestle. Set aside to cool.
Place the grilled endive on serving plates and drizzle with the hazelnut mixture. Top with carrots and serve immediately.

Stuffed Mushrooms

Preparation time 15 minutes
Cooking time 10 minutes
Wine *Cirò Rosato*

10 medium-sized mushrooms
juice of 1/2 lemon
5 oz (150 g) spinach, chopped
2 oz (50 g) mascarpone
3 slices sandwich bread, cubed
1 tsp truffle oil
salt and pepper
2 tbsps extra-virgin olive oil
1 garlic clove, smashed
1 tbsp grated Parmesan

664

Soak the mushrooms in water and the lemon juice for a few minutes.
Drain and remove the stems from the mushrooms.
Finely chop the mushroom stems. Mix with the spinach in a mixing
bowl. Stir in the mascarpone, bread cubes and truffle oil. Season the
mixture with salt and pepper to taste.
Heat the oil in a frying pan and sauté the garlic. Add the mushroom
tops, cover and cook for 3 minutes over high heat. Remove from the
heat and arrange the mushroom tops on a baking sheet.
Fill each mushroom with 1 tablespoon of the spinach filling and
sprinkle with grated Parmesan.
Brown the mushrooms under the broiler for a few minutes until the
cheese is crispy. Serve immediately.

Roast Vegetable Caponata

Note *Traditionally caponata, a Sicilian vegetable dish, is made with fried eggplant and celery with flavoursome additions like olives, capers, anchovies, chilli and vinegar. This lighter version includes eggplant as well as other vegetables, and is roasted in the oven instead of fried.*

Preparation time 10 minutes
Cooking time 25 minutes
Wine *Soave*

1 long eggplant
1 onion, diced
2 large carrots, peeled and
 thickly sliced
3 zucchini, thickly sliced
10 cherry tomatoes
salt and pepper
2 tbsps extra-virgin olive oil

665

Preheat oven to 425°F (220°C).
Quarter the eggplant and remove the seedy white centre. Slice lengthwise into wedges. Chop the wedges into cubes.
Mix the cubed eggplant, diced onion, carrot and zucchini slices and cherry tomatoes together in a large mixing bowl. Season to taste with salt and pepper. Drizzle with olive oil and toss to coat well.
Transfer the vegetables to a baking dish and bake for 25 minutes, stirring from time to time with a wooden spoon.
Remove from oven and let cool to room temperature. Serve, if desired, with toasted Altamura-style bread.

Cherry Tomatoes Stuffed with Curried Rice and Eggplant

Note *Use a mix of white Basmati and black Venere rice for a colourful variation. The addition of black rice also varies the texture and taste of the dish. Other seasonal vegetables may be added to the filling.*

Preparation time 15 minutes
Cooking time 25 minutes
Wine *Sicilia Chardonnay*

3/4 cup (5.5 oz or 150 g) Basmati rice
salt and pepper
20 large cherry tomatoes
2 tbsps extra-virgin olive oil
1 tsp sweet curry powder
1/2 eggplant, peeled and diced
parsley, chopped

666

Boil the rice in lightly salted water for 18 minutes. Drain and rinse with cold water until cool.
Cut the cherry tomatoes in half and remove the seeds and pulp. Discard the seeds and pulp and set the tomatoes aside.
Heat 1 tablespoon of olive oil in a frying pan and sauté the cooked rice. Sprinkle with curry powder and stir to coat evenly. Sauté the rice until the grains begin to pop open. Remove from heat and transfer to a bowl.
Heat the remaining olive oil in the frying pan and add the eggplant. Season with salt and pepper and sauté until the eggplant is tender. Fill the tomato halves with the curried rice and top with the sautéed eggplant. Sprinkle with chopped parsley and serve immediately.

Broccoli-Stuffed Onions

Preparation time 25 minutes
Cooking time 15 minutes
Wine *Cirò Bianco*

8 medium-sized onions
2½ cups (7 oz or 250 g) broccoli
 florets
5 tbsps grated Parmesan
1 egg, separated
salt and pepper
1 knob of butter
3 slices sandwich bread
2 tbsps grated Emmenthal
 cheese
1/2 cup (120 ml) water

Preheat oven to 400°F (200°C).
Roast the onions for 30 minutes. Remove from the oven and cool. Peel
the onions, slice a lid off the top, scoop out some of the centre of the
onions and reserve. Chop the reserved onion and set the shells aside.
Boil the broccoli florets until tender. Drain and coarsely chop. Add to the
chopped onion. Mix in the Parmesan and egg yolk and season to taste
with salt and pepper.
Beat the egg white to stiff peaks and fold into the broccoli mixture.
Stuff the onion shells with the broccoli filling and place them on a
buttered baking dish.
Blend the Emmenthal and bread in a food processor and sprinkle the
mixture over the onions. Add the water to the baking dish and bake for
15 minutes.
Remove from the oven and let cool before serving.

Spinach with Sweet and Sour Onions

Note *When buying fresh spinach, make sure that the leaves are a uniform bright green colour and that the stems are firm. Spinach may be washed, dried and stored in a plastic bag in the refrigerator for a few days or blanched and frozen for longer periods of time.*

Preparation time 15 minutes
Cooking time 10 minutes
Wine *Trebbiano d'Abruzzo*
♟

1 tbsp raisins
4 tbsps vin santo or other sweet
 wine
3½ tbsps butter
2 yellow onions, thinly sliced
1 tbsp pine nuts
1 tsp white wine vinegar
salt and pepper
2 handfuls of spinach

668

Soak the raisins in the vin santo and a little warm water for 5 minutes. Drain and squeeze out the excess liquid.
Melt the butter in a frying pan. Sauté the sliced onions over low heat until soft. Add the pine nuts and raisins and sauté for 1 minute. Add the white wine vinegar and let evaporate. Season to taste with salt and pepper. Add a little water to the frying pan and continue cooking over low heat.
Meanwhile steam the spinach, remove from heat and squeeze out any excess water. Season with salt to taste.
Place 4 round cookie cutters on individual serving plates and fill with the steamed spinach. Remove the cookie cutters and top the spinach with the sautéed onion mixture. Serve immediately.

Roast Pepper Rolls with Anchovies

Preparation time 15 minutes
Cooking time 20 minutes
Wine *Colli di Conegliano Verdiso*

1 red bell pepper
1 yellow bell pepper
3 tbsps extra-virgin olive oil
1 garlic clove, halved
5 salted capers, rinsed and
  chopped
3 tbsps breadcrumbs
parsley
salt and pepper
12 anchovy fillets in oil

669

Preheat oven to 400°F (200°C).
Halve the peppers and remove the seeds and white pith. Roast
the pepper halves in the oven or over an open flame until the
skin begins to blacken. Place the peppers in a plastic bag and
let steam for 10 minutes. Remove from the bag, peel and slice to
obtain 12 thick strips.
Heat the olive oil in a frying pan and sauté the garlic halves. Add
the capers and breadcrumbs. Toast the mixture over low heat for a
few minutes, stirring often. Add the minced parsley and season to
taste with salt and pepper. Remove and discard the garlic.
Drain the anchovy fillets and place 1 fillet on each pepper slice.
Cover with the toasted breadcrumb mixture and roll up each
pepper slice. Close each roll with a toothpick and place on a
baking sheet. Bake for 4 minutes and serve immediately.

Wild Nettle Tart

Preparation time 20 minutes
Cooking time 45 minutes
Wine *Val d'Aosta Pinot Bianco*

2 tbsps extra-virgin olive oil
1.75 lbs (800 g) wild nettles,
 roughly chopped
salt and pepper
1 lb (400 g) ricotta
3 tbsps grated Parmesan
1 egg
9 oz (250 g) puff pastry
(see recipe p. 1092)

670

Preheat oven to 350°F (180°C).
Heat the olive oil in a frying pan and add the nettles. Sauté for
a few minutes over high heat. Lower the heat and cook for 10
minutes. Season to taste with salt and pepper. Transfer the cooked
nettles to a mixing bowl and add the ricotta, grated Parmesan and
egg. Carefully mix with a wooden spoon to combine the ricotta
and eggs. Adjust the salt and pepper to taste.
Line a lightly oiled round tart tin with the puff pastry. Pour in the
nettle filling and fold over any extra crust. Bake for 30 minutes.
Remove from the oven and serve immediately.

Brie-Stuffed Artichokes

Note *Brie is a soft French cheese with an edible white rind. There are many varieties of Brie: Brie de Meaux, which has a delicate flavor; stronger Brie de Melun; Brie Fermier; Brie Noir, aged for up to a year; and Brie de Chevre (goat's milk Brie).*

Preparation time 25 minutes
Cooking time 20 minutes
Wine *Fiano di Avellino*

8 small artichokes
3.5 oz (100 g) Brie cheese
3 tbsps heavy cream
1 egg yolk
5 tbsps grated Parmesan
5-6 thyme sprigs, chopped
3 tbsps ground almonds
2 tbsps extra-virgin olive oil

671

Preheat oven to 325°F (170°C).
Trim the artichoke stems and remove the tough outer leaves. Loosen the inner leaves and remove the choke with a pairing knife, leaving a small opening at the centre of the artichoke for the filling. Blanch the artichokes for a few minutes in boiling water. Set aside to dry.
Trim off the crust from the Brie and chop the cheese into small pieces. Melt the cheese with the cream over low heat to form a smooth, velvety mixture. Remove from the heat and stir in the egg yolk, 4 tablespoons of grated Parmesan cheese, the chopped thyme leaves and the ground almonds.
Fill each blanched artichoke with 1-2 tablespoons of the Brie mixture. Place the stuffed artichokes upright in a lightly oiled baking dish and top with the remaining Parmesan cheese.
Bake for about 10 minutes or until the artichokes are golden-brown on top. Remove from the oven and serve immediately.

Fried Artichokes with Spicy Salsa

Note *When buying baby artichokes make sure that the leaves at the bottom of the artichoke are closed tightly. The external leaves should be dark green in colour and the inner leaves should be tender. The stem should not be discoloured or bruised.*

Preparation time 25 minutes
Cooking time 15 minutes
Wine *Lagrein Rosato*

ARTICHOKES
6 baby artichokes
sunflower oil

BATTER
1½ cups plus 1½ tbsps
 (7 oz or 200 g) plain flour
7 tbsps milk
1/2 cup (120 ml) white wine
2 eggs
salt and pepper

SALSA
1/2 green bell pepper, deseeded
 and diced
1/2 onion, minced
1 garlic clove, minced
1 chilli pepper, minced
1 medium tomato, diced
2 tbsps lemon juice
3 tbsps extra-virgin olive oil
1/2 tsp ground coriander
salt and pepper

Trim the artichoke stems and remove the tough outer leaves. Boil the artichokes for 15 minutes. Drain, slice in half and remove the choke.
Mix together the flour, milk and wine. Add eggs and season with salt and pepper. Let rest for 20 minutes.
Mix together the green bell pepper, onion, garlic, chilli pepper and tomato. Add the lemon juice, olive oil and ground coriander. Season with salt and pepper.
Heat the sunflower oil in a saucepan. Dip the artichoke halves in the batter and fry until golden-brown. Drain on paper towels using a slotted spoon. Serve immediately, accompanied by the tomato-pepper salsa.

Glazed Pearl Onions

Preparation time 15 minutes
Cooking time 25 minutes
Wine *Lambrusco di Sorbara*

2 cups (500 ml) water
4 sage leaves
1 rosemary sprig
20 pearl onions, peeled
3 carrots, peeled and julienned
6 tbsps balsamic vinegar
1 tsp sugar
salt and pepper

Heat the water, sage and rosemary in a saucepan. Place the onions is a steaming basket and steam for 15 minutes over the herb-infused water. Remove from the heat.
Place the carrots in the steaming basket and steam for 4-5 minutes. Remove from the heat and set aside.
Heat the balsamic vinegar and sugar in a small saucepan and reduce to a syrupy consistency. Pour the syrup over the onions and season with salt and pepper.
Serve the glazed onions with the carrots.

Chickpea Quenelles

Preparation time 15 minutes
Cooking time 20 minutes
Wine *Bianco d'Alcamo*

1 cup (7 oz or 200 g) chickpeas
1 bay leaf
2 eggplant, halved lengthwise
5 tbsps extra-virgin olive oil
salt and pepper
parsley, chopped
4 slices crusty bread, toasted

Preheat oven to 400°F (200°C). Boil the chickpeas with the bay leaf until soft. Drain the chickpeas and set aside. Meanwhile, score the top of the eggplants. Drizzle with oil and bake until soft. Remove from the oven and scoop out the pulp into a food processor. Puree the eggplant with the chickpeas (remove the bay leaf first). Sieve the mixture, then stir in 2 tablespoons olive oil. Season with salt, pepper and parsley.
Using 2 spoons, form the puree into quenelles. Place 1 quenelle on each slice of bread and serve.

673

Spicy Sautéed Chicory
(LÁZIO)

Note *This is a traditional way of preparing chicory which highlights its simple yet bold flavours. This cooking method works with any other strongly flavoured, robust greens, like broccoli rabe or turnip tops.*

Preparation time 20 minutes
Cooking time 1 hour 10 minutes
Wine *Aprilia Trebbiano*

Serves 6

2.2 lbs (1 kg) dark-green chicory
salt
4 tbsps extra-virgin olive oil
2 garlic cloves, minced
1/2 red chilli pepper, chopped

674

Wash the chicory under cold running water. Drain and wrap in a clean kitchen towel to dry.
Boil the chicory in salted water for 40 minutes. Drain, squeeze out the excess water and chop the chicory.
Heat the olive oil in a frying pan and add the minced garlic. When the garlic begins to brown add the chilli pepper. Sauté briefly and then add the chicory. Season to taste with salt.
Mix with a wooden spoon and continue cooking over medium heat for 15 minutes. Serve immediately.

Frittedda
(SICILY)

Preparation time 10 minutes
Cooking time 30 minutes
Wine *Bianco d'Alcamo*

4 small artichokes
juice of 1 lemon
1.75 lbs (800 g) pea pods
3 lbs (1.5 kg) fresh fava bean
 pods
6 tbsps extra-virgin olive oil
1 onion, minced
salt and pepper
1/2 tbsp sugar
2 tbsps vinegar

Trim the artichoke stems and remove the tough outer leaves and
the choke. Cut the artichokes into wedges or slices. Soak the
artichokes in cold water and lemon juice.
Meanwhile, shell the peas and favas and peel the fava beans.
Heat the olive oil in a large frying pan. Add the onion and sauté
until soft. Add the drained artichokes and cook for a few minutes.
Add the peas and favas. Season to taste with salt and pepper.
Add a little water, lower the heat and cook until the artichokes are
tender, adding more water if necessary.
When the artichokes are cooked, add the sugar and vinegar, mix
well and remove from heat. Cool the frittedda and serve.

675

Sweet-Corn Fritters

Preparation time 15 minutes
Cooking time 10 minutes
Wine *Etna Bianco*

1 cup (3.5 oz or 100 g) chickpea
 flour
1/4 cup (1 oz or 30 g) plain
 flour
1 tsp baking powder
parsley, minced
salt and pepper
1/2 cup (120 ml) water
1½ cups (14 oz or 400 g) drained
 canned sweet corn, rinsed,
sunflower oil

676

Mix together the chickpea flour, plain flour, baking powder, parsley
and pinches of salt and pepper. Stir in the water a little at a time to
form a smooth batter. Add the corn and adjust the salt. Mix well.
Heat the sunflower oil in a large frying pan. Drop spoonfuls of
the corn mixture into the hot oil. Working in batches, fry the corn
fritters for 1-2 minutes. When golden-brown on both sides, drain
the fritters on paper towels. Place the fritters on a plate and serve
immediately.

Spring Vegetable Tart

Preparation time 30 minutes
Cooking time 40 minutes
Wine *Gambellara*
♟

1 lb (500 g) pie crust dough (see p.
 1093)
3½ tbsps butter
1 shallot, minced
2 medium zucchini, deseeded
 and chopped
vegetable broth
extra-virgin olive oil
4 cups (9 oz or 250 g) snow peas,
 trimmed and blanched
1 cup (5.5 oz or 150 g) green
 beans, trimmed and blanched
salt and pepper
3 hard-boiled eggs, shelled
 and sliced

677

Preheat the oven to 350°F (180°C).
Roll out the pie crust into a very thin sheet, about 1/5 inch
(1/3 cm) thick. Line a buttered and floured pie pan with the crust.
Bake for 25 minutes. Remove the crust from the oven and let cool
completely.
Heat half of the butter in a non-stick frying pan and add the
shallot. Sauté briefly then add the zucchini and a little broth. Cook
for 10 minutes. Remove from the heat and puree the mixture with
a little olive oil to form a thick sauce. Add more broth if necessary.
Heat the remaining butter in the frying pan and sauté the blanched
snow peas and green beans for a few minutes. Season to taste
with salt and pepper.
Pour the zucchini puree into the pie crust, top with the snow peas
and green beans and finish with the egg slices. Serve at room
temperature.

Smoked Ham Salad

Preparation time 15 minutes
Wine *Ortrugo*

1 head romaine lettuce,
 shredded
15-20 canned baby corn spears,
 drained and rinsed
2 white button mushrooms,
 thinly sliced
7 oz (200 g) smoked ham,
 sliced into thin strips
salt and pepper
2 tbsps balsamic vinegar
2 tbsps extra-virgin olive oil

678

Place the lettuce on serving
plates. Arrange the baby corn
spears and sliced mushrooms
on top of the lettuce and top
with the strips of smoked ham.
Season with salt and pepper
and drizzle with balsamic
vinegar and olive oil. Serve
immediately.

Note *Smoked ham is
sometimes called Black Forest
ham in the United States, and
prosciutto di Praga (Prague
ham) in Italy.*

Artichoke Salad

Preparation time 15 minutes
Wine *Lugana*

3 baby artichokes
juice of 1/2 lemon
salt and pepper
4 tbsps extra-virgin olive oil
5-6 romaine lettuce leaves
2 celery stalks, chopped
8 slices grilled eggplant in oil,
 drained and chopped
2 oz (60 g) Parmesan, shaved

Remove the tough outer leaves
and stem from the artichokes.
Cut in half, remove the choke
and thinly slice the artichoke
halves. Place the artichoke
slices in a bowl, add the lemon
juice and season with salt and
pepper. Drizzle with olive oil and
mix to combine.
Tear up the lettuce and divide
between serving plates. Top
with celery and then the
eggplant. Place a few spoonfuls
of the artichokes on the salad
and season with salt. Drizzle
with olive oil and sprinkle with
Parmesan shavings.

Potatoes with Salsa Verde

Preparation time 15 minutes
Cooking time 10 minutes
Wine *Lacryma Christi Bianco*

POTATOES
3 cups (750 ml) water
2 rosemary sprigs
5-6 yellow-fleshed potatoes,
 peeled and sliced

SALSA VERDE
1 egg, hard boiled
1 bunch parsley
1 garlic clove
salt and pepper
6 tbsps extra-virgin olive oil
juice and grated zest of 1 lemon
ground chilli pepper

Bring the water to a boil with the rosemary. Steam the potato slices in a metal steaming basket over the rosemary-infused water until tender. Peel the egg and separate the white from the yolk. Place the parsley, garlic, egg white and salt and pepper in a food processor. Add the oil and blend until smooth. Add the lemon juice and zest and ground chilli pepper and blend. Plate the potatoes and drizzle the salsa verde over them.

Pea Puree

Preparation time 10 minutes
Cooking time 30 minutes
Wine *Alto Adige Sauvignon*

PUREE
3 tbsps corn oil
1 garlic clove
2 spring onions, thinly sliced
2⅔ cups (14 oz or 350 g) peas
salt
1 cup (250 ml) vegetable broth

GARNISH
chives, chopped

679

Heat the corn oil in a saucepan and add the garlic clove, sauté briefly them add the spring onions. Cook until soft. Add the peas and a pinch of salt. Stir and cover with broth. Cover and cook for 25 minutes over medium heat.
Puree the mixture in a food processor or blender to form a thick sauce. Season to taste with salt and pepper. Serve with chopped chives.

Note *Corn oil can be stored for long periods of time. It should not be used for frying.*

Chickpea-Stuffed Zucchini

Note *The Ronde de Nice variety of zucchini is round and pale green, and excellent for stuffing.*

Preparation time 25 minutes
Cooking time 25 minutes
Wine *Ortrugo*

2 tbsps extra-virgin olive oil
1 shallot, minced
3/4 cup (7 oz or 200 g) drained
 canned chickpeas
1 rosemary sprig
1/2 cup (120 ml) water
1/2 tsp curry powder
salt and pepper
4 round zucchini

680

Preheat oven to 400°F (200°C).
Heat the olive oil in a frying pan. Sauté the minced shallot until soft. Add the drained chickpeas, rosemary sprig and water and cook over medium heat for 15 minutes. Remove the rosemary sprig, add the curry powder and season to taste with salt and pepper to taste. Transfer the mixture to a blender and puree until smooth.
Trim the zucchini, slice in half and scoop out the seedy centre to form 8 small cups. Steam the zucchini for 5 minutes, and set on a paper towel to dry.
Fill the zucchini with the chickpea puree and place on a baking sheet. Bake for 5 minutes. Remove from the oven and let cool slightly before serving.

Artichokes Stuffed with Olives and Mushrooms

Preparation time 25 minutes
Cooking time 30 minutes
Wine *Alto Adige Pinot Bianco*

ARTICHOKES
12 small, round artichokes
juice of 1 lemon
vegetable broth

STUFFING
2 small yellow-fleshed potatoes
salt and pepper
4.5 oz (130 g) mixed wild
 mushrooms preserved in oil

1/2 cup (2 oz or 60 g) pitted
 black olives
3 tbsps extra-virgin olive oil
1 garlic clove, smashed
parsley, chopped
10 cherry tomatoes, deseeded
 and chopped
1 egg yolk

681

Preheat oven to 350°F (180°C).
Trim the artichokes and remove the tough outer leaves and the
choke. Place the artichokes in a bowl and cover with cold water and
lemon juice.
Boil the potatoes in salted water until tender. Drain, peel and mash
with a fork or potato ricer.
Drain the mushrooms and chop them together with the black olives.
Heat the olive oil in a large frying pan with the smashed garlic clove.
Sauté briefly until the garlic begins to brown then add the potatoes
and parsley. Cook for a few minutes, and mix well. Season to taste
with salt and pepper. Remove from heat and add the tomatoes and
egg yolk. Mix well and set aside.
Bring the vegetable broth to a boil and add the artichokes. Cook for
3-4 minutes and drain. Fill the artichokes with the potato mixture and
place in a baking dish. Bake for 15 minutes. Remove from the oven
and serve immediately.

Asparagus and Emmenthal Flan

Preparation time 20 minutes
Cooking time 15 minutes
Wine *Alto Adige Sauvignon Riserva*

**15 aspargus spears
(about 10 oz or 300 g)
2 tbsps extra-virgin olive oil
1/2 onion, minced
4 eggs
1/2 tsp ground nutmeg
salt and pepper
5 tbsps grated Parmesan
4 oz (120 g) Emmenthal, grated
1 knob of butter**

682

Preheat oven to 350°F (180°C).
Trim the asparagus, peeling the woody stems, and slice the spears.
Heat the olive oil in a frying pan and add the onion. Sauté until the onion begins to soften and then add the asparagus. Sauté for a few minutes and remove from the heat.
Beat the eggs in a mixing bowl. Add the nutmeg and season with salt and pepper. Mix in the grated Parmesan and Emmenthal. Stir the mixture well then add the sautéed asparagus.
Butter a ceramic loaf pan or soufflé dish. Pour in the asparagus mixture and bake for 15 minutes.
Unmould and serve the asparagus flan with a green salad, if desired.

Mozzarella-Stuffed
Squash Blossoms

Preparation time 20 minutes
Cooking time 20 minutes
Wine *Tocai Friulano*

SQUASH BLOSSOMS
1 medium potato
salt and pepper
1 cow's milk mozzarella, diced
2 anchovy fillets, chopped
chives, chopped
12 squash blossoms
sunflower oil

BATTER
1 cup (4.5 oz or 125 g)
 plain flour
salt
2/3 cup (150 ml) beer
2 tbsps extra-virgin olive oil
2 eggs, separated

683

Boil the potato in salted water until tender. Drain, peel and mash
the potato with a fork or potato ricer. Mix in the mozzarella,
anchovies and chives. Season with salt and pepper.
Mix together the flour and salt. Whisk in the beer, olive oil and egg
yolks.
Beat the egg whites to stiff peaks and fold into the batter.
Carefully clean the squash blossoms with a damp paper towel.
Remove the pistils without breaking the flower petals. Fill each
blossom with a spoonful of the mozzarella mixture. Twist the top of
the blossom to close.
Heat the sunflower oil in a saucepan.
Dip each blossom in the batter and fry until golden-brown on all
sides.
Drain using a slotted spoon and place on paper towels. Season
with salt and serve with a green salad or tomato sauce, if desired.

Escarole with Olives

Preparation time 15 minutes
Cooking time 20 minutes
Wine *Bolgheri Bianco*

4 tbsps extra-virgin olive oil
1 small onion, minced
4 tomatoes
salt and pepper
4 heads of escarole, quartered
1/2 cup (120 ml) white wine
1/3 cup (2 oz or 50 g) pitted
 black olives
parsley, chopped

Heat 3 tablespoons olive oil in
a frying pan and add the onion.
Sauté until soft.
Blanch the tomatoes for 1
minute, then grain, peel and
chop. Add the tomatoes to the
onion and season with salt and
pepper. Add the escarole and
pour over the white wine. Cook
over low heat for 10 minutes.
Add the black olives and
parsley and cook for another 5
minutes.
Place the escarole on individual
serving plates and drizzle with
olive oil. Serve immediately.

Zucchini Tortes Tatin

Preparation time 20 minutes
Cooking time 35 minutes
Wine *Roero Arneis*

1 garlic clove
1 tbsp extra-virgin olive oil
3 zucchini, julienned
salt and pepper
4 tbsps corn oil
2 tbsps sliced almonds
5 oz (150 g) mild pecorino,
 shaved
9 oz (250 g) puff pastry

Preheat oven to 375°F (190°C).
Brown the garlic in a frying pan
with the oil. Add the zucchini
and sauté over high heat for 5
minutes. Season with salt and
pepper.
Brush 4 ramequins with corn oil.
Divide the almonds between the
ramequins. Add the zucchini and
pecorino.
Roll out the puff pastry and cut
out 4 rounds that are slightly
larger than the ramequins. Cover
the zucchini with the pastry
rounds and tuck in the edges.
Bake the tarts for 15 minutes.
Run a knife around the edge of
the ramequins and invert onto
individual serving plates.

684

Pear and Walnut Salad with Camembert

Preparation time 10 minutes
Wine *Colli Perugini Rosso*
♟

VINAIGRETTE
3 tbsps raspberry vinegar
1 tsp spicy mustard
sugar
3 tbsps walnut oil
3 tbsps sunflower oil
salt and pepper
1 bunch mixed herbs, chopped

SALAD
1 large fennel bulb
juice of 1 lemon
1 small bunch of grapes
1/2 head Lollo Biondo lettuce
1 large pear, thinly sliced
1 kiwi, peeled and thinly sliced
1 spring onion, chopped
1/2 cup (2 oz or 50 g) chopped
 walnuts
9 oz (250 g) Camembert cheese,
 cut into thin wedges

685

In a small bowl, whisk together the vinegar, mustard and a pinch of sugar for the vinaigrette. Whisk in the walnut and sunflower oils to emulsify and season to taste with salt and pepper. Add the chopped mixed herbs and stir to combine. Set the dressing aside.

Trim and thinly slice the fennel bulb using a mandoline or very sharp knife. Blanch in boiling water and lemon juice for 2-3 minutes. Drain the fennel slices and let cool completely.

Peel and halve the grapes. Remove the seeds, if using a seeded variety.

Wash the lettuce and wrap it in a clean kitchen towel. Refrigerate for 5 minutes to crisp. Tear up the lettuce leaves and place them on individual serving plates. Add the blanched fennel and arrange the pear and kiwi slices around the lettuce. Top with grape halves. Sprinkle with chopped spring onion and walnuts. Distribute wedges of Camembert between the plates of salad. Finally, whisk the vinaigrette to recombine and then drizzle it over the salad plates. Serve immediately.

Steamed Vegetable Salad with Tahini-Yogurt Dressing

Note *Tahini is made by smashing toasted sesame seeds into a thick paste. It is widely used in Middle Eastern and Greek cuisine. Tahini is available from most supermarkets.*

Preparation time 25 minutes
Cooking time 20 minutes
Wine *Sorni Bianco*

686

SALAD
juice and peel of 1 lemon
2 potatoes, peeled and diced
2 carrots, peeled and diced
2 turnips, peeled and diced
5-6 asparagus spears, peeled and diced
2 zucchini, trimmed, deseeded and diced
1 heart of romaine lettuce, thinly sliced
salt and pepper

DRESSING
1 tbsp plain yogurt
2 tsps tahini
2 tbsps extra-virgin olive oil

Heat a small amount of water and the lemon juice in a wide saucepan. Add the lemon peel to the water. Bring to a boil and place the steaming basket over the pan.
Add the potatoes and carrots to the steaming basket. Cover and let cook for a few minutes and then add the turnips. Next add the asparagus and zucchini. Steam briefly until the vegetables are just tender. Remove the vegetables from the heat and cool completely. Whisk together the yogurt, tahini and olive oil to form a creamy dressing.
Mound the lettuce on individual serving plates. Top with the steamed vegetables. Drizzle over the tahini dressing and season to taste with salt and pepper.

Vegetable Terrine

Preparation time 20 minutes
Cooking time 5 minutes
Wine *Alto Adige Müller Thurgau*

1 head Belgian endive
2 carrots, peeled and thinly
 sliced
10 cherry tomatoes, quartered
 and deseeded
2 new potatoes, peeled and
 thinly sliced
1 bunch arugula, chopped
3 tbsps extra-virgin olive oil
1 tbsp balsamic vinegar
salt

Remove the leaves from the
Belgain endive and layer them
into the bottom of a loaf pan
or terrine. Season with salt and
pepper. Make layers of carrots,
tomatoes, potatoes and arugula,
seasoning each layer with
salt and drizzling with olive oil.
Continue until the vegetables are
finished. Press down to compact
the layers and cover with plastic
wrap. Refrigerate for 1 hour.
Whisk together the oil, balsamic
vinegar and salt.
Invert the terrine onto a serving
plate and drizzle with the
dressing. Serve immediately.

Zucchini and Goat Cheese Tart

Preparation time 10 minutes
Cooking time 30 minutes
Wine *Pinot Grigio*

2 garlic cloves
3 tbsps extra-virgin olive oil
2 medium zucchini, diced
salt and pepper
4 eggs
2 tbsps grated Parmesan
3/4 cup plus 1 tbsp (200 ml) milk
7 tbsps heavy cream
3.5 oz (100 g) fresh goat's milk
 cheese, diced
9 oz (250 g) pie crust dough
 (see p. 1093)
1/4 cup (1 oz or 30 g) pine nuts

Preheat oven to 325°F (170°C).
Sauté garlic cloves in the oil until
they begin to brown. Add the
zucchini and season with salt.
Cook until tender. Remove garlic
cloves and cool.
Beat the eggs and Parmesan
together. Add the milk and cream
and season with salt and pepper.
Puree the zucchini with the goat
cheese. Add to the egg mixture.
Roll out the pie crust and place it
in a tart tin. Pour in the zucchini
filling and trim excess dough.
Sprinkle the tart with pine nuts
and bake for 25-30 minutes.

687

Grilled Eggplant, Zucchini and Mozzarella Bake

Note *Eggplants arrived in Italy from the Middle East, and are used today primarily in southern Italian cooking. Eggplants are very versatile and can be baked, fried, sautéed, dried, preserved in oil or grilled, as in this recipe.*

Preparation time 3 minutes
Cooking time 15 minutes
Wine *Verdicchio di Matelica*
♟

1 large eggplant, peeled and thinly sliced
2 medium zucchini, thinly sliced lengthwise
3 tbsps extra-virgin olive oil
2 medium tomatoes, thinly sliced
12 oz (350 g) buffalo mozzarella, thinly sliced
8-10 basil leaves
salt and pepper

688

Preheat oven to 350°F (180°C).
Heat a cast-iron grill pan over high heat and grill the eggplant slices.
Blanch the zucchini slices in boiling water for 1 minute. Drain the zucchini on a clean kitchen towel and let cool.
Oil a baking dish and make layers of grilled eggplant, zucchini, tomato, mozzarella and basil leaves, seasoning with salt and pepper to taste. Finish with a layer of eggplant and then a layer of mozzarella.
Bake for 5 minutes or until the mozzarella is completely melted and has formed a golden-brown crust. Garnish with a few basil leaves and serve.

Vegetable Millefeuille with Basil Sauce

Note *Pine nuts are the seeds of mature pine cones. They are an important ingredient in Mediterranean cuisine, used in both sweet and savoury dishes. Take care when storing pine nuts as they become rancid quickly due to their high fat content.*

Preparation time 15 minutes
Cooking time 18 minutes
Wine *Val d'Aosta Pinot Bianco*
♟

MILLEFEUILLE
5 yellow-fleshed potatoes,
 peeled and very thinly sliced
5 carrots, peeled and sliced
6 large zucchini, sliced
salt and pepper

BASIL SAUCE
15 basil leaves
1 tbsp pine nuts
salt
4 tbsps extra-virgin olive oil

689

Line a loaf pan with plastic wrap. Make layers of potatoes, carrots and zucchini, seasoning each layer with a little salt and pepper. Press down to compact the vegetables and then cover with another sheet of plastic wrap to seal.
Steam the millefeuille for about 18 minutes. Remove from the heat and remove the top layer of plastic wrap. Invert the pan onto a serving dish. Let cool completely and then remove the remaining plastic wrap.
Place the basil leaves in a mortar and mash with the pestle. Add the pine nuts, a pinch of salt and the oil and continue pounding to obtain a smooth cream.
Slice the millefeuille into thick slices and place on individual serving plates. Drizzle over the basil sauce and serve immediately.

Rustic Salad with Flowers

Note *In Italy a clear sign that spring has arrived are the wild flowers that bloom in uncultivated fields. Edible flowers are picked and used for salads, omelettes and liqueurs. Nasturtiums, violets, rose petals, borage, dandelions and caper flowers could be used in this recipe.*

Preparation time 10 minutes
Cooking time 30 minutes
Wine *Riesling Renano*

4 medium potatoes
salt and white pepper
4 oz (120 g) Emmenthal cheese, sliced
2 slices of ham, diced
1/4 head of escarole or frisée lettuce, chopped
extra-virgin olive oil
edible flowers, such as nasturtiums

690

Boil the potatoes in salted water. Let cool, peel and slice. Place the potatoes, cheese and ham in a bowl and add the escarole or frisée.
Whisk together the olive oil, salt and white pepper. Pour the dressing over the salad and toss to coat. Let sit for at least 5 minutes.
Mix in the flowers just before serving so that they do not wilt. Serve immediately.

Spring Vegetable Baskets with Balsamic Reduction

Preparation time 20 minutes
Cooking time 15 minutes
Wine *Frascati*

3 zucchini
3 carrots, peeled
3 yellow-fleshed potatoes,
  peeled
7-8 basil leaves
6 tbsps grated Parmesan
3 tbsps balsamic vinegar

Carve the zucchini, carrots and potatoes into small, uniform balls using a melon baller or paring knife. Place the vegetable balls in a steaming basket.

Fill a shallow saucepan with water, add the basil leaves and bring to a boil. Place the steaming basket over the saucepan and steam the vegetables until tender.

Meanwhile, sprinkle a thin layer of Parmesan cheese into a small non-stick frying pan. Melt the Parmesan over medium heat. Remove from heat and run a spatula around the cheese circle to free the edges. Flip the Parmesan round onto an upside-down glass and shape to form a small cup. Repeat to make 3 more Parmesan cups. Let cool completely.

Bring the balsamic vinegar to a boil in a small saucepan over low heat and reduce to form a syrup. Remove from heat and let cool. Place the steamed vegetables in the Parmesan cups and top with the balsamic reduction.

Cumin Carrot Toasts

Note *Spread goat's cheese over the toasts before topping with the carrots for a delicious and light snack or appetizer.*

Preparation time 10 minutes
Cooking time 6 minutes
Wine *Alto Adige Gewürztraminer*

1/2 tsp cumin seeds
5 large carrots, peeled and
 trimmed
juice of 1/2 lemon
parsley, chopped
salt and pepper
3 tbsps extra-virgin olive oil
1 French baguette, sliced

692

Toast the cumin seeds in a small frying pan over high heat until they are browned. Grind in a mortar and pestle and set aside. Steam the whole carrots for 6 minutes in a steaming basket. Remove from the heat and let cool completely. Sprinkle over the lemon juice.
Julienne the carrots and place them in a bowl. Add the cumin and chopped parsley and season to taste with salt and pepper. Pour over the olive oil and toss to evenly coat the carrots.
Toast the bread under the broiler until golden-brown. Let the toasts cool completely and then top with the marinated carrots. Serve immediately.

Chocolate Cream Puffs
(Campania)

Preparation time 50 minutes
Cooking time 20 minutes

Serves 6

12.3 oz (350 g) dark chocolate
8.4 fl oz (250 ml) whipping cream
1½ tbsps water
1.6 fl oz (50 ml) milk
1 tbsp butter
1/3 cup plus 2 tbsps
 (1.7 oz or 50 g) plain flour
2 eggs

Preheat oven to 425°F (220°C).
Melt 8.8 oz (250 g) chocolate in a double boiler.
Whip the whipping cream to stiff peaks and then fold it into the chocolate. Set the chocolate cream aside.
Bring the water, milk and butter to a boil in a saucepan. Remove from heat and sift in the flour, stirring constantly with a wooden spoon. Return the saucepan to the stove and cook the mixture for 2 minutes, stirring constantly.
Let the mixture cool and then add the eggs, one at a time, stirring to incorporate completely.
Butter and flour a baking sheet. Transfer the batter to a pastry bag and form beignets or doughnut shapes. Bake for 6-7 minutes until the beignets are puffy and reduce the oven temperature to 375°F (190°C). Bake until cooked through.
Fill the cream puffs with chocolate cream.
Melt the remaining chocolate and drizzle over each cream puff.

Strawberry Mousse with Chocolate Sauce

Preparation time 30 minutes
Cooking time 10 minutes
Wine *Alto Adige Malvasia Passita*

Serves 8

5 oz (150 g) strawberries,
 hulled
1/3 cup (2.1 oz or 60 g) sugar
1 tbsp white rum
1 gelatin sheet
9.4 fl oz (280 ml) whipping
 cream
7 oz (200 g) chocolate sauce

696

Add half the strawberries and the sugar to a frying pan and sauté for a few minutes. Add rum and cook for a few minutes. Remove from heat.

Soak the gelatin in cold water. Drain and squeeze out the excess water. Add the gelatin to the cooked strawberries. Add the uncooked strawberries and puree.

Whip the whipping cream to stiff peaks and fold into the strawberry mixture. Refrigerate.

Coat the inside of 20 wax paper cups with chocolate sauce. Refrigerate the cups until the chocolate hardens then remove from the paper.

Fill the chocolate cups with strawberry mousse and drizzle with chocolate sauce. Chill before serving.

Wheat Tart with Ricotta and Lemon

Preparation time 40 minutes
Cooking time 30 minutes
Wine *Asti Moscato Spumante*

2 tbsps (1 oz or 30 g) butter
1 egg
2 tbsps sugar
1¼ cup (5.2 oz or 150 g)
 plain flour
4.2 oz (120 g) cooked wheat
2.3 fl oz (70 ml) milk
2 tbsps honey
peel of 1/2 organic lemon
3.5 oz (100 g) ricotta
1 handful pine nuts
icing sugar

697

Preheat oven to 350°F (180°C).
Melt the butter in a double boiler. Let cool.
Beat the egg and sugar together. Add the butter and flour and mix until the dough is smooth and elastic. Refrigerate for 30 minutes.
Heat the cooked wheat, milk, honey and lemon peel. Simmer the mixture until the milk has been absorbed by the wheat. Remove from heat and let cool.
Remove the lemon peel and add the ricotta, mixing with a wooden spoon.
Roll out the dough into a thin sheet and cut out 4 rounds.
Place the rounds on the bottom of 4 individual tart tins. Use the remaining dough to cut out 4 strips. Place the strips around the edges of the tins and press down to seal the bottom and sides.
Pour the cooked wheat filling into the tarts and top with the pine nuts.
Bake for 25 minutes. Sprinkle with icing sugar before serving.

Chocolate Cakes with Strawberry Filling

Note *To make strawberry jam wash and hull 7 lbs (3 kg) of strawberries. Dice the strawberries and add the juice of 1 lemon. Let sit for 2 hours. Cook the strawberries with 3.3 lbs (1.5 kg) sugar for 1 hour. Transfer the hot jam to sterilized jars and seal tightly. Store the jam in a dark place.*

Preparation time 15 minutes
Cooking time 15 minutes
Wine *Banyuls*

Serves 6

1.7 oz (50 g) extra-dark chocolate, chopped
1 tbsp whipping cream
3½ tbsps (2.4 oz or 70 g) strawberry jam
3.5 oz (100 g) dark chocolate
3 tbsps (2.8 oz or 80 g) butter
2 eggs
1/3 cup (2.4 oz or 70 g) sugar
2 tbsps plain flour

698

Preheat oven to 400°F (200°C).
Melt the extra-dark chocolate with the cream in a double boiler. Add the strawberry jam and mix well. Transfer to the freezer and let harden slightly.
Melt the dark chocolate with the butter and let cool slightly.
Beat the eggs and sugar until thick and creamy. Fold in the chocolate and butter mixture.
Butter and flour 6 ramequins. Fill the ramequins two-thirds-full with the chocolate batter.
Remove the chocolate-jam mixture from the freezer. Scoop out 6 balls and drop 1 ball into the center of each ramequin. Top with remaining batter.
Bake for 12 minutes. Cool slightly and invert onto serving plates.

Ricotta Mousse with Kiwis

Preparation time 25 minutes
Wine *Gewürztraminer Vendemmia Tardiva*

8.8 oz (250 g) ricotta
2 tbsps sugar
1 tsp vanilla extract
4-5 mint leaves, finely chopped
2 lemons
3 tbsps chocolate puffed rice
3 ripe kiwis, peeled
 and thinly sliced
toasted hazelnuts

Mix the ricotta with the sugar, vanilla and mint. Add the grated zest of 1 lemon and the puffed rice.
Line the bottom of a baking dish with half of the kiwis. Add the ricotta mixture and top with remaining kiwis.
Julienne the zest of the remaining lemon and chop the toasted hazelnuts. Decorate the mousse with lemon zest and hazelnuts.

Chocolate Mousse with Strawberries

Preparation time 15 minutes
Wine *Barolo Chinato*

8.8 oz (250 g) dark chocolate
5 fl oz (150 ml) whipping cream
2 gelatin sheets
5 tbsps white rum
2 egg whites
salt
2 tbsps sugar
2 small baskets of strawberries,
 hulled and sliced

Melt the chocolate in a double boiler. Remove from heat and let cool.
Whip the cream and fold it into the chocolate.
Soak the gelatin in cold water. Drain and squeeze out the excess water.
Add the gelatin and the rum to the chocolate mixture.
Beat the egg whites with a pinch of salt until foamy. Add the sugar and beat to stiff peaks. Fold the egg whites into the mousse.
Refrigerate for 4 hours and decorate with sliced strawberries.

699

Ricotta Quenelles with Kiwi and Raspberries

Preparation time 25 minutes
Cooking time 40 minutes
Wine *Trentino Moscato Rosa*
👨‍🍳

QUENELLES
11 tbsps (5.2 oz or 150 g) butter
1/4 cup (1.4 oz or 40 g) sugar
2 eggs, separated
1 tsp vanilla extract
zest of 1 lemon
ground cinnamon
8.8 oz (250 g) ricotta
1/3 cup (1 oz or 30 g)
 ground almonds

1⅔ cups (6.3 oz or 180 g)
 breadcrumbs

SAUCE
3 large kiwis, peeled
1.6 fl oz (50 ml) maple syrup
1½ tbsps kiwi liqueur
1 tsp lime juice
1/2 cup (1.7 oz or 50 g)
 raspberries
icing sugar

700

Mix 4 tablespoons of butter with the sugar, egg yolks and vanilla. Add a little lemon zest, cinnamon and the ricotta.
Beat the egg whites to stiff peaks. Fold the egg whites into the ricotta mixture and then add the almonds and 2/3 cup (2 oz or 60 g) of breadcrumbs. Let rest for 2 hours.
Dice 1 kiwi and puree 2 kiwis. Strain the kiwi puree and add the maple syrup, liqueur and lime juice. Mix well. Add the diced kiwi and whole raspberries.
Melt the remaining butter in a frying pan and add the remaining breadcrumbs. Toast the breadcrumbs until they are golden-brown and remove from heat.
Bring a saucepan of water to a simmer.
Form 12 quenelles with the ricotta mixture. Place the quenelles in the simmering water and cook for 10 minutes. Remove with a slotted spoon and shake off excess water. Roll the quenelles in the browned breadcrumbs. Place the quenelles on a serving plate and sprinkle with icing sugar. Serve with the kiwi-raspberry sauce.

Strawberries on Brioche with Crème Anglais

Preparation time 25 minutes
Cooking time 20 minutes
Wine *Moscato Passito di Pantelleria*

1 basket of strawberries, hulled and diced
1 tbsp sugar
2 mint leaves, finely chopped
4 slices of brioche bread
3.5 oz (100 g) dark chocolate
17 fl oz (500 ml) milk
grated zest of 1 lemon
4 egg yolks
2/3 cup (4.4 oz or 125 g) sugar
1 tsp corn flour
1 tbsp whipping cream

Mix the strawberries, sugar and mint leaves together and let sit.
Cut the brioche bread slices into 4 rounds and toast them slightly.
Melt the chocolate in a double boiler and dip the toasted bread in
the chocolate. Set the chocolate coated bread on a sheet of wax
paper and let harden.
Heat the milk and lemon zest.
Beat the egg yolks and sugar with the corn flour. Whisk the hot
milk into the eggs and then transfer the mixture back to the
saucepan. Cook the cream over low heat until it coats the back of
a wooden spoon. Place the saucepan in a cold water bath and let
the cream cool completely.
Place the chocolate-covered brioche on individual serving
plates. Place a round cookie cutter on the bread and fill with the
strawberry mixture. Carefully remove the cookie cutter so that the
strawberries hold their shape.
Top with cold crème anglais and a little cream.

Pistachio Semifreddo

Preparation time 25 minutes
Cooking time 3 minutes

**1.4 oz (40 g) extra-dark
 chocolate
2 cups (2.1 oz or 60 g)
 chocolate puffed rice
7 oz (200 g) pistachio ice cream
3.4 fl oz (100 ml) whipping cream
4 sprigs blackcurrants
 or redcurrants
dark chocolate**

702

Line a baking sheet with plastic wrap. Place 4 individual spring
form moulds (without the bottom) on the baking sheet.
Melt the chocolate in a double boiler. Pour the melted chocolate
over the puffed rice and mix well.
Place 1 tablespoon of the rice mixture in each spring-from mould.
Use a spatula to make an even layer.
Place the ice cream in a bowl and mix it with a spatula until creamy.
Whip the whipping cream and incorporate it into the ice cream. Fill
the spring-form moulds with the ice cream mixture and refrigerate
for 30 minutes.
Remove from the refrigerator and unmould the semifreddos.
Place each semifreddo on a serving plate and decorate with
currant sprigs and chocolate shavings.

Renette Apple Mousse with Chocolate Sauce

Preparation time 1 hour
Cooking time 25 minutes
Wine *Erbaluce di Caluso Passito*
♟ ♟

MOUSSE
2 tbsps butter
3/4 cups (5.2 oz or 150 g) sugar
1 lb (500 g) Renette apples,
  cored and diced
2 fl oz (60 ml) brandy
6.7 fl oz (200 ml) milk
2 gelatin sheets

2 eggs
5 fl oz (150 ml) whipping cream

MERINGUE CUPS
1¼ cups (5.2 oz or 150 g)
 plain flour
1½ cups (5.2 oz or 150 g)
 icing sugar
4 egg whites
11 tbsps (5.2 oz or 150 g) butter

CHOCOLATE SAUCE
3.5 oz (100 g) dark chocolate
1 tbsp water

Preheat oven to 350°F (180°C).
Melt the butter and a third of the sugar in a large frying pan and add the apples and brandy. Sauté briefly and remove from heat. Transfer the apples to a mixing bowl.
Soak the gelatin in cold water, drain and squeeze out.
Bring the milk to a boil. Whisk the eggs and remaining sugar together. Mix in the boiling milk and gelatin and add to the apples. Whip the cream to stiff peaks and fold into the apples. Pour the mixture into ramequins and refrigerate for 1 hour.
Meanwhile, mix the flour, icing sugar, egg whites and butter until smooth. Pour some of the mixture onto a non-stick baking sheet and spread it out using to back of a spoon to form a 4-inch (5 cm) round. Repeat until the batter is finished (6-8 rounds). Bake for 5 minutes. Remove from the oven and using a spatula lift each round off the baking sheet and place on overturned teacups. Mould the round over the teacups and cool completely.
Melt the chocolate with the water. Spoon the mousse into the meringue cups and drizzle with chocolate sauce.

Sicilian Cassata

Preparation time 40 minutes
Wine *Zibibbo*

CASSATA
14 oz (400 g) ricotta
2 cups (7 oz or 200 g)
 icing sugar
7 oz (200 g) candied fruit,
 chopped
3.5 oz (100 g) dark chocolate,
 chopped
vanilla extract
4 tbsps rum
1 lb (500 g) round of sponge
 cake

GLACÉ
2 cups (7 oz or 200 g)
 icing sugar
juice of 1/2 lemon

Sieve the ricotta into a bowl. Add the icing sugar, half the candied fruit and all the chocolate. Add the vanilla extract and the rum and mix well.
Cut the sponge cake into 2 rounds. Slice 1 round into strips and line the edges of a deep cake pan with the strips. Fill the pan with the ricotta mixture and place the remaining sponge cake round over the top of the filling. Refrigerate for a few hours.
Prepare the glacé by mixing the icing sugar, lemon juice and a little hot water to form a thick syrup.
Unmould the cassata on a serving dish and cover with the glacé. Decorate with the remaining candied fruit.

Arezzo-Style Chocolate Roll
(TUSCANY)

Preparation time 30 minutes
Cooking time 15 minutes
Wine *Vin Santo*
♟ ♟

CAKE
2 eggs
3/4 cup (3.5 oz or 150 g) sugar
2 tbsps milk
1/2 cup (2.1 oz or 60 g)
  plain flour
1/2 cup (2.1 oz or 60 g)
  corn flour

zest of 1 lemon
1 tsp baking powder
4 tbsps Alchermes liqueur
4 tbsps vin santo or other sweet
  wine

FILLING
1 batch pastry cream
  (see p. 1100)
3.5 oz (100 g) dark chocolate

TOPPING
icing sugar

705

Preheat oven to 300°F (150°C).
Beat the eggs and sugar until thick and creamy. Add the milk
(at room temperature), flour, corn flour, lemon zest and baking
powder. Mix to form a smooth batter.
Line a rectangular baking dish with parchment paper and pour the
batter into the pan. The dish should be large enough to make a
1/2-inch (1 cm) layer of batter.
Bake for about 15 minutes, or until the cake begins to colour.
Shave the chocolate into the warm pastry cream.
Remove the cake from the oven and let cool slightly. Carefully
invert the cake onto a clean kitchen towel and remove the
parchment paper. Brush the cake with vin santo and Alchermes.
Frost with the chocolate pastry cream. Using the kitchen towel, roll
up the cake like a jelly roll. Twist the ends of the towel to tighten
the roll.
Refrigerate until firm and then remove the cake from the towel.
Place on a serving dish and sprinkle with icing sugar.

Rice Pudding with Banana Sabayon

Preparation time 1 hour
Cooking time 20 minutes
Wine *Asti Moscato Spumante*

706

PUDDING
17 fl oz (500 ml) milk
3/4 cup (5.2 oz or 150 g)
 Originario rice
salt
1 knob of butter
2 eggs, separated
1/3 cup (2.1 oz or 60 g) sugar
1 tsp vanilla extract

SABAYON
2 bananas
2 egg yolks
2 tbsps sugar
1/2 cup (120 ml) sweet wine
grated zest of 1/2 organic lemon

Preheat oven to 350°F (180°C).
Bring the milk to a boil in a saucepan and then add the rice, a pinch of salt and butter. Cook the rice until it is very soft and then transfer it to a bowl to cool.
Beat the egg yolks with the sugar and vanilla. Add to the rice.
Whip the egg whites to stiff peaks and fold into the rice.
Butter 4 ramequins and coat with sugar. Pour the rice mixture into the ramequins and place them in a baking dish. Fill the baking dish half full with hot water and bake the puddings for 35 minutes.
Meanwhile, puree the banana. Beat the egg yolks, sugar, sweet wine and lemon zest until frothy. Place in a double boiler and cook over low heat, whisking constantly, until the mixture is thick and has doubled in size. Remove from heat and whisk in the banana puree.
Serve the rice puddings with the hot banana sabayon.

Apple Fritters with Grappa

Preparation time 15 minutes
Cooking time 15 minutes
Wine *Asti Moscato Spumante*
♟ ♟

3 eggs
1 cup (4.4 oz or 125 g)
 plain flour
salt
4 tbsps grappa
milk
5 Renette apples
sunflower oil
icing sugar

Beat the eggs with the flour and pinch of salt. Add the grappa. Mix the batter, adding milk, until it is quite thin. Let rest for 15 minutes. Peel and core the apples leaving them whole and then slice them into thin rings.
Heat the sunflower oil in a saucepan.
Dip the apple rings in the batter and fry until golden-brown. Drain on paper towels. Sprinkle with icing sugar and serve very hot.

Chocolate Bundt Cake

Preparation time 15 minutes
Cooking time 45 minutes
Wine *Asti Moscato Spumante*

6 tbsps (2.8 oz or 80 g)
 butter, softened
3/4 cup (5.2 oz 150 g) sugar
2 eggs
1/2 cup (120 ml) milk
1¼ cups (5.2 oz or 150 g)
 plain flour
3/4 cup (3.5 oz or 100 g) corn flour
salt
2 tsps baking powder
1/4 cup (2 oz or 60 g) chocolate
 chips
2 small pears
icing sugar

Preheat oven to 300°F (150°C).
Cream the butter and sugar
together. Add the eggs, milk,
flour, corn flour and a pinch of
salt. Add the baking powder and
chocolate chips and mix well.
Peel, core and dice the pears
and add them to the batter.
Butter a Bundt pan and coat
with sugar. Pour the batter into
the pan and bake for 45 minutes.
Let cool completely and sprinkle
with icing sugar.

Hazelnut Cookies with Chocolate

Preparation time 30 minutes
Cooking time 20 minutes
Wine *Colli di Parma Malvasia
Dolce*

1⅔ cups (7 oz or 200 g)
 plain flour
14 oz (400 g) margarine
1 cup (7 oz or 200 g) sugar
2⅔ cups (7 oz or 200 g)
 ground hazelnuts
1/4 cup (0.8 oz or 25 g) cocoa
 powder
1/2 cup (3.5 or 100 g) raw sugar
1 tbsp rum

Preheat oven to 375°F (190°C).
Mix the flour with half the
margarine. Add the sugar and
the hazelnuts. Mix well.
Roll the dough into small balls
and place them on a parchment
paper-lined baking sheet. Bake
for 20 minutes.
Meanwhile, mix the remaining
margarine, cocoa, raw sugar and
rum together to form a cream.
Let the cookies cool completely
and then spread the bottom of 1
cookie with chocolate cream and
stick it to another cookie to form
a sandwich.

708

Sicilian Cannoli

Preparation time 25 minutes
Cooking time 10 minutes
Wine *Moscato Passito di
Pantelleria*

CANNOLI SHELLS
3/4 cup plus 2 tbsps
 (3.5 oz or 100 g) plain flour
1 tsp cocoa powder
1 tsp instant coffee granules
1 tbsp sugar
1 tbsp melted butter
salt
white wine
1 egg white
sunflower oil

FILLING
5.2 oz (150 g) ricotta
1/2 cup (1.7 oz or 50 g)
 icing sugar
1 oz (30 g) candied citron
 and orange, chopped
1 oz (30 g) chocolate chips
1 tsp orange flower water

GARNISH
icing sugar

Mix together the flour, cocoa powder, instant coffee, sugar, melted
butter and a pinch of salt. Add enough wine to make a smooth
and elastic dough. Knead into a ball, cover and refrigerate for 30
minutes.
Roll out the dough into a very thin sheet. Cut out circles with a
cookie cutter. Elongate the circles from both sides to form ovals
and roll the dough around a cannoli mould or small stainless-steel
cylinder. Seal the cannolo using a little bit of egg white.
Heat the sunflower oil in a saucepan. Fry the cannoli (on their
moulds) until they are crunchy. Drain on paper towels and remove
the cannolo mould. Let cool.
Sieve the ricotta and then mix it with the icing sugar, candied fruit,
chocolate chips and orange flower water. Fill the cannoli shells with
the ricotta and sprinkle with icing sugar.

Fruit Tart

(see p. 1092)

Note *To avoid fresh fruit from discolouring, brush the top of the tart with a neutral-flavoured jelly.*

Preparation time 40 minutes
Cooking time 35 minutes
Wine *Asti Moscato Spumante*

17 fl oz (500 ml) milk
4 eggs, separated
2/3 cup (4.2 oz or 120 g) sugar
2 tsps vanilla extract
6½ tbsps (1.8 oz or 50 g)
 plain flour
8.8 oz (250 g) pâte sablée
 (see p. 1092)
1 knob of butter
fresh fruit

710

Preheat oven to 350°F (180°C).
Bring the milk to a simmer.
Beat the egg yolks with the sugar and vanilla extract and add the flour. Whisk in the hot milk and return the mixture to the saucepan. Cook over low heat, stirring constantly, until the cream thickens. Remove from heat.
Butter and flour a round tart tin.
Roll out the pâte sablée and line the tin with the dough. Cut off any excess dough and pierce the surface of the dough with a fork. Bake for 25 minutes and let cool.
Wash and slice the fresh fruit.
Pour the pastry cream into the baked crust and decorate with fresh fruit. Chill until serving.

Cherry Clafoutis

Preparation time 10 minutes
Cooking time 20 minutes
Wine *Cartizze*

3/4 cup plus 1 tbsp
 (3.5 oz or 100 g) plain flour
2 eggs
1/3 cup (2.8 oz or 80 g) sugar
2 tsps vanilla extract
salt
8.4 fl oz (250 ml) milk
1 knob of butter
1 lb (450 g)
 black cherries, pitted
icing sugar

Preheat oven to 425°F (220°C). Mix the flour, eggs, sugar, vanilla and a pinch of salt in a mixing bowl. Slowly whisk in the milk, being careful not to let lumps form. The batter should be smooth and creamy. Butter a deep, heavy baking dish and fill it two-thirds-full with the batter. Add the cherries and the remaining batter. Bake for at least 20 minutes. The cake should be a deep golden-brown colour. Sprinkle with icing sugar and serve hot or cool.

Sicilian Nut Brittle

Preparation time 15 minutes
Cooking time 10 minutes
Wine *Zibibbo*

2⅓ cups (8.8 oz or 250 g)
 slivered almonds
1 tsp sunflower oil
2/3 cup (4.2 oz or 120 g) sugar
1/2 tsp glucose syrup
1 tbsp water
3/4 cup (3.5 oz or 100 g)
 pistachios, chopped

Preheat oven to 400°F (200°C). Toast the almonds in a frying pan for 4 minutes, stirring frequently. Line a baking sheet with parchment paper and brush with sunflower oil. Caramelize the sugar with the glucose syrup and water over low heat. Add half the almonds and mix well. Pour onto the baking sheet and spread with a spatula. Top with remaining almonds and the pistachios. Lay over more parchment paper and press down to form an even layer. Let cool completely. Cut into squares. Store in an air-tight container.

711

Coffee Cream Millefeuille

Preparation time 15 minutes
Cooking time 1 hour 10 minutes
Wine *Marsala Dolce*

712

8.8 oz (250 g) puff pastry
10 fl oz (300 ml) milk
1 tsp instant coffee granules
4 egg yolks
1/2 cup (3.5 oz or 100 g) sugar
1/4 cup (1 oz or 30 g)
 plain flour
3.4 fl oz (100 ml) whipping cream
icing sugar
shaved chocolate

Preheat oven to 400°F (200°C).
Roll out the puff pastry into a thin sheet. Pierce the dough with a
fork and then cut out 12 rounds, 3 inches (8 cm) in diameter. Place
them on a baking sheet and bake for 5 minutes. Let cool.
Heat the milk with the coffee granules. Beat the egg yolks with the
sugar and add the flour. Whisk in the hot milk and return to the
saucepan. Cook over low heat, stirring constantly, until the cream
thickens. Let cool.
Whip the whipping cream and fold it into the coffee cream.
Cover 1 pastry round with cream, top with another pastry round
and top with cream. Top with the final pastry round. Repeat 3
more times to make 4 millefeuilles.
Sprinkle with icing sugar and chocolate shavings.

Mini Fruit Tarts

Note *Kiwi fruit are native to China, but Italy is now the world's leading producer. Kiwi have very high levels of vitamin C and are rich in fiber.*

Preparation time 30 minutes
Cooking time 30 minutes
Wine *Cartizze*

8.4 fl oz (250 ml) milk
2 egg yolks
1/3 cup (2.1 oz or 60 g) sugar
vanilla extract
3 tbsps plain flour
8.8 oz (250 g) pâte sablée
 (see p. 1092)
2 kiwis, peeled and sliced
raspberries

Preheat oven to 325°F (170°C).
Bring the milk to a boil in a saucepan.
Beat the egg yolks with the sugar and vanilla extract. Sift in the flour and whisk in the milk. Return the mixture to the saucepan and cook over low heat, stirring constantly, until the cream thickens. Remove from heat, transfer to a bowl and let cool.
Roll out the pâte sablée and cut out several small circles. Butter and flour individual tart tins and line with the dough rounds. Pierce the surface of the dough and then bake for 14 minutes. Remove from the oven and cool completely. Fill with cream and top with kiwi slices and raspberries.

Chocolate Tart with Pastry Cream

Preparation time 30 minutes
Cooking time 45 minutes
Wine *Albana di Romagna Dolce*

PASTRY CREAM
17 fl oz (500 ml) milk
2 tsps vanilla extract
4 egg yolks
2/3 cups (4.4 oz or 125 g) sugar
1/2 cup (2 oz or 55 g)
 plain flour

CRUST
11 tbsps (5.6 oz or 160 g) butter
2⅔ cups (11.6 oz or 330 g)
 plain flour
3/4 cup (5.6 oz or 160 g) sugar
1 egg
2 egg yolks
1/3 cup (1 oz or 30 g) cocoa powder
1 tbsp pine nuts

714

Bring the milk and vanilla extract to a boil.
Beat the egg yolks with the sugar and add the flour. Whisk the milk into the eggs and return to the saucepan. Bring to a boil over low heat, stirring constantly, until the cream thickens. Remove from heat and let cool.
Cut the butter into small pieces. Pour the flour into a mixing bowl and add the butter, sugar, egg yolks, egg and cocoa. Mix well to form a uniform dough. Cover the dough and refrigerate for 1 hour. Preheat oven to 350°F (180°C).
Butter and flour a tart tin.
Roll out the dough into 2 thin sheets and line the tin with 1 sheet of dough. Pour in the pastry cream and then cover with the second sheet of dough. Press down the dough to seal, cutting off any extra dough if necessary. Top with pine nuts and bake for 35 minutes. Let cool completely before serving.

Chocolate Puddings with Bananas

Preparation time 25 minutes
Cooking time 15 minutes
Wine *Ruby Port*
♟ ♟

BANANAS
4 small bananas
1 tbsp butter
juice of 1 lime
1/2 cup (3.5 oz or 100 g) raw sugar
2 fl oz (60 ml) rum
1/2 tsp ground cinnamon

TART
7 tbsps (3.5 oz or 100 g) butter
3.5 oz (100 g) dark chocolate
2 eggs
2 egg yolks
2/3 cup (4.4 oz or 125 g) raw sugar
salt
1/4 cup (1 oz or 30 g)
 plain flour
1/3 cup (1 oz or 30 g)
 ground almonds

715

Preheat oven to 400°F (200°C).
Peel the bananas and slice them lengthwise into thirds.
Melt the butter in a frying pan and sauté the bananas with the lime juice. Transfer the bananas to a plate.
Caramelize the sugar in the same pan and add the rum. Add the cinnamon and whisk until the sugar dissolves. Return the bananas to the pan and sauté them in the caramel for another 2 minutes. Remove from heat and set aside.
Melt the butter and chocolate.
Beat the eggs, egg yolks, sugar and a pinch of salt together. Continue whisking until the mixture is thick and creamy. Add the melted butter and chocolate and mix well. Sift in the flour and the ground almonds. Butter 4-6 ramequins and coat with sugar. Pour the chocolate batter into the ramequins and bake for 15 minutes. Meanwhile, slice the cooked bananas into rounds.
Invert the tarts onto serving plates and top with the bananas and caramel. Serve immediately.

Coconut Cream Millefeuille

716

Preparation time 20 minutes
Cooking time 35 minutes
Wine *Brachetto d'Acqui*

8.8 oz (250 g) puff pastry
1 egg, beaten
1/2 cup (1.7 oz or 50 g)
 grated coconut
6.7 fl oz (200 ml) milk
3.4 fl oz (100 ml) coconut milk
1/2 vanilla bean
3 egg yolks
1/3 cup (2.8 oz or 80 g) sugar
1/3 cup (1.7 oz or 50 g) corn flour
6.7 fl oz (200 ml) whipping cream
icing sugar
coconut flakes

Preheat oven to 400°F (200°C).
Line a baking sheet with parchment paper.
Cut the puff pastry into 4 rectangles and pierce the surface with a
fork. Place the puff pastry on the baking sheet. Brush with egg wash
and sprinkle with the grated coconut. Bake for 20 minutes.
Meanwhile, bring the milk, coconut milk and vanilla bean to a boil.
Beat the egg yolks with the sugar. Add the corn flour and then whisk
in the hot milk. Return the mixture to the saucepan and cook over
medium heat, stirring constantly, until the cream thickens. Remove
the vanilla bean, transfer the cream to a bowl and let cool.
Mix the whipping cream into the pastry cream.
Make layers of puff pastry and pastry cream, finishing with puff pastry.
Sprinkle the final layer with icing sugar and coconut flakes. Slice the
millefeuille and serve.

Amaretto Truffles

Preparation time 25 minutes
Cooking time 15 minutes
Wine *Marsala Dolce*

3.5 oz (100 g) dark chocolate,
 chopped
3.4 fl oz (100 ml) whipping cream
1¼ cups (3.5 oz or 100 g)
 crushed graham crackers
2 fl oz (60 ml) Amaretto liqueur
2/3 cup (2.1 oz or 60 g)
 icing sugar
1/2 cup (1.7 oz or 50 g)
 cocoa powder

Melt the chocolate with the
cream in a saucepan. Remove
from heat and add the graham
crackers, Amaretto liqueur and
the icing sugar. Mix well and
refrigerate the mixture for 10
minutes.
Roll the mixture into balls and
dust them with cocoa powder.
Place the truffles in paper
baking cups and refrigerate.
Remove the truffles from the
refrigerator 10 minutes before
serving.

Yogurt Cake

Preparation time 25 minutes
Cooking time 15 minutes
Wine *Malvasia dei Colli Piacentini
Dolce*

4 eggs
1 cup (7 oz or 200 g) raw sugar
1 tsp malt
salt
3/4 cup (7 oz or 200 g) plain yogurt
2 cups (8.8 oz or 250 g)
 plain flour
5 tbsps (2.8 oz or 80 g) butter,
 melted
2 tsps baking powder
grated zest of 1 lemon
icing sugar

Preheat oven to 325°F (170°C).
Beat the eggs and the sugar
and add the malt and a pinch
of salt. Add the yogurt and flour
and whisk in the melted butter.
Mix carefully and add the
baking powder. Add the lemon
zest and pour the batter into a
cake pan. Bake for 40 minutes.
Remove from the oven, let cool
and invert the cake onto a wire
rack. Flip the cake over onto a
serving plate and sprinkle with
icing sugar.

Apple Tarts with Calvados Sauce

Preparation time 45 minutes
Cooking time 30 minutes
Wine *Montecarlo Vin Santo*

TARTS
1/4 cup (1.4 oz or 40 g) raisins
1.3 lbs (600 g) Renette apples
1/3 cup (1.4 oz or 40 g) slivered
 almonds
1 tsp cinnamon
grated zest of 1 lemon
1 egg

1/3 cup (2.1 oz or 60 g) sugar
2 tsps vanilla extract
6.7 fl oz (200 ml) whipping cream

SAUCE
6.7 fl oz (200 ml) milk
1/2 vanilla bean
1/4 cup (60 ml) Calvados
2 egg yolks
1/4 cup (1.7 oz or 50 g) sugar
8.8 oz (250 g) pâte sablée
 (see p. 1092)

718

Preheat oven to 300°F (150°C).
Soak the raisins in warm water for a few minutes. Drain and
squeeze out the excess water.
Peel, core and dice the apples. Add the almonds, raisins,
cinnamon and lemon zest.
Beat the egg with the sugar, vanilla extract and cream and add to
the apples.
Make the sauce: Bring the milk, vanilla bean and Calvados to a
boil in a saucepan.
Beat the egg yolks and sugar in a bowl. Whisk in the milk and
return the mixture to the saucepan. Cook over low heat, stirring
constantly, until the sauce thickens. Remove the vanilla bean and
let cool.
Butter and flour small tart tins.
Roll out the pâte sablée into a thin sheet. Line the tart tins with the
dough and fill with the apple mixture and 1 tablespoon of Calvados
cream.
Bake for 30 minutes. Serve with the Calvados cream.

Ricotta Cream Tart

Note *Gianduiotti chocolates were created for Turin's 1867 Carnival by the chocolatiers Cafferel and Prochet. The shape of chocolate was supposed to resemble the hat of the fictional character Gianduiotto, an important figure in Turin's carnival traditions.*

Preparation time 30 minutes
Cooking time 35 minutes
Wine *Moscato di Sicilia*

8.8 oz (250 g) pâte sablée
 (see p. 1092)
1 handful raisins
1/4 cup (1 oz or 30 g)
 plain flour
2 eggs
1/3 cup (2.4 oz or 70 g) sugar
14 oz (400 g) ricotta
ground cinnamon
20 gianduiotti chocolates, chopped
icing sugar

Preheat oven to 320°F (160°C).
Butter and flour a spring-form pan and line with the pâte sablée. Pierce the surface of the dough with a fork.
Soak the raisins in a little warm water. Drain and squeeze out the excess water. Dust the raisins with flour.
Beat the egg with the sugar until thick and creamy. Add the ricotta and a pinch of cinnamon and mix well. Finally add the raisins and the chopped chocolates.
Pour the mixture over the dough. Make a lattice design on top of the filling with any leftover dough. Bake for 35 minutes. Sprinkle with icing sugar.

Yogurt Cake with Apples

Preparation time 15 minutes
Cooking time 35 minutes
Wine *Colli di Parma Malvasia Dolce*

3 eggs, separated
3/4 cups (5.2 oz or 150 g) sugar
1/2 cup (4.4 oz or 125 g) plain
 low-fat yogurt
2 cups (8.8 oz or 250 g)
 plain flour
7 tbsps (3.5 oz or 100 g) butter
2 tsps baking powder
2 tsps vanilla extract
1/2 tsp ground cinnamon
3 apples

Preheat oven to 350°F (180°C).
Beat the egg yolks with the sugar
and then add the yogurt, flour,
butter, baking powder, vanilla
extract and cinnamon.
Beat the egg whites to stiff peaks
and fold them into the batter.
Peel, core and thinly slice the
apples.
Butter and flour a round cake
pan and pour in the batter. Layer
the apples in concentric circles
over the batter. Bake for 35
minutes.
Let cool slightly before serving.

Cornmeal Cake

Preparation time 15 minutes
Cooking time 20 minutes
Wine *Friuli Malvasia Spumante*

4 eggs, separated
3/4 cup (5.2 oz or 150 g) sugar
7 tbsps (3.5 oz or 100 g) butter,
 softened
1¼ cups (7 oz or 200 g) cornmeal
salt
zest of 1 lemon
zest of 1 orange
2 tsps baking powder
3.4 fl oz (100 ml) milk

Preheat oven to 350°F (180°C).
Beat the egg yolks and the
sugar until thick and creamy.
Add the butter and whisk in the
cornmeal, salt and the lemon
and orange zest. Dissolve the
baking powder in a little milk
and add to the batter. If the
batter is too thick, add a little
more milk.
Beat the egg whites to stiff
peaks and fold them into the
batter.
Pour the batter into 10 very
small ramequins and bake for
20 minutes.

720

Ricotta Cake

Preparation time 15 minutes
Cooking time 45 minutes
Wine *Asti Moscato Spumante*

1/3 cup (1.7 oz or 50 g) raisins
10.5 oz (300 g) ricotta
3 eggs, separated
3/4 cup (5.2 oz or 150 g) sugar
grated zest of 1 lemon
grated zest of 1 orange
2 cups (8.8 oz or 250 g)
 plain flour
1 tsp baking powder
2 tbsps rum

Preheat oven to 350°F (180°C).
Soak the raisins in a little hot water. Drain and squeeze out the
excess water. Roll the raisins in a little flour to coat.
Sieve the ricotta. Beat the egg yolks with the sugar. Add the
ricotta, orange and lemon zest, the remaining flour, baking powder
and raisins. Mix well and add the rum.
Beat the egg whites to stiff peaks and fold into the batter.
Line a loaf pan with parchment paper and pour in the batter.
Bake for 45 minutes. Serve the cake warm or at room
temperature.

Sweet Ravioli
(LIGURIA)

Preparation time 1 hour 30 minutes
Cooking time 20 minutes
Wine *Cinque Terre Sciacchetrà*

PASTA
4¾ cups (1.3 lb or 600 g)
 plain flour
4 eggs
3/4 cups (5.2 oz or 150 g) sugar
9 tbsps (4.4 oz or 125 g) butter,
 softened
grated zest of 1/2 orange
grated zest of 1/2 lemon
1 tsp baking powder

FILLING
3.1 oz (90 g) extra-dark chocolate
1 candied citron
12.3 oz (350 g) ricotta
1/2 cup (3.1 oz or 90 g) sugar
2 tbsps pine nuts
1/2 tsp ground cinnamon
2 fl oz (60 ml) orange liqueur

GARNISH
icing sugar
whipped cream

722

Mound the flour on a work surface and make a well in the center.
Add the eggs and sugar and mix. Add the butter, orange and
lemon zest and baking powder and continue kneading until the
dough is smooth. Let the dough rest.
Meanwhile, chop the chocolate and the citron peel and sieve the
ricotta. Mix the ricotta with the sugar in a bowl. Add the chocolate,
citron, pine nuts, cinnamon and liqueur. Mix until smooth.
Knead the dough for a few minutes. Lightly flour a work surface
and roll the dough into 2 thin rectangular sheets. Drop the filling
by rounded teaspoonfuls along the center of the sheet, at least
2 inches (5 cm) apart. Cover with the second sheet of pasta and
press down along the edges and between each round of filling.
Cut into ravioli.
Butter a baking sheet and place the ravioli on the sheet. Bake for
20 minutes and cool completely. Sprinkle with icing sugar and
serve with whipped cream.

Cicerchiata
(Umbria)

Note *Cicerchiata is a typical Umbrian sweet; a cake made of tiny fried cookies coated in honey and candied fruit.*

Preparation time 30 minutes
Cooking time 20 minutes
Wine *Sagrantino di Montefalco Passito*

Serves 6

2 cups (8.4 oz or 240 g)
 plain flour
1 knob of butter
2 tbsps sugar
2 eggs
1 tbsp white wine
sunflower oil
1/2 cup (3.5 oz or 100 g) sugar
1/3 cup (3.5 oz or 100 g) honey
diced candied fruit

Mound the flour on a work surface and make a well in the center. Add the butter, sugar, eggs and wine. Mix to incorporate then knead to form a smooth dough. Roll the dough into tiny chickpea-sized balls.

Heat the sunflower oil and fry the balls until they are golden-brown. Remove from the oil with a slotted spoon and drain on paper towels.

Caramelize the sugar and the honey over low heat. Add the fried cookies and mix with a wooden spoon. Add the candied fruit and mix.

Pour the mixture out onto a sheet of wax paper and shape it into a doughnut or a rectangular mound. Let cool until the cake sets.

Borricche Fritters
(TUSCANY)

Preparation time 20 minutes
Cooking time 5 minutes
Wine *Vin Santo*

724

4 eggs
1 tbsp sugar
3¼ cups (14 oz or 400 g)
 plain flour
6.7 fl oz (200 ml) extra-virgin
 olive oil
2 fl oz (60 ml) Cognac
vanilla extract
grated zest of 1 lemon
icing sugar

Beat the eggs with the sugar in
a mixing bowl.
Mound the flour on a work
surface and make a well in the
center. Add the egg mixture,
2 tablespoons of oil, Cognac,
vanilla extract and the lemon
zest. Mix to form a smooth
dough. Cover and let rest for 30
minutes.
Flour the workspace and roll the
dough out into a sheet 1/5-inch
(1/2 cm) thick. Using a cookie
cutter, cut out oval shapes.
Fry the fritters in the remaining
olive oil. Drain on paper towels
and sprinkle generously with
icing sugar.

Chocolate
Cherries (TUSCANY)

Preparation time 25 minutes
Cooking time 10 minutes

7 oz (200 g) dark chocolate
1 cup (7 oz or 200 g) sugar
3 tbsps water
3 tbsps kirsch liqueur
16 small cherries preserved
 in alcohol

Chop two thirds of the
chocolate and melt it in a
double boiler, stirring frequently.
Remove from heat, add the
remaining chocolate and mix
until smooth.
In a small saucepan dissolve
the sugar in the water and
liqueur over low heat.
Add the cherries to the syrup
and coat them evenly. Remove
from the syrup and refrigerate
for 30 minutes.
Dip the cherries in the melted
chocolate one by one and let
cool on a baking sheet lined
with parchment paper.

Anise Cookies
(UMBRIA)

Preparation time 10 minutes
Cooking time 10 minutes

4 fl oz (120 ml) of wine
1 tbsp sugar
1 tbsp anise seeds
1 tbsp extra-virgin olive oil
plain flour

Prepare a wood fire.
Mix the wine, sugar, anise seeds and oil in a large bowl. Whisk in enough flour to form a smooth batter.
Heat the iron panicocoli mould in the fire and pour in 1 tablespoon of batter. Place the iron panicocoli mould over the fire for 1 minute, flip and cook for 1 more minute. Repeat until the batter is gone. Serve the cookies plain or fill them with jam or cream to make little sandwich cookies.

Note *In Umbria, these cookies, called* panicocoli, *are traditionally prepared for the festival of St. Nicholas in December. The cookies are cooked over a wood fire using special long tongs made of cast iron with two cast-iron plates attached to the ends.*

Torcetti Cookies
(PIEDMONT)

Preparation time 20 minutes
Cooking time 15 minutes
Wine *Bracchetto d'Acqui*

Serves 6-8

2 cups (8.8 oz or 250 g) plain flour
1¼ cups (8.8 oz or 250 g) sugar
salt
11 tbsps (5.2 oz or 150 g) butter, softened
baking powder
5 egg yolks
5 tbsps milk

725

Preheat oven to 450°F (230°C).
Mix the flour, sugar and a pinch of salt in a large bowl. Add the butter, a pinch of baking powder, the egg yolks and milk. Mix well to form a smooth dough.
Roll the dough into ropes 4 inches (10 cm) long.
Sprinkle a cutting board with sugar and roll the ropes in the sugar to coat completely.
Twist each rope into a heart shape.
Place the torcetti on a buttered a baking sheet. Bake until the cookies are golden-brown. Let cool completely and serve.

Lavender Puddings

Note *Lavender oil strengthens the immune system, helps with insomnia and has important antiseptic qualities. When cooking with essential oils it is important to use small doses and to dissolve the oils in milk, yogurt or cream.*

Preparation time 5 minutes
Cooking time 10 minutes

10 fl oz (300 ml) whole milk
1/4 cup (1.5 oz or 45 g) sugar
2 tsps vanilla extract
1 tbsp agar agar powder
5 drops of lavender oil
1 tbsp plus 1/2 tsp raw sugar

Heat the milk, sugar and vanilla. Add the agar agar and dissolve in the milk. Cook over low heat stirring constantly for 5 minutes.
Let cool slightly and then add the lavender oil and 1/2 teaspoon raw sugar.
Pour the pudding into individual moulds and let cool.
When cool refrigerate for another 2 hours.
Sprinkle with the remaining tablespoon of raw sugar before serving.

summer

Light dishes to enliven summer lunches and dinners with originality and flair. Salads of pasta, rice, vegetables and fish for easy and quick cold appetizers and first courses. Aromatic herbs and fragrant spices season meat and fish, to make every dish special. And for a sweet finish, creamy, icy, vividly coloured desserts.

Chardonnay-Steamed Lobster with Vanilla Sauce

Preparation time 20 minutes
Cooking time 15 minutes
Wine *Sicilia Chardonnay*
♟♟

2 small lobsters
3 tbsps extra-virgin olive oil
1 shallot, chopped
1 celery stalk, chopped
1 carrot, chopped
3/4 cup plus 1 tbsp (200 ml) Chardonnay wine
1/2 vanilla bean, halved
1 ripe tomato, chopped
3/4 cup plus 1 tbsp (200 ml) very cold water
corn flour
salt and pepper

Remove the heads from the lobsters and cut the heads in half. Heat the oil in a saucepan and sauté the shallot, celery and carrot. Add the lobster heads and brown for 3 minutes, then pour over 1/2 the wine. Let evaporate, then add the vanilla, tomato and water. Bring to a boil and let reduce to 1/3 of the original volume. Strain, crushing the heads against the strainer to extract all the flavour from them.

Dissolve a pinch of corn flour in 1 tablespoon cold water and whisk into the broth to thicken. Season the sauce with salt and pepper to taste.

Reduce the remaining wine in a saucepan, and when the alcohol has cooked off, add a little water. Place the lobster tails and claws in a metal steaming basket and steam, covered, over the water and wine for 9-10 minutes.

Serve the lobster hot, with the Chardonnay-vanilla sauce.

Mussel and Prawn Croquettes

Preparation time 30 minutes
Cooking time 30 minutes
Wine *Malvasia Istriana*

3 yellow-fleshed potatoes
salt
12 large mussels
2 tbsps extra-virgin olive oil
1 garlic clove, smashed
1/2 dried red chilli pepper
5-6 jumbo prawns, shelled
 and deveined
2 eggs
1¼ cups (5.5 oz or 150 g)
 breadcrumbs
2 tbsps pine nuts
sunflower oil
salad leaves

732

Place the potatoes in cold salted water and bring to a boil. Cook until tender, then drain (reserving a little of the cooking water), peel and mash.
Wash the mussels well; soak and debeard them.
Heat the oil and sauté the garlic and chilli. Add the mussels and cook, covered, over high heat for 2-3 minutes. Add the prawns and cook for another 3 minutes. Remove from the heat, shell the mussels and dice the prawns, and place in a bowl. Add some of the potato cooking water, 1 egg and a few teaspoons of breadcrumbs, if necessary to bind the mixture.
Beat the remaining egg in a bowl and blend the remaining breadcrumbs and pine nuts in a food processor.
Form little balls from the prawn-potato mixture with a mussel in the centre of each one. Roll between the palms of the hands, dip in the remaining beaten egg, and then the pine nut-breadcrumb mixture.
Heat the sunflower oil until very hot and fry the croquettes. Drain on paper towels, salt and serve hot, garnished with salad leaves.

A P P E T I Z E R

Baked Salmon-Trout Parcels

Preparation time 40 minutes
Cooking time 30 minutes
Wine *Alto Adige Terlaner*
♔♔

DOUGH
4 cups (1 lb or 500 g)
 plain flour
2/3 cup (150 ml) extra-virgin olive oil
2/3 cup (150 ml) warm water
salt

FILLING
1 small cauliflower
salt and white pepper
3 tbsps white wine

6 tbsps extra-virgin olive oil
1 garlic clove, smashed
3 cups (7 oz or 200 g) shredded
 Savoy cabbage
1 shallot, minced
parsley, minced
10.5 oz (300 g) salmon trout fillet
1 egg, beaten

733

Preheat oven to 400°F (200°C).
Mix together the flour, oil, warm water and pinch of salt to form a
dough and knead until elastic. Form a ball, wrap in plastic wrap and
refrigerate.
Cut the cauliflower into small florets and blanch them in boiling salted
water with the wine for 5 minutes. Drain and cool in a bowl of ice water.
Heat 3 tablespoons oil in a frying pan with the garlic and sauté the
cabbage. Season with salt and pepper to taste and set aside.
Heat the remaining oil in a frying pan and sauté the shallot with a little
water and a pinch of parsley.
Remove the skin and bones from the fish and dice the flesh.
Roll out the dough with a rolling pin until 1/5-inch (1/2 cm) thick. Cut
out 2-inch (5 cm) squares. Place a spoonful of cabbage, a few trout
pieces and a cauliflower floret in the centre of each one, top with a
teaspoon of shallot and bring the edges together like a little purse.
Brush with beaten egg and bake for 20 minutes. Serve hot.

Herb Omelettes with Prawns

Preparation time 10 minutes
Cooking time 20 minutes
Wine *Metodo Classico
Franciacorta Brut*

2 tbsps extra-virgin olive oil
2/3 cup (3.5 oz or 100 g)
 minced shallot
12.5 oz (350 g) shelled prawns
salt and pepper
3/4 cup (180 ml) white wine
6 eggs
2 tbsps milk
chervil and chives, minced

Heat 1 tabespoon oil and sauté the shallot until soft. Add the prawns and brown for a few minutes. Season with salt and pepper, add wine and cook for 3-5 minutes.
Beat the eggs in a bowl with the milk, salt, chervil and chives.
Heat the remaining oil in a crêpe pan and make individual little omelettes until the eggs are finished. Arrange on a serving plate and top with the prawns.

Tomato Bruschetta

Preparation time 10 minutes
Cooking time 5 minutes
Wine *Fiano di Avellino*

1 garlic clove, thinly sliced
5-6 tomatoes, thickly sliced
salt and pepper
15 basil leaves
8 slices crusty bread
3 tbsps extra-virgin olive oil

Place 1 slice of garlic on each tomato slice and lightly season with salt and pepper. Grill on a cast-iron grill pan for 1 minute on each side, placing a basil leaf on top after turning the first time.
Toast the bread on the grill pan, then lay the grilled tomato slices on each slice of toasted bread.
Drizzle with oil and serve immediately.

734

Bresaola Rolls with Zucchini

Preparation time 30 minutes
Cooking time 20 minutes
Wine *Valcalepio Bianco*

1 eggplant, very thinly sliced
5 zucchini, sliced lengthways
oregano
salt and pepper
1 small yellow bell pepper
3 tbsps extra-virgin olive oil
20 slices of bresaola

Preheat oven to 375°F (190°C). Grill the eggplant and zucchini slices on a cast-iron grill pan. Season with oregano, salt and pepper and let cool.
Halve the pepper, remove the white pith and seeds, brush with a little oil and bake for around 20 minutes. Close in a plastic bag and let sweat for 10 minutes, then peel. Puree the flesh with the remaining oil.
Roll the eggplant and zucchini slices in the bresaola and serve with the yellow-pepper sauce.

Spicy Grouper Salad

Preparation time 10 minutes
Cooking time 20 minutes
Wine *Bolgheri Bianco*

5 tbsps extra-virgin olive oil
1 garlic clove, sliced
1 dried red chilli pepper
1 grouper fillet
 (around 14 oz or 400 g)
4-5 cherry tomatoes, halved
salt and pepper
1 head iceberg lettuce, shredded
10 sun-dried tomatoes in oil,
 chopped

735

Heat a large non-stick pan with 4 tablespoons oil, garlic and crumbled chilli pepper. Add the grouper and cook over low heat, turning often. After a few minutes add the tomatoes and season with salt and pepper. Toss the lettuce with oil and salt and arrange on serving plates. Top with sun-dried tomatoes. Once cooked through, let the fish cool and cut into chunks. Add to the salad and serve.

Fried Cassatedde with Tuma
(SARDINIA)

Preparation time 20 minutes
Cooking time 15 minutes
Wine *Torbato di Alghero*

4 cups (1 lb or 500 g)
 plain flour
salt
6 salted anchovies
3 tomatoes, peeled and chopped
parsley, minced
9 oz (250 g) tuma
 (goat's milk cheese), chopped
salt and pepper
sunflower oil

736

Mound the flour on a work surface and make a well in the middle.
Add a pinch of salt and enough water to mix a smooth and quite
elastic dough. Form a ball and let rest for 1 hour.
Meanwhile remove any bones from the anchovies and rinse the
anchovies well under cold running water. Chop them and place in
a bowl with the tomatoes, parsley, tuma and pinches of salt and
pepper and mix well.
Roll the dough out into a thin sheet and cut out disks with a
cookie cutter. Place 1 tablespoon of filling in the middle of each
one and fold over to form half-moons.
Heat the oil until very hot and fry the half-moons until golden, then
drain and dry on paper towels. Serve hot or warm, according to
taste.

Swordfish Involtini
(SICILY)

Preparation time 15 minutes
Cooking time 20 minutes
Wine *Regaleali Rosato*

extra-virgin olive oil
1 small onion, minced
parsley, minced
3/4 cup (3.5 oz or 100 g)
 breadcrumbs
3.5 oz (100 g) swordfish fillet,
 chopped
salt and pepper
3.5 oz (100 g) spicy provolone,
 diced
1 egg
4 thin slices swordfish

737

Heat a little oil in a frying pan and sauté the onion with the
parsley. Add the breadcrumbs and brown, then add the chopped
swordfish. Season with salt and pepper and cook over low heat
for 5 minutes, then puree in a food processor and place in a bowl.
Mix in the provolone and egg and stir with a wooden spoon.
Pound out the swordfish slices with a meat tenderizer and divide
the filling between them, then roll up into involtini and secure with
toothpicks.
Cook the involtini on a grill or a grill pan, turning as little as
possible, until cooked through. Season with salt and pepper to
taste and serve.

738

Swordfish Tartare with Mint Vinegar

Preparation time 15 minutes
Cooking time 15 minutes
Wine *Metodo Classico Franciacorta Rosé*

3/4 cup (180 ml) white wine
 vinegar
1 garlic clove
mint
2 spring onions, sliced
salt and pepper
4 tbsps extra-virgin olive oil
1 eggplant, diced
1 lb (500 g) swordfish, diced
juice of 1/2 lemon
1 tbsp capers

Bring the vinegar to a boil with the garlic, mint, spring onions and a little salt and reduce to 1/2 the original volume.
Heat 2 tablespoons oil in a frying pan and sauté the eggplant until tender. Salt and let cool. Strain the vinegar and pour over the eggplant. Let marinate for 1 hour.
Toss the swordfish with the remaining oil, salt, lemon juice and capers. Add the eggplant and mix well. Serve garnished with a few mint leaves.

Anchovy and Roast Pepper Bruschetta

Preparation time 20 minutes
Cooking time 10 minutes
Wine *Falanghina del Sannio*

4 slices crusty bread
4 tbsps extra-virgin olive oil
1 red bell pepper
1 yellow bell pepper
1 green bell pepper
4 tomatoes, thinly sliced
oregano
salt and pepper
3.5 oz (100 g) anchovies

Preheat the broiler and preheat oven to 425°F (220°C).
Lay the bread on a baking sheet and drizzle with some oil. Toast under the broiler for 2-3 minutes.
Roast the peppers in the oven for 8-10 minutes, close in plastic bag to steam for a few minutes then peel. Cut into quarters and remove the seeds. Top the bread with the tomato slices, season with oregano, salt, pepper and a drizzle of oil, then top with peppers and a few anchovy fillets. Drizzle with oil, sprinkle with oregano and serve.

Mussel Bruschetta

Preparation time 15 minutes
Cooking time 10 minutes
Wine *Bianco d'Alcamo*

10.5 oz (300 g) mussels
2 tbsps extra-virgin olive oil
1 garlic clove
1/2 dried red chilli pepper
2 tomatoes
parsley, minced
salt and pepper
6 slices crusty bread

Wash, soak and debeard the mussels. Heat the oil, garlic and chilli in a frying pan and add the mussels. Cover and cook over high heat for 5 minutes, until the mussels open.
Blanch the tomatoes, drain and cool in ice water. Peel, deseed and chop the flesh.
Shell the mussels and strain their cooking liquid. Place the mussels and liquid in a small saucepan with the parsley and cook down until the liquid is reduced. Mix in the tomatoes, salt and pepper and keep warm.
Cut the bread into pieces, toast and top with the mussels and tomatoes.

Ricotta and Anchovy Crostini

Preparation time 5 minutes
Cooking time 5 minutes
Wine *Frascati*

3½ tbsps ricotta
1½ cups (5.5 oz or 150 g) grated
 Pecorino Romano cheese
1 egg
1 egg yolk
2 tbsps white wine
8 anchovy fillets, 4 chopped
 and 4 whole
thyme and parsley, minced
2 garlic cloves, smashed
salt and pepper
4 slices ciabatta bread

739

Sieve the ricotta into a bowl. Stir in the grated cheese, egg, egg yolk and white wine and mix well. Stir in the chopped anchovies, herbs and garlic and season with salt and pepper. Toast the bread slices, then spread with the cheese mixture, having removed the garlic. Broil until golden. Top each crostino with 1 whole anchovy fillet and serve.

Octopus Salad with Croutons

Preparation time 20 minutes
Cooking time 35 minutes
Wine *Tocai Friulano*

1 octopus (around 1 lb or 500 g)
1 garlic clove
1 dried red chilli pepper
2 carrots, peeled and diced
3/4 cup (3.5 oz or 100 g)
 spring peas
salt and pepper
2 slices crusty bread, cubed
4 tbsps extra-virgin olive oil
1 sprig rosemary
10 cherry tomatoes, quartered

740

Boil the octopus with the garlic and chilli for 35 minutes, then let cool in the water.
Boil the carrots and peas in salted water and drain when al dente.
Toss the bread with a little salt, oil and the rosemary leaves. Toast in the oven or in a non-stick frying pan.
Drain the octopus and thinly slice. Arrange on plates with the carrots and peas, season with salt and pepper and drizzle with oil. Top with cherry tomatoes and croutons.

Spicy Seafood Sauté

Preparation time 20 minutes
Cooking time 10 minutes
Wine *Ischia Bianco*

9 oz (250 g) cockles
9 oz (250 g) clams
7 oz (200 g) mussels
salt
3 tbsps extra-virgin olive oil
2 garlic cloves, 1 minced
 and 1 halved
parsley, minced
1 dried red chilli pepper
1/2 cup (120 ml) white wine
5 cherry tomatoes, quartered
4 slices crusty bread

741

Wash the shellfish well, scrubbing the clams and removing any brown fibers from the mussels.
Place the cockles, mussels and clams in 3 separate bowls with salted water to purge them and let sit for 30 minutes.
Heat the oil in a saucepan. Sauté the minced garlic and a little parsley and crumble in the chilli pepper.
Add the clams, raise the heat and cook for 3 minutes. Pour over the wine and add the mussels and cockles. Bring to a boil, add the tomatoes and more parsley and continue cooking, covered, until all the shellfish are open. Discard any which do not open.
Toast the bread, rub it with the halved garlic and place in shallow soup bowls.
Top the bread with the hot shellfish and serve immediately.

Frise
(PUGLIA)

Note *In the past frise, or freselle, were one of the staple foods for Puglian peasants. This simple but tasty dish is still much appreciated today, and is part of a balanced Mediterranean diet.*

Preparation time 20 minutes
Cooking time 30 minutes
Wine *Leverano Bianco*

1 tbsp (12 g) active dry yeast
4 cups (1 lb 0.4 oz or 500 g) plain flour
1 tsp salt
1¼ cups (300 ml) water

742

Preheat oven to 400°F (200°C).
Dissolve the yeast in a little warm water.
Mound the flour on a work surface, form a well in the middle and pour in the yeast, salt and water. Knead vigorously to obtain a smooth, uniform dough. Form into a loaf shape, cover with a clean kitchen towel and leave to rise for 15 minutes.
Divide the dough into loaves weighing around 2 oz (50 g) each and arrange on a parchment paper-lined baking sheet. Bake for around 20 minutes. Remove from the oven, cut in half horizontally, arrange the halves in a single layer and return to the oven until golden brown. Let cool and serve with olive oil, chopped tomatoes, garlic or soft cheeses, as desired.

Romagna-Style Piadina
(EMILIA-ROMAGNA)

Note *Piadina is a classic flatbread from Romagna, the eastern half of the central Italian region of Emilia-Romagna. It is usually served with pancetta, sausage, squacquerone cheese and arugula, but the fillings can vary greatly. In the past they were cooked on a stone heated over coals, but nowadays a simple griddle or cast-iron frying pan is used.*

Preparation time 30 minutes
Cooking time 10 minutes
Wine *Trebbiano di Romagna Spumante*

Serves 6

8 cups (2.2 lb or 1 kg)
 plain flour
3/4 cup (5.3 oz or 150 g) lard,
 in pieces
salt
milk

Mound the flour on a work surface and make a well in the middle. Place the lard and a pinch of salt in the well, and mix with enough milk or water necessary to obtain a smooth, uniform and firm dough. Form into a ball and leave to rest for 1 hour, covered with a clean kitchen towel.
Divide the dough into many little balls and roll out with a rolling pin to obtain piadinas (similar to tortillas) of around 10-12 inches (25-30 cm) in diameter.
Heat a cast-iron griddle until very hot and cook the piadinas for just a few minutes, turning them clockwise, poking the top with a fork so the inside cooks well and flipping often.
Serve hot, filled with fresh soft cheese or cured meats as desired and folded in half.

Summer Crostoni

Preparation time 10 minutes
Cooking time 5 minutes
Wine *Alto Livenza Müller Thurgau*

5.5 oz (150 g) crusty
 Altamura-style bread
3 tbsps extra-virgin olive oil
1 large melon
9 oz (250 g) mascarpone
2 tbsps heavy cream
salt and pepper
4 oz (120 g) sliced prosciutto

Preheat oven to 350°F (180°C).
Cut the bread into thick slices,
then in half. Drizzle with 2
tablespoons oil and toast in the
oven for about 5 minutes.
Deseed the melon and cut into
balls with a melon baller.
Mix the mascarpone, cream, 1
tablespoon oil and pinches of
salt and pepper in a bowl. Beat
to a thick cream. Place in a
pastry bag with a ridged tip.
Arrange the bread on serving
plates and pipe over the cream.
Serve with melon balls and
prosciutto slices.

Tuna and Sweet Onion Canapés

Preparation time 15 minutes
Wine *Cirò Bianco*

1 sweet red onion,
 very thinly sliced into rings
1 tbsp extra-virgin olive oil
salt and pepper
7 oz (200 g) tuna in oil, drained
 and crumbled
2 tbsps mayonnaise
1 tbsp yogurt
8 slices soft olive bread
10 basil leaves, chopped

Place the onion rings in a bowl
and toss with a little oil, salt and
pepper. Let sit for 10 minutes.
Place the crumbled tuna in a
bowl and add the mayonnaise
and the yogurt. Beat with a fork
until the mixture is smooth and
quite uniform.
Spread the tuna mixture on
the olive bread, and top with a
few rings of marinated onion.
Garnish with chopped basil.

744

A P P E T I Z E R

Stuffed Cherry Tomato Skewers

Preparation time 15 minutes
Wine *Roero Arneis*

7 oz (200 g) soft fresh cheese
basil, minced
salt and freshly ground pepper
20 cherry tomatoes

Beat the cheese until creamy
then stir in the basil and a pinch
of salt. Grind in a little fresh
pepper.
Cut the cherry tomatoes in half,
remove the seeds and scoop
out a little of the flesh. Fill with
the cheese and reassemble
them. Thread onto wooden
skewers and refrigerate until
serving.

Note *The cheese filling can be
replaced with a mixture of 1 can
of tuna in brine or water, drained
and beaten until smooth with
a few spoonfuls of mayonnaise
and some minced parsley.*

Toasted Focaccia with Ricotta

Preparation time 10 minutes
Cooking time 5 minutes
Wine *Cinque Terre*

7 oz (200 g) sheep's milk ricotta
5-6 basil leaves, minced
salt and pepper
9 oz (250 g) Ligurian focaccia
4 anchovy fillets in oil
7 capers in brine
8 black olives, pitted

Preheat oven to 350°F (180°C).
Beat the ricotta with the basil,
salt and pepper until smooth
and creamy.
Cut the focaccia into 1½-inch (4
cm) strips and toast in the oven
for 3-4 minutes, then remove
from the oven and let cool.
Drain the anchovy fillets and
rinse the capers and squeeze
out excess liquid. Finely mince
the olives and anchovies
together with the olives.
Spread a little of the ricotta
cream on each piece of
focaccia, then sprinkle with
the anchovy mixture. Serve
immediately.

Eggplant Flans with Cherry-Tomato Sauce

Note *Despite its now-crucial role in Italian cuisine, the tomato is a recent introduction to the country. Originally from America, the fruit was introduced to Europe in the mid-16th century but at first was believed to be poisonous and used only for decoration. Its culinary value was discovered during the 18th century, particularly in Naples.*

746

Preparation time 35 minutes
Cooking time 45 minutes
Wine *Alto Adige Pinot Bianco*

FLAN
4 tbsps extra-virgin olive oil
1 garlic clove
dried oregano
1 large eggplant, diced
salt and pepper
3.5 oz (100 g) mild scamorza
 cheese, diced
1 egg
1 egg yolk
3 tbsps grated pecorino cheese

SAUCE
3 tbsps extra-virgin olive oil
1 garlic clove, smashed
5 oregano sprigs, chopped
2 cups (10.5 oz or 300 g) cherry
 tomatoes, quartered
1 tbsp capers in salt, rinsed
salt and pepper

Preheat oven to 350°F (180°C).
Heat the oil for the flan with the garlic and dried oregano until the garlic browns. Add the eggplant, sauté for 2 minutes, season with salt and pepper and cook for another 5 minutes.
Fill a baking dish halfway with water and place in the oven.
Mix the eggplant, scamorza, egg, egg yolk and pecorino. Fill small oiled moulds with the mixture. Bake in the bain-marie for 30 minutes.
Meanwhile heat the oil for the sauce with the garlic and oregano, then add the tomatoes. Lower the heat, cover and cook for 5 minutes.
Push through a sieve to remove the seeds and skin. Add the capers, simmer for 2 minutes then add salt and pepper to taste.
Remove the flans from the oven, unmould and serve with the sauce.

Provola and Basil Frittata

Preparation time 10 minutes
Cooking time 10 minutes
Wine *Verdicchio dei Castelli di Jesi*

5 tbsps extra-virgin olive oil
2 spring onions, thinly sliced
6 eggs
salt and pepper
2 tbsps grated Parmesan
3.5 oz (100 g) provola cheese, diced
4-5 basil leaves, chopped
lettuce leaves

Heat the oil in a frying pan and sauté the spring onions until soft.
Meanwhile beat the eggs with pinches of salt and pepper and stir in the Parmesan, provola and basil. Stir in the spring onions, then return to the same frying pan. Cook until the underside is cooked through, then flip over and cook for a few more minutes. Serve sliced, with a few lettuce leaves.

Zucchini and Rice Fritters

Preparation time 10 minutes
Cooking time 15 minutes
Wine *Lagrein Rosato*

1¾ cup (12.5 oz or 350 g) Carnaroli rice
2 eggs
salt and pepper
5 tbsps plain flour
1 tbsp dry active yeast
7 tbsps milk
1 large zucchini, grated
3 dill sprigs, minced
1 onion, minced
sunflower oil

Boil the rice until tender.
Beat the eggs with salt and pepper and sift in the flour with the yeast. Pour the milk in a thin stream, mixing constantly, to obtain a thick batter. Stir in the grated zucchini, dill, cooked rice and onion.
Heat the sunflower oil in a frying pan until very hot, then fry spoonfuls of the rice mixture. Fry for 2 minutes on each side, drain, dry on paper towels and salt before serving.

Ricotta, Walnut
and Arugula Crostini

Note *Walnuts are of Asian origin and are much used in Italian cooking, particularly in baking and for pasta sauces in certain regions, like Liguria. Usually it is a good idea to remove the dark skin from the shelled walnuts, as it impedes cooking and gives a bitter taste to the final dish.*

Preparation time 15 minutes
Cooking time 5 minutes
Wine *Colli Euganei Bianco*

9 oz (250 g) sheep's milk ricotta
1/2 cup (2 oz or 50 g) walnuts,
 crushed
1 egg
5 tbsps grated Parmesan
salt and pepper
1 baguette
1 bunch arugula, chopped

748

Sieve the ricotta into a glass mixing bowl and stir in the walnuts, egg, Parmesan, salt and pepper. Mix well with a wooden spoon to obtain a smooth and uniform cream.
Cut the baguette into rounds about 1 inch (2 cm) thick and toast under the broiler for 5 minutes or until golden-brown.
Place the ricotta cream in a pastry bag and pipe a 1½-inch (3-4 cm) thick layer on each toast.
Top with the chopped arugula. Serve immediately.

APPETIZER

Sea Bass Tartare Crostone

Preparation time 30 minutes
Cooking time 6 minutes
Wine *Roero Arneis*
♟♟

7 oz (200 g) sea bass fillet
srated zest and juice of 1/2
 organic lemon
1 tbsp pink peppercorns
6 oregano sprigs
salt and pepper
9 tbsps extra-virgin olive oil
1 large zucchini, diced
4 slices sandwich bread
 (around 3.5 oz or 100 g)
1 garlic clove

Remove the skin from the fish fillet and mince the flesh finely. Toss
with the grated lemon zest, the lemon juice, pink peppercorns,
the leaves of 3 oregano sprigs and a pinch of salt, then chop
everything together to obtain a smooth mixture. Stir in 3
tablespoons olive oil. Use a round cookie cutter to form disks of
the sea bass tartare.
Heat 3 tablespoons oil in a frying pan and brown the zucchini.
Season with salt and pepper and cook for 5 minutes. Add the 3
remaining oregano sprigs and continue cooking until tender but
still al dente.
Meanwhile cut the bread into 4-inch (10 cm) diameter circles. Heat
3 tablespoons oil in a frying pan and when hot, brown the garlic
clove, then sauté the bread circles until golden.
Arrange the bread circles on serving plates, top with the circles of
tartare and garnish with the sautéed zucchini. Drizzle with olive oil
and serve.

Parma-Style Fritters
(Emilia-Romagna)

Preparation time 15 minutes
Cooking time 5 minutes
Wine *Colli di Parma Rosso*

Serves 4-6

**4 cups (1 lb or 500 g)
 plain flour
3 tbsps extra-virgin olive oil
salt
lard**

750

Mound the flour on a work surface, make a well in the centre and add in the oil, a pinch of salt and enough warm water to form a soft dough. Knead until the dough is uniform and without lumps. Roll the dough into a 1-inch (3 cm) thick sheet and cut out small diamond shapes

Melt abundant lard in a saucepan over high heat, and as soon as it is very hot, fry the dough, turning so it browns on both sides. Once golden, drain with a slotted spoon and let dry on paper towels. Serve the fritters while hot and crunchy, paired with thinly sliced cured meats or soft cheeses as desired.

Fava Panelle
(SICILY)

Preparation time 5 minutes
Cooking time 40 minutes
Wine *Regaleali Bianco Spumante*

Serves 6-8

1.3 lb (600 g) dried fava beans
salt
2 tbsps extra-virgin olive oil
1 onion, minced
sunflower oil

Boil the favas in abundant salted water until they are almost falling apart. Drain.
Heat the olive oil in a frying pan and sauté the onion until golden.
Add the favas and cook until they become a uniform, thick puree.
As soon as this happens, pour the puree out onto a work surface, spread into an even layer with a spatula and leave to cool.
Once cooled, cut into irregular pieces and fry in very hot sunflower oil. When the panelle are golden-brown on both sides, transfer to a paper, towel-lined plate using a slotted spoon.
Serve the panelle very hot.

751

752

Smoked Salmon Frittata

Preparation time 15 minutes
Cooking time 50 minutes
Wine *Bianco d'Alcamo*

Serves 6

FRITTATA
12 eggs
5 tbsps grated Parmesan
1½ cups (350 ml) heavy cream
9 oz (250 g) smoked salmon,
 chopped
6 spring onions, thinly sliced
3.5 oz (100 g) fresh goat's
 cheese

GARNISH
slices of smoked salmon

Preheat oven to 350°F (180°C).
Beat the eggs with the
Parmesan, cream, chopped
smoked salmon, spring onions
and goat's cheese.
Line a spring-form pan with
parchment paper, pour in the
egg mixture and bake for 50
minutes. Remove from the
oven, unmould and serve
sliced, garnished with slices of
smoked salmon.

Octopus Involtini

Preparation time 30 minutes
Cooking time 12 minutes
Wine *Colli del Trasimeno Bianco*

2.2 lb (1 kg) octopus
salt and pepper
3/4 cup (180 ml) white wine
1 rosemary sprig
1/2 organic lemon
3 red bell peppers
4 tbsps extra-virgin olive oil
1 tbsp white wine vinegar
dried red chilli pepper flakes
1 tbsp capers in vinegar
marjoram, rosemary and parsley

Boil octopus with salt, wine,
rosemary sprig and lemon half for
40 minutes. Let cool 30 minutes.
Cut the peppers into 1-inch (2
cm) long strips.
Reserve and strain 1/2 cup
(120 ml) cooking water. Cut
the octopus tentacles into
small pieces. Wrap each in a
pepper strip and fix close with a
toothpick.
Heat the oil and brown the
involtini. Add the vinegar,
reserved cooking water, salt,
pepper and chilli flakes and
continue cooking. Mix in capers
and minced herbs, then serve.

Robiola and Eggplant Canapés

Preparation time 10 minutes
Wine *Bolgheri Bianco*

8 oz (220 g) robiola cheese
1 tsp oregano
salt and pepper
6-8 slices sandwich bread
10 slices grilled eggplant in oil

Beat the robiola with the oregano, salt and pepper to obtain a smooth, soft cream. Cut the crusts off the bread and spread the slices with the robiola cream.
Drain the eggplant from the oil and lay over the bread without leaving any spaces. Cut into squares and serve.

Note *The eggplant could be replaced by zucchini or bell peppers, grilled and preserved in oil, and the robiola could be replaced by fresh goat's cheese or crescenza.*

Mozzarella and Pesto Canapés

Preparation time 20 minutes
Cooking time 2 minutes
Wine *Bianco d'Alcamo*

8 slices multi-grain bread
9 oz (250 g) buffalo mozzarella, thinly sliced
4 tbsps Genoan-style pesto (see p. 1098)
2 tomatoes

Cut an X in the bottom of each tomato and blanch in boiling salted water. Drain, immerse in ice water, then peel. Cut into 4 wedges, remove the seeds and dice the flesh.
Lay the mozzarella slices on the bread. Top with a little pesto and the tomatoes. Cut as desired, and serve.

Note *For a lighter dish with more subtle flavours, the pesto can be replaced by a mixture of 2 tbsps oregano and 5 tbsps extra-virgin olive oil.*

753

Zucchini and Feta Terrine

Note *Feta is a Greek cheese made from cow's and goat's milk. It is semi-hard and is traditionally preserved in brine in rectangular or cylindrical forms.*

Preparation time 30 minutes
Cooking time 10 minutes
Wine *Cirò Bianco*

2 firm zucchini, thickly sliced
8 oz (220 g) feta cheese
6.5 oz (180 g) fresh goat's cheese
salt and pepper
5-6 mint leaves, minced
4 sheets of gelatin
7 tbsps heavy cream
2 red tomatoes
2 tbsps extra-virgin olive oil

754

Steam the zucchini slices for 5 minutes then cool in the refrigerator.
Beat the feta with the goat's cheese, salt, pepper and mint until smooth and creamy.
Soak the gelatin in cold water, drain and squeeze out then dissolve in a small saucepan with the cream over low heat. Add the cream and gelatin to the cheeses and stir well.
Line a rounded terrine mould or loaf pan with plastic wrap and place a layer of zucchini slices in the bottom. Pour in 1/2 the cheese mixture, layer in the rest of the zucchini, and top with the rest of the cheese mixture, levelling out the surface with spatula. Cover with plastic wrap and refrigerate for 1 hour 30 minutes.
Blanch and peel the tomatoes, cut into wedges and remove the seeds. Chop the flesh and toss with oil, salt and pepper.
Serve the terrine unmoulded and sliced, with the tomatoes.

Tuna-Filled Zucchini Rolls

Preparation time 20 minutes
Cooking time 15 minutes
Wine *Soave Classico*

3 large zucchini, sliced
 lengthwise
6.5 oz (180 g) tuna in oil, drained
1 spring onion, chopped
1 tbsp extra-virgin olive oil
8 capers in salt, rinsed
 and chopped
6 pitted olives, chopped
1 leek, cut into thin strips
5 basil leaves

Grill the zucchini slices.
Beat the tuna with the spring
onion and oil, then stir in the
capers and olives. Place a
spoonful of the mixture on each
zucchini slice and roll up.
Blanch the leek strips in boiling
salted water for a few minutes,
then drain and use to tie closed
the zucchini rolls. Let rest for
30 minutes, chill and serve.
Garnish with basil leaves.

Prosciutto and Melon with Thyme

Preparation time 10 minutes
Wine *Trentino Nosiola*

1 firm melon
4 oz (120 g) prosciutto
fresh thyme, minced

Remove the seeds from the
melon and cut into balls with a
melon baller. Refrigerate until
using.
Finely slice the prosciutto,
removing any excess fat. Cut
into strips 1/2-inch (1 cm) wide
and wrap each one around a
melon ball, then sprinkle with
thyme. Thread the melon balls
onto toothpicks and serve as a
snack with drinks before dinner.

Note *Canteloupe melons are
traditionally used for this simple
appetizer, but may be replaced
with other kinds of melon, or figs.*

755

Marinated Anchovies
(SICILY)

Preparation time 20 minutes

1 lb (500 g) very fresh anchovies
2 garlic cloves
1 bunch parsley
1/2 dried hot red chilli pepper
1/2 tsp oregano
salt
juice of 2 lemons

Wash the anchovies well under cold running water and remove the head, guts and backbone, taking care not to break them. Dry and set aside.
Mash together the garlic, parsley and chilli with a mortar and pestle, then add the oregano, a pinch of salt and the lemon juice. Pour the marinade over the anchovies and let sit for at least 3 hours. Serve at room temperature.

756

Tomato and Bread Soup
(TUSCANY)

Preparation time 25 minutes
Cooking time 1 hour 30 minutes
Wine *Elba Rosso*

1.3 lb (600 g) tomatoes,
 chopped
1 carrot, chopped
1 onion, chopped
1 celery stalk, chopped
5 tbsps extra-virgin olive oil
salt and pepper
1 lb (500 g) stale Tuscan-style
 bread
2 garlic cloves
basil
6 cups (1.5 l) water

757

Place the tomatoes, carrot, onion and celery in a saucepan and
bring to a boil. Cook until soft, then pass through a sieve or food
mill and return to the pan with some oil, salt and pepper and
continue cooking.
Cut the bread into slices or cubes and place in a saucepan with
abundant olive oil, garlic, basil, salt, pepper and the water. Bring
a boil and stir frequently, breaking up the bread. Add the tomato
sauce and continue to simmer for 1 hour, adding a little water if
necessary.
Serve the soup hot or cold, as desired.

Grilled Eggplant and Provola Rolls

Preparation time 15 minutes
Cooking time 8 minutes
Wine *Cirò Rosato*

1 large, long eggplant,
 thinly sliced
12.5 oz (350 g) mild provola
 cheese
2 tomatoes, peeled, deseeded
 and diced
10 pitted black olives
basil
salt and pepper
3 tbsps extra-virgin olive oil

758

Preheat oven to 425°F (220°C).
Grill the eggplant slices on a cast-iron grill pan until tender and set aside.
Cut the cheese into the same number of pieces as the number of eggplant slices, and grill the cheese cubes.
Wrap each cube of cheese in a slice of eggplant and roll it up.
Place in a small baking dish and top with tomatoes, olives and basil. Season with salt and pepper and bake for 5 minutes. Serve drizzled with olive oil.

Warm Bresaola Involtini

Preparation time 15 minutes
Cooking time 5 minutes
Wine *Valcalepio Bianco*

3.5 oz (100 g) fresh goat's
 cheeese
chives, minced
1 zucchini, green part only,
 julienned
salt and pepper
12 slices bresaola
4 tbsps extra-virgin olive oil
1 shallot, minced
juice of 1 lemon
Worcester sauce

Beat the cheese with the chives, zucchini, salt and pepper.
Spread the bresaola slices with the cheese mixture and roll up into involtini.
Heat the oil and sauté the shallot until soft. Dissolve a pinch of salt in the lemon juice, season with a drop of Worcester sauce and pepper, stir in the sautéed shallot and whisk in the oil to make an emulsified sauce. Serve warm over the involtini.

Mozzarella and Anchovy Toasts

Preparation time 15 minutes
Cooking time 8 minutes
Wine *Etna Bianco*

12 1/2-inch (1 cm) thick slices
 of Tuscan-style bread
7 oz (200 g) cow's milk
 mozzarella
salt and pepper
5 salted anchovies
3 tbsps butter
parsley, minced

Preheat oven to 350°F (180°C). Thread 3 slices of bread on each skewer and lay 1 slice of mozzarella on the middle piece of bread. Sprinkle with salt and pepper and toast in the oven until the cheese melts and the bread is crunchy.
Meanwhile, soak the anchovies in cold water for a few minutes. Drain and chop. Melt the butter in a frying pan and add the anchovies and a pinch of pepper. Remove the skewers from the oven and sprinkle with parsley and the anchovies. Serve with the anchovy pan juices on the side.

Lecce-Style Pizzi
(PUGLIA)

Preparation time 30 minutes
Cooking time 20 minutes
Wine *Lizzano Bianco Spumante*

Serves 6

6 tbsps extra-virgin olive oil
5 tomatoes, peeled
 and chopped
3/4 cup (3.5 oz or 100g) pitted
 black olives
dried red chilli pepper flakes
2 onions, minced
salt
2.2 lb (1 kg) plain flour
2 tbsps (0.9 oz or 25 g)
 active dry yeast

Mix 4 tablespoons oil, the chopped tomatoes, olives, a pinch of
chilli flakes and onions and season to taste with salt. Stir with
a wooden spoon until uniform, then add the flour and yeast
dissolved in a little warm water. Mix to obtain a smooth dough,
adding extra oil or water if necessary. Form a loaf and let rise until
doubled in volume.
Preheat oven to 475°F (240°C).
Roll the dough out thinly with a rolling pin, roll up like a jelly roll and
slice to obtain snail-like rolls. Arrange them on a lightly oiled baking
sheet and bake for around 20 minutes, until golden. Serve warm
or cooled.

A P P E T I Z E R

Sfincione
(SICILY)

Preparation time 15 minutes
Cooking time 40 minutes
Wine *Inzolia*

Serves 6

2 lb (900 g) prepared bread
 dough
1/2 cup (120 ml) extra-virgin
 olive oil
1 lb (500 g) tomatoes
1 onion, sliced
salt
12 salted anchovies
3.5 oz (100 g) Ragusano cheese
 or provolone, grated
8 tbsps breadcrumbs

761

Preheat oven to 425°F (220°C).
Knead the bread dough with 3 tablespoons of olive oil.
Blanch the tomatoes, peel, deseed and coarsely chop.
Heat 2 tablespoons oil in a frying pan and sauté the onion for 8
minutes over low heat. Add the tomatoes, season with salt and
cook for 10 minutes.
Rinse the anchovies under running water to remove the salt. Dry,
debone and mince, then add to the tomatoes together with the
grated cheese.
Divide the bread dough into 4 parts. Roll each part out to a
thickness of 1 inch (3 cm) and lay them out on baking sheets,
oiled with 1 tablespoon oil. Divide the tomato mixture between
each one, top with breadcrumbs and the remaining oil and bake
for 20 minutes or until the dough is cooked through. Serve hot.

Black Rice Wafers with Prawns and Tomatoes

Preparation time 15 minutes
Cooking time 30 minutes
Wine *Terre di Franciacorta Bianco*

1/4 cup (1.8 oz or 50 g)
 Roma rice
3 cups (1.5 l) water
salt and pepper
1/2 tsp nero di seppie (squid ink)
10 medium-small prawns
2 tomatoes
2 tbsps extra-virgin olive oil
1 sprig dill, minced

Preheat oven to 350°F (180°C).
Place the rice in a saucepan and cover with the water. Lightly salt and cook for 25 minutes, adding the nero di seppie halfway through. The rice should be overcooked.
Puree the rice with a immersion blender to obtain a sticky cream.
Spread a little of the cream on a parchment paper-lined baking sheet with the back of a tablespoon to form 4 rounds and bake for around 12 minutes.
Meanwhile steam the prawns and shell them.
Blanch the tomatoes and peel, deseed and dice. Toss the tomatoes with oil, salt, pepper and dill.
Chop the prawns and add to the tomatoes.
Serve the tomato-prawn mixture on top of the rice wafers.

762

Tomato Caponata
(CAMPANIA)

765

Note *To enrich this recipe, add slices of hard-boiled egg to the caponata, or olives, capers, tuna in oil, anchovies or other ingredients, as desired. Freselle are a kind of crisp, hard bread, almost like a rusk, typical to Campania. They are available as toasts or rounds, and come in regular and whole-wheat versions.*

Preparation time 15 minutes
Wine *Falerno del Massico Bianco*

2 whole-wheat freselle or large rusks
2 tbsps extra-virgin olive oil
4 ripe tomatoes, thinly sliced
1 garlic clove, minced
oregano
4 basil leaves, chopped
salt

Quickly dip the freselle in cold water to soften them slightly, without letting them disintegrate. Drain and cut into large pieces. Place in a large salad bowl and toss with oil, tomatoes, garlic, a pinch of oregano and the basil.
Season with salt to taste and stir well. Let sit for a few minutes before serving.

Fried Pizzas with Clams and Tomatoes

Note *Ingredients can be fried with a coating, such as a batter, or without a coating. The latter is suitable only for ingredients which, thanks to the presence of albumin, starch or sugar, can form their own external crust during the frying process.*

Preparation time 20 minutes
Cooking time 10 minutes
Wine *Greco di Tufo*

2.2 lb (1 kg) clams
salt and pepper
parsley, minced
1 garlic clove
6 tbsps extra-virgin olive oil
14 oz (400 g) tomatoes
basil, minced
9 oz (250 g) prepared pizza
  dough (see p. 1093)
sunflower oil

766

Wash the clams well and soak in salted water for 30 minutes to purge.
Drain and place in a frying pan with the parsley, garlic and 2 tablespoons olive oil. Cover and cook for 5 minutes, until the clams open. Drain and shell the clams.
Blanch the tomatoes, drain, peel and chop the flesh.
Heat the remaining olive oil in a frying pan and sauté the shelled clams, tomatoes and basil. Season with salt and pepper.
Roll the pizza dough out thinly and cut out small disks. Heat the sunflower oil until very hot and fry the disks for a few minutes. Drain and dry on paper towels.
Arrange the disks on a serving plate and top with the clam and tomato mixture. Serve immediately.

A P P E T I Z E R

Stuffed Zucchini with Crunchy Squash Blossoms

Preparation time 25 minutes
Cooking time 25 minutes
Wine *Terre di Franciacorta Bianco*

4 large zucchini
2 tbsps extra-virgin olive oil
2 garlic cloves, smashed
dried red chilli pepper flakes
6 capers
10 black olives, pitted
basil, torn by hand
2 tbsps breadcrumbs
1 egg
1 tbsp poppy seeds
6½ tbsps plain flour
ice-cold sparkling water
8 squash blossoms
sesame oil

767

Preheat oven to 350°F (180°C).

Top and tail the zucchini, and using an apple corer, scoop out the inside flesh, keeping the outside intact. Chop the zucchini flesh and reserve the shells.

Heat the oil in a large frying pan and sauté the garlic and a pinch of chilli flakes. Add the chopped zucchini, capers, olives and basil. Sauté over high heat for 10 minutes, adding a little water if necessary. Remove the garlic and puree the rest in a food processor with the breadcrumbs and egg.

Steam the zucchini shells for 5 minutes, then stuff with the chopped zucchini mixture. Lay on a baking sheet and bake for 10 minutes.

Meanwhile make a batter with the poppy seeds, flour, a pinch of salt and enough cold sparkling water to make a fluid mixture. Dip the squash blossoms in the batter, drain off any excess and fry them in hot sesame oil.

Serve the zucchini with the hot crunchy squash blossoms.

Mediterranean Strudel

Preparation time 30 minutes
Cooking time 30 minutes
Wine *Greco di Tufo*

9 oz (250 g) puff pastry
7 oz (200 g) mild provolone,
 sliced
7 oz (200 g) vine-ripened
 tomatoes, peeled and chopped
3 tbsps capers, rinsed
 and chopped
3 tbsps pitted green olives,
 chopped
4 salted anchovy fillets, rinsed
 and chopped
oregano
salt and pepper

Preheat oven to 375°F (190°C).
Roll the puff pastry out on a
floured work surface. Cover
with a layer of provolone slices.
Sprinkle over the tomatoes,
capers, olives, anchovies,
oregano, salt and pepper. Roll
up the pastry and carefully seal
the ends.
Place on an oiled baking
sheet and bake for around 30
minutes. Serve warm or cooled.

Octopus Vol-au-Vents

Preparation time 20 minutes
Cooking time 30 minutes
Wine *Pinot Bianco del Piave*

10.5 oz (300 g) octopus
1 bay leaf
1/2 cup (120 ml) white wine
1/4 small celeriac (celery root),
 peeled
1/2 fennel bulb
2 potatoes
parsley, minced
3 tbsps pitted black olives,
 chopped
2 tbsps capers, chopped
salt and pepper
4 tbsps extra-virgin olive oil
20 small ready-made
 vol-au-vents

Boil the octopus with the bay,
wine, celeriac, fennel and
potatoes for 30 minutes. Let cool
in the cooking water.
Cut the octopus into small
chunks. Peel and dice potatoes.
Dice celeriac and fennel.
Mix octopus, potatoes, celeriac
and fennel with parsley, olives
and capers. Season with salt and
pepper and toss with the oil.
Heat the vol-au-vents in the
oven, let cool slightly and fill with
the octopus mixture.

Mediterranean Stuffed Zucchini

Preparation time 15 minutes
Cooking time 5 minutes
Wine *Alto Adige Sylvaner*

4 round zucchini
9 oz (250 g) tuna fillet in oil,
 drained
1 bunch mixed salad leaves,
 shredded finely chopped
5-6 cherry tomatoes, quartered
1 tbsp black olives, chopped
1 tbsp capers, rinsed
 and chopped
1 spring onion, thinly sliced
2 tbsps extra-virgin olive oil
1 tbsp balsamic vinegar
salt and pepper

Slice the top off the zucchini
with a serrated knife to form a
lid. Scoop out the white flesh
from inside, leaving a 1/5-inch
(1/2 cm) thick shell. Steam for
about 5 minutes then let cool.
Mix the tuna, salad, tomatoes,
olives, capers and spring onion
and dress with oil, vinegar, salt
and pepper.
Fill the cooled zucchini shells
with the salad and serve.

Mozzarella Skewers

Preparation time 15 minutes
Cooking time 5 minutes
Wine *Fiano di Avellino*

1/2 yellow bell pepper
16 mini cow's milk mozzarella
 balls (bocconcini)
8 anchovy fillets
16 pitted black olives, halved
16 cherry tomatoes, halved
salt
fresh oregano
1 tbsp extra-virgin olive oil

Roast the pepper half over an
open flame, close in a plastic
bag to steam for a few minutes,
then peel, deseed and cut into
8 strips.
Wrap 8 mozzarella balls with
1 anchovy fillet each, and 8
mozzarella balls with 1 pepper
strip each.
Prepare 16 skewers by
threading each one with an
olive half, a tomato half, 1
anchovy-wrapped mozzarella or
1 pepper-wrapped mozzarella,
a tomato half and an olive half.
Arrange the skewers on a
plate. Sprinkle with a little salt,
abundant fresh oregano leaves
and a drizzle of oil.

Taralli

(PUGLIA)

Note *To give the taralli more flavour, add some fennel seeds to the dough, or, if you prefer, a pinch of dried chilli pepper flakes, oregano, sesame seeds or dried onion. Use 0.2 oz (5 g) of flavouring per 2 lb (1 kg) of dough.*

Preparation time 30 minutes
Cooking time 45 minutes
Wine *Locorotondo Spumante*

Serves 6-8

2.2 lb (1 kg) plain flour
1¼ cups (300 ml) dry white wine
1 cup (250 ml) extra-virgin
  olive oil
1 tsp salt

770

Mound the flour on a work surface and make a well in the centre. Add the wine, oil and salt and work vigorously to obtain a smooth, uniform and quite elastic dough. Cover with a clean kitchen towel and let rest for 20 minutes.
Preheat oven to 400°F (200°C).
Divide the dough into portions and from each one form little ropes about 1/2 inch (1 cm) in diameter and 3 inches (8 cm) long. Form them into rings by pressing the ends together.
Bring a large pot of salted water to a boil and boil the taralli in batches. As soon as they come to the surface, drain them with a slotted spoon and dry on a clean kitchen towel.
Arrange the boiled taralli on a lightly oiled baking sheet and bake for around 40 minutes, until golden.

Crispeddi
(SICILY)

Preparation time 30 minutes
Cooking time 30 minutes
Wine *Regaleali Bianco Spumante*

14 oz (400 g) prepared bread
 dough
lard
10 anchovy fillets, deboned
 and rinsed
oregano

Mix 1 tablespoon lard into
the bread dough and knead
vigorously by hand. Form a
loaf shape and leave to rise for
around 1 hour, covered with a
clean kitchen towel.
Form the dough into flat, long
rolls and place an anchovy fillet
and a pinch of oregano inside
each one. Lay the crispeddi on
a cloth and let rise for another
30 minutes.
Heat abundant lard in a large
saucepan and when it is very
hot, fry the crispeddi one at a
time. Drain as soon as they are
golden, dry on paper towels
and serve very hot.

Sardinian Crackers (SARDINIA)

Preparation time 2 minutes
Cooking time 5 minutes
Wine *Vermentino di Gallura*

4 sheets pane carasau
salt
2 tbsps extra-virgin olive oil

Preheat oven to 400°F (200°C).
Cut the pane carasau into
pieces, place on a baking sheet
and season with a pinch of
salt and a drizzle of oil. Bake
for around 5 minutes. Remove
from the oven and serve when
golden and crunchy. Pair with
soft cheeses or cured meats if
desired.

Note *Pane carasau is a thin,
crisp Sardinian bread, almost
like a cracker. It can sometimes
be found in specialty Italian
markets, or can be made at
home. Mix 2.2 lbs (1 kg) flour
with enough water to obtain a
firm dough. Roll the dough out
into very thin disks and leave
to rest. Bake until they start to
expand, then cut incisions in
the edges and bake again until
golden.*

Lardo di Colonnata Crostini
(TUSCANY)

Note *Lardo di Colonnata is lard cured in herbs and spices and aged in marble containers, from a small mountain village in Tuscany, and is eaten thinly sliced. These crostini can be varied by replacing the tomato and rosemary with a mix of minced spring onion, celery, carrot, garlic and rosemary.*

772

Preparation time 10 minutes
Cooking time 3 minutes
Wine *Morellino di Scansano*

1/2 loaf Tuscan-style bread,
 thinly sliced
10.5 oz (300 g) lardo
 di Colonnata, thinly sliced
10 cherry tomatoes, quartered
1 sprig rosemary
freshly ground pepper
2 tbsps new harvest extra-virgin
 olive oil

Toast the bread on a hot cast-iron grill pan for 3 minutes.
Top each slice with some slices of lardo, some tomato wedges,
a few rosemary leaves, freshly ground pepper and a drizzle of oil.
Serve immediately, to appreciate the contrast between the hot
bread and the cold lardo.

A P P E T I Z E R

Campania-Style Caprese Salad

Preparation time 10 minutes
Wine *Capri Bianco*

1 lb (500 g) buffalo mozzarella
1 lb (500 g) fresh tomatoes
4 tbsps extra-virgin olive oil
salt
oregano
basil leaves

Slice the mozzarella and tomatoes into fairly thick slices. Arrange the slices on a serving plate, either covering the tomatoes with mozzarella or alternating the slices. Dress with oil, a pinch of salt and abundant oregano. Serve immediately, decorating the plate with a few basil leaves.

Note *The buffalo mozzarella can be replaced with regular cow's milk mozzarella.*

Adda-Style Bresaola (LOMBARDY)

Preparation time 10 minutes
Wine *Valcalepio Rosso*

3½ tbsps butter, softened
2 oz (50 g) Gorgonzola
12 slices bresaola
parsley, minced

Beat the softened butter and Gorgonzola in a bowl with a wooden spoon until smooth and creamy.
Lay the bresaola slices on a serving plate and spread each one with the Gorgonzola mixture. Roll them up like cigars and dip each end into the minced parsley. Arrange on a plate and serve.

773

Clam Soup with Celery, Tomato and Carrots

Note *It is important to know the provenience of your clams, as they can absorb toxins and pollution from the water.*

Preparation time 25 minutes
Cooking time 35 minutes
Wine *Colli di Luni Bianco*

774

2.2 lb (1 kg) clams
salt and pepper
3 tbsps extra-virgin olive oil
1 garlic clove
1 leek, thinly sliced
1 medium potato (about 7 oz or 200 g), diced
2 carrots, diced
3 celery stalks, cut into sticks
1⅓ cup (7 oz or 200 g) cherry tomatoes, quartered
4 cups (1 l) fish broth
1 pinch saffron
parsley, minced

Let the clams soak in salted water for 30 minutes to purge them, then rinse and drain. Place them in a saucepan with 2 tablespoons oil and the garlic and cook over high heat until open. Reserve 1/3 of the clams with their shells. Shell the remaining 2/3. Strain the cooking liquid and set aside.

Heat the remaining oil in a saucepan and sauté the leek until soft. Add the potato, carrot, celery and tomatoes. Pour over the fish broth and clam cooking liquid. Cover and cook over low heat for 30 minutes.

Dissolve the saffron in a little warm water and add to the soup. Season with salt and pepper and add all the clams. Sprinkle with parsley, let cook for a few more minutes, then serve hot, with sliced of grilled bread if desired.

Spicy Yogurt Spread

2 cups (1 lb or 500 g)
 plain yogurt
1 spring onion, chopped
2 celery stalks, fibers
 removed and cut into chunks
dried red chilli pepper flakes
salt
4 tbsps extra-virgin olive oil
2 tbsps white wine vinegar
1 sprig dill, chopped
4 slices sandwich bread
2 tbsps minced mixed herbs
1 sprig wild fennel or dill,
 chopped

775

Blend the yogurt with the spring onion, celery, a pinch of chilli
flakes and 1/2 teaspoon salt in a food processor or blender. Puree
to obtain a smooth cream then add the oil, vinegar and dill. Blend
for a few more seconds then refrigerate the spread until serving.
Sprinkle the bread with the mixed herbs, and roll gently with a
rolling pin so they adhere. Cut into rounds with a cookie cutter and
toast under the broiler for a few minutes.
Serve the yogurt cream cold, sprinkled with wild fennel and
accompanied by the herbed toasts.

Herb-Steamed Scallop Dumplings

Preparation time 20 minutes
Cooking time 8 minutes
Wine *Alto Adige Pinot Bianco*
Riserva

1/2 cup (2.8 oz or 80 g) rice flour
5½ tbsps plain flour
12 large scallops
1 sprig marjoram
1 sprig parsley
1 sprig tarragon
5-6 tbsps soy sauce
2 tbsps extra-virgin olive oil

776

Mix together the flours and add enough cold water to mix a
dough. Knead for a long time so the plain flour binds the dough.
Let rest in the refrigerator for 20 minutes, then divide the dough
into 12 portions and roll each one out thinly, ideally with a pasta
machine.
Wash the scallops well, remove any dark fibers and dry on paper
towels. Place 1 scallop on each piece of dough and close carefully,
cutting around the edges with a rolling pasta cutter.
Place the parcels in a steamer basket (preferably a bamboo one)
and set over a saucepan containing 1½ cups (350 ml) water and
the herbs. Cover and cook for 7-8 minutes, until the dough starts
to become transparent and the scallop is slightly firm.
Meanwhile reduce the soy sauce over very low heat and set aside
to cool.
Serve the dumplings lightly glazed with the soy sauce reduction
and with a drizzle of olive oil.

Cold Sardinian Gnocchetti in Zucchini Puree

Preparation time 20 minutes
Cooking time 15 minutes
Wine *Torbato di Alghero*

2 tbsps extra-virgin olive oil
1 garlic clove, peeled and
 smashed
3 young zucchini, thickly sliced
salt and pepper
1/2 cup (120 ml) vegetable broth
12.5 oz (350 g) ridged, durum-wheat
 Sardinian gnocchetti
3-4 basil leaves
7-8 cherry tomatoes, quartered
1 tbsp pine nuts

Heat the oil and garlic in a frying pan and sauté the zucchini.
Season with salt and pepper. When browned, add the broth and
cook, covered, until tender, then cool.
Meanwhile bring a pan of salted water to a boil and cook the
gnocchetti until al dente. Cool under running water.
Discard the garlic from the zucchini and puree the zucchini in a
food processor with the basil.
Toast the pine nuts, then chop them.
Mix the gnocchetti with the zucchini puree, stir in the tomatoes
and top with pine nuts. Serve immediately.

777

Livorno-Style Fish Soup
(TUSCANY)

Note *This soup is known as* caciucco, *from the Turkish* küküt, *meaning odds and ends, or a mixed catch of little fish. This dish is typical of Livorno, on the Tuscan coast, which since the 16th century has been an important commercial port with strong international ties.*

Preparation time 35 minutes
Cooking time 1 hour
Wine *Bolgheri Bianco*

3.3 lb (1.5 kg) assorted seafood (cuttlefish, tub gurnard, swallowfish, dogfish, mullet, hake, prawns, mussels, cockles)
4 tbsps extra-virgin olive oil
3 garlic cloves, 2 minced and 1 halved
1 dried red chilli pepper
sage leaves
4 cups (1 l) red wine
1⅔ cups (10.5 oz or 300 g) crushed tomatoes
salt and pepper
8 slices crusty bread
parsley, minced

Clean and descale the large fish and cut them into pieces.
Cut the cuttlefish into pieces, leave the prawns whole, and wash the mussels well, removing any fibers.
Heat the oil in a saucepan and sauté the minced garlic, chilli and sage leaves. Add the cuttlefish, cook off any liquid they give off, then add the red wine. When the wine has cooked down, add the tomatoes, season with salt and pepper and cook for 20 minutes.
Cook the mussels in a covered saucepan until they open.
Add all the other fish to the soup and cook for 10-15 minutes, then add the mussels.
Toast the bread and, rub with the remaining garlic. Lay the slices in terracotta serving dishes, pour over the soup and sprinkle with parsley.

778

Rigatoni and Mediterranean Vegetable Gratin

Preparation time 25 minutes
Cooking time 35 minutes
Wine *Pavese Rosso*
♟

4 tbsps extra-virgin olive oil
1 garlic clove, minced
6 tbsps minced onion
1 small eggplant, julienned
1 medium zucchini, sliced
2-3 celery stalks, sliced
2 medium tomatoes
1/2 cup (120 ml) red wine

thyme
salt and pepper
10.5 oz (300 g) rigatoni
3½ tbsps butter
1 cup (3.5 oz or 100 g) grated
 Pecorino Romano cheese
3/4 cup plus 1 tbsp (200 ml)
 heavy cream
3 egg yolks
1 tbsp mixed minced parsley,
 rosemary and celery leaves
nutmeg, grated

Preheat oven to 400°F (200°C).
Heat the olive oil and sauté the garlic and onion. Add the eggplant,
zucchini and celery and brown over high heat for 5 minutes.
Blanch the tomatoes, peel and deseed them and dice the flesh. Add
them to the vegetables with the wine and season with thyme, salt and
pepper. Cook, uncovered, until the wine has evaporated by 1/2 the
original volume.
Bring a large pot of salted water to a boil and cook the rigatoni until al
dente. Drain and toss with the vegetables, then transfer to a buttered
baking dish.
Mix together the grated cheese, cream, egg yolks, minced herbs, salt,
pepper and nutmeg. Pour the sauce over the pasta and bake for about
15 minutes.
Melt the remaining butter and pour over the pasta halfway through
cooking.
Remove from the oven when the surface is golden, and serve hot.

Umbrian-Style Spaghetti
(UMBRIA)

Preparation time 10 minutes
Cooking time 20 minutes
Wine *Colli Perugini Rosato*

2 medium tomatoes
3 tbsps extra-virgin olive oil
1 onion, minced
3.5 oz (100 g) pancetta, diced
salt and pepper
marjoram
14 oz (400 g) spaghetti
pecorino, grated (optional)

780

Blanch the tomatoes in a pot of boiling water. Peel and slice.
Heat the oil in a wide frying pan and sauté the onion until golden-
brown. Add the pancetta and sauté until the fat is rendered
and the meat is crispy and brown. Add the tomatoes. Continue
cooking, seasoning to taste with pinches of salt, pepper and
marjoram, until the tomatoes are cooked and the sauce has
thickened.
Bring a large pot of salted water to a boil and cook the spaghetti
until al dente. Drain and toss with the tomato sauce in the frying
pan until well coated.
Serve sprinkled with grated pecorino, if desired.

Crêpes with Ricotta and Tomatoes

Preparation time 15 minutes
Cooking time 30 minutes
Wine *Terlaner*
♟♟

Serves 6

CRÊPES

1½ cups (7 oz or 200 g)
 plain flour
2 cups (500 ml) milk
salt
2 eggs
oil

FILLING

5 ripe San Marzano or plum
 tomatoes
salt and pepper
2 large cow's milk mozzarellas,
 diced
basil, minced
10.5 oz (300 g) sheep's milk
 ricotta
2 tbsps extra-virgin olive oil
1½ cups (5.5 oz or 150 g)
 grated Parmesan

Mix the flour, milk and salt in a bowl until smooth. Beat the eggs separately, then add to the mixture. Cover and let rest for 30 minutes. Preheat oven to 350°F (180°C).
Meanwhile blanch, peel and deseed the tomatoes and crush them, then season with salt and pepper.
Lightly oil a non-stick frying pan. Pour 1 ladleful of the crêpe batter into the pan, spreading quickly to form a very thin layer. Cook for 1 minute on each side and transfer to a plate. Continue making crêpes until the batter is finished.
Mix together the mozzarella, basil and ricotta until uniform. Spread on the crêpes and roll them up, then cut into 1-inch (2 cm) thick slices and arrange them in a baking dish. Top with tomatoes, olive oil, basil and Parmesan and bake for 30 minutes.

Zucchini Gnocchi with Monkfish

Preparation time 45 minutes
Cooking time 30 minutes
Wine *Bolgheri Bianco*

GNOCCHI
1 lb (500 g) potatoes
2 zucchini, green part only, diced
1 cup plus 3 tbsps (5.3 oz or 150 g)
 plain flour
1 egg
nutmeg, grated
salt

SAUCE
2 large tomatoes
4 tbsps extra-virgin olive oil
1 garlic clove
1 bay leaf
3.5 oz (100 g) pancetta, diced
14 oz (400 g) monkfish fillet,
 chopped
2-3 sprigs marjoram, leaves only,
 minced
1/2 cup (120 ml) white wine
salt and pepper

782

Boil the potatoes and let cool.
Blanch the green part of the zucchini for 1 minute, drain and let cool.
Peel the potatoes and mash them with a potato ricer. Mix the potato puree with flour, zucchini, egg, a pinch of nutmeg and salt to obtain a uniform dough. Form the dough into ropes about 1/2-inch (1 cm) thick, then cut into gnocchi about 1/2-3/4-inch (1-2 cm) long. Roll each one over the tines of a fork so they become ridged and slightly flattened. Lay them on a floured tray and refrigerate.
Blanch the tomatoes, peel, deseed and dice.
Heat the oil and brown the garlic and bay leaf. Add the pancetta and monkfish and brown. Add the marjoram and wine, let reduce, then add the tomatoes and adjust the salt and pepper.
Bring a large pot of salted water to a boil and cook the gnocchi. Drain, toss with the sauce, and serve immediately.

Spicy Bucatini with Tomatoes, Prawns and Mozzarella

Preparation time 20 minutes
Cooking time 35 minutes
Wine *Sicilia Chardonnay*

1.3 lb (600 g) tomatoes
5 tbsps extra-virgin olive oil
1 small onion, sliced
1-2 garlic cloves, sliced
2 red chilli peppers, minced
1 tbsp tomato paste
salt and pepper
1/2 tsp sweet paprika
1 tbsps minced basil
16 prawns, shelled
12.5 oz (350 g) bucatini
9 oz (250) cow's milk mozzarella,
  cubed
thyme

783

Blanch the tomatoes, peel, deseed and strain the juices. Dice the flesh.

Heat 2 tablespoons oil in a large, oven-proof frying pan and sauté the onion, garlic and chilli. Add the diced tomatoes, then the tomato juices and tomato paste, a pinch of salt, pepper and paprika. Cook for 20 minutes then stir in the basil.

Clean and devein the prawns, leaving the shell on the very end of the tail. Heat the remaining oil and brown the prawns on both sides. Season with salt and pepper.

Bring a large pot of salted water to a boil and cook the bucatini until al dente. Drain into the tomato sauce, toss, then add the prawns and mozzarella. Place under the broiler for a few minutes to brown, then sprinkle over some thyme leaves and serve.

Naked Ricotta and Nettle Ravioli
(Tuscany)

784

Note *These tender* gnudi *— or nude ravioli! — are missing their pasta "clothes".*

Preparation time 25 minutes
Cooking time 20 minutes
Wine *Elba Bianco*

Serves 6

GNUDI
1 lb (500 g) ricotta
10.5 oz (300 g) edible nettle
  shoots, chopped
8 tbsps grated Parmesan
4 eggs
nutmeg, grated
salt and pepper
7 tbsps plain flour

SAUCE
12 squash blossoms
extra-virgin olive oil
1 onion, thinly sliced
3/4 cup plus 1 tbsp (200 ml) milk
3 tbsps pine nuts
salt and pepper

Mix all the gnudi ingredients, except for the flour, together in a bowl. Stir to obtain a smooth mixture and form it into balls, not too large, or into quenelles, using 2 spoons.
Wash the squash blossoms and dry them carefully on paper towels. Heat a drizzle of oil in a saucepan and sauté the onion and squash blossoms (setting aside a few for garnish) for a few minutes, then add the milk and pine nuts. Let cook very briefly then remove from the heat and puree in a blender or food processor. Adjust salt and pepper and set aside.
Bring a large pot of salted water to a boil, dust the gnudi with flour and cook. Drain as soon as they rise to the surface and toss with the sauce. Serve with a grinding of fresh pepper and the reserved squash blossoms.

Sea Bass-Filled Maremmani with Prawns (TUSCANY)

Preparation time 40 minutes
Cooking time 15 minutes
Wine *Bolgheri Bianco*

4 cups (1 lb or 500 g)
 plain flour
3 eggs
1/2 cup (120 ml) water
1 slice sandwich bread
milk
10.5 oz (300 g) sea bass fillet,
 diced
2 egg yolks
1 tbsp heavy cream
1/2 tsp minced marjoram
salt and pepper
nutmeg, grated
3 tbsps extra-virgin olive oil
30 prawns, shelled
3/4 cup (180 ml) white wine

785

Mound the flour on a work surface, make a well in the centre and break in the eggs. Mix a dough, adding water little by little, until smooth and uniform. Let rest in a dry place.

Meanwhile soften the bread in a little milk, squeeze out the excess liquid and mix with the sea bass, egg yolks, cream, marjoram, a pinch of salt, pepper and a little nutmeg. Stir well.

Roll the dough out into 2 very thin sheets of the same size. Form the filling into hazelnut-sized balls, arrange them on 1 pasta sheet and cover with the other sheet. Press down around the filling then cut out with a rolling pasta cutter. Lay on a floured work surface and cover with a clean kitchen towel.

Heat the olive oil and sauté the prawns with the wine, salt and pepper. Cook for around 5 minutes then set aside.

Bring a large pot of salted water to a boil and cook the maremmani for around 10 minutes. Serve hot with the prawn sauce.

Baked Seafood Crêpes in Tomato Sauce

Note *The tomato sauce can be replaced by a creamy sauce, made by reducing the seafood cooking juices with 7 tbsps heavy cream over moderate heat for 5 minutes. Pour the sauce over the crêpes and bake, then serve garnished with diced fresh tomatoes.*

786

Preparation time 30 minutes
Cooking time 15 minutes
Wine *Soave Superiore*
𝒫𝒫𝒫

CRÊPES
1 egg
1 cup (250 ml) milk
3/4 cup (3.5 oz or 100 g)
 plain flour
oil
butter

FILLING
1 lb (500 g) mixed seafood
 (mussels, clams, cockles, etc.)
1 cuttlefish, chopped
3 tbsps extra-virgin olive oil
1 garlic clove
1/2 dried red chilli pepper
1 cup (6.5 oz or 180 g)
 crushed tomatoes
basil
salt and pepper

Beat the egg and milk together and slowly add flour to make a batter. Let rest for 30 minutes.
Meanwhile wash the seafood. Heat the oil, garlic and chilli in a frying pan and add the seafood. Cook, covered, until the shellfish are open. Remove the shells and mince the meat.
Heat a non-stick pan with a little oil and butter. Wipe out with a paper towel then pour in a ladleful of batter. Roll the pan around to form an even layer, cook for 2 minutes and flip over carefully. Cook for another minute. Let cool. Continue until all the batter has been used up.
Place the seafood on half the crêpe and roll up. Place in a baking dish. Heat the tomatoes and basil and cook down until slightly thickened. Season with salt and pepper, then pour over the crêpes. Broil for 10 minutes and serve.

Rice Gnocchi with Basil-Arugula Pesto

Preparation time 20 minutes
Cooking time 8 minutes
Wine *Cinque Terre*

GNOCCHI
3.5 oz (100 g) rice flour
7 tbsps plain flour
1 ¼ cups (300 ml) water
1 knob of butter
salt

PESTO
1 bunch basil
1 bunch arugula
2 tbsps pine nuts

1 tbsp walnuts
1 tbsp hazelnuts
3 tbsps extra-virgin olive oil

Sift the 2 flours together.
Heat the water with the butter in a small saucepan. Bring to a boil, season with salt, then sprinkle in the flours, stirring constantly. When the mixture becomes elastic, remove from the heat and pour onto a work surface. Knead with a little flour for a few minutes, then form a soft, smooth ball and let cool.
Form the dough into small ropes of pasta by hand. Cut them into gnocchi 1/2-3/4 inch (1-2 cm) long and roll over the tines of a fork to give them ridges and a slightly flattened shape.
Bring a large pot of salted water to a boil and cook the gnocchi.
When they start to rise to the surface, continue cooking for another 2 minutes then drain.
Puree the basil, arugula, nuts and oil in a blender or food processor to make the pesto.
Serve the gnocchi hot, with the pesto.

Pasta Salad with Vegetables

Preparation time 20 minutes
Cooking time 20 minutes
Wine *Alto Adige Terlaner*

salt and pepper
13.5 oz (380 g) farfalle
1/2 red bell pepper, cut into strips
1 eggplant, sliced
1 red onion, sliced
4 tbsps extra-virgin olive oil
5.3 oz (150 g) feta, cubed
basil, julienned

Bring a large pot of salted water to a boil, cook the farfalle until al dente, drain and cool under running water.
Grill the pepper strips, starting with the skin side down, on a barbecue or cast-iron grill pan, then close in a plastic bag to steam. Grill the eggplant and onion slices over low heat until tender. Let cool. Peel the pepper and slice into thin strips. Mix all the vegetables together, season with salt and pepper, and stir in the oil and cold farfalle. Just before serving, stir in the feta and garnish with julienned basil.

Fusilli with Ratatouille

Preparation time 15 minutes
Cooking time 25 minutes
Wine *Roero Arneis*

2 tbsps extra-virgin olive oil
1 onion, minced
2 celery stalks
1 carrot, diced
2 zucchini, diced
1/2 turnip, diced
salt and pepper
5 basil leaves, chopped
5.3 oz (150 g) aged ricotta
6 oz (170 g) whole-wheat farro (emmer) fusilli
6 oz (170 g) corn fusilli
1/4 cup (1 oz or 30 g) slivered almonds

Sauté the onion in the oil, add the vegetables and sauté, adding 1 tablespoon water. Salt and pepper to taste and add the basil.
Beat the ricotta with a fork, adding a little warm water, to make a cream.
Bring a large pot of salted water to a boil, cook the fusilli, drain and toss with the vegetables and ricotta cream. Let cool, and garnish with almonds before serving.

788

Black Gnocchetti

Preparation time 15 minutes
Cooking time 20 minutes
Wine *Vermentino di Sardegna*

2 small cuttlefish with ink sacs
2 tbsps extra-virgin olive oil
1 shallot, minced
1 red chilli pepper, minced
15 fresh pea pods
3/4 cup (180 ml) fish broth
salt and pepper
13.5 oz (380 g) Sardinian
 gnocchetti (small gnocchi)
thyme and parsley, minced

Clean the cuttlefish and cut into strips, reserving ink sacs without breaking them.
Heat the oil in a frying pan and sauté the shallot and chilli until golden. Shell the peas and add to the shallot and chilli with the broth. Cook, covered, until tender, adding the cuttlefish halfway through.
Mix the cuttlefish ink with a little broth and add to the sauce with salt and pepper.
Bring a large pot of salted water to a boil and cook the gnocchetti until al dente. Drain and toss with the sauce and the minced herbs

Buckwheat Salad

Preparation time 15 minutes
Cooking time 20 minutes
Wine *Bardolino Chiaretto*

1 tbsp pine nuts
2 cups (1 oz or 30 g) basil
 leaves
3 tbsps extra-virgin olive oil
7 oz (200 g) buckwheat
 berries
2 cups (500 ml) water
1/2 fennel bulb, diced
salt and pepper
10 cherry tomatoes, quartered

Toast the pine nuts and puree them with the basil and olive oil to obtain a smooth pesto.
Boil the wheat berries for 20 minutes in the water, adding the fennel after 10 minutes. Drain off any excess water. Season with salt and pepper and let rest.
Drain the buckwheat and fennel, toss with the tomatoes and dress with the pesto. Serve warm.

Acqua Cotta Soup
(TUSCANY)

Preparation time 20 minutes
Cooking time 35 minutes
Wine *Rosso di Montalcino*

Serves 6

2 large ripe tomatoes
3 medium onions, thinly sliced
8 tbsps extra-virgin olive oil
1 bay leaf
4-5 basil leaves
1 celery stalk, sliced
6 cups (1.5 l) vegetable broth
6 slices Tuscan-style bread
salt and pepper
6 eggs
5 tbsps grated mild pecorino

790

Preheat oven to 350°F (180°C).
Blanch the tomatoes in boiling water for a few seconds. Drain, peel, cut into quarters and deseed.
Place the onions in a saucepan with the oil and bay leaf and sauté for 5-7 minutes over low heat. Add the basil, tomatoes and celery. Cook for a few minutes then add the broth and simmer for 20 minutes.
Toast the bread in the oven for 5 minutes. Remove and keep warm.
Season the soup with salt and a little pepper, remove from the heat and break the eggs into the pan. Keep them whole and poach, while stirring quickly to form a vortex.
Place 1 slice of bread in each of 6 terracotta bowls (or shallow soup bowls) and sprinkle with pecorino. Fill with soup and place 1 egg in each bowl. Serve immediately.

Scammaro Vermicelli
(CAMPANIA)

Preparation time 10 minutes
Cooking time 15 minutes
Wine *Vesuvio Bianco*

1 tbsp capers
2 salted anchovies
1 tbsp raisins
6 tbsps extra-virgin olive oil
1 garlic clove
3/4 cup (3.5 oz or 100 g) black
 Gaeta olives, pitted and finely
 sliced
1 tbsp pine nuts
3 tbsps breadcrumbs
salt
14 oz (400 g) vermicelli
parsley, minced

791

Rinse the capers and pound them with a mortar and pestle.
Wash the anchovies under cold running water, debone and chop.
Soak the raisins in warm water, drain and squeeze out excess
liquid.
Heat the oil in a wide frying pan and sauté the garlic until golden.
Add the anchovies and smash them with a wooden spoon. Add
the capers, olives, raisins and pine nuts. Cook for a few minutes
then remove the garlic and stir in the breadcrumbs.
Boil the pasta in abundant salted water until al dente, drain and
toss in the frying pan with the sauce, stirring well to distribute it
evenly. Top with a sprinkling of parsley and, if desired, another
spoonful of breadcrumbs. Serve hot.

Pasta Salad with Eggplant

Preparation time 15 minutes
Cooking time 15 minutes
Wine *Trebbiano di Romagna*

10.5 oz (300 g) rigatoni
3 tbsps extra-virgin olive oil
1 jar grilled peppers in oil,
 drained and chopped
1 eggplant, thinly sliced
salt and pepper
3 basil leaves, minced
3 mint leaves, minced

Boil the rigatoni until al dente,
drain and cool under running
water. Toss with 1 tablespoon
oil and the grilled peppers.
Heat the remaining oil in a non-
stick frying pan and sauté the
eggplant slices until tender,
turning often so they brown
on both sides. Season with
salt and pepper to taste then
sprinkle with the herbs. Stir into
the pasta, adjust the salt and
serve.

Penne Caprese with Pesto

Preparation time 20 minutes
Cooking time 15 minutes
Wine *Falanghina del Sannio*

12.5 oz (350 g) mezze penne
salt
2 ripe tomatoes
1 bunch basil
4 anchovy fillets in oil
1 tbsp pine nuts
1 tbsp capers
2 tbsps extra-virgin olive oil
9 oz (250 g) cow's milk
 mozzarella, diced

Boil the mezze penne in salted
water until al dente, drain and
cool under running water.
Blanch the tomatoes for 2
minutes, cool in a bowl of ice
water and peel. Deseed and
chop the flesh.
Puree the basil, anchovies,
pine nuts, capers and oil in a
blender or food processor.
Stir the pasta, tomatoes and
mozzarella together in a bowl
and dress with pesto.

792

Cold Summer Farfalle

Preparation time 15 minutes
Cooking time 18 minutes
Wine *Bianco dei Colli Romani*

4 tomatoes
1/2 sweet red onion, minced
4 tbsps extra-virgin olive oil
salt and pepper
basil, chopped
12.5 oz (350 g) farfalle
7 oz (200 g) tuna in oil, drained
 and chopped
1 yellow bell pepper, diced
2 boiled eggs, cut into wedges

Blanch the tomatoes for a few
minutes, drain, peel and puree
the flesh. Pour into a bowl and
mix with the onion, oil, salt,
pepper and basil. Refrigerate.
Bring a large pot of salted
water to a boil and cook the
pasta until al dente. Drain and
cool under running water.
Add the pasta to the tomatoes
and carefully stir in the tuna,
bell pepper and eggs.

Reginette with Langoustines

Preparation time 15 minutes
Cooking time 15 minutes
Wine *Val d'Aosta Chardonnay*

14 oz (400 g) langoustines
1¼ cups (5.5 oz or 160 g)
 minced onion, carrot and celery
1 garlic clove, smashed
3 tbsps extra-virgin olive oil
1/2 dried red chilli pepper
3 young zucchini, cut into strips
salt and pepper
8 squash blossoms, chopped
12.5 oz (350 g) reginette pasta

793

Shell the langoustines, reserving
the heads and shells. Chop the
meat.
Brown the heads and shells in a
frying pan with the onion, carrot
and celery, cover with water and
cook for 1 hour. Strain the broth.
Sauté the garlic in the olive oil
and add crumbled chilli pepper.
Add the zucchini, season with
salt and pepper, and add the
langoustine meat. Sauté briefly
and add broth, squash blossoms
and salt and pepper.
Bring a pot of salted water to a
boil, cook the reginette until al
dente, drain and toss with the
sauce.

Orecchiette with Tomato Sauce and Cacioricotta (Puglia)

Note *Cacioricotta is a typical Puglian cheese, made with sheep's milk. It has a strong flavour and firm texture, though it is often only aged for few months. It is eaten grated over pasta.*

Preparation time 10 minutes
Cooking time 30 minutes
Wine *Salice Salentino Rosato*

2 tbsps extra-virgin olive oil
1 onion, minced
1 lb (500 g) canned, peeled plum
 tomatoes
salt
14 oz (400 g) orecchiette
6 tbsps grated cacioricotta
 cheese
basil leaves (optional)

Heat the oil in a large frying pan and sauté the onion until golden-brown. Add the plum tomatoes, season with salt and cook down to obtain a smooth, thick sauce.
Bring a large pot of salted water to a boil and cook the orecchiette until al dente. Drain and toss with the tomato sauce in the pan until coated completely. Sprinkle with cacioricotta and serve immediately. Garnish with basil leaves, if desired.

Pasta alla Norma
(Sicily)

Preparation time 20 minutes
Cooking time 40 minutes
Wine *Etna Bianco Superiore*

Serves 4-6

3 eggplants, diced
salt and pepper
2 lb (1 kg) ripe tomatoes
3 tbsps extra-virgin olive oil
1 onion, minced
2 garlic cloves, minced
1 tsp sugar
6 basil leaves, chopped
1 lb (500 g) fresh pasta
 (rigatoni or spaghetti)
8 tbsps grated aged ricotta
 salata

795

Sprinkle the eggplant with salt and leave to drain in a colander for
30 minutes.
Blanch, peel and deseed the tomatoes, and chop the flesh.
Heat 1 tablespoon oil in a frying pan and sauté the garlic and onion
until golden. Add the tomatoes and sugar and stir well. Season
with salt and pepper, add the basil and cook for a few more
minutes.
Heat the remaining oil in another frying pan and fry the eggplant.
Drain and dry on paper towels.
Bring a large pot of salted water to a boil and cook the pasta until
al dente. Drain and toss with the tomato sauce. Stir in the eggplant
and sprinkle with ricotta salata. Stir and serve immediately.

Pasta Salad with Marinated Vegetables

Preparation time 15 minutes
Cooking time 10 minutes
Wine *Torbato di Alghero*

1 carrot, diced
2 celery stalks, diced
1¼ cup (5.3 oz or 150 g) diced
 mixed red, yellow and green
 bell peppers
1⅓ cups (3.5 oz or 100 g)
 chopped mushrooms
1/3 leek, thinly sliced
2 garlic cloves, smashed
2 tbsps extra-virgin olive oil
parsley, basil and thyme, minced
salt and pepper
10.5 oz (300 g) short pasta
(like penne or fusilli)

Mix the carrot, celery, bell peppers, mushrooms, leek, garlic, olive oil, minced herbs, salt and pepper in a bowl. Let sit for 2 hours. Bring a large pot of salted water to a boil and cook the pasta until al dente. Drain and rinse under cold running water. Drain well and add to the vegetables. Let sit for 1 hour and serve.

Black Rice with Artichokes and Baby Squid

Preparation time 30 minutes
Cooking time 30 minutes
Wine *Malvasia Istriana*

1/2 cup (3.5 oz or 100 g)
 black Venere rice
2 tbsps extra-virgin olive oil
1 shallot, minced
3 artichokes
1/2 cup (120 ml) vegetable broth
lemon thyme
5.5 oz (150 g) baby squid
herbed salt for fish

797

Boil the rice for 20 minutes.
Trim the artichokes, removing the hard external leaves and choke,
leaving only the heart. Slice thinly.
Heat the oil in a frying pan and sauté the shallot until soft.
Add the artichokes to the shallot and sauté for a few minutes, then
add the broth and cook until tender.
Drain the rice and rinse under cold running water. Mix with thyme
and the artichokes, then divide between 4 serving plates.
Heat a non-stick frying pan and sauté the baby squid for 30
seconds. Add a drizzle of oil, a pinch of herbed salt, and serve
immediately over the rice.

Bucatini with Spicy Stockfish
(CALABRIA)

Note *Mammola is a town near Reggio Calabria, known for its stockfish (dried cod), which is produced artisanally and is highly prized for its quality.*

Preparation time 15 minutes
Cooking time 30 minutes
Wine *Melissa Bianco*

798

Serves 4-6

2 tbsps extra-virgin olive oil
1 onion, minced
1 garlic clove, minced
2 lb (1 kg) Mammola stockfish, already soaked and chopped
salt
1 lb (500 g) canned, peeled plum tomatoes, chopped
1 red chilli pepper, minced
14 oz (400 g) bucatini
parsley, minced

Heat the oil in a saucepan and sauté the onion and garlic until soft. Add the stockfish and season with salt to taste. Cook for a few minutes, then remove the stockfish and set aside. Add the tomatoes and chilli and cook until thickened, then return the stockfish to the pan and continue cooking.
Bring a large pot of lightly salted water to a boil and cook the bucatini until al dente. Drain and toss in the saucepan with the sauce. Sprinkle with parsley and serve hot.

Trebua Farro
(UMBRIA)

Preparation time 15 minutes
Cooking time 1 hour 30 minutes
Wine *Colli Perugini Rosso*

2 tbsps extra-virgin olive oil
1 onion, minced
1 celery stalk, minced
3.5 oz (100 g) smoked pancetta,
 diced
2 potatoes, diced
1/2 cup (3.5 oz or 100 g)
 canned, peeled plum tomatoes,
 chopped
salt
3/4 cup (5.5 oz or 160 g) farro
 (emmer wheat)
1 cup (3.5 oz or 100 g) grated
 pecorino
parsley, minced

Heat the oil in a saucepan and
sauté the onion and celery until
golden. Add the pancetta, let
brown, then add the potatoes.
Brown slightly, then add the
tomatoes and salt to taste. Add
abundant water and bring to a
boil. Add the farro and cook for
around 1 hour, stirring every so
often to make sure it does not
stick to the bottom of the pan.
When the farro is soft sprinkle
with pecorino and serve hot,
garnished with parsley.

Umbrian-Style Acquacotta

Preparation time 15 minutes
Cooking time 40 minutes
Wine *Colli Perugini Rosso*

Serves 6

4 onions, minced
2 lb (1 kg) canned, peeled plum
 tomatoes, sliced
mint, chopped
salt and pepper
1 cup (250 ml) vegetable broth
dry, crusty bread, sliced
4 tbsps extra-virgin olive oil
4 tbsps grated Parmesan

Place the onions, tomatoes,
mint and a little salt in a
saucepan and pour over the
broth. Cook over medium heat
for about 30 minutes, stirring
every so often and adding broth
when necessary.
Heat a non-stick pan and toast
the bread slices in it.
Lay 1 slice of bread each in
shallow soup bowls, drizzle with
oil, season with salt and pepper
and pour over 1 ladleful of the
tomato soup. Sprinkle with
Parmesan and serve hot.

Orecchiette with Tomato, Arugula and Ricotta Salata

Note *The ricotta can be replaced with shavings of pecorino cheese.*

Preparation time 15 minutes
Cooking time 25 minutes
Wine *Ribolla Gialla*

3 tbsps extra-virgin olive oil
1 garlic clove, minced
20 cherry tomatoes, quartered
salt and pepper
14 oz (400 g) fresh orecchiette
1 bunch arugula, destemmed
 and chopped
3.5 oz (100 g) ricotta salata,
 1/2 grated and 1/2 shaved

800

Heat the oil in a large frying pan and add the garlic. Sauté until golden-brown. Add the quartered cherry tomatoes. Cook for 5 minutes over medium heat and season with salt and pepper to taste.

Bring a large pot of salted water to a boil. Add the orecchiette and cook until al dente, drain and toss with the tomatoes. Add the arugula and toss to coat. Sprinkle over the grated ricotta salata. Divide between 4 plates and top with the shavings of ricotta salata. Serve immediately.

Red, White and Green Gnocchi with Seafood

Preparation time 45 minutes
Cooking time 1 hour 10 minutes
Wine *Val d'Aosta Chardonnay*
♟♟

Serves 6-8

GNOCCHI
1.5 lb (700 g) starchy potatoes
2 cups (8.8 oz or 250 g)
 plain flour
1/2 cup (3.5 oz or 100 g)
 semolina flour
1 egg
salt
2⅔ cups (3 oz or 80 g) spinach
1 tbsp tomato paste

SAUCE
3 tbsps extra-virgin olive oil
1 garlic clove, minced
1 large spring onion, sliced
1 medium carrot, minced
1-2 celery stalks, minced
basil and thyme, minced
1 dried red chilli pepper
1/2 cup (120 ml) white wine
1 lb (500 g) clams
7 oz (200 g) squid, thinly sliced
salt and pepper
4 oz (120 g) small prawns
1 tbsp capers

Preheat oven to 400°F (200°C).
Wrap the potatoes in aluminum foil and bake for 1 hour. Remove from the oven, peel and mash. Mix the mashed potatoes with the flours, egg and salt to form a dough. Divide into 3 parts.
Blanch the spinach, drain, squeeze out excess water and puree in the food processor. Mix into one of the dough portions.
Mix the tomato paste into another dough portion.
Form the dough into different coloured gnocchi.
Heat the oil in a saucepan and sauté the garlic and spring onion. Add carrot, celery, basil, thyme, chilli and wine. Add the clams and squid, season with salt and pepper and cook, covered, for 5 minutes. Add the prawns and capers and cook for another 5 minutes.
Bring a large pot of salted water to a boil and cook the gnocchi. Drain into the sauce, adjust salt and pepper and serve.

Rice Salad

Preparation time 10 minutes
Cooking time 10 minutes
Wine *Bianco di Valdichiana*

5 tbsps extra-virgin olive oil
1 eggplant, diced
salt and pepper
1½ cups (10.5 oz or 300 g)
 parboiled rice
5.5 oz (150 g) ham, cubed
3 oz (80 g) smoked provola
 cheese, cubed
3/4 cup (3.5 oz or 100 g)
 mushrooms in oil, drained
1/2 cup (4 oz or 120 g) canned
 sweet corn, drained
3/4 cup (3.5 oz or 100 g)
 peppers in oil, drained
 and chopped
juice of 1 lemon
parsley, minced

Heat 2 tablespoons oil in a frying
pan. Add the eggplant and sauté
for 5-10 minutes. Salt to taste.
Boil the rice until al dente, drain
and cool.
Mix the rice in a bowl with
eggplant, ham, provola,
mushrooms, sweet corn and
peppers. Dress with remaining
oil, lemon juice, parsley, salt and
pepper. Mix well and let sit for 10
minutes before serving.

Rigatoni with Basil and Zucchini

Preparation time 10 minutes
Cooking time 15 minutes
Wine *Gambellara*

6 tbsps extra-virgin olive oil
1 garlic clove, thinly sliced
1 small zucchini, chopped
4 tbsps julienned basil
salt and pepper
12.5 oz (350 g) rigatoni
2 oz (50 g) Fiore Sardo cheese,
 grated
2 tbsps grated Parmesan

Heat the oil in a frying pan and
brown the garlic and zucchini
for 2-3 minutes. Lower the
heat, add the basil and sauté
for a few seconds, then remove
from the heat.
Bring a large pot of salted
water to a boil and cook the
rigatoni until al dente. Drain and
toss with the sauce, returning
the pan to the heat, and stir
until well mixed. Season with
a little salt and pepper and
the grated cheeses. Serve
immediately.

802

Blueberry Risotto

Preparation time 10 minutes
Cooking time 15 minutes
Wine *Nebbiolo d'Alba*

3½ tbsps butter
1⅓ cups (10 oz or 280 g)
 Carnaroli rice
1/2 cup (120 ml) white
 Fragolino wine
1 cup (3.5 oz or 100 g)
 Concord grapes, deseeded
1/3 cup (2 oz or 50 g) blueberries
4 cups (1 l) milk
2/3 cup (4.5 oz or 130 g) sugar

Melt the butter in a saucepan and toast the rice. Add the wine, grapes and blueberries and reduce slightly. Add the milk and sugar and continue cooking until all the liquid has been absorbed and the rice is done.
Fill several different flower-shaped moulds of various sizes with the risotto, then refrigerate for 2 hours.
Unmould and arrange in a pyramid on a serving plate. Serve decorated with strawberries, if desired.

Pasta Wheels with Tomato Puree

Preparation time 10 minutes
Cooking time 10 minutes
Wine *Lugana*

salt and pepper
10.5 oz (300 g) ruote
 or rotelle pasta
3 tbsps extra-virgin olive oil
15 tomatoes, chopped
fresh aromatic herbs
10 basil leaves
1 spring onion, thinly sliced

Bring a large pot of salted water to a boil and cook the ruote until al dente. Drain and let cool, tossing with 1 tablespoon oil to prevent sticking.
Puree the tomatoes, remaining oil, herbs and basil in a food processor until smooth. Season with salt and pepper and toss with the cooled pasta. Garnish with spring onion and serve.

Fisherman's Scialatielli
(Campania)

Note *Scialateielli is a handmade pasta, typical of Campania, which resembles fat spaghetti. It is often served with seafood sauces like this one.*

Preparation time 5 minutes
Cooking time 30 minutes
Wine *Greco di Tufo*

804

7 oz (200 g) mussels
4 tbsps extra-virgin olive oil
1 garlic clove, minced
parsley, minced
3.5 oz (100 g) small shrimp
7 oz (200 g) clams
3.5 oz (100 g) squid, sliced into
 rings
3/4 cup (180 ml) white wine
3 tbsps tomato sauce
salt and pepper
12.5 oz (350 g) scialatelli,
 fettuccine or tagliatelle

Cook the mussels in a covered pan until they open.
Heat the oil in a large frying pan and sauté the garlic until golden.
Add the parsley (reserving a little for garnish), then add the
prawns, clams, squid and cooked mussels. Pour over the wine
and as soon as it has evaporated add the tomato sauce and
continue cooking for around 15 minutes over medium heat.
Bring a large pot of salted water to a boil and cook the scialatelli.
Drain and toss in the frying pan with the seafood. Stir well and
serve hot, sprinkled with pepper and the remaining parsley.

Scottiglia
(TUSCANY)

Preparation time 30 minutes
Cooking time 2 hours 20 minutes
Wine *Rosso di Montalcino*

Serves 4-6

6 tbsps extra-virgin olive oil
1 onion, minced
1 carrot, minced
1 celery stalk, minced
1 garlic clove
7 oz (200 g) lean beef for stew, cubed

7 oz (200 g) rabbit meat, cubed
7 oz (200 g) chicken thigh meat, cubed
7 oz (200 g) turkey thigh meat, cubed
7 oz (200 g) pork loin, cubed
7 oz (200 g) lamb shoulder meat, cubed
1¾ cups (400 ml) red wine
1 lb (500 g) canned, peeled plum tomatoes, chopped
salt and pepper
Tuscan-style bread, sliced

805

Heat 3 tablespoons oil in a large frying pan and sauté the onion, carrot and celery with the garlic until soft. Add all the meat. As soon as it is slightly browned, add the wine and let reduce for a few minutes. Add the tomatoes, season with salt and pepper and continue cooking, over low heat, for 2 hours. If the sauce dries out, add a little broth or water.
Grill or toast the bread with the remaining oil on a cast-iron grill pan or in a non-stick frying pan.
Serve the scottiglia on the slices of bread, arranged on serving plates.

Cold Pasta Salad

Note *The ham could be replaced with smoked ham, the mozzarella with smoked scamorza and the pine nuts with coarsely chopped almonds, for a more distinctive flavour.*

Preparation time 30 minutes
Cooking time 14 minutes
Wine *Etna Bianco*

806

salt
4 oz (120 g) farfalle
1/2 cup (2.5 oz or 70 g) peas
2½ tbsps pine nuts, chopped
5.5 oz (150 g) mozzarella, diced
3 oz (80 g) ham, diced
2½ tbsps brined capers
1/3 cup (2 oz or 50 g) diced red
 bell pepper
1/3 cup (2 oz or 50 g) diced
 yellow bell pepper
2½ tbsps pitted olives, sliced
1/2 cup (3 oz or 80 g) cherry
 tomatoes, quartered
7-8 basil leaves, minced, plus
 extra for garnish
juice of 1/2 lemon
5 tbsps extra-virgin olive oil

Preheat oven to 350°F (180°C).
Bring a pot of salted water to a boil and cook the farfalle. Just before they reach al dente, add the peas and blanch with the pasta for 1 minute. Drain and rinse under cold water to stop cooking.
Spread the chopped pine nuts on a baking sheet and toast in the oven for 5 minutes.
Mix the pasta and peas with the mozzarella, ham, capers, peppers, olives, tomatoes, minced basil and pine nuts. Dress with lemon juice, olive oil and a pinch of salt.
Serve garnished with basil leaves.

Paccheri with Langoustines and Eggplant

Note *Paccheri are Campania's most typical pasta shape. In the past they were known as the poor people's pasta, because it did not take very many to fill the plate. They are traditionally served with a San Marzano tomato sauce, but these days they are often found with fish and other seafood.*

Preparation time 20 minutes
Cooking time 1 hour 30 minutes
Wine *Cirò Bianco*
♟♟

15 small langoustines
3 tbsps extra-virgin olive oil
1¼ cup (5.5 oz or 150 g)
 minced celery, carrot and onion
1/2 cup (120 ml) white wine
salt
14 oz (400 g) paccheri
1 small eggplant, deseeded
 and diced
sunflower oil
1 shallot, minced
1/2 dried red chilli pepper
10 cherry tomatoes, chopped
parsley, minced

807

Slice the langoustine tails lengthwise and extract the tail meat. Reserve shells and heads.
Heat 1 tablespoon olive oil and sauté celery, carrot and onion. Add shells, heads and wine. Reduce and cover with cold water. Simmer for 1 hour 30 minutes. Pass through a food mill and season with salt.
Bring a pot of salted water to a boil and cook the paccheri until al dente, then drain.
Fry the eggplant in the sunflower oil.
Heat the remaining olive oil and sauté the shallot and chilli. Add the tomatoes and sauté briefly. Add the langoustines, the fried eggplant, parsley and some langoustine broth. Lower the heat and add the paccheri. Sauté briefly, adding more broth if necessary, then serve.

Red Rice Salad with Ham

Preparation time 15 minutes
Cooking time 20 minutes
Wine *Orvieto Classico*

1 cup (7 oz or 200 g) parboiled rice
1/2 cup (3.5 oz or 100g) red rice
5.5 oz (150 g) ham, diced
1/3 cup (3.5 oz or 100 g) canned
  sweet corn, drained and rinsed
1 spring onion, minced
1 bunch arugula, shredded
3 tbsps shelled pumpkin seeds
2 tomatoes, diced
salt and pepper
2 tbsps extra-virgin olive oil

Boil the red and white rice
separately and drain as soon
as al dente. Cool under running
water.
Mix both types of rice in a bowl
with the ham, sweet corn,
spring onion, arugula, pumpkin
seeds and tomatoes.
Season to taste with salt and
pepper and drizzle with oil.
Let sit for 30 minutes before
serving.

Pasta with Peppers and Ricotta

Preparation time 20 minutes
Cooking time 15 minutes
Wine *Elba Bianco*

1/2 red bell pepper
1/2 yellow bell pepper
1 bunch arugula
salt and pepper
10.5 oz (300 g) ruote or rotelle
 pasta
2 tbsps extra-virgin olive oil
2 oz (60 g) aged ricotta salata,
 shaved

Roast the peppers over an
open flame until they are
completely blackened. Close in
a plastic bag to steam.
Meanwhile refresh the arugula
by soaking in cold water.
Bring a large pot of salted
water to a boil and cook the
pasta until al dente, then drain
and cool under cold running
water.
Drain and dry the arugula and
tear into pieces.
Peel the peppers and cut into
thin strips.
Mix together all the ingredients,
top with ricotta shavings and
seasoning with salt and pepper
to taste.

808

Ligurian-Style Rice Sedanini

Preparation time 10 minutes
Cooking time 10 minutes
Wine *Riviera Ligure di Ponente Pigato*
♟

4 tbsps extra-virgin olive oil
1 garlic clove, peeled and
 smashed
1 tbsp toasted pine nuts
15 Taggiasca olives, pitted
 and chopped
10 cherry tomatoes, halved
basil, minced
salt and pepper
12.5 oz (350 g) rice sedanini
 or small penne
chives, minced
1 carrot, peeled and grated

Heat the oil and sauté the garlic
until golden. Add the pine nuts,
olives, tomatoes and basil. Salt
to taste and add a little hot
water. Cook for 5 minutes then
adjust salt and pepper.
Bring a large pot of salted
water to a boil and cook the
sedanini until al dente. Drain
and toss in the pan with the
sauce. Stir in the chives and
divide between serving plates.
Top with grated carrot and
serve.

Mediterranean Spaghetti

Preparation time 15 minutes
Cooking time 10 minutes
Wine *Aglianico del Taburno*
♟

1 red bell pepper
9 oz (250 g) San Marzano
 or plum tomatoes
extra-virgin olive oil
1 garlic clove
basil leaves
dried red chilli pepper flakes
salt
11.5 oz (320 g) spaghetti

809

Roast the pepper over an open
flame, then close in a plastic
bag to steam. Peel, deseed
and cut into strips.
Blanch the tomatoes, peel,
deseed and cut into strips.
Heat some olive oil in a frying
pan with the garlic, basil and
a pinch of chilli flakes. Add the
tomatoes and peppers, season
with salt and sauté over high
heat for about 6-7 minutes.
Bring a large pot of salted
water to a boil and cook the
spaghetti. Drain and toss in
the pan with the sauce, adding
extra basil and a little olive oil.

Syracusan-Style Spaghetti
(SICILY)

Preparation time 20 minutes
Cooking time 40 minutes
Wine *Carricante*

2 salted anchovies
5 tbsps pitted black olives
2½ tbsps capers
1 lb (500 g) ripe tomatoes
2 eggplants, peeled and diced
2 bell peppers
6 tbsps extra-virgin olive oil
1 garlic clove, peeled and
 smashed
salt and pepper
basil, chopped
14 oz (400 g) spaghetti
4 tbsps grated pecorino cheese

810

Rinse the anchovies and remove any bones. Finely mince them together with the olives and capers.
Peel the tomatoes and pass through a sieve.
Place the eggplant in a bowl and sprinkle with salt. Let sit until it gives off water, then drain and rinse.
Roast the peppers over an open flame, close in a plastic bag to steam, then peel, deseed and slice.
Heat the oil and sauté the garlic until golden. Remove from the pan and add the eggplant. Cook for a few minutes, then add the tomatoes. Season with salt and pepper and add the peppers, olives, capers and anchovies together with some basil. Continue cooking until the sauce thickens.
Bring a large pot of salted water to a boil and cook the spaghetti until al dente. Drain and place in bowl, then dress with the sauce and sprinkle with pecorino. Serve immediately.

Reggio Calabrian-Style Tagliatelle
(CALABRIA)

Preparation time 20 minutes
Cooking time 30 minutes
Wine *Donna Camilla Rosato*

2 sweet bell peppers
2 tbsps extra-virgin olive oil
2 garlic cloves, minced
1 onion, minced
1 large zucchini, diced
salt and pepper
2 tbsps tomato sauce
14 oz (400 g) tagliatelle
basil, chopped
4 tbsps grated pecorino cheese

Roast the peppers over an open flame then close in a plastic bag to sweat. Peel, deseed and cut into thin strips.
Heat the oil in a saucepan and sauté the garlic and onion until soft. Add the pepper strips and zucchini. Season with salt and pepper and add tomato sauce. Cook over low heat to obtain a thick sauce.
Bring a large pot of salted water to a boil and cook the tagliatelle until al dente. Drain and toss in the pan with the sauce. Season with some basil and sprinkle with grated pecorino. Serve immediately.

Quick Paella

812

Preparation time 20 minutes
Cooking time 20 minutes
Wine *Prosecco di Conegliano Brut*

4 tbsps extra-virgin olive oil
1 garlic clove, smashed
15 mussels
1/2 white onion, minced
1 sausage, peeled
2 cups (14 oz or 400 g) Patna rice
vegetable broth
1¼ cups (5.5 oz or 150 g) peas
10 prawns, shelled
9 oz (250 g) squid, sliced into rings
2 tsps paella spice mix
5 cherry tomatoes, quartered
parsley, minced
grated zest of 1 organic lemon
salt

Preheat oven to 450°F (230°C).
Heat 2 tablespoons oil in a frying pan and sauté the garlic until golden. Add the mussels and cover. Cook until opened, then remove from the heat and cool. Remove the shells, reserving the cooking juices.
Heat the remaining oil and sauté the onion until soft. Crumble in the sausage meat and add the rice. Toast over high heat, then start adding broth. After 5 minutes, add the peas, and after another 5 minutes the prawns, squid and spice mix. Continue cooking, adding broth little by little together with the mussel cooking liquid.
As soon as the rice is al dente, add the shelled mussels, tomatoes, parsley and grated lemon zest. Adjust the salt and transfer to a large non-stick oven-proof dish. Finish cooking for 5 minutes in the oven.

Ponente-Style Pennette

Preparation time 10 minutes
Cooking time 20 minutes
Wine *Colli di Luni Bianco*

5.5 oz (150 g) salted anchovies
4 tbsps extra-virgin olive oil
1 garlic clove, halved
2/3 cup (3.5 oz or 100 g) capers
3/4 cup (3.5 oz or 100 g)
 pine nuts
1/3 cup (2 oz or 50 g) whole
 peeled almonds, finely chopped
1 cup (5.5. oz or 150 g) pitted
 black olives, minced
3/4 cup (200 ml) tomato sauce
salt
14 oz (400 g) ridged penne
4 tbsps Genoan pesto (see p. 1089)

Rinse the excess salt from the anchovies, rubbing it off by hand.
Heat the oil in a wide frying pan and sauté the garlic until golden.
Remove garlic and add the capers, pine nuts, almonds, olives and
anchovies and brown for 1 minute. Add the tomato sauce, stir
well, and cook for 10 minutes. Adjust the salt.
Bring a large pot of salted water to a boil and cook the penne until
al dente. Drain, reserving some of the cooking water, and toss with
the sauce in the pan. Add 2-3 tablespoons of cooking water and
the pesto and stir well. Serve hot.

Messina-Style Swordfish Pie
(SICILY)

Preparation time 1 hour
Cooking time 2 hours 10 minutes
Wine *Catarratto*

DOUGH
3 cups (12. 3 oz or 350 g)
 plain flour
3/4 cup (7 oz or 200 g) butter,
 softened
2 egg yolks
1 tsp sugar
salt

FISH
1.3 lb (600 g) swordfish
plain flour
1 large onion, minced

1 carrot, minced
1/2 celery stalk, minced
3/4 cup plus 1 tbsp (200 ml)
 extra-virgin olive oil
14 oz (400 g) ripe tomatoes,
 balnched, peeled and deseeded
1/3 cup (2 oz or 50 g) pitted
 black olives
2½ tbsps salted capers, rinsed
3½ tbsps pine nuts
3 tbsps raisins, soaked in water
 and squeezed out
salt and pepper
2 bay leaves

814

Mound flour on a work surface and make a well. Add the butter, egg
yolks, sugar and a pinch of salt. Mix well. Cover and let rest.
Cut the swordfish into bite-sized pieces. Dust with flour.
Sauté the onion, carrot and celery with the oil until soft. Add swordfish
and brown over low heat for a few minutes. Add the tomatoes, olives,
capers, pine nuts and raisins. Adjust salt and pepper and cook,
covered, for 1 hour 30 minutes, adding water or broth if too dry.
Preheat oven to 350°F (180°C).
Roll out the dough into 3 sheets. Butter and flour a baking dish, and
line with 1 sheet of dough. Pour in half the swordfish mixture and add
1 bay leaf, then cover with another dough sheet. Spread over the
remaining swordfish and top with another bay leaf, then cover with the
remaining sheet of dough, sealing the edges.
Bake for about 30 minutes and serve.

Arezzo-Style Pappardelle
(Tuscany)

Preparation time 40 minutes
Cooking time 1 hour
Wine *Chianti Classico*
♔♔

1 duck
10.5 oz (300 g) tomatoes
4 tbsps butter
salt
1/2 onion, minced
1/2 carrot, minced
1/2 celery stalk, minced
1.5 oz (40 g) prosciutto, diced
nutmeg, grated
2 cups (500 ml) beef broth
3 oz (80 g) beef spleen
14 oz (400 g) pappardelle

Carefully clean the duck. Chop the liver and reserve
Blanch the tomatoes, drain, peel and pass through a sieve.
Melt the butter in a saucepan and brown the duck, turning
frequently, until evenly coloured. Remove from the heat and cut
into pieces. Season with salt.
In the same pan, sauté the onion, carrot, celery, prosciutto and
tomatoes with a grating of nutmeg and add the duck pieces.
Continue cooking over low heat for 40 minutes, stirring often and
adding broth when necessary.
Clean the beef spleen and chop. Boil in a saucepan, then drain
and add to the sauce together with the chopped liver and continue
cooking for a few minutes.
Bring a large pot of salted water to a boil and cook the
pappardelle. Drain and add to the sauce. Serve hot.

Radiatori with Fresh Anchovies, Zucchini and Arugula

Note *If desired, you can add a handful of toasted pine nuts or 2 minced sun-dried tomatoes to the sauce.*

Preparation time 15 minutes
Cooking time 15 minutes
Wine *Alto Adige Pinot Bianco*

20 fresh anchovies
2 tbsps extra-virgin olive oil
1 garlic clove, minced
1/2 dried red chilli pepper
8 small young zucchini,
  quartered lengthways
1 tomato, deseeded and
  chopped
1/2 bunch broad-leaved arugula,
  finely chopped
salt and white pepper
1 oregano sprig, minced
13.5 oz (380 g) dried egg
  radiatori pasta

816

Wash the anchovies and open them like a book, removing the head and backbone.
Heat the oil in a frying pan with the garlic and chilli. Add the zucchini and sauté for 2 minutes. Add the anchovies and sauté briefly then add the tomato and arugula. Season with white pepper and oregano.
Bring a large pot of salted water to a boil and cook the radiatori until al dente. During the cooking add a few spoonfuls of the cooking water to the sauce.
Drain the pasta and toss with the sauce in the pan, then serve.

Rice Salad with Ham and Melon

Note *The parboiled rice can be replaced by another variety, such as Basmati.*

Preparation time 35 minutes
Cooking time 20 minutes
Wine *Trentino Müller Thurgau*

1¾ cups (12.5 oz or 350 g)
  parboiled rice
1 small melon
7 oz (200 g) ham, diced
1 bunch wild arugula,
  destemmed
4 tbsps extra-virgin olive oil
salt and freshly ground pepper

817

Boil the rice until al dente, about 20 minutes.
Meanwhile cut the melon in half, remove the seeds, peel and chop the flesh into bite-sized cubes.
When the rice is cooked, drain and rinse under cold water to remove the starch. Place in a large salad bowl. Stir in the melon, ham and arugula, reserving a few leaves for garnish. Dress with oil and season with salt and freshly ground pepper to taste. Stir to evenly coat the rice with the dressing and let sit for at least 15 minutes before serving.
Garnish with arugula leaves and serve immediately.

Whole-Wheat Spaghetti with Tuna, Eggplant and Peppers

Preparation time 20 minutes
Cooking time 20 minutes
Wine *Bolgheri Bianco*

4 tbsps extra-virgin olive oil
2 garlic cloves, smashed
1 spring onion, finely sliced
1 eggplant, diced
1 red bell pepper, diced
5.5 oz (160 g) canned tuna
 in water, drained
1/2 cup (120 ml) white wine
salt and freshly ground pepper
12.5 oz (350 g) whole-wheat
 spaghetti
1 bunch parsley, minced

818

Heat the oil and sauté the garlic and spring onion. Add the eggplant and pepper and sauté over high heat. Crumble in the tuna. Add the wine and season with salt and pepper to taste. Bring a large pot of salted water to a boil and cook the spaghetti until al dente. Drain and add to the saucepan with a little cooking water and sauté to mix well.
Remove the heat and stir in a handful of parsley, a little freshly ground pepper and a drizzle of oil. Serve immediately.

Summer Vegetable Lasagna

Preparation time 45 minutes
Cooking time 15 minutes
Wine *Etna Bianco*
♟♟

DOUGH
2⅓ cups (10.5 oz or 300 g)
 plain flour
1 tbsp extra-virgin olive oil
3 eggs
salt

FILLING
4 tbsps extra-virgin olive oil
2 onions, thinly sliced

2 large eggplants, sliced
salt and pepper
8 firm, ripe tomatoes, thickly
 sliced
1 bunch basil
4 tbsps grated Parmesan
7 oz (200 g) fresh goat's cheese,
 chopped
2 tbsps melted butter

819

Preheat oven to 400°F (200°C).
Mix together the dough ingredients to form a smooth, uniform dough.
Cover with plastic wrap and refrigerate for about 30 minutes.
Heat 2 tablespoons oil in a frying pan and sauté the onions with a little
water so they soften without colouring.
Heat the remaining 2 tablespoons oil in another frying pan and sauté
the eggplant slices with pinches of salt and pepper.
Grill the tomato slices on a cast-iron grill pan.
Bring a large pot of salted water to a boil. Roll the dough into thin
sheets and cut into rectangles. Boil for 3 minutes and cool under cold,
running water.
Oil a baking dish. Start with a layer of pasta, top with some eggplant,
basil leaves, Parmesan, onions, tomatoes and goat's cheese and top
with another layer of pasta. Continue until all the ingredients have been
used up, finishing with a layer of pasta. Brush with melted butter and
sprinkle with Parmesan. Bake for 10 minutes. Let cool slightly before
serving.

Ziti and Tuna Salad

Preparation time 15 minutes
Cooking time 10 minutes
Wine *Ciró Bianco*

salt and pepper
10.5 oz (300 g) ziti-type pasta
1 tomato, cut into thin wedges
1 bunch mixed salad (butter
  lettuce, frisée, radicchio,
  romaine), chopped
1 tsp oregano
7 oz (200 g) tuna fillet in oil
3 tbsps extra-virgin olive oil

820

Bring a large pot of salted water to a boil and cook the ziti until just al dente. Drain and cool under running water. Cut the ziti into 1½-inch (4 cm) lengths and place in a bowl. Mix in the tomato, lettuces and oregano. Arrange on a serving plate and crumble over the tuna. Dress with oil, salt and pepper and serve.

Spaghetti al Cartoccio

Preparation time 25 minutes
Cooking time 20 minutes
Wine *Metodo Classico
Franciacorta Brut*

3 tbsps extra-virgin olive oil
1 garlic clove
3.5 oz (100 g) prawns,
  shelled and deveined
4 cherry tomatoes, halved
1/2 cup (3 oz or 80 g) pitted
  black olives
salt and pepper
parsley, minced
12.5 oz (350 g) spaghetti
1 cup (3.5 oz or 100 g)
  grated Parmesan

Preheat oven to 350°F (180°C). Heat the oil in a frying pan and sauté the garlic. Add the prawns and sauté for 2 minutes. Add the tomatoes and olives and sauté for 2 minutes. Season with salt and pepper and add the parsley. Bring a pot of salted water to a boil. Blanch spaghetti for 2 minutes. Drain and mix with the sauce and Parmesan.
Lay out 4 sheets of aluminum foil. Place the pasta on the foil and close tightly. Bake until the spaghetti is soft.

Tagliolini with Shellfish

Preparation time 20 minutes
Cooking time 15 minutes
Wine *Pigato*

♟

1 lb (500 g) mixed shellfish
 (cockles, clams, mussels)
3 tbsps extra-virgin olive oil
1 garlic clove
1/2 red chilli pepper, deseeded
 and minced
parsley, minced
1 tomato, deseeded and diced
salt
14 oz (400 g) egg tagliolini

Wash the shellfish, debearding the
mussels and soaking the clams in
cold, salted water for 30 minutes
to remove any sand.
Heat the oil in a frying pan with the
garlic and chilli. Add the cockles
and cook, covered, over medium
heat. After 5 minutes add the
clams, and then the mussels,
and cook until opened. Sprinkle
with parsley and add the tomato.
Lightly season with salt.
Bring a large pot of salted water to
a boil and cook the tagliolini until
al dente. Drain and toss with the
sauce, letting the pasta soak up
some of the cooking juices.
Serve hot.

Spicy Spaghetti

Preparation time 5 minutes
Cooking time 10 minutes
Wine *Aprilia Bianco*

♟

3 tbsps extra-virgin olive oil
2 garlic cloves, thinly sliced
2 fresh red chilli peppers,
 minced
1 cup (2 oz or 50 g) minced
 parsley
salt
14 oz (400 g) spaghettini
 (thin spaghetti)
1 cup (3.5 oz or 100 g) grated
 Parmesan

Heat the oil in a frying pan and
sauté the garlic and most of the
chilli for 5 minutes. Add parsley
and remove from heat.
Bring a large pot of salted
water to a boil and cook the
spaghettini until al dente, about
5 minutes. Drain and toss with
the garlic and chilli mixture,
stirring well to mix thoroughly.
Sprinkle with Parmesan and
remaining chilli and serve
immediately.

Cavatelli with Chickpeas
(PUGLIA)

Preparation time 20 minutes
Cooking time 50 minutes
Wine *Orta Nova Rosato*

SAUCE
1½ cups (10.5 oz or 300 g) dried
 chickpeas
1 bay leaf
1 garlic clove
2 tbsps extra-virgin olive oil
1 onion, minced
1 dried red chilli pepper
10.5 oz (300 g) tomatoes, chopped
salt

CAVATELLI
2 cups (14 oz or 400 g)
 semolina flour
salt

822

Soak the chickpeas in cold water overnight. Drain and place in a
saucepan with abundant water, bay and garlic and simmer over
medium heat for about 50 minutes, then drain.
Meanwhile heat the oil in a large frying pan and sauté the onion.
Crumble in the chilli and add the tomatoes. Cook over low heat for
around 30 minutes, and adjust the salt.
Mix the semolina flour for the pasta with enough water and a pinch
of salt to form a smooth dough of average consistency. Roll the
dough into small, hazelnut-sized balls, and form each one into a
cavatello by rolling it on a work surface with a finger tip, forming a
little cavity in the middle.
Boil the cavatelli in abundant salted water. Drain and place in a
bowl. Mix with the chickpea sauce and serve immediately.

Cercivento-Style Plum Gnocchi
(Friuli-Venezia Giulia)

Preparation time 10 minutes
Cooking time 10 minutes
Wine *Collio Goriziano Sauvignon*

GNOCCHI
1.3 lb (600 g) potatoes
2⅓ cups (10.5 oz or 300 g)
 plain flour
4 eggs
salt
ground cinnamon
20 fresh plums or prunes,
 halved and pitted

SAUCE
2/3 cup (5.5 oz or 150 g) butter
5 sage leaves
3.5 oz (100 g) aged latteria
 cheese, grated

823

Boil the potatoes until tender but not falling apart. Drain, peel and
pass through a sieve. Once cooled, mix with the flour (reserving a
small amount), eggs, salt and a pinch of cinnamon.
Form the dough into egg-sized portions. Divide each portion in
half, place a plum or prune half in the middle, and close with the
other half of the dough.
Melt the butter in a non-stick saucepan with the sage leaves and
let simmer gently.
Bring a large pot of salted water to a boil and cook the gnocchi for
3 minutes. When they float, drain carefully with a slotted spoon.
Serve with the sage butter and grated cheese.

Grilled Gnocchi with Tomatoes and Basil

Preparation time 10 minutes
Cooking time 25 minutes
Wine *Fiano di Avellino*

824

GNOCCHI
1 lb (500 g) yellow-fleshed
 potatoes
3/4 cup plus 1 tbsp (3.5 oz
 or 100 g) plain flour
2 eggs
2 tbsps grated Parmesan
salt

SAUCE
4 tbsps extra-virgin olive oil
2 garlic cloves, halved
10 cherry tomatoes, halved
salt and pepper
basil, chopped
2 oz (60 g) smoked provola
 cheese, diced
1 knob of butter
2 tbsps grated Parmesan

Boil the potatoes, drain, peel and mash. Mix in the flour, eggs, Parmesan and salt to form a smooth dough. Roll into 1/2-inch (1/2 cm) thick ropes, then cut into gnocchi.
Heat the oil in frying pan and sauté the garlic. Add the tomatoes and sauté for 2 minutes. Season with salt and pepper.
Bring a large pot of salted water to a boil and cook the gnocchi. Drain into the pan with the tomatoes and add the basil and provola. Adjust the salt. Fill 4 buttered individual moulds with the gnocchi mixture and top with Parmesan. Grill for 10 minutes.

Spaghetti with Prawns

Preparation time 10 minutes
Cooking time 15 minutes
Wine Friuli Collio Pinot Grigio

salt and pepper
14 oz (400 g) spaghetti alla
 chitarra
6 tbsps extra-virgin olive oil
2 garlic cloves
1/2 dried red chilli pepper
1 eggplant, deseeded and diced
12.5 oz (350 g) prawns, shelled
 and chopped
parsley, minced
2 tomatoes, deseeded and diced
basil, chopped

Bring a large pot of salted
water to a boil and start
cooking the spaghetti.
Meanwhile heat the oil in a
frying pan and sauté the garlic
and chilli. Add the eggplant
and sauté for 5 minutes. Add
the prawns, parsley and a little
of the pasta cooking water.
Season with salt and pepper
and add the tomatoes. Cook
for another 3 minutes, stirring in
the basil. Drain the pasta when
al dente, and toss in the frying
pan with the sauce.

Baked Ziti

Preparation time 15 minutes
Cooking time 20 minutes
Wine Verduzzo del Piave

3 tbsps extra-virgin olive oil
2 garlic cloves, unpeeled and
 smashed
10.5 oz (300 g) canned, peeled
 plum tomatoes
salt and pepper
14 oz (400 g) ziti
7 oz (200 g) fresh provola
 cheese, diced
1 cup (3.5 oz or 100 g) grated
 aged pecorino

Preheat oven to 425°F (220°C).
Heat the oil in a saucepan and
sauté the garlic until golden.
Add the tomatoes and crush
with a spoon. Cook over
medium heat wooden for 6-7
minutes and season with salt
and pepper.
Bring a large pot of salted
water to a boil and cook the
ziti. Drain and toss with the
tomatoes. Stir in the provola
and half the pecorino. Place
the pasta in a baking dish and
sprinkle with the remaining
pecorino. Bake for 5 minutes
and serve.

Cold Torchietti with Peas, Roast Pepper and Bacon

Preparation time 25 minutes
Cooking time 15 minutes
Wine *Lagrein Rosato*

1/2 red bell pepper, halved
1/2 yellow bell pepper, halved
1½ cups (7 oz or 200 g) peas
salt and pepper
2 tbsps extra-virgin olive oil
6 thin slices bacon, 2 minced
 and 4 whole
10.5 oz (300 g) egg torchietti
 or conchiglie pasta
5 mushrooms, peeled and thinly
 sliced
mint leaves

826

Roast the peppers directly over a flame or under the broiler, set on high. Close them in a plastic bag to steam, then peel and deseed. Cut into strips and then dice.
Meanwhile blanch the peas for 3 minutes in boiling salted water. Heat the oil in a frying pan and sauté the mushrooms until browned and crispy. Drain on paper towels.
Fry the minced bacon in a frying pan. Add the peas and roast peppers and cook for a few seconds. Season with salt and pepper.
Bring a large pot of salted water to a boil and cook the torchietti until al dente. Drain and cool under running water. Mix together with the mushrooms, peas, peppers and a few mint leaves.
Fry the remaining slices of bacon in a non-stick frying pan over high heat.
Serve the cold pasta topped with the crispy bacon slices.

Parsley Maltagliati with Lobster and Shallot Oil

Preparation time 30 minutes
Cooking time 20 minutes
Wine *Gewürztraminer*
👨‍🍳👨‍🍳

SHALLOT OIL
1 shallot, minced
extra-virgin olive oil

MALTAGLIATI
3/4 cup (3.5 oz or 100 g)
 plain flour
1 cup (7 oz or 200 g) semolina
 flour
3 eggs
parsley, minced

SAUCE
1 small lobster
 (around 1.3 lb or 600 g)
vegetable broth
salt and peppercorns
bay leaves
cloves
3/4 cup (180 ml) white wine
extra-virgin olive oil
1 shallot, minced
1 zucchini, green part only,
 cut into matchsticks
1 carrot, peeled and cut into
 matchsticks
1 spring onion, sliced

Make the shallot oil by mixing the shallot with some oil. Let sit for a few hours and strain.
Mix together all the maltagliati ingredients into a smooth dough. Let rest for 30 minutes, then roll out into a thin sheet, let dry slightly then cut into maltagliati, irregular squares.
Blanch the lobster for a few minutes in boiling salted vegetable broth with some peppercorns, bay leaves, cloves and the wine. Drain, remove the shell and dice the lobster meat.
Heat some oil in a frying pan and sauté the minced shallot until soft. Add the lobster meat and brown. Season with salt and pepper and set aside.
Sauté the zucchini, carrot and spring onions individually in a frying pan with a little oil, keeping them crunchy. Season with salt.
Bring a large pot of salted water to a boil and cook the maltagliati. Drain and toss in a frying pan with the lobster, zucchini, carrots and spring onions. Drizzle with shallot oil.

Spaghetti with Lobster and Tomato

Note *Be careful not to overcook the lobster, as the meat can lose its characteristic elasticity and become floury.*

Preparation time 10 minutes
Cooking time 30 minutes
Wine *Torbato di Alghero Spumante*
♟

extra-virgin olive oil
1/2 onion, minced
1 carrot, minced
7 oz (200 g) canned, peeled
 plum tomatoes, chopped
1 live lobster
 (around 1.5 lb or 700 g)
salt
14 oz (400 g) spaghetti

828

Heat a drizzle of oil in a large saucepan and sauté the onion and carrot until soft. Add the tomatoes and cook over moderate heat for 15 minutes. Add the whole lobster, still alive, to the pan. Cover, lower the heat and cook for about 10 minutes. Remove the lobster from the pan, cut into pieces using poultry scissors, return to the pan and cook for another 8 minutes.
Bring a large pot of salted water to a boil and cook the spaghetti until al dente. Drain and toss in the pan with the sauce. Serve hot.

Cold Sedanini with Baby Squid and Tomatoes

Preparation time 20 minutes
Cooking time 7 minutes
Wine *Castel del Monte Rosato*
♟

salt and pepper
10.5 oz (300 g) durum-wheat
 ridged sedanini or penne
3 tbsps extra-virgin olive oil
2 ripe tomatoes
parsley, minced
7 oz (200 g) baby squid
1/2 garlic clove, finely minced

Bring a large pot of very salty water to the boil and cook the
sedanini for just 4-5 minutes. Drain and cool under cold running
water. Toss with a little olive oil and set aside.
Blanch the tomatoes and immerse in cold water. Peel, deseed and
dice. Season with salt and pepper and sprinkle over the parsley.
Steam the baby squid for 2 minutes, mix with a little minced garlic
and stir into the pasta with the tomatoes. Mix well and serve.

831

Summer Orecchiette with Caper Pesto

Preparation time 35 minutes
Cooking time 15 minutes
Wine *Cirò Bianco*

CAPER PESTO
3 bunches basil, destemmed
1 bunch parsley, destemmed
4 tbsps brined capers, drained
4 tbsps green olives, pitted
 and chopped
4 tbsps pine nuts
1/2 garlic clove
4 tbsps grated Parmesan
7 tbsps extra-virgin olive oil
salt and pepper

PASTA
1 medium zucchini, diced
2 large carrots, diced
13 oz (360 g) orecchiette
4.5 oz (130 g) cow's milk
 mozzarella, diced
2 cups (9 oz or 260 g) cherry
 tomatoes, quartered
1/2 cup (3.5 oz or 100 g) cooked
 chickpeas
5-6 basil leaves, minced
2 tbsps extra-virgin olive oil
salt and pepper

832

Place the basil and parsley leaves, capers, olives, pine nuts, garlic, Parmesan, oil, salt and pepper in a food processor and blend until smooth.
Blanch the zucchini and carrots for 3-4 minutes, drain and cool, reserving the cooking water.
Bring the cooking water to a boil and use it to cook the orecchiette, for about 8 minutes. Drain and place in a bowl with the zucchini, carrots, mozzarella, tomatoes, chickpeas and minced basil. Toss with oil and pinches of salt and pepper. Arrange in serving plates, drizzle with the pesto and serve.

Barley with Caramelized Peppers and Mixed Seafood

Preparation time 40 minutes
Cooking time 50 minutes
Wine *Colli di Luni Bianco*
♟♟

3/4 cup (5.5 oz or 150 g) pearled
  barley
9 tbsps extra-virgin olive oil
salt and pepper
1 lb (500 g) red and yellow bell
  peppers, deseeded and cut into
  strips

1 tbsp sugar
3 tbsps white wine vinegar
10.5 oz (300 g) baby octopus
9 oz (250 g) baby cuttlefish, cut
  into strips
12.5 oz (350 g) baby squid
1 lb (450 g) monkfish fillet,
  cut into bite-sized chunks
10.5 oz (300 g) prawns, shelled
parsley, minced
1 garlic clove, minced

833

Boil the barley for 15 minutes. Drain, place in a bowl and dress with 3 tablespoons oil and pinches of salt and pepper.

Heat 2 tablespoons oil in a frying pan and sauté the pepper strips for 2 minutes. Sprinkle over the sugar. When the sugar has dissolved and started to caramelize, add the vinegar and cook for another 10 minutes. Salt to taste.

Bring 3 pots of water to a boil. Boil the octopus for 25-30 minutes, the cuttlefish for 20 minutes and the squid for 5 minutes, each in a separate pot. Drain and mix together in a bowl.

Bring another pot of water to a boil and blanch the monkfish for 5 minutes. Drain, reserving the water, and add the monkfish to the other cooked seafood. Use the same water to blanch the prawns for 2 minutes, then drain and add to the bowl. Dress all the seafood with the parsley, garlic, oil, salt and pepper.

Arrange the barley on serving plates and top with peppers and seafood.

Spaghetti with Clams and Bottarga
(SARDINIA)

Note *Bottarga is cured mullet or tuna roe, much used in Sardinian cooking. Traditionally spaghetti is flavoured with a simple sauce of oil and garlic and topped with abundant grated bottarga.*

Preparation time 5 minutes
Cooking time 20 minutes
Wine *Vermentino di Sardegna*

1.3 lb (600 g) clams
salt
2 tbsps extra-virgin olive oil
2 garlic cloves, minced
2 bunches parsley, minced
14 oz (400 g) spaghetti
6 tbsps grated bottarga

834

Soak the clams in salted water for 1-2 hours so they expel any sand. Drain and wash well under cold running water.
Heat the olive oil in a large frying pan and sauté the garlic until golden-brown. Add the clams, cover, and cook over medium heat until they open. Discard any of the clams that stay closed and then season to taste with salt and sprinkle with parsley.
Bring a large pot of salted water to the boil and cook the spaghetti until al dente. Drain and add the pasta to the pan with the clams. Toss the spaghetti to coat evenly with the clam sauce. Serve hot in shallow soup bowls, topped with grated bottarga.

Cavatieddi in Tomato Sauce
(SICILY)

Note *Cavatieddi is the Sicilian name for cavatelli, which are typical to Puglia and Basilicata. For a richer dish, serve the cavatieddi in a meat ragù.*

Preparation time 30 minutes
Cooking time 25 minutes
Wine *Etna Rosato*

CAVATIEDDI
2⅓ cups (10.5 oz or 300 g) plain flour
salt
1 tbsp extra-virgin olive oil

SAUCE
2 tbsps extra-virgin olive oil
1 onion, minced
1 garlic clove, minced
3/4 cup (200 ml) tomato sauce
salt
5 tbsps grated pecorino cheese

835

Mound the flour on a work surface and make a well in the centre. Add a pinch of salt, the oil and enough warm water to mix a smooth, uniform dough with a firm texture.
Divide the dough into small portions, roll them by hand into little ropes and cut into 1/2-inch (1 cm) lengths. Press each little piece with a finger tip to form a cavity in the middle. Arrange the cavatieddi on a floured work surface and let rest for around 30 minutes.
Heat the oil in a large frying pan and sauté the onion and garlic until golden. Add the tomato sauce and cook down until thickened, adding salt if necessary.
Bring a large pot of salted water to a boil and cook the cavatieddi until al dente. Drain and toss with the tomato sauce in the pan. Serve hot, sprinkled with pecorino.

Creamy Pasta Salad

Preparation time 20 minutes
Cooking time 30 minutes
Wine *San Colombano*

836

salt
7 oz (200 g) ridged pennette
2⅓ cups (10.5 oz or 300 g)
 peas
2 medium tomatoes
1 tbsp extra-virgin olive oil
2 oz (50 g) prosciutto, diced
2 large spring onions, sliced
2 small carrots, peeled and
 diced
3 oz (80 g) Gruyère cheese, cut
 into matchsticks
3 oz (80 g) strong Gorgonzola
 cheese, diced
parsley, minced
1/2 cup (3.5 oz or 100 g)
 mayonnaise
3½ tbsps yogurt
wine vinegar
Cayenne pepper

Bring a large pot of salted water to a boil and cook the pennette
until al dente. Drain and rinse under cold running water to cool.
Boil the peas for 8 minutes, then drain, rinse under cold running
water, and set aside.
Blanch the tomatoes, peel and chop.
Heat the oil until very hot and brown the prosciutto and spring
onions for 1-2 minutes. Add the carrots and cook over low heat
for 5 minutes.
Mix the pasta, peas, tomatoes, prosciutto and carrots, cheeses
and parsley in a bowl.
Mix the mayonnaise, yogurt, vinegar to taste, a pinch of salt and
some Cayenne in a bowl, and use the sauce to dress the pasta.

Tagliatelline with Bottarga, Zucchini and Prawns

Preparation time 20 minutes
Cooking time 15 minutes
Wine *Torbato di Alghero*

4 vine-ripened tomatoes
4 baby zucchini with flowers
 attached
5 tbsps extra-virgin olive oil
1 shallot, minced
1 garlic clove, smashed
salt and pepper
10.5 oz (300 g) red prawns,
 shelled and diced
12.5 oz (350 g) tagliatelline
 (thin tagliatelle)
basil, julienned
4 tbsps grated bottarga, grated

Blanch the tomatoes, peel, deseed and dice.
Remove the flowers from the zucchini and julienne them, reserving
a few whole flowers for garnish. Slice the zucchini.
Heat the oil and sauté the shallot and garlic until soft. Add the
zucchini, season with salt and sauté over high heat for 2-3
minutes. Add the tomatoes and let cook for 5 minutes. Add the
prawns, remove from the heat and keep warm.
Bring a large pot of salted water to a boil and cook the tagliatelline
until al dente. Drain and add to the pan with the sauce, together
with a little cooking water. Add the basil, sprinkle with bottarga
and season with pepper to taste. Drizzle with a little oil, sauté for
a couple of minutes over high heat, then serve, garnished with the
reserved flowers.

Trofie with Monkfish and Lemon Thyme

Note *Trofie are a typical Ligurian pasta from the are a around the town of Recco. They look like little gnocchi and are excellent with Genoan pesto or other Ligurian sauces.*

Preparation time 30 minutes
Cooking time 20 minutes
Wine *Metodo Classico Franciacorta Rosé*
♟♟

3 tbsps extra-virgin olive oil
1 garlic clove
2 spring onions, minced
3-4 sprigs lemon thyme
1 lb (450 g) monkfish fillet,
 cut into bite-sized chunks
salt and pepper
1/2 cup (120 ml) white wine
1 medium zucchini, diced
1 large red bell pepper, diced
3 small carrots, diced
1½ celery stalks, diced
1/2 cup (3 oz or 80 g) peas
13 oz (360 g) trofie pasta
parsley, minced

838

Heat the oil in a frying pan, sauté the garlic and spring onions, then add the lemon thyme. Brown the monkfish chunks, season with salt and pepper and add the white wine. Let reduce, then add the vegetables, adjust the salt, and add a little water if necessary. Continue cooking until the vegetables are tender.
Bring a large pot of salted water to a boil and cook the trofie for 8-9 minutes. Drain and toss with the sauce. Sprinkle with parsley and serve immediately.

Pasta with Pesto and Tomatoes

Preparation time 10 minutes
Cooking time 10 minutes
Wine *Gambellara*

2 tomatoes
salt
thyme leaves, minced
3 bunches basil
2 tbsps pine nuts
1 tbsp walnuts
6 tbsps extra-virgin olive oil
11.5 oz (320 g) spaghetti

Place the food-processor bowl and blade in the refrigerator for 20 minutes, to avoid heating the basil while making the pesto.
Blanch the tomatoes in boiling water for 2 minutes, immerse in cold water then peel and dice. Place in a bowl with a pinch of salt and the thyme.
Puree the basil, pine nuts, walnuts and oil in the food processor, pulsing it so the blade does not over heat.
Bring a large pot of salted water to a boil and cook the spaghetti until al dente. Drain and toss with the tomatoes and pesto, then serve immediately.

Millet with Squash Blossoms

Preparation time 15 minutes
Cooking time 35 minutes
Wine *Friuli Collio Chardonnay*

1 cup (6.5 oz or 180 g) millet
2 tbsps extra-virgin olive oil
1/2 onion, minced
1/4 red bell pepper, diced
1/4 green bell pepper, diced
1/2 cup (120 ml) white wine
salt and pepper
10 squash blossoms, pistils
 removed
2 tbsps slivered almonds

839

Place the millet in a saucepan with double its volume of cold water and bring to a boil. Cook until tender.
Meanwhile heat the oil in a frying pan and sauté the onion. Add the peppers and wine. Season with salt and pepper and add the squash blossoms. As soon as the millet is cooked, drain and toss with the vegetables. Adjust the salt. Fill 4 individual moulds with the mixture and top with almonds. Cook under the broiler for 5 minutes, and serve.

San Vito-Style Fish Couscous
(SICILY)

Preparation time 45 minutes
Cooking time 1 hour 40 minutes
Wine *Catarratto*

Serves 10

4 cups plus 2½ tbsps
 (1.75 ibs or 800 g) durum-wheat
 semolina flour
extra-virgin olive oil
salt and pepper
2.2 lb (1 kg) mixed fish for
 soup (grouper, scorpion fish,

amberjack)
2 large onions, 1 minced
 and 1 quartered
3 garlic cloves, minced
2 tbsps tomato paste
bay leaves
6 cups (1.5 l) water
2.2 lb (1 kg) vegetables
 (bell peppers, zucchini,
 eggplant, peas), diced
dried red chilli pepper flakes
parsley, minced

840

Place the semolina flour in a saucepan and work it with the hands,
adding a drizzle of oil, a little warm water and a pinch of salt, to obtain
small balls. Leave to dry for 1 day.
Clean the fish, cutting it into fillets and reserving the scraps.
Heat some oil, fry the fish fillets, drain and keep warm.
Heat a drizzle of oil in a saucepan and sauté the minced onion and
garlic. Add the tomato paste. Add some water and the fried fish and let
cook for 30 minutes.
Place the fish scraps, onion quarters and bay leaves with the water in
steaming pot. Cook the couscous in a steaming basket over the water
for around 30 minutes.
Meanwhile heat some more oil and fry the mixed vegetables. Drain.
Mix together the couscous, fish, vegetables and a little of the strained
steaming broth. Mix well, let sit to meld the flavours, then serve with a
pinch of chilli pepper flakes and parsley.

Imbrecciata
(UMBRIA)

Preparation time 10 minutes
Cooking time 1 hour 30 minutes
Wine *Montefalco Rosso*

1/3 cup (2.5 oz or 70 g) farro
 (emmer wheat)
1/3 cup (2.5 oz or 70 g) pearled
 barley
6 cups (1.5 l) vegetable broth
salt and pepper
1/4 cup (2.5 oz or 70 g) cooked
 borlotti beans
3 tbsps cooked sweet corn
4 tbsps cooked chickpeas
4 tbsps cooked lentils
3 tbsps dried fava beans,
 cooked
2 tbsps extra-virgin olive oil
3.5 oz (100 g) pancetta, diced
1 onion, minced
3/4 cup (200 ml) crushed tomatoes
marjoram

841

Place the farro and barley in a large saucepan with about 4 cups
(1 l) broth and cook, covered, over medium heat for about 1 hour,
adding more broth if necessary. Season with salt and pepper and
add the borlotti beans, sweet corn, chickpeas, lentils and fava
beans.
In another saucepan heat the oil and sauté the pancetta and
onion. As soon as the onion is golden, add the tomato and cook
for around 15 minutes. Add this mixture to the grains and beans
and continue cooking for 10 minutes. Season with marjoram, a
pinch of salt and pepper to taste, and serve hot, drizzled with olive
oil if desired.

Black Tagliolini with Bottarga Pesto and Cherry Tomatoes

Preparation time 40 minutes
Cooking time 5 minutes
Wine *Riviera Ligure di Ponente*
Pigato
😋😋😋

TAGLIOLINI
4 cups (1 lb plus 1.6 oz or 500 g)
 plain flour
4 eggs
1 egg yolk
2 tbsps extra-virgin olive oil
2 tbsps squid ink
salt

SAUCE
1 bunch parsley, destemmed
1 garlic clove
3 tsps powdered tuna bottarga
9 tbsps extra-virgin olive oil
salt and pepper
2 1/3 cups (12.5 oz or 350 g)
 cherry tomatoes, diced

842

Mix together all the tagliolini ingredients to obtain a smooth dough.
Wrap in plastic wrap and refrigerate for 15 minutes.
Meanwhile prepare the pesto by pureeing the parsley, garlic,
1 teaspoon bottarga, 4 tablespoons oil and pinches of salt and
pepper in a food processor.
Place the tomatoes in a large bowl and toss with a pinch of salt
and 5 tablespoons oil.
Roll out the pasta dough, cut into large strips, then use a pasta
machine to cut into 1/5-inch (1/2 cm) wide tagliolini.
Bring a large pot of salted water to a boil and cook the tagliolini
for about 5 minutes. Drain and toss with the pesto and tomatoes.
Sprinkle with the remaining bottarga and serve immediately.

Tagliolini with Prawns and Clam Ragù

Preparation time 30 minutes
Cooking time 15 minutes
Wine *Elba Bianco*

TAGLIOLINI
2⅓ cups (10.5 oz or 300 g)
 plain flour
2 eggs
1 egg yolk
2 tsps extra-virgin olive oil
salt

SAUCE
4 tbsps extra-virgin olive oil
2 garlic cloves

1 large carrot, diced
1 large celery stalk, diced
2 spring onions, chopped
14 oz (400 g) small prawns,
 shelled and chopped
salt and pepper
1/2 cup (120 ml) white wine
2.2 lb (1 kg) clams
6-7 small basil leaves
1⅔ cups (9 oz or 250 g)
 cherry tomatoes, quartered

843

Mix the flour with the eggs, yolk, oil and a pinch of salt to make a smooth and compact dough. Wrap in plastic wrap and refrigerate for at least 20 minutes.

Heat the oil and sauté 1 garlic clove until golden. Add the carrot, celery and spring onions and sauté until soft. Add the prawns and cook for 3-4 minutes. Season with salt and pepper and add the wine. Let reduce.

Wash the clams and place in a frying pan with 1 garlic clove and 3 basil leaves. Cover and cook until the clams open. Remove from their shells and strain the cooking liquid.

Add the clams and cooking liquid to the prawns and stir.

Roll out the pasta and cut out tagliolini about 1/5-inch (1/2 cm) wide. Bring a large pot of salted water to a boil and cook them for 5 minutes. Drain and toss with the prawns and clams. Sauté together, then add the tomatoes and the rest of the basil and stir with a wooden spoon. Serve immediately.

Spaghetti with Garlic, Oil and Chilli

Note *This is the traditional recipe for this classic, simple dish: While the spaghetti cook, mince 2 garlic cloves and heat some extra-virgin olive oli in a frying pan. When they start to colour, add as much dried red chilli flakes as desired and 2 tbsps minced parsley, then after a few seconds, 1 ladleful of pasta cooking water. Drain the spaghetti al dente and finish cooking in the frying pan with the sauce.*

844

Preparation time 5 minutes
Cooking time 7 minutes
Wine *Bianco d'Alcamo*

3 garlic cloves
8 tbsps extra-virgin olive oil
1 mild red chilli pepper
12.5 oz (350 g) spaghetti alla
 chitarra
salt

Peel the garlic cloves, remove the inner shoot, and puree in a food processor with 3 tablespoons oil. Let sit for 1 day in a cool place, then strain.
Remove the white pith and seeds from the chilli, mince and cook in a small saucepan with 3 tablespoons oil until it dissolves and becomes a paste.
Boil the spaghetti alla chitarra in abundant salted water until al dente, drain and divide between 3 small bowls.
Dress 1/3 of the spaghetti with the garlic oil, 1/3 with the chilli paste and 1/3 with the remaining olive oil.
Divide the spaghetti between 4 plates, forming small nests of each type of spaghetti, so that each plate has one of each flavour.

Spicy Greek-Style Penne

Preparation time 10 minutes
Cooking time 10 minutes
Wine *Sicilia Chardonnay*

7-8 cherry tomatoes, quartered
extra-virgin olive oil
salt
dried hot red chilli pepper
oregano
7 oz (200 g) feta cheese,
 thinly sliced
3/4 cup (3.5 oz or 100 g)
 black olives, pitted
basil, chopped
10.5 oz (300 g) ridged penne

Toss the tomatoes with a few
spoonfuls of oil, a pinch of salt,
some crumbled chilli pepper
and a pinch of oregano. Let sit
to marinate.
Mix the feta with the olives and
basil.
Bring a large pot of salted
water to a boil and cook the
penne until al dente. Drain and
mix with all the ingredients.
Serve hot or cold.

Scafata (Umbria)

Preparation time 15 minutes
Cooking time 35 minutes
Wine *Friuli Collio Chardonnay*

1⅔ cups (9 oz or 250 g) fresh
 shelled fava beans
salt and pepper
4 tbsps extra-virgin olive oil
2 spring onions, sliced
1 bunch wild fennel or dill,
 chopped
3.5 oz (100 g) guanciale, diced
9 oz (250 g) Swiss chard,
 chopped
8 cherry tomatoes, diced
1 bunch mint, chopped

Blanch the favas in boiling
salted water for a few minutes,
then drain and peel.
Heat the oil in a saucepan and
sauté the spring onions until
golden. Add the fennel and
guanciale and sauté for a few
minutes. Add the favas and
chard and cook, covered, for
10 minutes. Add the tomatoes
and continue cooking, adding
a little water when necessary.
Season with salt and pepper
and add the mint.

845

Grilled Chianina Steak
(TUSCANY)

Note *The Chianina breed of cattle is one of Italy's oldest and most important. Their beef is traditionally used for the classic* bistecca fiorentina *steak.*

Preparation time 15 minutes
Cooking time 10 minutes
Wine *Brunello di Montalcino*

3/4 cup (3.5 oz or 100 g) salted capers, rinsed and minced
2 tbsps Tuscan extra-virgin olive oil
7 oz (200 g) red and yellow grilled or roasted peppers, chopped
salt and pepper
1 Chianina steak (around 2.2 lb or 1 kg, 2 inches (4-5 cm) thick
coarse salt
5.5 oz (150 g) long green pickled peppers, chopped

846

Mix the capers with a little oil. Mix the roast peppers with salt, pepper and a little oil.

Preheat a barbecue, with the grill 2 inches (5 cm) from the hot coals, or preheat a cast-iron grill pan.

Make little cuts along the fat of the steak and near the bone, to stop it curling up and to help it cook evenly.

Grill on the hot barbecue for 5 minutes on each side, seasoning it with coarse salt. If using a grill pan, sprinkle the pan with salt before putting on the steak.

Thickly slice the steak and serve, drizzled with olive oil, with the capers and peppers on the side.

Ancona-Style Stockfish
(MARCHE)

Preparation time 30 minutes
Cooking time 30 minutes
Wine *Verdicchio dei Castelli di
Jesi Riserva*

Serves 6-8

2.5 lb (1.2 kg) stockfish
 (dried cod), pre-soaked
4 cups (1 l) milk
6 tbsps extra-virgin olive oil
4 carrots, minced
2 celery stalks, minced
4 garlic cloves (preferably red
 garlic), peeled
2/3 cup (150 ml) white wine
3 tbsps tomato sauce
1.3 lb (600 g) tomatoes,
 deseeded and cut into strips
salt and pepper
1.75 lb (800 g) potatoes, peeled
 and cubed
parsley, minced

847

Remove the skin and any bones from the stockfish, and cut into
2-inch (5 cm) cubes. Place in a bowl, cover with milk, and let sit
overnight. Drain and pat dry.
Heat the oil and sauté the carrot and celery until soft. Add the
stockfish and garlic and cook over low heat for about 10 minutes.
Add the wine, let cook off, then add the tomato sauce and enough
warm water to cover the fish. Continue cooking, and when most
of the water has evaporated, remove the garlic and add the
tomatoes. Adjust salt and pepper, then add the potatoes. Bring to
a boil over medium heat, then cook until the potatoes are tender.
Remove the stockfish and potatoes and keep warm. Strain the
cooking liquid and use as a sauce to serve with the stockfish and
potatoes, sprinkled with parsley.

Braised Rabbit with Pantelleria Capers

Note *Capers are the pickled or salted flower buds of the caper shrub. Capers from the windy, rugged island of Pantelleria of the coast of Sicily are some of the best in the world.*

Preparation time 15 minutes
Cooking time 45 minutes
Wine *Sicilia Chardonnay*

848

4 tbsps butter
2 tbsps extra-virgin olive oil
1 rabbit (around 2.5 lb
 or 1.2 kg), cut into pieces
1 tbsp plain flour
3/4 cup (180 ml) red wine
1½ cups (350 ml) broth from
 a stock cube
1 bunch mixed herbs
 (parsley, sage, rosemary),
 coarsely chopped
salt
dried red chilli pepper flakes
1.5 oz (40 g) dried porcini
 mushrooms
1 garlic clove
6 tbsps Pantelleria capers, rinsed
2 anchovy fillets in oil, drained

Heat 1 tablespoon butter and the oil in a saucepan and brown the rabbit pieces.
Add the flour, red wine, broth, herbs, salt and chilli to the pan, and cook for around 30 minutes over medium heat.
Meanwhile soak the porcini in hot water until soft, drain and squeeze out excess water. Chop them, then sauté in a frying pan with the remaining butter and garlic.
Transfer the rabbit to a terracotta casserole dish. Strain the cooking liquid and pour over the rabbit. Add capers, porcini mushrooms and anchovies. Cover and cook for another 5 minutes over medium heat. Serve hot.

Beef Fillet al Cartoccio

Preparation time 35 minutes
Cooking time 20 minutes
Wine *Trebbiano di Romagna*

1.3 lb (600 g) beef or veal fillet,
 sliced
2 tbsps paprika
salt and pepper
3.5 oz (100 g) pickles, drained
 and julienned
1 red bell pepper
5 basil leaves
thyme and parsley
4 tbsps white wine
4 tbsps extra-virgin olive oil

849

Preheat oven to 400°F (200°C).
Lay the beef slices on a large tray. Season with paprika, a pinch of salt and some pepper. Sprinkle over the pickles.
Roast the pepper in the oven until the skin is charred. Close in a plastic bag to steam, then peel, deseed and cut into thick strips. Spread over the beef.
Lower the oven temperature to 350°F (180°C).
Mince together the basil, thyme and parsley and set aside.
Take 4 sheets of aluminum foil and divide the beef slices and their toppings between them. Add white wine, olive oil and the herbs to each portion, then lay over 4 more sheets of foil. Fold in the edges towards the centre to seal the packages.
Lay the packages on a baking sheet and bake for 15 minutes.
Remove from the oven and serve.

Chicken in Lemon Leaves with Tomatoes au Gratin

Preparation time 20 minutes
Cooking time 10 minutes
Wine *Bolgheri Bianco*

850

TOMATOES
4 ripe, firm tomatoes
salt
3 tbsps extra-virgin olive oil
2 garlic cloves
15 salted capers, rinsed
1¼ cups (5.5 oz or 150 g)
 breadcrumbs
basil, minced

CHICKEN
14 oz (400 g) ground chicken
 (breast and thigh)
seasoned salt for grilled meat
salt and pepper
20 organic lemon leaves

Halve the tomatoes horizontally and scoop out the seeds. Lightly salt the interior and turn upside-down on paper towels to drain. Heat the oil in a frying pan and brown the garlic. Add the capers and cook briefly, then add the breadcrumbs and toast slightly. Remove the garlic and add the basil.
Fill the tomato halves with the breadcrumbs, pressing down to compact.
Mix the chicken with a pinch of seasoned salt, regular salt and pepper, and form round balls. Wrap each one in a lemon leaf and secure with a toothpick.
Cover a cast-iron grill pan in aluminum foil to distribute the heat evenly and cook the chicken until cooked through to the centre. Meanwhile broil the tomatoes for around 5 minutes.
Serve the chicken with the tomatoes.

Beef Roll with Spinach Sauce

Preparation time 25 minutes
Cooking time 30 minutes
Wine *Dolcetto di Dogliani*
♟ ♟

2 slices beef sirloin or rump
 (around 10.5 oz or 300 g)
3 carrots
8 asparagus spears
salt and pepper
1 egg
7 oz (200 g) spinach
4 tbsps extra-virgin olive oil
2 garlic cloves, minced
nutmeg, grated
sage and rosemary, chopped

Preheat oven to 400°F (200°C).
Pound out the beef slices with a meat tenderizer.
Blanch the carrots and asparagus separately in boiling salted water, then drain when they are al dente. Cut the carrots and asparagus into matchsticks.
Boil the egg for 5 minutes and peel it.
Blanch the spinach, drain and squeeze out excess water. Heat a little oil in a frying pan with the minced garlic and sauté the spinach for a few minutes. Puree in a blender or food processor with the nutmeg and boiled egg, adding a drizzle of oil if necessary.
Lay out a sheet of aluminum foil on a cutting board and sprinkle with sage and rosemary. Drizzle with oil and lay the beef slices in a single layer. Spread the carrots and asparagus on top, season with salt and pepper and roll up like a Swiss roll. Close the foil, twisting at both ends, and bake for 25 minutes. Remove from the oven and let rest before unwrapping the foil and slicing. Serve with the spinach sauce.

851

Beef Carpaccio

Preparation time 15 minutes
Cooking time 15 minutes
Wine *Soave*

5.5 oz (150 g) arugula
salt and pepper
12 thin slices of beef or veal
 fillet
5 tbsps extra-virgin olive oil
juice of 1/2 lemon
2 tbsps green olives, pitted and
 sliced
2 oz (50 g) sun-dried tomatoes,
 chopped
1 celery stalk, sliced
1 tbsp capers

852

Tear the arugula by hand and
divide between serving plates,
seasoning with a little salt.
Pound the fillet slices between
2 sheets of wax paper without
tearing the meat, then lay the
fillet over the arugula.
Mix the oil, lemon juice, salt
and pepper in a bowl. Add the
olives, sun-dried tomatoes,
celery and capers. Use the
mixture to dress the carpaccio
and serve.

Chicken Kebabs with Prosciutto

Preparation time 30 minutes
Cooking time 25 minutes
Wine *Bardolino Chiaretto*

1 large red bell pepper
1 chicken breast
3.5 oz (100 g) prosciutto, sliced
20 small sage leaves
5.5 oz (150 g) feta cheese, diced
salt and pepper
2 tbsps extra-virgin olive oil

Cut the pepper in half and
remove the seeds. Grill or broil
for 7 minutes on each side.
Close in a plastic bag until cool,
then peel, deseed and cut into
strips.
Cut the chicken into bite-sized
chunks. Cut each prosciutto
slice in half to make 2 long
strips. Place a sage leaf on
each piece of chicken and
wrap each one in a strip of
prosciutto. Thread them onto
metal skewers and set aside.
Mix the peppers with the feta
and dress with salt, pepper and
olive oil.
Grill the skewers on a barbecue
or cast-iron grill pan. Serve with
the pepper and feta salad.

Roast Rabbit with Thyme

Preparation time 5 minutes
Cooking time 25 minutes
Wine *Solopaca Rosso*

4 rabbit legs (around 5.5 oz
  or 150 g each)
salt and pepper
4 tbsps extra-virgin olive oil
1 garlic clove, peeled
4 thyme sprigs
3/4 cup (180 ml) dry white wine
juice and zest of 1 organic
  lemon

Preheat oven to 350°F (180°C).
Season the rabbit with salt and
pepper. Lay in a roasting pan
with the oil, garlic and thyme
and place in the oven. When
browned, pour over the wine,
then 5 minutes later the lemon
juice.
Baste the rabbit frequently with
the pan juices throughout the
roasting time. When the rabbit
is cooked through (at least 25
minutes), add the lemon zest,
cut into strips. Serve hot.

Grilled Beef with Salsa Verde

Preparation time 15 minutes
Cooking time 10 minutes
Wine *Brunello di Montalcino*

1 egg
1 lb (500 g) lean beef fillet
1 garlic clove
1 bunch parsley, destemmed
salt
4 tbsps extra-virgin olive oil

Boil the egg for 5 minutes.
Cut the beef fillet into 4
medallions, and tie a piece of
kitchen string tightly around
each one to keep its shape
during cooking.
Shell the boiled egg and place
the yolk in a food processor.
Remove the green shoot from
the garlic and add the rest of
the clove to the yolk, together
with the parsley, salt and oil.
Puree, pulsing, leaving the
sauce somewhat coarse.
Cook the beef fillets on a cast-
iron grill pan or a barbecue for
3 minutes on each side, leaving
the inside rosy and rare. Serve
topped with a little salsa verde.

Spoleto-Style Pork Chops
(UMBRIA)

Preparation time 15 minutes
Cooking time 30 minutes
Wine *Torgiano Rosso*

854

OLIVE PUREE
3 tbsps green olives
dried red chilli pepper flakes
1 garlic clove
1 bunch parsley, destemmed
juice of 1/2 lemon
5 tbsps extra-virgin olive oil

PORK CHOPS
4 pork chops with bone
2 tbsps plain flour
4 tbsps extra-virgin olive oil
2 bay leaves
1 rosemary sprig
3/4 cup (180 ml) white wine
6 tbsps green olives, pitted
dried red chilli pepper flakes
salt and pepper

Puree the olives with a pinch of chilli flakes, garlic, parsley, lemon juice and oil.
Pound the pork chops out with a meat tenderizer. Cut incisions with a sharp knife around the edges and dust with flour on both sides.
Heat the oil in a large frying pan and brown the meat together with bay and rosemary. Pour over the wine and let evaporate slowly over medium heat.
Add the olives, a pinch of chilli flakes and 2 tablespoons of the olive puree, adjust salt and pepper and continue cooking the chops, turning occasionally until cooked through.
Serve hot with the pan juice.

Traditional Vitello Tonnato
(PIEDMONT)

Preparation time 25 minutes
Cooking time 20 minutes
Wine *Gemme*

Serves 6

1 carrot, chopped
1 celery stalk, chopped
1 onion, chopped
1 rosemary sprig
bay leaves
sage
10.5 oz (300 g) top-loin veal
salt and pepper
3 eggs
juice of 1 lemon
extra-virgin olive oil
11.5 oz (320 g) tuna in oil,
  drained
1 tbsp capers
2 anchovies

855

Preheat oven to 400°F (200°C).
Line a baking dish with parchment paper and place the carrot,
celery, onion, rosemary, bay and sage in it, then lay the veal on
top, seasoning lightly with salt and pepper.
Roast for 20 minutes, turning the meat every so often.
Meanwhile, prepare the mayonnaise. Break the eggs in a bowl,
add a pinch of salt and the lemon juice. Whisk vigorously while
pouring in a thin stream of olive oil to make a loose mayonnaise.
Remove the veal from the oven and set aside to cool.
Puree the roast vegetables with the pan juices together with the
tuna, capers and anchovies. Fold into the mayonnaise.
Slice the cooled veal, lay on a serving dish and cover with the tuna
mayonnaise. Serve cold.

Speck ham and Eggplant Involtini

Note *Typical of Trentino-Alto Adige in the northwest of Italy, speck ham is a cured meat similar to prosciutto, but with more flavour as it is cured with many different aromatic herbs and spices and smoked.*

Preparation time 25 minutes
Cooking time 10 minutes
Wine *Alto Adige Pinot Nero*

coarse salt
2 long eggplants, thinly sliced
  lengthwise
1 lb (450 g) beef rump or sirloin,
  sliced
salt and pepper
6 tbsps extra-virgin olive oil
3.5 oz (100 g) speck ham, thinly
  sliced
2 garlic cloves, smashed
3 tbsps extra-virgin olive oil
rosemary

Preheat oven to 375°F (190°C).
Heat a cast-iron grill pan and sprinkle some coarse salt over the surface. Grill the eggplant slices on the very hot surface for a couple of minutes on each side.
Pound the beef slices with a meat tenderizer and trim to make rectangles. Season with salt and pepper and lay 1 eggplant slice on each one. Brush with a little olive oil then lay 1 slice of speck ham on top. Roll up to form involtini.
Arrange the involtini in an oiled baking dish together with the garlic and rosemary. Bake for 10 minutes. Serve immediately.

Turkey Burgers with Eggplant

Preparation time 5 minutes
Cooking time 10 minutes
Wine *Colli Piacentini Gutturnio*

4 turkey burgers
 (3.5 oz or 100 g each)
4 tbsps extra-virgin olive oil
salt and pepper
1 rosemary sprig
sage leaves
4 slices peeled eggplant, ½-inch
 (1 cm) thick
1 medium tomato, peeled
 and diced
3 oz (80 g) cow's milk mozzarella,
 diced

Season the burgers with
oil, salt, pepper, rosemary
and sage.
Grill the eggplant slices on a
hot cast-iron grill pan for 2
minutes on both sides.
Grill the burgers on the grill
pan. Arrange on plates, cover
with an eggplant slice each and
top with tomato and mozzarella.
Serve hot.

Roast Pork with Plums and Port

Preparation time 30 minutes
Cooking time 25 minutes
Wine *Refosco dal Peduncolo Rosso*

1.3 lb (600 g) pork loin
salt and pepper
4 sweet red plums
4 tbsps extra-virgin olive oil
2 bay leaves
1/2 cup (120 ml) Ruby Port wine
1/2 cup (120 ml) water

Preheat oven to 425°F (220°C).
Season the pork with salt and
pepper and tie with kitchen
string like a roast.
Cut the plums into quarters,
remove the pit, then halve the
quarters.
Oil a medium-small baking dish.
Roll the pork loin in the oil then
lay it in the dish with the plums
and bay. Roast for 10 minutes,
then pour over the port.
Continue cooking for 5 minutes,
then pour over the water and
turn the meat. Cook for another
8 minutes, then remove from
the oven, untie and let rest for
5 minutes. Slice and serve with
the plums and pan juices.

Beef and Vegetable Gratin

Preparation time 30 minutes
Cooking time 45 minutes
Wine *Alto Adige Pinot Bianco*
♟ ♟

1/2 cup (3.5 oz or 100 g)
 Superfino rice
salt and pepper
5 tbsps butter
2/3 cup (3.5 oz or 100 g) minced
 onion
1 large leek, thinly sliced
14 oz (400 g) ground beef or veal
1 egg
basil, chopped
1 large zucchini, thinly sliced
2 large tomatoes, thinly sliced
6 tbsps grated Parmesan

858

Preheat oven to 400°F (200°C).
Boil the rice in a saucepan of lightly salted boiling water until
tender, then drain.
Melt 3 tablespoons butter in a frying pan and gently sauté the
onion and leek until soft. Add the ground meat and brown for 1-2
minutes, stirring constantly.
Transfer the meat to a bowl and mix with the cooked rice, egg,
salt, pepper and basil and mix well.
Butter a baking dish and line the bottom with a layer of zucchini
slices. Spread over the meat mixture, then cover with a layer of
overlapping zucchini and tomatoes. Sprinkle with 1 tablespoon of
butter in small pieces, season with salt and pepper and bake for
20 minutes. Top with Parmesan and another tablespoon of butter
and return to the oven for another 20 minutes. Serve.

Roast Beef Salad

Preparation time 10 minutes
Cooking time 20 minutes
Wine *Piemonte Chardonnay*

Serves 6

ROAST BEEF

2 lb (900 g) beef entrecôte
2 rosemary sprigs, minced
4-5 sage leaves, minced
salt and freshly ground pepper
6 tbsps extra-virgin olive oil
2 garlic cloves
3/4 cup (180 ml) white wine

SALAD

4 small carrots
4 oz (120 g) mixed salad leaves
3.5 oz (100 g) arugula
2 celery stalks, thinly sliced
9 oz (250 g) small mozzarella
 balls (bocconcini)
5 tbsps Parmesan shavings

DRESSING

6 tbsps extra-virgin olive oil
juice of 1 lemon
1 tbsp mustard
salt and pepper

Preheat oven to 350°F (180°C).
Tie the beef with kitchen string like a roast and season with
rosemary, sage, salt and freshly ground pepper.
Heat the oil with the garlic and brown the meat for 5 minutes on
all sides. Place in a baking dish and roast for 15 minutes, basting
with the wine halfway through. Remove from the oven and let cool.
Cut the carrots in half lengthwise then slice into half-moons and
boil until al dente. Drain and cool.
Tear the salad leaves and arugula by hand and place in a bowl.
Mix with the carrots, celery, mozzarella and Parmesan.
Mix the dressing ingredients together and use to dress the salad.
Thinly slice the roast beef and arrange on plates next to the salad.
Serve immediately.

Tuscan Rabbit alla Cacciatora

Note *This recipe can be varied by adding a handful of black olives along with the tomatoes.*

Preparation time 35 minutes
Cooking time 1 hour 30 minutes
Wine *Vernaccia di San Gimignano*

1 rabbit
extra-virgin olive oil
2 garlic cloves
rosemary
3/4 cup (200 ml) white wine
1 lb (500 g) tomatoes
salt and pepper

860

Cut the rabbit into pieces, reserving the heart and liver.
Heat a drizzle of olive oil in a large saucepan and sauté the garlic with rosemary leaves until golden-brown. Add the rabbit pieces and brown. Add the white wine and let evaporate.
Blanch the tomatoes in abundant water for a few minutes. Drain, peel, deseed and chop, then add to the rabbit. Season to taste with salt and pepper.
After 45 minutes, add the heart and liver. Continue cooking for another 45 minutes. Adjust the salt and pepper and serve hot with the pan juices.

Friccò
(UMBRIA)

Note *Instead of chicken, this recipe can be made with a mix of veal, duck, rabbit and lamb.*

Preparation time 20 minutes
Cooking time 50 minutes
Wine *Colli Perugini Rosato*

Serves 4-6

6 tbsps extra-virgin olive oil
rosemary
sage
2 garlic cloves
1 chicken (around 2.5 lb
 or 1.2 kg), cut into pieces
salt and pepper
1½ cups (350 ml) white wine
1/2 cup (120 ml) white wine
 vinegar
3 ripe tomatoes, deseeded

861

Heat the olive oil, rosemary, sage and garlic in a Dutch oven or terracotta baking dish. Add the chicken and brown, turning often. Season to taste with salt and pepper. As soon as the meat is evenly browned, add the white wine and vinegar and adjust the salt and pepper. Cover and continue cooking over low heat. When the meat is tender and starts to pull away from the bone, add the tomatoes and continue cooking for another 10 minutes. Serve the chicken with the pan juices. The friccò may be accompanied by potatoes or steamed vegetables, if desired.

Grilled Chicken Salad with Sun-Dried Tomatoes

Preparation time 20 minutes
Cooking time 15 minutes
Wine *Siclia Chardonnay*

1 chicken breast
salt and pepper
1 bunch aromatic herbs
(sage, rosemary, thyme),
destemmed and finely minced
1 head frisée
extra-virgin olive oil
15 sun-dried tomato halves in
oil, drained and chopped
20 lupini beans, cooked
and peeled

862

Cut the chicken breast in half, removing the central bone. Slice the 2 parts horizontally to obtain 4 fillets. Salt and pepper them and dip in the minced herbs.
Grill the chicken on a barbecue or cast-iron grill pan, then cut into strips.
Tear the frisée into pieces and dress with salt, pepper and oil.
Compose plates of salad with the frisée, chicken, sun-dried tomatoes and lupini beans.

Arrosticini Kebabs
(ABRUZZO)

Note *This is a simple but very tasty dish, typical of the southern Italian region of Abruzzo. They are often cooked at village festivals, and served with garlic bruschetta.*

Preparation time 15 minutes
Cooking time 10 minutes
Wine *Montepulciano Cerasuolo*

Serves 6-8

1.5 lb (700 g) mutton
 (or lamb shoulder)
salt

Prepare the barbecue or grill.
Cut the mutton into small, 1/2-inch (1 cm) cubes, then thread the cubes onto wooden skewers.
Cook the skewers on a grill over hot coals for about 10 minutes, turning often so they cook evenly, and taking care not to overcook and dry out the meat.
Once cooked, salt them generously and serve very hot, accompanied, if desired, by slices of grilled bread brushed with olive oil.

865

Chicken Kebabs with Pistachios

Preparation time 15 minutes
Cooking time 5 minutes
Wine *Ribolla Gialla*

2 tomatoes
1 chicken breast, cut into
 bite-sized pieces
1 egg white
salt
3/4 cup (3.5 oz or 100 g)
 pistachios, minced
basil leaves
rosemary, chopped
3 tbsps extra-virgin olive oil
juice of 1/2 lemon

866

Blanch the tomatoes, drain, immerse in ice water, then peel. Cut into quarters, deseed and refrigerate until cold.
Beat the egg white with a little salt. Dip 2/3 of the chicken pieces in the egg white then roll in the minced pistachios. Press down on the coated chicken to make the nuts stick. Thread all the coated chicken pieces on wooden skewers, alternating with the tomato wedges, uncoated chicken pieces and basil leaves. Sprinkle the skewers with chopped rosemary.
Cook the skewers on a barbecue or a cast-iron grill pan for 1 minute on each of the 4 sides. Drizzle with a little oil and lemon juice and serve.

Chicken and Olives al Cartoccio

Preparation time 30 minutes
Cooking time 20 minutes
Wine *Trebbiano di Romagna*

4 chicken breasts
 (5.5 oz or 150 g each)
8 anchovy fillets
10.5 oz (300 g) sun-dried
 tomatoes
3/4 cup (3.5 oz or 100 g) black
 olives
4 rosemary sprigs
1 organic lemon, sliced
salt and pepper
4 tbsps extra-virgin olive oil

Preheat oven to 400°F (200°C).
Cut 2 incisions in the top part of each chicken breast with a sharp
knife, and insert 1 anchovy fillet in each incision.
Lay out 4 sheets of aluminum foil. Divide the sun-dried tomatoes
and olives between each sheet, together with 1 chicken breast,
1 rosemary sprig and 1 lemon slice each. Season with salt and
pepper and drizzle with olive oil. Cover with 4 more sheets and
fold the edges in to form a sealed package.
Lay the packages on a baking sheet and place in the oven. After a
few minutes lower the temperature to 325°F (170°C). Cook for 20
minutes.
To serve, place each package on a plate and open with scissors
or knife. Serve immediately.

868

Chicken Salad with Pesto

Preparation time 15 minutes
Cooking time 30 minutes
Wine *Friuli Collio Pinot Grigio*

5 potatoes
salt and pepper
1 red onion, thinly sliced into
 rings
7 tbsps vinegar
1 tsp sugar
1 chicken breast
2 rosemary sprigs, minced
6 sage leaves, minced
3 lettuce leaves
1 tbsp extra-virgin olive oil
2 tbsps Genoan pesto
 (see p. 1098)

Place the potatoes in cold salted
water and bring to a boil. Cook
until tender.
Place the onion in a bowl, toss
with vinegar and sugar and let sit.
Meanwhile cut the chicken breast
in half and roll in the minced herbs.
Season with salt and pepper.
Grill the chicken on a cast-iron grill
pan until cooked, then slice.
Peel the boiled potatoes and slice.
Plate the salad with the potatoes,
lettuce, chicken and the onion
slices, drained and squeezed out.
Dress with oil, pepper and pesto.

Veal Scallops with Almonds

Preparation time 5 minutes
Cooking time 7 minutes
Wine *Chianti Colli Aretini*

1/4 cup (2 oz or 50 g) almonds
4 slices veal rump
 (3 oz or 80 g each)
salt and pepper
2 tbsps butter
2 tbsps extra-virgin olive oil
2 tbsps plain flour
1/2 cup (120 ml) white wine
8 basil leaves

Toast the almonds in a non-
stick pan, then chop finely.
Thinly pound out the veal slices
with a meat tenderizer and
season with salt and pepper.
Melt the butter and oil in a
frying pan, dust the veal with
flour and sauté for 3 minutes
on each side letting the meat
brown slightly. Pour over the
wine and let reduce, then add
the basil and toasted, chopped
almonds. Cook for 3-4 minutes,
adjust salt and serve with pan
juices.

Roman-Style Straccetti
(LAZIO)

Preparation time 20 minutes
Cooking time 5 minutes
Wine *Orvieto Classico*

14 oz (400 g) milk-fed veal,
 sliced
3 tbsps extra-virgin olive oil
1 garlic clove, peeled
 and sliced
1/4 cup (60 ml) white wine
salt and pepper
20 cherry tomatoes,
 halved
1 bunch arugula, chopped

Cut the meat into irregular strips and set aside.
Heat the oil in a large non-stick frying pan and sauté the garlic until golden-brown. Remove the garlic from the pan and discard. Add the veal strips and raise the heat to the highest setting. Let brown for a few seconds then pour over the white wine. Let the wine evaporate. Season to taste with salt and pepper, add the tomatoes and cook for 1 minute. As soon as the meat is almost cooked through, about 3 minutes, add the chopped arugula and finish cooking. Serve, if desired, with radish slices.

Olivetan-Style Tripe
(SICILY)

Preparation time 20 minutes
Cooking time 50 minutes
Wine *Nerello Mascalese*

870

Serves 6

1 lb (500 g) tomatoes
1 small eggplant (about 10.5 oz
  or 300 g), cut into strips
salt and pepper
extra-virgin olive oil
1 onion, minced
1.75 lb (800 g) pre-cooked tripe,
  cut into strips
3 eggs
3.5 oz (100 g) fresh caciocavallo
  cheese, sliced
5 tbsps grated pecorino
nutmeg, grated
cloves

Preheat oven to 350°F (180°C).
Blanch the tomatoes, peel and pass through a sieve.
Sprinkle the eggplant with salt and leave to drain in a colander for 1
hour. Drain and fry in a little oil. Drain and dry on paper towels.
Heat a drizzle of oil in a frying pan and sauté the onion until golden.
Brown the tripe in the pan for a few minutes then add the tomato
pulp. Adjust salt and pepper and cook for around 15 minutes.
Meanwhile beat the eggs with pinches of salt and pepper in a bowl.
Lightly oil a baking dish and line it with a layer of tripe. Cover with a
layer of eggplant, slices of caciocavallo, a sprinkling of pecorino and
grated nutmeg and a few cloves. Pour over a little of the beaten eggs
and continue with the layers until all the ingredients have been used
up. Bake for about 20 minutes, until the top is golden-brown.
Serve hot, directly from the baking dish.

Spoleto-Style Mixed Kebabs
(UMBRIA)

Preparation time 30 minutes
Cooking time 15 minutes
Wine *Rubesco*

5.5 oz (150 g) chicken breast,
 cubed
3.5 oz (100 g) pork loin, cubed
4 slices pork liver, cubed
8 slices pancetta
4 lamb chops
sage leaves
salt and pepper
rosemary sprigs
juniper berries
white wine
extra-virgin olive oil

Thread the meats onto 4 skewers, alternating cubes of chicken, pork and liver with pancetta slices, lamb chops and sage leaves. Season with salt and pepper.
Place in a container with rosemary and juniper berries and cover with wine. Let marinate for 5-6 hours.
Drain from the marinade and cook the skewers on a grill or in a frying pan over medium heat, turning occasionally. Finish with a drizzle of oil and serve hot.

Roast Beef, Robiola and Eggplant Involtini

Note *Robiola is the name for several different kinds of fresh cheeses made in Lombardy and Piedmont, all small and round. They can be covered with a layer of white mould or by a red bloom, and are made with varying proportions of cow's, goat's and sheep's milk.*

872

Preparation time 15 minutes
Cooking time 10 minutes
Wine *Lagrein Rosato*

1/2 eggplant, sliced
3 tbsps extra-virgin olive oil
salt and pepper
3.5 oz (100 g) robiola cheese
5 tbsps pine nuts, toasted
 and chopped
1 tbsp salted capers, rinsed
 and chopped
celery leaves, minced
12 slices roast beef

Grill the eggplant slices on a very hot grill, on a cast-iron grill pan or under a broiler. Season with 1 tablespoon oil, salt and pepper and set aside.
Beat the robiola into a smooth cream in a bowl, then add the pine nuts, capers, celery leaves and the remaining oil. Season with salt and pepper to taste and stir well.
Lay the roast beef slices out on a work surface. Top with the eggplant slices and spread with the robiola mixture. Roll the beef slices up and cut in half. Arrange on a serving plate and garnish with a crunchy salad, if desired.

Herbed Bresaola with Seasonal Vegetables

Preparation time 15 minutes
Cooking time 5 minutes
Wine *Trebbiano d'Abruzzo*
♟

BRESAOLA
1 medium red bell pepper, diced
1 medium yellow bell pepper, diced
1 medium zucchini, thickly sliced
 into half-moons
2 small carrots, peeled and thickly
 sliced into half-moons
2 spring onions, julienned
1 large celery stalk, thickly sliced
5.5 oz (150 g) bresaola, sliced
mixed aromatic herbs (thyme,
 chives, parsley, oregano), minced

DRESSING
juice of 1/2 lemon
6 tbsps extra-virgin olive oil
1 tbsp mustard seeds
2 tbsps white wine vinegar
salt and pepper

873

Place the vegetables in a saucepan of lightly salted boiling water and boil for 2-3 minutes (they should remain al dente). Drain and cool.
Squeeze the lemon juice in a bowl and add the oil, mustard seeds, vinegar and pinches of salt and pepper. Mix well.
Arrange the bresaola in circles on a serving plate and sprinkle with the minced herbs. Arrange the blanched vegetables in the middle and drizzle over the dressing. Serve.

Lamb Buglione
(TUSCANY)

Preparation time 20 minutes
Cooking time 1 hour 10 minutes
Wine *Bolgheri Sassicaia*

Serves 4-6

4 tbsps extra-virgin olive oil
3 garlic cloves, 2 unpeeled
 and 1 halved
1 rosemary sprig
2.2 lb (1 kg) lamb, cut into large
 pieces
3/4 cup (200 ml) white wine
1.75 lb (800 g) canned, peeled
 tomatoes
dried red chilli pepper flakes
salt and pepper
4 slices stale Tuscan-style bread

874

Heat the olive oil with 2 unpeeled garlic cloves and the rosemary.
Brown the lamb pieces, turning so they colour evenly. Add the
wine and let evaporate. Add the canned tomatoes, 1 ladleful of
warm water (or broth) and chilli flakes. Season to taste with salt
and pepper. Let cook, uncovered, over medium heat for about 1
hour, stirring occasionally.
Near the end of the cooking time, toast the bread in a toaster or
under the broiler. Peel the remaining garlic clove and cut in half.
Rub the toasted bread with the cut side of the garlic clove. Place
the bread on individual serving plates and top with the hot lamb
and its pan juices. Serve immediately.

Fried Citrus Chicken

Preparation time 20 minutes
Cooking time 20 minutes
Wine *Alto Adige Pinot Bianco*

1 large chicken breast
juice of 1 organic lemon
grated zest of 1 organic lime
salt and pepper
sunflower oil
3/4 cup (3.5 oz or 100 g)
 plain flour
2 tbsps rice flour
1/2 tsp baking soda
sparkling water
1 tbsp poppy seeds
lemon leaves

Cut the chicken into small pieces, around 1 inch (2 cm) each, and place in a bowl with the lemon juice, grated lime zest and pepper. Marinate in the refrigerator for 4 hours.
Heat a wok or large frying pan with abundant sunflower oil.
Sift the 2 flours into a bowl with the baking soda. Beating constantly with a fork or a whisk, pour in enough sparkling water to make a smooth and quite fluid batter. Stir in the poppy seeds
Drain the chicken and dry on paper towels. Dip the pieces in the batter, tapping on the side of the bowl to remove any excess. Fry in the hot oil until golden. Drain on paper towels and lightly salt.
Serve hot, garnished with lemon leaves.

Herbed Sea Bass with Vegetable Caponata

Preparation time 15 minutes
Cooking time 15 minutes
Wine *Alto Adige Pinot Bianco*

4 sea bass fillets
 (3.5 oz or 100 g each)
thyme, basil and parsley, finely
 minced
3 tbsps extra-virgin olive oil
1 shallot, diced
1 carrot, peeled and diced
1 celery stalk, diced
1 zucchini, diced
1 tomato, deseeded and diced
salt and pepper

876

Remove any bones from the fish with kitchen tweezers, trim with a sharp knife and cut into diamond shapes.
Mix the minced herbs with 2 tablespoons oil in a bowl.
Add the fish, stir well, cover with plastic wrap and refrigerate for 10 minutes.
Heat a non-stick frying pan with the remaining tablespoon of oil. Add the shallot and sauté, then add the carrot and celery. A few minutes later add the zucchini, and then the tomatoes. Season with salt and pepper. Cook until the vegetables are tender.
Cook the sea bass fillets in a non-stick frying pan with no oil, or in the oven at 400°F (200°C) for 5 minutes. Serve with the vegetable caponata.

Eggplant-Stuffed Squid

Preparation time 15 minutes
Cooking time 30 minutes
Wine *Greco di Tufo*
♟

8 medium squid
extra-virgin olive oil
1 onion, minced
1 eggplant, chopped
salt and pepper
1 handful small prawns,
  chopped
parsley, minced
1 egg
1 tbsp grated Parmesan
breadcrumbs

Wash the squid under running water and remove the bone. Detach and chop the tentacles.

Heat some oil in a frying pan and sauté the onion until soft. Add the eggplant and cook until tender. Season with salt and pepper then puree in a blender or food processor for a few minutes. Return to the frying pan.

Stir the chopped tentacles and prawns into the eggplant puree and cook for about 5 minutes, then remove from the heat. Add the parsley, egg and Parmesan and mix well.

Stuff the squid with the eggplant mixture and close with a toothpick. Place in an oiled baking dish, sprinkle with salt, pepper and breadcrumbs and broil for about 10 minutes. Serve warm.

Mediterranean-Style Grouper

Note *Grouper belong to the sea bass family, and are found in the Atlantic and Gulf of Mexico. The fish has a lean, firm flesh which is very versatile in the kitchen. The skin should always be removed before cooking.*

Preparation time 5 minutes
Cooking time 20 minutes
Wine *Bianco d'Alcamo*

1 tbsp pine nuts
2 garlic cloves
2 tbsps extra-virgin olive oil
1 tbsp salted capers, rinsed
1 tbsp black olives
3 anchovy fillets in oil
4 cups (1 l) water
salt and pepper
basil leaves
1 grouper (1.3 lb or 600 g),
  cleaned and filleted

878

Toast the pine nuts in a non-stick frying pan until golden-brown and crunchy.
Peel the garlic cloves and smash them lightly with the palm of the hand.
In another frying pan, heat the oil and sauté the garlic until golden. Add the capers, olives, anchovies and pine nuts. Stir well and cook for a few minutes, then add the water and bring to a boil. Season with salt and pepper and add the basil.
Cut incisions in the grouper fillets and add to the frying pan. Cook over low heat for 20 minutes, then serve.

Baby Squid with Roast Zucchini

Preparation time 10 minutes
Cooking time 13 minutes
Wine *Malvasia Istriana*

1 large pale green zucchini
3 tbsps extra-virgin olive oil
salt and pepper
9 oz (250 g) baby squid
juice of 1/2 lemon
10 Taggiasca olives, pitted
 minced

Preheat oven to 425°F (220°C).
Cut the zucchini into chunks
and toss with 2 tablespoons oil
and salt and pepper to taste.
Roast in the oven for about 12
minutes.
Meanwhile wash the baby
squid, removing the transparent
skin and bone. Blanch in water
with a little lemon juice for 1
minute, then drain and place in
a bowl.
Mix the olives with the
remaining tablespoon of oil.
Arrange the zucchini on serving
plates and top with the squid.
Drizzle with the olives in oil and
serve.

Red Prawn Carpaccio

Preparation time 15 minutes
Cooking time 10 minutes
Wine *Friuli Collio Tocai Friulano*

6 tbsps extra-virgin olive oil
1 spring onion, minced
4 small zucchini, cubed
8 red prawns, shelled and
 deveined
1 tbsp mild paprika
juice of 1/2 lemon
1 piece ginger, grated
salt and pepper

879

Heat 1 tablespoon oil and
sauté the spring onion until
soft. Add the zucchini and cook
briefly, then add 2 tablespoons
water. Continue cooking for 10
minutes over medium heat.
Lay the prawns on a lightly
oiled sheet of plastic wrap.
Beat them out gently with a
meat tenderize. Sprinkle with
paprika.
Mix the lemon juice, ginger,
salt and pepper and whisk in 4
tablespoons oil to emulsify.
Serve the prawns over the
zucchini, drizzled with the
lemon-ginger dressing.

Sardinian-Style Lobster

Preparation time 20 minutes
Cooking time 20 minutes
Wine *Nasco di Cagliari*

2 lobsters
salt and pepper
extra-virgin olive oil
vinegar
juice of 1 lemon

880

Tie the lobsters with kitchen string so the tail is folded in towards
the head. Boil them in abundant salted water for about
20 minutes. Drain and let cool.
Cut off the lobster tails and remove the meat, taking care not to
break it. Slice the tails into 1/2-inch (1 cm) thick slices and arrange
on a serving plate.
Remove all the meat remaining in the heads and the body cavity
and puree it with any roe in a food processor with a drizzle of oil,
a few drops of vinegar and lemon juice and pinches of salt and
pepper. Add as much oil and lemon juice as necessary to make a
smooth sauce.
Drizzle the lobster tail meat with the sauce. Garnish with lettuce
leaves, if desired, and the lobster claws.

Mediterranean Breaded Oysters

Preparation time 25 minutes
Cooking time 15 minutes
Wine *Metodo Trento Talento Extra Brut*

1 garlic clove
5 tbsps extra-virgin olive oil
1 anchovy fillet in oil, drained
10 Pantelleria capers, rinsed
 and minced
2 organic lemon leaves or grated
 lemon zest
7 tbsps breadcrumbs
parsley, minced
salt and white pepper
4-5 cherry tomatoes, diced
12 large oysters

Preheat oven to 425°F (220°C).
Peel and halve the garlic, removing the internal shoot.
Heat the oil in a frying pan and sauté the garlic and anchovy until the garlic is golden and the anchovy disintegrates. Remove the garlic and add the capers. Add the lemon leaves or zest, sauté briefly, then add the breadcrumbs, parsley, salt and pepper, sauté until toasted then set aside to cool.
Dry the diced tomatoes on paper towels and mix into the breadcrumb mixture. Remove the lemon leaves.
Shuck the oysters with an oyster knife or a teardrop-shaped Parmesan knife. Roll each oyster in the flavoured breadcrumbs then lay on a baking sheet. Bake for 4 minutes then serve.

Tea-Steamed Lobster with Eggplant Puree and Crispy Prosciutto

Preparation time 15 minutes
Cooking time 20 minutes
Wine *Cirò Rosato*

salt and pepper
1 eggplant, sliced
3 tbsps extra-virgin olive oil
1/2 onion, minced
2 small lobsters
1 tbsp green tea
3 oz (80 g) prosciutto, diced

882

Generously salt the eggplant slices, then place in a colander with a weight on top so they give off their liquid. Leave for 30 minutes. Rinse the eggplant and pat dry with a clean kitchen towel.
Heat the oil in a saucepan and sauté the onion gently until soft. Add the eggplant slices and cook, covered, for 7-8 minutes, stirring frequently. As soon as they are cooked, puree into a smooth cream and adjust salt and pepper.
Steam the lobsters over 2½ cups (600 ml) water with the tea. As soon as they are cooked through remove from the heat and let cool. Break the shell to extract the meat. Chop the meat.
Brown the prosciutto in a non-stick frying pan until crunchy.
Divide the eggplant puree between serving plates and top with the lobster meat. Sprinkle with prosciutto and serve.

Ancona-Style Sardines
(Marche)

Preparation time 30 minutes
Cooking time 40 minutes
Wine *Verdicchio di Matelica*

extra-virgin olive oil
salt and pepper
1 onion, minced
7 tbsps white wine
4 large tomatoes, finely
 chopped
2.2 lb (1 kg) sardines
3 tbsps breadcrumbs
parsley, minced

Heat a little olive oil in a frying pan and sauté the onion until soft.
Add the white wine and let reduce. Add the tomatoes and cook
until thickened, around 30 minutes. Season with salt and pepper
to taste.
Preheat oven to 350°F (180°C).
Meanwhile clean the sardines, gut them and open like a book. Dry
well with paper towels and lay on a lightly oiled baking dish. Spoon
over the tomato sauce, sprinkle with breadcrumbs and parsley,
drizzle with oil and bake for around 10 minutes, until golden-brown
on top. Serve immediately.

Lobster Catalana

Preparation time 20 minutes
Cooking time 25 minutes
Wine *Metodo Classico
Franciacorta Extra Brut*
♟ ♟

1 lb (500 g) coarse salt
thyme and marjoram, minced
2 medium lobsters
2 celery stalks, sliced
1 fennel bulb, sliced
1 shallot, sliced
2 carrots, sliced
1 bunch radishes, sliced
salt
1 tbsp balsamic vinegar
4 tbsps extra-virgin olive oil

Preheat oven to 400°F (200°C).
Mix together the coarse salt,
thyme and marjoram. Place the
lobsters in a baking dish and
cover with the herb salt. Bake
for 20-25 minutes.
Shell the lobsters and extract
the meat from the tail and
claws. Slice the meat and
arrange on a platter with the
sliced, raw vegetables.
Dissolve a little salt in the
vinegar and whisk in the oil to
emulsify. Drizzle the dressing
over the lobster and vegetables
and serve.

Chardonnay Prawns

Preparation time 10 minutes
Cooking time 10 minutes
Wine *Friuli Collio Chardonnay*
♟

12 jumbo prawns
2 tbsps extra-virgin olive oil
1²/₃ cups (7 oz or 200 g) diced
 celery, carrot and shallot
parsley, minced
1/2 cup (120 ml) Chardonnay wine
salt

Shell the prawns, reserving
heads and shells.
Heat the olive oil in a large
saucepan and brown the
prawns heads and shells, then
add the diced celery, carrot
and shallot. Cover with cold
water and bring to a boil.
Add the minced parsley and
cook down to 1/2 the original
volume. Strain the mixture,
pushing down with the back
of a spoon to extract all of the
liquid. Return the broth to the
stove, bring to a boil and add
the wine. Add the prawns and
adjust the salt. Let cook for
4 minutes, then serve.

884

Grilled Cuttlefish with Green Tomatoes

Preparation time 20 minutes
Cooking time 15 minutes
Wine *Montecarlo Bianco*

6 tbsps extra-virgin olive oil
1 garlic clove, minced
1 red chilli pepper, minced
7 oz (200 g) broccoli rabe
 or turnip tops
juice and grated zest
 of 1/2 organic lemon
salt and pepper
8 fresh, medium sizod cuttlefish
4 green tomatoes, sliced
5 tbsps breadcrumbs

Heat 3 tablespoons the oil in a frying pan and sauté the garlic and chilli. Add the broccoli rabe and sauté, then pour over 1 ladleful of hot water and continue cooking, covered, until tender.
Meanwhile mix the remaining oil with lemon juice and zest, salt and pepper.
Clean and gut the cuttlefish and slice along their backs. Place in the oil mixture for 5 minutes, then drain.
Season the tomato slices with salt and dip in breadcrumbs.
Grill the cuttlefish and tomatoes on a barbecue or cast-iron grill pan.
Stuff the cuttlefish with the broccoli rabe and serve.

885

Grilled Calamari on Arugula

Preparation time 20 minutes
Cooking time 5 minutes
Wine *Greco di Tufo*
♟

4 tomatoes
1 celery stalk, diced
3 tbsps salted capers, rinsed
juice of 1 lemon
salt and pepper
6 tbsps extra-virgin olive oil
8 medium squid
2 bunches arugula
ground chilli pepper

886

Blanch the tomatoes, peel, deseed and dice. Mix in a bowl with the celery, capers, lemon juice and salt, and cover with olive oil. Clean the squid and open so they form a kind of square. Remove the bladder, eyes and teeth from the tentacles, and rinse.
Using a sharp knife, make a series of diagonal incisions 1/2 inch (1 cm) apart across the inside of the squid, going first one way and then the other, so that it is covered in a diamond pattern.
Season the squid with salt and pepper and cook in a very hot cast-iron grill pan or non-stick frying pan for 4-5 minutes. They are cooked when they start to roll up.
Tear the arugula by hand and divide between serving plates. Top with the squid and drizzle over the tomato mixture. Sprinkle with ground chilli pepper and serve.

Sole Fillets with Mint

Preparation time 30 minutes
Cooking time 20 minutes
Wine *Sicilia Chardonnay*

4 sole fillets (8 oz or 220 g each)
2 tbsps plain flour
2 tbsps extra-virgin olive oil
1 garlic clove, peeled
salt and pepper
zest of 1/2 organic lemon,
 cut into matchsticks
juice of 1 lemon
1/2 cup (120 ml) white wine
2⅔ cups (14 oz or 400 g)
 cherry tomatoes, quartered
10 mint leaves, 6 chopped
 and 4 whole

887

Remove the skin from the sole fillets and slice them into long, thin strips. Braid the strips and fix them with a toothpick at either end. Cover with plastic wrap and refrigerate for 10 minutes.
Dust the sole with flour. Heat the oil and garlic in a frying pan and brown the sole. Season with salt and pepper and add the lemon zest, lemon juice and white wine. Let reduce, then remove the sole from the frying pan and set aside. Add the tomatoes to the frying pan with the chopped mint, stir, adjust salt and pepper and cook for 2-3 minutes.
Arrange the sole on serving plates and top with the tomato sauce. Garnish each plate with a mint leaf and serve.

Langoustines in Tomato-Brandy Sauce (Veneto)

Note *This is an ancient Venetian dish of Dalmatian origin, though the tomatoes are a fairly recent addition. It is called scampi alla bùsara.*

Preparation time 20 minutes
Cooking time 10 minutes
Wine *Lison-Pramaggiore Pinot Bianco Spumante*

888

16 langoustines
extra-virgin olive oil
1 onion, minced
1 garlic clove, minced
3 tbsps brandy
2 tomatoes, peeled and sliced
7 tbsps white wine
salt and pepper
3 tbsps butter
1 tbsp plain flour
parsley, minced

Make an incision along the back of the langoustines.
Heat a little oil in a saucepan and sauté the onion and garlic. Add the langoustines and brown for a few minutes. Add the brandy and flame it to cook off the alcohol. Add the tomatoes, wine, salt and pepper and cook for a few minutes.
Remove the langoustines from the pan and arrange on a serving plate. Keep warm.
Mix the butter and flour and whisk into the tomato mixture.
Cook until thickened, then pour the sauce over the langoustines.
Sprinkle with parsley and serve, accompanied by soft or grilled polenta if desired.

Buridda
(Liguria)

889

Note *Different kinds of fish can be used for this recipe, particularly salt cod (in which case take care not to add too much extra salt) or conger eel.*

Preparation time 15 minutes
Cooking time 30 minutes
Wine *Colli di Luni Vermentino*

Serves 6

6 tbsps extra-virgin olive oil
1 garlic clove
1 onion, minced
3 tomatoes, sliced
2 anchovies in oil, drained
parsley, minced
3/4 cup (180 ml) white wine
3.3 lb (1.5 kg) monkfish,
 cut into pieces
1 bay leaf
salt
crusty bread

Heat the olive oil in a large saucepan and sauté the garlic and onion until they begin to soften. Remove the garlic and discard. Add the sliced tomatoes, anchovies and minced parsley. Add the white wine and let reduce slightly, then add the monkfish, and bay leaf and season with a pinch of salt. Cook, uncovered, over low heat for 20 minutes.
Meanwhile, slice the crusty bread and toast under the broiler until golden-brown.
Serve the buridda accompanied by toasted crusty bread.

Hake Fillets with Sun-Dried Tomato Pesto

Preparation time 10 minutes
Cooking time 12 minutes
Wine *Malvasia Istriana*

PESTO
1¼ cups (7 oz or 200 g) cherry
  tomatoes, quartered
3.5 oz (100 g) sun-dried
  tomatoes in oil, sliced
2 tbsps pesto
2 tbsps balsamic vinegar
2 tbsps extra-virgin olive oil
salt and pepper

HAKE
8 small hake fillets
salt
2/3 cup (150 ml) white wine
2 tbsps extra-virgin olive oil
1 bunch parsley, chopped
1 dill sprig, chopped
1 thyme sprig, chopped
2 garlic cloves, sliced

GARNISH
fresh dill

890

Preheat oven to 350°F (180°C).
Mix the cherry tomatoes, sun-dried tomatoes, pesto, balsamic vinegar and oil in a bowl. Season with salt and pepper and set aside.
Lay the hake fillets in a baking dish. Lightly salt and drizzle with the white wine and 2 tablespoons olive oil. Sprinkle with the herbs and garlic, and bake for 12-15 minutes.
Remove from the oven, arrange the fish on plates and strain the cooking juices directly into the tomato mixture. Stir, then pour over the fish. Garnish with dill and serve immediately.

Red Mullet, Potato, Arugula and Black Olive Terrine

Preparation time 20 minutes
Cooking time 25 minutes
Wine *Etna Bianco*
♟ ♟

10 cherry tomatoes
1 garlic clove, sliced
2 tbsps extra-virgin olive oil
3 large yellow-fleshed potatoes,
 peeled and very thinly sliced
salt
8 red mullet, filleted
 and deboned
15 pitted black olives in oil,
 drained and finely chopped
1 bunch arugula, chopped

Preheat oven to 400°F (200°C).
Place the tomatoes in a baking dish with the garlic and oil and roast for 25 minutes to concentrate the flavour but without letting them disintegrating. Remove from the oven, drain and smash to make a sauce.
Line a terrine mold with plastic wrap and alternate layers of potato slices, a little salt, mullet fillets, olives and a little arugula until all the ingredients have been used up. Press down well and close with more plastic wrap.
Steam for 22-25 minutes. Unmold and serve sliced into 4 portions, accompanied by the tomato sauce.

Warm Squid and Tomato Salad

Preparation time 15 minutes
Cooking time 7 minutes
Wine *Tocai Friulano*

14 oz (400 g) fresh,
 medium-sized squid
1 red tomato
4 tbsps mild extra-virgin olive oil
1 spring onion, chopped
1 bunch parsley, minced
1 bunch basil, minced
1 lemon thyme sprig, minced
salt and pepper

892

Wash the squid and peel off
the skin and remove the central
bone and ink sac. Rinse and
cut the squid into rings.
Blanch the tomato, immerse in
cold water then peel, deseed
and dice. Place in a bowl and
add the oil, spring onion, herbs,
salt and pepper. Let sit for 10
minutes.
Steam the squid for 7 minutes,
then immediately dress it with
the tomato dressing.

Neapolitan-Style Sea Bream

Preparation time 25 minutes
Cooking time 30 minutes
Wine *Greco di Tufo*

4 cups (1 l) water
1 tomato, chopped
1 garlic clove
1 tsp oregano
salt and pepper
1⅓ lb (600 g) sea bream,
 cleaned, washed and descaled
2 tbsps extra-virgin olive oil

Preheat oven to 375°F (190°C).
Place the water, tomato, garlic,
oregano and a pinch of salt in
a large, oven-proof frying pan
and bring to a boil over medium
heat. Add the sea bream and
transfer to the oven for 25
minutes.
Fillet the fish and serve with
the tomato drained from the
cooking water. Season with salt
and pepper and drizzle with
olive oil.

Mussel and Prawn Sauté

Preparation time 15 minutes
Cooking time 5 minutes
Wine *Alto Adige Pinot Bianco*
♟

7 oz (200 g) clams
9 oz (250 g) Spanish mussels
16 medium prawns
3 tbsps extra-virgin olive oil
1 garlic clove, minced
1 red chilli pepper, minced
10 cherry tomatoes, halved
parsley, minced
4 slices crusty bread

Soak the clams in a bowl of salted water for 30 minutes. Wash the mussels, removing any external fibers. Shell the prawns, leaving the final part of the tail.
Heat the oil in a frying pan and sauté the garlic and chilli. Add the clams, then after a short time the mussels. Cover and cook for 2 minutes. Add the tomatoes and prawns, sprinkle with parsley, and cook for another 3 minutes.
Serve the prawns and mussels over slices of toasted bread, drizzled with the pan juices.

Swordfish Carpaccio

Preparation time 10 minutes
Cooking time 10 minutes
Wine *Riviera Ligure di Ponente Pigato*
♟

10 basil leaves
10 mint leaves
2-3 marjoram sprigs
1/2 cup (120 ml) extra-virgin olive oil
juice of 2 lemons
salt and pepper
14 oz (400 g) swordfish, very thinly sliced
1 small baguette, sliced

893

Preheat oven to 400°F (200°C). Puree the basil, mint, marjoram, oil, lemon juice, a large pinch of salt and a little pepper in a food processor or blender to obtain a thick, smooth sauce.
Lay the swordfish on a serving plate and pour over the sauce. Let marinate for about 15 minutes.
Meanwhile, toast the baguette slices in the oven until golden. Serve the carpaccio with the toasted bread.

Warm Cuttlefish Salad with Wild Arugula

Note *Cuttlefish are very similar to squid but have a shorter and more stocky body. They also have a sac of black ink, used in nature as a defensive tool, which can be cooked in sauces, pastas and risottos.*

Preparation time 10 minutes
Cooking time 15 minutes
Wine *Colli di Luni Bianco*

8 oz (220 g) fresh, small cuttlefish
salt and pepper
2 bunches wild arugula
juice of 1 lemon
6 tbsps extra-virgin olive oil
15 cherry tomatoes, quartered

894

Bring a large pot of salted water to a boil and add the cuttlefish. Cook for about 15 minutes and then drain and thinly slice.
Soak the arugula in a bowl of ice water to crisp it.
Squeeze the lemon juice into a bowl, mix in pinches of salt and pepper, then whisk in the oil in a thin stream to emulsify.
Drain the arugula and spin in a salad spinner. Wrap in a clean kitchen towel to dry completely.
Arrange the arugula on serving plates, top with cuttlefish rings and cherry tomatoes and adjust the salt and pepper. Drizzle with the lemon dressing. Serve immediately.

Zucchini-Wrapped Sea Bream with Lemon Sauce

Preparation time 20 minutes
Cooking time 10 minutes
Wine *Gambellara*

4 sea bream fillets
 (4 oz or 110 g each)
salt and pepper
2 small young, firm zucchini,
 thinly sliced
5 tbsps extra-virgin olive oil
2 garlic cloves, unpeeled
 and halved
1 bay leaf
5 peppercorns
juice of 1 lemon
sugar
2 tbsps heavy cream

895

Preheat oven to 375°F (190°C).
Wash the sea bream fillets and remove any bones with kitchen tweezers. Lightly season with salt and pepper. Wrap each fillet with the zucchini slices, overlapping slightly. Drizzle with 2 tablespoons oil and place on a wax paper-lined baking dish.
Heat the remaining 3 tablespoons oil in a small saucepan with the garlic, bay leaf and peppercorns. Squeeze in the lemon juice, season with salt and a pinch of sugar and let cook down until reduced. Strain and let cool.
As soon as the lemon mixture is cooled, beat it with the cream with an immersion blender or a small whisk.
Bake the fish for 10 minutes and serve with the lemon sauce.

Fish in Carpione
(LOMBARDY)

Note *This recipe from Lake Como can be served as a main course or an appetizer.*

Preparation time 15 minutes
Cooking time 40 minutes
Wine *Oltrepò Pavese Chardonnay*

Serves 6

2.2 lb (1 kg) freshwater fish
   (such as bleak and shad)
3 tbsps plain flour
8 tbsps extra-virgin olive oil
salt and pepper
1 garlic clove
1 onion, minced
1 carrot, minced
1/2 celery stalk, minced
parsley, minced
2 cloves
thyme
2 bay leaves
3/4 cup (180 ml) vinegar
3/4 cup (180 ml) white wine

896

Clean and gut the fish and wash and dry. Flour on both sides and fry them in 6 tablespoons of hot olive oil in a large frying pan, turning and cooking on all sides until a golden crust is formed. Drain, salt and dry on paper towels.
In a separate frying pan heat 2 tablespoons oil and sauté the garlic until golden. Add the onion, carrot, celery, parsley, a pinch of pepper, cloves, thyme and bay and cook until the vegetables are golden, then add the vinegar and wine and bring to a boil.
Arrange the fish in a large container. Pour over the boiling hot marinade. Let cool and leave to marinate for a day. Serve cold.

Piedmontese Salt Cod

Preparation time 15 minutes
Cooking time 20 minutes
Wine *Grignolino d'Asti*

Serves 6

1.75 lb (800 g) salt cod, desalted
milk
plain flour
4 tbsps extra-virgin olive oil
1 knob of butter
2-3 anchovies
1 garlic clove, minced
vegetable broth
parsley, minced
juice of 1 lemon

Soak the salt cod in milk for 2 days, keeping it covered and refrigerated.
Drain well and chop into large pieces. Dust with flour and set aside.
Heat the oil and butter in a non-stick frying pan. Add the anchovies and garlic. Sauté then add the salt cod pieces and brown. Add a little vegetable broth if needed. Let cook slowly for 15 minutes. Serve the salt cod with its cooking liquid, minced parsley and a squeeze of lemon juice.

Brustico
(UMBRIA)

Preparation time 10 minutes
Cooking time 30 minutes
Wine *Orvieto Classico*

4 pike
4 tbsps extra-virgin olive oil
salt and pepper

Grill the whole pike over charcoals, cooking on both sides until a crust forms and the fish is cooked through. Remove from the heat, scrape off the scales and remove the guts. Cut fillets and arrange on a serving dish. Serve warm, drizzled with olive oil and seasoned with salt and pepper.

Note *This dish, part Tuscan and part Umbrian, originates from an ancient, perhaps Etruscan, recipe based on perch. There are few ingredients so it is crucial that they be of the highest quality.*

Sicilian Swordfish

Preparation time 25 minutes
Cooking time 25 minutes
Wine *Friuli-Aquileia Verduzzo*

5 tbsps minced onion
2 garlic cloves, minced
6 tbsps extra-virgin olive oil
5 tbsps minced parsley
4 basil leaves, minced
3 oregano sprigs, minced
4 slices swordfish
 (around 1.5 lb or 700 g)
grated zest of 5 organic lemons
6 round tomatoes
salt and pepper

898

Preheat oven to 350°F (180°C).
Mix together the onion and garlic. Spread a spoonful of the mixture over the bottom of a baking dish, then drizzle over 2 tablespoons of olive oil.
Mix the parsley, oregano and basil with the rest of the garlic and onion mixture.
Remove the skin from the swordfish and arrange the slices on a plate. Sprinkle the fish with some of the grated lemon zest on both sides.
Arrange the swordfish in the baking dish and sprinkle over some of the herb mixture.
Blanch the tomatoes in boiling water, peel and dice. Sprinkle over the swordfish together with the rest of the grated lemon zest and the herb mixture. Season with salt and pepper and drizzle over the rest of the oil. Bake for 25 minutes. Remove from the oven and serve.

Tuna Loaf with Tuna Sauce

Preparation time 15 minutes
Cooking time 40 minutes
Wine *Bianco d'Alcamo*

TUNA LOAF
10.5 oz (300 g) tuna in oil,
 drained
3 eggs
3 tbsps grated Parmesan
3 tbsps breadcrumbs
3 tbsps extra-virgin olive oil
2 cups (500 ml) milk
1 garlic clove
2 bay leaves

SAUCE
2 eggs
3.5 oz (100 g) tuna in oil, drained

Finely chop the tuna for the loaf and mix with the 3 eggs,
Parmesan and breadcrumbs to form a smooth mixture. With damp
hands, form into a meatloaf shape. Wrap in gauze and twist and
close at both ends with kitchen string.
Place the oil in a saucepan, add the loaf and cover with the milk.
Add the garlic and bay. Cook, covered, for 40 minutes, until the
milk has reduced. Remove the loaf from the pan and let cool.
Remove the bay and garlic from the saucepan. Add the 2 eggs
and tuna and stir vigorously over very low heat until the sauce
comes together. Beat with an immersion blender to form a
smooth, creamy sauce.
Unwrap the loaf and slice.
Serve the slices with the sauce, and capers, extra-virgin olive oil
and a few drops of lemon juice, if desired.

Baby Squid with Zucchini Velouté

Preparation time 20 minutes
Cooking time 20 minutes
Wine *Malvasia Istriana*
🍳

4 tbsps extra-virgin olive oil
1 shallot, minced
1 yellow-fleshed potato, peeled
 and thinly sliced
2 zucchini, thickly sliced
2 cups (500 ml) hot vegetable
 broth
salt and pepper
10.5 oz (300 g) fresh baby squid
4 basil leaves
grated zest of 1 organic lemon

900

Heat 3 tablespoons oil in a saucepan and sauté the shallot gently until soft. Add the potato and zucchini slices and brown for 2 minutes. Cover with hot broth, season with salt and pepper and let cook, covered, until the potatoes are al dente.
Meanwhile peel the baby squid under running water and gut them, also removing the central bone. Cut into rings and steam in a steaming basket for about 10 minutes.
As soon as the vegetables are done remove from the heat. Add the basil and lemon zest and puree in a food processor or blender until smooth. Divide between shallow soup bowls and top with the warm squid. Drizzle with a little oil and serve.

Fried Umbrine Parcels with Spicy Tomatoes

Preparation time 25 minutes
Cooking time 10 minutes
Wine *Metodo Classico*
Franciacorta Rosé

14 oz (400 g) umbrine or sea
 bass fillet
8 basil leaves
salt and pepper
4 sheets phyllo dough
2 tomatoes, chopped
2 tbsps extra-virgin olive oil
1 dried red chilli pepper
sunflower oil

Cut the umbrine into 4 pieces and slice each one in half
horizontally. Place 1 basil leaf on each piece of fish, season with
salt and pepper and roll up the fillets.
Cut the phyllo dough into rectangles and wrap up the fillets,
sealing the edges well.
Drain any excess liquid from the tomatoes. Heat the olive oil with
the crumbled chilli and add the tomatoes. Heat through then
transfer to a bowl and let sit.
Heat the sunflower oil and fry the parcels. Drain and serve with the
tomatoes.

901

Mediterranean Mackerel Salad

Preparation time 15 minutes
Wine *Trentino Nosiola*

1 small head lettuce
1 large cucumber
3 salad tomatoes
4 mackerel fillets in oil, drained
4 tbsps black Gaeta olives
 in brine, drained and rinsed
extra-virgin olive oil
sesame oil
salt

902

Shred the lettuce and set aside.
Peel the cucumber and thinly
slice both the cucumber and
tomatoes.
Arrange the lettuce, cucumber
and tomatoes between 4 small
serving plates and top with the
crumbled mackerel fillets and
black olives. Drizzle with olive
oil, sesame oil and salt. Serve
with toasted crusty bread if
desired.

Herbed Turbot Fillets

Preparation time 10 minutes
Cooking time 10 minutes
Wine *Bianco di Custoza*

6 tbsps breadcrumbs
mixed aromatic herbs
 (thyme, parsley, rosemary),
 finely minced
salt and pepper
extra-virgin olive oil
8 turbot fillets

Preheat oven to 400°F (200°C).
Mix the breadcrumbs, herbs,
salt and pepper.
Lightly oil the fillets then
dip them in the herbed
breadcrumbs. Arrange on a
parchment paper-lined baking
sheet and bake for 10 minutes.
Serve hot, accompanied by a
mixed salad, if desired.

Note *The turbot can be
replaced by fillets of hake or sea
bream.*

Zucchini-Stuffed Cuttlefish

Preparation time 20 minutes
Cooking time 30 minutes
Wine *Vermentino della Riviera Ligure di Ponente*
♟ ♟

2 tbsps extra-virgin olive oil
1 garlic clove
5 zucchini, sliced
15 hazelnuts
2 slices sandwich bread
1/2 cup (120 ml) milk
5 basil leaves
salt and pepper
8 medium cuttlefish

Preheat oven to 375°F (190°C).
Heat the oil in a frying pan and
sauté the garlic until golden.
Remove the garlic and add the
zucchini. Sauté briefly then add
the hazelnuts and 2 tablespoons
water. Cook for 10 minutes.
Soak the bread in the milk,
squeeze out and transfer the
bread to a food processor
with the basil and the cooked
zucchini. Puree and adjust the
salt and pepper.
Clean the cuttlefish, removing
the head and fins. Stuff with the
zucchini mixture and arrange
in a baking dish. Bake for 20
minutes.

Breaded Cuttlefish with Herbs

Preparation time 15 minutes
Cooking time 10 minutes
Wine *Malvasia Istriana*
♟

14 oz (400 g) medium-small
 cuttlefish
mixed lettuce leaves
1¼ cups (5.5 oz or 150 g)
 breadcrumbs
1 bunch aromatic herbs
 (thyme, parsley, tarragon), minced
4 tbsps extra-virgin olive oil
salt and pepper
juice of 1 lemon

Preheat oven to 375°F (190°C).
Wash the cuttlefish and clean
well. Cut into medium-sized
pieces and set aside.
Tear the lettuce by hand and
divide between serving plates.
Mix the breadcrumbs with the
minced herbs and 1/2 the oil.
Season with salt and pepper
and mix by hand.
Thread the cuttlefish onto
skewers and dip them in the
breadcrumb mixture.
Press well to adhere.
Bake for 8-10 minutes
and serve over the salad,
sprinkled with lemon juice
and the remaining oil.

Sardines in Saor
(VENETO)

Preparation time 30 minutes
Cooking time 15 minutes

14 oz (400 g) large sardines
2/3 cup (3 oz or 80 g)
  plain flour
1½ cups (360 ml) sunflower oil
1.75 lb (800 g) onions, thinly
  sliced
3/4 cup plus 1 tbsp (200 ml)
  white wine vinegar
1/3 cup (80 ml) white wine
5 tbsps raisins
5 tbsps pine nuts

904

Descale the sardines, remove the head and wash well under running water. Lightly dust with flour. Heat the sunflower oil until very hot and fry the sardines until almost cooked, about 5 minutes. Remove from the pan, leaving the oil, and set aside.
Pour off most of the sunflower oil. Use the remaining part to sauté the onions until soft. Add the vinegar and wine and reduce. Add the raisins and pine nuts and stir well.
Arrange a layer of fried sardines in a container and top with the still-hot onion mixture, so that the fish continues cooking. Continue forming more layers of sardines and onions, until the ingredients are used up. Cover with plastic wrap and let marinate in a cool place for 2 days before serving.

Prawns alla Rossini
(MARCHE)

Preparation time 20 minutes
Cooking time 20 minutes
Wine *Bianchello del Metauro*

Serves 6

2 cups (500 ml) white wine
1/2 carrot
1 celery stalk
1/2 onion
3.3 lb river prawns, shelled
7 tbsps extra-virgin olive oil
10.5 oz (350 g) new chicory
juice of 1 lemon
salt and pepper

Heat the wine with a little water, the whole carrot, celery and
onion. Bring to a boil and add the shelled prawns. Boil until
cooked through and then drain. Set the prawns aside
Arrange a layer of chicory in an oiled saucepan. Top with a layer
of prawns and continue layering chicory and prawns until the
ingredients are finished. Cover and cook over medium heat until
the chicory is wilted.
Meanwhile, whisk together 6 tablespoons oil, the lemon juice and
pinches of salt and pepper to make a dressing.
Divide the prawns and chicory between 6 serving plates
and drizzled with the dressing. Serve immediately.

White Bream with Marinated Peppers and Eggplant

Note *There are several different sizes of white bream available. It is best on the grill, baked, or, as in this recipe, pan-fried.*

Preparation time 20 minutes
Cooking time 15 minutes
Wine *Torbato di Alghero*

VEGETABLES
1 eggplant
salt and pepper
1 red bell pepper
oregano
4 tbsps extra-virgin olive oil

BREAM
4 white bream fillets
 (4.5 oz or 130 g each)
pepper
2 tbsps extra-virgin olive oil
2 garlic cloves, smashed

GARNISH
arugula
extra-virgin olive oil
salt

906

Halve the eggplant lengthwise then cut into 1/2-inch
(1 cm) thick slices. Grill and season with salt.
Roast the pepper, close in a plastic bag to steam, then peel,
deseed and cut into strips. Add to the eggplant, sprinkle with
pepper and oregano, drizzle with olive oil and let sit to marinate.
Remove any bones from the white bream and wash the fillets.
Season with pepper. Heat the 2 tablespoons oil in a frying pan
with the garlic, then sauté the fish.
Dress the arugula with oil and salt.
Serve the fish over the arugula with the marinated eggplant
and peppers, drained of any excess oil.

Swordfish Steak al Cartoccio

Preparation time 15 minutes
Cooking time 12 minutes
Wine *Falanghina del Sannio*

1¼ cups (6.5 oz or 180 g) diced
 red, yellow and green bell
 peppers
2 small carrots, diced
1 small zucchini, diced
1 cup (3.5 oz or 100 g) green
 beans, chopped
1 leek, diced
salt and pepper
4 swordfish steaks (1.3 lb
 or 600 g), skin removed
1/2 organic lemon, sliced
4 basil leaves
4 tbsps extra-virgin olive oil

Preheat oven to 350°F (180°C).
Blanch the vegetables in boiling
salted water for 3 minutes. Drain,
cool in cold water, and dry.
Sprinkle the swordfish with salt
and pepper.
Divide the vegetables between
4 sheets of aluminum foil and
top with 1 swordfish steak, 1
lemon slice, 1 basil leaf and 1
tablespoon oil each. Season with
salt and pepper. Fold the edges
of the foil in to form a package.
Lay on a baking sheet and bake
for 12 minutes.

Herb-Marinated Tuna

Preparation time 20 minutes
Cooking time 10 minutes
Wine *Sicilia Chardonnay*

salt and pepper
juice of 1 lemon
14 oz (400 g) fresh tuna fillet,
 sliced
5 tbsps extra-virgin olive oil
1 shallot, minced
1 garlic clove, sliced
1 tsp peppercorns
rosemary and minced thyme,
 minced

Bring a saucepan of salted
water to a boil, acidulated with
the lemon juice. Steam the tuna
slices in a steaming basket
covered in plastic wrap over the
water for around 10 minutes.
Heat the oil and gently sauté
the shallot.
Add the peppercorns and
herbs. Let sit for a few minutes
to meld the flavours.
Arrange the tuna in a container
and pour over the herb mixture.
Let marinate for 6 hours in the
refrigerator, covered with plastic
wrap, before serving.

Tiger Prawn Carpaccio with Olives and Caperberries

Note *Caperberries are the fruit of the caper shrub, while capers are the unopened buds of the same plant.*

Preparation time 10 minutes
Cooking time 4 minutes
Wine *Vermentino di Gallura*

CARPACCIO
2 vine-ripened tomatoes
5 tbsps black olives, pitted
 and chopped
5 tbsps caperberries
1 bunch wild arugula, chopped
1 lb (450 g) tiger prawns, shelled
2 tbsps extra-virgin olive oil
salt

DRESSING
juice of 1 lemon
salt and pepper
5 tbsps extra-virgin olive oil

908

Blanch the tomatoes in boiling water for 30 seconds, peel, deseed, dice and place in a bowl. Add the olives, caperberries and arugula.
Cut the prawns in half lengthwise and pound them out lightly with a meat tenderizer. Brush a serving plate with oil and lay the prawns on it. Lightly salt them and cover with the tomato mixture.
Mix the lemon juice, salt and pepper and whisk in the olive oil in a thin stream to emulsify. Drizzle over the prawns. Let sit a few minutes before serving.

Livorno-Style Dogfish
(TUSCANY)

Preparation time 15 minutes
Cooking time 25 minutes
Wine *Bolgheri Rosato*

2 tbsps extra-virgin olive oil
1 garlic clove
2¼ cups (14 oz or 400 g)
 crushed tomatoes
dried red chilli pepper flakes
parsley, minced
1.75 lb (800 g) dogfish fillet,
 sliced
1/2 onion, minced
1/3 cup (1.5 oz or 40 g) peas
salt and pepper

Heat a tablespoon of olive oil in a large frying pan and sauté the
garlic, tomatoes, a pinch of chilli and the minced parsley. Add the
dogfish to the tomato sauce and sauté over medium heat for a few
minutes.
Heat a tablespoon of olive oil in another frying pan and sauté the
onion. When the onion is soft, but not brown, add the peas and
cook for around 15 minutes. Add a little water if the peas become
too dry and then add the mixture to the tomatoes and dogfish.
Season to taste with pinches of salt and pepper.
Continue cooking until the dogfish is cooked through and serve hot.

Spinach-Stuffed Cuttlefish

Note *If you can't find cuttlefish, this recipe can also be made with squid, as long as they are not too small for stuffing.*

Preparation time 20 minutes
Cooking time 15 minutes
Wine *Orvieto Classico*

1 tbsp raisins
2 handfuls spinach
1 knob of butter
2 tbsps extra-virgin olive oil
1 shallot, minced
1 tbsp pine nuts
salt and pepper
1 tomato, diced
1 tbsp breadcrumbs
8 very fresh, medium-sized
 cuttlefish

910

Soak the raisins in warm water. Wash the spinach, leaving a little water on the leaves.
Heat the butter and oil in a saucepan and sauté the shallot until golden, then add the pine nuts and the spinach. Cook for 5 minutes then drain raisins, squeeze out excess water, and add to the pan. Season with salt and pepper. Remove from the heat As soon as the spinach is slightly cooled, stir in the tomato and breadcrumbs.
Wash the cuttlefish, gut them and remove the external film. Stuff with the spinach mixture, season with salt and grill. Turn and continue cooking until done. Let rest for 1 minute before serving.

Prawn Kebabs

Preparation time 30 minutes
Cooking time 20 minutes
Wine *Prosecco di Conegliano
e Valdobbiadene Brut*

1 yellow bell pepper
1 zucchini, cut into chunks
4 ripe tomatoes
4 tbsps extra-virgin olive oil
1 garlic clove
8 mushrooms
salt and pepper
12 jumbo prawns (preferably
 black tiger), shelled
basil leaves
2 tbsps minced mixed herbs
(parsley, dill, thyme)

911

Roast the pepper over an open flame or under a broiler, peel, deseed and cut into 8 strips.
Blanch the zucchini in boiling salted water for 3 minutes. Drain with a slotted spoon and set aside reserving the water. Bring the same water back to a boil and blanch the tomatoes for 30 seconds. Peel, deseed and cut into quarters.
Heat 2 tablespoons oil with the garlic and sauté the mushrooms whole. Season with salt and let cook for 10 minutes, covered.
Cut the prawns into chunks. Form kebabs by threading them onto skewers alternating with the vegetables and basil leaves.
Heat the remaining oil in a frying pan and sauté the skewers for 4-5 minutes, turning so they cook evenly. Season with salt and pepper and sprinkle with herbs.
Serve hot, accompanied by a seasonal salad, if desired.

Seared Tuna with Crunchy Salad

Note *Fennel is low in calories and an excellent source of vitamins and minerals, particularly potassium. The green leaves can be used to make herbal teas which make good digestifs.*

Preparation time 15 minutes
Cooking time 4 minutes
Wine *Greco di Tufo*

14 oz (400 g) fresh tuna fillet
salt and pepper
1 lemon thyme sprig, minced
2 carrots, peeled and julienned
1/2 fennel bulb, julienned
1 celery stalk, julienned
1 zucchini julienned
4 tbsps extra-virgin olive oil
1 garlic clove, smashed
juice of 1/2 lemon

912

Cut the tuna into two 1-inch (2 cm) thick slices and season with a little salt, pepper and lemon thyme.
Soak the carrots, fennel, celery and zucchini in a bowl of ice water so they stay crunchy.
Heat a non-stick frying pan with the oil and garlic and sear the tuna for 2 minutes on each side, keeping the inside pink. Slice and let cool.
Whisk together the lemon juice, salt and pepper and whisk in the olive oil in a thin stream until emulsified.
Drain the vegetables and quickly dry on paper towels. Toss with the lemon dressing, then arrange on the plates and top with the cooled tuna slices. Drizzle over a little of the pan juices.

Swordfish and Eggplant Involtini with Two Tomato Sauces

Preparation time 20 minutes
Cooking time 10 minutes
Wine *Metodo Classico Franciacorta Rosè*

4 garlic cloves, 2 whole
  and 2 smashed
4 tbsps extra-virgin olive oil
1 medium eggplant (about 14 oz
  or 400 g), peeled and diced
salt and pepper
14 oz (400 g) swordfish
rosemary
2 large tomatoes
  (about 14 oz or 400 g)
1 tsp sugar
basil, chopped
20 cherry tomatoes

913

Sauté 2 whole garlic cloves in 1 tablespoon of olive oil and add the eggplant. Cook over high heat until browned. Season with salt and pepper then puree.
Slice the swordfish into thin slices, pound out with a meat tenderizer and season with salt.
Spread the eggplant puree on the slices and fold into a little parcel, securing it with a toothpick.
Heat the oil with the rosemary and cook the involtini, covered, for 5-7 minutes.
Blanch the tomatoes, drain, peel, pass the pulp through a food mill and season it with sugar, salt, pepper and basil.
Remove the involtini from the frying pan and add the smashed garlic and the cherry tomatoes. Crush them with the back of a spoon and sauté for a few minutes.
Place a spoonful of blanched tomato sauce on each plate, top with involtini and cherry tomato sauce. Garnish with basil and serve warm.

Scallop Skewers

Preparation time 20 minutes
Cooking time 15 minutes
Wine *Metodo Classico
Franciacorta Rosé*

20 scallops
3 tbsps extra-virgin olive oil
salt and pepper
juice of 1/2 lemon
8 baby zucchini with flowers
 attached
10 cherry tomatoes, halved
1 tbsp balsamic vinegar

Toss the scallops with 1
tablespoon oil, salt, pepper
and lemon juice and let sit to
marinate.
Detach the flowers from the
zucchini and remove the
pistils. Cut the zucchini in half
lengthwise and then horizontally.
Thread the scallops, zucchini,
zucchini flowers and cherry
tomatoes on wooden skewers.
Grill, turning often, until evenly
cooked through. Season with
salt and pepper and serve with
a drizzle of oil and balsamic
vinegar.

Mussel Impepata
(Campania)

Preparation time 5 minutes
Cooking time 15 minutes
Wine *Fiano di Avellino*

Serves 4-6

1 garlic clove
2 tbsps extra-virgin olive oil
1 lb (500 g) mussels, cleaned
parsley, minced
freshly ground pepper

Sauté the garlic in the oil in a
large frying pan. As soon as it is
golden, add the mussels, shake
the pan and cook until they
open. Discard any which stay
closed. Serve, sprinkled with
parsley and abundant pepper.

Note *To clean the mussels,
wash them under cold running
water, remove the beard (the
external fibers) and scrub them
with a brush to remove any dirt.*

914

Florentine-Style Salt Cod (Tuscany)

Preparation time 20 minutes
Cooking time 15 minutes
Wine *Montecarlo Bianco*

1.75 lb (800 g) pre-soaked
 salt cod
plain flour
extra-virgin olive oil
2 garlic cloves, smashed
salt and pepper
3/4 cup (180 ml) tomato sauce

Cut the salt cod into fairly large
cubes. Dust lightly with flour on
all sides and set aside.
Heat abundant oil in a frying
pan with the garlic. When it
is golden, add the salt cod
and brown evenly on all sides.
Season with salt to taste, add
a little pepper, and finally the
tomato sauce. Continue to
cook for a few minutes.
Serve hot, sprinkled with
minced parsley if desired.

Salmoriglio Swordfish (Campania)

Preparation time 10 minutes
Cooking time 5 minutes
Wine *Bianco di Enotria*

juice of 1 lemon
oregano
salt and pepper
6 tbsps extra-virgin olive oil
1 lb (500 g) swordfish
parsley, minced

Mix together the lemon juice,
oregano, salt and pepper and
whisk in the olive oil to emulsify.
Cut the swordfish into 1-inch
(2 cm) thick slices and marinate
in the sauce for about 1 hour.
Cook the fish on a grill, a cast-
iron grill pan or a non-stick frying
pan for about 5 minutes, turning
every so often and brushing with
the marinade. Once cooked
through, arrange on a serving
plate, pour over any remaining
marinade, and sprinkle with
parsley.

915

Calabrian-Style Pizza with Capers and Eggplant

Preparation time 20 minutes
Cooking time 15 minutes
Beer *Italian Lager*

10.5 oz (300 g) prepared pizza
 dough (see p. 1093)
1 eggplant, thinly sliced
10 oz (280 g) buffalo mozzarella,
 cubed
1 tbsp salted capers, rinsed
20 cherry tomatoes, quartered
3 tbsps extra-virgin olive oil
salt and pepper
basil leaves

916

For round pizzas, divide the dough into 4 balls, and for a flat pizza,
spread all the dough out in an oiled, rectangular baking sheet.
Cover with a damp cloth and let rise again.
Preheat oven to 450°F (230°C).
Meanwhile, heat a ridged cast-iron grill pan and grill the eggplant
slices for 2 minutes on each side.
Roll out the pizza dough and top with mozzarella cubes, capers
and tomato wedges. Drizzle with oil and season with salt and
pepper.
Bake for 8 minutes, adding the eggplant halfway through.
The edges of the crust should be golden-brown and crunchy.
Remove the pizza from the oven, sprinkle with fresh basil
and serve immediately.

Robiola with Pistachios
and Spiced Honey

Preparation time 15 minutes
Wine *Verduzzo di Ramandolo*

2 tbsps raisins
1 gelatin sheet
1/4 cup (1 oz or 30 g) shelled
  pistachios
12.5 oz (350 g) robiola cheese
2 tbsps milk
2/3 cup (150 ml) heavy cream
5 tbsps confectioners' sugar
1/3 cup (3.5 oz or 100 g) honey
1 tsp mixed ground spices
  (cardamom, cinnamon, cloves,
  cumin, pepper)

917

Soak the raisins in warm water, and soak the gelatin sheet in cold
water.
Blanch the pistachios in boiling water for 1 minute, drain and
remove the skins. Toast them in the oven or in a frying pan.
Grind them with a mortar and pestle or chop finely with a knife.
Beat the robiola in a bowl until soft then stir in the pistachios.
Drain the gelatin and dissolve it in the milk in a small saucepan.
Let cool for a few minutes then stir the milk and gelatin into the
cheese.
Whip the cream and the confectioners' sugar to soft peaks,
then fold into the cheese mixture. Cover and refrigerate.
Heat the honey with the ground spices, the drained and squeezed-
out raisins and 1 tablespoon water.
Using 2 tablespoons form the cheese mixture into quenelles.
Drizzle with the spiced honey and serve.

Eggplant Parmigiana
(CAMPANIA)

Preparation time 15 minutes
Cooking time 1 hour
Wine *Falanghina*

3 eggplants, sliced lengthwise
salt
5 tbsps extra-virgin olive oil
2 garlic cloves, minced
3 cups (700 ml) crushed
 tomatoes
4 basil leaves, chopped
5 tbsps grated Parmesan
9 oz (250 g) cow's milk
 mozzarella, sliced

918

Place the eggplant slices in a colander, sprinkle with salt and let sit
for 30 minutes, then drain and squeeze out excess liquid.
Preheat oven to 400°F (200°C).
Heat a little olive oil in a large frying pan until very hot and fry the
eggplant slices, in batches if necessary.
In another frying pan heat a drizzle of oil and sauté the garlic until
golden. Add the tomato and cook down until thickened. Remove
from the heat, add the basil and salt to taste, then pass through
a food mill.
Spread a layer of eggplant in an oiled baking dish. Top with
1 ladleful of tomato sauce, sprinkle with Parmesan and cover with
mozzarella slices. Continue making layers until all the ingredients
have been used up. Finish with a layer of tomato sauce, drizzle
with oil and bake for around 45 minutes.
Serve hot.

'Ndjua Pizza
(CALABRIA)

Preparation time 10 minutes
Cooking time 20 minutes
Beer *Lager*

DOUGH
1 tbsp (0.4 oz or 12 g) active
 dry yeast)
3/4 cup (200 ml) warm water
salt
1 tsp sugar
3 tbsps extra-virgin olive oil
3 cups plus (14 oz or 400 g)
 all-purpose flour

TOPPING
2 Tropea or other sweet red
 onions, very thinly sliced
salt
2 tbsps extra-virgin olive oil
7 oz (200 g) buffalo mozzarella,
 diced
1 cup (7 oz or 200 g) crushed
 tomatoes
5.5 oz (150 g) 'nduja (soft, spicy
 salami)

919

Dissolve the yeast in the warm water. Add salt, sugar and oil and
stir well. Mound the flour on a work surface, make a well in the
middle and pour in the yeast mixture. Knead vigorously to obtain
a smooth dough. Dust with flour and leave to rise for 2 hours in
a large, floured bowl, covered with a cloth. Form the dough into
many small balls, cover and let them rise again for 1 hour.
Knead all the dough balls together and spread on a round, oiled
baking sheet, pushing out with fingertips. Cover and let rise
for 25 minutes.
Preheat oven to 400°F (200°C).
Mix the onions with salt and the oil.
Dry the mozzarella with paper towels.
Top the pizza with crushed tomatoes, the onions, the mozzarella
and the 'nduja, broken into pieces. Bake for around 20 minutes.
Serve hot.

Asiago in a Hazelnut Crust

Preparation time 15 minutes
Cooking time 2 minutes
Wine *Lagrein Dunkel*

1/2 cup (2 oz or 60 g) hazelnuts,
 peeled
10.5 oz (300 g) Asiago cheese,
 sliced and cut into triangles
1 small head green lettuce,
 chopped
10 cherry tomatoes, quartered
salt
3 tbsps extra-virgin olive oil

Toast the hazelnuts for a few
minutes in a non-stick frying
pan. Let cool, then grind them
in a food processor.
Dip the cheese in the ground
hazelnuts, pressing well so they
adhere. Heat a grill or cast-iron
grill pan, and cook the cheese
until golden-brown on both
sides.
Meanwhile divide the lettuce
between serving plates and top
with the tomatoes. Dress with a
little salt and olive oil. Place the
grilled cheese on top and serve
immediately.

Cherry Tomato and Arugula Pizza

Preparation time 10 minutes
Cooking time 15 minutes
Beer *Italian Pilsner*

14 oz (400 g) prepared pizza
 dough (see p. 1093)
all-purpose flour
extra-virgin olive oil
10.5 oz (300 g) cow's milk
 mozzarella, sliced
20 cherry tomatoes, halved
salt
2 bunches arugula, chopped
5.5 oz (150 g) Parmesan, shaved

Preheat oven to 425°F (220°C).
Roll out the dough into a
thin sheet on a floured work
surface. Place on an oiled
baking sheet.
Top the dough with the
mozzarella and then scatter
over the tomatoes. Season with
salt.
Bake the pizza for 15 minutes,
until the crust is golden-brown
and crispy.
Remove from the oven, top with
arugula, Parmesan shavings
and a drizzle of oil and serve.

M A I N   C O U R S E S

Shrimp and Mushroom Pizza

Preparation time 20 minutes
Cooking time 15 minutes
Beer *Irish Stout*

10 oz (280 g) prepared pizza
 dough (see p. 1093)
4 tbsps extra-virgin olive oil
7 oz (200 g) cow's milk
 mozzarella, chopped
15 shrimp, shelled and deveined
20 black olives, pitted
4 white mushrooms, peeled and
 sliced
salt and pepper
1 bunch arugula, chopped

Preheat oven to 450°F (230°C).
Form the dough into 4 balls.
Cover with a damp cloth and
let rise again in a warm place
for 30 minutes.
Roll out the dough and place
on an oiled baking sheet.
Top the pizza with the
mozzarella, shrimp, olives,
mushrooms, 2 tablespoons
oil, salt and pepper. Bake for
around 8 minutes.
Remove from the oven and top
with the arugula, a drizzle of oil
and a little salt.

Radicchio Frittata

Preparation time 10 minutes
Cooking time 25 minutes
Wine *Prosecco di Valdobbiadene Brut*

1 tbsp extra-virgin olive oil
2 Tropea or other sweet red
 onions, sliced
2 heads Treviso radicchio,
 shredded
salt and pepper
3/4 cup (180 ml) white wine
2 eggs
3 tbsps grated Parmesan

Heat the oil and sauté the
onions over low heat for 10
minutes. Add the radicchio and
brown briefly. Season with salt
and pepper then add the wine
and let reduce.
Beat the eggs with the
Parmesan, salt and pepper.
Pour the eggs over the
radicchio, stir briefly then let
cook over low heat. Once
the underside is cooked, flip
with the help of the pan lid,
and continue cooking until
firm in the middle. Serve cut
into wedges, hot or at room
temperature.

Neapolitan-Style Pizzas
(Campania)

Preparation time 40 minutes
Cooking time 10 minutes
Beer *Light Beer*

Serves 6

Dough
1 tbsp plus 1 tsp (0.6 oz or 16 g)
 active dry yeast
1 cup plus 1 tbsp (250 ml) warm
 water
2 tsps salt
1 tsp sugar
4 tbsps extra-virgin olive oil

2⅓ cups (10.5 oz or 300 g)
 all-purpose flour
1½ cups plus 1½ tbsps (7 oz
 or 200 g) enriched white flour

Topping
4 tomatoes, blanched, peeled
 and sliced
extra-virgin olive oil
basil and oregano

922

Dissolve the yeast in a little warm water. Add the salt, sugar and
oil. Mound the 2 flours on a work surface and make a well in the
middle. Pour the yeast mixture in the middle and mix a smooth,
uniform dough, adding as much of the remaining warm water as
necessary. Let rise for 2 hours.
Divide the dough into many small balls and let rise for another
hour.
Preheat oven to 350°F (180°C).
Roll the dough out, not too thinly, and form many little pizzas.
Top each one with a drizzle of oil, some tomato slices, a few
leaves of basil and a pinch of oregano.
Bake for 10 minutes. Serve hot.

Sardinian-Style Pizza

Preparation time 10 minutes
Cooking time 10 minutes
Wine *Nuragus di Cagliari*

4 sheets pane carasau
 (or Armenian cracker bread)
1/2 cup (120 ml) crushed
 tomatoes
9 oz (250 g) cow's milk
 mozzarella, diced
2 tbsps capers
1/3 cup (2 oz or 50 g) black
 olives
oregano
salt
4 tbsps extra-virgin olive oil
3.5 oz (100 g) Sardinian
 pecorino, shaved

Preheat oven to 400°F (200°C).
Spread the tomatoes evenly over each sheet of bread. Top each
one with mozzarella, capers, olives, oregano, a pinch of salt,
a drizzle of olive oil and a layer of pecorino shavings.
Place on baking sheets and bake for around 10 minutes.
Serve immediately.

Eggplant Caponata
(SICILY)

Preparation time 10 minutes
Cooking time 1 hour 10 minutes
Wine *Bianco d'Alcamo*

924

5 medium eggplant, cubed
salt
3 tbsps extra-virgin olive oil
3/4 cups (3.5 oz or 100 g) green
 olives
1 tbsp capers, rinsed
1 celery stalk, finely chopped
1 lb (500 g) ripe tomatoes, sliced
4 tbsps sugar
4 tbsps vinegar

Salt the eggplant and leave to drain in a colander for 30 minutes
to give off water.
Heat the oil in a large saucepan and brown the eggplant cubes.
Add the olives, capers and celery and cook for 10 minutes.
Add the tomatoes and cook for 1 hour. Add the sugar and vinegar,
stir, remove from the heat and let cool slightly before serving.
The caponata can also be canned in sterilized glass jars.

Grilled Tomatoes with Thyme Oil

Preparation time 20 minutes
Cooking time 15 minutes
Wine *Sicilia Chardonnay*

4 tbsps extra-virgin olive oil
2 lemon thyme sprigs
2 garlic cloves
coarse salt
8 firm, ripe tomatoes, halved

Heat the oil in a small saucepan with the thyme and garlic without
letting it get too hot, then remove from the heat and let cool
Salt the tomato halves with a little coarse salt so they give
off some liquid.
Grill them on a charcoal grill 2 inches (5 cm) from the coals,
starting with the cut side down and turning after 6 minutes.
Move them away slightly from the center of the coals and continue
cooking for another 3-4 minutes.
Place on a serving plate, drizzle with the thyme oil and season
with salt and pepper to taste.
Let sit for 5 minutes and serve.

925

Lettuce Parcels Filled with Leek and Potato

Preparation time 30 minutes
Cooking time 30 minutes
Wine *Malvasia dei Colli Piacentini*

2 large potatoes
1 large head of lettuce,
 leaves separate
1 tbsp extra-virgin olive oil
1 garlic clove
1 leek, thinly sliced
1 tbsp minced parsley
1 egg
1 tbsp corn flour
1 tbsp grated Parmesan
salt and pepper
2 tomatoes, diced
1 tbsp pine nuts, toasted
basil leaves

926

Boil the potatoes, peel and cut into small chunks.
Meanwhile blanch the lettuce leaves for a few seconds and immerse them immediately in ice water, being careful to not break them.
Heat the oil and garlic and sauté the leek and potatoes. Add the parsley and cook over medium heat for 10-15 minutes, stirring frequently. Drain off any excess oil and transfer to a bowl. Stir in the egg, corn flour, Parmesan, salt and pepper and mix well. Preheat the grill.
Lay the lettuce leaves out on a clean kitchen towel, arranging them in clusters like the petals of a flower. Place a few spoonfuls of the leek and potato mixture in the centre of each cluster, then roll up like a spring roll.
Place the parcels on a baking sheet and broil for 6 minutes under a very hot grill. Serve garnished with tomatoes, pine nuts and basil leaves.

Carrot Flans with Parmesan Zucchini

Preparation time 25 minutes
Cooking time 1 hour
Wine *Trebbiano d'Abruzzo*
🍷🍷

Serves 6

FLAN
3 tbsps extra-virgin olive oil
1/3 leek (1 oz or 30 g), sliced
4 small carrots (10.5 oz
 or 300 g), halved lengthwise
 then thinly sliced
salt and pepper
7 tbsps heavy cream
3/4 cup (200 ml) vegetable broth

3/4 cup (200 ml) béchamel
 (see p. 1096)
2 eggs
5 tbsps grated Parmesan
nutmeg, grated

ZUCCHINI
3½ tbsps butter
1 lb (450 g) zucchini, peeled and
 sliced 1/5-inch (1/2 cm) thick
3 thyme sprigs
4 tbsps grated Parmesan
salt and pepper

927

Preheat oven to 350°F (180°C).
Heat the oil and sauté the leek. Add the carrots and season
with salt and pepper. Add the cream and broth and cook for 10
minutes over high heat until the liquid has completely evaporated.
Puree the mixture with an immersion blender or food processor,
then stir in the béchamel, eggs, 4 tablespoons Parmesan and a
grating of nutmeg.
Place a baking dish half-filled with water in the oven.
Butter and sprinkle with Parmesan 6 individual aluminum moulds.
Pour in the carrot mixture, place in the water and bake for 40
minutes.
Meanwhile melt the butter in a frying pan and sauté the zucchini
with the thyme. Cook for 5-7 minutes, add the Parmesan and
season with salt and pepper to taste.
Unmould the flans on serving plates and serve immediately,
accompanied by the zucchini.

Tomato and Ricotta Salad

Note *Though ricotta made from cow's milk is now the most common type, it was traditionally made with sheep's milk, which has a stronger, more distinctive flavour.*

Preparation time 10 minutes
Wine *Trentino Müller Thurgau*

4 ripe, red tomatoes, cut into
  wedges
dried oregano
salt and pepper
5-6 lettuce leaves, shredded
7 tbsps extra-virgin olive oil
7 oz (200 g) sheep's milk ricotta
1 bunch basil, chopped

928

Season the tomatoes with oregano, salt and pepper. Dress the lettuce with 2 tablespoons oil and a pinch of salt.
Beat the ricotta with a little oregano, salt and 2 tablespoons oil.
Place the tomatoes on a bed of lettuce, top with spoonfuls of ricotta and the basil. Drizzle with 3 tablespoons oil and oregano.

Calabrian Peperonata

Preparation time 20 minutes
Cooking time 40 minutes
Wine *Bianco di Enotria*

1 lb (500 g) eggplant, cubed
salt
4 tomatoes
extra-virgin olive oil
1.75 lb (800 g) bell peppers,
 chopped
basil, chopped
oregano

Place the eggplant in a colander and sprinkle with salt. Let sit for 30 minutes.

Blanch the tomatoes for a couple of minutes, peel, deseed and chop the flesh.

Drain the eggplant and squeeze out excess liquid. Heat abundant oil in a saucepan and fry the eggplant cubes until golden. Scoop out with a slotted spoon and set aside. Fry the peppers, drain and set aside.

Heat a drizzle of oil in another saucepan, sauté the tomatoes and add the eggplant and peppers. Stir and salt to taste. Add some basil and a pinch of oregano, leave for a few minutes and serve hot.

931

Caponata with Thyme

Preparation time 15 minutes
Cooking time 20 minutes
Wine *Alto Adige Terlaner*

1/2 red bell pepper
1/2 yellow bell pepper
2 tbsps extra-virgin olive oil
1/2 onion, diced
1 carrot, diced
1 celery stalk, diced
1 eggplant, deseeded and diced
salt and pepper
1 zucchini, diced
thyme leaves

Remove the seeds and white pith from inside the peppers, then dice. Heat the oil in a saucepan and sauté the onion. Add the peppers, carrot and celery and continue cooking. Add the eggplant, lightly season with salt and pepper and cook, covered, for 5 minutes. Just before the vegetables are done add the zucchini. Stir in the thyme. Serve in small bowls.

Onions with Herb Butter

Preparation time 15 minutes
Cooking time 10 minutes
Wine *Vermentino di Gallura*

5 sage leaves, finely minced
1 rosemary sprig, finely minced
1/3 cup (2.8 oz or 80 g) butter, softened
4 red onions
4 white onions
salt and pepper

Mix the sage and rosemary with the butter and spread on a piece of parchment paper. Roll the paper into a cylinder, then refrigerate until firm.
Peel the onions and blanch them in salted water for about 10 minutes. Drain and immerse in cold water. Cut in half or thickly slice, and lightly season with pepper.
Cook on a cast-iron grill pan for 5 minutes on each side.
Lightly salt the onions and serve topped with slices of the herb butter, so that it melts from their heat.

932

Nettle Frittata

Preparation time 10 minutes
Cooking time 20 minutes
Wine *Ortrugo*

4 oz (120 g) edible nettle leaves
salt
6 eggs
3 tbsps grated Parmesan
1 tbsp extra-virgin olive oil

Preheat oven to 350°F (180°C).
Blanch the nettles in boiling
salted water for 2-3 minutes.
Drain and roughly chop.
Beat the eggs in a bowl with
the Parmesan and a pinch of
salt. Add the nettles and mix
well.
Pour the mixture into an oiled
baking dish and bake for 15-20
minutes. Flip the frittata and
bake for another 1-2 minutes.
Serve immediately, with a green
salad dressed with salt, oil and
balsamic vinegar, if desired.

Fried Vegetables with Salad

Preparation time 20 minutes
Cooking time 10 minutes
Wine *Alto Adige Müller Thurgau*

2 bunches mixed lettuce leaves
10 cherry tomatoes, quartered
8 squash blossoms
3/4 cup (3.5 oz or 100 g)
 plain flour
2 tbsps fine cornmeal
sparkling water
2 large zucchini, cut into 2-inch
 (5 cm) matchsticks
1 eggplant, cut into 2-inch
 (5 cm) matchsticks
sunflower oil
3 tbsps extra-virgin olive oil
salt

Plate the salad and top with
tomatoes.
Remove the pistils from the
blossoms.
Mix flour and cornmeal in a bowl
and whisk in enough sparkling
water to make a fluid batter.
Whisk until smooth.
Heat sunflower oil in a frying pan.
Dip the zucchini, eggplant and
blossoms in the batter. Fry in the
hot oil until golden.
Dress the salad with oil and salt.
Top with the fried vegetables.

933

Tomato and Caper Flan

Note *The tomatoes can be replaced with thinly sliced zucchini.*

Preparation time 15 minutes
Cooking time 25 minutes
Wine *Etna Bianco*

4 ripe tomatoes
extra-virgin olive oil
2 garlic cloves, minced
1 spring onion, minced
salt and pepper
2 eggs
1/3 cup (80 ml) heavy cream
2 tbsps salted capers, rinsed
 and chopped
basil, chopped
2 oz (60 g) pancetta or prosciutto,
 diced
1 tbsp butter

934

Preheat oven to 325°F (170°C).
Blanch the tomatoes in boiling water, drain and immerse in ice water. Peel, deseed and dice.
Heat a little oil in a frying pan and sauté the garlic and spring onion. Add the tomatoes, season with salt and pepper and cook over low heat for 5 minutes.
Beat the eggs and cream in a bowl and stir in the capers and a little basil.
Brown the pancetta in a non-stick frying pan over high heat. Drain off the fat and add the pancetta to the tomatoes. Season with salt and pepper to taste. Remove from the heat and let cool.
Mix the tomato mixture with the eggs and cream, stirring well. Divide the mixture between 4 buttered individual baking dishes. Bake for 20 minutes. Let cool for 30 minutes before serving.

Sweet and Sour Eggplant Involtini

Preparation time 30 minutes
Cooking time 15 minutes
Wine *Alto Adige Pinot Bianco*

6 tbsps raisins
1 small eggplant (about 10.5 oz
 or 300 g), thinly sliced
4 tbsps extra-virgin olive oil
salt and pepper
1 garlic clove
1 small red bell pepper, cut into
 matchsticks
1 small yellow bell pepper, cut
 into matchsticks
1 small green bell pepper, cut
 into matchsticks
1 medium zucchini, cut into
 matchsticks
5 tbsps pine nuts
chives, minced

935

Soak the raisins in a hot water, drain and squeeze out excess water.
Drizzle a little oil over the eggplant and sprinkle with salt. Cook on a very hot cast-iron grill pan.
Heat the remaining oil in a frying pan until very hot and sauté the garlic until golden. Add the peppers and zucchini and sauté for 3-4 minutes over high heat. Season with salt and pepper. Add the pine nuts and raisins and cook for another 4 minutes. Stir in the chives.
Put a spoonful of the vegetable mixture on each eggplant slice and roll up. Secure with a toothpick if necessary. Arrange on plates with the rest of the sautéed vegetables. Sprinkle with some more chives and serve immediately.

Millet and Pepper Gratin

Note *Millet is an ancient cereal, not so commonly eaten in Europe and the United States, but an important staple of many Asian and North African diets. It is high in protein and rich in iron, phosphorous and B vitamins, and can help protect the skin, hair, nails and tooth enamel.*

Preparation time 15 minutes
Cooking time 40 minutes
Wine *Trentino Pinot Grigio*

3/4 cup (5.5 oz or 150 g) pearled millet
salt
6 tbsps extra-virgin olive oil
1 garlic clove, sliced
2 yellow bell peppers, cut into strips
2 tomatoes, diced
1 egg
3/4 cup (3.5 oz or 100 g) grated Parmesan
dried red chilli pepper flakes
1 bunch parsley, minced
8-10 basil leaves, minced
3 tbsps breadcrumbs

Preheat oven to 350°F (180°C).
Cook the millet in boiling salted water for 15 minutes.
Heat a little oil in a saucepan and sauté the garlic until golden. Add the peppers and cook over high heat for 5 minutes. Add the tomatoes, season with salt and continue cooking for 10 minutes over medium heat.
Drain the millet and mix with the egg, 1/2 the Parmesan and a pinch of chilli flakes in a bowl.
Form the mixture into walnut-sized balls using a tablespoon.
In another bowl, mix the minced herbs, breadcrumbs, the remaining Parmesan and the remaining oil and stir well.
Spread the peppers and tomatoes in a baking dish, top with the millet balls and sprinkle over the herbed breadcrumbs. Bake for 10 minutes.

Zucchini Gratin with Pecorino

Preparation time 15 minutes
Cooking time 30 minutes
Wine *Colli Euganei Bianco*

🍳

1 knob of butter
3 medium zucchini, thinly sliced
salt and pepper
7 tbsps grated pecorino cheese
1 tbsp breadcrumbs
thyme leaves

Preheat oven to 400°F (200°C).
Butter a baking dish and
arrange the zucchini slices
in layers. Season with salt
and pepper and top with the
remaining butter.
Mix the grated pecorino with
the breadcrumbs. Sprinkle the
mixture over the zucchini.
Bake the gratin for 10 minutes
until golden on top.
Remove from the oven, sprinkle
with thyme and serve.

Robiola and Bell Pepper Salad

Preparation time 15 minutes
Cooking time 10 minutes
Wine *Cirò Bianco*

🍳

SALAD
1/2 red bell pepper
1/2 yellow bell pepper
extra-virgin olive oil
1 eggplant, peeled and diced
salt and pepper
1 heart of lettuce, shredded
2 tbsps silvered almonds,
 toasted
5.5 oz (150 g) robiola cheese

DRESSING
4 tbsps extra-virgin olive oil
salt and pepper

Roast the peppers over a
low flame. Close in a plastic
bag, seal to steam, then peel,
deseed and cut into strips.
Heat a little oil in a frying pan
and sauté the eggplant until
tender. Season with salt and
pepper and let cool.
Mix together the lettuce,
almonds, peppers, pieces of
robiola and eggplant. Dress
with oil, season with salt and
pepper to taste and serve.

Puglian Caponata

Preparation time 25 minutes
Cooking time 50 minutes
Wine *Gioia del Colle Bianco*

Serves 4-6

3 tbsps extra-virgin olive oil
1 large eggplant, diced
2 carrots, diced
2 celery stalks, diced
1 large zucchini, diced
1 red bell pepper, diced
1 onion, minced
2 San Marzano or plum
  tomatoes, diced
1 tbsp capers
1 round, red chilli pepper
1 tbsp sugar
vinegar
salt
mint
oregano

938

Heat the oil in a frying pan until very hot and sauté the eggplant, then add the carrots, celery, zucchini and bell pepper. Cook for a few minutes all together, until the vegetables are browned and crisp, stirring every so often and adding more oil when necessary. Drain the vegetables with a slotted spoon and set aside. Add the onion to the same pan and sauté, then add the tomatoes, capers and chilli, then all the sautéed vegetables. Add the sugar, a few drops of vinegar, a pinch of salt and the mint. Let cook for a few minutes then transfer to a bowl. Sprinkle with oregano and cool before serving.

Greek Salad

Preparation time 25 minutes
Cooking time 15 minutes

1/2 red bell pepper
1/2 yellow bell pepper
3 tbsps extra-virgin olive oil
1 heart of lettuce, chopped
1 cucumber, peeled and sliced
1 handful black olives
salt and pepper
7 oz (200 g) fresh feta cheese,
 diced

Preheat oven to 400°F (200°C).
Cut the peppers in half, remove the white pith and seeds, brush
with oil and roast in the oven for 15 minutes. Close in a plastic bag
to steam until completely cool.
Meanwhile mix together the lettuce, cucumber and black olives.
Lightly season with salt.
Peel the roasted peppers and cut into small squares. Add to the
salad together with the feta, and dress with oil and pepper. Serve
immediately.

Cucumber and Feta Salad

Preparation time 20 minutes
Wine *Bianchello del Metauro*

6 cucumbers, 4 chopped
 and 2 sliced
salt and pepper
10.5 oz (300 g) feta cheese,
 cubed
4 giant green olives, pitted
 and sliced
6 tbsps extra-virgin olive oil
oregano
1 cup (9 oz or 250 g) yogurt
1 mint sprig
1/2 garlic clove

Place the chopped cucumber
in a bowl and season with a
pinch of salt. Stir and let sit for
10 minutes. Quickly rinse and
drain, then mix in a bowl with
the feta and olives. Dress with 2
tablespoons oil, oregano and a
pinch of pepper.
Blend the yogurt with the mint,
garlic, 2 tablespoons oil, salt
and pepper in a blender or food
processor. Dress the salad with
the yogurt dressing, drizzle
with oil and garnish with the
cucumber slices.

Vegetable Fritters

Preparation time 15 minutes
Cooking time 10 minutes
Wine *Prosecco di Conegliano
e Valdobbiadene Brut*

1 large yellow-fleshed
 potato, peeled and cut into
 matchsticks
1 cup (5.3 oz or 150 g)
 plain flour
1/3 cup (1.8 oz or 50 g) fine
 cornmeal
sparkling water
2 carrots, peeled and cut into
 matchsticks
2 zucchini, cut into matchsticks
sunflower oil
salt

Soak the cut potatoes in a bowl
of cold water for 10 minutes.
Mix the flour and cornmeal in
a bowl and pour in sparkling
water in a thin stream, whisking
constantly, to obtain a fluid batter.
Drain the potatoes and add to
the batter with the carrots and
zucchini.
Heat the oil until very hot. Using
2 forks or a pair of tongs, take
small amounts of the vegetable
mixture and fry in the oil. Drain on
paper towels, salt and serve.

940

Mixed Salad with Mozzarella

Preparation time 15 minutes
Wine *Pagadebit di Romagna*
♟

1 eggplant, thinly sliced
2 tomatoes, sliced
5 mushrooms, peeled and thinly
 sliced
1 head curly leaf lettuce, leaves
 torn into pieces
2 carrots, peeled and thinly
 sliced
1 rectangular mozzarella, thinly
 sliced
extra-virgin olive oil
salt and pepper
oregano

Heat a cast-iron grill pan until
very hot then grill the eggplant
slices. Grill the tomato slices.
Compose the salad by
alternating slices of raw
mushrooms, grilled eggplant,
lettuce, raw carrots, grilled
tomato slices and mozzarella
slices.
Dress the salad with olive oil,
salt, pepper and oregano.

Panzanella Salad

Preparation time 20 minutes
Wine *Morellino di Scansano*
♟

4 cups (1 l) water
3 tbsps white wine vinegar
salt and pepper
1 lb (500 g) dry Tuscan-style
 bread
1 cucumber, sliced
3 ripe tomatoes, cut into thin
 wedges
1/2 yellow bell pepper, deseeded
 and sliced
1 red onion, sliced into rings
3 celery stalks, sliced
basil, chopped
4 tbsps extra-virgin olive oil
1 head of green lettuce,
 shredded

Place the water in a bowl with
the vinegar and a little salt.
Break the bread into pieces
and soak them for about 10
minutes. Drain, squeeze out
and transfer to another bowl.
Add the cucumber, tomatoes,
bell pepper, onion, celery and
basil to the bread and dress
with oil, salt and pepper.
Refrigerate for 30 minutes.
Serve the salad over a bed of
lettuce.

Mint-Marinated Grilled Peppers

Note *There are over
600 different varieties of
mint, but the two most
commonly used for
cooking are peppermint
and spearmint. In Italy, the
three most common mints
are piperita, romana and
mentuccia.*

Preparation time 20 minutes
Cooking time 15 minutes
Wine *Alto Adige Sauvignon*

1 red bell pepper
1 yellow bell pepper
10 mint leaves
5 tbsps extra-virgin olive oil
salt and pepper
grated zest of 1 organic lemon
1 garlic clove (preferably pink
  garlic), sliced

942

Halve the peppers and remove the seeds and white pith. Cut
them in half again and cook the strips on a cast-iron grill pan for
6 minutes on the skin side and 4 minutes on the other side. Seal
them in a plastic bag so they can steam, and leave for 15 minutes.
Remove from the bag, peel and cut into thinner strips.
Meanwhile crush the mint with the oil and pinches of salt and
pepper in a mortar and pestle and stir in the lemon zest.
Place the peppers in a bowl and drizzle with the mint oil. Add the
garlic, cover with plastic wrap, and let sit for 4 hours in a cool
place to marinate. Remove the garlic before serving.

Pepper, Olive and Grouper Timbale

Preparation time 20 minutes
Cooking time 25 minutes
Wine *Trentino Nosiola*
♟ ♟

3 bell peppers (red and yellow)
6 tbsps extra-virgin olive oil
1⅔ cups (7 oz or 200 g) diced
 celery, carrot and onion
3/4 cup (180 ml) white wine
10.5 oz (300 g) grouper fillet
1 shallot, minced
salt and pepper
3 tbsps heavy cream
1 egg white
parsley, minced
grated zest of 1 organic lemon
2 tbsps minced Taggiasca olives
4 anchovy fillets in oil

943

Preheat oven to 400°F (200°C).
Halve the peppers and remove the seeds. Brush with a little oil
and broil until roasted. Close in a plastic bag to steam until cooled,
then peel. Dice 1 pepper and cut the others into strips.
Meanwhile heat the diced celery, carrot and onion with water. As
soon as it reaches a boil, add the wine. Poach the grouper in the
broth for 5 minutes then drain. Remove any bones from the fish.
Heat a little oil in a saucepan and sauté the shallot gently, with a
little water. Add the grouper and the diced pepper, cook briefly and
adjust the salt and pepper to taste. Let cool, then puree in a food
processor with the cream, egg white, minced parsley and lemon
zest. Adjust salt, pepper and oil as needed.
Line 4 metal moulds with the pepper strips. Fill each one halfway
with the puree. Place 1/2 tablespoon of olives in the middle, then
top up with the remaining puree.
Bake for 18 minutes. Unmould onto serving plates and top with an
anchovy fillet.

Roast Pepper and Mozzarella Terrine

Preparation time 30 minutes
Cooking time 15 minutes
Wine *Torbato di Alghero*

2 red bell peppers
2 yellow bell peppers
0.7 oz (20 g) gelatin in sheets
1¼ cups (300 ml) hot vegetable broth
14 oz (400 g) buffalo mozzarella, sliced
4-5 basil leaves, chopped
3/4 cup (3.5 oz or 100 g) Taggiasca olives, pitted and chopped
4 tbsps extra-virgin olive oil
salt
dried red chilli pepper flakes
oregano

944

Roast the peppers over an open flame. Peel, deseed, cut into strips, wash and dry on a kitchen towel.

Soak the gelatin in cold water, then drain and squeeze out excess liquid. Dissolve in the hot broth.

Pour a shallow layer of broth into a terrine mould. Make a layer of red pepper strips, pour in a little more broth, then top with a layer of mozzarella and some basil.

Continue with a layer of yellow pepper strips, a little broth, mozzarella and basil and continue until the terrine is full.

Refrigerate until firm, at least 2 hours.

Meanwhile mix the olives with the oil, salt, chilli flakes and oregano to make a sauce.

Serve the terrine, unmoulded and sliced, accompanied by the olive sauce and, if desired, a fresh seasonal salad.

Summer Vegetable Bake

Preparation time 30 minutes
Cooking time 35 minutes
Wine *Colli di Parma Malvasia Secca*

6 tbsps extra-virgin olive oil
1/3 cup (2 oz or 50 g) pitted
 green olives, sliced
1 garlic clove
1⅓ cups (9 oz or 250 g)
 crushed tomatoes
salt and pepper
5 basil leaves, finely minced
1 red bell pepper
1 yellow bell pepper
2 eggplants, sliced
1 large zucchini, sliced
1/2 cup (2 oz or 50 g) grated
 Parmesan
10.5 oz (300 g) cow's milk
 mozzarella, thinly sliced

945

Preheat oven to 350°F (180°C).
Heat 5 tablespoons oil in a saucepan and sauté the olives and garlic clove until the garlic is golden. Remove the garlic and add the tomatoes. Salt and pepper to taste and cook for 10 minutes. Add the basil and stir.
Roast the peppers over an open flame for 2-3 minutes to char the skin. Immerse in a bowl of cold water, then peel, halve and deseed them. Cut into strips.
Heat a cast-iron grill pan and grill the eggplant and zucchini slices. Oil a baking dish and arrange a layer of eggplant in the bottom. Cover with a few spoonfuls of tomato sauce and a sprinkling of Parmesan. Create a second layer of pepper strips and top with mozzarella. Cover with zucchini, spread over some more tomato sauce and more Parmesan. Continue making layers until the ingredients have been used up. Top with more basil. Drizzle with oil and bake for 15 minutes. Remove from the oven and serve.

Vegetable Salad with Potatoes

Preparation time 15 minutes
Cooking time 35 minutes
Wine *Bardolino Chiaretto*

3 large yellow-fleshed potatoes
salt and pepper
2 carrots, peeled and sliced
  or julienned
1 red onion, thinly sliced into
  rings
2 zucchini, sliced or julienned
2 San Marzano or plum
  tomatoes, chopped
3 tbsps extra-virgin olive oil

946

Place the potatoes in a
saucepan, cover with cold
salted water and bring to a boil.
Cook until they are still firm in
the centre. Drain and let cool.
Peel the cooled potatoes and
chop or slice them.
Mix together the carrots, onion,
zucchini and tomatoes in a
bowl. Toss with oil and season
with salt and pepper to taste.
Serve with the potatoes.

Pineapple and Endive Salad

Preparation time 20 minutes
Wine *Prosecco di Conegliano Dry*

1 head Belgian endive, chopped
4-5 Romaine lettuce leaves,
  chopped
extra-virgin olive oil
salt
1/4 pineapple, peeled, sliced
  and cut into fan-shaped
  wedges
2 kiwis, peeled and sliced
  vertically into wedges
10 cherry tomatoes, halved
  or quartered
1 small spring onion, thinly
  sliced

Toss the chopped Belgian
endive and Romaine lettuce
with a little oil and season with
salt to taste.
Divide the endive and Romaine
between serving plates.
Attractively arrange the
pineapple, kiwi and cherry
tomatoes on top of the salads
and then sprinkle each one with
a little spring onion.

Crudités with Chickpea Dip

Preparation time 25 minutes
Cooking time 1 hour 15 minutes
Wine *Lagrein Rosato*

CHICKPEA DIP
1/2 onion, minced
1¼ cups (9 oz or 250 g)
 cooked chickpeas
1¼ cups (300 ml) vegetable
 broth
3 tbsps extra-virgin olive oil
salt and pepper
1 rosemary sprig

VEGETABLES
2 carrots, quartered lengthwise
4 celery stalks
12 radishes
1 fennel bulb, cut into wedges
2 heads radicchio, cut into
 wedges

Heat the onion, chickpeas and broth in a saucepan and cook for 15 minutes. Puree to obtain a smooth cream. Add oil and season with salt and pepper to taste.
Arrange the vegetables on a serving plate or in a salad bowl. Place the chickpea dip into small bowls, garnish with rosemary leaves, and serve.

Eggplant Rolls in Tomato Sauce

Preparation time 20 minutes
Cooking time 10 minutes
Wine *Sicilia Chardonnay*

salt and pepper
1 long eggplant, sliced
 lengthwise
2 tbsps extra-virgin olive oil
1 garlic clove, smashed
1¼ cups (7 oz or 200 g) crushed
 tomatoes
3.5 oz (100 g) fresh spinach
 leaves, chopped
4 oz (120 g) fontina cheese,
 chopped

947

Lightly salt the eggplant and let sit for 30 minutes to purge. Pat dry with paper towels and grill for 30 seconds on each side on a hot cast-iron grill pan.
Heat the oil in a frying pan and sauté garlic. Add the tomatoes, cook for 5 minutes and season with salt and pepper.
Place some spinach and fontina on each eggplant slice and roll up, closing with a toothpick. Place them in a parchment paper-lined baking dish. Pour over the tomatoes and grill for 10 minutes under the grill on the highest setting. Serve hot.

Beans al Fiasco
(TUSCANY)

Note *Traditionally these beans are cooked in a Chianti wine bottle (fiasco) with a wide mouth, made of thick, heat-resistant glass and closed with a damp cloth tied with string. It is then placed in the hot ashes of a fireplace for around 5 hours.*

Preparation time 10 minutes
Cooking time 3 hours

1¾ cups (14 oz or 400 g) dried
 cannellini beans
4 garlic cloves, peeled
 and smashed
sage
6 tbsps extra-virgin olive oil
 (preferably Tuscan)
salt

948

Soak the beans overnight in warm water. Drain.
Place the beans in a large saucepan with the garlic, sage, olive oil and a pinch of salt. Cover with hot water up to 2 inches (5 cm) over the beans. Place in a double boiler and cover. Simmer for 3 hours.
Serve the beans drizzled with more extra-virgin olive oil, accompanied by tuna fillets in olive oil if desired.

Peperonata
(SICILY)

Preparation time 15 minutes
Cooking time 40 minutes
Wine *Sicilia Chardonnay*

4 medium tomatoes
 (around 14 oz or 400 g)
3 tbsps extra-virgin olive oil
1 onion, minced
4 bell peppers, deseeded and
 chopped
1 1/3 cups (3.5 oz or 100 g)
 pitted green olives
salt and pepper

Blanch the tomatoes in boiling
water for a few minutes. Drain,
peel, deseed and chop.
Heat the oil and sauté the onion
until golden. Add the peppers
and sauté until soft. Add the
tomatoes, olives, salt and
pepper and cook, covered, over
medium heat for 30 minutes.
Serve hot.

Salsa Verde
(LOMBARDY)

Preparation time 20 minutes
Cooking time 5 minutes

Serves 6

crusty bread, crust removed
white wine vinegar
2 bunches parsley, minced
capers
2 anchovies
1 garlic clove
1 hard-boiled egg, yolk only
6 tbsps extra-virgin olive oil

949

Soak the bread in a little
vinegar for a few minutes, then
drain and squeeze out excess
liquid. In a food processor, or
with a mortar and pestle, puree
the parsley with a few capers,
the anchovies, garlic, bread,
hard-boiled egg yolk and olive
oil until thoroughly combined.

Green Bean Flan

Preparation time 30 minutes
Cooking time 1 hour
Wine *Valle d'Aosta Bianco*

950

Serves 6

BEANS
3.3 lb (1.5 kg) green beans,
  trimmed
salt
3 tbsps butter
1 onion, minced
2 eggs
4 tbsps grated Parmesan
7 oz (200 g) grated Emmenthal
  cheese

BÉCHAMEL
3 tbsps butter
5 tbsps flour
2 cups (500 ml) warm milk
2 tbsps grated Parmesan
salt
nutmeg, grated

Preheat oven to 350°F (180°C).
Boil the green beans in abundant salted water and drain when
tender.
Melt the butter and sauté the onion until soft. Add the beans and
sauté for 5 minutes. Season with salt.
Make the béchamel: melt the butter in a small saucepan over
medium heat. Sprinkle in the flour, whisking constantly, and then
the warm milk. Add the Parmesan, season with salt and grate in
some nutmeg. Cook for 5-10 minutes, whisking continuously, until
thickened. Add the green beans, eggs, Parmesan and Emmenthal.
Pour into a buttered mould and bake for 30 minutes. Unmould and
serve warm.

Summer Vegetable Quiche

Preparation time 30 minutes
Cooking time 45 minutes
Wine *Metodo Classico*
Franciacorta Brut
ℜ

Serves 8

1 mcdium tomato
3 tbsps extra-virgin olive oil
1/2 onion, thinly sliced
1 cup (3 oz or 80 g) thinly sliced
 mushrooms
1 small zucchini, thinly sliced
salt and pepper
sage and thyme, minced
9 oz (250 g) pie crust dough
 (see p. 1093)

1 cup (3.5 oz or 100 g) grated
 aged pecorino cheese
3 eggs
nutmeg, grated
1 garlic clove, minced
2 cups (500 ml) heavy cream
2/3 cup (150 ml) milk

951

Preheat oven to 350°F (180°C).
Blanch the tomato for a few minutes, drain and cool under cold
running water. Peel and cut into wedges.
Heat the oil in a frying pan then add the onion, mushrooms, zucchini
and tomatoes and cook for 2-3 minutes. Adjust salt and pepper and
stir in the sage and thyme. Let cool.
Roll the dough out to a thickness of 1/5 inch (1/2 cm). Use it to line
a pie dish, then fill with the sautéed vegetables and sprinkle over the
pecorino.
Beat the eggs with salt, pepper, a grating of nutmeg and the minced
garlic. Stir in the cream and milk and whisk everything together.
Pour the mixture over the vegetables and bake for 50 minutes.
During the last 5 minutes raise the oven temperature to 375°F
(190°C). Serve hot or warm.

Zucchini and Basil Flan with Tomato Sauce

Preparation time 20 minutes
Cooking time 45 minutes
Wine *Alto Adige Pinot Bianco*

nutmeg, grated
3-4 basil leaves, minced
1 knob of butter
1 tbsp plain flour

FLAN
4 tbsps extra-virgin olive oil
2 garlic cloves
1 large zucchini (around 10.5 oz
 or 300 g), sliced
salt and pepper
4 eggs
4 tbsps grated Parmesan
3/4 cup plus 1 tbsp (200 ml)
 heavy cream

TOMATO SAUCE
4 vine-ripened tomatoes
3 tbsps extra-virgin olive oil
2 basil leaves
salt

GARNISH
basil leaves
extra-virgin olive oil

Preheat oven to 350°F (180°C).
Heat the oil and sauté the garlic. Add the zucchini, season with salt, add 2 tablespoons of water and cook for 10 minutes. Puree the zucchini and place in a bowl to cool.
Stir the eggs, Parmesan and cream into the pureed zucchini. Season with pepper and nutmeg and adjust the salt. Stir in the basil and pour into buttered and floured moulds. Bake for 35 minutes.
Blanch the tomatoes for 30 seconds, peel, deseed and puree with oil, basil and salt.
Unmould the flans and serve warm with the tomato sauce. Garnish with basil leaves and drizzle with olive oil.

Stuffed Zucchini with Peppers and Tuna

Preparation time 25 minutes
Cooking time 25 minutes
Wine *Locorotondo Riviera*

6 round zucchini
salt and pepper
3 tbsps extra-virgin olive oil
1 shallot, minced
1/2 yellow bell pepper, diced
1/2 red bell pepper, diced
1 tsp sugar
1 tbsp capers
2 tbsps white wine vinegar
5.5 oz (150 g) tuna in oil, drained
parsley, minced
2-3 basil leaves, julienned

953

Preheat oven to 350°F (180°C).

Cut the top part off 4 of the zucchini. Scoop out the interior using a spoon, leaving a 1/5-inch (1/2 cm) thick shell. Boil the shells and lids in salted water for 6-7 minutes, drain and let dry on a wire grill. Dice the remaining 2 zucchini.

Heat 1 tablespoon oil in a saucepan and sauté the shallot until soft. Add the peppers and brown over high heat for 5 minutes. Add the diced zucchini. Sprinkle with sugar, season with salt and add the capers, vinegar and 2 tablespoons water. Cook over medium heat for 10 minutes.

Just before the cooking is finished, crumble in the tuna. Stir in the parsley and mix well.

Fill the zucchini with the mixture, arrange in an oiled baking dish and bake for 10 minutes. Serve the zucchini hot, garnished with basil and a little pepper.

Bavarian Cream with Raspberries

Preparation time 20 minutes
Cooking time 15 minutes
Wine *Trentino Moscato Rosa*

954

6.7 fl oz (200 ml) milk
1 vanilla bean, halved
 lengthwise
6 oz (170 g) white chocolate
2 gelatin sheets
2 egg yolks
3/4 cup (5.2 oz or 150 g) sugar
8.4 fl oz (250 ml) whipping cream
1 basket of raspberries

Heat the milk and vanilla bean. Let cool slightly, scrape out the
vanilla seeds from the bean and add them to the milk. Discard the
bean.
Chop the chocolate and dissolve it in the warm milk.
Soak the gelatin in cold water. Drain, squeeze out the excess
water and add to the milk and chocolate. Stir to dissolve the
gelatin.
Beat the egg yolks with the sugar until thick and creamy. Whisk
the warm milk mixture into the eggs and let cool.
Whip the whipping cream to stiff peaks and fold into the chocolate
cream. Add the raspberries.
Line a loaf pan with plastic wrap and pour the cream into the pan.
Refrigerate for at least 3 hours. Slice and serve.

Mascarpone Cream in Wafer Cups

Preparation time 45 minutes
Cooking time 10 minutes
Wine *Vernaccia di Serrapetrona*
♟ ♟

WAFER CUPS
4 tbsps (2 oz or 60 g) butter,
 softened
1/2 cup (2 oz or 60 g)
 plain flour
2/3 cups (2 oz or 60 g)
 icing sugar
1 tsp vanilla extract
2 egg whites

MASCARPONE CREAM
3 egg yolks
1/2 cup (3 oz or 90 g) sugar
9 oz (250 g) mascarpone

GARNISH
1 knob of butter
2 peaches, sliced
1 tbsp sugar
ground cinnamon
juice of 1/2 lemon

Preheat oven to 375°F (190°C).
Cream the softened butter with the flour, icing sugar, vanilla and egg whites until smooth.
Line a baking sheet with parchment paper. Pour 1 tablespoon of batter onto the baking sheet and spread into a 5-inch (12 cm) diameter circle using the back of a spoon. Bake for 5-6 minutes. Place the hot wafer over the back of a ladle or teacup to form a little bowl. Repeat until the batter is finished.
Beat the egg yolks with the sugar and add the mascarpone. Mix until smooth.
Melt the knob of butter in a non-stick frying pan and add the peaches, sugar, cinnamon and lemon juice. Sauté for a few minutes and remove from heat.
Fill the wafer cups with the cream and top with peaches and cooking liquid.

Apricots in Sauternes Aspic

Preparation time 10 minutes
Cooking time 5 minutes

⚜

2 tbsps (1 oz or 30 g) sugar
2 tbsps Grand Marnier
12 firm apricots, halved
 and pitted
3 gelatin sheets
10 fl oz (300 ml) Sauternes wine
1/3 cup (1 oz or 30 g) sliced
 almonds, toasted

Heat the sugar, Grand Marnier
and 1 tablespoon water in a
frying pan and add the apricots.
Sauté over high heat for 2
minutes.
Soak the gelatin in water, drain
and squeeze out the excess
water. Dissolve the gelatin in
the wine.
Pour a quarter of the wine into
a soufflé dish to form a single
layer and chill until firm.
Cut the apricot halves into
slices, place the slices on the
gelatin and top with the toasted
almonds. Cover with the
remaining gelatin and refrigerate
for 3 hours. Unmould the aspic
and serve.

Nectarines with Sauternes

Preparation time 20 minutes
Cooking time 10 minutes
Wine *Sauternes*

⚜

2 firm white nectarines, thinly
 sliced
3.4 fl oz (100 ml) Sauternes wine
2 tbsps raisins
5 amaretto cookies
mint leaves

Place the nectarine slices in
a bowl with the Sauternes
and raisins. Stir and leave to
marinate for 30 minutes.
Drain the nectarines, reserving
the Sauternes marinade, and
divide them between 4 wine
glasses. Top with crushed
amaretto cookies.
Cook the reserved marinade
over medium heat until reduced
in volume. Pour the reduced
syrup over the nectarines and
garnish with mint leaves.

956

Summer Fruit Cup

Preparation time 15 minutes
♟

8.4 fl oz (250 ml) whipping cream
icing sugar
2 peaches
2 apricots
2 loquats
2 French plums
4 ladyfingers
Grand Marnier liqueur

Whip the whipping cream with
a pinch of icing sugar.
Pit and slice all the fruit.
Soak ladyfingers in the Grand
Marnier.
Line 4 small serving bowls with
a third of the ladyfingers and
top with whipped cream. Add
some of the fruit. Make 2 more
layers, finishing with whipped
cream. Sprinkle with icing
sugar, and serve.

Raspberry Vanilla Coulis

Preparation time 20 minutes
Cooking time 15 minutes
Wine *Moscato Passito*
di Pantelleria
♟

2 tbsps sugar
3.4 fl oz (100 ml) water
1 vanilla bean
1 basket of raspberries

Bring the sugar, water and
vanilla bean to a boil. Reduce
heat and simmer for 5 minutes.
Remove the vanilla bean and
slice it in half lengthwise. Return
the bean to the pan and reduce
the syrup for another few
minutes.
Remove from heat and remove
the vanilla bean. Scrape out the
seeds and return them to the
pan. Discard the bean.
Puree the raspberries, adding
the syrup slowly.
Serve the coulis with ice cream
or cheesecake as desired.

Apricot Canederli
(TRENTINO-ALTO ADIGE)

Preparation time 40 minutes
Cooking time 50 minutes
Wine *Alto Adige Moscato Giallo
Spumante*

Serves 6

CANEDERLI
12 apricots
4 medium potatoes
salt
1 knob of butter
1⅔ cups (7 oz or 200 g)
 plain flour
2 eggs, beaten

BROWN BUTTER
10 tbsps butter (5.2 oz or 150 g)
2/3 cup (2.4 oz or 70 g)
 breadcrumbs
sugar

958

Remove the pits from the apricots without cutting the apricots in half completely.
Boil the potatoes in salted water. Drain, peel and mash the potatoes with a potato ricer. Add the butter to the potatoes and sift in the flour. Mix well and then add the beaten eggs and a pinch of salt. Mix the dough until it is smooth and divide it into 12 portions. Roll each bit of dough into a ball. Make an indentation in the dough and push in an apricot. Cover the apricot with the dough.
Bring a pot of salted water to a boil and carefully add the canederli. Boil until the dumplings come to the surface.
Brown the butter in a frying pan and transfer the canederli from the boiling water to the pan using a slotted spoon. Sauté for 2 minutes and sprinkle with breadcrumbs. Place on a serving dish and sprinkle generously with sugar.

Buckwheat Cake
(TRENTINO-ALTO ADIGE)

Preparation time 40 minutes
Cooking time 45 minutes
Wine *Alto Adige Moscato Giallo*

Serves 6

1⅓ cups (10.5 oz or 300 g)
 butter, softened
1½ cups (10.5 oz or 300 g) sugar
6 eggs, separated
2 tsps vanilla extract
2½ cups (10.5 oz or 300 g)
 buckwheat flour
3 tbsps plain flour
2 tsps baking powder
blackcurrant or blueberry jam
icing sugar

Preheat oven to 350°F (180°C).
Cream the butter and sugar. Add the egg yolks one at a time and
then the vanilla and mix until creamy. Sift in the flours and baking
powder.
Beat the egg whites to stiff peaks and fold into the batter.
Butter and flour a cake pan and pour in the batter. Bake for 45
minutes. Remove from the oven and let cool. Cut the cake in half
horizontally to form 2 rounds. Spread the jam over one round and
top with the remaining round. Sprinkle with icing sugar and serve.

Basil Chantilly Cream

Preparation time 30 minutes
Cooking time 25 minutes

Serves 6

17 fl oz (500 ml) milk
zest of 1 lemon
12 basil leaves
2 egg yolks
1/2 cup (3.8 oz or 110 g)
 plus, 1 tsp sugar
 1/3 cup (1.4 oz or 40 g)
 plain flour
1 basket of raspberries
8.4 fl oz (250 ml) water
3 tbsps whipping cream
9 ladyfingers

960

Heat the milk with the lemon zest. Add the basil and let sit for 2 hours. Strain the milk and bring to a boil.

Beat the egg yolks with the sugar and then add the flour. Whisk in the boiling milk and transfer the mixture back to the saucepan. Cook over low heat for 10 minutes. Remove from heat and let cool.

Place the raspberries, water and 1 teaspoon of sugar in a small saucepan and cook over high heat. When the sugar begins to caramelize remove from heat and puree the mixture.

Whip the whipping cream to stiff peaks and fold it into the cooled pastry cream.

Dip the ladyfingers in the raspberry sauce.

Pour the remaining raspberry sauce into a trifle bowl, line the bowl with the ladyfingers and top with the Chantilly cream.

Cold Melon and Strawberry Soup

Preparation time 20 minutes
Cooking time 15 minutes
Wine *Ruby Port*

WAFERS
1 knob of butter
2 tbsps raw sugar
3 tbsps plain flour
1 tbsp honey

SOUP
1½ cups (8 oz or 230 g)
  strawberries, hulled
1/2 small melon, peeled,
  deseeded and diced
1/3 cup (2.8 oz or 80 g) sugar
2 tbsps ruby port wine
3.4 fl oz (100 ml) water

Preheat oven to 325°F (170°C).
Mix the butter, sugar, flour and honey until it forms a smooth dough. Refrigerate.
Puree three-quartess of the strawberries and melon in the blender.
Heat the sugar in a saucepan until it begins to caramelize. Add the port and water and reduce to a thin syrup. Let cool.
Pour the cooled syrup over the pureed fruit and puree again. Refrigerate.
Meanwhile, roll the wafer dough into balls and place the balls on a parchment paper-lined baking sheet. Flatten the balls into disks and bake for 8-9 minutes. Remove from the oven and mould the hot wafers over a teacup or ladle to form small cups. Let cool.
Fill the wafer cups with the remaining strawberries and melon.
Puree the fruit soup one more time to emulsify and then pour it into shallow bowls. Place 1 fruit basket in each bowl. Serve immediately.

Pine Nut Wafers with Steamed Apricots

Preparation time 15 minutes
Cooking time 15 minutes
Wine *Trentino Moscato Rosa*

APRICOTS
8 small apricots, halved and
 pitted
2 cinnamon sticks
4 mint leaves

WAFERS
7 tbsps (3.5 oz or 100 g) butter
2 egg whites

1 cup (3.5 oz or 100 g)
 icing sugar
1/2 cup (2.4 oz or 70 g)
 plain flour
1/4 cup (1 oz or 30 g) ground
 pine nuts

GARNISH
2 tbsps sweetened plain yogurt
mint leaves
ground cinnamon

962

Preheat oven to 400°F (200°C).
Place the apricots, cinnamon and mint in a ziploc plastic bag and
steam for 15 minutes. Let cool.
Melt the butter and cool.
Meanwhile, beat the egg whites and the icing sugar to very soft
peaks. Whisk in the cooled, melted butter, flour and ground pine
nuts. Refrigerate for 10 minutes.
Line a baking sheet with parchment paper.
Place teaspoonfuls of dough on the baking sheet. Using the back
of a spoon, spread the dough to form rounds. Bake for 5 minutes
or until the wafers begin to colour. Remove from the oven and
mould the hot wafers over teacups to form little bowls.
Once the apricots are cool, fill each wafer bowl with an apricot
half. Top with a dollop of yogurt and a mint leaf. Sprinkle with
cinnamon.

Sebadas
(SARDINIA)

Preparation time 40 minutes
Cooking time 30 minutes
Wine *Nasco di Cagliari Liquoroso Dolce*
♟ ♟

Serves 8

FILLING
2.2 lb (1 kg) soft mild cheese
4.2 fl oz (125 ml) warm water
1 tbsp vanilla extract
zest of 1 orange
1/3 cup plus 2 tbsps
 (1.7 oz or 50 g) plain flour

DOUGH
2.2 lb (1 kg) plain flour
1 cup (7 oz or 200 g) lard
salt

FRYING
sunflower oil

GARNISH
bitter honey (such as chestnut)

965

Slice the cheese and place in a saucepan with the water, vanilla and orange zest. Cook over medium heat until the cheese melts. Remove from heat and whisk in the flour.
Divide the cheese mixture into walnut-sized balls and place them on a damp cutting board. Press down on the balls to flatten and set aside. Meanwhile, pour the flour for the dough onto a work surface and work in the lard and salt. Slowly add enough warm water to form a smooth, elastic dough.
Roll out the dough into a thick sheet. Using a cookie cutter, cut out several circles. Place 1 piece of the cheese filling on half of the dough circles. Cover with the remaining circles of dough. Press down around the edges to seal.
Heat the oil in a saucepan and fry the sebadas until they are golden-brown. Drizzle with honey.

Melon and Vodka Aspic

Preparation time 15 minutes
Cooking time 5 minutes
Wine *Gewürztraminer Vendemmia Tardiva*
♟

1 yellow melon
3 gelatin sheets
1/2 cup (3.5 oz or 100 g) sugar
3.4 fl oz (100 ml) late-harvest
 Gewürztraminer wine
2 tbsps melon-flavoured vodka
6.7 fl oz (200 ml) water

966

Halve and deseed the melon.
Make melon balls with a melon baller.
Soak the gelatin sheets in cold water. Drain and squeeze out the excess water.
Heat the sugar, wine and vodka in a frying pan. Add melon balls and sauté for 2-3 minutes. Add the water and continue cooking for another 3 minutes. Remove from heat and add the gelatin.
Pour the mixture into 4 small, square moulds and let cool.
Once cool refrigerate for 2 hours.
Dip the moulds in hot water, unmould and serve immediately.

Cold Melon-Port Soup

Preparation time 10 minutes
Wine *Ruby Port*
♟

1 melon
6 tbsps sugar
2 fl oz (60 ml) ruby port wine
mint leaves

Peel, seed and dice the melon.
Puree with the sugar.
Transfer the puree to a bowl and slowly mix in the port.
Pour the mixture into individual serving bowls and refrigerate until serving. Garnish with mint leaves.

Note *Port is a sweet, fortified wine originally from the Douro Valley in Portugal. There are serverd kinds, like tawny, ruby and white. Port and melon is a classic Mediterranean pairing.*

Sauternes Jellies with Blackberries

Preparation time 15 minutes
Cooking time 2 minutes
Wine *Sauternes*

10 fl oz (300 ml) Sauternes wine
1 tsp lemon juice
1 tbsp sugar
1 tsp agar agar
4 mint sprigs
4 blackberries

Heat the wine in a saucepan over low heat. Add lemon juice, sugar and agar agar powder. Dissolve, stirring frequently, and cook for 2 minutes until the liquid is smooth.
Cut a sheet of wax paper into 4 triangles. Roll each triangle around a rolling pin to form a cylinder and tape it closed. Place the wax paper cylinders in narrow glasses and pour the wine mixture into the waxed-paper moulds. Refrigerate until firm. Remove the glasses from the refrigerator and unwrap the jelly.
Place the jellies on a plate and decorate with mint leaves and blackberries.

Coconut-Almond Granita

Preparation time 15 minutes

3.4 fl oz (100 ml) coconut milk
6.7 fl oz (200 ml) almond milk
2 tbsps sugar
1¼ cups (3.5 oz or 100 g) coconut shavings
chocolate shavings

Strain the coconut milk and pour it into a bowl. Stir in the almond milk. Add the sugar and stir until it dissolves and then add the coconut shavings. Freeze the mixture for about 3 hours.
Remove from the freezer and place the frozen mixture in a food processor. Pulse the mixture to break up the ice into a slushy consistency.
Decorate the granita with chocolate shavings and serve immediately.

Peach Semifreddo

Preparation time 30 minutes
Cooking time 10 minutes
Wine *Zibibbo*

968

SEMIFREDDO
4 ripe peaches, peeled and
 diced
1/3 cup (2 oz or 60 g) sugar
juice of 1/2 lemon
fruity white wine
1 gelatin sheet
5 fl oz (150 ml) whipping cream

JELLY
3 passion fruits
2 tsps apple juice concentrate
1.6 fl oz (50 ml) water
1 tsp lemon juice
1 gelatin sheet

Sauté the peaches in a frying pan with the sugar and lemon juice.
Add some wine when the peaches are hot and cook over low heat
until just tender. Transfer to a blender and puree.
Soak the gelatin in cold water. Drain and squeeze out the excess
water. Add the gelatin to the peach puree. Chill the puree.
Whip the whipping cream and fold it into the puree.
Line a small rectangular baking dish with parchment paper and
pour in the peach mixture. Freeze until firm.
Meanwhile, remove the pulp from the passion fruits and place it
in a saucepan with the apple juice concentrate, water and lemon
juice. Cook over medium heat for a few minutes.
Soak the gelatin sheet in cold water. Drain and squeeze out the
excess water. Add the gelatin to the passion fruit mixture and let
cool slightly. Pour the mixture over the peach cream and return it
to the freezer.
Cut the peach cream into small rectangles and serve with chopped
hazelnut pralines, if desired.

Coffee Ice Cream Soufflés

Preparation time 25 minutes
Cooking time 10 minutes
Wine *Marsala Dolce*

4 egg yolks
2/3 cup (4.4 oz or 125 g) sugar
1 tbsp coffee liqueur
2 fl oz (60 ml) strong coffee
2 egg whites
6 fl oz (180 ml) whipping cream
1 tsp cocoa powder

Prepare the soufflé cups by cutting out 4 strips of aluminum foil. The strips should be at least 2 inches wider than the height of individual ramequirs. Line the edges of 4 ramequins with the aluminum foil. Secure the foil with tape. Place the ramequins in the refrigerator.

Beat the egg yolks with half of the sugar in a double boiler. Cook the mixture, stirring constantly, until it is dense and foamy. Remove from heat and add the coffee liqueur and coffee. Pour the mixture into a bowl and refrigerate.

Meanwhile, whip the egg whites to stiff peaks. Add the remaining sugar and then fold into the coffee mixture.

Whip the whipping cream to stiff peaks. Fold it into the coffee mixture. Spoon the coffee cream into the ramequins and refrigerate overnight. Remove the aluminum foil before serving and sprinkle with cocoa powder.

Creamy Coffee Granita

Preparation time 10 minutes

12 ice cubes, chopped
8.4 fl oz (250 ml) coffee, cooled
3 tbsps simple syrup
4 tbsps whipping cream

Place half the chopped ice in the blender. Add the cold coffee and the simple syrup.
Blend for 1 minute. While blending, pour in the whipping cream.
Place the remaining ice in glasses or cups and pour the coffee granita over the ice.
Serve immediately.

Note *In Sicily coffee granita is served with whipped cream and sweet brioche for breakfast in the summer.*

Strawberry and Apricot Mousse

Preparation time 20 minutes
Cooking time 10 minutes
Wine *Asti Moscato Spumante*

10 strawberries, hulled and diced
6 apricots, peeled, pitted and sliced
3 gelatin sheets
4 fl oz (125 ml) water
1 cup (7 oz or 200 g) sugar
10 fl oz (300 ml) whipping cream

Puree strawberries and apricots separately and refrigerate.
Soak gelatin in cold water, drain and squeeze out excess water.
In a small saucepan heat the water and sugar then add the gelatin. Let simmer for 10 minutes and remove from heat.
Let cool and then refrigerate.
Whip the cream to stiff peaks.
Add half the sugar syrup to the apricots and half to the strawberries. Fold half the cream into each of the fruit mixtures.
Layer the mousses in a single mould and refrigerate for 2 hours.
Unmould and serve.

970

Berry Tarts with Ricotta Cream

Preparation time 30 minutes
Cooking time 8 minutes
Wine *Verduzzo di Ramandolo*
♟ ♟

10.5 oz (300 g) puff pastry
2 tbsps sugar
5.2 oz (150 g) ricotta
2.8 oz (80 g) mild goat's cheese
3.5 oz (100 g) fresh cow's
 cheese
2.8 oz (80 g) mascarpone
2 tbsps icing sugar,
 plus more for garnish
7 oz (200 g) mixed berries
zest of 1 lime

Preheat oven to 425°F (220°C).
Roll out puff pastry into a thin
sheet. Pierce surface with a fork
and then cut into small squares.
Place the squares on a
parchment paper-lined baking
sheet. Sprinkle with sugar and
bake for 8 minutes. Let cool.
Beat the ricotta, cheeses and
mascarpone until smooth. Mix in
the sugar then sieve the mixture.
Toss berries with lime zest.
Make sandwiches with the pastry
squares, cheese cream and
berries. Sprinkle the sandwiches
with icing sugar.

Lemon and Basil Sorbet

Preparation time 10 minutes
Cooking time 2 minutes
♟

10 fl oz (300 ml) water
1 cup (7 oz or 200 g) sugar
3 lemons
2 fl oz (60 ml) vodka
10 basil leaves, chopped, plus
 more for garnish
1 egg white

Boil the water and sugar with
the peel of 1 lemon for 2
minutes. Remove and discard
the lemon peel and let the
syrup cool.
Stir the juice from the remaining
lemons, vodka and chopped
basil into the syrup.
Beat the egg white until it forms
stiff peaks and fold it into the
syrup. Freeze the mixture for 2
hours.
Transfer the mixture to an ice-
cream maker or blender. Blend
until creamy.
Garnish the sorbet with
whole basil leaves and serve
immediately.

Maritozzi

(Lazio)

Note *These sweet rolls originated in Roman times. In the Middle Ages maritozzi were a concession to fasting during the Lent period. Today maritozzi are a popular morning snack and can be filled with pastry cream or whipped cream.*

Preparation time 40 minutes
Cooking time 10 minutes
Wine *Cesanese di Affile Spumante Dolce*

Serves 6

2/3 cup (3.5 oz or 100 g) raisins
1 lb (500 g) yeast bread dough
4 tbsps extra-virgin olive oil
1/3 cup (1.7 oz or 50 g) candied citron, chopped
1/3 cup (1.7 oz or 50 g) pine nuts
4 tbsps sugar
salt
whipped cream

972

Soak the raisins in warm water for 10 minutes. Drain and carefully squeeze out the excess water.
Place the prepared bread dough on a work surface and knead in the oil, raisins, candied citron, pine nuts, 2 tablespoons sugar and a pinch of salt. Knead vigorously to obtain a smooth dough. Divide the dough into 20-24 equal pieces. Form oval-shaped rolls with the dough pieces. Let the rolls rise in a warm place for 2 hours.
Preheat oven to 485°F (250°C).
Oil a baking sheet and place the rolls on the sheet. Bake for 7 minutes. Meanwhile, dissolve the remaining 2 tablespoons sugar in a little water. Remove the rolls from the oven, brush them with the syrup and bake for 2 more minutes.
Serve the maritozzi filled with whipped cream.

Chiavari Cake
(LIGURIA)

Preparation time 25 minutes
Cooking time 1 minute
Wine *Riviera Ligure di Ponente
Ormeasco Sciacchetrà*

Serves 6

1 square sheet of sponge cake
2 fl oz (60 ml) Curaçao liqueur
33 fl oz (1 l) whipping cream
3 egg yolks
2 tbsps sugar
4.2 fl oz (125 ml) Marsala wine
6 amaretto cookies
2 fl oz (60 ml) rum
2 tbsps butter, melted
25-30 langues de chat cookies

Slice the sponge cake in half horizontally to form 2 thin rectangular sheets. Reserve any crumbs. Brush the sponge cake with Curaçao.
Meanwhile, toast the sponge cake crumbs and push then through a sieve to make a fine powder.
Whip the whipping cream to stiff peaks and set aside. In another mixing bowl, beat the egg yolks, sugar and Marsala wine until thick and foamy.
Place the first layer of sponge cake in the centre of a serving plate. Frost the sponge cake with layers of whipped cream (reserve a quarter of the whipped cream) and Marsala mixture, finishing with a final layer of whipped cream. Crumble the amaretto cookies over the whipped cream and sprinkle with rum. Top with the second sheet of sponge cake. Frost the second layer with the remaining whipped cream and the powder made from the sponge cake crumbs. Brush the sides of the cake with butter and stick the langues de chat cookies to the sides. Refrigerate before serving.

Watermelon and Mint Granita

Preparation time 15 minutes

10 oz (300 g) watermelon
juice of 1/2 lemon
10 mint leaves, plus extra
 for garnish

Chop the watermelon flesh into
chunks, removing the seeds.
Freeze the watermelon chunks
until hard.
Remove from the freezer and
pour over the lemon juice.
Place in a food processor and
add the mint leaves. Pulse the
mixture until slushy.
Transfer the granita to wine or
martini glasses. Garnish with
the extra mint leaves and serve
immediately.

White Chocolate-Berry Mousse

Preparation time 20 minutes
Cooking time 10 minutes

7 oz (200 g) mixed berries
zest of 1 lemon
3 tbsps malt extract
1/2 tsp agar agar powder
3.5 oz (100 g) white chocolate
3.4 fl oz (100 ml) whipping cream
round wafers cookies

Cook the berries with the lemon
zest, malt extract and agar agar
then let cool.
Melt the chocolate over a
double boiler. Remove from
heat and stir until cool.
Whip the whipping cream
to stiff peaks and fold it into
the chocolate. Add the berry
mixture and fold.
Refrigerate for 1 hour. Serve the
mousse with wafer cookies.

974

Strawberry Sorbet

Preparation time 30 minutes
Cooking time 10 minutes

6.7 fl oz (200 ml) water
2 tbsps sugar
juice and peel of 1 lemon
1 basket wild strawberries
1/2 tsp agar agar
3 tsps strawberry-flavoured
  vodka
1 green apple, sliced
4 scoops lemon sorbet

Bring the water, sugar, lemon juice and a piece of lemon peel to a boil.
Add the wild strawberries to the saucepan and cook for 10 minutes.
Strain the mixture and add the agar agar. Stir to dissolve. Add the vodka, pour the mixture into wine or martini glasses and refrigerate.
Decorate each glass with apple slices and top with a scoop of lemon sorbet. Serve immediately.

Tiramisù with Wild Strawberries

Preparation time 15 minutes
Cooking time 10 minutes
Wine *Prosecco di Valdobbiadene Brut*

Serves 8-10

8 oz (250 g) strawberries, halved
juice of 1 lemon
1¼ cups (8.8 oz or 250 g) sugar
2 fl oz (60 ml) Cognac
2 fl oz (60 ml) strawberry liqueur
6 eggs, separated
17 oz (500 g) mascarpone
14 oz (400 g) ladyfingers
2 small baskets of wild
  strawberries

975

Place the strawberries, lemon juice, 1/2 cup (3.5 oz or 100 g) sugar, Cognac and strawberry liqueur in a saucepan. Simmer for 10 minutes. Puree. Let cool.
Beat egg whites to stiff peaks. Beat egg yolks with remaining sugar, add mascarpone and fold in the egg whites.
Dip the ladyfingers in the strawberry puree. In a rectangular baking dish layer the ladyfingers and cream. Top with wild strawberries and refrigerate until serving.

Brigidini di Lamporecchio
(TUSCANY)

Note *Local legend says that these Tuscan sweets were first made by the nuns at the Lamporecchio convent of Saint Brigit. An error was made in the preparation of the holy host and the nuns, not wanting to waste the batter, invented this delicious sweet.*

Preparation time 15 minutes
Cooking time 10 minutes

5 eggs
1 cup (7 oz or 200 g) sugar
3 tbsps anise seeds
1 tsp vanilla extract
3¼ cups (14 oz or 400 g) plain flour
salt

976

Preheat oven to 425°F (220°C).
Beat the eggs and sugar until creamy. Add the anise seeds and vanilla and sift in the flour and a pinch of salt. Knead the mixture until smooth. Divide the dough into little balls and roll out each ball with a rolling pin.
Place the cookies on an oiled baking sheet and bake until golden-brown.

Strawberry Mousse in Cookie Shells

Preparation time 30 minutes
Cooking time 10 minutes
Wine *Asti Moscato Spumante*
♟ ♟ ♟

MOUSSE
3 gelatin sheets
10 fl oz (300 ml) whipping cream
14 oz (400 g) strawberries,
 hulled
1/2 cup (3.5 oz or 100 g) sugar
grated zest of 1/2 lemon

COOKIES
4 tbsps butter

1/2 cup (1.7 oz or 50 g)
 icing sugar
2 egg whites
2 tsps vanilla extract
1/3 cup plus 2 tbsps
 (1.7 oz or 50 g) plain flour

STRAWBERRY SAUCE
7 oz (200 g) strawberries, diced
1 knob of butter
2 tbsps sugar

977

Preheat oven to 400°F (200°C).
Soak the gelatin in cold water. Drain and squeeze out the excess
water. Dissolve the gelatin in 1 tablespoon of whipping cream.
Puree the strawberries and mix with gelatin, sugar and lemon zest.
Whip the remaining cream to stiff peaks and fold into the strawberries.
Pour the mousse into a loaf pan. Refrigerate for 1 hour.
Meanwhile cream the butter, icing sugar, egg whites, vanilla and flour.
Mix until smooth.
Place several round metal cookie cutters, 4 inches (10 cm) in
diameter, on a baking sheet. Pour some of the batter into each one,
forming a thin layer. Bake for 4-5 minutes. Remove from the oven and
cool slightly. Remove the cookies from the cookie cutters and pinch
the edges of one side together to form a shell shape.
Sauté the diced strawberries with butter and sugar for 3-4 minutes.
Place the cookie shells on serving plates and fill with the mousse. Top
with warm strawberries and sprinkle with icing sugar.

Peaches and Cream

Preparation time 40 minutes
Cooking time 25 minutes
Wine *Malvasia delle Lipari*

ALMOND BRITTLE
3/4 cups (100 g) almonds
1/2 cup (1.7 oz or 100 g) sugar
3 tbsps water

CREAM
3 gelatin sheets
10 fl oz (300 ml) milk
zest of 1 lemon
1 vanilla bean
3 egg yolks
1/2 cup (3.8 oz or 110 g) sugar
8.4 fl oz (250 ml) whipping cream

PEACHES
2 peaches, peeled and sliced
2 tbsps butter
1/4 cup (1.7 oz or 50 g) sugar
zest of 1 lemon

978

Soak the gelatin in cold water. Drain and squeeze out the excess water.
Simmer the milk and lemon zest with the vanilla bean.
Beat the egg yolks and sugar until thick and then whisk in the strained hot milk. Add the gelatin and mix well. Let cool.
Whip the whipping cream to stiff peaks and fold it into the cooled cream. Pour the mixture into individual ramequins and refrigerate for 1 hour.
Place the almonds, sugar and water into a saucepan. Cook over medium heat until the mixture caramelizes and continue cooking until it turns a deep amber-brown colour. Remove from heat and pour onto a parchment paper-lined baking sheet.
When the brittle is cool, break it into small pieces.
Sauté the peaches with the butter, sugar and lemon zest for 5 minutes.
Invert the ramequins onto serving plates and top with warm peaches and almond brittle.

Melon and Port Wine Sorbet

Preparation time 10 minutes
Cooking time 10 minutes
♟

10 fl oz (300 ml) water
3/3 cups (5.6 oz or 160 g) sugar
10.5 oz (300 g) melon
2 tsps port wine
1.6 fl oz (50 ml) dextrose syrup
3 tbsps poppy seeds
mint leaves

Boil the water and sugar in a saucepan for 7-8 minutes until syrupy.
Peel, seed and dice the melon. Puree the melon with the port and then add the hot syrup. Mix in the dextrose syrup. Let cool slightly and freeze the sorbet in an ice-cream machine.
Sprinkle the sorbet with poppy seeds and mint leaves and serve.

Raspberry and Blueberry Sorbet

Preparation time 20 minutes
Cooking time 1 minute
♟

10.5 oz (300 g) blueberries
10.5 oz (300 g) raspberries
8.4 fl oz (250 ml) water
1½ cups (10.5 oz or 300 g) sugar
mint leaves

Puree the blueberries and raspberries.
Heat the water in a saucepan without boiling. When the water is hot add the sugar and dissolve. Remove from heat and add the berry puree. Place the pan in ice water to cool quickly. Once cool refrigerate the mixture for 2 hours.
Place the berry mixture in an ice-cream machine and follow manufacturers' instructions for sorbet. Freeze until serving. Garnish with mint leaves.

979

Grape Schiaccia
(Tuscany)

Preparation time 30 minutes
Cooking time 1 hour
Wine *Moscato Bianco Passito*

1 lb (500 g) black or red grapes
2½ tsps dry active yeast
1/2 cup (120 ml) warm water
4 cups (17.6 oz or 500 g)
 plain flour
1½ cups (10.5 oz or 300 g) sugar
1 tbsp extra-virgin olive oil
1 knob of butter

980

Preheat the oven to 300°F (150°C).
Remove the grapes from the stems, taking care not to break them.
Dissolve the yeast in the warm water.
Mound the flour on a work surface and make a well in the centre.
Add half the grapes, the yeast water, sugar and olive oil. Mix well
and then knead for 10 minutes. If the dough becomes too sticky
add a little flour.
Form the dough into a ball and cover it with a kitchen towel. Let
rise for 1 hour in a cool dry place.
Butter and flour a baking sheet. Place the dough on the baking
sheet and spread out the dough by hand, pressing with fingertips,
until it covers most of the pan.
Distribute the remaining grapes over the dough. Sprinkle
generously with sugar. Bake for 1 hour.

Sugal di Ferrara
(EMILIA ROMAGNA)

Note *The traditional recipe for this pudding calls for a sauce made from freshly crushed wine grapes. For the best results, use wine grapes in this recipe.*

Preparation time 40 minutes
Cooking time 1 hour 30 minutes
♟ ♟

sweet red grapes
cornmeal
1 tbsp sugar

Cook the grapes in a saucepan for 30 minutes. Transfer the cooked grapes to a mixing bowl, cover with a kitchen towel and refrigerate for 24 hours.
Strain the grapes with a fine mesh sieve. Add 1/3 cup (1.7 oz or 50 g) of cornmeal for every 4 cups (1 liter) of juice obtained. Mix in the cornmeal and sugar and cook over medium heat until the mixture is thick and smooth. Reduce the heat when the mixture comes to a boil and cook for 1 hour. Divide the sugal into serving bowls and let cool until firm.
The sugal may be preserved in the refrigerator for 2-3 days.

Mascarpone and Cherry Semifreddo

Preparation time 30 minutes
Cooking time 25 minutes
Wine *Metodo Classico*
Franciacorta Rosé
♟ ♟

SEMIFREDDO
1 knob of butter
10.5 oz (300 g) cherries, halved
 and pitted
5 egg yolks
1/3 cup (80 g) sugar
3.4 fl oz (100 ml) milk
zest of 1 lemon
10 fl oz (300 ml) whipping cream

GARNISH
8.8 oz (250 g) mascarpone
1 tbsp powdered sugar
2 tbsps plain yogurt
1 knob of butter
1/3 cup (2 oz or 60 g) sugar
7 oz (200 g) cherries, halved
 and pitted

982

Heat the butter in a frying pan, add the cherries and sauté for 2-3 minutes.
Beat the egg yolks with the sugar, milk and lemon zest. Transfer to a double boiler and cook over medium heat, whisking constantly, until thick and creamy. Add the cherries to the egg mixture and stir to incorporate. Remove from heat and let cool.
Whip the whipping cream and fold into the cooled egg mixture. Transfer the mixture to a bowl and freeze for 3 hours.
Meanwhile, beat the mascarpone with the sugar and yogurt. Heat the butter and sugar in a frying pan, add the cherries and let caramelize for 5-6 minutes. Remove from heat and let cool.
Slice the semifreddo and place on individual serving plates.
Top with mascarpone cream and caramelized cherries. Serve immediately.

Ricotta Cake with Wild Strawberries

Preparation time 30 minutes
Cooking time 5 minutes
Wine *Verduzzo di Ramandolo*
♟ ♟

Serves 6-8

4.2 oz (120 g) graham crackers
1/3 cup (1.7 oz or 50 g)
 hazelnuts
11 tbsps (5.2 oz or 150 g) melted
 butter

1/2 cup (3.5 oz or 100 g) sugar
12.3 oz (350 g) ricotta
6.7 fl oz (200 ml) whipping cream
3 eggs, separated
zest of 1 lemon
4 gelatin sheets
2 tbsps brandy
10.5 oz (300 g) wild strawberries,
 nulled
3 tbsps redcurrant jelly
2 tbsps water

Pulse the graham crackers and the hazelnuts in a food processor. Add the melted butter and 1/3 cup (2.8 oz or 80 g) of sugar and pulse to combine. Line the bottom of a spring-form pan with the graham-cracker mixture and refrigerate until firm.

Mix the ricotta, whipping cream and the remaining sugar. Add the egg yolks and lemon zest.

Soak the gelatin sheets in cold water. Drain and squeeze out the excess water. Dissolve the gelatin in the brandy and add to the ricotta mixture.

Whip the egg whites to stiff peaks and fold into the ricotta mixture. Pour half of the ricotta filling over the graham cracker crust and top with wild strawberries. Top with the remaining ricotta filling and refrigerate for 2 hours.

Heat the redcurrant jelly in a small pan with the water. Brush the top of the cake with the currant glaze and return to the refrigerator. Chill before serving.

Pear and Apricot Tart

Preparation time 30 minutes
Cooking time 45 minutes
Wine *Metodo Classico*
Franciacorta Rosé Demi-Sec
♟ ♟

Serves 6

TART
1 cup plus 2 tbsps
 (8.8 oz or 250 g) butter
1¼ cups (8.8 oz or 250 g) sugar
2 eggs
4 cups (17 oz or 500 g)
 plain flour

zest of 1 lemon
2 tsps baking powder

FILLING
3 large pears, sliced
1/4 cup (1 oz or 30 g) pine nuts
3/4 cup (8.8 oz or 250 g) apricot
 jam

GARNISH
pine nuts
ground cinnamon

984

Cream the butter and then gradually add the sugar, eggs, flour,
lemon zest and baking powder. Mix to form a smooth dough. Roll
the dough into a ball, cover and refrigerate for 15 minutes.
Preheat oven to 350°F (180°C).
Blanch the pears in boiling water for 3 minutes. Drain and cool.
Line a tart tin with parchment paper. Roll out three-quarters of
the dough and line the tin. Layer the pears and pine nuts over the
dough. Roll out the remaining dough and slice it into thin strips.
Using the dough strips, form a lattice over the top of the tart.
Bake for 30 minutes. Remove the tart from the oven and add the
apricot jam to the spaces between the lattice top. Return to the
oven and bake for another 10 minutes.
Let cool and decorate with pine nuts and ground cinnamon.

Blackberry Cake with Chocolate Sauce

Preparation time 25 minutes
Cooking time 10 minutes
Wine *Alto Adige Moscato Rosa*

zest of 1 lemon
1 tsp vanilla extract
2 fl oz (60 ml) whipping cream

GARNISH
20 blackberries

CAKE
1 basket of blackberries
2 tbsps sugar
5 fl oz (150 ml) water
4 rounds of sponge cake
5.2 oz (150 g) mascarpone
5.2 oz (150 g) ricotta
2 tbsps icing sugar

CHOCOLATE SAUCE
3.5 oz (100 g) milk chocolate
2 fl oz (60 ml) whipping cream

Place the berries in a saucepan with the sugar and water. Bring to a boil and cook for 8 minutes. Remove from heat and puree the cooked berries.
Slice each sponge cake round in half horizontally. Brush the 8 sponge cake rounds with berry puree.
Beat the mascarpone and ricotta with the icing sugar, lemon zest and vanilla extract. Whip the whipping cream to stiff peaks and fold into the mascarpone mixture.
Fill a pastry bag with the mascarpone filling. Pipe the filling between each layer of cake, and frost the top with the filling. Decorate with blackberries.
Heat the chocolate and whipping cream in a double boiler. Stir until melted and remove from heat.
Serve the cake with the chocolate sauce.

Banana Tart

Preparation 30 minutes
Cooking time 40 minutes
🍳 🍳

Serves 6

DOUGH
4 eggs, separated
3/4 cup (5.2 oz or 150 g) sugar
1 cup (4.2 oz or 120 g)
 corn flour
juice of 1/2 lemon
1 knob of butter

CREAM
8.4 fl oz (250 ml) milk
2 tsps vanilla extract
2 eggs, separated
1/3 cup (2 oz or 60 g) sugar
2 bananas
2 tbsps Maraschino liqueur

GARNISH
1 banana, sliced
icing sugar

986

Preheat oven to 320°F (160°C).
Mix the egg yolks and sugar, then add the corn flour and lemon juice.
Beat the egg whites to stiff peaks and fold into the egg yolk mixture.
Butter a tart tin and line with parchment paper. Pour the batter into the tin and bake for 30 minutes. Remove from the oven and let cool.
Meanwhile, heat the milk and vanilla extract in a saucepan.
Beat the egg yolks and sugar in a double boiler and whisk in the milk. Cook over low heat until the mixture is thick and creamy. Let the mixture cool.
Whip the egg whites to stiff peaks and fold into the cooled cream.
Mash the bananas with a fork and mix in the Maraschino. Fold into the cream.
Fill the tart crust with the banana cream and refrigerate. Decorate with slices of banana and icing sugar.

Raspberry and Ricotta Pastries

Preparation time 25 minutes
Cooking time 25 minutes
Wine *Verduzzo di Ramandolo*
👨‍🍳 👨‍🍳

DOUGH
1½ cups (6.3 oz or 180 g)
plain flour
1/3 cup (2.4 oz or 70 g) sugar
2 fl oz (60 ml) warm milk
1 egg yolk

FILLING
3.5 oz (100 g) ricotta
3.5 oz (100 g) cream cheese
1 tbsp icing sugar plus
 extra for decoration
vanilla extract
grated zest of 1 lemon
1 basket of raspberries
melted butter

Preheat oven to 350°F (180°C).
Mix the flour and sugar together and whisk in the warm milk and
egg yolk. Place on a work surface and knead to form an elastic
dough. Cover with plastic wrap and let rest for 30 minutes in a
cool place.
Beat the ricotta and cream cheese with 1 tablespoon of icing
sugar, vanilla extract and lemon zest. Set aside.
Butter and flour 4 individual tart tins.
Roll out the dough into a thin sheet and cut out 4 squares, slightly
larger than the tart tins.
Line the tins with the dough. Fill with the ricotta mixture and top
with raspberries. Fold the corners of the dough over the top of
the filling and pinch together to seal. Brush with melted butter and
bake for 25 minutes.
Sprinkle the pastries with icing sugar and serve.

Chocolate Cups with Mascarpone Cream

Preparation time 30 minutes
Cooking time 5 minutes
♟ ♟

988

CHOCOLATE CUPS
1 egg white
3/4 cup (2.8 oz or 80 g)
 icing sugar
1 tsp dark rum
6 tbsps melted butter
1/3 cup plus 2 tbsps
 (2.8 oz or 80 g) plain flour
4 tbsps cocoa powder

CREAM
4.2 oz (120 g) mascarpone
3.5 oz (100 g) cream cheese
1 tbsp icing sugar
1 tsp vanilla extract

DECORATION
1 basket of raspberries
mint leaves

Preheat oven to 400°F (200°C).
Beat the egg white and icing sugar in a bowl and add the rum and melted butter. Sift in the flour and cocoa powder and mix to form a sticky, elastic dough. Refrigerate for 20 minutes.
Line a baking dish with parchment paper. Using the back of a spoon, spread the dough into 2½-inch (5 cm) diameter circles. Bake for 5 minutes. Remove from the oven and mould the chocolate rounds over a teacup or in a muffin tin. Let sit for 1 minute, thenremove the chocolate cups.
Beat the mascarpone and cream cheese with icing sugar. Place in a pastry bag and fill each chocolate cup. Top with 1 raspberry and 1 mint leaf. Serve immediately.

Fruit Tart with Apple Cream

Preparation time 20 minutes
Cooking time 25 minutes
Wine *Asti Moscato Spumante*

DOUGH
2¼ cups (10.5 oz or 300 g)
 plain flour
3 tbsps malt extract
2 tbsp sesame oil
8.4 fl oz (250 ml) apple juice
zest of 1 lemon
1 tsp baking powder

APPLE CREAM
2 Golden Delicious apples,
 sliced
1 tbsp malt extract
1 vanilla bean
2 tbsp almond paste

TOPPING
sliced fresh fruit

GLAZE
1 tsp corn flour
4 tbsps apple juice

Mix the flour, malt extract, sesame oil, apple juice, lemon zest and baking powder to form a smooth dough. Refrigerate for 30 minutes.

Sauté the apples with the malt extract and vanilla bean until soft. Discard the vanilla bean and puree the apples with the almond paste.

Roll out the dough and place it in a parchment paper-lined pie pan. Cover the dough with another layer of parchment paper and fill with pie weights or dried beans. Bake for 15 minutes. Remove the crust from the oven and remove the parchment paper and pie weights. Bake for another 5 minutes.

Let the crust cool completely and then cover with a thin layer of apple cream. Top with sliced fresh fruit.

Dissolve the corn flour in the apple juice and cook over medium heat for 3 minutes. Brush the tart with the apple juice glaze. Refrigerate for 30 minutes and serve.

Mini Ice Cream Bombes

Preparation time 35 minutes
Cooking time 30 minutes

990

1 knob of butter
plain flour
3 eggs
1/3 cup (2.6 oz or 75 g) sugar
zest of 1 lemon
salt
2/3 cup (2.6 oz or 75 g)
 plain flour
blackberry liqueur
7 oz (200 g) blackberry ice
 cream
7 oz (200 g) pine nut or hazelnut
 ice cream
2 tbsps toasted pine nuts,
 chopped
1 basket blackberries, chopped

Preheat oven to 375°F (190°C).
Butter and flour a round cake pan.
Beat the eggs and sugar with the lemon zest and a pinch of salt
with an electric mixer for 15 minutes. Sift the flour over the egg
batter and then carefully fold in the flour until incorporated. Pour
the batter into the prepared cake pan and bake for 30 minutes.
Let cool and slice into 1/4-inch (1/2 cm) thick rounds. Dilute the
blackberry liqueur with a little water and brush over the sponge
cake rounds. Line 4 round moulds with the sponge cake.
Beat the ice creams separately with a spatula until soft and fill 2 of
the moulds with blackberry ice cream and the other 2 moulds with
pine nut ice cream. Freeze for 2 hours.
Meanwhile mix the pine nuts and blackberries
Invert the ice cream bombes onto individual serving plates and
serve with the pine nuts and blackberries.

Prosecco Sabayon
with Strawberries

Preparation time 20 minutes
Cooking time 5 minutes
Wine *Metodo Classico*
Franciacorta Demi Sec

8.4 fl oz (250 ml) prosecco
2 egg yolks
1 egg
1/3 cup (2 oz or 60 g) sugar
6.7 fl oz (200 ml) whipping cream
2 baskets of strawberries
2 tbsps raw sugar

Simmer the prosecco in a saucepan until the alcohol has evaporated, about 3-4 minutes.

Beat the egg yolks with the egg and the sugar in a double boiler. Add the prosecco and continue beating until the mixture is light and creamy.

Transfer to a bowl and let cool.

Whip the whipping cream to stiff peaks and fold into the prosecco sabayon.

Puree half the strawberries with the raw sugar.

Layer the strawberries sauce and prosecco cream in small glass serving bowls. Refrigerate until firm. Decorate with the remaining strawberries and sauce.

991

Peach Clafoutis

Preparation time 20 minutes
Cooking time 40 minutes
Wine *Moscato Passito di
Pantelleria*

2 tbsps plain flour
2 tbsps malt extract
salt
2 eggs
17 fl oz (500 ml) milk
4 tbsps grappa
1 vanilla extract
2.2 lbs (1 kg) peaches, peeled
 and sliced
2 tbsps sesame seed oil

Preheat oven to 375°F (190°C).
Sift the flour into a mixing bowl and add 1 tablespoon malt extract
and a little salt. Stir in the eggs, milk, grappa and vanilla extract.
Mix well to form a smooth batter.
Sauté the peach slices with the remaining tablespoon of malt
extract in a frying pan over low heat for around 5 minutes.
Oil with sesame oil and flour a round baking dish.
Pour the batter into the baking dish and then add the peaches.
Bake for 40 minutes, until the top of the clafoutis is golden-brown.
Serve hot or at room temperature.

Hazelnut Cake with Nectarines

Preparation time 20 minutes
Cooking time 50 minutes
Wine *Malvasia Dolce*
♟♟

Serves 8

3/4 cup (1.7 oz or 50 g) ground
 hazelnuts
1 cup (7 oz or 200 g) sugar
grated zest of 1 lemon
5 amaretto cookies
3 eggs
5 tbsps margarine
1/2 cup (4.4 oz or 125 g) plain
 yogurt
1 cup (7 oz or 250 g) plain
 flour
2 tsps baking powder
4 large nectarines, thinly sliced

Preheat oven to 350°F (180°C).
Blend the hazelnuts, sugar and
lemon zest in a food processor.
Transfer the hazelnut mixture to
a bowl and add the crumbled
amaretto cookies, eggs,
margarine and yogurt. Whisk
the batter until smooth. Sift in
the flour and baking powder.
Butter and flour a cake pan and
pour in the batter. Place the
nectarines on top in concentric
circles. Bake for 50 minutes.

Carrot Cake with Chocolate

Preparation time 20 minutes
Cooking time 30 minutes
Wine *Prosecco di Valdobbiadene
Extra Dry*
♟

3 eggs
1⅔ cups (7 oz or 200 g)
 plain flour
3/4 cups (3.5 oz or 100 g)
 coconut flour
3/4 cup (5.2 oz or 150 g) sugar
5 tbsps sesame seed oil
3 tbsps milk
2 tsps vanilla extract
1 tsp baking powder
3/4 cups (5.2 oz or 150 g)
 grated carrots
3.5 oz (100 g) chocolate, chopped

Preheat oven to 350°F (180°C).
Mix together the eggs, flours,
sugar, oil, milk, vanilla extract,
baking powder and grated
carrots and stir well until all the
ingredients are incorporated.
Pour the batter into a cake
pan. Add the chocolate pieces
and stir them in with a wooden
spoon.
Bake for 30 minutes. Serve
warm.

Kiwis with Melon Mousse

Preparation time 20 minutes
Cooking time 5 minutes

MOUSSE
2 gelatin sheets
1 yellow melon
1/2 cup (3.5 oz or 100 g)
 raw sugar
juice of 1 lemon
5 fl oz (150 ml) whipping cream
4 firm kiwis

GARNISH
mixed berries

994

Soak the gelatin in cold water. Drain and squeeze out the excess water.
Peel, deseed and dice the melon and place in a saucepan with the raw sugar and lemon juice. Cook the melon for 5 minutes, slightly caramelizing the sugar. Remove from heat and dissolve the gelatin in the melon mixture. Let cool.
Whip the whipping cream to stiff peaks and fold it into the melon mixture.
Cut the kiwis in half and scoop out some of the pulp. Fill the kiwi halves with melon mousse. Refrigerate for 2 hours. Decorate with berries before serving.

Fruit Salad with Coconut

Preparation time 30 minutes
Cooking time 15 minutes

7 tbsps sugar
6 tbsps water
2 pears, peeled and sliced
6 fl oz (180 ml) white wine
7 oz (200 g) cherries, pitted
4 tbsps kirsch liqueur
8 apricots, pitted and sliced
1 banana, sliced
3.5 oz (100 g) fresh coconut, shaved
1 cup (8.8 oz or 250 g) yogurt

Dissolve 2 tablespoons of sugar in 2 tablespoons of water in a frying pan and add the pears. Sauté for 2 minutes and add the white wine.
Place the cherries in a saucepan with 2 tablespoons of sugar, 2 tablespoons water and the kirsch. Cook over high heat for 10 minutes. Strain the cherries.
Sauté the apricots with the remaining 3 tablespoons of sugar and the remaining 2 tablespoons water.
Mix the pears, cherries, apricots, banana and the coconut shavings in a large bowl and serve with yogurt.

995

Melon Sorbet with Poppy Seeds

Note *The best time of year for melons is in late summer and early autumn. Test for ripeness by smelling the blossom end. It should give off a sweet, fragrant perfume. Unripe melons can be stored at room temperature until slightly soft, but they will never be as good as those picked at the peak of ripeness.*

Preparation time 10 minutes
Cooking time 10 minutes

10 fl oz (300 ml) water
3/4 cup (5.6 oz or 160 g) sugar
10 oz (300 g) melon
1 tbsp port wine
3 tbsps dextrose syrup
3 tbsps poppy seeds
mint leaves

Bring the water and sugar to a boil in a saucepan and cook for 7-8 minutes, until syrupy.
Dice the melon and puree with the port wine. Add the hot sugar syrup and then the dextrose. Let cool and freeze in an ice-cream machine following the manufacturers' instructions. Serve the melon sorbet with poppy seeds and mint leaves.

Yogurt Sorbet with Currant Sauce

Preparation time 35 minutes
Cooking time 20 minutes
♟ ♟

Serves 6

SORBET
10 fl oz (300 ml) whipping cream
vanilla bean
3 tbsps glucose syrup
2/3 cup (4.5 oz or 130 g) sugar
3/4 cup (6.3 oz or 180 g) plain
 yogurt

SAUCE
1 tbsp sugar
1 basket of red currants,
 destemmed
4 tbsps dry sparkling wine
8.4 fl oz (250 ml) water

GARNISH
6 small sponge cake rounds

997

Mix the whipping cream, vanilla bean, glucose syrup and sugar in
a saucepan and heat to 180°F (80°C).
Remove the vanilla bean and pour the mixture over the yogurt.
Mix well and pour into an ice-cream maker. Freeze following the
manufacturers' instructions.
Meanwhile, caramelize the sugar and currants in a saucepan over
low heat. Add wine and water. Reduce the liquid by half, remove
from heat and cool.
Pour the currant mixture into 6 shallow bowls, place a round of
sponge cake in the centre and top with sorbet.

Berry and Mascarpone Tart

Preparation time 30 minutes
Cooking time 25 minutes
Wine *Trentino Moscato Rosa*
♟

Serves 8

DOUGH
2 cups (8.8 oz or 250 g)
 plain flour
2/3 cup (4.4 oz or 125 g) sugar
10 tbsp (4.7 or 135 g) butter
1 egg
1 egg yolk
grated zest of 1 lemon
salt

FILLING
4.2 oz (120 g) mascarpone
vanilla extract
3 tbsps icing sugar
2.7 fl oz (80 ml) whipping cream

GARNISH
7 oz (200 g) mixed berries
1/2 tbsp icing sugar

998

Preheat oven to 350°F (180°C).
Quickly mix together the flour, sugar, butter, egg, egg yolk, lemon zest and a pinch of salt to form a smooth dough. Roll the dough into a ball and cover with plastic wrap. Refrigerate for 30 minutes. Lightly flour a work surface and roll out the dough to a 1/4-inch (1/2 cm) thick sheet. Line a tart tin with the dough and bake for 20-25 minutes.
Meanwhile, mix together the mascarpone, vanilla and the icing sugar.
Whip the cream to stiff peaks and fold it into the mascarpone mixture.
Fill the cooled tart with the mascarpone cream and top with the berries. Sprinkle with icing sugar and refrigerate until firm. Serve cold.

Citrus Tart with Limoncello Sauce

Preparation time 20 minutes
Cooking 25 minutes
Wine *Vin Santo*
♟

Serves 10

DOUGH
4 cups (1 lb or 500 g)
 plain flour
14 tbsps (7 oz or 200 g) butter
1 cup (7 oz or 200 g) sugar
2 egg yolks
2 eggs
1 tsp vanilla extract
zest of 1 lemon

FILLING
3.5 oz (100 g) ricotta
2 eggs
1/3 cup plus 2 tbsps
 (2.8 oz or 80 g) sugar
zest of 1 orange
zest of 1 lemon
zest of 2 grapefruit

LIMONCELLO SAUCE
1/3 cup (2.4 oz or 70 g) sugar
1 tbsp water
2.4 fl oz (80 ml) limoncello
 liqueur
2 tbsps lemon marmalade

999

For the crust, quickly mix together the flour, butter, sugar, egg yolks, eggs, vanilla extract and lemon zest to form a smooth dough. Roll the dough into a ball, cover with plastic wrap and refrigerate for 30 minutes.
Preheat the oven to 350°F (180°C).
Butter and flour a tart tin, roll out the dough and line the tin.
For the filling, sieve the ricotta. Beat the eggs and sugar together and add the ricotta. Add the citrus zest and mix well.
Pour the filling into the tart tin and bake for 20 minutes.
For the sauce, caramelize the sugar and water in a small saucepan. Remove from heat and add the limoncello. Mix well. In a double boiler heat the lemon marmalade until it becomes liquid. Strain the hot marmalade and add to the limoncello syrup.
Serve the tart with the limoncello sauce.

Banana Tiramisù

Preparation time 30 minutes
Cooking time 5 minutes

Serves 8

1/3 cup (1.7 oz or 50 g) raisins
2 fl oz (60 ml) rum
1/2 cup (3.5 oz or 100 g) sugar
4 fl oz (125 ml) water
juice of 2 lemons
6 bananas
6.7 fl oz (200 ml) whipping cream
30 ladyfingers

1000

Soak the raisins in the rum. Drain the raisins, reserving the rum. Dissolve the sugar in the water over medium heat, stirring constantly until the mixture comes to a boil. Remove from heat and let cool. Add the juice from 1 lemon and the reserved rum. Puree the bananas with the remaining lemon juice in a food processor.
Whip the whipping cream to stiff peaks and fold into the banana puree. Add the raisins.
Dip the ladyfingers in the rum syrup and layer a third of the ladyfingers in the bottom of a rectangular baking dish. Top with a third of the banana cream. Make 2 more layers, finishing with the cream. Cover with plastic wrap and refrigerate until firm.

Ricotta and Blueberry Pastries

Preparation time 25 minutes
Cooking time 25 minutes
Wine *Alto Adige Moscato Rosa*
♟

PASTRIES
10.5 oz (300 g) puff pastry
5.2 oz (150 g) ricotta
seeds from 1 vanilla bean
2 tbsps sugar
zest of 1 lemon
1/2 basket of blueberries
1 egg, beaten

BLUEBERRY SAUCE
1/2 basket of blueberries
2 tbsps water
1 tbsp honey

1001

Preheat oven to 375°F (190°C).
Roll out the puff pastry and cut it into 4 rectangles, 1½ inches by 3 inches (4 by 8 cm).
Beat the ricotta with the vanilla, sugar and lemon zest. Place the filling on half of each rectangle. Add a few blueberries and fold in half. Pinch the edges closed to seal.
Brush the pastries with the beaten egg. Make a few diagonal incisions on the top of each pastry.
Bake for 20 minutes.
Meanwhile, heat the remaining blueberries with the water and the honey. Once the berries are soft, remove from heat and puree the sauce.
Serve the warm pastries with the blueberry sauce.

Berry Cake with Mascarpone

Preparation time 35 minutes
Cooking time 40 minutes
Wine *Piemonte Moscato Passito*
👨‍🍳

CAKE
3/4 cup plus 2 tbsps (6.3 oz
 or 180 g) plain flour
3/4 cups (5.3 oz or 150 g) sugar
1/2 cup (1.7 oz or 50 g) chopped
 almonds
grated zest of 1 lemon
ground cinnamon
2 tsps baking powder
3 egg yolks
1/2 cup plus 2½ tbsps
 (5.3 oz or 150 g) butter, softened
juice of 1 orange

3.4 fl oz (100 ml) milk
4 nectarines, sliced
1⅔ cups (7 oz or 200 g)
 raspberries
2/3 cup (3.5 oz or 100 g)
 blueberries
1 cup (3.5 oz or 100 g) wild
 strawberries
1/4 cup (0.8 oz or 25 g) sliced
 almonds

FROSTING
8.8 oz (250 g) mascarpone
2 tsps vanilla
1/4 cup (1 oz or 30 g)
 icing sugar
2 egg whites

1002

Preheat oven to 325°F (170°C).
Mix together the flour, sugar, almonds, lemon zest, cinnamon and
baking powder. Add the egg yolks and softened butter. Add enough
orange juice to form a very thick batter. Mix in the milk.
Butter a cake pan and pour in 3/4 of the batter. Place the nectarine
slices on top of the batter in concentric circles and then top with 3/4
of the berries. Pour the remaining batter into the cake pan and top
with sliced almonds. Bake for 40 minutes.
Meanwhile mix the mascarpone, vanilla and icing sugar.
Beat the egg whites to stiff peaks and fold into the mascarpone.
Remove the cake from the oven and frost with the mascarpone
cream. Top with remaining berries and icing sugar.

Apricot Tart with Yogurt Cream

Preparation time 45 minutes
Cooking time 30 minutes
Wine *Moscato Passito di Pantelleria*

Serves 8

8.8 oz (250 g) puff pastry
3 tbsps sugar
3/4 cup (7 oz or 200 g) plain
 yogurt
3.5 oz (100 g) ricotta
2 tbsps icing sugar
50 ml whipping cream
12.3 oz (350 g) preserved apricot
 halves in syrup, drained
1.7 oz (50 g) amaretto cookies,
 crushed

Preheat oven to 400°F (200°C).
Roll out the puff pastry and pierce it with a fork. Sprinkle with sugar and cut in half. Bake for 20 minutes.
Meanwhile, beat the yogurt and the ricotta with the icing sugar until smooth and creamy.
Whip the whipping cream to stiff peaks and fold into the yogurt mixture. Spread the yogurt cream on the puff pastry, top with apricot halves and crushed amaretto cookies. Place the second puff pastry sheet on top and decorate with yogurt cream and apricots. Refrigerate until firm. Slice and serve.

Lemon-Grass Mint Jellies with Pineapple

Preparation time 15 minutes
Cooking time 15 minutes

10 fl oz (300 ml) water
4 tbsps sugar
1 lemongrass shoot, smashed
1/4 pineapple
1 tbsp mint syrup
1 tsp agar agar
mint leaves

Bring the water and sugar to a boil with the lemongrass.
Peel, core and dice the pineapple.
Add the pineapple trimmings to the lemongrass syrup and simmer until reduced to approximately 7 fl oz (200 ml).
Strain the mixture and add the mint syrup and agar agar. Return to heat and simmer until the agar agar dissolves.
Pour the mixture into dome-shaped moulds and add a few pieces of pineapple to each one. Top off the moulds with any remaining liquid. Refrigerate for 2 hours.
Unmould the jellies onto serving plates and decorate with mint leaves.

Peach and Basil Phyllo Rolls

Preparation time 30 minutes
Cooking time 10 minutes

2 tbsps raw sugar
1 mint sprig
6 basil leaves
zest of 1 lime
3 ripe peaches, peeled and
 diced
4 loquats, peeled and pitted
4 sheets of phyllo dough
1 egg yolk
1 tbsp sugar
1 tbsp grappa
sunflower oil

1005

Mix the raw sugar, mint and basil leaves and lime zest with the peaches and refrigerate for 30 minutes.
Puree the loquats and set aside.
Slice each sheet of phyllo dough into 4 strips. Place 1 tablespoon of peaches on each strip. Carefully fold in the sides and roll up the dough. Brush with a little water to seal.
Whisk the loquat puree with the egg yolk, sugar and grappa.
Transfer to a double boiler and continue beating over medium heat until the mixture is thick and foamy. Remove from heat and cool in a water bath.
Fry the peach rolls in hot sunflower oil until golden-brown and drain on paper towels. Serve warm with the loquat sauce.

Melon and Kiwi Salad

Preparation time 20 minutes
Cooking time 10 minutes

1/4 watermelon
1 white-fleshed melon
2 yellow-fleshed melons
2 kiwis, peeled and sliced
juice of 1 lemon
juice of 1 orange
1/4 cup (1.7 oz or 50 g) sugar
2 tbsps water
mint leaves
1/2 vanilla bean

1006

Cut the watermelon and white melon into balls using a melon baller. Cut the yellow melons in half and remove the seeds. Carve out melon balls leaving the outer melon shell intact. Mix together the kiwi slices and melon balls and add the lemon and orange juice.
Dissolve the sugar in the water and cook over medium heat. Add the mint leaves and the seeds from the vanilla bean. Pour the mixture over the fruit. Fill the melon shell with the fruit salad and refrigerate until serving.

Spiced Melon Balls with Port

Preparation time 15 minutes

1.6 fl oz (100 ml) white port wine
1 mint sprig, destemmed and
 chopped
1 star anise
1 tbsp honey
2 vanilla beans, halved
 lengthways
2 cantaloupe melons
amaretto cookies

Mix together the port, mint leaves, star anise, honey and vanilla beans. Mix well and let sit for 30 minutes.
Meanwhile halve the melons and remove the seeds. Cut the melons into balls using a melon baller. Add the melon balls to the port marinade and refrigerate for 3 hours. Sprinkle the melon balls with crushed amaretto cookies and drizzle over a little of the marinade.

Peach Smoothie with Vodka

Preparation time 15 minutes

2 tbsps raw sugar
zest and juice of 1 lemon
2 mint sprigs, leaves only, plus
  extra for garnish
3 peaches, peeled and diced
2 tbsps vodka

Mix the sugar, lemon zest and mint leaves with the diced peaches in a bowl.
Sprinkle the lemon juice over the peaches.
Stir the vodka into the mixture and refrigerate overnight.
Remove the mint leaves and blend the mixture until creamy and smooth in a blender.
Serve immediately, garnished with mint leaves.

Peach and Berry Skewers

Preparation time 20 minutes
Cooking time 10 minutes
Wine *Asti Moscato Spumante*

3 tbsps sugar
1 tbsp balsamic vinegar
8.4 fl oz (250 ml) water
1/2 tsp agar agar powder
1 peach, peeled and cubed
1 nectarine, peeled and cubed
12 raspberries
5 strawberries

Caramelize the sugar with the balsamic vinegar and slowly add the water. Return to a boil and add the agar agar and dissolve slowly. Pour into a baking dish and refrigerate. Thread the peach and nectarine cubes with raspberries and strawberries onto skewers. Break up the gelatin using a fork. Roll the skewers in the gelatin to coat with gelatin bits. Serve the skewers with cookies.

Yogurt and Peach Frappé with Redcurrants

Preparation time 15 minutes

Serves 2

1 ripe yellow peach, peeled and diced
1 tsp lemon juice
1 tbsp raw sugar
5.2 oz (150 g) plain frozen yogurt
3.4 fl oz (100 ml) milk
2-3 ice cubes
2 sprigs fresh redcurrants

1008

Mix the diced peach, lemon juice and sugar together in a bowl and refrigerate for 20 minutes.
Place the frozen yogurt in a blender with the milk and ice cubes. Blend for 1 minute until creamy.
Place the marinated peaches in the bottom of 2 wine or martini glasses.
Pour the yogurt frappé over the peaches and top with the redcurrant sprigs.

Lemon Bavarian Creams
with Pineapple

Note *The pineapple should be prepared 1 day in advance.*

PINEAPPLE
17 fl oz (500 ml) water
3⅓ cups (1.5 lb or 670 g) sugar
1/2 pineapple

BAVARIAN CREAM
1 sheet gelatin
2.7 fl oz (80 ml) milk
3 tbsps sugar
zest of 1 lemon
1 egg yolk
1.6 fl oz (100 ml) whipping cream

Preparation time 20 minutes
Cooking time 5 hours
🎩 🎩 🎩

Heat the water and sugar in a saucepan until it reaches 86°F (30°C). The sugar should dissolve and the liquid should become syrupy without colouring.
Peel the pineapple and slice it thinly on a mandoline. Place the pineapple slices in a baking dish and pour over the sugar syrup.
Marinate the pineapple for 12 hours.
Preheat the oven to 210°F (100°C).
Drain the pineapple and place the slices on a parchment paper-lined baking sheet.
Bake for 4-5 hours.
Soak the gelatin in cold water. Drain and squeeze out the excess water. Bring the milk, 1 tablespoon sugar and lemon zest to a boil. Beat the egg yolk with the remaining sugar. Whisk the hot milk into the egg mixture and transfer the mixture to a double boiler. Cook until the mixture reaches 180°F (82°C). Add gelatin and stir, them remove from heat.
Whip the whipping cream to stiff peaks and fold it into the warm mixture.
Pour the mixture into 4 ramekins and refrigerate for 2 hours.
Unmould the Bavarian creams and serve with the pineapple slices.

Plum Mousse

Preparation time 15 minutes
Cooking time 10 minutes

5 yellow plums, peeled and
 pitted
5 red plums, peeled and pitted
3 gelatin sheets
4.2 fl oz (125 ml) water
3/4 cups (5.2 oz or 150 g) sugar
10 fl oz (300 ml) whipping cream
2 passion fruits
1-2 plums, sliced

1010

Slice the plums into wedges. Puree the red plums and the yellow
plums separately. Refrigerate.
Soak the gelatin in cold water. Drain and squeeze out the excess
water. Melt the gelatin sheets in a small pan over low heat.
Heat the water and the sugar in a small pan and simmer for 10
minutes.
Whip the whipping cream to stiff peaks and fold half into each
plum puree. Then fold half of the water-sugar mixture into each
puree. Layer the red and yellow plum mixtures into individual
ramekins and freeze for 2 hours. Decorate the plum mousse with
passion fruit pulp and plum slices.

Yellow Peach Sorbet

Preparation time 10 minutes
Cooking time 2 minutes

♔

10 fl oz (300 ml) water
2 tbsps malt extract
3 yellow peaches, peeled and
  diced
juice of 1/2 lemon
1 egg white

Heat the water and malt extract in a saucepan and add the peaches and lemon juice. Cook for 2 minutes. Remove from heat and let cool. Puree the peaches.
Beat the egg white to soft peaks and fold into the peaches. Freeze for 3 hours. Remove from the freezer and blend the sorbet before serving.

Frozen Yogurt with Mandarin

Preparation time 10 minutes
Cooking time 5 minutes

♔

5 fl oz (150 ml) rice milk
2 tsps agar agar
3 tbsps malt extract
1½ cups (350 g) low-fat yogurt
2 tbsps mandarin orange jam

Heat the rice milk over low heat, add the agar agar and stir until dissolved. Add the malt extract and let cool. Add the yogurt.
Pour the mixture into a rectangular container and freeze.
Puree the mandarin jam and pour it over the frozen yogurt mixture. Refrigerate for 3 hours. Cut into cubes and serve.

1011

Babà
(CAMPANIA)

Preparation time 3 hours 20 minutes
Cooking time 30 minutes

Serves 6

STARTER DOUGH
1 tsp dry active yeast
1 tbsp warm water
1 tsp sugar
3 tbsps enriched white flour

SYRUP
17 fl oz (500 ml) water
1½ cups (10.5 oz or 300 g) sugar
zest of 1 lemon
rum

BABÀ
1⅔ cups (7 oz or 200 g) enriched
  white flour
3 tbsps sugar
3 eggs
7 tbsps butter
salt

1012

Dissolve the yeast in the warm water. Add the sugar and flour and let rise in a warm dry place for 2 hours.
Meanwhile, prepare the syrup. Bring the water, sugar and lemon zest to a boil and cook for 15 minutes. Let cool and add as much rum as desired.
Transfer the starter dough to a large bowl and add the flour, sugar, eggs, 4 tablespoons of butter and a pinch of salt. Knead the dough until smooth. Cover the bowl with a kitchen towel and let rise until doubled in volume.
Preheat oven to 350°F (180°C).
Butter babà moulds (or mini brioche tins) with the remaining butter and add the dough to the moulds. Brush with the rum syrup and bake for 20 minutes.
Remove from the oven and fill the babà with lemon pastry cream or whipped cream if desired.

festive menus

Rich and sumptuous holiday feasts offer cooks a chance to really experiment and be creative in the kitchen. The following dishes are a mix of unusual recipes with exotic ingredients together with the classics of traditional Italian regional cuisine.

Sea Bream Carpaccio with Arugula and Cherry Tomatoes

Note *Any very fresh white fish can be used for this appetizer. The arugula salad may be substituted with white Zolfini beans. Soak the dried beans overnight and then boil for 1 hour. Season with salt, pepper and a little extra-virgin olive oil.*

Preparation time 15 minutes
Wine *Greco di Tufo*

10 Pachino cherry tomatoes
1 bunch arugula, chopped
salt and pepper
1 tsp lemon juice
4 tbsps delicate extra-virgin olive oil
12 oz (350 g) sea bream fillets

1014

Slice the tomatoes in half and remove the seeds.
Toss the tomatoes with the arugula, season to taste with salt and pepper and add lemon juice. Drizzle with olive oil and toss to coat. Arrange the arugula salad on 4 individual serving plates.
Using a very sharp knife, slice the fish fillets into very thin, almost transparent sheets. Place the carpaccio on the arugula salad, season with salt and pepper and drizzle with olive oil.

Liver Pâté with Mushrooms on Polenta

Preparation time 30 minutes
Cooking time 30 minutes
Wine *Cabernet di Breganze*

♟ ♟

POLENTA
3½ cups (800 ml) water salt
1⅔ cups (200 g) instant
 polenta cornmeal
sunflower oil

PÂTÉ
5 chicken livers
2 tbsps white wine vinegar
1½ cups (5.5 oz or 150 g)
 mixed wild mushrooms

salt and pepper
4 tbsps butter
1 small onion, diced
1 carrot, peeled and diced
1 celery stalk, diced
hot vegetable broth
1 tbsp capers

1015

Bring the water to a boil in a saucepan, season with salt and whisk in the polenta. Cook for 10 minutes, stirring constantly, then pour into a rectangular baking dish to cool.
Wash the chicken livers and soak them in cold water and vinegar. Rinse and pat dry with a paper towel.
Blanch the mushrooms in salted water and finely chop.
Heat the butter in a frying pan and add the onion, carrot and celery. Sauté briefly and add the chicken livers. Cook for 3-4 minutes and add the mushrooms. Cook for 5-6 minutes, adding a little hot broth and the capers. Cook for another 4-5 minutes, season with salt and pepper and remove from heat.
Puree the mixture until smooth and creamy.
Cut the polenta into circles with a cookie cutter and fry in hot sunflower oil until golden-brown. Spread the pâté on the polenta rounds and serve.

Potato and Anchovy Flan with Pesto

Preparation time 25 minutes
Cooking time 15 minutes
Wine *Elba Bianco*

FLAN
3 yellow-fleshed potatoes
1/2 red bell pepper
1/2 yellow bell pepper
6 tbsps extra-virgin olive oil
1 garlic clove, smashed
2 tbsps milk
1 egg
salt and pepper
20 fresh anchovies

PESTO
1 handful fresh basil leaves
1 tbsp pine nuts
3 tbsps extra-virgin olive oil
salt

DECORATION
1 leek, thinly sliced
plain flour
sunflower oil
16 cherry tomatoes

1016

Preheat oven to 350°F (180°C).
Boil potatoes in salted water until just tender. Drain, peel and mash.
Roast the peppers, close in a plastic bag to steam, peel and dice.
Heat oil in a non-stick frying pan with the garlic and add peppers.
Sauté briefly and remove the garlic clove. Add the mashed potatoes and milk. Mix well and remove from heat.
When cool, stir in the egg and season with salt and pepper.
Clean and gut the fish. Remove the head and spine and slice the flesh into rectangular fillets.
Oil 4 ramequins and line with anchovies, making sure that the skin side of each fillet is touching the ramequin. Fill with potato-pepper mixture and bake for 20 minutes.
Roast the cherry tomatoes.
Puree the basil, pine nuts, olive oil and a pinch of salt.
Dust the leek with flour. Fry the leek in the sunflower oil until crispy.
Remove the flans from the oven and invert onto serving dishes. Top with pesto and crunchy leeks. Garnish with roasted tomatoes.

A P P E T I Z E R

Beef Tartare with Mustard and Leeks

Preparation time 20 minutes
Cooking time 20 minutes
Wine *Nebbiolo d'Alba*

LEEKS
extra-virgin olive oil
1 large leek, thinly sliced
3-4 tbsps hot water
salt and pepper

TARTARE
1 lb (500 g) beef fillet, trimmed
1 tbsp salted Pantelleria capers,
 rinsed
salt and pepper
3 tbsps delicate extra-virgin olive oil

SAUCE
2 egg yolks
1/2 tsp Dijon mustard

Heat the olive oil in a frying pan and add the leek. Let cook over low heat until soft, adding a little hot water if necessary. Season with salt and pepper and let cool.
Thinly slice the beef fillet and then cut into julienne strips. Cut the strips crosswise into a fine dice. Chop the capers and add them to the beef. Season with salt and pepper and drizzle with olive oil. Beat the egg yolks with the mustard.
Form the tartare into quenelles using 2 spoons and place on a serving plate. Top with the mustard sauce and leeks.

Braised Beef Cappelletti in Broth

Preparation time 30 minutes
Cooking time 30 minutes
Wine *Lambrusco di Sorbara*

BROTH
1/2 free-range chicken
10.5 oz (300 g) mixed fresh herbs,
 coarsely chopped
1 tomato, quartered

PASTA DOUGH
2½ cups (10.5 oz or 300 g)
 plain flour

2 eggs
2 egg yolks
salt

FILLING
9 oz (250 g) braised beef with
 cooking juices
5 oz (150 g) ricotta
1 tbsp grated Parmesan
salt and pepper

GARNISH
Parmesan shavings

1018

Place the chicken, herbs and tomato in a pot of cold water and
bring to a boil. Cook for 1 hour. Let cool and strain the broth.
Reserve cooked chicken for another use.
Mound the flour on a work surface and make a well in the centre.
Add the eggs and egg yolks to the centre with a pinch of salt and
mix to form a smooth dough. Refrigerate for 30 minutes.
Blend the beef and cooking juices in a food processor and add the
ricotta and Parmesan. Season with salt, pepper and nutmeg.
Roll out the dough into 2 thin sheets. Place spoonfuls of filling at
1-inch (2½ cm) intervals along the pasta. Cover with the second
sheet of pasta and cut out rounds using a pasta cutter or cookie
cutter.
Boil the cappelletti in half the chicken broth until they rise to the
surface. Transfer the cappelletti and broth to shallow serving bowls
and pour over the remaining, heated broth. Garnish with shaved
Parmesan and serve.

Saffron Prawns with Potato Gnocchi

Preparation time 10 minutes
Cooking time 10 minutes
Wine *Friuli Isonzo Sauvignon*

6 tbsps extra-virgin olive oil
2 garlic cloves, smashed
1/2 red chile pepper, minced
12.5 oz (350 g) prawns, shelled
2 tbsps brandy
salt
3 tbsps tomato sauce
1/4 tsp ground saffron
2/3 cup (150 ml) heavy cream
white pepper
1 lb (440 g) small potato gnocchi

Heat the olive oil in a frying pan and add the garlic and chile pepper.
Slice the prawns in half lengthwise, add to the pan and sauté for a few minutes. Add the brandy and season with salt. Transfer the prawns to a plate and cover to keep warm. Add the tomato sauce, cook for 3-4 minutes and then add the saffron and cream. Mix carefully and remove from heat. Season with salt and pepper. Bring a large pot of salted water to a boil and cook the gnocchi until they rise to the surface. Drain the gnocchi with a slotted spoon and transfer directly to the tomato sauce. Sauté briefly. Plate the gnochetti and top with prawns. Serve immediately.

Pecorino and Chestnut Tortelli

Preparation time 25 minutes
Cooking time 15 minutes
Wine *Chardonnay*

PASTA DOUGH
1⅔ cups (7 oz or 200 g)
 plain flour
1/2 cup (2 oz or 60 g) chestnut flour
3 eggs
salt
1 tbsp extra-virgin olive oil

FILLING
1/4 cup (1 oz or 30 g) walnuts
7 oz (200 g) ricotta

6 tbsps grated pecorino cheese
1 egg yolk
salt and pepper

ARTICHOKES
4 small artichokes
extra-virgin olive oil
1 garlic clove

GARNISH
butter
2 tbsps grated Parmesan

1020

Mix the 2 flours with the eggs, salt and oil. Knead to form a
smooth dough. Cover and let rest for 30 minutes.
Toast the walnuts and chop finely.
Mix the ricotta with the pecorino and egg yolk. Add the walnuts
and season with salt and pepper.
Roll out the pasta dough and make tortelli with the walnut filling.
Place the tortelli on a floured baking sheet.
Cut the stalks off the artichokes and trim them, removing the hard
external leaves and the choke. Quarter and thinly slice.
Sauté the artichokes with the oil and whole garlic clove. Season
with salt, cover and cook for 10 minutes.
Boil the tortelli in salted water for 3-4 minutes.
Meanwhile, brown the butter in a frying pan.
Drain the tortelli and transfer them to a serving bowl. Add the
brown butter and top with artichokes and grated Parmesan.

Leek and Asiago Lasagna

Preparation time 30 minutes
Cooking time 25 minutes
Wine *Bardolino Chiaretto*
♟ ♟

LASAGNA
1 knob of butter
1 tbsp extra-virgin olive oil
1 leek, sliced
salt
1.25 lb (550 g) fresh egg pasta
 sheets (see p. 1094)
2 tbsps grated Parmesan

BÉCHAMEL
2 cups (500 ml) milk
3 tbsps butter
5 tbsps plain flour
nutmeg, grated
salt
9 oz (250 g) Asiago cheese,
 chopped

1021

Preheat oven to 375°F (190°C).
Heat the butter and olive oil in a frying pan and add the leek.
Sauté over low heat until soft. Season with salt.
Meanwhile, make the béchamel. Heat the milk in a saucepan. In another saucepan melt the butter and mix in the flour. Cook until the flour begins to brown and then whisk the flour and butter into the boiling milk. Continue mixing until the béchamel thickens. Season with nutmeg and salt. Pour into a bowl and let cool slightly. Add the Asiago and stir until cheese melts.
Boil the pasta sheets in salted water for 1 minute. Drain and place the pasta on a clean kitchen towel to dry.
Butter a baking dish and layer in the pasta, leeks and béchamel. Add a final layer of leeks and sprinkle with Parmesan. Bake for 20 minutes and serve.

Sweet and Sour Baccalà

Preparation time 25 minutes
Cooking time 30 minutes
Wine *Ribolla Gialla*

1.3 lb (600 g) pre-soaked salt cod
plain flour
4 tbsps extra-virgin olive oil
2 garlic cloves, unpeeled
 and lightly smashed
1 cup (7 oz or 200 g) peeled,
 canned plum tomatoes
5.5 oz (150 g) unsweetened
 chocolate, shaved
2 tbsps white wine vinegar
1 tbsp pine nuts
2 tbsps raisins, soaked
 in warm water

Cut the salt cod into large chunks and dust with flour.
Heat the oil in a frying pan with the garlic cloves and brown the
salt cod briefly, until it is golden on all sides.
Add the tomatoes and crush them in the pan with a wooden
spoon. Cook over low heat for about 10 minutes.
Place the chocolate shavings in a small, non-stick frying pan and
gently heat. When the chocolate starts to melt, start whisking it,
and add the vinegar in a thin stream, whisking constantly, until it is
all incorporated and the mixture is fluid and creamy.
Add the chocolate mixture to the salt cod together with the pine
nuts and drained raisins. Remove from the heat and let sit for 20
minutes before serving.

Bollito Misto with Mostarda

Note *Mostarda is a typical preserve from Cremona in Northern Italy, a mixture of spiced fruit preserved in a thick sugar syrup seasoned with mustard. Mostarda can be found in specialty stores or Italian food markets.*

Preparation time 20 minutes
Cooking time 1 hour
Wine *Oltrepò Pavese Barbera*
♟

2 celery stalks
2 carrots
1 tomato
2 onions
1/2 chicken
10.5 oz (300 g) beef chuck or flat rib
7 oz (200 g) pork head meat
salt and pepper
2 tbsps extra-virgin olive oil
mostarda

1023

Fill a large pot with water and add the celery stalks, carrots, tomato and onions. Lightly salt the water and then add the whole pieces of meat. Gently simmer for 1 hour, skimming off the foam that rises to the top.
Let the meat cool in the broth, and then drain. Reserving the broth for another use.
Slice the meat and serve it with the mostarda.

Braised Beef

Preparation time 15 minutes
Cooking time 1 hour 10 minutes
Wine *Chianti Classico*

1.5 lb (700 g) beef brisket
salt and pepper
2 tbsps plain flour
4-5 tbsps extra-virgin olive oil
4 garlic cloves, smashed
3/4 cup (4 oz or 120 g) diced onion
3 bay leaves
1 rosemary sprig
2 cups (500 ml) Merlot wine
4 cups (1 l) beef broth
3¼ cups (1.75 lb or 800 g)
 tomato sauce
nutmeg, grated
2 cloves

1024

Tie brisket with kitchen string tied at 2-inch (5 cm) intervals.
Season with salt and pepper and dust with flour.
Heat the olive oil in a pot and add the garlic and onion. Sauté
briefly and add the bay leaves and rosemary. When the onion
begins to brown add the meat and brown evenly on all sides for
about 10 minutes. Add the red wine and reduce. When the pan
juices are thick add the broth, tomato sauce, nutmeg and cloves.
Season with salt and cover. Cook over low heat for 1 hour 10
minutes.
Slice the beef and serve with its pan juices.

Tongue with Leek and Caper Sauce

Note *Leek and caper sauce may be substituted* with *bagnetto verde green sauce. Prepare the bagnetto by pureeing parsley, oil, garlic and 1 hard-boiled egg white.*

Preparation time 20 minutes
Cooking time 1 hour 20 minutes
Wine *Enfer d'Arvier*

TONGUE
1 carrot, peeled
1 onion
2 celery stalks
1 tomato
1 garlic clove
1 lb (500 g) beef tongue
salt and pepper

SAUCE
3 tbsps extra-virgin olive oil
1 large leek, thinly sliced
1 tbsp salted capers, rinsed

1025

Add the vegetables and garlic to a large pot of water and bring to a boil. Lightly salt the broth and cook for 30 minutes.
Add the tongue and simmer for 1 hour 20 minutes. Let the meat cool in the broth, about 3 hours.
Heat the olive oil in a frying pan and add the leek. Cook until tender, adding a little water if necessary. Mince the capers and add to the leeks. Remove from heat.
Drain, peel and thinly slice the tongue. Season with salt and pepper and drizzle with olive oil. Serve the tongue with the leek sauce.

Sweet Salami

Preparation time 30 minutes
Cooking time 15 minutes
Wine *Moscato di Pantelleria*

Serves 6

5 fl oz (150 ml) whipping cream
1/2 panettone
7 oz (200 g) white chocolate
3/4 cup (8.8 oz or 250 g)
 chocolate sauce
1/2 cup (2 oz or 60 g) pine nuts

Whip the whipping cream to soft peaks. Crumble the panettone into the whipping cream and let sit until soft.
Melt the white chocolate in a double boiler and fold it into the panettone and cream mixture.
Line a cylindrical terrine pan with plastic wrap and pour the mixture into the pan. Press the mixture into the pan until compact and seal tightly with the plastic wrap. Refrigerate for 15 minutes.
Heat the chocolate sauce.
Remove the salami from the refrigerator and place on a wire rack. Pour the chocolate sauce over the salami to coat completely and sprinkle with pine nuts. Slice the salami and serve.

1026

Crunchy Walnut Brittle

Preparation time 10 minutes
Cooking time 5 minutes
Wine *Moscato di Pantelleria*

1⅓ cups plus 2 tbsps
 (9.8 oz or 280 g) sugar
2 tbsps water
1¼ cups (9 oz or 250 g)
 walnut halves
1 tbsp lemon juice

Heat the sugar and water over low heat until caramelized. Toast the walnuts briefly and rub them with a clean kitchen towel to remove the skin. Add lemon juice to the caramel and then the walnuts. Pour the mixture onto a parchment paper-lined baking sheet and spread the brittle with an oiled spatula. Let cool and break into pieces.

Note *Walnuts can be substituted with any other chopped nuts.*

Ice Cream-Filled Mini Panettones

Preparation time 15 minutes
Wine *Asti Moscato Spumante*

Serves 8

4 miniature panettones
1 lb (500 g) ice cream
 (vanilla, chocolate and/
 or rum-raisin)

Cut an opening in the top of each panettone with a cookie cutter and remove a kind of lid. With fingers, scoop out some of the interior crumb. Reserve the lids. Work the ice cream with a spatula until creamy and then fill the panettones with the ice cream. Top with the panettone lids and press down to cover the ice cream. Freeze the panettones for a few minutes until the ice cream is firm. Serve immediately.

Chantilly and Chocolate Cream Millefeuille

Preparation time 20 minutes
Cooking time 30 minutes
Wine *Asti Moscato Spumante*

17 fl oz (500 ml) milk
2 tsps vanilla extract
4 egg yolks
2/3 cup (4.5 oz or 125 g) sugar
1/2 cup (2 oz or 55 g)
 plain flour
1/2 pandoro
5 fl oz (150 ml) whipping cream
2 oz (50 g) dark chocolate, grated

1028

Preheat oven to 250°F (120°C).
Heat the milk and vanilla in a saucepan. Beat the egg yolks with the sugar and then sift in the flour. Whisk the boiling milk into the egg mixture and then return to the saucepan. Cook over low heat until the cream thickens. Transfer to a bowl to cool.
Meanwhile, slice the pandoro into thin slices and toast in the oven for 12 minutes. Remove from the oven and cut each slice into thirds.
Whip the whipping cream to stiff peaks and fold it into the pastry cream. Fold in three-quarters of the chocolate and transfer the cream to a pastry bag with a wide tip.
Make a small mound of Chantilly cream in the centre of each serving plate. Top with a piece of pandoro and then with Chantilly cream. Make 3 or 4 layers and top with the remaining chocolate.

Chocolate Truffles

Preparation time 20 minutes
Cooking time 10 minutes
Wine *Zibibbo*

TRUFFLES
1/2 pandoro
6.7 fl oz (200 ml) milk
Amaretto liqueur
1.5 oz (50 g) amaretto cookies
3 oz (80 g) dark chocolate
3 tbsps whipping cream

GARNISH
1/2 cup (2 oz or 60 g)
 unsalted pistachios
1/4 cup (0.7 oz or 20 g)
 sliced almonds

1031

Dice the pandoro and soak it in the milk and a little Amaretto liqueur. Let sit for 5 minutes. Squeeze out the excess liquid and transfer the soaked pandoro to a bowl. Crumble in the amaretto cookies and mix well. Roll small quantities of the mixture into balls. Cover and refrigerate until firm.
Melt the chocolate in a double boiler with the whipping cream. Mix well and let cool.
Finely chop the pistachios in a food processor and toast the almond slices.
Drizzle the chocolate sauce over the truffles and sprinkle with the pistachios and almonds.

Salmon Mousse on Rye Toasts

Preparation time 20 minutes
Cooking time 10 minutes
Wine *Alto Adige Metodo*
Classico Brut

1/2 cup (4.2 oz or 120 g) butter
2 shallots, minced
10.5 oz (300 g) salmon fillet, cubed
salt
2 tbsps vodka
1 bunch parsley
1 bunch thyme
4 slices rye bread
pink peppercorns, crushed

Heat 1 tablespoon butter in a large frying pan and add the shallots. Sauté for 5 minutes. Add the salmon, season with salt and then add the vodka. Cover and cook for 6-7 minutes. Remove from heat and let cool.

Place the cooled salmon mixture in a food processor with the remaining butter, parsley and thyme. Season with salt. Blend until smooth. Refrigerate for 10 minutes.

Meanwhile, cut out the bread using star-shaped cookie cutters. Toast the bread. Using a pastry bag, pipe the mousse onto the toast. Sprinkle with pink peppercorns and serve.

1032

APPETIZER

Chicken and Vegetable Aspic

Preparation time 30 minutes
Cooking time 40 minutes
Wine *Metodo Trento Talento*
Extra Brut

1 onion
1 celery stalk, trimmed
1 tomato
salt and pepper
1/2 free-range chicken
1 carrot, peeled and diced
1 small winter squash, peeled
 and diced
1 tsp agar agar powder

Fill a large pot with cold water and add the onion, celery and
tomato. Bring to a boil and season with salt. Add the chicken and
cook for 40 minutes. Let the chicken cool in the broth.
Remove the chicken from the broth and take the meat off the
bones. Chop the meat.
Meanwhile, strain the broth and boil 4 cups (1 l) in a saucepan.
When the broth has been reduced to half its original volume, add
the carrot, squash and salt and pepper to taste. Stir in the agar
agar powder until dissolved.
Pour the broth into 4 ramequins and add the chicken meat. Cover
with any remaining broth and refrigerate for at least 3 hours.
Unmould the aspics and serve.

Moulded Trout Mousse with Celeriac

Preparation time 30 minutes
Cooking time 10 minutes
Wine *Alto Adige Pinot Bianco*

♟ ♟

MOUSSE
2/3 cup (150 ml) fish broth
5 oz (150 g) trout fillets
juice of 1/2 lemon
3 gelatin sheets
salt and pepper
2/3 cup (150 ml) whipping cream
12.5 oz (350 g) smoked salmon,
 thinly sliced

CELERIAC
1 celeriac (celery root), peeled
 and julienned
juice of 1 lemon
3 tbsps balsamic vinegar
salt and pepper
6 tbsps extra-virgin olive oil
parsley, minced

1034

Bring the fish broth to a boil and add the trout. Reduce heat and simmer for 10 minutes.
Remove the trout from the broth and transfer to a food processor. Puree the trout and pass through a sieve. Add the lemon juice and let cool.
Soak the gelatin sheets in cold water. Drain and squeeze out the excess water and then dissolve the gelatin in a little hot fish broth. Add the gelatin to the pureed trout. Season with salt and pepper.
Whip the whipping cream to stiff peaks and fold it into the trout mixture. Line 4 ramequins with smoked salmon slices. Pour the trout mixture into the ramequins. Top with smoked salmon and refrigerate for 4 hours.
Soak the celeriac in cold water and lemon juice.
Mix the vinegar, salt and pepper in a bowl. Whisk in the olive oil to emulsify and then add the parsley. Dress the celeriac with the vinaigrette.
Invert the ramequins onto plates and serve with the celeriac.

A P P E T I Z E R

Prawn Cocktail in Pastry Shells

Note *For a thicker sauce, add 1 hard-boiled egg white before blending the sauce.*

Preparation time 15 minutes
Cooking time 5 minutes
Wine *Metodo Classico Franciacorta Rosé*

7 oz (200 g) prawns, heads
 removed
salt and white pepper
6 cherry tomatoes
2 tbsps heavy cream
lemon thyme
1/4 tsp Tabasco sauce
12 puff pastry shells
chives, chopped

Boil the prawn tails in salted water for 5 minutes. Drain and remove the shells.
Halve the tomatoes and remove the seeds.
Place the prawn tails, tomatoes, cream and lemon thyme in a blender. Season with salt and pepper and puree. Add the Tabasco sauce and mix well. Refrigerate.
Heat the puff pastry shells. Fill the shells with the prawn mixture. Top with chives and serve.

Porcini Soup with Passatelli

Preparation time 20 minutes
Cooking time 20 minutes
Wine *Rossese di Dolceacqua*

PASSATELLI
2 eggs
1½ cups (5 oz or 150 g)
 grated Parmesan
3 cups (10.5 oz or 300 g)
 breadcrumbs
salt
1/3 cup (1.8 oz or 50 g) plain
 flour

SOUP
1 knob of butter
1 tbsp extra-virgin olive oil
1/2 yellow onion, diced
1/2 dried red chile pepper, seeded
2 small yellow-fleshed potatoes,
 peeled and sliced
2½ cups (600 ml) hot vegetable broth
3 large fresh porcini mushrooms
salt and pepper
1 rosemary sprig
1 thyme sprig

1036

Mix the eggs with the Parmesan cheese, breadcrumbs and a
pinch of salt.
Pour the flour onto a work surface and make a well in the centre.
Pour the egg mixture into the well and mix by hand to form a
smooth dough. Cover and set aside.
Heat the butter and oil in a wide saucepan. Add the onion and
cook over low heat for a few minutes. Crumble in the chile pepper
and then add the potatoes. Add a little hot broth and let cook.
Meanwhile, chop the mushrooms, add them to the pan and
season with salt and pepper. Pour over the boiling broth and add
the rosemary sprig and thyme leaves. Adjust the salt and pepper.
Cook for 15 minutes over medium heat. Remove the rosemary
sprig and puree.
Bring a large pot of salted water to a boil. Push the passatelli
dough through a potato ricer directly into the boiling water. When
the passatelli rise to the surface, drain using a slotted spoon.
Pour the porcini soup into soup bowls and top with passatelli.

Tagliatelle with Roast Beef

Note *Fresh porcini may be substituted with 1 oz (30 g) of dried porcini mushrooms. Soak the mushrooms in warm water before using.*

Preparation time 20 minutes
Cooking time 1 hour 30 minutes
Wine *Dolcetto di Dogliani*

1 beef roast (2.2 lbs or 1 kg)
plain flour
3 tbsps extra-virgin olive oil
mustard
1 onion
5 fresh porcini mushrooms, sliced
7 tbsps milk
1 knob of butter
salt
9 oz (250 g) egg tagliatelle

Dust the roast with flour. Heat the olive oil in a large pot and brown the roast evenly on all sides. Add the mustard and whole onion and cover. Cook over low heat for 1 hour. Remove the roast from the pot and cover to keep warm.
Add the mushrooms to the pan juices. Cook until the mushrooms are tender. Add the milk. If the sauce seems too thin add a little flour. Remove from heat and stir in the butter. Season with salt.
Cook the tagliatelle for a few minutes in boiling salted water. Drain and top with the mushroom sauce. Serve the pasta with slices of the beef roast.

Black Rice Timbales with Curried Prawns

Preparation time 15 minutes
Cooking time 20 minutes
Wine *Metodo Classico*
Franciacorta Rosé

1 knob of butter
1 shallot, minced
1¾ cups (10 oz or 280 g)
 black Venere rice
6 cups (1.5 l) fish broth
12 oz (350 g) large prawns
6 tbsps extra-virgin olive oil
1/2 Golden Delicious apple,
 peeled and diced
1 tbsp brandy
salt
1/2 tsp saffron
1 tsp curry
7 tbsps heavy cream

1038

Heat the butter in a large saucepan, add half of the shallot and
sauté. When the shallot is transparent, add the rice and toast over
high heat for 3-4 minutes. Add the fish broth to the rice a little at a
time, letting the broth absorb completely before adding more.
While the rice cooks peel the prawns, leaving the tails attached.
Heat the oil in a frying pan and add the remaining shallot and
apple. Add the prawns and brown evenly on both sides. Add the
brandy and season with salt. Remove the prawns from the pan
and set aside. Cover to keep warm.
Dissolve the saffron and curry in a little hot fish broth and add
to the pan juices. Reduce the sauce over low heat and add the
cream. Keep warm.
Once the rice is cooked (40-50 minutes), fill 4 ramequins with the
rice and invert them onto serving plates. Top the timbales with the
prawns and sauce. Serve immediately.

Porcini and Chestnut Soup with Walnuts

Preparation time 20 minutes
Cooking time 40 minutes
Wine *Lago di Caldaro*

10 chestnuts
3 tbsps extra-virgin olive oil
1 shallot, minced
1/2 carrot, minced
1 celery stalk, minced
2 medium porcini, diced
6 cups (1.5 l) vegetable broth
salt and pepper
2 slices crusty bread
5 walnut halves, chopped

Boil the chestnuts until tender and peel them.
Heat the oil in a large saucepan and sauté the shallot, carrot and celery. Add the porcini and cook until they have released their liquid.
Crumble the chestnuts into the pan and after a few minutes, add the broth. Season with salt and pepper and simmer for about 25 minutes.
Puree the soup and adjust the salt and pepper.
Dice the bread and toast it for a few minutes in a non-stick pan.
Serve the soup with the croutons and chopped walnuts.

1039

Grilled Cotechino with Lentil Cream

Preparation time 30 minutes
Cooking time 1 hour
Wine *Gutturnio Classico*

3/4 cup (5.5 oz or 150 g) lentils
salt and pepper
2 extra-virgin olive oil
1 shallot, minced
1 garlic clove
2 sage leaves
3/4 cup (200 ml) beef broth
1 pre-cooked cotechino

1040

Rinse the lentils, boil in lightly salted water until tender and drain. Heat the olive oil in a saucepan and add the shallot. Add the whole garlic clove, sage leaves and lentils. Cook for 1 minute and then add the broth. Cook for 6 minutes and then remove the garlic clove. Season with salt and pepper. Blend the mixture and set aside in a warm place.
Meanwhile, bring a large pot of water to a boil and add the cotechino, still in its cooking bag. Boil until heated through. Remove the cotechino, skim the fat off and let cool slightly. Cut into thick slices. Grill the cotechino slices in a non-stick pan until browned.
Pour the lentil cream into shallow soup bowls and serve with the grilled cotechino slices.

Beef Fillet with Taleggio Sauce

Preparation time 20 minutes
Cooking time 15 minutes
Wine *Brunello di Montalcino*

BEEF
1.5 lbs (700 g) beef fillet
8 thin slices of pancetta
4 bay leaves
salt and pepper
4 large porcini mushrooms,
 stalks removed
3 tbsps extra-virgin olive oil

SAUCE
1 knob of butter
3 tbsps milk
3.5 oz (100 g) taleggio cheese,
 chopped

1041

Cut the fillet into 4 thick steaks and wrap each one with 2 slices of pancetta. Place 1 bay leaf on top of each steak and tie with kitchen string. Season with salt and pepper.
Heat a cast-iron grill pan and cook the fillets.
Meanwhile melt the butter with the milk in a saucepan. Add the taleggio and stir until smooth and creamy.
Grill the porcini mushrooms.
Plate the fillets, season with pepper and drizzle with olive oil.
Top with 1 grilled porcini mushroom. Serve the fillets with a little taleggio sauce.

Pork Tenderloin with Mirto Liqueur

Preparation time 30 minutes
Cooking time 25 minutes
Wine *Refosco dal Peduncolo Rosso*

1.5 lb (700 g) pork tenderloin
salt and pepper
4 tbsps extra-virgin olive oil
2 garlic cloves, smashed
3 fresh porcini mushrooms, sliced
parsley, minced
3 tbsps mirto liqueur
1/2 cup (120 ml) Vermentino wine
1 bay leaf

Preheat oven to 375°F (190°C).
Butterfly the pork loin and pound out gently with a meat tenderizer. Season with salt and pepper.
Heat 1 tablespoon olive oil in a non-stick frying pan and add 1 garlic clove. Add the mushrooms and cook over high heat. Add the parsley, salt and pepper. When the mushrooms are browned and crispy remove from heat and transfer to a bowl.
Stuff the pork with mushrooms. Roll up and tie with kitchen string. Heat the remaining olive oil in an oven-proof pan and add the remaining garlic clove. Add the pork loin and brown evenly on all sides. Add the mirto, let evaporate and then add the wine and bay leaf. Transfer the pan to the oven and roast for 18 minutes.
Slice the pork loin and serve with the cooking juices.

Roasted Quails with Artichoke Salad

Preparation time 10 minutes
Cooking time 20 minutes
Wine *Oltrepò Pavese Pinot Nero*

6 quails
salt and pepper
3 tbsps extra-virgin olive oil
5 baby artichokes
juice of 1/2 lemon
2 oz (50 g) Grana Padano cheese,
 shaved

Preheat oven to 375°F (190°C).
Season the quails with salt, pepper and a little olive oil. Roast for 20 minutes.
Remove from the oven, cool slightly and remove the meat from the bones.
Cut the stalks off the artichokes and trim the artichokes, removing the hard external leaves and the choke. Thinly slice the artichokes and transfer to a bowl.
Whisk together the lemon juice, salt and pepper and slowly add the remaining olive oil to emulsify. Pour the dressing over the artichokes and add the Grana Padano.
Place the artichoke salad in 4 small serving bowls and top with quail meat.

1043

Pumpkin-Seed Cookies

Preparation time 20 minutes
Cooking time 50 minutes
Wine *Vin Santo*
♟

Serves 4-6

8 tbsps peanut oil
1/2 cup (5 oz or 150 g) acacia honey
1¾ cups (6.5 oz or 180 g)
  multi-grain muesli
3 tbsps plain flour
1/4 cup (1.5 oz or 40 g)
  unsalted peanuts
3 tbsps coconut flakes
1 cup (2 oz or 60 g) unsalted
  pumpkin seeds
1/2 tsp anise seeds, ground

1044

Preheat oven to 250°F (120°C).
Heat the oil and honey in a saucepan until thin. Add the muesli,
flour, peanuts, coconut, pumpkin seeds and anise. Mix well with a
wooden spoon.
Pour the mixture onto a sheet of parchment paper. Form
cherry-sized balls with well-oiled hands. Place the cookies on a
parchment paper-lined baking sheet and bake for 40-50 minutes.
Let the cookies cool and store in an air-tight container.

Panettone Flan with Raisins

Preparation time 15 minutes
Cooking time 20 minutes
Wine *Marsala Dolce*

Serves 6

10 fl oz (400 ml) milk
6.7 fl oz (200 ml) whipping cream
2 tsps vanilla extract
4 egg yolks
2/3 cups (4 oz or 120 g) sugar
1 tsp corn flour
2 tbsps raisins
2 tbsps Marsala wine
butter
1/2 panettone, diced

Preheat oven to 350°F (180°C).
Heat milk, cream and vanilla.
Beat egg yolks, sugar and corn
flour. Whisk in the hot millk and
return to the pan. Cook over low
heat until the cream coats the
back of a spoon. Let cool.
Soak the raisins in the Marsala
wine and a little water.
Line 6 buttered ramequins with
the panettone. Divide the raisins
and soaking liquid between
the ramequins. Top with any
remaining panettone. Pour the
pastry cream into the ramequins.
Bake for 12 minutes and serve.

Stuffed Dates with Pistachios

Preparation time 10 minutes
Wine *Marsala Dolce*

3.5 oz (100 g) mascarpone
3.5 oz (100 g) ricotta
1 tbsp confectioners' sugar
1/2 tsp orange flower water
16 pitted dates
1/4 cup (1 oz or 30 g)
 unsalted pistachios

Beat the mascarpone and
ricotta with the confectioners'
sugar until smooth.
Sieve the mixture to eliminate
any lumps. Stir in the orange
flower water and transfer the
mixture to a pastry bag with a
small round tip.
Slice open the dates and fill
with the mixture. Close the
dates.
Finely chop the pistachios in
a food processor. Sprinkle the
dates with the pistachios and
refrigerate until serving.

Amaretto Cookies

Preparation time 20 minutes
Cooking time 30 minutes
Wine *Moscato Passito
di Pantelleria*

**2 cups (10.5 oz or 300 g) peeled
almonds**
1¾ cups (12 oz or 350 g) sugar
3 egg whites
zest and juice of 1 lemon
salt
1 tbsp plain flour
1 tsp corn flour
almond extract
confectioners' sugar

1046

Blend the almonds in a food processor with a few tablespoons of
sugar.
Beat the egg whites, 1 teaspoon lemon juice and a pinch of salt
to stiff peaks. Add the ground almonds and remaining sugar to
the egg whites and sift in the flour and corn flour. Mix carefully and
then add the almond extract.
Butter and flour a baking sheet. Drop spoonfuls of the batter onto
the baking sheet. Sprinkle with confectioners' sugar and let rest for
4-5 hours.
Preheat the oven to 210°F (100°C).
Bake the cookies for 30 minutes.
Remove from the oven and transfer the hot cookies to a wooden
cutting board to cool. Once cool the cookies can be stored in an
airtight tin.

Caprese Cake

Preparation time 20 minutes
Cooking time 55 minutes
Wine *Aleatico*

2 cups (10.5 oz or 300 g) almonds
1 cup (7 oz or 200 g) sugar
5 eggs
10 oz (280 g) dark chocolate
7 tbsps (3.5 oz or 100 g) butter
2 fl oz (60 ml) Amaretto liqueur
1 tsp almond extract
2 tsps vanilla extract
3 tbsps corn flour
salt
2 tsps baking powder
confectioners' sugar

1047

Preheat oven to 350°F (180°C).
Blend the almonds in a food processor with the sugar to the consistency of coarse meal. Transfer to a mixing bowl and stir in the eggs.
Melt the chocolate and butter together and let cool slightly.
Add the Amaretto liqueur, vanilla and almond extracts, corn flour and a pinch of salt to the egg mixture. Add the chocolate to the egg mixture and stir to combinate. Sift in the baking powder and mix to incorporate.
Butter and flour the sides of a 9-inch (22 cm) spring-form pan.
Cut out a 9-inch (22 cm) round of parchment paper and line the bottom of the pan. Pour the cake batter into the pan and bake for 45 minutes.
Sprinkle the cake with confectioners' sugar and serve warm.

Blueberry Cheesecake

Preparation time 20 minutes
Wine *Malvasia di Bosa*

Serves 6-8

10.5 oz (300 g) graham crackers
7 tbsps melted butter
6 oz (180 g) sheep's milk ricotta
6 oz (180 g) cream cheese
4 oz (120 g) mascarpone
5 tbsps confectioners' sugar
zest of 1 lemon
2 tsps vanilla extract
2 gelatin sheets
2 tbsps Cognac
7.5 fl oz (220 ml) whipping cream
2 baskets of blueberries

1048

Blend the graham crackers in a food processor, add the melted butter and pulse until the mixture holds its shape.
Line the bottom of a 9-inch (22 cm) spring-form pan with parchment paper. Press the graham cracker mixture in to form a uniform crust. Refrigerate until firm.
Meanwhile, sieve the ricotta, cream cheese and mascarpone. Beat the mixture together with the confectioners' sugar, lemon zest and vanilla extract.
Soak the gelatin in cold water, drain and squeeze out the excess water. Dissolve the gelatin in the Cognac and add to the ricotta mixture.
Whip the whipping cream to stiff peaks and fold into the ricotta. Pour the filling into the graham cracker crust or pipe it in using a pastry bag. Refrigerate until firm, about 2 hours. Decorate with whole blueberries or blueberry puree.

Gianduia Tart

Preparation time 30 minutes
Cooking time 25 minutes
Wine *Asti Moscato Spumante*
♟

Serves 6

DOUGH
2½ cups (10.5 oz or 300 g)
 plain flour
3/4 cup (6 oz or 170 g) butter,
 diced
1 egg
1 egg yolk
2 tsps vanilla extract
3/4 cups (5 oz or 150 g) sugar
salt

FILLING
4 oz (120 g) gianduia chocolate
1/4 pandoro
2 fl oz (60 ml) whipping cream

Mound the flour onto a work surface and place the butter in the centre. Add the egg, egg yolk, vanilla extract, sugar and a pinch of salt. Mix together quickly with fingertips until all the flour has been incorporated and the dough is smooth. Roll into a ball and cover with plastic wrap. Refrigerate for 40 minutes.
Preheat oven to 325°F (170°C).
Butter and flour a round cake pan. Roll out the dough into a thin sheet and place it in the cake pan. Pierce the dough with a fork. Cover the dough with parchment paper and fill with pie weights or dried beans. Bake for 20 minutes. Remove from the oven and let cool.
Melt the chocolate in a double boiler and let cool.
Crumble the pandoro into a mixing bowl. Whip the whipping cream to stiff peaks and fold it into the chocolate. Add the pandoro and mix to combine. Pour the filling over the crust and set aside until firm.

Artichokes Stuffed with Sausage and Pecorino

Preparation time 20 minutes
Cooking time 50 minutes
Wine *Alto Adige Santa Maddalena*

8 artichokes
juice of 1 lemon
6.5 oz (180 g) luganega sausage
1 medium potato, boiled
3.5 oz (100 g) pecorino cheese, shaved
salt and pepper
6 tbsps breadcrumbs
2 tbsps extra-virgin olive oil

Preheat oven to 375°F (190°C).
Cut the stalks off the artichokes and trim the artichokes, removing the hard external leaves and the choke. Place the artichokes in cold water and add half the lemon juice.
Bring a pot of salted water to a boil and add the remaining lemon juice. Add the artichokes and blanch for 3 minutes. Drain with a slotted spoon and let dry on paper towels.
Meanwhile, remove the casing from the sausage and crumble it into a non-stick pan. Brown over medium heat.
Peel and mash the potato with a fork and add it to the sausage. Remove from heat, add the pecorino and season with salt and pepper. Mix well to combine.
Stuff the artichokes with the sausage filling and sprinkle with breadcrumbs. Drizzle with olive oil. Place the artichokes on an oiled baking sheet and bake for 20 minutes.

1050

Acorn Squash and Artichoke Fritters

Preparation time 15 minutes
Cooking time 5 minutes
Wine *Prosecco di Valdobbiadene Brut*

1 lb (400 g) acorn squash
5 baby artichokes
juice of 1 lemon
1 cup plus 3 tbsps (5.3 oz or 150 g)
 plain flour
2 tbsps finely ground semolina flour
1 tsp baking powder
1 egg
sparkling water
sunflower oil
salt and pepper

Peel, deseed and julienne the squash.
Cut the stalks off the artichokes and trim the artichokes, removing the hard external leaves and the choke. Thinly slice the artichokes and transfer to a bowl with cold water and lemon juice.
Mix the flour, semolina flour and baking powder in a bowl and add the egg. Add enough sparkling water to make a batter of medium consistency. Let rest for 30 minutes.
Add the artichokes to the batter and mix well to coat uniformly.
Heat the sunflower oil in a saucepan and fry the artichokes until golden-brown. Drain on paper towels and season with salt and pepper. Serve immediately.

Crescenza Fritters with Mortadella

Preparation time 15 minutes
Cooking time 5 minutes
Wine *Metodo Classico*
Franciacorta Dosaggio Zero

6.5 oz (180 g) crescenza cheese
1¾ cups (8 oz or 220 g)
 plain flour
2 tsps baking powder
2-3 sage leaves, minced
sunflower oil
salt
5 oz (150 g) mortadella, thinly sliced

Beat the crescenza cheese with a fork and add a little warm water to thin the consistency.
Add the flour and baking powder and mix to obtain a smooth, thick batter. Add the sage and cover with aluminum foil. Let rest for 40 minutes.
Heat the sunflower oil and drop spoonfuls of batter into the oil. Fry until golden-brown and drain on paper towels. Season with salt and serve with the mortadella.

1052

A P P E T I Z E R

Venison Tartare with Butternut Squash and Broccoli Rabe

Preparation time 15 minutes
Cooking time 20 minutes
Wine *Alto Adige Pinot Nero*

1 rosemary sprig
3/4 cup (200 ml) extra-virgin
 olive oil
sunflower oil
5 oz (150 g) butternut squash,
 peeled, deseeded and diced
2 garlic cloves, smashed
1 chile pepper
12 oz (350 g) broccoli rabe,
 tough stalks removed
salt and pepper
8.5 oz (240 g) venison, minced

Coarsely chop the rosemary and mix with half the olive oil.
Heat the sunflower oil in a saucepan and fry the squash. Drain on paper towels.
Heat the remaining olive oil in a frying pan and add the garlic and chile pepper. Sauté for a few minutes and add the broccoli rabe. Cover and cook for 10-15 minutes adding a little water if necessary.
Mix the venison and squash in a bowl with the rosemary oil. Season with salt and pepper.
Place the broccoli rabe on serving plates. Use a round cookie cutter to mould the tartare and place on top of the broccoli rabe.

1053

Robiola-Stuffed Spinach Pasta Rolls

Note *Robiola di Roccaverano is made in the valleys surrounding the city of Asti in Piedmont, the only Italian goat's milk cheese to have a DOP classification. It is a raw milk cheese that can be eaten just a week after production or aged for up to 1 month.*

1054

Preparation time 40 minutes
Cooking time 20 minutes
Wine *Erbaluce di Caluso*

PASTA
2 cups (2 oz or 50 g) spinach
salt
1⅔ cups (7 oz or 200 g)
 plain flour
2 eggs
1 tbsp extra-virgin olive oil

FILLING
9 oz (250 g) Robiola di Roccaverano
 cheese
6 tbsps grated Parmesan
1 tbsp extra-virgin olive oil
ground nutmeg
salt and pepper
milk

Preheat oven to 340°F (170°C).
Blanch the spinach in salted water. Drain, squeeze out and finely chop. Mound the flour on a work surface and make a well in the centre. Add the eggs, spinach and olive oil. Mix to form an elastic dough. Cover with plastic wrap and refrigerate.
Mix the Cheese with 4 tablespoons Parmesan, the oil and a pinch of ground nutmeg until smooth and creamy. Season with salt and pepper. If the mixture is too dry add 2 tablespoons of milk.
Roll out the pasta into a thin sheet. Spread the cheese filling over the pasta and roll up like a canellone. Cut the roll into 4-inch (10 cm) lengths and pinch the ends to seal closed.
Place the rolls in an oiled baking dish and sprinkle with remaining Parmesan. Bake for 15 minutes and then grill for a final 3 minutes.

Gnocchi alla Caprese

Preparation time 20 minutes
Cooking time 50 minutes
Wine *Capri Rosso*

Serves 6-8

3 tbsps extra-virgin olive oil
1/2 onion, minced
5 oz (150 g) ground beef
2 lbs (1 kg) peeled, canned tomatoes
basil leaves
salt
2.5 lbs (1.2 kg) potato gnocchi
9 oz (250 g) cow's milk mozzarella,
 chopped
4 tbsps grated Parmesan,

Preheat oven to 350°F (180°C).
Heat the olive oil in a large frying pan and add the onion. Sauté briefly and add the beef. Brown the meat and then add tomatoes and a few basil leaves. Reduce the heat and simmer for 30 minutes.
Bring a large pot of salted water to the boil and cook the gnocchi until they rise to the surface. Using a slotted spoon drain half of the gnocchi directly into a well-oiled baking dish. Top with half of the chopped mozzarella and then add the remaining gnocchi. Add the remaining cheese and cover with the beef sauce. Sprinkle with Parmesan cheese and bake for 5-10 minutes until the top is golden-brown. Remove from the oven and serve immediately.

Roast Pork with Grapes

Preparation time 20 minutes
Cooking time 50 minutes
Wine *Morellino di Scansano*

2 rosemary sprigs
5 sage leaves
salt and pepper
1 centre-cut pork loin
4 slices of pancetta
4 tbsps extra-virgin olive oil
2 shallots, coarsely chopped
3/4 cup (180 ml) rosé wine
1 bunch of red grapes
4 bay leaves

1056

Preheat oven to 350°F (180°C).
Mince together the rosemary and sage leaves.
Salt and pepper the meat and rub with the herb mixture. Wrap in
the pancetta and tie with kitchen string.
Heat the olive oil in a frying pan and add the shallots. Add the
meat and brown evenly on all sides. Add the wine and remove
from heat. Transfer the meat and pan juices to a baking dish and
add the grapes and bay leaves. Bake for 45 minutes.

Pork Chops Stuffed with Walnuts and Acorn Squash

Preparation time 30 minutes
Cooking time 15 minutes
Wine *Cirò Rosso*
♟ ♟

FILLING
extra-virgin olive oil
1/2 acorn squash, peeled and sliced
1/4 cup (1 oz or 30 g) chopped
 walnuts

PORK CHOPS
4 thick pork chops
salt and pepper
4 sage leaves, minced
3 tbsps extra-virgin olive oil
2 garlic cloves, smashed

GARNISH
1/4 cup (1 oz or 30 g) chopped
 walnuts
balsamic vinegar

1057

Preheat oven to 350°F (180°C).
Place the squash slices on an oiled baking sheet and bake for 25 minutes.
Meanwhile, make a horizontal incision in the pork chops to form a little pocket. Sprinkle minced sage, salt and pepper on the pork chops and inside the pocket.
Mash the squash and stir in the walnuts. Stuff the pork chops with the squash mixture.
Heat the oil and garlic cloves in a non-stick frying pan. Add the pork chops and brown evenly on both sides. Cook for another 5 minutes per side.
Top the pork chops with the remaining walnuts and a drizzle of balsamic vinegar.

Lamb Chops with Zolfini Bean Puree

Preparation time 20 minutes
Cooking time 2 hours
Wine *Rosso di Montalcino*

1058

BEAN PUREE
1/2 cup (3.5 oz or 100 g)
 dried Zolfini beans
2 garlic cloves
2 star anise seeds
3 tbsps extra-virgin olive oil
salt and pepper

LAMB CHOPS
8 lamb chops
salt and pepper
2 tbsps plain flour
1 egg, lightly beaten
2/3 cup (6 oz or 180 g) breadcrumbs
sunflower oil
fleur du sel

Soak the Zolfini beans overnight.
Place the beans, garlic cloves, star anise and 1 tablespoon of olive oil in a terracotta pot and cover with 3 fingers of water. Cook over medium heat for 1 hour 45 minutes.
Trim any excess fat off of the lamb chops. Season the chops with salt and pepper and coat with flour. Dip the lamb chops in the egg and then coat with breadcrumbs. Press down with hands to adhere.
Drain the beans (reserving a little cooking liquid) and discard the garlic and star anise. Puree the beans with a little cooking liquid and remaining olive oil. Season with salt and abundant pepper.
Heat the sunflower oil in a large frying pan. Add the lamb chops and fry until golden brown. Drain on paper towels. Serve the lamb chops with the bean puree and top with fleur de sel.

Couscous-Stuffed Squid

Preparation time 15 minutes
Cooking time 10 minutes
Wine *Etna Bianco*

1 shallot, minced
4 tbsps extra-virgin olive oil
boiling water
1 garlic clove, smashed
20 cherry tomatoes, sliced
10 basil leaves, chopped
3/4 cup (5 oz or 150 g) couscous
salt and pepper
1 egg white
4 medium-large squid

Sauté the shallot in 1 tablespoon of olive oil. Add the couscous and toast briefly. Add enough boiling water to cover. Place a lid on the pan and remove from heat.

Heat 1 tablespoon olive oil in a frying pan and add the garlic. Add half the tomatoes and sauté briefly. When the tomatoes are tender add the basil leaves and couscous. Season with salt and pepper. Remove from heat and let cool. Mix in the egg white.

Clean the squid and cut off the tentacles. Fill the squid with the couscous mixture.

Heat the remaining olive oil in a frying pan and add the squid and remaining tomatoes. Cook, covered, until the squid is tender. Season with salt and pepper and serve immediately.

Lemon Cream Profiteroles

Preparation time 30 minutes
Cooking time 20 minutes

Serves 4-6

BEIGNETS
2 organic lemons
17 fl oz (500 ml) milk
4 egg yolks
2/3 cups (4.5 oz or 125 g) sugar
1/3 cup plus 2 tbsps (2 oz or 55 g)
 plain flour
20-25 ready-made beignets

CARAMEL
3/4 cup (5 oz or 150 g) sugar
2 tbsps water

1060

Peel the lemons using a potato peeler.
Heat the milk and lemon peel. When the milk reaches a boil
remove from heat and set aside for 10 minutes.
Meanwhile, beat the egg yolks with the sugar until thick. Sift in the
flour and mix well.
Strain and reheat the milk. Whisk the hot milk into the egg mixture
and then return the saucepan. Cook over low heat, stirring
constantly, until the cream thickens. Transfer to a bowl and let cool
completely.
Place the cream in a pastry bag. Slice open the beignets. Fill with
the lemon cream and refrigerate.
Meanwhile, heat the sugar and water in a saucepan and cook over
low heat until it begins to colour. Remove from heat and let cool
just until the caramel falls in thread-like ribbons from a spoon.
Assemble the beignets into a pyramid shape and drizzle over the
caramel. Let sit for 5 minutes before serving.

Champagne Cream with Raspberries

Preparation time 20 minutes
Cooking time 5 minutes
Wine *Champagne Crémant*

CHAMPAGNE CREAM
8.5 fl oz (250 ml) Champagne
2 egg yolks
1 egg
1/3 cup (2 oz or 60 g) sugar
6.7 fl oz (200 ml) whipping cream

RASPBERRY SAUCE
2 baskets of raspberries
2 tbsps raw sugar

GARNISH
1 basket raspberries

1061

Reduce the Champagne in a small pan over low heat for 3-4 minutes.
Meanwhile, beat the egg yolks with the egg and add the sugar.
Whisk in the Champagne reduction and transfer to a double boiler.
Cook over low heat, whisking constantly until the sauce is thick and foamy. Let cool.
Whip the whipping cream to stiff peaks and fold into the Champagne sauce.
Puree half the raspberries with the raw sugar.
Layer the champagne cream and raspberry puree (reserving some for garnish) in 4 glass bowls and refrigerate until firm.
Decorate with a drizzle of raspberry puree and the remaining raspberries.

Chocolate Roll with Cream

Preparation time 20 minutes
Cooking time 15 minutes

Serves 6-8

SPONGE CAKE
3 eggs
3/4 cups plus 2 tbsps
 (4.7 oz or 135 g) sugar
4 tbsps (1 oz or 30 g)
 plain flour
1/4 cup (1 oz or 25 g)
 cocoa powder

CREAM
10 fl oz (300 ml) whipping cream
5 fl oz (150 ml) sweetened
 condensed milk

1062

Preheat oven to 400°F (200°C).
Using an electric beater with the whisk attachment, beat the eggs with 1/2 cup (3.5 oz or 95 g) sugar. When the mixture lightens in colour and begins to form ribbons carefully fold in the sifted flour and cocoa powder. Pour the batter into a parchment paper-lined rectangular baking sheet. Spread the batter with a spatula to form a uniform layer. Bake for 15 minutes.
Meanwhile, place a clean kitchen towel on a work surface and top with paper towels. Sprinkle the remaining sugar over the paper towels. Invert the hot sponge cake onto the paper towels and roll up the sponge cake like a jelly roll.
Whip the whipping cream to stiff peaks and add the sweetened condensed milk.
Unroll the sponge cake, spread the cream over the cake and re-roll the cake. Cover the cake and refrigerate until firm. Slice the chocolate roll and serve.

Salmon and Arugula Spread

Preparation time 20 minutes
Cooking time 15 minutes
Wine *Torbato di Alghero Brut*

1 lb (500 g) salmon fillet
juice of 1/2 lemon
1 tbsp extra-virgin olive oil
salt
pink peppercorns, crushed
2 bunches arugula, chopped
3 tbsps mayonnaise
chives and dill, chopped
1 baguette

Remove the skin and any bones from the salmon. Place in a steamer basket and place the basket in a pan with 2 inches (5 cm) of water. Cover and steam until tender.
Remove from heat and let cool. Crumble up the salmon with fingertips, removing any bones or scales. Smash with a fork, add a little lemon juice and oil and season with salt and pink pepper. Chill the salmon and then stir in the arugula, mayonnaise, chives and dill.
Slice the baguette and toast.
Using 2 spoons make salmon quenelles and place on the warm toast. Serve immediately.

1065

Tiger Prawns on Porcini Carpaccio

Preparation time 25 minutes
Cooking time 15 minutes
Wine *Metodo Classico*
Franciacorta Dosaggio Zero

2 yellow-fleshed potatoes
salt and pepper
1/2 tsp saffron
4 cups (1 l) water
zest and juice of 1 lemon
3 mint sprigs
3 fresh porcini mushrooms
4 tablespoons extra-virgin olive oil
1.3 lb (600 g) tiger prawns
 or jumbo prawns, shelled
 and deveined

1066

Boil the potatoes in salted water with the saffron. Drain, peel and dice the potatoes.

Heat the water with the lemon zest and 2 mint sprigs.

Clean the mushrooms with a damp paper towel and thinly slice. Arrange the mushrooms on a serving plate.

Mix the lemon juice with salt and pepper. Whisk in the olive oil to emulsify. Mince the remaining mint and add it to the vinaigrette. Set aside.

Place the prawns in a steaming basket and steam over the lemon-mint infusion until cooked through.

Arrange the steamed prawns on the porcini and drizzle with the mint vinaigrette. Add the saffron potatoes and serve.

APPETIZER

Creamy Baccalà with Broccoli-Walnut Croquettes

Preparation time 25 minutes
Cooking time 30 minutes
Wine *Alto Adige Sauvignon*
♟ ♟

BACCALÀ
2 tbsps butter
1 shallot, minced
12.5 oz (350 g) pre-soaked
 salt cod
2 cups (500 ml) milk

CROQUETTES
1¼ cups (5 oz or 150 g)
 plain flour
1 tsp baking powder
1/2 cup (2 oz or 50 g) chopped
 walnuts
salt and pepper
1 head of broccoli
sunflower oil

LAMPASCIONI
20 lampascioni (or pearl onions)
1 tbsp mirto liqueur
2 tbsps balsamic vinegar

Heat the butter in a saucepan, sauté the shallot until soft and then add the salt cod. Cover with milk and let cook slowly over low heat. Meanwhile, mix together the flour, baking powder and walnuts and blend in a food processor. Season with salt and pepper. Add enough water to the mixture to form a smooth batter of medium consistency. Steam the broccoli florets until tender and cool in ice water. Drain, coarsely chop and add to the batter. Let the batter rest for 1 hour. Blanch the lampascioni for 2 minutes in salted water. Transfer to a hot frying pan and brown for 1 minute. Add the mirto liqueur and let evaporate. Add the balsamic vinegar and remove from heat.
Remove any bones from the fish and pass the mixture through a sieve to obtain a smooth puree.
Heat the sunflower oil in a saucepan. Drop spoonfuls of the broccoli batter into the oil and fry until golden-brown. Drain on paper towels and season with salt.
Place the salt-cod puree in shallow bowls and serve with the broccoli croquettes and galzed lampascioni.

Eggplant Cannelloni with Cabbage and Lonzino

Preparation time 40 minutes
Cooking time 45 minutes
Wine *Lagrein Rosato*

3 tbsps extra-virgin olive oil
1 shallot, minced
1 eggplant, peeled and diced
1 egg
thyme leaves
2 tbsps breadcrumbs
salt and pepper
1/4 Savoy cabbage, julienned
1/2 onion, minced
4 cups (1 l) vegetable broth
9 oz (250 g) egg pasta sheets
1 knob of butter
3 oz (80 g) lonzino, thinly sliced

1068

Preheat oven to 350°F (180°C).
Heat the olive oil in a pot and add the shallot. Sauté for a few minutes and add the eggplant. Cook over high heat, stirring frequently, for 15 minutes. Puree the mixture and add the egg, thyme and breadcrumbs. Season with salt and pepper.
Meanwhile, wilt the cabbage with the onion over medium heat. Add the vegetable broth and cook for 20 minutes. Remove from heat and let cool. Puree the mixture.
Trim the pasta sheets to 3½-inch by 5-inch (8 by 10 cm) rectangles. Boil the pasta sheets and rinse with cold water. Dry on a clean kitchen towel.
Spread the pasta sheets with the eggplant puree and roll into cannelloni. Place the cannelloni in a buttered baking dish and top with small pieces of butter. Bake for 8 minutes.
Meanwhile, fry the lonzino slices in a non-stick pan until crispy.
Serve the cannelloni with the cabbage puree and crispy lonzino.

Baked Tagliolini with Porcini Ragù

Preparation time 20 minutes
Cooking time 40 minutes
Wine *Alto Adige Pinot Nero*

TAGLIOLINI
2⅓ cups (10.5 oz or 300 g)
 plain flour
3 eggs
1 tbsp extra-virgin olive oil
salt

PORCINI RAGÙ
4 tbsps extra-virgin olive oil
1 shallot, minced
2 garlic cloves
4 fresh porcini mushrooms,
 thinly sliced
salt and pepper
3 tbsps grated Parmesan
2 tbsps butter

1069

Preheat oven to 350°F (180°C).
Mix together the flour, eggs, oil and a pinch of salt. Knead to form a smooth and elastic dough. Roll the dough into a ball, cover and refrigerate for 20 minutes.
Heat 2 tablespoons of olive oil with the shallot and garlic and sauté the mushrooms until soft. Season with salt and pepper.
Roll out the pasta into thin sheets. Roll up the pasta and slice thinly to form tagliolini. Dust a wooden cutting board with flour and toss the tagliolini in the flour. Let the pasta dry.
Bring a large pot of salted water to a boil. Boil the tagliolini for a few minutes and drain. Drizzle 2 tablespoons of oil over the pasta. Butter a soufflé dish. Pour in half the tagliolini and top with 1/2 the mushroom ragù, 1 tablespoon of Parmesan and 1 tablespoon of butter. Mix to combine and form a second layer with the remaining pasta, ragù, butter and Parmesan. Bake for 15 minutes.

Sea Bass in a Salt Crust with Mandarin Oil

Preparation time 20 minutes
Cooking time 30 minutes
Wine *Bianco d'Alcamo*
♟

1 sea bass (about 2.2 lb or 1 kg)
1 rosemary sprig
2.2 lbs (1 kg) sea salt
grated zest of 3 mandarins
white pepper
1 egg white
5 tbsps extra-virgin olive oil

Preheat oven to 375°F (190°C).
Wash the fish and remove the gills. Place the rosemary in the stomach cavity.
Pour the salt into a large bowl and add the zest of 2 mandarins, freshly ground white pepper and egg whites. Mix well.
Place one-third of the salt mixture on a baking sheet. Spread out the salt to form an even layer. Place the fish on top of the salt and cover with the remaining salt. Pack the salt over the fish by hand, pressing down to adhere.
Bake for 30 minutes.
Meanwhile, mix the remaining mandarin zest with the olive oil.
Remove the fish from the oven and crack open the salt shell. Fillet the fish and serve with the mandarin oil.

1070

Prawn and Mediterranean Vegetables in Cartoccio

Preparation time 20 minutes
Cooking time 30 minutes
Wine *Metodo Classico Franciacorta Rosé*
♟

1 red bell pepper
1 yellow bell pepper
3 tbsps extra-virgin olive oil
2 garlic cloves
1 eggplant, peeled, deseeded and julienned
3 zucchini, julienned
salt and pepper
16 jumbo prawns
parsley, chopped

Preheat oven to 400°F (200°C).
Cut the bell peppers in half and remove the seeds and white membrane.
Grill the peppers on a cast iron grill-pan and transfer to a plastic bag. Let the peppers steam for 10 minutes. Peel and thinly slice the peppers.
Heat the olive oil in a non-stick pan with the garlic. Add the eggplant and sauté for 5 minutes. Add the peppers and zucchini. Season with salt and pepper.
Line a baking dish with a large sheet of parchment paper. Transfer the vegetables to the baking dish, add the prawns and sprinkle with parsley. Fold the parchment paper over the top and twist to close. Bake for 20 minutes. Open the parchment paper at the table and serve.

Baked Tub Gurnard with Potatoes

Preparation time 15 minutes
Cooking time 25 minutes
Wine *Bolgheri Bianco*

1 tub gurnard (about 1.75 lb
 or 800 g)
salt and pepper
6 yellow-fleshed potatoes, peeled
 and thickly sliced
3 garlic cloves
10 cherry tomatoes
1 1-inch (2 cm) piece of fresh
 ginger root, thinly sliced
1 lemon, 1/2 juiced and 1/2 sliced
oregano
3 tbsps extra-virgin olive oil

1072

Preheat oven to 400°F (200°C).
Wash and gut the fish and season the inner cavity with salt.
Layer the potatoes in the bottom of a baking dish and place the
fish on top of the potatoes. Add the garlic cloves, cherry tomatoes,
ginger, lemon juice and lemon slices. Add enough water so the
liquid covers about a third of the fish. Season with salt and pepper
and sprinkle with oregano. Cover with aluminum foil and bake for
25 minutes. Remove the foil and cook for another 15 minutes.
Drizzle the fish with olive oil and serve.

Potato Cream with Cuttlefish

Note *Nero di seppie can purchased in Italian specialty stores.*

Preparation time 15 minutes
Cooking time 15 minutes
Wine *Riviera Ligure di Ponente Pigato*

POTATO CREAM
3 tbsps extra-virgin olive oil
1 shallot, minced
1/2 chile pepper
4 medium white-fleshed potatoes,
 peeled and thinly sliced
4 cups (1 l) hot vegetable broth
salt and pepper
parsley, minced

CUTTLEFISH
2 cuttlefish
1 tbsp nero di seppie (squid ink)
white wine
3 tbsps extra-virgin olive oil
2 garlic cloves, smashed
salt and pepper

Heat the olive oil in a pot and add the shallot. Sauté for a few minutes and then add the chile pepper and potatoes. Sauté for another 3-4 minutes and cover with boiling hot broth. Season with salt and pepper. Cook for another 7-8 minutes, remove from the heat and puree.
Wash and thinly slice the cuttlefish.
Dilute the nero di seppie with a little white wine.
Heat the remaining oil in a large frying pan with the garlic cloves. Add the cuttlefish and sauté for 2 minutes. Add the diluted nero di seppie. Season with salt and pepper.
Serve the cuttlefish with the potato puree and garnish with parsley.

Bavarian Creams with Berry Sauce

Preparation time 45 minutes
Cooking time 15 minutes
Wine *Moscato Passito*

👨‍🍳 👨‍🍳

BAVARIAN CREAMS
5 tbsps milk
1/2 vanilla bean
2 egg yolks
1/2 cup (3.5 oz or 100 g) sugar
3 gelatin sheets
8.5 fl oz (250 ml) whipping cream
8.8 oz (250 g) ricotta

WAFERS
3½ tbsps butter, softened
1/2 cup (1.7 oz or 50 g)
 confectioners' sugar

1/3 cup plus 2 tbsps (1.7 oz
 or 50 g) plain flour
2 egg whites

SAUCE
2 baskets of mixed berries
1 lb (500 g) raspberries
1 lb (500 g) sugar
juice of 1 lemon
2 tbsps water

DECORATION
cocoa powder
confectioners' sugar

1074

Heat the milk with the vanilla bean.
Beat egg yolks with half the sugar in a double boiler. Whisk in hot milk. Remove from heat and add gelatin. Let cool completely.
Whip the cream and half the sugar to stiff peaks. Fold into the pastry cream with the ricotta. Pour into 4 ramequins. Refrigerate for 2 hours.
To make the wafers, mix the softened butter with the sugar and flour. Add the egg whites and mix well. Refrigerate for 1 hour.
Preheat oven to 350°F (180°C).
Roll out the dough and cut out 4 triangles. Lay on an oven-proof silicon mat and bake for 6-7 minutes.
Cook the berries with the sugar, lemon juice and water for a few minutes. Sieve the mixture.
Unmould the creams onto serving plates. Garnish with the wafers and berry sauce. Dust with cocoa powder and confectioners' sugar.

Raspberry Cream Puffs

Note *The fresh raspberry sauce can be replaced with raspberry jam. Fold the whipped cream directly into the jam.*

Preparation time 10 minutes
Cooking time 3 minutes
Wine *Trentino Moscato Rosa*

CREAM PUFFS
1⅔ cups (7 oz or 200 g) raspberries
1/3 cup (2 oz or 60 g) sugar
7 fl oz (200 ml) whipping cream
12 ready-made beignets

CHOCOLATE SAUCE
3.5 oz (100 g) dark chocolate
6 tbsps whipping cream
1/3 cup (2 oz or 60 g) sugar crystals

1075

Puree the raspberries with the sugar.
Whip the whipping cream with a wire whisk and fold in the raspberry puree.
Transfer the cream to a pastry bag and fill the beignets.
Melt the chocolate with the cream in a double boiler. Remove from heat and let cool.
Coat the beignets with chocolate sauce and sprinkle with sugar crystals.
Refrigerate at least 1 hour before serving.

Chocolate Heart Cake

Preparation time 30 minutes
Cooking time 1 hour
Wine *Banyuls*

Serves 6-8

3 oz (80 g) dark chocolate
10 tbsps (5 oz or 150 g) butter
4 medium-sized (25 g) butter
 cookies
1½ cups (7 oz or 200 g) almonds
2 eggs, separated
2/3 cups (4.2 oz or 120 g) sugar
salt
1 tbsp Strega liqueur
7 fl oz (200 ml) whipping cream
2 tbsps confectioners' sugar
1/2 tsp vanilla extract
cocoa powder

1076

Melt the chocolate in a double boiler with 3 tablespoons of butter
and 2 tablespoons of water, stirring frequently.
Blend the cookies and almonds in a food processor.
Beat the egg yolks with the sugar until thick and light in colour.
Work the remaining butter with a spatula until creamy and add it
to the yolks. Whisk in the chocolate mixture, almond mixture and
liqueur.
Whip the egg whites with a pinch of salt to stiff peaks and fold into
the batter.
Butter and flour a heart-shaped cake pan and pour in the batter.
Bake for 1 hour. Invert onto a wire rack to cool.
Whip the remaining whipping cream with the confectioners' sugar
and vanilla extract.
Slice the cake into 2 layers and spread 1 layer with the whipped
cream. Top with the second layer and sift the cocoa powder over
the top. Refrigerate until serving.

Vanilla Tiramisù

Note *If desired, the dessert can be enriched by sprinkling grated dark chocolate over every layer.*

Preparation time 25 minutes
Cooking time 5 minutes

CREAM
8.5 fl oz (250 ml) milk
1 vanilla bean, sliced in half
 lengthwise
2 egg yolks
1/3 cup (2 oz or 60 g) sugar
3 tbsps plain flour
1.7 oz (50 g) robiola cheese
1.7 oz (50 g) ricotta
5 tbsps whipping cream

CAKE
7 fl oz (200 ml) water
3 tbsps sugar
5 tbsps Alchermes liqueur
1 round of sponge cake

GARNISH
amaretto cookies

1077

Heat the milk with the vanilla bean.
Beat the egg yolks with the sugar and sift in the flour. Whisk in the hot milk and return to the saucepan. Cook over low heat until the cream thickens. Remove the vanilla bean, pour into a bowl and let cool. Add the robiola and ricotta and mix until creamy.
Whip the whipping cream to stiff peaks and fold into the pastry cream.
Bring the water and sugar to a boil and add the Alchermes. Remove from heat and cool. Soak the sponge cake in the cooled sugar syrup. Cut the sponge cake into rounds that fit into the serving dishes.
Layer the sponge cake and pastry cream in the serving dishes.
Top with crumbled amaretto cookies and serve.

This practical appendix serves as reference for basic recipes, definitions of kitchen tools and terms and an introduction to the diverse world of Italian wines.

The chapter begins with a description of kitchen tools, describing the uses for many of the common and not-so-common utensils, tools and appliances referred to in the recipes throughout the book.

The next section is dedicated to foundation recipes which form the base of Italian cuisine: puff pastry, egg pasta and pizza doughs, simple pasta sauces and flavoured oils.

A guide to setting the table includes handy tips and original decorating ideas, as well as guidelines for wine pairings and wine glasses.

Nearly every recipe in this book comes with a suggested wine or other beverage to pair with it. In the appendix you'll find "The Wine List", with brief descriptions provided for the most important Italian wines as well as suggested foods and serving temperatures.

"Cooking Terms" offers a comprehensive glossary of cooking terms, some uniquely Italian and others which form part of any cook's repertoire.

Finally the index offers a navigational guide to *La Cucina d'Oro* to help you find exactly the recipe you want.

Kitchen Tools

bamboo steaming basket (4)
The basket is placed directly over a pot of boiling water so the steam penetrates the basket and cooks the food inside. Steaming basket sets include several stacked baskets for steaming different foods with different cooking times.

boule
Similar to an egg white bowl but with one long handle. Can be used on its own or together with a double boiler. The rounded bottom makes this pan perfect for whipped sauces.

cannoli moulds (24)
Straight, seamless tubes made of stainless steel, for making cylindrical pastry shells.

cheese grater (26)
An indispensable kitchen tool for grating hard cheeses or dry bread. A wide variety of graters are available: microplane, box and electric.

cheese knife (7)
Long curved blade ending in two sharp points.

cheese plane (3)
Similar to a truffle plane, the cheese plane shaves or slices hard or medium-hard cheeses.

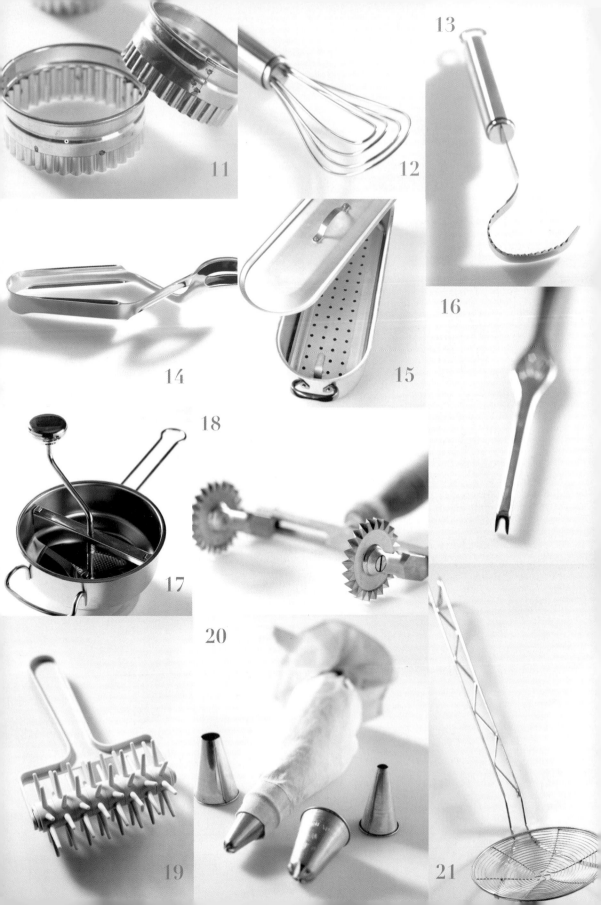

11

12

13

14

15

16

17

18

19

20

21

chef's knife
Flat-bladed knife (6-12 inches or 15-30 cm), the classic multipurpose kitchen knife for cutting raw meat and vegetables. A similar longer bladed knife (8-14 inch or 21-35 cm) is used for cutting large pieces of meat.

chinois sieve
A fine, conical sieve for straining broth or other thin liquids. The shape means the liquid can be sieved directly into a small bowl or pan.

citrus zesters (10)
Three different utensils for removing the peel and zest from citrus.

cookie cutter (11)
Made in steel or stainless steel, they come in various shapes and sizes. In Italian cooking the coppapasta (pasta cutter) is round, can be fluted, and is used to cut out pasta and other types of dough. It can also be used as a mould to shape meat or vegetables when presenting a finished dish.

crab fork (16)
Used for removing the meat from the claws or legs of crabs or other shellfish. When setting the table, crab forks should be placed on the outer side of the fish knife.

cream whipper
Bottle-shaped container with nitrous oxide cartridges that aerate and whip cream.

crêpe pan (37)
Small, shallow, non-stick pan used to make crêpes. The low sides help with flipping the crêpes.

1083

deep fryer
The simple version is a large wire-mesh basket which can be dipped into boiling hot oil or fat, holding the foods to be fried. If you fry a lot of foods, consider investing in a convenient electric deep fryer.

digital thermometer
Gives an instant reading for the internal temperature of meat, fish or poultry.

double boiler ceramic bowl (5)
A ceramic bowl made to fit inside a double boiler, useful for melting chocolate. The thick ceramic bowl keeps the temperature even and the chocolate liquid.

egg beater
Two whisks that rotate by turning a handle. Useful for beating batters or creams as well as eggs.

egg slicer (2)
A slotted dish for holding a hard-boiled egg with hinged wires which close to slice.

egg white bowl
A copper mixing bowl with two handles. This bowl can be set directly on the stove top or used with its metal base.

escargot tongs (14)
Flat, 6-inch (15 cm) tongs hold escargot firmly while serving and eating.

fish flatware (31)
The fish knife has a flat curved blade ending in a sharp point that can be used to remove scales or skin. The fork has 4 tines, one of which is sharpened for cutting fish fillets without using a knife.

fish poacher (15)

An oblong saucepan made of stainless steel or copper with 2 handles and a lid. The pot contains a removable wire rack to keep the fish from touching the bottom of the pan.

fish scaler (13)

This tool removes the scales from fish without damaging the skin or meat.

flat spatula (29)

Used for spreading creams or thick sauces or for scraping batter out of pans or bowls. Spatulas are made in a variety of materials.

flat whisk (12)

For mixing small quantities, this whisk is perfect for emulsifying vinaigrettes or for omelets.

food mill (17)

The food mill can be electric or manual and is used to puree or strain foods with a low liquid content. Interchangeable discs with larger or smaller holes mean the puree's thickness can be regulated.

immersion blender

A hand-held blending device, often with various attachments for whipping, chopping and pureeing.

knife steel (1)

Traditional tool used for sharpening knives, available in many sizes.

mandoline

A kitchen utensil made up of a flat surface with a mounted blade. The mandoline allows fruit and vegetables to be sliced in a variety of shapes and sizes. Unlike a knife, the mandoline is held still while the fruit or vegetable is moved across the blade. Particularly useful for hard vegetables like fennel or carrots.

meat cleaver
The wide rectangular blade of this knife is ideal for cutting through bone. The wide blade may also be used as a meat tenderizer.

meat fork
A large sharp-tined fork used while cooking or carving large pieces of meat or fish.

meat scissors
For cutting meat, fish or poultry quickly and easily.

melon baller (23)
Used to cut fruits and vegetables into balls.

mister
Used to spray any liquid, can be gas-propelled or manual, and in plastic, aluminum or glass. Used to moisten dough or grease a baking sheet precisely or evenly.

moulds
Individual molds can be of different shapes, sizes and materials and are used for sweet and savoury tarts, flans and cakes.

mortar and pestle
A thick stone, wood or bronze bowl with a masher used to crush, pulverize or mix sauces, spices or nuts.

oyster knife (8)
Short knife with blade protection and a thick tear-drop-shaped blade.

paring knife (30)

Short, curved blade, used for peeling, shaving or trimming fruit and vegetables.

pasta cutter (18)

For cutting fresh pasta dough or pastry. Rolling cutters can have one or more wheels. Multi-wheeled cutters can be regulated and serve to make uniform strips of pasta.

pasta pot

A large saucepan with a built-in colander so pasta can be quickly drained in a single movement. It can also be used to steam or blanch vegetables.

pastry bag (20)

Plastic or cloth triangular bag with removable metal tips. A pastry bag is used to decoratively pipe out cream or frosting or to fill beignets.

perforated ladle

Used for skimming fat off of liquids and draining solids from liquids.

ramequins

Small round baking cups which are used to make individual tarts, creams and soufflés. Ceramic and stainless steel ramequins are common and can be purchased in many sizes.

ravioli cutter (36)

Small round utensil, similar to a cookie cutter, used for cutting out ravioli. May be square or round.

ravioli moulds (35)

Similar to an ice-cube tray, these metal moulds help make regular-shaped ravioli. Place a sheet of pasta over the mold, add filling and top with a second sheet. Roll a rolling pin over the dough and remove the excess pasta.

scoring tool (19)
A spiked rolling cutter, used to pierce unbaked pastry crust to prevent air bubbles from forming during baking or to score pastry like shortbread.

sculpting knives (9)
Knives for making incisions, carving or detailed cutting, useful for creating decorative garnishes.

seafood cracker (22)
Used for cracking the tough outer shell of crabs, lobster and other shellfish. On a set table, the seafood cracker should be placed to the left of the plate on the outside of the fish fork.

serving spatula (28)
Indispensable for flipping or serving, these spatulas are made in may shapes and sizes and from a variety of materials, most commonly metal and plastic.

serving tongs
Small tongs for serving beignets, petit-fours, canapés or croquettes.

shaker (33)
A practical dispenser for sugar, icing sugar or cocoa or other ingredients.

silicone baking mat
Nonstick sheet that is both heat and cold resistant.

skimmer (21)
A ladle made of concentric wire circles, primarily used for draining fried foods or ravioli-type pasta.

spaghetti measurer (32)
Stainless steel, with two holes of different sizes to measure out 1 or 2 portions of spaghetti.

spring-form pan (27)
A two-piece pan with detachable, round base and an interlocking band 2-3 inches (5-8 cm) high forming the sides, with a latch for opening and closing.

strainer (6)
Kitchen tool made of a wire or nylon mesh of varying thickness, used to filter liquids, or to separate solids from liquids.

utility knife
Thin flat-bladed knife (9-14 inches or 23-36 cm) with a rounded tip. Good for slicing meat or cured meats.

whisk (34)
Used to blend ingredients until smooth or incorporate air into creams, sauces or other liquids.

wok (25)
An all-purpose pan traditionally used in Asian cuisine. The bowl-like wok has high, sloping sides which help to evenly distribute heat.

1089

22

28

27

26

23

24

25

29

34

35

30

33

36

31

32

37

Basic *techniques*

Basic pastry doughs for *sweet* and *savory recipes*
The three most common pastry doughs in Italian cuisine are pasta frolla, *pâte sablée or shortbread;* pasta sfoglia, *puff pastry; and* pasta brisée, *savoury pie crust.*
A recipe for pizza and focaccia dough is also included here.

Pâte Sablée (Pasta Frolla)

One of the most commonly used doughs in Italian cooking, pâte sablée is the base for most sweet Italian tarts, and is also used for cookies.
Ingredients for 1 lb (500 g) pâte sablée. *1⅔ cups (7 oz or 200 g) plain flour - 7 tbsps (3.5 oz or 100g) butter, softened - 1/2 cup (3.5 oz or 100 g) sugar - 2 egg yolks - grated zest of 1 lemon - salt*
Mound the flour on a work surface and make a well in the centre. Add the butter, sugar, egg yolks, lemon zest and a pinch of salt to the well. Quickly mix the ingredients together. When the dough is smooth and elastic, form a ball and cover with plastic wrap. Refrigerate for at least 30 minutes.

Puff Pastry (Pasta Sfoglia)

This light and flaky dough is the base for many sweet and savoury dishes.
Ingredients for 1 lb (500 g) puff pastry: *1⅔ cups (7 oz or 200 g) plain flour - 3.4 fl oz (100 ml) water - salt - 1 cup plus 1 tbsp (8.8 oz or 250 g) butter*
Mound the flour on a work surface and place the water and a pinch of salt in the centre. Mix well to form an elastic dough. Wrap in a clean

1092

kitchen towel and let rest for 20 minutes. Roll out the dough into a very thin rectangular sheet (1/5 inch or 1/2 cm). Thinly slice the butter and place it in the centre of the dough. Fold the sides over the butter and then fold the remaining 2 sides in. Roll out the dough very lightly with a rolling pin and then wrap in aluminum foil and refrigerate for 5 minutes.

Begin the first round of rolling out the dough. Place the dough on a floured work surface and roll out the dough in one direction until it makes a 1/2-inch (1 cm) thick rectangle. Fold the dough in thirds horizontally to obtain a brick. Turn the dough 90 degrees. Start the second round of rolling out the dough. Roll out the dough in the same direction, fold into thirds, wrap in aluminum foil and refrigerate for 30 minutes. Repeat this operation twice, turning and folding the dough a total of 6 times. After the final round, refrigerate for 1 hour before using.

Pie Crust (Pasta Brisée)

A salted dough for savoury preparations like tarts and quiches.

Ingredients for 14 oz (400 g) pie crust: *2¹/₃ cups plus 2 tbsps (10.5 oz or 300 g) plain flour - salt - 1 egg - 5 tbsps (2.5 oz or 70 g) butter, diced*

Mound the flour on a work surface and make a well at the centre. Add a pinch of salt and then the egg and butter. Mix to form a smooth dough. Cover with plastic wrap and refrigerate at least 20 minutes.

Pizza and Focaccia Dough

Ingredients for 1.75 lbs (700 g) of dough: *2½ tsps dry active yeast - 8.4 fl oz (250 ml) water - 2 tsps salt - 1 tsp sugar - 4 tbsps extra-virgin olive oil - 2¹/₃ cups plus 2 tbsps (10.5 oz or 300 g) plain flour - 1²/₃ cups (7 oz or 200 g) enriched white flour*

Dissolve the yeast in lukewarm water and add the salt, sugar and oil. Mix well to combine. Mound the flour on a work surface and make a well in the centre. Pour the yeast mixture into the well and mix to combine. Knead until the dough is smooth and elastic. Place the dough in a floured plastic bowl and cover with a clean kitchen towel. Let rise for 2 hours, punch down and divide into 5 or 6 balls. Cover and let rise for 1 hour.

Fresh Pasta Doughs

Egg Pasta Dough

1²/₃ cups (7 oz or 200 g) plain flour - 2 eggs - salt

Mound the flour on a work surface and make a well in the centre. Add the eggs and a generous pinch of salt. Mix to combine and then knead for 10 minutes. If the dough seems to dry add a few teaspoons of water; if too wet add a few teaspoons of flour. Roll the dough into a ball and let rest for 15 minutes. Roll out the dough with a pasta machine or rolling pin and then cut out pasta. For a rich, bright yellow pasta, double the eggs.

Lasagna Dough

2¹/₃ cups plus 2 tbsps (10.5 oz or 300 g) plain flour - 3 eggs - 1 tbsp extra-virgin olive oil

Mound the flour on a work surface and form a well in the centre. Add the eggs and mix well. Knead the dough for 10 minutes and roll into a ball. Let rest for 30 minutes. Roll out the dough with a pasta machine or rolling pin. Cut into rectangles of 2 inches by 4 inches (5 cm by 10 cm). Bring a large pot of salted water to a boil and add 1 tablespoon of olive oil. Cook the pasta sheets for 1 minute and drain with a slotted spoon. Dry the cooked pasta on a clean kitchen towel.

Tortelloni Dough

2 cups (8.8 oz or 250 g) plain flour - 1 egg - 3 egg yolks - salt

Mound the flour on a work surface and make a well in the centre. Add the egg, egg yolks and salt and mix to combine. Knead to form a smooth and elastic dough. Cover with plastic wrap and let rest for 30 minutes. Roll out the dough into thin sheets with a pasta machine or rolling pin. Place spoonfuls of filling on the dough at 1½-inch (3 cm) intervals. Top with a second sheet of dough and press down around each mound of filling to seal. Cut out the tortelloni with a pasta wheel or tortelloni cutter.

Potato Gnocchi

1 lb (500 g) yellow-fleshed potatoes - salt - 3/4 cup (3.5 oz or 100 g) plain flour - 2 eggs - 2 tbsps grated Parmesan

Boil the potatoes in salted water until tender and mash with a potato ricer. Mix in the flour (the amount of flour will vary depending on the amount of starch in the potatoes), eggs and Parmesan. Mix to combine the ingredients without overworking the dough. Roll the dough into ropes about 1/2-inch (1 cm) thick. Cut into 1-inch (2 cm) long dumplings. Press the centre of each dumpling with the thumb and roll on a floured board.

Sauce Bases and *Broths* - Serves 4

Brown Sauce

Brown sauce is used as a base for many other sauces.

4 tbsps extra-virgin olive oil - 2 lbs (1 kg) beef bones and fat - 1 cup (3.5 oz or 100 g) chopped onion - 1 cup (3.5 oz or 100 g) chopped celery - 1 cup (3.5 oz or 100 g) chopped carrot - 1 cup (250 ml) red wine - 4 cups (1 l) beef broth - 2 tbsps butter - 2 tbsps plain flour - salt

Preheat oven to 400°F (200°C). Heat the olive oil in an oven-proof pan and add the beef bones and chopped vegetables. Add the wine and cook off most of liquid. Bake in the oven for 30-40 minutes. When the vegetables start to caramelize remove the pan from the oven and place it on the stovetop. Deglaze the pan with the broth over medium heat. Simmer the broth until the sugars in the broth are dissolved. Strain the broth and season with salt. Return the broth to the saucepan and reduce over low heat. Mix the butter and flour together with fingertips and whisk into the reduced broth. Cook the sauce until the flour is incorporated and the sauce thickens.

Béchamel

Ingredients *4 tbsps butter - ½ cup (2 oz or 50 g) plain flour - 2 cups (500 ml) hot milk - 1 tsp salt - nutmeg - pepper*
Melt the butter in a saucepan over low heat. Whisk in the flour and stir until smooth, cooking briefly without browning. Add the hot milk little by little. Add the salt and season with freshly ground nutmeg and pepper. Bring the mixture to a simmer, stirring constantly, and cook until the béchamel reaches the desired thickness.

Beef Broth

2.5 lbs (1.25 kg) beef (brisket or sirloin) - 1 large onion, coarsely chopped - 2 celery stalks, coarsely chopped - 1 carrot, coarsely chopped - 1 garlic clove - sea salt and peppercorns - 16 cups (4.5 l) water
Cut the beef into large chunks. Place the beef in a large pot with the onion, celery, carrot and whole garlic clove. Add a pinch of sea salt and a few peppercorns and cover with the water. Bring to a simmer and cook for 3 hours, skimming off the foam from time to time. Remove from heat and strain the broth. Adjust the salt and pepper. Once the broth is cool refrigerate. Remove any fat from the cold broth.

Vegetable Broth

1 knob of butter - 1 onion, coarsely chopped - 1 leek, coarsely chopped - 2 celery stalks, coarsely chopped - 1 carrot, coarsely chopped - 6 cups (1.5 l) water - salt and peppercorns - 1 bunch of parsley

Heat the butter in a large pot and add the chopped vegetables. Cook for 15 minutes and then add water. Season with salt and peppercorns and simmer for 1 hour. Strain the broth and refrigerate. Skim off any excess fat before using.

Fish Broth

3 tbsps extra-virgin olive oil - 1 small onion, coarsely chopped - 1 carrot, coarsely chopped - 1 celery stalk, coarsely chopped - 6 cups (1.5 liters) water - salt and peppercorns - 1 bouquet garni - 1 lb (500 g) fish for broth, washed and gutted

Heat the olive oil in a large pot and add the vegetables. Sauté for a few minutes and then add the water. Season with salt and pepper and add the bouquet garni. When the broth begins to simmer add the fish. Skim the broth from time to time. Simmer until the fish is still tender but cooked through. Remove the fish from the broth with a slotted spoon and puree with a food mill, adding a little broth if necessary. Remove the bouquet garni; return the puree to the broth and strain. For a lighter broth refrigerate and skim off any fat before using.

Flavoured Oils and *Pasta Sauces*

The best type of oil for dressing salads is without a doubt extra-virgin olive oil. Olive oil may be hearty or delicate depending on its origin. Olive oils from Liguria or Garda in the north of Italy are more subtle, while those from the regions of Tuscany, Umbria, Lazio, Puglia and Sicily tend to be more robust.

Olive oil absorbs flavours very well and can be infused with many different herbs and spices. To preserve an infusion, store it in a glass bottle with a tight-fitting lid or cork and keep in a cool, dark place. The oil can be infused for 3-6 weeks depending on the desired strength of the flavour. Strain before using.

Basil Oil

6 basil sprigs, 2 cups (500 ml) extra-virgin olive oil. For pasta, tomato or potato salads.

Oregano and Marjoram

2 sprigs oregano, 2 sprigs marjoram, 2 sprigs wild fennel or dill, 4 white peppercorns, 2 cups (500 ml) extra-virgin olive oil. For salads with cheese or for fish.

Chilli Pepper

4 red chilli peppers, 3 garlic cloves, 1 bay leaf, 1 sprig rosemary, 2 cups (500 ml) extra-virgin olive oil. For pasta, bean, rice or barley salads.

Vinaigrette

The basic recipe for this simple salad dressing is 3 parts olive oil to 1 part vinegar with pinches of salt and pepper. It may be whisked to emulsify or shaken. It is important to dissolve the salt in the vinegar, then add the oil and finally the pepper. A close relative of the vinaigrette is citronette, using strained lemon juice instead of vinegar. Citronette pairs well with vegetable salads, blanched vegetables and cold fish dishes. Herbs and spices may be added to dressings as desired.

Genoan Pesto

1 bunch of basil, destemmed - 2 tbsps pine nuts - 1 garlic clove - salt - 4 tbsps grated Parmesan - 1 tbsp grated pecorino cheese - 5 tbsps extra-virgin olive oil

Wash the basil in cold water, dry with a paper towel and place in a mortar and pestle, blender or food processor. Add the pine nuts, garlic, salt and 3 tablespoons olive oil and blend. When the nuts are completely blended, add the cheeses and continue blending until the pesto is smooth. Add the remaining olive oil and mix well.

Walnut Sauce

3½ tbsps butter - 3 sage leaves - 2 cups (7 oz or 200 g) chopped walnuts - 1 tbsp heavy cream - salt - 3.5 oz (100 g) sheep's milk ricotta

Heat the butter in a saucepan and add the sage and chopped walnuts. Toast briefly. Remove the sage leaves and add a few tablespoons of water. Cook for 5 minutes. Add the cream, remove from heat and let cool. Season with salt and mix in the sheep's milk ricotta until smooth and creamy.

Tomato Sauce

Serves 6-8 *2 tbsps extra-virgin olive oil - 2 medium stalks celery, finely diced - 2 small carrots, finely diced - 1 medium yellow or white onion, finely diced - 3 lbs (1½ kg) crushed tomatoes - sugar - basil leaves - salt and pepper*

Heat the oil in a saucepan and add the diced vegetables. Sauté until soft. Add the crushed tomatoes, a pinch of sugar and basil leaves. Season with salt and pepper and simmer for 30 minutes, until thickened. Remove from heat and pass the tomato sauce through a sieve.

Bolognese Ragù

4 tbsps butter - 10.5 oz (300 g) ground beef - 1 onion, finely chopped - 1 carrot, finely chopped - 1 celery stalk, finely chopped - 3.5 oz (100 g) pancetta, diced - 2 cloves - 1/2 cup (120 ml) beef broth - 3 tbsps tomato sauce - salt and pepper - 1/2 cup (100 ml) heavy cream

Heat the butter in a saucepan and add the onion, carrot, celery and pancetta. Add the ground beef and cloves and cook for a few minutes. Pour in the broth little by little, letting it cook off slightly before adding more. Add the tomato sauce and season with salt and pepper. Add enough water to cover the meat. Place a lid on the pot and cook over low heat until all of the liquid has been absorbed. Stir in the cream and remove from heat.

Lemon Cream Sauce

1/2 cup (100 ml) milk - juice and grated zest of 1 organic lemon - 1 bay leaf - 4 peppercorns - 3 tbsps heavy cream - 1/2 tsp cornstarch - 4 tbsps butter, diced - salt

Simmer the milk and grated lemon zest together in a saucepan for 10 minutes. Meanwhile, strain the lemon juice into another saucepan. Add the bay leaf and peppercorns and reduce slightly. Strain the milk into the lemon mixture and then add the cream. Cook for 2 minutes and add the cornstarch and butter. Remove the peppercorns and bay leaf and puree the sauce. Season with salt. This sauce is ideal for steamed fish or grilled vegetables.

Dessert Sauces and Creams

There are many different dessert sauces and creams, used for different purposes: icing and filling cakes, filling tarts and cream puffs, serving with fresh fruit or to be enjoyed on their own. Here are a few of the most common.

Pastry Cream

17 fl oz (500 ml) milk - 1 vanilla bean - 4 egg yolks - 2/3 cup (4.5 oz or 125 g) sugar - 1/3 cup plus 2 tbsps (1.7 oz or 50 g) plain flour

Bring the milk and vanilla bean to a boil. Beat the egg yolks and the sugar until they are light in color and creamy. Sift in the flour and mix to incorporate. Whisk in the hot milk and return the mixture to the saucepan. Bring to a boil over low heat and stir constantly until the mixture thickens. Pour the cream into a bowl to cool and cover with plastic wrap. Pastry cream is ideal for filling beignets, cannoli, fruit tarts or profiteroles. If serving the pastry cream on its own, try mixing in a little Alchermes liqueur and whipped cream (in equal parts) for Pompadour cream.

Crème Anglais

Serves 6. *17 fl oz (500 ml) milk - 1 vanilla bean, sliced in half lengthwise - 4 egg yolks - 2/3 cups (4.5 oz or 125 g) sugar*

Heat the milk and vanilla bean. Beat the egg yolks with the sugar until light and creamy. Whisk in the milk and return the mixture to the saucepan. Cook over low heat until the cream thickens. Stir constantly, and do not let the cream boil. Remove from heat and pass through a chinois sieve. Pour the mixture into a chilled bowl. This cream pairs well with chocolate mousse and can also be used as a gelato base. The vanilla may be substituted with cinnamon, coffee or Grand Marnier.

Chantilly Cream

Serves 6. *peel of 1 lemon - 17 fl oz (500 ml) milk - 4 egg yolks - 1/2 cup (3.5 oz or 100 g) sugar - 2/3 cup (2.5 oz or 75 g) plain flour - 5 tbsps whipping cream*

Thinly slice the lemon peel. Heat the milk and lemon peel. Beat the egg yolks with the sugar until thick and creamy. Sift in the flour and mix to combine. Remove the lemon peel from the milk and whisk the milk into the egg mixture. Transfer the mixture back to the saucepan and cook over low heat until the cream thickens. Strain the cream and let cool. Whip the whipping cream to stiff peaks and fold it into the cooled cream. Chantilly cream can be eaten on its own or with fresh fruit.

Cooking Techniques

Pasta Cooking Secrets

The secret to perfect pasta is not just in using the best possible ingredients, but also depends greatly on the cooking. Here are a few simple rules for cooking perfect pasta:

1. Always use a large pot for cooking pasta. This helps to keep the water temperature constant and stops the pasta becoming gluey. Use at least 4. cups (1 l) of water for every 3.5 oz or 100 g) of pasta.

2. When the water reaches a full boil add coarse salt (1 tsp per 3.5

oz/100 g of pasta). Let the salt dissolve.

3. Add the pasta to the water when it has begun to boil again. Adding the pasta lowers the water temperature so it is best to turn up the heat immediately afterwards. Long pasta, like spaghetti or fettuccine, should be placed in the pot and then fanned out, never broken. Short pasta, such as penne or rigatoni, should be poured into the water so it doesn't collect in the bottom of the pan and stick together. Pasta or pasta that is dried in a bird's nest shape should be immersed in boiling water and then gently separated with a large fork or wooden spoon.

4. Mix the pasta carefully and frequently during the first few minutes of cooking, until the pasta stops sticking together. Then leave the pasta to cook stirring only from time to time for the rest of the cooking time.

5. Drain the pasta and then transfer to a bowl with the sauce. Mix to coat the pasta uniformly. If the recipe calls for the pasta to be sautéed in the sauce, drain the pasta one minute before the cooking time is finished and transfer to the saucepan. Sauté the pasta and sauce over high heat for the final minute of cooking.

6. Generally pasta should never be rinsed under cold water as this removes the starchy film that helps the pasta and sauce combine. Pasta salads and certain pastas with butter-based sauces may be rinsed.

Frying

Frying is a complex cooking technique. Here are a few pointers for mastering fried foods:

1. The food to be fried should be dry to prevent the oil from splattering. Make sure that the foods to be fried are at room temperature so as not to lower the temperature of the oil.

2. Oil should never be used more than once for frying. Abundant oil should be used and kept at the correct temperature, otherwise the ingredients will burn quickly.

3. Frying should be done in several small batches, never leaving the hot

oil without a small piece of food cooking, even just a piece of bread. The oil should never be heated beyond the smoking point, when wisps of smoke rise off the oil surface. For foods with a high moisture content (fish, fresh fruit and vegetables) the ideal oil temperature is between 320-350°F (160-180°C). For meat, breaded fish or fritters, the oil should be between 375-425°F (190-220°C). The hottest frying, used for shrimp, potatoes and croquettes, requires a temperature of 580°F (280°C).

Steaming

Steaming is usually used for fish, vegetables and other particularly delicate foods. It gently cooks foods that wouldn't survive more aggressive techniques, as well as helping to maintain nutrients that would be lost during boiling.

This simple cooking technique requires a covered pot and steamer basket. The steamer basket may be substituted with a wire mesh colander. Fill a saucepan with water (broth or herb-infused water may also be used) and place the basket in the pot. The water level should be low enough that the steamer basket does not touch the liquid.

Follow these guidelines while steaming:

1. It is important that the food in the steamer basket never comes in contact with the cooking liquid.

2. Cover the pot to retain the steam, allowing for uniform cooking.

3. Ingredients to be steamed should be about the same size to facilitate even cooking, and if foods have different cooking times, remember to add the ingredients to the steamer basket in several batches, according to the various cooking times.

4. Remember to turn the food halfway through

Grilling

A quick and simple way of cooking that maintains flavor without adding fat. For best results, keep in mind the following suggestions:

1. It is important that the hot grill be slightly oiled and wiped with a damp towel to prevent food from sticking.

2. The fire or charcoal briquettes should be lit at least 1 hour before cooking. The coals or embers should be white before beginning to grill.

3. Small items should be cooked closer to the heat source while larger foods should be cooked from a greater distance.

4. Season grilled foods after cooking to avoid excess liquid from dripping on the coals and also to prevent foods from becoming too tough.

5. If cooking with a fire, use wood chips to enhance flavors, or aromatic herbs such as rosemary, thyme, sage and bay, which can be added to the coals for increased flavor.

Trimming and *Cutting Vegetables*

There are various ways to trim and cut vegetables. Below, some of the simplest techniques for daily cooking and garnishing:

Julienne

Cut the vegetables into 2½-3-inch (5-6 cm) lengths. Slice each piece in half lengthwise. Place the vegetables, cut side down, on the cutting board. Cut lengthwise into very thin, even slices, then cut the slices into thin strips. For greater regularity in slicing use a mandoline with a julienne attachment. When cooking julienned ingredients, take care to follow correct cooking times so the strips do not fall apart.

Dice

A dice is made from julienned vegetables chopped into tiny cubes. Cut the vegetables into 2½-3-inch (5-6 cm) lengths. Cut in half lengthwise and thinly slice, then cut the slices into strips. Bunch the strips together evenly and cut into 1/4-inch (7 mm) cubes.

Brunoise

A very fine dice of 1/16-inch (3 mm) cubes. Usually used for carrots, celery, onions or leeks. Julienne the vegetable, turn the julienne 90 degrees and dice and then dice again.

Mirepoix

A fine dice of onion, carrot and celery, usually equal parts of onion and carrot and half as much celery. The carrot and celery are sautéed in butter or oil, and the onion is added after a few minutes. The mirepoix should cook until softened and beginning to colour. Mirepoix is the base of many recipes.

Guide to *Table Setting* and *Decoration*

Whatever the occasion — a birthday, a family lunch, Christmas or a romantic dinner for two to celebrate something special — good preparation of the table is fundamental to entertaining your guests. It is especially worth paying attention to the choice of china, glasses, tablecloth, candles and flowers, remembering the importance of visual stimuli when it comes to dining. Thinking about coordinating colours, materials and styles even before you lay the table means that if something is missing and you have to buy candles or flowers, all the details will still be composed harmoniously. The secret is to make your guests feel special, creating a unique atmosphere for them. There are many ways to change the look of everyday table linens, china and flatware that you already have: a new napkin-folding technique, matching a tablecloth with different napkins, rediscovering dishes forgotten in a corner of the kitchen, tying a ribbon around a carafe or at the base of an otherwise plain wine glass. Even just putting a napkin of a contrasting

colour under a plate, directly on the tablecloth or between plates can bring a touch of freshness to the most ordinary table setting. Take your main inspiration from the season, and give free rein to creativity and imagination. Even if you are not used to thinking about details — all those things that work to improve a good menu — you can still enhance the table in a special way with minimal effort. Remember, the most important thing is to start, and then one idea will naturally follow after another.

Below is a guide to different seasons and occasions. Use it as a starting point to invent your own personal style.

Practical *Advice*
the *menu*

Once the guests have been invited, establish the style of the meal, based on their tastes and the occasion. An informal supper normally requires a simple table setting and menu, while a special occasion lends itself to a more sophisticated menu and a greater display of imagination in preparing the table and other details. For example, decide in advance if you want to compose individual plates of food in the kitchen or bring a big serving dish to the table, perhaps with the food arranged in an attractive way. Remember that good service is not a prerogative of restaurants.

When creating the menu, you must above all respect the seasonality of the ingredients in the recipes. While fruits and vegetables in particular will taste better when they are in season, there are also cooking techniques which are more suited to specific times of the year. Soups, stews, roasts and other slow-cooking dishes are best for the winter, while summer is the time for grilling, salads, cold pastas and fresh fruit. For important celebrations like Christmas, Easter or birthdays, it is always appropriate to follow tradition and prepare classic dishes. Even better on these occasions are time-honoured family recipes. These might be jealously guarded secrets,

time-honoured family recipes. These might be jealously guarded secrets, but if not you could have them written out in calligraphy and present them to interested guests at the end of the meal as an original gift.

the *order*

Typically Italian meals follow a strict pattern. One always starts with *l'antipasto*. Once upon a time it was hot broth to "open the stomach" and stimulate the appetite. Now it's more likely to be some kind of finger food, a hot or cold appetizer with a fairly light flavour, so as not to ruin the palate for the following dishes. The next course, the *primo*, could be a soup or risotto, or one of the many possible variations on pasta. For the *secondo*, the main course, fish is considered the midway point of the meal, served hot, perhaps with a few vegetables. After this, a refreshing sorbet could be offered to cleanse the palate, followed by a substantial meat-based dish, with a side, or *contorno*. If there is more than one dessert, *dolce*, start with the plated dessert, and finish with cookies or other baked goods.

To finish, fruit, *frutta*, preferably already peeled and cut into wedges, or in a salad; and cheese, *formaggio*, at least three to five different kinds, maybe paired with some preserves.

a *dinner* book

To make your dinners truly unique, you should keep a dinner book, where you can write notes on the event: the tablecloth, plates and glasses used, and of course the menu. If you like, include the names of the guests, so you can use the same table settings for different guests. Avoiding repetition requires just a few small changes — perhaps only a square of coloured paper under a plate or new napkin rings.

cutlery

Even though the trend is towards meals at home becoming more informal and creative, the arrangement of the cutlery should be kept traditional:

1108

forks on the left, knives and spoons on the right. Special pieces of cutlery for fish should follow the same pattern. Then set them in the order of the dishes they will be used for, starting with the furthest out for the appetizer and moving towards the plate for successive courses.

Fruit and dessert cutlery goes above the plate, with handles pointing to the right or the left depending on use. If there is a fruit knife, the fork goes to the left and the knife to the right. Spoons always point with the handle to the right.

flowers

To make a meal special, a flower arrangement at the centre of the table or in a corner of the dining room creates the perfect festive atmosphere. Arranging can be the very simple task of placing a bunch of flowers in a vase, or it could involve a careful study of colour coordination and formal composition. The first factors to consider are the seasonality of the flowers, the size of the vase, selection of complementary foliage and matching the colours to the tablecloth, napkins and plates. If the composition is going on a set table, be sure to choose unscented flowers, so as not to interfere with the food's own aromas, and keep them low so guests can still carry on face-to-face conversations.

seating

Whether the meal will be served in the kitchen, dining room or living room, imagine your house as a space for movement.

If you table happens to be too small for the number of guests, use it to set out a buffet. Arrange chairs, cushions and other improvised seats around the house so everyone can sit down, or use a different surface for serving the food. Reinventing spaces adds a note of creativity to your event, and will also help your guests get in the right spirit for a successful party. If you are using a traditional table but do not have enough matching chairs for the guests, don't worry; the chairs can still look good if matched tastefully, or given identical cushions, or, if you are very organized, matching slipcovers. Focus on the arrangement of people. While a little old-fashioned, the classic system of assigning places puts guests at ease and resolves any anxieties about choosing a neighbour. Plus if you know your guests' personalities you can help create balanced conversation. If possible, alternate men and women, and put people with common interests together.

There are many ways to mark places: a simple white card with the name written on it, a leaf, photos of the guests, a coloured ribbon, flowers on women's plates or vice versa; personalized candles for men and women; and so on. Here you can really play around and let your creativity loose.

lighting and *music*

Arrigo Cipriani, the renowned restaurateur and man of the world, once said that yellow tablecloths reflect an unflattering light on women's faces. Some other color, like pink, is better. Lighting on and around the table is a detail not to be underrated, and often assists greatly in creating the right atmosphere for a lunch or dinner.

Good lighting can lift the spirits of the party, and should always be arranged with the aim of creating a pleasant atmosphere. Plan the lights on a par with the menu, tablecloth, dishes, drinks and the rest. For dinner, use a combination of candles and electric lights, perhaps leaving some lamps on in dark corners to create a warm and welcoming atmosphere. Candles should not be scented, and their colour should harmonize with the rest of the table.

A not-too-invasive musical background underscores the importance of the arrival of the guests, and is the right complement to a pre-dinner drink and to the end of the meal.

Seasonal Tables

Our recipes are organized according to the seasons, Autumn, Winter, Spring and Summer, based on seasonal ingredients and what cooking techniques are best adapted to different times of the year.

We suggest that you also use the seasons as a guide to setting your table, using the materials and products which are readily available. With just a little creativity and inspiration, certain products can acquire a completely different meaning and be seen in a new light.

Don't make the assumption that setting the table in an artistic and original way must necessarily be elaborate or expensive. Often excellent results can be obtained simply using everyday, ordinary materials, even more so if they happen to be seasonal. With a few simple ideas and some inspiration, you can completely change the look of your table, using items like fresh fruits and vegetables and seasonal flowers to enliven your dinners, parties, family lunches or banquets in a unique way.

autumn

During this season the feelings to convey to your guests are warmth and intimacy, though perhaps with a fresh, light touch in memory of summer. Play around with the symbols of autumn, which is after all the harvest season. This is when the grapes are picked to be turned into wine, so use vine shoots, maybe with a few grapes still attached, to tie napkins. The napkins should be in warm, vivid autumnal colors like red, forest green and brown, and should be in harmony with the tablecloth. Use a burgundy-coloured pen to write your guests' names on new corks to make simple and original place markers. An elevated fruit-plate or cake-stand with some overflowing bunches of grapes makes an excellent centrepiece, while thin vines can be wrapped around wine glasses and a decanter to complete the autumnal theme.

winter

Again, warmth and intimacy are the watchwords for this season. Naturally, the high points of this time of year are Christmas and New Year's Eve. For parties, create a beautiful centrepiece by starting with some simple, wide candles, preferably all the same colour (like white) but of different heights and varying shapes. Arrange the candles on an oval mirror in the centre of the table, representing winter ice. Scatter some small coloured crystals on the mirror around the base of the candles to create new lighting effects and sparkling reflections. Plates should be porcelain, snow-white and without any pattern, as should the tablecloth. If you want to add a subtle note of color, use ornate wine glasses in different shades.

spring

The spring table should be inspired by freshness, lightness and colour, and absolutely must feature flowers. Spring is the season of rebirth, and the table should be set simply, for example with a simple tablecloth in pure cotton with white and green checks, classic and simple wine glasses, china with a floral pattern and vases of seasonal flowers like tulips, peonies, daffodils and hyacinths. Here is an unusual and creative idea for a special occasion centrepiece: take two dozen roses with strong stems, a cube of floral foam and a large transparent glass vase. Soak the foam then drain off excess water. Cut the roses all to the same length, around 3 inches (8 cm). Make six holes in the sides of the cube and three on the top and bottom. Insert a rose in every hole, pushing in up to the bud. You will have a kind of sphere of roses (see photo, right), which can be placed in a glass vase or on a fruit-stand.

summer

Here you can really play with strong colours and also the idea of lightness, perhaps setting the table in the garden, if possible. Naturally the colours to choose are ones which are clear and light. For a radiant table, use a bright-yellow tablecloth with coordinating coloured napkins and plates. For a point of interest on the table and to break up the dominant colour, create an aromatic pyramid centrepiece using three terracotta pots of different sizes, and seasonal aromatic herbs. Compose a pyramid by lining the bottom of each pot with floral foam, then stacking them up in order of size to form a tower. Insert sprigs of different aromatic herbs like rosemary, thyme and marjoram (ideally in flower) in the spaces between each pot, perhaps finishing with a few radishes. To complement the dominant yellow and green of the table, use green glasses or green crystal goblets to echo the centrepiece. Finally, give a touch of humour to the table by presenting guests with a menu written on a piece of parchment paper, rolled up, tied with a ribbon and placed into the neck of a bottle as though it was a message from a desert island.

Suggestions *for* Good *Drinking*

1114

table water

Make everyone happy with both sparkling and still mineral water on the table. If you don't like the look of bottles as part of your your table setting, serve the water in two pitchers, identified with different coloured ribbons tied to the handles, and tell your guests which is which.

to every *food* its *wine*

When friends and family come to your house for a meal, it is important to pair beverages with the food which are suitable for the mood of the event.

Drawing up a guide to choosing wines is very difficult and complex. Every person has their own tastes and inclinations which you often may not know. So how can you get the marriage between dishes and bottles right?

First of all some general advice.

Never offer exclusive or very expensive wines and remark on the fact to your guests; it will make them embarrassed.

Do not show off about your knowledge of wine. It might be a conversation topic of little interest to your guests. If someone asks you about one of the bottles, answer simply and concisely, avoiding any technical terminology.

If a guest chooses a glass of Prosecco instead of elegant Champagne, turn a blind eye, and refrain from launching into a discourse on the differences between where they come from, the grapes used, production methods, and particularly price.

Do not serve your wines in carafes. A labelled bottle is always preferable, so guests can see the name and alcohol level. Decanters can be used only when your guests are close friends and if the bottle requires it (i.e. complex, aged red wines which need a long breathing period).

Do not serve wines you have bottled yourself or bought directly from a winemaker without a label. These are not suitable for the occasion and should only be consumed privately.

Now we come to the choice of wine.

These days we seem to have moved beyond pairing a particular wine for each dish, particularly at home. There is no need to change wines for each course; because of this, it is important to choose a wine which is pleasant and pairs fairly well with each dish. There are still some rules which should be followed.

antipasti Depending on the appetizers, antipasti or finger food, offer a good aperitivo wine. White wines are certainly very agreeable, whether sparkling Metodo Classico or Prosecco (Charmat method) or still wines with aromatic notes like Gewürztraminer, Riesling or native varieties like Nosiola from Trentino or Inzolia and Carricante from Sicily. There are many choices on the market. Choose something you like, making sure it is light. Do not offer heavy wines at the start of a meal.

As far the serving temperature is concerned remember that sparkling wines should be served cold at 6°C and still, aromatic whites at 10-12°C.

first *courses* Italian cuisine offers such a range of first courses, from risottos to filled pastas, with a thousand different sauces, that it is difficult to offer general guidelines to follow.

Always pair to the filling or the sauce. If subtle, with vegetables or seafood, choose a white wine with average structure and intensity, not too rich or opulent; if the sauce is heavier, with stronger flavours, like a meat ragù, choose a young, fresh red.

Avoid heavy wines with a high alcohol level, and serve the first course wines at a temperature of around 12-14°C for whites and 16-18°C for reds. Some soups can be interesting with a rosé.

Some suggestions of Italian wines for first courses:
soups: Montecarlo Bianco, Colli di Luni Bianco, Lagrein Rosato, Verduzzo del Piave, Riesling Renano, Bianco di Custoza, Gambellara
filled egg pastas: Lugana, Alto Adige Pinot Bianco, Dolcetto d'Asti, Erbaluce di Caluso, Albana di Romagna, Ortrugo
durum-wheat pastas: Malvasia Istriana, Alto Adige Sylvaner, Bianco d'Alcamo, Bardolino Chiaretto, Bianco dei Colli Albani, Val d'Aosta Pinot Grigio, Trentino Nosiola

main *courses* Dishes based on fish or delicate white meats require important white wines, with good structure and long persistence. Based on cooking techniques and ingredients try wines of varying intensity, remembering that there is no single rule. Generally, for their enjoyability and ease of pairing, we recommend Chardonnay or Sauvignon Blanc.

For rich dishes of roasted, braised or stewed meats choose red wines with marked and distinctive character. The great Tuscan and Piedmontese reds are the most prestigious, but the wines of Friuli, Alto Adige and southern Italy can also be very agreeable.

Some suggestions of Italian wines for main courses:

seafood or vegetables: Fiano di Avellino, Etna Bianco, Bolgheri Bianco, Friuli Collio Sauvignon, Alto Adige Pinot Bianco, Vermentino di Gallura, Cinque Terre, Frascati, Chardonnay del Piave, Cirò Bianco

meats: Nebbiolo d'Alba, Rosso di Montalcino, Friuli Collio Merlot, Lagrein Dunkel, Nero d'Avola, Oltrepò Pavese Barbera, Lambrusco di Sorbara, Cabernet di Breganze

desserts and *fruit* Fruit is hard to pair with wine, though some fruit salads can go well with Cartizze (the best variety of Prosecco from Conegliano and Valdobbiadene).

For cakes and cookies we recommend liqueur-like passito wines, as well as sweet sparkling wines like Asti Moscato Spumante or Metodo Classico Demi-Sec.

Spoon sweets made with chocolate often go better with dry spirits like clear grappa or fortified wines like Barolo Chinato

Some suggestions of Italian wines for desserts:

Marsala Dolce, Zibibbo, Moscato Passito di Pantelleria, Malvasia Dolce Frizzante, Recioto della Valpolicella, Verduzzo di Ramandolo, Alto Adige

Moscato Rosa, Gewürztraminer Vendemmia Tardiva, Vin Santo, Aleatico
Some suggestions of non-Italian wines for desserts: Port, Madeira, Banyuls

Foods Not to Pair with *Wines*

When choosing wines to pair with dishes it is worth remembering that some ingredients, if predominant, can be hard to pair with wine because the taste will be unpleasantly altered. This the case with lemon, not so much if used in small quantities as a flavouring, but more so if used for lengthy marinades. In this case any wine will accentuate the acidic taste of the dish. However if you enjoy a light sharpness, pair a wine with fruity notes. Vinegar has the same problems: It is hard to pair a wine to a dish like

1118

sardines in saor (see p. 904), while if vinegar is not the main ingredient you can choose a wine which softens its sharpness. It can be hard to find a harmonious match for certain vegetables, particularly when they are served raw. These include artichokes, asparagus and fennel. If you do not want to deprive yourself of the pleasure of a glass of wine with these vegetables, it is best to serve them cooked with other ingredients, to mitigate their effects and make the pairing easier.

If offering a semifreddo or ice cream at the end of the meal, remember that there should not be too much difference between the temperature of the dish and the wine, so that it can be fully savoured. For fruits, strawberries and cherries are only good with wine if they have been macerated in the that same wine.

Now that we have provided a few guidelines for wine pairings, all that remains is for you to choose which wines to serve. The list which follows, while in no way claiming to be exhaustive, is another tool to help you with this delicate task. All the wines indicated come with a description of their characteristics and suggestions on serving temperatures. Remember, however, that these are just suggestions, as the season and type of dish can influence your wine's ideal serving temperature.

the *right* glass

Every dish has its serving plate, and every wine and spirit has its glass. Here is some advice on setting your table with the right glasses.

complete set (1). From left: glass for soft, balanced red wines like Nebbiolo, Rosso di Montepulciano, Pinot Nero and Morellino di Sanscano; glass for full-bodied, structured whites like Chardonnay and Sauvignon Blanc and aromatic wines like Gewürztraminer and Riesling; low water glass (which could also be different from the wine glass set); tall flute for aperitivo, particularly sparkling Metodo Classico and Champagne.

set for white *wines* (2) These are defined by a wide base and a progressive closing towards the top, allowing appreciation of the range of fragrances which typify white wines. From left: glass for whites with significant structure and body; tall glass for aromatic whites; glass for young, fruity and fresh whites.

set for red *wines* (3) These are marked by a large size and different openings. From left: balloon glass for soft, balanced reds like Brunello di Montalcino, Taurasi and many Cabernet Sauvignons; glass for noble, elegant reds (Barolo, Barbaresco, Amarone, Sangre de Toro and Syrah); glass for reds with important structure like Barbera d'Asti, Sagrantino di Montefalco, Aglianico and Nero d'Avola.

glasses for spirits *and* fortified wines (4) From left: low glass for whisky or bourbon; low glass for aged, fortified or passito wines (Marsala, port, Madeira and sherry); high glass for spirits with ethereal bouquets (aged aromatic grappas, Calvados); bulging glass for spirits with delicate fruity aromas (young aromatic grappas, slivovitz, maraschino); classic glass for Cognac and brandy.

1120

1

2

3

4

The *Wine List*

1122

Albana di Romagna White wine from the Albana grape, produced in Emilia-Romagna around Forlì, Ravenna and Bologna. A simple wine that pairs well with appetizers, egg-based dishes, risottos, fish soups, fried fish and cheeses. The sweet wines produced from this grape variety, Amabile and Passito, pair well with desserts or can be served as a digestif. Serve at 46-53°F (8-12°C).

Aleatico di Puglia Typical red wine from the Puglia region made from the Aleatico grape. A stronger liqueur-style wine is also produced from the same variety. This wine is full-bodied and sweet. Ideal with desserts or as a digestif. Serve at 57-64°F (14-18°C).

Alto Adige Chardonnay Chardonnay produced in the mountainous Alto Adige region. A dry white wine that makes an excellent aperitif and also pairs well with delicate fish-based appetizers, shellfish, soups, risottos or fish mains courses. Serve at 46-53°F (8-12°C).

Alto Adige Gewürztraminer White wine made from the Traminer grape variety, traditionally grown in the Alto Adige region. This wine is full-bodied and aromatic with a slightly bitter finish. Excellent as an aperitif or with delicate appetizers, soufflés, flans, fish with white sauces and other white meats. Serve at 46-50°F (8-10°C).

Alto Adige Moscato Rosa This wine is produced almost exclusively from the Moscato Rosa grape variety, from the area around the city of Bolzano. A sweet wine that pairs well with desserts. Serve at 53-64°F (12-14°C).

Alto Adige Pinot Bianco One of the best-adapted grape varieties to the Alto Adige region, wines made from Pinot Bianco grapes are dry and crisp. They pair well with refined appetizers, omelets, vegetable flans, soft cheeses, risottos and seafood. Serve at 46-53°F (8-12°C).

Alto Adige Pinot Nero The most elegant of the Alto Adige wines, Pinot Nero (Pinot Noir) is a dry and full-bodied red. It may be served with white or red meats, cured meats, game and aged cheeses. Serve at 60- 64°F (16-18°C).

Alto Adige Santa Maddalena This red wine is produced in and around the town of Santa Maddalena, near Bolzano in the far northeast of Italy. An important red wine from the region, it is known as the "Prince of Reds". Santa Maddalena is a full-bodied, dry wine with hints of almond. It can accompany fish, meat, soups and soft cheeses. Serve at 60-64°F (16-18°C).

Alto Adige Sauvignon A dry white wine with hints of fruit. Pairs well with cured meats, cream soups, vegetable risottos, cheeses, egg-based dishes and fish. Serve at 46-53°F (8-12°C).

Amarone della Valpolicella Traditional red wine from the Verona area made from Corvina, Rondinella, and Molinara variety grapes. Full-bodied and dry, this red wine pairs best with red meats, especially roast game, and cured meats. Serve at 64-68°F (18-20°C).

Asti Moscato Spumante Made exclusively from white Moscato grapes grown near the towns of Asti, Cuneo and Alessandria in the northwestern Piedmont region. This sparkling white wine is sweet and crisp with a smooth finish. Pairs well with desserts, fruit and citrus. Serve at 43-48°F (6-9°C).

Barbaresco Made from the Nebbiolo grape, Barbaresco is an important red wine from the Langhe area of Piedmont. The wine is noted for its ruby-red colour, delicate scent and smooth dry taste. Serve with roasts, game and aged cheeses. Serve at 64-68°F (18-20°C).

Bardolino Chiaretto and Bardolino Classico Produced in the town of Bardolino near Verona, both wines are pale pink in colour. Dry and savoury with a slightly bitter finish these wines pair well with a variety of dishes, from soups to white meat. Bardolino Chiaretto is the traditional accompaniment to fish from nearby Lake Garda. Serve at 53- 64°F (12-14°C).

Barolo The king of Italian wines, Barolo is made from the Nebbiolo grape around the villages of Barolo, Serralunga d'Alba, La Morra and Grinzane Cavour in the Langhe hills of Piedmont. Barolo is aged for at least 3 years in oak or chestnut barrels, and once bottled should age at least 8 years before drinking. Ruby red in colour, Barolo is a heavy, full-bodied wine with a velvety finish. Pairs well with red meats, game and aged cheeses. Aged Barolo should be opened and decanted at least 1 hour before serving. Ideal drinking temperature is 68°F (20°C).

Bianco d'Alcamo Sicilian white wine produced in and around Alcamo, mainly using the Cataratto grape. This crisp, fruity wine is very versatile and pairs well with appetizers, soups and Sicilian fish dishes such as beccafico sardines. Serve at 46-50°F (8-10°C).

Bianco dei Colli Albani White wine produced in the Lazio region. Bianco dei Colli Albani comes in three types: Novello, Superiore and sparkling. The wine is pale yellow in colour, has a delicate fruity taste and is slightly sweet. The Novello and Superiore should be served at 46-50°F (8-10°C) and the sparkling wine at 42-46°F (6-8°C).

Bolgheri Bianco Tuscan white wine produced in Bolgheri, a small village near Castagneto Carducci, from the Trebbiano grape. A dry, fruity wine which can be served as an aperitif or to accompany an entire meal. Serve at 46-50°F (8-10°C).

Brachetto d'Acqui Typical sweet, sparkling Piedmontese red wine from the town of Acqui Terme, near Alessandria, and also produced around Asti. Serve Brachetto with desserts or non-citrus fruit. Still Brachetto should be served at 53-60°F (12-16°C) and sparkling Brachetto at 46-50°F (8-10°C).

Brunello di Montalcino This prestigious Tuscan wine is known for its austerity and ability to age well. Made from the Sangiovese grape in and around Montalcino, near Siena, Brunello has an intense red colour. As it ages, it tends towards garnet and becomes drier. A robust, tannic wine, to be served with beef roasts, grilled red meats, roast game or aged cheeses. Serve at 64-68°F (18-20°C).

Cabernet di Breganze Red wine produced in the province of Vicenza from Cabernet Franc and/or Cabernet Sauvignon grapes. A dry robust wine which pairs well with red and white meats, cured meats and aged cheeses. Serve around 64°F (18°C).

Cartizze White wine made from the Prosecco grape variety in the Valdobbiadene area. This dry and harmonious wine is lightly effervescent. A pleasant wine to serve as an aperitif, it also pairs well with delicate soups, vegetables and soft cheeses. Serve at 42-46°F (6-8°C).

Chianti Classico Produced in and around Siena and Florence, Chianti has a bright ruby-red colour with a dry, tannic flavour. It is a strong wine that should be paired with grilled or roasted prime beef cuts, game or aged cheeses. Serve at 64-68°F (18-20°C).

Cinque Terre White wine made around La Spezia and the Cinque Terre villages on the Ligurian coast. Dry and lightly aromatic, this wine may be served as an aperitif or with appetizers, Ligurian pasta dishes, fried fish and grilled shellfish. Serve at 50-53°F (10-12°C).

Cirò Rosato Calabrian white wine produced in and around the towns of Cirò and Cirò Marina. A tannic yet harmonious wine, it pairs well with meats, cheeses and stronger fish dishes. Serve at 53-64°F (12-14°C).

Colli di Luni Bianco Produced in Colli di Luni, the hilly area between La Spezia in Liguria and Massa Carrara in Tuscany, this wine is made from Vermentino and Trebbiano grapes. A dry white wine, it makes an excellent aperitif and pairs well with appetizers and fish dishes from the region. Serve at 50-53°F (10-12°C).

Colli di Parma Red wine made from Barbera and Bonarda grapes. Dry and slightly sparkling, this wine pairs well with cured meats and pasta dishes from Emilia-Romagna. Serve at around 60°F (16°C).

Colli di Parma Malvasia Produced in the Apennine region near Parma from Malvasia and Candia Aromatica grapes. Both still and sparkling versions of this white wine are available. It wine pairs well with vegetables, eggs and lighter appetizers and can be served with desserts. Serve at 50-53°F (10-12°C).

Colli Piacentini Malvasia Dolce A sweet white wine made in the Piacenza area. This aromatic wine lends itself to pastries and other desserts. Serve at 42-46°F (6-8°C).

Colli Piacentini Sauvignon White wine from the Piacenza area made exclusively from Sauvignon Blanc grapes. This dry wine is smooth and balanced, and sometimes sparkling. Pairs well with appetizers, soups, vegetable risottos and seafood. Serve at 50-53°F (10-12°C).

Cortese di Gavi Dry, light and crisp white wine made in the Gavi area in the Alessandria province of Piedmont. An excellent wine to serve as an aperitif or with appetizers, shellfish, soups or white fish. Serve at 46-53°F (8-12°C).

Dolcetto d'Alba Dolcetto is grown throughout the Langhe zone of Piedmont, but Dolcetto d'Alba is the best-known version. This dry, full-bodied wine has a bright ruby-red colour. It is an ideal accompaniment for salami, carpaccio, stuffed vegetables, mushrooms, truffled cheeses and white meats. Serve at 60-68°F (16-20°C).

Dolcetto d'Asti This Dolcetto is produced in the Asti area. It has an intense red colour and smooth taste. Serve at 60-68°F (16-20°C).

Elba Bianco White wine made on the island of Elba from the Tuscan Trebbiano grape. A crisp, dry wine that can be served as an aperitif or throughout a meal. Pairs best with soups, fish stews and grilled fish. Serve at 46-53°F (8-10°C).

Erbaluce di Caluso This historic sweet white wine has been produced for centuries. Today both Champagne-style wine and sweet Passito are made in the Piedmont region. The latter is a sweet, deep-yellow wine that lends itself to desserts. Serve the Passito around 50-53°F (10-12°C) and the sparkling wine at 57-64°F (14-18°C).

Etna Bianco Sicilian white wine produced in the area around Catania. This crisp dry wine pairs well with appetizers, fried fish and pasta dishes. Serve at 46-53°F (8-10°C).

Etna Rosso Produced in the Sicilian province of Catania. Match this dry red wine with durum-wheat pasta or beef roasts. Serve at 64-68°F (18-20°C).

1128

Falanghina White wine made from the Falanghina grape variety popular in and around Naples. This soft dry wine best accompanies shellfish, pasta and rice with fish, or grilled fish. Serve at 46-53°F (8-10°C).

Fiano di Avellino From the Fiano grape variety produced around Avellino, this white wine has a distinctive dryness. Best served with shellfish, grilled fish and vegetables. Serve at 46-53°F (8-12°C).

Frascati Produced in the Lazio region, this soft, pale-yellow white wine can be either still or sparkling. It best accompanies fish or vegetable dishes. Serve at 46-53°F (8-12°C).

Freisa d'Asti Red wine produced in the hills around the town of Asti. Still, sparkling and sweet sparkling wines are all made from the Freisa grape. Still and sparkling Freisa pair well with cured meats, cheeses, stuffed vegetables, poultry, rabbit and goat. The sweet sparkling Freisa is best for desserts. Still Freisa should be served at 60-68°F (16-20°C), sparkling Freisa at 57-60°F (14-16°C) and the sweet sparkling Freisa at 46-50°F (8-10°C).

Friuli Collio Merlot Friulian red wine produced in Collio, in the Gorizia province of Friuli-Venezia Giulia. This dry and harmonious wine pairs well with ravioli-type pastas, roasted white meats, light beef dishes and cheeses. Serve at 60-64°F (16-18°C).

Friuli Collio Sauvignon Produced in Collio in the province of Gorizia. This white wine is dry with a slightly bitter finish. May be served as an aperitif or with appetizers, soups, sautéed fish and white meat. Serve at 50-54°F (10-12°C).

Friuli Isonzo Pinot Bianco White wine produced around Isonzo in the province of Gorizia, near Collio. This crisp white wine pairs well with fish-based appetizers, fish stews, fried fish and vegetarian dishes. Serve at 50-54°F (10-12°C). The sparkling Pinot Bianco should be served 43-46°F (6-8°C).

Gambellara Produced in the Veneto region, this white wine is made from a blend of Garganega, Trebbiano and Soave grapes. Gambellara typically has a dry and slightly bitter taste and makes a great aperitif. Serve with appetizers, egg- and vegetable-based dishes and freshwater fish. Serve at 50-54°F (10-12°C).

Greco di Tufo White wine from Campania produced in the Tufo area in the Avellino province. A full-bodied fruity wine which may be served as an aperitif or with delicate appetizers, shellfish and fish main courses. Serve at 50-54°F (10-12°C).

Grignolino d'Asti Produced in and around Asti, this red wine is dry and tannic with a pleasantly bitter finish. Grignolino is a table wine that can be served throughout the entire meal. Pairs particularly well with Piedmontese appetizers, thick soups, roast poultry and fried foods like the traditional fritto misto. Serve at 59-61°F (15-16°C).

Grignolino del Monferrato Red wine from the Grignolino grape in the Monferrato area of the province of Alessandria in northwestern Italy. Dry Grignolino del Monferrato pairs well with cured meats, poultry and roast rabbit. Serve at 61-64°F (16-18°C).

Gutturnio Classico Made from Barbera and Bonardo grapes in the hills around Piacenza, this ruby-red coloured wine can be either still or sparkling and is generally dry and slightly sweet. A full-bodied wine that can be served with Emilian cured meats, braised beef or game. Serve at around 64°F (18°C).

1130

Inzolia Sicilian wine produced near Trapani. A full-bodied dry white which best accompanies shellfish, spaghetti alla marinara, baked fish and soft cheeses. Serve at 50-54°F (10-12°C).

Lago di Caldaro Schiava Red wine made from the Schiava grape in the zones around Bolzano and in a few towns in the Trento province. A soft table wine with hints of almond which can be served throughout a meal. May be served with cured meats, such as speck, as well as delicate appetizers, soufflés, flans and white meats. Serve at 57- 64°F (14-18°C).

Lagrein Dunkel e Lagrein Rosato Lagrein is a typical grape variety from Alto Adige. The Rosato (rosé) is partially vinified like a white wine, while the Dunkel (dark) is vinified like a red wine. Rosato has a light ruby colour, while Dunkel has an intense ruby colour. It is a soft, pleasant and balanced wine. The Rosato is good with speck and other typical Alto Adige cured meats, while the Dunkel is the perfect match for pork, beef or aged cheeses. Serve the Rosato around 54-57°F (12-14°C) and the Dunkel around 61-64°F (16-18°C).

Lambrusco di Sorbara Produced in the Sobara area of the province of Modena, this red table wine is dry and sparkling. Pairs well with salami, roast white meats and vegetable dishes with cheese. Serve at 54-57°F (12-14°C).

Lugana Produced in the hills around the southern part of Lake Garda. A fresh and acidic wine to serve as an aperitif or with appetizers, regional specialties from Lake Garda and freshwater fish. Serve at 46°-54°F (8-12°C).

Malvasia delle Lipari This sweet white wine is produced an the island of Lipari off the coast of Sicily. Sweet, Passito and liqueur-style wines are made. The sweet Malvasia and Passito may be served with meals or desserts while the liqueur-style is best reserved for desserts or as a digestif. Serve at 54-57°F (12-14°C).

Malvasia Istriana del Collio White wine produced in and around the Gorizia province in the Friuli region. A well-rounded wine that is ideal with soups, vegetable soufflés, soft cheeses and fish. Serve at 46-54°F (8-12°C).

Marsala Dolce Produced in the province of Trapani, Marsala wine is categorized by the number of years that it is aged, from 1 to 10. Golden, amber, white and red Marsala are not aged. Characteristically sweet and dry, this wine offers many possibilities, from appetizers and cheeses to desserts. Marsala is frequently used in cooking. Serve at 54-57°F (12-14°C).

Metodo Trento Talento Brut This Champagne-style wine is produced in the Trento region. An elegant wine with a delicate, Trento Talento Brut may be served as an aperitif, with appetizers and shellfish or throughout an entire light meal. Serve at around 43°F (6°C).

Metodo Classico Franciacorta The Franciacorta area in the province of Brescia, in Lombardy, produces large quantities of delightful Champagne-style white wine made from Chardonnay, Pinot Bianco and Pinot Nero grapes. There are 3 main types of sparkling Franciacorta: Dosaggio 0, the driest Franciacorta, to be served with fish-based appetizers, shellfish, vegetables and cheeses; Satèn, made exclusively from white grapes, may be served as an aperitif or paired with appetizers, fish-based dishes, white meats or vegetables; Brut, often strengthened with Pinot Nero grapes, can be paired with pasta with fish, grilled fish, fresh cheeses or fried foods. The wine temperature when serving should be around 43°F (6°C).

Montefalco Rosso Umbrian red wine made in the Montefalco area from Sangiovese grapes. A smooth yet dry wine that pairs well with typical Umbrian dishes, thick soups, stewed white meats and salami. Serve around 64°F (18°C).

Montepulciano d'Abruzzo Produced throughout the region of Abruzzo, this is a dry and full-bodied red wine that may be served throughout a meal when young. When aged this wine should be reserved for robust red meats or game. Serve at 61-64°F (16-18°C).

Morellino di Scansano Made from a blend of Scansano, Magliano, Grosseto and Sangiovese grapes. A dry and harmonious red wine that is ideal for beef or game main dishes. Ideally served around 64°F (18°C).

Moscato Passito di Pantelleria Produced on the Sicilian island of Pantelleria from the Zibibbo grape after it has been dried to concentrate the sugars. This sweet wine has a golden colour and may be served with fruit or desserts. Serve at 46-54°F (8-12°C).

Nebbiolo d'Alba This red wine is produced near Alba in the Langhe hills of Piedmont. Still, Champagne-style and sweet versions of Nebbiolo are available. This full-bodied wine is dry and smooth, sometimes with a little sweetness. The driest Nebbiolos pair well with roasted meats. The wine temperature when serving should be around 64°F (18°C). Sparkling should be served at 46-50°F (8-10°C).

Nero d'Avola One of the best-known wines produced in Sicily, this full-bodied red is intense and fruity. Its high alcohol content makes it a good choice to serve with prime beef cuts. Serve at a temperature of around 64°F (18°C).

Oltrepò Pavese Barbera Produced in the hills outside of Pavia, this red wine is a blend of Barbera and other local grape varieties. A well-structured dry wine that pairs well with cured meats, cheeses and braised or stewed meats. Serve around 64°F (18°C).

Ortrugo Produced in the hills surrounding Piacenza, this sparkling dry white has a slightly bitter finish. It is a pleasant table wine which pairs well with thick soups, fish, egg-based dishes and fresh cheeses. Serve at 50-54°F (10-12°C).

Orvieto Classico This white wine is one of the best known of the Italian peninsula. Produced in the Orvieto area, it is an elegant, fruity wine with a slightly bitter finish. May be served as an aperitif or to accompany an entire meal. The driest Orvieto Classico wines pair well with shellfish, baked or grilled fish and egg- and cheese-based dishes. Sweeter types may be served with creamy soups or pâté. Serve at 46-54°F (8-12°C).

Trentino Pinot Nero Red wine produced in the Trentino region. This dry and savoury wine is an excellent choice when serving meat dishes. It also pairs well with polenta, mushroom-based dishes and aged cheeses. Serve at 61-64°F (16-18°C).

Prosecco di Conegliano e Valdobbiadene Brut Produced in and around the towns of Conegliano and Valdobbiadene in the province of Treviso, in the northwest Veneto region. At least 90% of the grapes used to make this sparkling white wine are Prosecco. This straw-yellow wine can be dry or lightly sweet. Prosecco makes an ideal aperitif or it may be served with delicate appetizers, light soups, vegetable- or egg-based dishes and soft cheeses. Serve at 43-45°F (6-8°C).

Recioto della Valpolicella Full-bodied, sweet red wine with a soft finish. Both sparkling and liqueur-style wines are available. The sparkling Recioto pairs well with desserts while the liqueur-style should be served as an after-dinner drink. Serve at 54-57°F (12-14°C).

Refosco dal Peduncolo Rosso Friulian wine made in the areas near Pordenone and Udine from the red Refosco dal Peduncolo grape. This red wine is well-rounded with a pleasantly bitter finish. Pairs well with Friulian regional cuisine. The wine temperature when serving should be around 64°F (18°C).

Ribolla Gialla White made principally in the Udine area of the Friuli region, a full-bodied dry wine that makes an excellent aperitif and can also be served with appetizers, cream soups and most fish dishes. Serve at 50-54°F (10-12°C).

Riesling Renano Produced in several styles throughout northern Italy, Riesling is a dry and acidic white wine which pairs well with soups and fish. Serve at 46-54°F (8-12°C).

Riviera Ligure di Ponente Pigato Full-bodied white wine made in Liguria from the Pigato grape variety. An elegant white wine to serve throughout a meal or with Ligurian appetizers, soups, fish, egg-based dishes, vegetables and soft cheeses. Serve at 46-54°F (8-12°C).

Riviera Ligure di Ponente Vermentino This Ligurian white wine is made from Vermentino grapes. Crisp and dry, Ligurian Vermentino can accompany omelets, vegetables with cheese and fish. Serve at 46-54°F (8-12°C).

Roero Arneis Piemontese white wine made from Nebbiolo and Arneis grapes. This dry and harmonious wine pairs well with appetizers and fish. Serve at 46-50°F (8-10°C).

Rossese di Dolceacqua Produced in the Ligurian province of Ventimiglia with Rossese grapes. This red wine pairs well with roasts, grilled meats, fillets with sauces, game and medium-aged cheeses. The wine temperature when serving should be around 64°F (18°C).

Rosso Conero Riserva Made from Montepulciano and Sangiovese grapes in the province of Ancona in the central Marche region. This full-bodied, dry red wine is an excellent choice for main courses with red or white meats and aged cheeses. Serve at around 64°F (18°C).

Rosso di Montalcino Produced in Montalcino with Sangiovese and/ or Brunello grapes. This ruby-red wine is full-bodied and slightly tannic. It can be served throughout an entire meal and pairs well with regional cuisine from the Siena area, especially cured meats, poultry, pork and pan-fried red meats. Serve around 64°F (18°C).

Sicilia Chardonnay A full-bodied Sicilian white wine that can be served throughout an entire meal, or with appetizers, pastas and risottos with seafood and white meats. Serve at 46-50°F (8-10°C).

Soave White wine produced in the Veneto region from the Garganega grape variety. This crisp dry wine is can be served as an aperitif or with appetizers, risottos, fish and white meats with delicate sauces. Serve at 46-54°F (8-12°C).

1136

Taurasi One of the most important of the red wines produced in the Campania region. Taurasi is made from the Aglianico grape and is known for its dry and balanced flavour. Pairs well with red meat, game and aged cheeses. Serve at 64-68°F (18-20°C).

Terre di Franciacorta Bianco This soft white wine pairs well with appetizers, delicate soups and freshwater fish. Serve at 46-54°F (8-12°C).

Trebbiano d'Abruzzo Dry white table wine made from the Trebbiano grape. Ideal with fish-based appetizers, delicate soups, fish soups or white meat. Serve at 46-54°F (8-12°C).

Trebbiano di Romagna White wine produced in the provinces of Forlì, Ravenna and Bologna. A dry wine that may be served as an aperitif, throughout an entire meal or with grilled fish or shellfish. Serve at 46-54°F (8-12°C). Sparkling Trebbiano Romagnolo should be served between 43-46°F (6-8°C).

Trentino Chardonnay Both still and sparking versions of Trentino Chardonnay are available. This versatile white wine is smooth and dry. Pairs well with delicate appetizers, lightly sauced pastas, egg-based dishes, vegetables, cheese and white fish. Serve at 46-54°F (8-12°C) or 43-46°F (6-8°C) for sparkling.

Trentino Moscato Rosa Sweet rose wine produced in the Trento province. Pairs well with cookies and other regional desserts. Serve at 54-57°F (12-14°C).

Trentino Müller Thurgau Celebrated white wine from the Trentino region. The grape variety is named after German wine researcher Herman Müller Thurgau. Typically a crisp fruity wine that makes an excellent aperitif. Pairs well with fish-based appetizers and shellfish. Serve at 46-50°F (8-10°C).

Trentino Vin Santo Dessert wine produced in the province of Trento. This sweet wine requires at least 3 years of aging. Serve with desserts, strong cheeses or as an after-dinner drink. Serve at 46-54°F (8-12°C).

Val d'Aosta Chardonnay White wine produced in the Val d'Aosta in northern Italy. This Chardonnay is full-bodied and dry with woody hints. Pairs well with appetizers, pasta, risotto and white meat. Serve at 54-57°F (12-14°C).

Valcalepio Bianco A blend of Pinot Bianco, Chardonnay and Pinot Nero grapes produced in the Bergamo province. Dry and balanced, this white wine pairs well with soups, tortelli and freshwater fish. Serve at 54°F (12°C).

Valcalepio Rosso A blend of Merlot, Cabernet and Sauvignon made around Bergamo. This red wine is full-bodied and smooth. Pairs well with grilled, braised and boiled meats and polenta. Serve around 64°F (18°C).

Valle d'Aosta Nus Rosso Red wine produced in the Aosta province. A fruity table wine that can accompany cured meats, regional soups and main courses with meat. Ideal serving temperature is around 64°F (18°C).

Val D'Aosta Pinot Grigio Dry white wine produced in the Aosta province, this Pinot Grigio is golden-yellow with an intense perfume. Serve at 50-54°F (10-12°C).

1138

Verdicchio dei Castelli di Jesi White wine made from the Verdicchio grape in many villages around the town of Jesi in the Marche region. A crisp dry wine with a slightly bitter finish that best accompanies fish dishes. May also be paired with delicate cured meats, shellfish soups, risottos, vegetable flans and pâtés. The sparkling version makes an excellent aperitif. Serve at 46-54°F (8-12°C) or 43-46°F (6-8°C) for sparkling.

Verdicchio di Matelica Produced in the Marche region, this dry white wine has a slightly bitter finish. May be served as an aperitif or with fish, roast poultry or soft flavourful cheeses. Serve at 46-54°F (8-12°C).

Verduzzo di Ramandolo Produced in the province of Udine in the northeast of Italy from Verduzzo grapes. This sweet, velvety wine has an intense yellow colour and pairs well with desserts. Serve at 54-57°F (12-14°C).

Vermentino di Gallura Sardinian white wine produced on the north-eastern coast of the island. This wine is made from the Vermentino grape and has a dry, slightly bitter taste. Makes an excellent aperitif and pairs particularly well with fish and shellfish. Serve at 46-54°F (8-12°C).

Vermentino di Sardegna White wine from Sardinia. This wine should be drunk young and served with fish, fresh cheeses or vegetable dishes. Serve at 46-50°F (8-10°C).

Zibibbo Sweet liqueur-like wine from the Zibibbo grape produced on the Sicilian island of Pantelleria. Zibibbo is aged for at least 1 year in oak. This amber-coloured wine pairs well with desserts, nuts and dried fruit. The wine temperature when serving should be around 57°F (14°C).

Cooking Terms

acqua pazza "Crazy water" in Italian: a technique used for large fish, which are cooked in a pan with water, tomatoes, vegetables and herbs. The fish remains tender and absorbs the flavours of the aromatics.

al dente Literally "to the tooth". This term is used to describe pasta, rice or vegetables when cooked to the point of offering a little resistance when bitten into without being soft and overcooked.

bain-marie Cooking technique in which dishes are immersed in or placed just above another dish or pot of hot water. Ingredients are gently cooked (i.e. custards or flans) or heated without boiling (i.e. pastry creams, sabayon, chocolate).

bake To cook slowly in the oven.

bard To wrap meat with thin slices of lardo, pancetta or prosciutto usually tiedon with kitchen string. This technique keeps meats moist during cooking and enhances flavor.

baste To brush or spoon over liquids during cooking, particularly used with meat when in the oven to keep it moist and add flavour.

blanch To quickly boil a food in water to make it easier to peel or partially cook it, or to remove bitterness.

boil To cook in hot water (or another liquid) that has reached boiling point.

1140

braise To brown an ingredient and then continue cooking it with a liquid such as wine or broth, usually covered.

broil To grill food under a direct heat source such as a broiler or grill.

broth The flavoursome liquid obtained from cooking vegetables, meat, poultry or fish in water and then straining the mixture. Broth can be made from scratch, for example with a chicken carcass or shrimp shells, or from a stock cube (also known as a bouillon cube).

brown To quickly sauté meat or vegetables until they begin to colour. Frequently used for onions, shallots or garlic. When referring to meat, fish or poultry it means to cook over high heat until a crust forms around the meat, sealing in the juices. Cooking is usually completed with the addition of liquid.

bundt pan A circular baking pan with a hole in the middle used to make ring cakes.

butterfly To cut open a piece of meat or fish without cutting completely through, then opening it like a book.

caramelize To heat sugar until it melts and colours. This term is often used for vegetables and meat when they are cooked over high heat until a brown crust forms.

carpaccio Traditionally very thin slices of beef fillet, served raw with a dressing of olive oil, lemon juice or mayonnaise, but now used for any dish of thinly sliced meat or fish.

cartoccio Italian term for food (usually vegetables or fish) wrapped in a parcel of parchment paper or aluminum foil and baked. Flavour is retained and no fat needs to be added. In French the technique is called *en papillote*.

clarify To make a cloudy liquid clear. Butter can be clarified by heating it in a double boiler, without boiling, for about 1 hour. When all of the solid white matter has collected at the bottom of the pan the butter is strained through a fine mesh sieve.

court bouillon A vegetable broth, often with white wine, used for poaching seafood like lobsters.

debone fish To remove the bones from raw, cooked or preserved fish. When deboning raw fish it is best to use a very sharp fish knife and to cut the fish in half as if to fillet it. Very large fish to be cooked whole or stuffed should be deboned by cutting the fish open along the backbone, leaving the fish intact. Smoked fish, anchovies and sardines should be deboned.

debone meat To remove the bones from meat or poultry while leaving the meat intact. This technique requires a very sharp, thin-bladed knife. Butchers will generally debone larger pieces of meat, while smaller animals like chicken and quail may be deboned at home.

1142

deep fry To cook by submerging the ingredient in very hot fat, such as oil or melted lard.

deglazing Technique for making a simple sauce from pan juices or drippings. Pour wine, broth or other liquid into the hot pan and cook to dissolve the brown bits stuck to the pan, stirring with a wooden spoon.

dice To cut food into very small cubes.

double boiler A bain-marie, with one pot partially filled with water and another pot or a bowl set on top. As the water boils, the steam rises to cook the ingredients gently and evenly. Often used for melting chocolate and making pastry creams.

drizzle To pour a liquid like olive oil in a thin stream over a food, either before baking to moisten, or just before serving to add flavour and as a garnish.

emulsify To make into an emulsion, a smooth and uniform mixture of two or more liquids which usually would not combine. Vinaigrettes can be emulsified by mixing together the vinegar, salt and other flavourings, then whisking in the oil, adding it drop by drop or in a very thin stream, until the dressing is thick and glossy. Mayonnaise and hollandaise sauce are both emulsions.

fillet To cut the bones from a piece of meat or fish, creating boneless portions. Make sure to use a very sharp knife when filletting fish.

fillo see *phyllo dough*

flambé To cover a food with alcohol and light it on fire. Setting fire to the dish burns off most of the alcohol and also very briefly cooks the dish without losing flavour.

fold To carefully combine two mixtures using a spatula, usually a lighter, whipped ingredient like cream or egg whites with a thicker mixture, like custard.

fonduta Italian fondue, a rich cheese sauce with egg yolks.

garnish A decorative addition to a finished dish, such as herb leaves, fresh berries or croutons.

glaze To cover fruit, vegetables, meat or cakes with a liquid to make the food shine. Meat is usually glazed with its own sauce and then grilled briefly, while vegetables may be glazed with butter and stock, simmered until the liquid is absorbed and then sautéed to coat. Glaze can also refer to covering with a gelatin-based sauce.

gratiné To create a golden-brown crust over a dish. Ingredients may be cooked entirely this way, or previously cooked foods may be finished in the oven to create a crispy brown layer over the surface. Gratiné is usually a finishing technique as it is often difficult to cook the ingredients precisely.

grill To cook directly over a heat source, such as charcoals or a gas flame, usually outdoors. Can be replicated inside with a preheated, ridged cast-iron grill pan.

infuse To give flavour to a liquid by heating it with aromatic ingredients like herbs or tea. Infusions are often used for steaming, so they transmit extra flavours to the food being steamed.

julienne To cut into long, thin strips or matchsticks.

knead To work a dough until it comes together in a smooth, uniform, elastic mass. At home, often done by hand, using the heels of the hands to press the dough down and then away from the body, folding and turning the dough and repeating until it reaches the desired consistency.

lard To insert little pieces of lardo, pancetta or bacon into incisions in meat. During the cooking the fat melts, distributing flavour throughout the meat and helping to keep the meat tender. This technique is useful for meats that tend to dry out during cooking.

lardo A type of cured pork or boar meat made from the layer of back fat just under the skin and cured with salt, herbs and spices.

lardo di colonnata a type of lardo made in and around the town of Colonnata in Tuscany. The pork fat is seasoned with a mixture of sea salt, herbs and spices and layered into individual marble tubs. The meat is aged in the tubs for 6-10 months in a cave or cellar.

marinate To soak foods in a liquid to add flavour to, preserve or tenderize meat or vegetables. Marinating game, like wild boar, also helps to remove excessively gamey flavours. Marinades can be made with red or white wine, vinegar, oil, herbs and spices. Fish is usually marinated in white wine or white wine vinegar and herbs. Meat, fish and vegetables may also be breaded, fried and then preserved in a mixture of water, wine, vinegar and herbs, a common technique in Italy called *in carpione*.

mince To chop food very finely, particularly aromatic ingredients like onions, garlic and woody herbs like rosemary.

mounting A finishing technique which makes a dish creamy by stirring in butter, cheese or cream in the last few minutes of cooking. May also refer to finishing gelato.

nap To uniformly cover a dish with a sauce, ragù, gravy or gelatin. The term derives from the French *nappe* or tablecloth.

pan juices The liquid and/or fat left in a roasting dish, frying pan or pot after the food has been cooked. It is often added to a sauce or poured over the food to moisten and add flavour.

pasta board A wooden board used for preparing dough or pasta. Wooden boards and utensils should be kept in dry places so that the wood doesn't warp over time.

pesto Traditionally a blend of basil, pine nuts, oil and Parmesan cheese from Liguria, used to dress pasta, but can refer to any similar variant with herbs, nuts and/or cheese.

phyllo dough Phyllo dough comes from Greece and the name derives from the Greek word *fillo* or sheet, the name by which it is also known. Phyllo is very thin and has a short cooking time. It may be baked or deep fried for sweet or savoury preparations. Widely used in the Middle East and southern Mediterranean as a base for nut-filled sweets like baklava.

plate To plate food is to compose the dish on individual plates or bowls before serving, rather than placing a large serving dish on the table and having people help themselves.

poach To cook gently in hot water (or another liquid like broth or oil), just below the boiling point. Particularly used for eggs, chicken and fish, and fruits like pears in sugar syrup.

puree To grind or mash a food until smooth, whether with an immersion blender, food processor, blender or mortar and pestle.

quenelle Oval shapes made by forming ingredients using two spoons. May be sweet or savoury, cooked or raw.

ramequin Small, individual baking dish used for custards, flans etc.

reduce To cook down a liquid or sauce until it diminishes in volume, and sometimes thickens.

render To melt animal fat so that it leaves the meat crispy. Particularly used for pancetta or bacon.

riso carnaroli A medium grain rice native to the region of Piedmont. Carnaroli rice is favored for risotto because of its high starch content and firm texture and because it holds its shape better than other rice varieties during slow cooking.

rissole Small fried or baked croquette of minced ingredients with a breadcrumb or pastry crust.

roast To cook in the oven, uncovered and usually at high temperatures.

sabayon French for *zabaglione*, often used to refer to a sauce, sweet or savoury, made with egg yolks.

salame cotto A type of salami which is cooked or smoked before or after the curing process.

salsa verde Literally "green sauce": a finely chopped or pureed mixture of various herbs (always parsley, often with others), oil and other flavourings like capers, garlic, anchovies or vinegar.

sauté To cook a food quickly, usually in a frying pan with a little oil or other fat.

savarin A cake of French origin named after the renowned gastronome Brillat-Savarin (1725-1826). The traditional savarin is made from an egg-based batter baked in a Bundt pan. There are many sweet and savoury variations.

separating fat Removing extra fat from pan juices, sauces and broth. Very fatty meats usually cook off large amounts of fat. Fat can be separated off of sauces, broths and pan drippings with a fat separator or by chilling the liquid in the refrigerator until a layer of fat forms on top of the liquid. The fat can then be skimmed off with a spoon.

shave To cut into very thin slices, often with a vegetable peeler: used for chocolate and hard cheeses like Parmesan and pecorino.

shred To tear or cut into narrow strips, often used for lettuce and leafy greens like spinach and Swiss chard.

simmer The phase of cooking before a liquid boils. Irregular, tiny bubbles rise to the surface when water or liquid is at a simmer. A delicate cooking technique that lengthens the cooking time.

singe To remove any feathers or fine down that may be left on poultry. Particularly important for game. Pass the bird over an open flame to burn off any remaining feathers. When cooking game, it is advisable to rub a cut lemon over the skin after singeing.

skim To remove the foam or the fat off the top of broth. Metal ladles with holes can be used for skimming.

soften To sauté a vegetable over low heat until soft, without browning. Commonly used for aromatics such as onions or shallots.

spring-form pan A baking pan with a removable base for easy unmoulding.

1148

steam To cook over boiling water, or another liquid, in a covered pan. Good for delicate foods like fish.

stew To cook vegetables or meats very slowly with a little water or other liquid, until they become very tender. Good for tough cuts of meat.

tartare Coarsely ground or finely chopped raw meat or fish.

thicken To add a thickening agent (like flour, corn flour, gelatin) to a sauce, soup, mousse, etc. Often the agent must be dissolve in liquid or mixed with butter before being added so that it does not form lumps.

timbale A dish of cheese, chicken, fish or vegetables baked in a small mould.

toast Generally used to describe the heating of dry ingredients such as bread or nuts until they lose some moisture and turn golden-brown. This term is also used to describe the initial phase when cooking risotto, when the rice is added to the onion or vegetable base. The rice should be heated or toasted in the pan, stirring frequently, until it begins to brown and smells nutty. The toasting helps to keep the rice al dente throughout cooking.

toss To gently but thoroughly mix together two foods, such as a pasta and a sauce or a salad and a dressing.

trim To eliminate excess fat or gristle from meat before cooking. This term is also used for fish, fruit, vegetables and means removing any unwanted bits from the ingredients.

velouté A smooth white sauce made with stock, thickened with a roux, also used to refer to a smooth, creamy soup.

vinaigrette A mix of oil, vinegar and other seasonings, usually used to flavour a salad.

whip To vigorously beat ingredients like cream or egg whites until air becomes incorporated and they expand in volume and become fluffy and paler in colour. Generally they are beaten to soft peaks or stiff peaks, depending on the use, and often need to be folded into other ingredients carefully and gently so as not to lose their airiness.

zabaglione Dessert made by whisking together egg yolks, sugar, wine or liqueur over a double boiler.

zest The top layer of citrus rind, before the bitter white pith starts.

Recipe Index

with Zolfini Bean Puree 1058
Nervetti with Beans (Lombardy) 269
Oil-Mill Soup with Beans
 and Farro 308
Rustic Pizza 172
Shrimp and White Bean Salad 427
Vegetable and Bean Soup
 with Bread (Tuscany) 326

beans, cannellini
Cannellini Beans
 in Tomato Sauce 192
Cannellini Beans
 with Sautéed Greens 420
Pork Stew with Cannellini Beans 380
Shrimp and White Beans 530

beans, fava
Buckwheat Tagliatelle with Favas 566
Chicken with Favas 597
Farro and Fava Salad 559
Fava Flan with Onion Sauce 217
Fava Panelle (Sicily) 751
Fava Soup with Prosciutto 307
Frittedda (Sicily) 675
Giant Shrimp with Favas 641
Pennette with Langoustines,
 Favas and Wild Fennel 576
Ricotta and Fava Terrine 658
Saffron Garganelli
 with Tomatoes and Favas 552
Scafata (Umbria) 845
Trofiette with Favas 565

beans, green
Baked Winter Squash with Green
 Beans and Goat's Cheese 59
Corn Fusilli with Green Beans
 and Squash 553
Green Bean and Carrot Flan 425
Green Bean Flan 950
Green Beans in Tomato Sauce
 (Lombardy) 186
Green Beans with Red Cabbage 445
Penne with Green Bean Pesto 567
Scrambled Eggs
 with Green Beans and Ham 655

beef
Beef and Chicken Terrine
 with Sangiovese Sauce 359
Beef and Pecorino Involtini 140
Beef and Vegetable Gratin 858
Beef Broth 1096
Beef Carpaccio 852
Beef Carpaccio Skewers 511
Beef Carpaccio with Pears 26
Beef Entrecôte with Artichokes
 and Scamorza 127
Beef Fillet al Cartoccio 849
Beef Fillet with Red-Wine Sauce 609
Beef Fillet with Taleggio Sauce 1041
Beef Roll with Spinach Sauce 851
Beef Stew with Barolo
 (Piedmont) 379
Beef Stew with Speck
 and Onions 369
Beef Tartare with Mustard
 and Leeks 1017
Beef, Mushroom and Olive Stew 387
Boiled Beef Salad 361
Bollito Misto with Mostarda 1023
Braised Beef 1024
Braised Beef Cappelletti
 in Broth 1018
Breaded Beef with Nuts 368
Brescian-Style Ravioli (Lombardy) 83
Brisket with Barolo
 and Blueberries 369
Florentine-Style Stewed Beef
 (Tuscany) 382
Grilled Beef with Salsa Verde 853
Grilled Chianina Steak (Tuscany) 846
Meatballs with Salad 595
Roast Beef Salad 859
Roast Beef with Salt 150
Roast Beef, Robiola
 and Eggplant Involtini 872
Speck and Asiago Involtini 361
Spiced Beef Kebabs with Speck
 and Herb Mayonnaise 154
Steak with Chestnuts 151
Steaks with Mushrooms
 and Potatoes 614
Stuffed Roast Beef 126
Tagliatelle with Roast Beef 1037

couscous

Couscous-Stuffed Squid	1059
San Vito-Style Fish Couscous (Sicily)	840

creams

Basil Chantilly Cream	960
Chantilly and Chocolate Cream Millefeuille	1028
Chantilly Cream	1101
Chantilly Cream Cups with Chocolate Cookies	224
Chocolate Cream Puffs (Campania)	695
Cream Puffs	481
Crème Anglais	1101
Lomon Cream Profiteroles	1060
Pastry Cream	1100
Pastry Cream with Almond Brittle	467
Raspberry Cream Puffs	1075
Strawberries on Brioche with Crème Anglais	701

crème brûlée

Chocolate Crème Brûlée	461
Steamed Crème Brûlée	459

crêpes

Artichoke Crêpes	560
Baked Seafood Crêpes in Tomato Sauce	786
Crêpes with Ricotta and Gorgonzola	322
Crêpes with Ricotta and Tomatoes	781
Crêpes with Spinach, Ricotta and Taleggio	85
Pea Crêpes	514
Potato Crêpes with Broccoli and Mozzarella	90

crescenza

Crescenza Fritters with Mortadella	1052
Crescenza Tarts with Taggiasca Olives	33
Lettuce Soufflés with Crescenza Sauce	428
Mini Panini with Crescenza	37

croquettes

Asiago and Mushroom Croquettes	24
Chickpea and Shrimp Croquettes	31
Codfish Croquettes with Pesto and Olives	164
Creamy Baccalà with Broccoli-Walnut Croquettes	1067
Emmenthal and Potato Croquettes	175
Mussel and Shrimp Croquettes	732
Potato and Porcini Croquettes	42
Potato Croquettes with Artichokes	440
Pumpkin and Mozzarella Croquettes	188
Rice and Provola Arancini	497
Salt Cod and Potato Croquettes	496
Shrimp and Potato Croquettes	266
Spinach Croquettes	530
Swiss Chard and Mushroom Croquettes	206

crostini and crostoni

Crostini with Black Truffle Cream	35
Citrus Trout Crostini	278
Creamed Pea Crostini	501
Herb and Cheese Crostini	501
Lardo and Tomato Crostini	262
Lardo di Colonnata Crostini (Tuscany)	772
Mediterranean Crostini	518
Melted Brie and Porcini Crostone	36
Norcina Crostini (Umbria)	47
Pecorino and Mostarda Crostini	265
Radicchio Crostini with Ricotta Cream	259
Ricotta and Anchovy Crostini	739
Ricotta, Walnut and Arugula Crostini	748
Sea Bass Tartare Crostone	749
Spicy Crostini (Calabria)	523
Summer Crostoni	744

E

San Vito-Style Fish
 Couscous (Sicily) 840
Spicy Seafood Sauté 741
Tagliolini with Shellfish 821
Trieste-Style Fish Soup
 (Friuli-Venezia Giulia) 634

flans

Asparagus and Emmenthal Flan 682
Cardoon Flans with Bagna
 Caoda Sauce 453
Carrot Flans with Parmesan
 Zucchini 927
Chanterelle Flan 63
Chard Flan with Pine Nuts 431
Eggplant Flans
 with Cherry-Tomato Sauce 746
Fava Flan with Onion Sauce 217
Goose Breast with Radicchio
 Flan and Balsamic Vinegar 136
Green Bean and Carrot Flan 425
Green Bean Flan 950
Grilled Ostrich Fillets
 with Porcini Flans 135
Panettone Flan with Raisins 1045
Parmesan Flan with Arugula
 and Tomatoes 516
Pea Flan with Spinach Sauce 525
Polenta and Asiago Flans 48
Potato and Anchovy Flan
 with Pesto 1016
Potato and Ricotta Flan
 with Radicchio Sauce 38
Provolone and Barley Flan 103
Radicchio Flan with Balsamic
 Vinegar 270
Ricotta Flan with Radicchio Sauce 414
Tomato and Caper Flan 934

flowers

Rustic Salad with Flowers 690

focaccia

Genoa-Style Focaccia (Liguria) 522
Honey Focaccia 238
Pizza and Focaccia Dough 1093
Potato Focaccia with Scamorza 271
Toasted Focaccia with Ricotta 745

fontina cheese

Cabbage and Fontina Soup 302
Chard, Porcini and Fontina Tart 179
Eggs with Fontina Cheese
 (Valle d'Aosta) 174
Fonduta (Valle d'Aosta) 413
Fonduta Risotto 345
Gnocchi alla Bava
 (Valle d'Aosta) 328
Polenta with Fontina 416
Potato and Fontina Strata 439
Seuppa (Valle d'Aosta) 305
Valle d'Aosta-Style Beef
 with Fontina 373

fossa cheese

Tuscan Farrotto
 with Fossa Cheese 332

frittatas

Anchovy Frittata 503
Nettle Frittata 933
Provola and Basil Frittata 747
Radicchio Frittata 921
Smoked Salmon Frittata 752

fritters

Acorn Squash
 and Artichoke Fritters 1051
Apple Fritters with Grappa 707
Borricche Fritters (Tuscany) 724
Buffalo Mozzarella
 and Black Olive Panzerotti 508
Chocolate-Almond Fritters 482
Crescenza Fritters
 with Mortadella 1052
Crispeddi (Sicily) 771
Fava Panelle (Sicily) 751
Fried Cassatedde
 with Tuma (Sardinia) 736
Parma-Style Fritters
 (Emilia-Romagna) 750
Panzarotti (Campania) 28
Potato Fritters
 with Lumpfish Caviar 64
Ricotta and Potato Fritters 273
Roman-Style Panzerotti (Lazio) 29
Sebadas (Sardinia) 965

with Malaga Gelato	232
Frozen Yogurt with Mandarin	1011
Ice Cream-Filled Mini	
Panettones	1027
Lemon and Basil Sorbet	971
Melon and Port Wine Sorbet	979
Melon Sorbet with Poppy Seeds	996
Mini Ice Cream Bombes	990
Pear Gratin with Whisky Gelato	251
Raspberry and Blueberry Sorbet	979
Strawberry Sorbet	975
Vanilla and Orange Infused	
Pineapple with Sorbet	484
Yellow Peach Sorbet	1011
Yogurt Sorbet with Currant	
Sauce	997
Watermelon and Mint Granita	974

K

kebabs and skewers

Arrosticini Kebabs (Abruzzo)	865
Beef Carpaccio Skewers	511
Breaded Squid Skewer	629
Chicken Kebabs	370
Chicken Kebabs with Pistachios	866
Chicken Kebabs with Prosciutto	852
Cuttlefish and Roast Pepper	
Kebabs	642
Fried Potato and Cabbage	
Skewers	443
Gorgonzola Grape Skewers	45
Liver and Sweetbread Skewers	
(Liguria)	367
Mini Skewers with Clams	
and Polenta	62
Mozzarella Skewers	769
Peach and Berry Skewers	1007
Pecorino and Pear Skewers	
with Honey and Walnuts	293
Potato Skewers with	
Gorgonzola Sauce	426
Scallop Skewers	914
Shrimp Kebabs	911
Spiced Beef Kebabs with Speck	
and Herb Mayonnaise	154
Spoleto-Style Mixed Kebabs	

(Umbria)	871
Stuffed Cherry Tomato Skewers	745

kid goat

Kid Goat Alla Cacciatora	
(Sardinia)	133

kiwis

Kiwis with Melon Mousse	994
Melon and Kiwi Salad	1006
Ricotta Mousse with Kiwis	699
Ricotta Quenelles with Kiwi	
and Raspberries	700

L

lamb

Arrosticini Kebabs (Abruzzo)	865
Lamb Buglione (Tuscany)	874
Lamb Chops with Artichokes,	
Pistachios and Mint	605
Lamb Chops with Nero d'Avola	602
Lamb Chops with Red	
Wine Sauce	125
Lamb Chops with Zolfini	
Bean Puree	1058
Lamb with Egg and Cheese	
(Abruzzo)	373
Lamb with Mint and Ginger	608
Lamb with Pea and Potato	
Purees	601
Lamb with Pinot Noir	597
Roast Lamb Chops	153
Spring Lamb Stew	596
Spoleto-Style Mixed Kebabs	
(Umbria)	871

langoustines

Langoustine Carpaccio	519
Langoustines in Tomato-Brandy	
Sauce (Veneto)	888
Langoustines with Carrot Puree	539
Langoustines with Orange	294
Paccheri with Langoustinesand	
Eggplant	807
Pennette with Langoustines,	
Favas and Wild Fennel	576

Liver Pâté with Mushrooms
on Polenta 1015
Lobster Tortelli with Mushrooms 350
Mushroom and Bell
 Pepper Toasts 57
Mushroom and Leek Lasagna 115
Mushroom Tagliatelle 115
Mushroom Tart 191
Mushroom Toasts 45
Mushroom-Stuffed Squash
 Blossoms 170
Potato and Mushroom Bake 437
Potato and Mushroom Gratin 196
Shrimp and Mushroom Pizza 921
Steaks with Mushrooms
 and Potatoes 614
Stuffed Mushrooms 664
Swiss Chard and Mushroom
 Croquettes 206
Swiss Chard with Mushrooms 200
Turbot and Mushroom Soup 79
Turkey and Mushroom Rotolini 146
Veal and Mushroom Risotto 336

mushrooms, chanterelle
Chanterelle and Borage Mousse
 in Baskets 287
Chanterelle Flan 63
Creamy Chanterelle and Potato
 Soup 72
Pork Tenderloin in a Citrus
 Crust with Chanterelles 137
Walnut Cappellacci
 with Chanterelles 335

mushrooms, porcini
Baked Penne with Porcini
 and Four Cheeses 97
Baked Tagliolini
 with Porcini Ragù 1069
Bell Pepper and Porcini Tarts 198
Chard, Porcini and Fontina Tart 179
Grilled Ostrich Fillets
 with Porcini Flans 135
Maltagliati with Quails,
 Truffle and Porcini 347
Melted Brie and Porcini Crostone 36
Porcini and Chestnut Soup

with Walnuts 1039
Porcini and Hazelnut Risotto 95
Porcini and Potato Soup 306
Porcini Cappelletti in Truffle Broth 75
Porcini Ravioli with Bell
 Pepper Cream 99
Porcini Soup with Passatelli 1036
Porcini Tagliatelle with Swordfish 89
Porcini, Roasted Tomato
 and Ricotta Salad 214
Porcini-Stuffed Pork Fillet 144
Potato and Porcini Croquettes 42
Rigatoni with Porcini 95
Risotto with Treviso Radicchio,
 Porcini and Truffle 325
Steamed Sea Bream with Porcini 404
Tagliatelle with Porcini Ragù 114
Thyme and Porcini Lasagnas 88
Tiger Shrimp on Porcini
 Carpaccio 1066
Truffle and Porcini
 Mushroom Omelette 43
Truffle, Porcini and Pine
 Nut Spread 68
Winter Squash and Porcini
 Lasagna 96

mussels
Barley with Mussels
 and Spinach 588
Chickpea Gnocchetti
 with Mussels 572
Fried Mussels (Puglia) 635
Mussel and Shrimp Croquettes 732
Mussel and Shrimp Sauté 893
Mussel Bruschetta 739
Mussel Impepata (Campania) 914
Sautéed Clams and Mussels
 with Garlic and Parsley Sardinia) 649

N

nectarines
Hazelnut Cake with Nectarines 993
Nectarines with Sauternes 956

with Pecorino 104
Pecorino and Chestnut Tortelli 1020
Porcini Cappelletti in Truffle Broth 75
Porcini Ravioli with Bell
 Pepper Cream 99
Quail and Prune Ravioli 110
Radicchio Ravioli
 with Gorgonzola Sauce 316
Robiola-Stuffed Spinach
 Pasta Rolls 1054
Sea Bass-Filled Maremmani
 with Prawns (Tuscany) 785
Prawns and Potato Ravioli
 with Pea Sauce 577
Sweet Ravioli (Liguria) 722
Tortelloni Dough 1094
Walnut Cappellacci
 with Chanterelles 335
White Tortelli with Figs,
 Ricotta and Prosciutto 111
Whole-Wheat Broccoli Ravioli
 with Prawns 333
Winter Squash Ravioli (Veneto) 100

pastas, fresh
Baked Tagliolini
 with Porcini Ragù 1069
Black Tagliolini with Bottarga
 Pesto and Cherry Tomatoes 842
Buckwheat Tagliatelle
 with Favas 566
Campofilone Pasta in Capon
 Broth (Marche) 113
Cavatelli with Chickpeas (Puglia) 822
Cavatieddi in Tomato Sauce
 (Sicily) 835
Corzetti with Genoan-Style Sauce
 (Liguria) 580
Egg Pasta Dough 1094
First of May Maltagliati 556
Fresh Fettuccine with Asiago,
 Mushrooms and Tomatoes 92
Fresh Tagliolini with Radicchio
 and White Truffle 315
Fresh Trofie with Clams
 and Broccoli Rabe 579
Garlic Strichetti (Emilia-Romagna) 538
Green and Yellow Maltagliati 561

Maltagliati with Pheasant
 and Vernaccia Ragù 120
Maltagliati with Quails, Truffle
 and Porcini 347
Orecchiette with Tomato,
 Arugula and Ricotta Salata 800
Parsley Maltagliati with Lobster
 and Shallot Oil 827
Saffron Garganelli with
 Tomatoes and Favas 552
Tagliatelle with Porcini Ragù 114
Tagliolini and Scallops
 with Pinot Bianco 587
Tagliolini with Prawns
 and Clam Ragù 843
Trofie with Green Apple,
 Salama and Goat's Cheese 320
Valtellina-Style Buckwheat Pasta
 (Lombardy) 546
Whole-Wheat Pasta
 with Chickpeas and Sausage 107

pastas, dried
Arezzo-Style Pappardelle
 (Tuscany) 815
Asparagus and Saffron Farfalle 544
Baked Penne with Porcini
 and Four Cheeses 97
Baked Ziti 825
Bigoli with Tench and Rucola 586
Broccoli Carbonara 313
Broccoli-Bottarga Spaghettini 88
Bucatini with Guanciale (Lazio) 70
Bucatini with Sardines 341
Bucatini with Spicy Stockfish
 (Calabria) 798
Cerinole Pasta with Sausage
 and Mushrooms (Umbria) 101
Cold Orecchiette with Vegetable
 Caponata 558
Cold Pasta Salad 806
Cold Sedanini with Baby Squid
 and Tomatoes 831
Cold Summer Farfalle 793
Cold Torchietti with Peas,
 Roast Pepper and Bacon 826
Corn Fusilli with Green Beans
 and Squash 553

pâtés
Eggplant Rounds

Ricotta and Swiss
 Chard Dumplings (Piedmont)   547
Ricotta Cake   721
Ricotta Cake with Wild
 Strawberries   983
Ricotta Cream Tart   719
Ricotta Flan with Radicchio
 Sauce   414
Ricotta Mousse with Kiwis   699
Ricotta Quenelles with Kiwi
 and Raspberries   700
Ricotta with Radicchio and Honey   299
Ricotta, Chard and Hazelnut
 Rissoles   660
Ricotta, Walnut
 and Arugula Crostini   748
Ricotta-Stuffed Onions   208
Savory Tart with Ricotta
 and Radicchio   216
Toasted Focaccia with Ricotta   745
Tomato and Ricotta Salad   928
Wheat Tart with Ricotta
 and Lemon   697
White Tortelli with Figs,
 Ricotta and Prosciutto   111
Zucchini and Ricotta Strata   182

rissoles
Bean Rissoles
 with Spring Onions   446
Cauliflower Rissoles   422
Ricotta, Chard
 and Hazelnut Rissoles   660

risotto
Amarone Risotto   336
Artichoke and Saffron Risotto   551
Artichoke and Scallop Risotto   344
Artichoke Risotto   554
Asparagus and Robiola Risotto   564
Blueberry Risotto   803
Brown Rice Risotto with
 Walnuts and Winter Squash   105
Crispy Amarone Risotto
 with Quails   346
Fonduta Risotto   345
Monk's Risotto (Lombardy)   574
Novara-Style Risotto (Piedmont)   343

Oyster, Champagne and Orange
 Risotto   352
Pea and Prawns Risotto   583
Porcini and Hazelnut Risotto   95
Quail Risotto with Radicchio
 and Truffles   106
Radicchio Risotto (Veneto)   354
Risotto with Arugula   89
Risotto with Sea Bass   351
Risotto with Treviso Radicchio,
 Porcini and Truffle   325
Sausage Risotto   323
Spiced Risotto with Chicken
 Ragù (Marche)   591
Taleggio Risotto   331
Veal and Mushroom Risotto   336

robiola cheese
Asparagus and Robiola Risotto   564
Roast Beef, Robiola
 and Eggplant Involtini   872
Robiola and Arugula Linguine   545
Robiola and Bell Pepper Salad   937
Robiola and Eggplant Canapés   753
Robiola with Pistachios
 and Spiced Honey   917
Robiola-Stuffed Spinach
 Pasta Rolls   1054

rolls and involtini
Arezzo-Style Chocolate Roll
 (Tuscany)   705
Asparagus Involtini   619
Beef and Pecorino Involtini   140
Beef Roll with Spinach Sauce   851
Bresaola Involtini   500
Bresaola Rolls with Zucchini   735
Cabbage Involtini
 with Emmenthal   438
Cauliflower-Filled Zucchini Rolls   445

Chestnut and Cabbage Rolls
 with Parmesan Sauce   32
Chestnut and Ricotta Roll   241
Chocolate Roll with Cream   1062
Cod-Stuffed Cabbage Rolls   406
Eggplant Rolls in Tomato Sauce   947
Endive and Ham Involtini

Whole-Wheat Pasta with
Chickpeas and Sausage 107

scallops
Artichoke and Scallop Risotto 344
Ginger-Lime Scallops 532
Gratinéed Scallops 157
Gratinéed Scallops with
 Almonds and Thyme 282
Gratinéed Scallops with Ginger 625
Herb-Steamed Scallop Dumplings 776
Scallop Skewers 914
Scallops over Fennel 283
Scallops with Belgian Endive 289
Scallops with Salted Butter 277
Tagliolini and Scallops
 with Pinot Bianco 587
Venere Rice with Champagne
 and Scallops 334

sea bass
Herbed Sea Bass with Vegetable
 Caponata 876
Risotto with Sea Bass 351
Sea Bass Carpaccio 507
Sea Bass in a Salt Crust
 with Mandarin Oil 1070
Sea Bass Tartare Crostone 749
Sea Bass with Radicchio 399
Sea Bass with
 Saffron-Chardonnay Sauce 643
Sea Bass-Filled Maremmani
 with Prawns (Tuscany) 785
Seared Salmon and Sea Bass 622

sea bream
Neapolitan-Style Sea Bream 892
Sea Bream Carpaccio with Arugula
 and Cherry Tomatoes 1014
Sea Bream with Walnuts
 and Broccoli 397
Sea-Bream Sandwiches 167
Steamed Sea Bream with Porcini 404
Zucchini-Wrapped Sea Bream
 with Lemon Sauce 895

semifreddos
Mascarpone and Cherry

Semifreddo 982
Nut Semifreddo with Moscato
 and Chocolate Sauce 462
Peach Semifreddo 968
Pistachio Semifreddo 702

sesame
Eggplant and Sesame Tart 650
Potato and Sesame Croquettes 182
Sesame Tempura Squid with Salad 630
Prawns and Sesame Toasts 537

shrimps (see prawns)

snow peas
Warm Snow Pea and Lobster Salad
 with Balsamic Reduction 533
sole
Sole Fillets with Mint 887
Sole Sautéed in White Wine 163
Sole with Green Grape Sauce 158
Sole with Winter Squash Cream 166

sorbet - see ice cream

soufflés
Coffee Ice Cream Soufflés 969
Lettuce Soufflés with Crescenza
 Sauce 428

Mini Potato and Spinach
 Soufflés 432
Roquefort Soufflés 272

soups and stews
Acqua Cotta Soup (Tuscany) 790
Acquasale Soup (Basilicata) 349
Arezzo-Style Bean Soup
 (Tuscany) 356
Bean and Grain Soup 310
Beef Stew with Barolo (Piedmont) 379
Beef Stew with Speck
 and Onions 369
Buridda (Liguria) 889
Cabbage and Fontina Soup 302
Canederli Soup with Speck
 (Trentino-Alto Adige) 319
Carcerato (Tuscany) 71

tarts, savory

Bell Pepper and Porcini Tarts	198
Chard, Porcini and Fontina Tart	179
Cheese Tart with Chicken and Mushrooms	152
Chestnut, Ricotta and Speck Tartlets	61
Colorful Tartlets	69
Crescenza Tarts with Taggiasca Olives	33
Eggplant and Sesame Tart	650
Endive and Leek Tart	450
Endive Tarts with Ham	67
Mediterranean Onion Tart	209
Mushroom Tart	191
Potato and Pancetta Tart	275
Potato, Asiago and Pancetta Tart	503
Red Cabbage and Goat's Cheese Tart	297
Savory Spinach Tart (Trentino Alto Adige)	41
Savory Tart with Ricotta and Radicchio	216
Spring Vegetable Tart	677
Swiss Chard and Chestnut Tart	213
Tartlets with Bell Peppers and Potatoes	185
Wild Nettle Tart	670
Winter Squash, Carrot and Zucchini Tarts	212
Zucchini and Escarole Tart	202
Zucchini and Goat Cheese Tart	687
Zucchini Tarte Tatin	684

tarts, sweet

Apple Tarts with Calvados Sauce	718
Apricot Tart with Yogurt Cream	1003
Banana Tart	986
Berry and Mascarpone Tart	998
Blueberry Tartlets	480
Caramelized Fig Tart	247
Chestnut Tart with Dark Chocolate	237
Chocolate Tart with Pastry Cream	714
Citrus Tart with Limoncello Sauce	999
Fresh Fruit Tart	478
Fruit Tart	710
Fruit Tart with Apple Cream	989
Gianduia Tart	1049
Honey Tart	242
Mascarpone and Fig Tart	228
Mini Fruit Tarts	713
Neapolitan Ricotta Tart	240
Pear and Apricot Tart	984
Pear and Calvados Tarte Tatin with Acacia Honey	223
Pear Tart with Amaretto Cream	244
Plum Jam Tart	239
Ricotta and Gianduia Tart	483
Ricotta Cream Tart	719
Roasted Pepper and Potato Tartlets	421
Wheat Tart with Ricotta and Lemon	697

tea

Tea-Steamed Lobster with Eggplant Puree and Crispy Prosciutto	882

terrines

Beef and Chicken Terrine with Sangiovese Sauce	359
Chicken Liver and Mushoom Terrine on Mixed Greens	60
Pork Terrine with Savoy Cabbage and Carrots	49
Red Mullet, Potato, Arugula and Black Olive Terrine	891
Ricotta and Fava Terrine	658
Roast Pepper and Mozzarella Terrine	944
Salmon and Aspargus Terrine	647
Vegetable Terrine	687
Zucchini and Feta Terrine	754

thyme

Caponata with Thyme	932
Gratinéed Scallops with Almonds and Thyme	282
Grilled Tomatoes with Thyme Oil	925
Prosciutto and Melon with Thyme	755
Roast Rabbit with Thyme	853
Thyme and Porcini Lasagnas	88
Tomato and Thyme Soup with Tuna	543
Trofie with Monkfish	

and Lemon Thyme 838

timbales

Black Rice Timbales
with Curried Shrimp 1038
Pepper, Olive and Grouper
Timbale 943
Rice and Ham Timbale 563
Steamed Grouper and Zucchini
Timbales 534

tiramisù

Banana Tiramisù 1000
Tiramisù with Wild Strawberries 975
Vanilla Tiramisù 1077

tomatoes

Baked Gnocchi with Tomatoes
and Basil 824
Baked Seafood Crêpes
in Tomato Sauce 786
Black Rice Wafers
with Shrimp and Tomatoes 762
Black Tagliolini with Bottarga
Pesto and Cherry Tomatoes 842
Cannellini Beans in Tomato
Sauce 192
Cavatieddi in Tomato Sauce
(Sicily) 835
Cherry Tomato and Arugula Pizza 920
Cherry Tomatoes Stuffed
with Curried Rice and Eggplant 666
Chicken in Lemon Leaves
with Tomatoes au Gratin 850
Clam Soup with Celery,
Tomato and Carrots 774
Cold Sedanini with Baby Squid
and Tomatoes 831
Crêpes with Ricotta
and Tomatoes 781
Eggplant Flans with
Cherry-Tomato Sauce 746
Fresh Fettuccine with Asiago,
Mushrooms and Tomatoes 92
Fried Pizzas with Clams
and Tomatoes 766
Fried Umbrine Parcels
with Spicy Tomatoes 901

Green Beans in Tomato Sauce
(Lombardy) 186
Grilled Cuttlefish with Green
Tomatoes 885
Grilled Tomatoes with Thyme Oil 925
Langoustines in Tomato-Brandy
Sauce (Veneto) 888
Lardo and Tomato Crostini 262
Marinated Turkey with Tomatoes 616
Mini Pizzas with Spinach
and Tomatoes 39
Mint and Pecorino Ravioli
in Tomato Sauce (Sardinia) 112
Mullet-Stuffed Endive
with Tomato Sauce 402
Orecchiette with Tomato Sauce
and Cacioricotta (Puglia) 794
Orecchiette with Tomato,
Arugula and Ricotta Salata 800
Parmesan Flan with Arugula
and Tomatoes 516
Pasta Wheels with Tomato Puree 803
Pasta with Pesto and Tomatoes 839
Phyllo Triangles with Ricotta
and Tomatoes 498
Plaice Cakes with Tomato Sauce 645
Porcini, Roasted Tomato
and Ricotta Salad 214
Saffron Garganelli
with Tomatoes and Favas 552
Schiacciata with Oregano
and Tomatoes 654
Sea Bream Carpaccio with
Arugula and Cherry Tomatoes 1014
Spaghetti with Lobster
and Tomato 828
Spicy Bucatini with Tomatoes,
Shrimp and Mozzarella 783
Spinach-Tomato Canapés 507
Stuffed Cherry Tomato Skewers 745
Stuffed Squid with
Tomato Sauce 395
Swordfish and Eggplant Involtini
with Two Tomato Sauces 913
Tomato and Bread Soup
(Tuscany) 757
Tomato and Caper Flan 934
Tomato and Ricotta Salad 928

Printed in China in January 2008